© pfg powell 2024

Edited and produced by St Breward Press,

St Breward, Cornwall PL30 4NB.

Tel: +44 (0)1208 851023.

The Hemingway enigma

How did a middling writer achieve such global literary fame?

by pfg powell

Contents

Preface	11
THE WORK	22
Introduction	23
'Truth' in Hemingway	43
Subjectivity: is objective judgment possible?	59
What was it to be – 'artist' or 'celebrity'?	72
Personality, mental and physical health	89
The writer, journalist, 'insider' and expert	106
'Rules on writing' and the 'Theory of Omission'	118
The Sun Also Rises and the 'lost generation'	129
A modernist writer?	148
Hemingway theology – Round and round	167
Hemingway theology – The tyranny of 'meaning'	183
Caveat lector – Enter academia	196

Caveat lector – Erich von Däniken takes a bow	**213**
Caveat lector – The Rorschach effect	**226**
The suspected inferiority complex	**241**
The linguist	**248**
The unknown lover and sex roles in bed	**254**
A lifetime's work	**263**
Work published posthumously	**282**
In sum: chacun à son goût	**299**
THE LIFE	**310**
1899-1921 – The early years	**312**
1921-1924 – Paris and life are sweet	**322**
1924-1925 – Learning to be a success	**333**
1925-1926 – Finally on the literary map	**343**
1926-1927 – Out with the old, in with the new	**353**
1927-1929 – Fame and a comfortable life	**362**
1929-1934 – Becoming the legend	**372**
1934-1936 – Poor sales and growing depression	**382**

1936-1940 – Cuba and a second divorce	**399**
1940-1943 – Trying and failing to settle	**414**
1943-1944 – Lonely and the third marriage ends	**424**
1944-1945 – Playing soldier and wooing again	**433**
1945-1954 – Fourth marriage and infatuations	**442**
1954-1961 – Terminal decline and suicide	**465**
APPENDICES	**488**
An Essay On Criticism	**489**
An Old Newsman Writes	**495**
Who Murdered The Vets?	**501**
The Art Of The Short Story	**507**
ENDNOTES	**518**
BIBLIOGRAPHY	**564**

It is not he who forms idols in gold or marble that makes them gods, but he who kneels before them.

**Marcus Valerius Martialis,
the Roman poet known as Martial.**

Yet Hemingway did not progress from strength to strength. His best work was done before he was thirty... Nonetheless, he spoke with the confidence of success. Everything he did, everything he wrote, became important because he was Ernest Hemingway.

**Matthew J. Bruccoli Scott and Ernest: The
Authority of Failure and the Authority of Success.**

What other culture could have produced someone like Hemingway and not seen the joke?

**Gore Vidal, Pink Triangle And
Yellow Star, published in 1983.**

From his first emergence as one of the bright literary stars in Paris during the twenties – as a chronicler of the 'Lost Generation', which he was to immortalize – he almost single-handedly transformed the literature and the ways of thought of men and women in every country in the world.

John F. Kennedy, July 2, 1961.

It may even be that the final judgment on his work may come to the notion that what he failed to do was tragic, but what he accomplished was heroic, for it is possible that he carried a weight of anxiety with him which would have suffocated any man smaller than himself.

Norman Mailer, Cannibals And Christians.

Hemingway was strange, very strange. He was a strange man.

Juanito Quintana, hotel owner
Juanito Montoya In The Sun Also Rises.

NOTE: This book began life as a series of essays on a website that consisted of many pages. In each essay, facts, quotations, attributions and observations were often repeated for the sake of comprehension and context. That would be tiresome in a book whose chapters conventionally are read in sequence. Re-writing those essays for this book, I have tried to rid the text of all such repetitions. Some might remain, however, and for these all I can do is apologise.

Preface

This is the West, sir. When the legend becomes fact, print the legend.

> **Maxwell Scott, The Man Who Shot Liberty Valance (ironically, a fictional character).**

The most important author living today, the outstanding author since the death of Shakespeare . . .

> **John O'Hara, New York Times, Sept 10, 1950.**

Why the life of this rich libertine and destroyer of wildlife should be of such great and continuing public interest a decade following his suicide, we cannot and need not say.

> **Judge Charles L. Brieant Jr, Aug 3, 1976, dismissing an appeal by Doubleday over a libel suit brought by A.E. Hotchner. His ruling was overturned on appeal seven months later.**

To me, Across the River And Into the Trees is one of the saddest books I have ever read; not because I am moved to compassion by the conjunction of love and death in the Colonel's life, but because a great talent has come, whether for now or forever, to such a dead end.

> **J. Donald Adams, writing about Across The River And Into The Trees, New York Times, Sept 24, 1950.**

Yet Hemingway did not progress from strength to strength.

> *His best work was done before he was thirty, and he produced only one major novel — For Whom the Bell Tolls — after 1929. Nonetheless, he spoke with the confidence of success. Everything he did, everything he wrote, became important because he was Ernest Hemingway.*
>
> **Matthew J. Bruccoli, in Scott and Ernest: The Authority of Failure and the Authority of Success.**

I DON'T doubt that many reading what follows will react with disbelief and scorn, and some diehard Hemingway champions possibly even with horror. More than 50 years after his death, the name Ernest Hemingway is perhaps not as popularly known as once it was, but I suspect that most who hear it will still pronounce him to have been 'a great writer' or even 'one of the 20th century's greatest writers', mainly, perhaps, because that's what they were taught at school. One does come across readers who think he was little more than a boorish braggart and who regard his style as dull, flat and often banal; that they have probably not read much of his work is because what they had read did not encourage them to read much more of it. The novelist Vladimir Nabokov wrote off Hemingway as 'a writer for boys' and, at the extreme, was a comment by the American novelist and wit Gore Vidal who asked (about his home nation)

> *What other culture could have produced someone like Hemingway and not seen the joke?* [1]

Yet these were, and perhaps still are, decidedly minority views. In 1941 the Pulitzer Prize jurors unanimously wanted to honour Hemingway for his novel For Whom The Bell Tolls, and that he didn't get the award was down to the lobbying by a very influential pro-Franco and ring-wing Pulitzer board member. [2] The jurors responded and made their feelings known by not awarding the Pulitzer Prize for Fiction to anyone else. Twelve years later they *were* able to honour Hemingway and awarded him the Fiction prize for The Old Man And The Sea. Then, in 1954, came an even greater distinction when Hemingway was awarded the Nobel Prize for Literature.

So who is 'right': the champions or the sceptics? Frankly, no one is – the excellence or

---

[1] It has to be said that Vidal delighted in shocking and taking a contrarian view. In his collection of essays Pink Triangle And Yellow Star, published in 1983 from which this quote is taken, he was also exceptionally nasty about F. Scott Fitzgerald.

[2] Nicholas Murray Butler, president of Columbia University.

Preface

otherwise of Hemingway's writing and his greatness or otherwise or his literary status are matters of opinion not fact. [1]

In fairness there was – at least at first – a little more to Hemingway's fiction. Yet in hindsight there was also less to his writing, and in time a great deal less, than his champions – and Hemingway himself – insist. It would be a sweeping generalisation, but not untrue, to suggest that he began at the top and worked his way down. The print, broadcast and online media are often accused of working on the principle of 'first simplify, then exaggerate' [2] and adopting that principle one could even suggest – no doubt to the outrage of many – that Hemingway's literary success was something of a fluke. In response, the champions might choose to repeat their mantra 'but Ernest Hemingway was a leading modernist and one of our / America's / the English-speaking world's greatest writers!' Unfortunately, continual repetition doesn't necessarily make it true. Yet having established their devotion, the devotees will never, but never, allow themselves to be gainsaid: those who disagree either don't 'get' Hemingway and are obviously philistine, or quite possibly they are just being malicious. If only.

. . .

The reason this book is subtitled 'How did a middling writing achieve such global literary fame?' is simple: that is an enigma which has interested me ever since I came back to reading Hemingway's work. And he certainly did achieve global fame. I had previously – many years ago in my salad days – read the early two novels and Death In The Afternoon and some of the short stories, but despite being on an English degree course, I was not intellectually equipped to deal with much literature of any kind. I also accepted without question – as did and do many others at that age when they first encounter 'Hemingway' – the conventional view that he was 'a great writer'. Thus if I did not 'get' him or was not as engaged and impressed by the work as I believed I should have been, I assumed it was most certainly my fault. That, too, might be true of others at that younger age.

Hemingway did have a certain gift, but it was – as many commentators and reviewers have pointed out – for descriptive writing, especially about nature. Discussing Across

---

1   When reading this some might scoff 'well, that's just what *you* think'. I wonder whether they are aware of the irony implicit in their scorn? The distinction between what is and can be a 'fact' or an 'opinion' is crucial, and I touch upon it later. See p.59ff

2   This is said to have been serious advice given to his young journalists by Geoffrey Crowther, the Economist's editor from 1938 until 1956. I suggest that adopting that principle might prove helpful in the short run, but in the long run will only distort.

The River And Into The Trees which Hemingway published in 1950, the New York Times' columnist and former book reviews editor J. Donald Adams wrote

> *My own feeling about him has always been that he is one of the best descriptive writers in English, surpassed only by Kipling and a very few others; a master in the evocation of mood – most perfectly displayed in some of the short stories, and in certain situations of the novels. He is not, and never has been, a creator of character in the sense that novelists like Balzac and Tolstoy were, and has never come remotely near the understanding of human life and the values of which it is composed that are essential to great fiction.*

Other commentators and reviewers also pointed out that – fatally, one might think, for a writer of fiction – Hemingway was not at all good at characterisation, and one might be hard-pushed to think of more than a handful of his characters who escape two dimensions, especially his female protagonists. On learning more about his life, it often seems that Hemingway's main gift, one which drove his career far more than any putative excellence in writing, was not literary at all but a remorseless and competitive ambition sustained by a talent for self-promotion. Yet in literary terms he did leave his mark, as pointed out by the scholar Matthew J. Bruccoli:

> *More than any other writer Hemingway influenced what American writers were able to write about and the words they used.*

In a sense there is, at first blush, perhaps less to that achievement than we might think; obliquely pertinent might be the observation often made about innovative software, new car models and the latest development in technological hardware: never buy version one of anything. Over the millennia that men and women have been writing, there have been many turning points in literature – though as with many such changes, they came and come in fits and starts – and as a young man publishing his first volume of short stories, Hemingway was the catalyst for one such change. The irony was that other writers took his techniques, attitude and subject matter, and turned out rather more interesting work than he did. Dare I even claim 'better' work? No, I dare not, but not because I might be strung up from the nearest lamppost by Hemingway champions. It's because in many discussions, the words 'good' and 'bad' – and thus 'better' and 'worse' – are not just inappropriate, but pretty damn useless. They do nothing except signal the bias of whoever is using them; they tell us nothing about the work in question.

Over the intervening years, my confidence has become more robust, and I am far less

Preface

inclined to accept wholesale and without question. I have also read more widely and, crucially, developed more sceptical instincts, largely, I suspect, because I once worked as a newspaper journalist [1]. I have also come to appreciate the virtues of an 'open mind'; and as I read more about Hemingway, it was an odd, quasi-theistic, evangelical, blinkered devotion to the writer and his work which increasingly came to worry me. All too often articles in specialist publications and discussions in webinars strike a curious note of adulation, as though one were at a prayer meeting or a Britney Spears convention. [2] A curious campfire cosiness permeates far too many of the studies and articles I have read about Hemingway and his work.

. . .

This book began life as an entry intended for a blog. Several years ago and on a whim – and I can't remember why I even thought about doing so – I had re-read Ernest Hemingway's novel The Sun Also Rises. The blurb on the back of my paperback edition described the novel as 'a masterpiece' and Hemingway as 'a writer of genius', and when I had finished reading it, I was baffled by those claims. The novel was certainly no 'masterpiece' and its author seemed to be anything but 'a genius'.

The novel isn't bad and it is entertaining enough; and, certainly, the two claims owe a great deal to publishers' hyperbole, puffing up a 'product' to ensure it sells. But The Sun Also Rises struggles to justify the claims made for it as being in any way 'profound', and to regard Hemingway as 'a writer of genius' [3] is frankly ridiculous. When an academic – Philip Young in his 1952 book Ernest Hemingway – describes Hemingway as 'very likely the finest writer of American prose to come along since [Henry] Thoreau himself', you really do wonder what is going on. It came down to a simple question: did Young lose the plot or have I?

However, my scepticism about Hemingway's alleged 'genius' is definitely a minority view: despite a decline in his reputation and popularity since his suicide in 1961, Hemingway is still spoken of by many as 'a leading modernist writer', 'a stylistic innovator' and, most dangerously for a sceptic such as me, 'one of the greatest American

---

1   First as a reporter then as a sub-editor [US copy editor].

2   Britney Spears' heyday was in the 1990s and early 2000s. Readers are welcome to substitute the name of any other pop starlet, boy or girl, of their choice with whom they are more familiar. At the time of writing it might be Taylor Swift.

3   Little more than publishers' hyperbole it might be, but when you come across such a claim as a young student in a seminar or reading an academic tome, you are more likely than not to take it seriously and worry why you can't agree.

writers'. Is it really likely that most of the world – many biographers, academics in their hundreds, the Pulitzer Prize jurors and notably the Nobel Prize committee – were wrong in their evaluation of the man and his work, and that I am right? Intrigued and not a little concerned that I was risking making a fool of myself, I began by scouring the net for the views and opinions of those who might share my minority view. Almost immediately I came across reviews of a book published in 2016 by the New York writer and journalist Lesley M.M. Blume called Everybody Behaves Badly, subtitled The True Story Behind Hemingway's Masterpiece The Sun Also Rises. It was a serendipitous find: well-researched, extensively annotated, well-written and – not at all least – very entertaining, Ms Blume's book gave a full account of Hemingway's early years in Paris in the 1920s and of the week-long trip to the San Fermin fiesta in Pamplona in 1925 upon which he based his novel. Pertinently it provided many details for my intended blog entry about The Sun Also Rises. I was, incidentally, amused – and rather pleased – to learn that the title of the German translation of Ms Blume's book is *Und Alle Benehmen Sich Daneben: Wie Hemingway Seine Legende Erschuf*. The main title translates, as one might expect, as Everybody Behaves Badly; but tellingly, Blume's subtitle has been amended, and in English it translates as 'How Hemingway Created His Legend'. This insight by the German publisher reflects one of the conclusions I have come to. In fact, this book is essentially about the Hemingway legend and how he actively created it. And although Ms Blume refers to The Sun Also Rises as 'Hemingway's masterpiece', I suspect that choice of words was, like the subtitle, not hers but her publisher's, given that Ms Blume's account of Hemingway and the genesis of his novel is rather less admiring than the description 'masterpiece' might imply.

After I had read Ms Blume's book, I realised I had a problem. She referenced the several biographies of Hemingway and other books about the man, and increasingly I felt that to do justice to both my project and the writer, I was obliged to undertake more background reading. It also became obvious to me that when dealing with the phenomenon of 'Ernest Hemingway, a writer deemed worthy of a Nobel Prize', I should tread carefully. Knowing more about the man and his work – including reading more of the work – seemed not just necessary but a wise course to take. Thus what was set to become a short blog entry grew, both in intention and scope.

...

The first biography of Hemingway was published in 1967, six years after Hemingway's death. It was by Carlos Baker who had been nominated by Hemingway himself as his

Preface

'official biographer'.[1] Baker had the cooperation of Mary Welsh, the writer's widow, although having Welsh on his side was a double-edged sword. As Baker discovered in his research, Hemingway could be decidedly brutal, vindictive, cruel and in some ways thoroughly dishonest; but Baker had to tread carefully in his descriptions of the writer. Welsh was litigious and had already taken one writer, A.E. Hotchner, to court over his memoir of her husband (a suit she eventually lost). To ensure Welsh's continued help, Baker did not want to alienate her. His volume – very detailed, but a little dull – was the definitive work for 18 years until Jeffrey Meyers published his biography in 1985. Two years later, in 1987, came the first volume of Michael Reynolds eventual five-volume work, followed by Kenneth S. Lynn's take on Hemingway; and in 1992 James Mellow published his biography.

By 1985, 24 years after Hemingway's suicide, his work was undergoing re-assessment, and in tone the more recent biographies were more critical of both the man and his work than Baker could afford to be. (Mary Welsh died in 1986 at the age of 78.) In 2016, James Hutchisson published what he called A New Life, but in truth it strikes me as simply a general romp through what previous biographers had written. Despite claims made in some reviews, Hutchisson does not seem to have undertaken any new or original research. Furthermore, although nicely produced, it contains, inexplicably, several outright howlers.

Two years later, Mary Dearborn published her biography, and although she might well have undertaken additional research, her work does not add much to what previous biographers had written. On one or two matters she even contradicts them, though who is 'right' and who is 'wrong' is impossible to establish.[2] I did not bother reading A.E. Hotchner's memoir which, I had gathered, was distinctly hagiographic and which took as copper-bottomed 'fact' too many of the tall, often outrageous, stories Hemingway told about his life and experiences. Anthony Burgess' take on Hemingway makes some interesting points, but in form, style and content it is a coffee-table book for which he also seems to have done no original research. Then there's a curious volume by Richard Bradford, published in 2019, which is notable for its hostility to Hemingway and, which might warn us, was badly edited.

---

1   That Hemingway believed it necessary – or perhaps, more charitably, agreed – to nominate 'his official biographer' indicates what a high opinion he had of himself and his work. I have yet to nominate my 'official biographer'.

2   This has nothing to do with 'opinion' but with factual claims. Dearborn reports, for example, that Hemingway wrote the first draft of The Sun Also Rises on a typewriter. All the other biographers – if they mention it – say that what began as a short story and later evolved into the novel was written in a number of blue notebooks. So who got a 'fact' wrong?

Bernice Kert's The Hemingway Women was especially interesting, highlighting how much macho ol' Ernie relied heavily on his wives, not just for emotional support but in two cases also for their money. Gioia Diliberto's more recent work, Paris Without End, The True Story Of Hemingway's First Wife, provides an interesting picture of Hadley Richardson and corrects the often accepted view that she was essentially a doormat who gave in to her egocentric and domineering husband at every turn. [1] Although Hadley is the main focus of her book, Diliberto also illuminates Hemingway's character very well.

Very useful were Scott Donaldson's The Paris Husband which covers much the same ground, as well as his book on the friendship between Hemingway and F. Scott Fitzgerald. Then there are the comparatively short volumes on the writer and the man by Linda Wagner-Martin, Peter Griffin, Charles A. Fenton and Verna Kale. The Second Flowering, Malcolm Cowley's volume of essays, two of which are about Hemingway, provides useful considerations on what is referred to as 'the lost generation'.

. . .

The more I read, I also realised that given the standing Hemingway had and for many still has in modern literature, I would have to do more than simply examine The Sun Also Rises and question why it was and still is hailed as 'a masterpiece'. It seemed to me that the central conundrum was: just why and how did Hemingway, essentially a middling writer of some talent but of no more than many other writers, attain such extraordinary worldwide prominence? None of his peers came close to enjoying such global recognition. [2] On that question Leonard J. Leff's – rather luridly titled – Hemingway And His Conspirators: Hollywood, Scribner's And The Making Of American Celebrity Culture was especially interesting. It examines the growth of celebrity and pop culture in 1920s 'jazz age' America as well as developments in advertising and marketing, and how Ernest Hemingway and his literary career benefited.

In his career of just under 40 years, Hemingway did not write a great deal – in fact, compared with his contemporary writers, he wrote surprisingly little. Despite the acclamation his early work met, by the mid-1930s, after the publication of Death In The Afternoon (1932), Green Hills Of Africa (1935) and then To Have And Have Not (1937) his reputation was already in decline, and some critics began to have doubts about the *Wunderkind* of ten years earlier. With the exception of For Whom The Bell Tolls (1940),

---

1   Michael Reynolds records F. Scott Fitzgerald's wife Zelda as telling Hadley '*I notice that in the Hemingway family you do what Ernest wants*'.

2   Somerset Maugham had a similar name recognition, but he was born in 1874 and was arguably of the previous generation of writers. He was already over 50 when The Sun Also Rises was published.

which became a best-seller, not least because in the US it was chosen as a Book Of The Month, and 12 years later The Old Man And The Sea, another commercial success and which also appeared its entirety in Life magazine, [1] Hemingway's scant work from 1929 on was regarded as nothing remarkable to not very good at all.

. . .

As my project took shape it's focus changed: it was no longer to examine why The Sun Also Rises was and occasionally still is spoken of as 'a masterpiece' and Hemingway was and is hailed as 'a genius'. Broader questions presented themselves, questions which transcended Hemingway and his work. For example, on the back of Virginia Woolf's pithy remarks about critics (as part of her review of Men Without Women, Hemingway's second volume of short stories), I began to wonder whether objective judgment of a piece of writing – or of any work of art – is even possible. Why, almost without question, do we hold academia in such esteem and seem prepared to accept their – often very contradictory – pronouncements as far more worthwhile than our own? It seems, at times, as though we allow our English literature professors to adopt the role of druids, shamans, rabbis, mullahs, priests and preachers past and present to interpret the 'word of God' on our behalf, and the humble believer feels disinclined to challenge what they say. I also consider the commercial background and imperatives of the second decade of the 20th century and how innovative advertising and marketing techniques helped to ensure Hemingway's 'first' novel became success. There was the question of Hemingway's alleged 'modernism': why was – and still is – Hemingway touted as 'a modernist' writer when it soon became clear – to me, at least – that he had next to nothing in common the 'modernists' who had been working in many fields since the last decade of the 19th century. Then there was the puzzle of why and how it came to be believed – to this day – that The Sun Also Rises portrayed the 'despair' of a 'lost generation'. What are we to make of Hemingway's writing 'style'; and why was and is his 'iceberg theory' of writing celebrated and regarded – not least by Hemingway – as an 'innovation'.

Central to it all was the force and impact of Hemingway's personality on his rise to fame; so this book concludes with short accounts of Hemingway's life, distilled from the various biographies. They recount his youth, his early years in Paris and his life in the 1930s when he began to play the part of the celebrated 'Papa' Hemingway, the hard-drinking, hard-living, action-man writer; then came his brief 'war' in France and his slow disintegration. Incidentally, Hemingway awarded himself the sobriquet 'Papa',

---

[1] It is still often called 'a novel' but frankly it is simply a long short story.

and by the mid-1920s he encouraged everyone to address him with the name. No one knows quite where it came from and why he chose it, and why he often insisted he should he addressed a 'Papa'. [1] It did, though, help to perpetuate the image of 'the authority', 'the insider' and 'the expert' he wanted the public to accept.

. . .

When considering Hemingway the 'literary genius' and his worldwide fame, it might be worth noting the following observations. Both are pertinent to how he achieved the status of 'one of America's greatest writers'. The first is by Mario Menocal Jr, a son of one of Hemingway's Cuban friends who himself became a friend, writing in a letter to biographer Jeffrey Meyers. In view of what he says, it is worth stressing that he and Hemingway did not fall out as Hemingway had with many of his other friends, [2] and Menocal's comment was not intended to be hostile:

> *No one was more conscious than Ernest of the figure and image he possessed in the minds of the American press and reading public. He felt (I am sure) that this was an important matter to him in terms of dollars and cents in book sales or fees for articles. He deliberately set out to keep the legend and image alive in the form he wanted it.*

Then there is the observation Michael Reynolds makes in the second volume of his five-volume biography, In Hemingway: The Paris Years

> *Early in his career, Hemingway began revising and editing what would become his longest and most well-known work: the legend of his own life, where there was never a clear line between fiction and reality.*

It would not be too far-fetched to suggest that 'Papa Hemingway, the great writer', was a conscious construct, one distinct from the 'real Ernest Hemingway', and that

---

1   He did not like his given name 'Ernest' and is said to have detested being called 'Ernie', though his family, some friends and relatives did call him that.

2   Menocal and Hemingway's other rich Cuban friends were, however, appalled by how he embraced Fidel Castro and often commented that Cuba's revolution was all for the best. They themselves were forced to leave the country and were exiled abroad.

Preface

furthermore in time Hemingway lost control of that figure.[1] One psychoanalytical conclusion was that the difficulties he faced reconciling the 'real' Hemingway with the figure of the 'great writer' he had created finally overwhelmed him and contributed to his eventual mental disintegration which culminated in his suicide.[2]

I have not undertaken any original research, and the nature of what I write would seem to make it superfluous. I suspect that apart from the major biographers, neither have many of the academics and critics who have added their two ha'porth worth – an American might choose to describe it as adding their 'two cents worth' – to 'Hemingway scholarship'. In fact, it is astonishing how much they all accept as established fact much about Hemingway and his writing which is certainly contentious and, when they are not disagreeing, echo each other. All the views expressed here are my own.

---

1   See p.99ff for the conclusions of psychiatrist Irvin D. Yalom and his author and historian wife Marilyn.

2   There were certainly other factors, not least Hemingway's chronic heavy drinking and the brain damage inflicted on him in the several concussions he suffered.

THE WORK

Introduction

Tough talk is only talk, a product of Hemingway's imagined version of himself, the man he wanted to be. He went to many wars, but was never a soldier; saw many bullfights, but never killed a single bull. If he ever fathered an illegitimate child, neither mother nor child has ever pressed claims.

Michael Reynolds, Hemingway: The Homecoming.

After 1930, he just didn't have it any more. His legs began to go and his syntax became boring and the critics began to ask why he didn't put in a few subordinate clauses just to make it look good. But the bar-tenders still liked him and the tourists liked him too. He got more and more famous and the big picture magazines photographed him shooting a lion and catching a tuna and interviewing a Spanish Republican militiaman and fraternising with bullfighters and helping liberate Paris and always smiling bushily and his stuff got worse and worse. Mr Hemingway the writer was running out of gas, but no one noticed it because Mr Hemingway the celebrity was such good copy.

Dwight Macdonald, Encounter, Jan-Jun 1962.

Hemingway had come from nowhere to nascent prominence in a period defined not only by the sort of American journalism that Time [magazine] advocated, but also by the final stage of the conversion of 'readers' into 'markets'. Like cosmetics, automobiles or motion pictures, publishing was an industry whose future depended on turning out a product for mass audience. The author was part of the product, the more promotable the better.

Leonard J. Leff, Hemingway And His Conspirators.

At best, much of his life was only of passing notoriety – or so one would have thought – and yet the legend lives on, as tenacious as ever. How to account for it?

John Banville, The Nation, Oct 2017.

OH, WHAT a piece of work was Ernest Hemingway. Everywhere you land when you scour the internet, you will come across adulation of the man and his work. Dissent from such adulation and suggestions that in hindsight both Hemingway the writer and Hemingway the man were not quite the real deal are considerably rarer. Scouring the internet you will also find interpretations of his fictions, in-depth exegeses, annotations to his non-fiction and any number of commentaries, readings, learned essays and papers, dissertations, glossaries, analyses and a great many short nostalgic memoirs and blogs. The internet used-books store, Abebooks, lists almost 27,500 volumes with 'Hemingway' in the title. You will also find at least one Hemingway cookbook and a Hemingway range of furniture, Hemingway spectacle frames, Hemingway spirits (US liquors), Hemingway bedding, Hemingway sauces and Hemingway skincare. All these, though, tell us far more about the commercial world we live in, its venal pursuit of money and our unremitting desire to impress friends and neighbours than anything useful about the man and writer and his work.

The nostalgic memoirs and blogs are largely from men who are now – in 2023 – in their sixties, seventies and eighties, recalling the thrill of a moment in their salad days when they first came across the work of Hemingway and, pertinently, when his larger-than-life persona as an 'action man and writer' still commanded their innocent awe. Reading those memoirs, you begin to understand Russian novelist Vladimir Nabokov's gibe when he described Hemingway (and Joseph Conrad) as 'writers of books for boys'.[1] Nabokov had added

In neither of these two writers can I find anything that I would

---

1   Nabokov was responding to questions put to him in 1963 for a Playboy interview by the writer and 'futurist' Alvin Toffler. It was reprinted in 1990 in Strong Opinions, a collection Nabokov's views express in interviews and articles.

> *care to have written myself. In mentality and emotion, they are hopelessly juvenile . . .*

As you carry on scouring the internet, you might also – just – come across the less laudatory, more sceptical views of those who, like me, are unimpressed by Hemingway and his work, and who are bemused and baffled by the adulation. We dissenters certainly acknowledge that his, in its time unusual, style had an undoubted influence on the development of literature; but try as we might, we cannot budge from our suspicion that at the end of the day there really was less to Hemingway than his reputation would seem to promise. Perhaps those other sceptics would agree that despite the Nobel Prize For Literature, the Pulitzer Prize and, ironically, his literary influence on a new generation, Hemingway was very much 'in the first rank of the second-rate'.

. . .

That rather cutting judgment was first made by William Somerset Maugham, though he was not talking about Hemingway or anyone else but himself. Maugham was one of the few writers whose worldwide fame while he was still alive matched Hemingway's, yet he was as unalike Hemingway as it was possible to be. After studying medicine and qualifying as a doctor, Maugham had forged for himself a successful career as a novelist and playwright, but after World War I when his style of plays became unfashionable, he concentrated on writing novels and short stories. Like Hemingway, Maugham volunteered to drive Red Cross ambulances in World War I because, already 40 in 1914, he was considered to old to serve in the armed forces (and his active service with the Red Cross lasted rather longer than Hemingway's four weeks).

One essential difference between the two men – and there were many differences – was that Maugham's output in a working life of 55 years was, at 25 plays, 36 novels and 13 collections of short stories, prodigious and dwarfed that of Hemingway.[1] Another distinct difference is that Maugham seems to have been a far more self-aware, self-critical and, above all, a far more honest man than Hemingway; and although one suspects Maugham would have loved someone to have disagreed with him when he made that modest admission about his ranking as a writer, he knew it was partly true.[i]

Hemingway, on the other hand, was a mythomaniac of the first order. Even while he was still alive, he was caught out time and again telling outrageous fibs about himself, his experiences and his achievements, embellishing details of his life with stories that grew

---

1   In his 36-year career, Hemingway published just five novels, three collections of short stories, one play and two volumes of non-fiction. More work was published after he died, but some of it needed substantial editing. See p.282ff

ever more extravagant with the telling. Yet such was the heft of his personality and such was the awe with which he was regarded that his claims were accepted without question by his contemporaries. Even today many still accept various 'facts' about Hemingway's life that are fiction – that he ran away from home at the age of 14 and lived the life of hobo, that he fought bulls and had boxed professionally, that he was a womaniser, that he was an expert on food and wine, that he was an unrivalled sportsman, that he had landed on the Normandy beaches on D Day, that he 'liberated the Ritz in Paris' – the list of claims about the 'astonishing life of one of the world's greatest authors' is never ending. [ii]

One suggestion in Hemingway's defence has been that many claims he made as a very young man were told simply to amuse his friends. Yet the claims and fictions continued to be made until he died, and they all served to build up the image of a hard man he liked others to see. His left eye was not, for example, damaged in a street fight as he led people to believe: he was born with a 'bad' left eye and poor eyesight which kept him, in turn, out of the US Army, the US Navy and the US Marines when he considered trying to enlist after the US entered World War I. [iii]

. . .

Asking 'How did a middling writer achieve such global literary fame?' might seem to be provocatively contentious; but the question does neatly sum up what follows in these pages: it attempts to investigate what, for me at least, is 'truly' – one of Hemingway's favourite words – an enigma. Julian Symons, the British poet, writer and historian of crime fiction, perhaps indicated one aspect of the Hemingway enigma when he wrote that Hemingway

> *created a style but lacked suitable subjects*

and he added that Hemingway

> *had no interest in other people except so far as they affected himself, no political beliefs, little cultural background. His subject was himself and the physical actions, often including violence, that excited him.*

. . .

As I stress again and again throughout, it is important to distinguish – as every first-year philosophy student is invited to do – between 'knowledge' and 'belief' (and

Introduction

thus 'fact' and 'opinion'), and what Symons writes is simply what he believed to be true. Yet he makes a valid point: Hemingway's lifelong objection that his fiction was not autobiographical is, of course, strictly true; but 'Ernest Hemingway' in an idealised form – as the cynical, but noble Jake Barnes, the cynical but noble Frederic Henry, the expert and altruistic patriot Robert Jordan, the wise old soldier Richard Cantwell, 'the dogged old fisherman' who hunts marlin in the Gulf Stream, the painter Thomas Hudson, the writer David Bourne and in many stories as Nick Adams – is central in much of his fiction. Yes, there are exceptions, but it is difficult not to see the spirit of Hemingway in Krebs returning from war in Soldier's Home, in the man urging his partner to have an abortion in Hills Like White Elephants, the 'Mike' in Cross-Country Snow bemoaning the end of carefree bachelorhood, in Harry in The Snows Of Kilimanjaro and in Francis Macomber gunned down by his 'bitch' wife. [iv]

. . .

In today's age when being a 'celebrity' in whatever field, though usually in showbiz, film and television, is a legitimate 'career path', those under 30 might find it difficult to accept that in his day Hemingway's fame was, in the literal sense, extraordinary (as in 'extra-ordinary'). Yes, there had been celebrities throughout the ages: the violinist Paganini, who was said – probably by an astute concert promoter – to have sold his soul to the Devil, was one, as were Mozart, Liszt and Chopin; national and military heroes such as Garibaldi and Wellington were celebrities, and there were sporting heroes such as W.G. Grace and the British boxer Tom Sayers. The poet Lord Byron became a celebrity, although he was 'celebrated' as much for the scandal he created as for his poetry (and in Greece he was and is celebrated as a patriot and national hero). Later, after the 'Great War' (as then it was known) when substantial cultural and social changes were underway, stars of the silver screen such as Clara Bow, aviators such as Charles Lindburgh and sportsmen such as 'Babe' Ruth also became celebrities. But poets and novelists did not.

Certainly, to boost sales, publishers will trumpet their latest best-selling writer, and his or her name is on everyone's lips for a year or two, but their fame is restricted to those who read books. As a writer Hemingway was a notable exception: many of his contemporaries – or, as he saw them his 'rivals' – 'sold well' [1], often better than he did when he burst on to the scene; in the English-speaking world Sinclair Lewis, F. Scott Fitzgerald, Zane Grey, Booth Tarkington, John Galsworthy, Warwick Deeping, Anne Douglas Sedgwick, Thornton Wilder, Hugh Walpole, John Erskine, Kathleen Norris all

---

1   . . . and were far more prolific.

regularly made the best-sellers' list. Yet none became 'a personality' and a fixture of the news and gossip pages and eventually a star of the middle and down-market photo magazines as Hemingway did. His fame and name-recognition were unusual simply because quite soon they transcended the world of books and 'literature'. From the late 1920s until after his death in 1961, men and women who would have been hard-pressed to name just one novelist or poet had most certainly heard of Ernest Hemingway. In time Hemingway's fame became global: even in the non-English-speaking world his name became known, and pictures of the grizzled and bearded veteran 'Papa' Hemingway he became were recognisable on every continent. [1]

. . .

Hemingway's career and his first steps to becoming that famous figure worldwide began in the mid-1920s with the publication of his novel debut The Sun Also Rises. [2] After that, it was more or less a question of, metaphorically as well as literally, staying 'in the headlines', and that was the strategy he followed enthusiastically, despite his persistent pious claim that he had no interest in fame at all and only wanted to write. It was a convenient fiction he employed to bolster his status as 'a serious artist'. As Matthew J. Bruccoli observes in his introduction to Conversations With Ernest Hemingway

> *His fame was not accidentally acquired. Hemingway's greatest character was Ernest Hemingway. From boyhood he assiduously fictionalised himself. He was a dedicated careerist who skilfully nurtured an heroic public image until the vainglorious role took over the man and it became necessary for him to live up to it. The public Papa and the private writer were eventually undifferentiable.*

. . .

Hemingway had set his heart on becoming a writer in his late teens, much like many other young men and women. Initially the stories he wrote were conventional and derivative, and none of them was accepted by the magazines to whom they were

---

1   He shared that distinction with Charlie Chaplin and Vladimir Lenin, and later, Ernesto 'Che' Guevara and, courtesy of the artist Andy Warhol, the actress Marilyn Monroe.

2   Strictly speaking it was his second novel. His first longer work was a novella, The Torrents Of Spring, which he had written in under two weeks and in which he sent up the latest novel of his then friend and mentor, Sherwood Anderson.

Introduction

submitted. Then in 1922, married to a woman almost eight years older than he and newly settled in Paris, he came under the influence of the writer and poet Ezra Pound and of the wealthy art collector, some-time writer and self-declared genius Gertrude Stein. Both counted themselves firmly as 'modernists' and took Hemingway in hand to help shape his writing according to what they believed were modernist principles. Much to Hemingway's irritation Stein later even claimed [1] – after she and Hemingway had fallen out – that she had created him as a writer.

In Paris, Hemingway became well-known in the close-knit English-speaking artistic ex-patriate community which had based itself in the Montparnasse district, and he evolved into an assiduous networker [2]. Word of the young writer with a new and unusual style eventually reached the commercial publishers in New York, not least because F. Scott Fitzgerald [3], who had sought him out in Paris and – for a while – became a close friend, spread the word. One house, Boni & Liveright, after initially rejecting the work, was persuaded to publish In Our Time, a collection of his short stories [4]. Confusingly a limited edition of a slim volume of short stories also called *in our time*, though with lower case initial letters, had previously been privately published in Paris. [v] The commercial version received remarkable reviews and boosted Hemingway's profile, but it did not sell well. [5] Then after a distinctly murky to-do which involved Hemingway dashing off his short novella in just ten days, he managed to get his contract with Boni & Liveright scrapped, and he signed up with the more prestigious Charles Scribner's Sons, Fitzgerald's publishers. He remained with the house, usually referred to as Scribner's, for the rest of his life.

At Scribner's Hemingway was taken under the wing of Maxwell Perkins, the editor who had discovered and championed Fitzgerald, and who was keen to publish The Sun Also Rises. At 32, Perkins was one of the house's young Turks who had argued that Scribner's, by the 1920s widely regarded as a tad fusty and fuddy-duddy, needed authors

---

1   In her book, The Autobiography Of Alice B. Toklas. Toklas was her life-partner.

2   Hemingway was certainly acquainted with non-American and non-British writers, composers and artists, but the evidence is he spent most of his time in the company of ex-patriates and despite his later claims his command of French remained basic.

3   Fitzgerald had become very wealthy by the mid-1920s, and he and his wife Zelda moved to France, first to the South of the country, then to Paris.

4   Apparently, Boni & Liveright's readers did not think much of the work, but were persuaded to change their mind in part by Sherwood Anderson, one of the authors they published and an early Hemingway mentor who had got to know him in Chicago. Anderson just happened to be calling in on Boni & Liveright and by-the-by had inquired about the manuscript.

5   Hemingway blamed poor marketing. He might have been right: Boni & Liveright did not seem overly bothered with the collection or their new author.

such as Fitzgerald and Hemingway to attract younger readers. He had first worked Scribner's advertising department and was firmly in tune with then new marketing and advertising techniques. In preparation for the publication of The Sun Also Rises and knowing of Hemingway's fondness for hunting, fishing and bullfighting, he decided to market his new young author as a different kind of writer, an outdoors action man and the antithesis of the pale, sensitive, delicate soul buried away in solitude in a garret. The strategy worked. In her account Everybody Behaves Badly: The True Story Behind Hemingway's Masterpiece The Sun Also Rises, Lesley M.M. Blume records that

> *It quickly became apparent that the public's appetite for Hemingway [the man] was as great as that for his writing. Here was a new breed of writer – brainy yet brawny, a far cry from Proust and his dusty, sequestered ilk, or even the dandyish Fitzgerald.*

When The Sun Also Rises was published in 1926, most of the reviews were full of praise. A few were lukewarm, but that did not matter. Initial sales were not extravagant, but they were brisk and steady. Although the novel and its pre-marital sex and excessive drinking thoroughly shocked older, respectable Prohibition-era Americans, it delighted their sons and daughters. A few years earlier, younger Americans had taken their cue from F. Scott Fitzgerald's 'jazz age'. Imitating the protagonists of his debut novel, This Side Of Paradise (published in 1920) and especially those in its follow-up, The Beautiful And The Damned (1922), the young had become 'sheiks' and 'flappers' and given themselves over to illicit booze and hedonism. Now, ever keen for novelty, they had new kinds of heroes and a heroine to emulate when a few years on Hemingway created them in his novel: men and a woman who were – apparently – hard-bitten, cynical, immoral and hard-drinking. [1] Biographer Carlos Baker reports that Hemingway's Paris acquaintance and later champion Malcolm Cowley (who was living in the US once again when The Sun Also Rises was published)

> *discovered that winter that Hemingway's 'influence' was spreading far beyond the circle of those who had known him in Paris. Girls from Smith College, coming to New York, 'were modeling [sic] themselves after Lady Brett . . . Hundreds of bright young men from the Middle West were trying to be Hemingway heroes, talking in tough understatements from the one side of their mouths'.*

---

1   It is, though, certainly a moot point whether Hemingway actually and consciously intended his hero to have these attributes.

Introduction

Hemingway had arrived, but it was not just because of his new pared-back style and the 'shocking' content of his stories. The age's evolving commercial practices and social changes also played a large part. In many ways Hemingway, his persona and lifestyle made him the right man for the time. In Hemingway And His Conspirators, Leonard J. Leff sums it up

> *Hemingway had come from nowhere to nascent prominence in a period defined not only by the sort of American journalism that Time [magazine] advocated, but also by the final stage of the conversion of 'readers' into 'markets'. Like cosmetics, automobiles or motion pictures, publishing was an industry whose future depended on turning out a product for mass audience. The author was part of the product, the more promotable the better.*

As Max Perkins had realised, Hemingway was certainly 'promotable' and Hemingway knew it, too. [vi] Leff suggests that the first edition dust-jacket cover of The Sun Also Rises was carefully chosen by Scribner's to attract the young college generation: it featured a rather skimpily dressed young woman showing plenty of thigh. This appeared, note, in the somewhat puritanical America of the 1920s – and, says Leff, it

> *breathed sex yet also evoked classical Greece*

and was certainly intended to appeal to both 'lowbrows and highbrows' as Hemingway promised Max Perkins would his novel. [1] Though Hemingway ostensibly and ostentatiously eschewed the publicity game and proclaimed he wasn't interested in fame, how he reacted when he was finally able to step into the limelight told a different story. Still based in Paris, he took a keen interest in the sales figures and an active interest in the novel's marketing, supplying Perkins on request with pictures of himself and biographical details for the publicity department. To be kept informed whenever his name appeared in print, he subscribed to not one but two New York cuttings agencies. As Leonard Leff puts it

> *Again and again Hemingway professed that he hated the traffic in photographs, Book of the Month club editions, and stage or movie*

---

1   Specifically, in a letter to Perkins, Hemingway claimed his novel would be *'praised by highbrows and [could] be read by lowbrows'*. However, despite the – to my mind spurious – claims that The Sun Also Rises portrays the 'despair of a lost generation' notwithstanding, it is difficult to see what in the novel might interest 'highbrows'.

adaptations that could bring an author fame and fortune; he wrote, in other words, 'for the relief of [his] own mind and without thought of publication'. Certainly he wanted an audience to hear what he had to say about valour or love or the anatomy of fiction. And certainly he needed money to sustain the grand life he had after 1929. Beyond that, however, he radiated personality and cultivated publicity even as he pretended to scorn it. [1]

...

After The Sun Also Rises appeared in 1926, Hemingway published another collection of short stories, Men Without Women, the following year and a second novel, A Farewell To Arms, in 1929. By then he had divorced his first wife, Hadley Richardson and married his second, Pauline Pfeiffer. Both the collection of stories and the novel sold well, and consolidated his fame, especially when, in 1932, A Farewell To Arms was filmed with Gary Cooper as its hero Frederic Henry. Then, however, Hemingway's career began to stutter. To his editor Max Perkins' consternation, Hemingway insisted that his next book would be non-fiction, and in 1932 he published Death In The Afternoon, his guide to bullfighting and writing. It was followed a year later by his third – and final – collection of original short stories, Winner Take Nothing, and it did not find a great deal of favour; although sales were better than those of his bullfighting book, they were disappointing. A New York Times review of it stated that Hemingway had

> *lost something of the old urgency which impelled him to tell the world about it in good prose.*

In 1935, came a second book of non-fiction, Green Hills Of Africa, an account of going on safari in East Africa. Like the bullfighting book it, too, did not sell well, and the critics, who had expected so much from the bright new talent of the late 1920s, were at best bemused to be presented with it. Writing a few years after Green Hills Of Africa had appeared, Edmund Wilson, a one-time Hemingway champion, was scathing. He wrote

> *[Hemingway] has produced what must be one of the only books ever written which make Africa and its animals seem dull. Almost the only thing we learned about the animals is that Hemingway*

---

1 According to Leff, 'the artist' Ernest Hemingway even claimed the success of A Farewell To Arms left him '*embarrassed and uneasy and vaguely sick*'.

Introduction

wants to kill them. And as for the natives . . . the principal impression we get of them is that they were simple and inferior people who enormously admired Hemingway.

In a piece for the New York Times in July, 1999, biographer Michael Reynolds noted that

The American reading public, in the midst of the Depression, was unenthusiastic about Hemingway's non-fiction – Death In The Afternoon and Green Hills Of Africa did not sell well, barely making back the money Hemingway had received as an advance. Both books seemed a bit precious: who could afford to go to Spain for the bullfights or to Africa for a 'spot' of lion hunting?

It did not get better. By the mid-1930s, Hemingway was not only under pressure from Scribner's to submit more fiction after publishing two comparative duds, but with the US now in the depths of the Great Depression, the literary left were castigating him for not addressing social issues in his work. His reluctant response, in 1937, was To Have And Have Not, [1] but it was not quite the original work Scribner's were hoping for. Apparently out of ideas, Hemingway had cobbled the novel together from two previously published short stories and tacked on a longer third story, hoping to give the work some cohesion. It did nothing of the kind, and yet again the critics were unimpressed. The New York Times chief book reviewer, J. Donald Adams, remarked

[Hemingway] has moved steadily toward mastery of his technique, though that is by no means the perfect instrument it has been praised for being. Technique, however, is not enough to make a great writer, and that is what we have been asked to believe Mr. Hemingway was in process of becoming. The indications of such a growth are absent from this book, as they have been absent from everything Mr. Hemingway has written since A Farewell To Arms. There is evidence of no mental growth whatever; there is no better understanding of life, no increase in his power to illuminate it or even to present it. Essentially, this new novel is an empty book.

---

1 Ironically, when most people hear the title To Have And Have Not, they will recall the film of that name, nominally 'the film of the book', although the film and the novel have very little in common. The film, released in 1944 starring Humphrey Bogart and Lauren Bacall, became a classic. The novel did not.

By 1937 what might today be called 'the Hemingway brand' was sustained solely by his fame as a 'well-known' personality and memories of his past work. It was certainly not sustained by an increasingly threadbare literary reputation – but then came For Whom The Bells Toll, and it all started looking up. The novel not only made him a great deal of money, not least because three years later it was filmed with Gary Cooper and Ingrid Bergman, but it won back some, though not all, of the critics. Hemingway was riding high again.

. . .

In the public eye, though, it was now certainly 'Hemingway the personality' rather than 'Hemingway the writer' who figured. He began to feature more and more in the photo-spreads of middle-market magazines and was profiled extensively in pieces which were able to recycle all the old, usually untrue, anecdotes about him: thus the public got to know Hemingway the war hero, the bon vivant, the superb fisherman, the champion hunter, the womaniser, the hard man not averse to using his fists and the expert on more or less everything. What was less celebrated and often not even mentioned was his writing. For those who read about Hemingway in their magazine of choice – but had not necessarily read any of his work – the equation was obvious though simplistic: if Hemingway the writer was so good at all these tough-guy, manly activities, surely he must also be a great writer!

Rather to prove the point that Hemingway's literary reputation was now sustained by his celebrity status more than respect for his work was the reaction to his fourth novel which appeared ten years later. Across The River And Into The Trees, published in 1950, was a barely fictionalised fantasy about an affair between a 51-year-old former soldier – who closely resembled the 51-year-old author – and a beautiful 19-year-old Venetian aristocrat – who closely resembled a 19-year-old Italian woman the author had fallen for. It sold exceptionally well and topped the New York Times best-sellers' list for seven weeks. On the other hand it was ridiculed by the critics, upon whose judgment – for better or worse – Hemingway's literary reputation then still depended. His former confidant, the novelist John Dos Passos, was blunt and wondered in a letter to friend

> *How can a man in his senses leave such bullshit on the page?*

But Hemingway could and he had, and his literary standing slumped even further. Yet it did not in the slightest affect his public standing: Hemingway was still one of America's favourite celebrities; and he stood out because, unlike the nation's other favourite celebrities, he was not a film star or a sportsman or a politician – he was 'a writer'!

Introduction

For some critics, Hemingway's novella, The Old Man And The Sea, the last piece of original fiction he published in his lifetime, went some way towards redeeming the literary reputation he seemed to have squandered, though not for all critics. Some, perhaps tactlessly, pronounced that he was parodying himself – but then came the Nobel Prize for Literature.

Ironically, Hemingway was both pleased and a little upset by being awarded the prize. He was pleased because he had long craved it, and it confirmed his status – and self-image – as 'one of the world's greatest writers'. He was a little upset because he suspected the prize was only being awarded because the Nobel committee felt it best to do so while he was still alive: almost two years earlier while on his second East African safari he had almost died when he was involved in two plane crashes. [1] Yet for the magazine-reading public, if not for the critics, winning the Nobel Prize was further proof that Hemingway was – as some might put it today – 'the man'.

If his celebrity status had risen as his literary reputation slumped, over the next seven years it rose even higher as his physical and mental health declined. A lifetime of heavy drinking, a series of severe head injuries sustained over the years and what some think was a bi-polar condition saw him suffer ever more bouts of the deep depression that had afflicted him all his life. Finally, after two spells of psychiatric treatment which included electro-shock therapy, early on Sunday morning, July 2, 1961, just three weeks before his 62nd birthday, he stuck a shotgun in his mouth and blew off the top of his head. At first and for several years, his widow Mary Welsh – his fourth wife – insisted the death had been a tragic accident sustained while Hemingway was cleaning the shotgun. When she finally did admit that he had indeed killed himself, the public had long known it was a suicide. Their reaction was one of the final ironies of Hemingway's life: the public were disappointed that their 'celebrity', the man they had admired who had portrayed himself as strong enough to take whatever life threw at him, who had advocated stoicism, nobility and 'grace in pressure', had taken what he himself regarded as 'the coward's way out'.

. . .

A measure of Hemingway's continuing fame is that in the decades after his suicide in July 1961, Scribner's published more of his work: another two novels, two more works of non-fiction, his memoir A Moveable Feast and several repackaged collections of his fifty-odd short stories. Yet the posthumously published work, except for the memoir,

---

1   Hemingway was also worried because he believed no writer who had been awarded the Nobel Prize afterwards ever wrote anything worthwhile.

does not stand much scrutiny; despite brave claims from one or two Hemingway cheerleaders, the consensus was and is that the two novels and the non-fiction were not very good at all. To be in any shape for publication, the novels had to be drastically cut, and all four works needed substantial editing. The memoir is also problematic: it exists in two versions. The first was edited by Mary Welsh, and appeared in 1964. It was criticised because Welsh had in part excised Hemingway's glowing references to his first wife Hadley Richardson. [1] The second version was edited by his grandson, Sean, and was published in 2009. Scribner's, now owned by Simon & Schuster, also went on to publish collections of Hemingway's journalistic juvenilia – the short pieces he wrote for the Toronto Star and his later magazine work. Ironically, rather more of Hemingway's work has been published since his death than was during his lifetime; one does get the distinct impression that the publishers are trying to screw as many dollars out of the 'Ernest Hemingway' name as possible before his glory finally fades completely.

Yet that glory has not entirely faded. In the third decade of the 21st century, The Sun Also Rises, A Farewell To Arms and For Whom The Bell Tolls still enjoy steady sales, and for many Hemingway is still 'a great writer'. So if that puzzles you as it puzzles me, it is worth asking: how did that reputation come about in the first place and who decided he was 'great'? By what alchemy did the initial public celebrity transmute into exalted literary status? More broadly: how does a judgment come to be made about a writer that she or he – in this case Ernest Hemingway – is 'great'? There are further questions: if two critics disagree about 'how good' a work is, which are we to believe? Can one critic's judgment be more reliable than that of another? [2] If so, how is the 'ordinary reader' do decide which critic 'is right'?

In the first phase of Hemingway's career, roughly from 1925 until the late 1940s, he was just another, albeit increasingly famous, writer. [3] In the second, from the late 1940s until his death, the 'well-known writer' became 'an artist'. What brought about

---

1   For the rest of his life, Hemingway made no secret that he should never have separated from Richardson, and he kept in touch with her until he died. In A Moveable Feast Hemingway attempts to blame his then good friends John Dos Passos and Gerald and Sara Murphy – although they are not named in the memoir – for engineering the break-up. The impression given in the Welsh-edited version was that he was the innocent naïf in all their scheming.

2   John Banville's novel The Sea won the 2005 Booker Prize, but was also described by New York Times reviewer Michiko Kakutani as '*a stilted, claustrophobic and numbingly pretentious tale*'. So is it 'good' or 'bad'?

3   Nor was he without competition: between 1925 when Hemingway published In Our Time and 1929 when A Farewell To Arms appeared, 33 authors made it to the US best-sellers' list. Despite the commercial success of The Sun Also Rises and A Farewell To Arms, Hemingway was not one of them.

Introduction

that transmutation – the Nobel Prize nominating committee was certainly persuaded he was 'an artist', but why? We can point to one possible development which might help to explain Hemingway's promotion to that enhanced status: at the end of the 1940s academia gradually became involved; and more so than 'the critics' – academia's journeymen siblings – 'the academics' and their judgment had real clout. Yet rather than help to clarify why and how Hemingway came to be regarded as 'a great writer', we are faced with another equally intractable question: why was and is the verdict of the academic – even more so than the critic – so respected and thus influential?

...

Greg Clark was the Toronto Weekly Star features editor in 1920 when he met Hemingway. Hemingway was back from his 'war' in Europe – first driving an ambulance and then handing out cigarettes and chocolates to Italian soldiers – and had been taken on as a companion and mentor to the disabled son of a wealthy man. He lived with the family at their Toronto home for several months. His employer, Ralph Connable, who ran the F.W. Woolworth chain in Canada, knew one of the Toronto Star's executives, and following up on an introduction, Hemingway began badgering the Star for work. At the time the Weekly Star, a colourful, down-market paper which printed a great deal of fluff, relied on copy from freelancers. It paid them very little, just half a cent a word [1], but they could write about anything they liked: if the Weekly Star editor J. Herbert Cranston thought it would entertain his readers, he bought it and it was printed. [2] At their first meeting, Clark was unimpressed by the tall, dark-haired and red-cheeked young man who talked ten to the dozen about 'his experiences' in Europe, and he doubted many of them were true. By then Hemingway's 'war' had already evolved in the telling into having fought with a famed Italian regiment [3] as its youngest commissioned officer, being wounded and being decorated by the king of Italy himself. Clark, whose acquaintance with Hemingway was renewed three years later when Hemingway returned to Toronto from Paris in October 1923 as a staff reporter, had remarked after his first meetings with Hemingway on the incongruity he had noticed in the young man between a

> *quivering sensitiveness and violence.*

---

1   At $1 for 200 words, in 2023 that would be $23.69. In the US – and depending in which state you find yourself – a Starbucks grande latte will cost you between $3.61 and $4.89.

2   Hemingway's pieces ranged from how to get a free shave, the party games played by Toronto high society, the fight by department stores against shoplifters to what a newspaperman carries in his pockets.

3   This was the Arditi, a special forces troop of the then Royal Italian Army.

That strange juxtaposition of sensitivity and an interest in violence serves to highlight the many other oddities and contradictions in Hemingway's personality. His ostensible disdain for, but his assiduous pursuit of, fame was one. Equally pertinent was his lifelong practice of telling extraordinary lies about himself and his experiences while insisting that 'a writer's job is to tell the truth'. Hemingway will not have been the first dishonest writer – there will be as many dishonest writers are there are dishonest plumbers, chefs, doctors and cab drivers – and admirers would, no doubt, insist it was 'artistic truth' he was championing. Yet quite apart from the distinctly malleable nature of 'truth' and that the notion of 'artistic truth' is unhelpfully vague, we might look beyond such pseudo-metaphysics and Hemingway's hi-falutin' stance on 'truth'. We might ask ourselves whether Hemingway was even aware of the odd contradiction between the nobility of his artistic ideal and the huge lies he told about himself, his achievements and his experiences. If he was aware – and it seems safe to assume he was – here is another question: why did he tell them? Was he simply hypocritical? I suggest he was not: of all his faults recorded and listed by friends as well as his biographers, hypocrisy was not ever said to be one. I suspect the key to many of the contradictions and the other jarring aspects of Hemingway's personality was that he suffered from a deep inferiority complex. This is not a suggestion pulled out of thin air: both a school classmate with whom he fell in love – his puppy love was not reciprocated – and his first wife, Hadley Richardson, were also persuaded that Hemingway had an inferiority complex, and it would account for a great deal of his behaviour. Thus, counter-intuitively, the self-aggrandisement as, for example, promoting himself as a 'war hero' and more pertinently as 'a great writer' was not an end in itself. It was not vanity. It had a purpose: it contributed to helping him form the persona he wanted the world to acknowledge and accept, and to distract the world from the discovering the 'real' Ernest he feared he was. [vii]

Constructing a fictional version of himself began early in life and continued until the day he died. In Hemingway: The Homecoming Michael Reynolds reminds us that

> *Some in Paris thought that [Hemingway] earned side-money giving boxing lessons; others were sure he was buried four days at the front before being rescued. Several were certain he ran away from home early, spending his teen years on the road. Tough talk is only talk, a product of Hemingway's imagined version of himself, the man he wanted to be. He went to many wars, but was never a soldier; saw many bullfights, but never killed a single bull. If he ever fathered an illegitimate child, neither mother nor child has ever pressed claims.*

Introduction

The point to remember is that every one of these claims originated with Hemingway. Thus the unavoidable question is: did the ambitious young writer with a middling talent also – successfully it would seem – construct for himself the persona of 'one of America's greatest writers'?

...

Even at a distance one hears the outrage of scholars, academics and Hemingway 'aficionados' that such a suggestion is ludicrous! Well, not quite. When we look at a list of Hemingway's specific literary achievements, at how he insisted he was 'an artist' and a writer who 'worked hard' at creating serious literature, and then look at the work itself, his claims all begin to look far less convincing. His output is not just sparser than one might expect, but the quality ranges from, at best, satisfactory[1] to very poor indeed: for example, should anyone care to make a case that To Have And Have Not and For Whom The Bell Tolls are 'great literature', I would be happy to hear it; but I doubt any would seriously try and shall not be holding my breath in anticipation. This sceptic would again point out that in 35-year career Hemingway published just three collections of short stories[2], five novels, a novella and two turgid tomes of non-fiction, parts of which are so badly written that they are borderline incomprehensible. Some short stories work, some don't and one or two are awful. The novels consist of one rather sour, unromantic pot-boiler, three adventure stories and one onanistic middle-age fantasy. Finally, the novella The Old Man And The Sea: well, each to his own, but a growing consensus is that it is uncomfortably close to being sentimental twaddle and pretty much Hemingway by numbers. Shouldn't we expect rather more from a 'great writer'?

...

The outraged scholars, academics and aficionados might counter that my judgment is merely subjective. That's true and I agree – but so is their judgment. Whether you belong to those who insist Hemingway was 'a great writer' and 'a leading modernist', or whether like me you suspect he was a man of narrow talent who achieved prominence through an unusual combination of his various other gifts, an often unscrupulous ambition and the era in which he lived is neither here nor there. At the end of the day such judgments – all such judgments, whether from the private reader or from a highly respected Ivy League academic – are subjective: they cannot be objective. For example,

---

1 That is, 'middling'.
2 In total just under 60 short stories, few of which are not at all long.

when you insist that The Sun Also Rises is a 'masterpiece', I respond that irrespective of how 'different' it was and how 'modern' it seemed when it was published in 1926, a more sober assessment today would be that it is essentially a readable novel with a great deal less of the significance and profound meaning that is still attributed to it. I would point out that for a masterpiece there is a great deal of padding in the novel – why the descriptions of walking through Paris, meals taken and bus rides into the mountains?[viii] Padding, a Hemingway scholar might sniff, nonsense! Yet at the end of the day, neither or us is 'right' or 'wrong'. In such matters there can be no 'right' or 'wrong'. Thus a further, more fundamental question demands an answer: are 'objective' judgments of works of art even possible?

As for Hemingway's much-quoted 'theory of omission', even a loyalist such as Philip Young admitted there was less to it than met the eye (and certainly less than Hemingway believed). Young concedes that it amounted to little more than allowing us to 'read between the lines' and was a literary technique well known to writers long before Hemingway 'discovered' it. There might be more substance to Young's claim that Hemingway's short stories should be read as 'a whole' in order to understand what he was trying to do with the character – pretty much his alter ego – Nick Adams; but it is hard to resist responding with 'so what?' If the answer is offered 'because he was a great writer', we get our first glimpse into what seems to be a fatal circularity in the worship of Ernest Hemingway: *'This is important because it was written by Ernest Hemingway'* and *'Ernest Hemingway is important because he wrote this'*.

We might also question why Carlos Baker, Young and many other scholars feel obliged to find anything of much interest in such throwaway stories included in In Our Time as Mr And Mrs Elliot and the painfully bad A Very Short Story. As for the various dicta on writing that Hemingway laid down in Death In The Afternoon and Green Hills Of Africa, they are simply too vague to stand tall in any self-respecting intellectual discussion: what might – to paraphrase – 'truer than true' mean outside a discussion at a teenage slumber party? What keen and budding young author has not boasted – or, more modestly, told her or himself – that she or he wanted to write to convey an experience in such a way that the reader felt it had happened to her or – more likely, given Hemingway's studiedly masculine appeal – to him? What assured Hemingway – and convinced his academic champions that he had succeeded – that his readers also felt the emotion he had felt? When reading, say, his description of a bullfight or going trout-fishing, we might certainly – or, of course, not – 'feel an emotion'; but it is beyond impossible for Hemingway to know we had felt the emotion he intended us to feel or for us to know whether what we are feeling is what Hemingway had intended. Pertinently, these points are not in any way arcane, just simple observations. Ironically, they might even have raised a cheer from Hemingway himself who was – publicly at least – ostentatiously anti-intellectual. So, another question suggest itself: why does academia so wilfully and remorselessly attempt to mine every story and novel for 'meaning' and 'significance' merely because it was 'written by Hemingway'?

. . .

I have not set out to 'prove' Hemingway was merely a 'middling' and not a 'great' writer: opinions and judgments cannot be 'proved' one way or the other. We can outline – as I try to do in this book – why we believe what we believe, but it can never be a question of 'evidence' or 'proof'. Those who will insist I am 'wrong' about Hemingway, that I do not 'understand' the man and his work might point to the huge body of academic work which has gone into analysing, interpreting and evaluating his fiction. The men and women who produced that work are conventionally regarded as 'the experts' and – I might be assured – they certainly wouldn't waste their time on a writer who was merely 'middling'. I agree: they undertook and still undertake their work precisely because they believe Hemingway was 'a great writer', an outstanding 'artist' and a leading 'modernist', and, no doubt, they believe that 'he has something to tell us'. Yet the essential point is that their judgment as well as mine is subjective: they believe one thing, I believe another – there is no definitive judgment.

What we might agree on, however, is that a great deal about Hemingway – the bully loudmouth who got into fights but who was at heart said to be a generous and an essentially shy man; the reputed womaniser who quite likely didn't sleep with more than ten women in his life; the hard man who made such a fetish of portraying full-blooded machismo but who felt a kinship with lesbians and enjoyed role-reversal sex games with his wives – was certainly something of a puzzle. What do we make of the man who preached stoical resilience in life but who finally – like his father, his brother and a sister – killed himself? As biographer Jeffrey Meyers puts it in a piece he wrote for the Virginia Quarterly Review in autumn 1984:

> *In the last decades of his life, the Papa legend undermined the literary reputation and exposed the underlying fissure between the two Hemingways: the private artist and the public spectacle. When his writing slacked off and he attempted to live up to and feed on the legend, his exploits seemed increasingly empty. His shotgun blast shattered the heroic myth – and led to a different persona.*

Yet there is one aspect to Hemingway which cannot be gainsaid and which even we sceptics must concede. It is undeniable that his style did influence how some writers later chose to write; and whether or not Hemingway was 'a great writer', his name does deserve to be recorded in the history books of literature on that score.

There are thus three distinct elements to the 'Hemingway enigma': was he 'truly' [sic] a great writer? How did he achieve global fame, whether or not he was a great or merely a middling writer? And what effect did he have on all those writing in English who came after him? To a greater or lesser extent – my qualifications, literary, academic and personal are not as broad as they might be for such an undertaking – I shall attempt examine all three elements. Yet I must again stress, and shall be doing so throughout, that in these matters all judgments are subjective. Like it or not, there is not 'right' or 'wrong'.

'Truth' in Hemingway

A writer's job is to tell the truth. His standard of fidelity to the truth should be so high that his invention, out of his experience, should produce a truer account than anything factual can be.

Ernest Hemingway, introduction to Men At War.

Hemingway always embroidered the events of his life. His exaggerations, lies and heroic image were related to the traditions and myths of frontier humour that had inspired his youthful works. But he not only helped to create myths about himself, he also seemed to believe them . . . Given his predisposition to mythomania, his reluctance to disappoint either his own expectations or those of his audience, and the difficulty of refuting and verifying certain facts of his life, he felt virtually forced to invent an imaginative alternative to commonplace reality.

Jeffrey Meyers, Hemingway: A Biography, 1985.

With Hemingway there is no such thing as non-fiction; there are simply degrees of fiction, some events more fictional than others.

from Hemingway The Paris Years, by Michael Reynolds.

These memoirs [of Hemingway] allow us to trace the origin and evolution of the Hemingway legend but are a minefield rather than a path through the tangled woods of Hemingway's life. The scholar concerned with the truth finds himself lost in rumor and half-proved fact, in conflicting statements and pure fantasy. His study of these exercises in egoism requires the utmost scepticism and vigilance.

Jeffrey Meyers, Virginia Quarterly Review (VQR), Autumn 1984.

Good writing is true writing. If a man is making a story up it will be true in proportion to the amount of knowledge of life that he has and how conscientious he is; so that when he makes something up it is as it would truly be.

Ernest Hemingway, Monologue To The Maestro, Esquire, October 1835.

ANYONE familiar with Hemingway will also be familiar with what seem to be his favourite words – 'true' and 'truly'. Advising on writing, he insists that to get started on a piece of fiction

all you have to do is write one true sentence. Write the truest sentence that you know.

Yet what at first blush might seem to be a craftsman's sage and useful advice becomes less clear and less useful when you drill down even a little. What exactly is 'a true sentence'? What could it be? And what might 'the truest sentence that you know' be? You think you understand what is being said, but there again . . .

The words 'true' and 'truly' as well as 'fine' and 'good',[i] crop up time and again in Hemingway's writing and letters, and are integral to the image of the honest craftsman, the no-nonsense and experienced man-of-the-world, and, above all, the authoritative writer he wanted the world to see and no doubt as he saw himself. But anyone hoping to discover more about the man – quite apart from trying to evaluate his work – sooner or later faces the very real problem of just what to believe. Even the possible explanations for why he made fictional claims about himself and his experience confuse: the observation by James Dickey, a poet, essayist and author, is relevant here (although he was talking about poets)

The manner in which a man lies, and what he lies about – these things and the form of his lies – are the main things to investigate in a poet's life and work.

'Truth' in Hemingway

Many of Hemingway's friends testified to his mischievous sense of humour and that when strangers inquired about his life, he sometimes told tall stories as a joke. Given that some friends also insisted that despite the loud and forceful public persona Hemingway projected, he was, in fact, very shy, it is not at all impossible that this practice also functioned as a protective shield. There is a passage in Soldier's Home, one of the 'better' [1] short stories in In Our Time, in which Krebs, the central character who is finding life difficult after returning from fighting in the war, confesses

> *[he] found that to be listened to at all he had to lie and after he had done this twice he, too, had a reaction against the war and against talking about it. A distaste for everything that had happened to him in the war set in because of the lies he had told . . . His lies were quite unimportant lies and consisted in attributing to himself things other men had seen, done or heard of, and stating as facts certain apocryphal incidents familiar to all soldiers.*

It would be wisest to keep an open mind about how autobiographical the passage is, if only because we have no way of knowing; but it does add an interesting dimension to Hemingway's habit of telling tale stories. However, 'being something of a joker' cannot explain all of the instances when Hemingway 'revealed' facts about his life and experience: given the circumstances when these claims were made, they could certainly not all have been intended as 'jokes'. [2] And there seem to be no recorded instances of when Hemingway 'came clean' and admitted he had 'been joking.' So initially we can ask: just how credible – just how 'true' – were many of the hitherto accepted 'facts' of his life for which he himself was often the sole source? Given that a great many have been shown to be nonsense and that the falsehoods originated with and were perpetuated by Hemingway himself, we might then ask how the man who insisted that [3]

> *. . . a writer should be of as great probity and honesty as a priest of God. He is either honest or not, as a woman is either chaste or not, and after one piece of dishonest writing he is never the same again*

could reconcile that claim and his ostensible beliefs with his lifelong habit of telling

---

1 There, I've broken my own rule.

2 Hemingway was adept at sending up other people, often cruelly, and making them the butt a joke; but he was said to have been completely humourless when he was the butt of a joke.

3 In his introduction to, Men At War, an anthology of stories and other writing he edited.

extremely tall stories about himself?[1] A pedantic Hemingway champion might choose to argue that when Hemingway insisted on 'probity' and 'honesty' in a writer, the statement is qualified by his reference to 'dishonest writing': thus the stricture and imperative to be 'honest', it could be claimed, refer only to the man or woman 'as a writer' and to what they are writing. That is plausible enough, but Hemingway's uncompromising insistence that a writer *'is either honest or not, as a woman is either chaste or not'* [ii] does suggest he is referring to the moral qualities of the writer generally, not just what he or she produces; and if a would-be dissenter is obliged to resort to legalism to defend a hero, she or he is certainly already on the back foot.

Then there's the question: what does Hemingway actually mean by 'dishonest writing'? What might 'dishonest writing' be?[2] In his novel New Grub Street, George Gissing presents us with two writers: Edward Reardon, a novelist and a man of integrity who patently is 'suffering for his art' in that he lives in perpetual penury; and Jasper Milvain, a journalist and an 'alarmingly modern young man' who is a cynical opportunist said to despise the people he writes for. Reardon, we are led to believe, is incapable of 'dishonest writing', whereas Milvain lives a good life by producing hack journalism, surely a good example of 'dishonest writing' in anyone's book – he'll write anything for money. But if presented blind with work by both writers, would we – context apart – be able to identify what had been written by the man of integrity and what by the cynical opportunist? I doubt it. Isn't 'dishonest writing' more the kind of thing earnestly debated in a literature class rather than anything which might trouble us with insomnia?[iii] In Gissing's novel, the distinction between Reardon and Milvain is certainly not stark black and white: Reardon is something of a holy fool and in many ways Milvain is surprisingly honest, although as he is 'surprisingly honest' in admitting to his lack of scruples, his honesty is perhaps not what we are inclined to admire.

As for 'probity' and 'honesty', Hemingway certainly does not get an automatic pass. The degree of veracity of the facts of his life that Hemingway passed on might be gauged by his claim that in the early to mid-1920s in Paris he and his first wife Hadley had lived in poverty and that – presumably once he had given up his freelance work for the Toronto Star and returned to Paris to write full-time – he was often reduced to catching

---

1   Given Hemingway's complex personality, it is perfectly possible that he was able to live with, and was perhaps even unaware of, the contradiction. As I point out earlier, 'hypocrisy' is never among the faults attributed to him. He was certainly conscious of 'telling lies', but he had – as far as he was concerned – a perfectly rational explanation for why he did it.

2   That, too, might seem perfectly clear to those who declare themselves to be 'passionate about literature', but the more you examine the notion, the less clear it becomes.

pigeons in a nearby park for their supper. [1] This could well also have been a joke and, at a very narrow pinch, might even have been true: if Hadley's trust fund cheque was late, Hemingway was obliged to borrow money from friends. [2] But as Harold Loeb – Robert Cohn of The Sun Also Rises – points out, the problems presented by trying to catch pigeons in a public park make it very unlikely indeed that Hemingway ever attempted it, [3] and he and Hadley were never in any danger of starving. That colourful claim is far more likely to be just another piece of Hemingway myth-making, another pillar to support the Hemingway legend. As Loeb points out in his essay Hemingway's Bitterness [4]

> *Actually, Hemingway was not as poor, in my opinion, as he makes himself out to be in A Moveable Feast. . . For Hem in those days did not stint himself except in the matter of clothes. On one occasion he bought and paid for a Miro, and on many others we drank Pouilly Fuisse and ate oysters, Portugaises when we felt poor, Marennes when we were flush. Hem always paid for his share or tried to. Pouilly Fuisse is a costly wine and French oysters even then were more expensive than their American counterparts.*

In fairness, Loeb wrote his essay – which might well have been called 'Loeb's Bitterness' – 40 years after The Sun Also Rises had appeared in which he was made to look very silly, and he was still upset by that portrayal; and Hemingway paid for the Miro in instalments, though again the matter is not quite straightforward. Ostensibly he bought the painting, The Farm, as a birthday present for his wife Hadley, but when they split up, he somehow managed to keep it in his possession. When many years later she eventually asked him to return it, he simply refused, and the painting remained prominently displayed at

---

1   It is tempting to accept that Hemingway 'the dedicated artist' gave up his salaried job on the daily Toronto Star because he was keen to devote himself full-time to his writing. As I recount later, the truth was more prosaic; briefly his short tenure on staff at the paper – just over two months – was not a success, and de facto he was demoted to the weekly Star after falling out with his boss several times. See p.331ff.

2   There were also problems in the mid-1920s when the husband of one of Hadley's close friends who had been entrusted to look after the trust fund invested in stock which promptly fell in price and, far more seriously, apparently embezzled a substantial proportion of the fund.

3   He claims he waited until the gendarme on duty in the park had retired to a cafe for a glass of wine and then attracted the pigeons by scattering corn he had brought with him, caught one and wrung its neck, then hid the body among the blankets in his son Bumby's pram.

4   It appeared in the Connecticut Review, 1967. Loeb was certainly not poor: he was born into a wealthy New York family, his father was an investment banker with his own firm and Peggy Guggenheim was a cousin.

his Finca Vigia home on the outskirts of Havana in Cuba. [1] As for Hemingway being reduced to catching pigeons for his and Hadley's supper, Loeb also observes

> *I do not know why Hemingway told [early biographer and friend A.E. Hotchner] he was so poor that he often fed the family on pigeons captured in the park. I don't know why Hotchner relates the story as if it were true. With corn or bread for bait and tremendous patience, it might be possible now and again to grab and hold a city pigeon. But then to wring its neck and kill it in the Luxembourg Gardens with hundreds of people walking around, and to do this repeatedly without being noticed seems to me quite incredible.*

In fact, during his first years in Paris, from December 1921 until September 1923, when he was still selling stories to the Star, [2] the bulk of the household income came from Hadley's trust fund that paid around $3,500 to $4,000 a month. Taking inflation into account, that sum would (in 2023) be roughly the equivalent of between $59,565 and $68,074. [iv] Given the extremely attractive exchange rate of the franc to the dollar at the time – which Hemingway wrote about in one of his earliest submissions to the Weekly Star from Paris – that was more than enough on which a newly-married, childless couple could live comfortably. [3] In fact, it is by no means unlikely that when Ernest, an ambitious would-be writer in his early 20s, and Hadley, almost nine years older, decided to marry and move to Europe, it was the prospect of having a reliable and regular income from her trust fund which will have made their plans seem feasible. [4]

Hemingway's practice of inventing facts about his past made the task facing his biographers difficult. At first, Philip Young and particularly A.E. Hotchner, who came to fulfil the role of Hemingway's amanuensis and general dogsbody, accepted at face value what the writer told them, questioned none of it and repeated it all as true. In his somewhat adoring book The Art Of Ernest Hemingway, published in 1952, the British writer John Atkins even repeats the 'facts' that while living in Oak Park Hemingway twice ran away from home and that in World War II Hemingway had performed 'valuable' war work for the US navy hunting down German submarines off the coast of Cuba. In

---

1   It is now on display at the National Gallery of Art, Washington.

2   Contrary to the assumption of many, he was never on staff in Paris.

3   The dollar/franc exchange rate was so favourable for Americans and British that throughout the 1920s tens of thousands went to live in Paris and the South of France, their often modest income going a great deal further than it would back home.

4   The young couple had initially intended to move to Naples and only changed their minds when the novelist Sherwood Anderson persuaded them that Paris was where artistically it was all happening.

fact, he never ran away from home, and when in the early 1940s he persuaded the US ambassador in Havana, Spruille Braden, to back his 'submarine hunting', scheme, it is now accepted it was as much a ruse to obtain rationed diesel so he could carry on marlin fishing, although we cannot safely deny that Hemingway was not partly motivated by patriotism. [1] Pertinently, Atkins submitted his manuscript to Hemingway for approval before publishing his book, and unsurprisingly it passed muster. Equally pertinently, it would have been odd in the 1940s and 1950s while Hemingway was already celebrated as 'a great writer' to have questioned, seemingly gratuitously, whether 'Hemingway is telling the truth'.

When as Hemingway's nominated biographer Carlos Baker began researching the writer's life in 1962, he soon came across many inconsistencies in Hemingway's claims; but although Baker was certainly not as uncritical as Young, Hotchner and Atkins, he had to tread carefully. When further biographies began to appear in the mid-1980s – Mary Welsh, who jealously tended the 'Papa' flame, had by then died – their authors were far more sceptical. Michael Reynolds, for example, made a point (he informs us in his introduction to his second volume, Hemingway: The Paris Years) of not including any of the accepted 'facts' about Hemingway that he could not himself verify. One example he gives is that Hemingway claimed he rented a garret room in which to write in a hotel in the rue Descartes (where, Hemingway claimed, the poet Verlaine had died). Hemingway might well have rented the room, says Reynolds, but he could find not a single piece of independent verification for the claim and concludes it was possibly just another piece of Hemingway's perpetual legend-building.

If Hemingway did rent that room, [v] it would have been during his first stay Paris, because the claim is hard to reconcile with another account he gives that to keep warm – another hint that he and Hadley were 'living on the breadline' – he either stayed in bed to write or composed his stories in cafés and had to nurse a cup of coffee for hours [2] because he was short of money. Whatever is true or not, all three accounts help to burnish the image of Hemingway liked to promote of himself as the 'dedicated

---

1   His then wife Martha Gellhorn was convinced that was the only reason, but by then she was not unbiased. According to Ken Burns' and Lynn Novick's 2021 documentary Hemingway, his supply of diesel was 'unlimited', so it would seem Ambassador Braden believed Hemingway *was* doing useful war work.

2   While sitting at his table, he says, he resented the attention of friends and acquaintances who approached him while he was working – it 'bitched' his writing, he said. This image of 'the artist at work' in public for the world to view (and possibly admire) does, though, unfortunately recall the early short piece Hemingway wrote for the Weekly Star in which he scorned those 'bluffers and fakers' in Montparnasse who swanned around posing as artists. His gibe does come dangerously close to the pot calling the kettle black.

young writer' whose sole concern was the quality of his art and who 'worked hard' doing 'difficult work'; but these various accounts do somehow begin to mock Hemingway's pious and pompous insistence on a writer's necessary priest-like 'probity and honesty'.

. . .

As for the myth-making, it is certainly plausible that as a teenager known for his outgoing and gregarious nature Hemingway made up stories simply to entertain his friends. Yet from an early age he also seems to have intended his tales to be believed; and although that practice might be understandable in a lad in his pre-pubescent and early teenage years, as he grew older Hemingway's habit of making bizarre and quite startling claims – that in Spain he had been part of a Loyalist death squad which killed more than 100 Falangists in a mass execution and that in World War II he had flown a Hurricane fighter in missions for the British RAF [vi] – became ever more disconcerting for those who knew him and knew the stories to be wholly untrue. [vii] Even as a very young man, he lied to the British officer Eric 'Chink' Dorman-Smith, who was to become a lifelong friend and who had been wounded in World War I. They met in Milan while Hemingway was recovering from being blown up by a mortar just before his 19th birthday in July 1918. When Dorman-Smith, who had been 'mentioned in dispatches' three time and was awarded the Military Cross and Bar in 1915 for bravery under fire, asked his new young acquaintance how he had been wounded, Hemingway informed him he had been fighting with the Italian Arditi [1] troops and had been the youngest officer to lead one of its battalions into battle. The wonder is not just that Hemingway would dare tell such a blatant lie to a man already honoured for his bravery, but that Dorman-Smith, who was no fool, believed him, never seems to have questioned such an unlikely story and apparently carried on believing the claim until Hemingway's death. Perhaps he simply liked Hemingway and his company so much that he chose not to confront him about the untruth.

Although Hemingway never stopped telling outright and outrageous lies about himself, his life and his experiences until he died, a charitable explanation might be that this tendency was exacerbated by his heavy drinking which became alcoholism and, in his last 15 years, as his mental health deteriorated badly. By most accounts, from the early 1940s on he was rarely sober except for brief interludes in the 1950s when obeying doctors' orders to try to bring down his very high blood pressure, he restricted himself

---

1   Italian Army 'shock' troops whose units were formed in 1917 to be deployed when fighting had reached a stalemate.

to just one glass of whisky and one glass of wine at supper.[1] But inevitably he was soon back off the wagon, mainly because such comparative sobriety made him morose and life dull.

The central question is, though: does any of this matter? And of course it does not matter at all – who cares whether Hemingway, still regarded by many as a writer of genius, told lie upon lie about himself and his experiences? It might have some bearing upon Hemingway the man, but it has – and can have – no bearing upon Hemingway the writer and, crucially, the work he produced. A composer might be a rapist, but his talent neither excuses his crime and nor do his crimes diminish the quality of his music: the two are separate and distinct. Yet there is something disconcerting that a man who time and again insisted on 'truth' in fiction and, pertinently, on 'probity' and 'honesty' in writers played fast and loose with truth in real life.

What is almost certain is that Hemingway was well aware that the claims he made about himself and his experiences were nonsense. In her book The Mystery Of The Ritz-Hotel Papers, Jacqueline Tavernier-Courbin quotes Hemingway as saying that

> *It's not unnatural that the best writers are liars. A major part of the trade is to lie or invent and they will lie when they are drunk, or to themselves, or to strangers. They often lie unconsciously and then remember their lies with deep remorse. If they knew all other writers were liars too, it would cheer them up . . . A liar in full flower . . . is as beautiful as cherry trees, or apple trees, when they are in blossom. Who should ever discourage a liar?*

Quite apart from Hemingway's conceit in tacitly and without a second thought ranking himself among 'the best writers', what he writes is, at best, disingenuous and, at worst, very confused and misleading.[2] The 'lying' he is describing is not what might be regarded as good-natured blarney exchanged by writers 'off-duty', intended to amuse and entertain each other and which assumes no one will take it seriously. Hemingway is taking it far further than that: he is amalgamating the 'writer as man or woman' and 'the writer as artist' and pronouncing that the dishonesty of their private lives is not just 'part' of their 'trade' as a writer, but a 'major' part of it, presumably – or so it reads – *sine qua non*. This is taproom blather and certainly unworthy of a 'great writer'. If

---

1 Although while in Europe ostensibly covering the progress of World War II after D Day he – and, it seems, everyone else – drank a great deal, the story that when 'in the field' attached to the 22nd Infantry Regiment, part of the 4th Division, he carried a canteen of gin and another of vermouth is untrue and, unusually, did not originate with Hemingway, who condemned it as rubbish.

2 His confident claim that 'all other' writers are liars is also at the very least questionable.

'the best writers are liars', how did Hemingway square that with insisting they should possess a priest-like 'probity and honesty'. He can't, of course, and frankly the error is ours for even bothering to give Hemingway the benefit of doubt and taking either pronouncement seriously. As for conflating 'lying' with 'invention', that, too, is at best, disingenuous and, at worst, nonsense: 'invention' is certainly essential to 'lying', but they are not, as Hemingway seems to suggest, identical. Here we might remind ourselves of the distinction between Greeks and Athenians. Furthermore, any instance where an individual is both an habitual liar and is also 'a writer' would be wholly coincidental: to suggest there is a causal relationship, as Hemingway does, would be unworthy of a fifth-former or a sophomore, let alone a 'great writer'.

In fact, Tavernier-Courbin's version might not be quite what Hemingway wrote; perhaps he wrote two versions or both are derived from an original, but were variously edited. Item 845 in the JFK Library Hemingway Collection in Boston is a scrap of paper in Hemingway's writing – but which otherwise remains unidentified – in which the writer claims that

> *It's not unnatural that the best writers are liars. A major part of the trade is to lie or invent and they will lie when they are drunk, or to themselves, or to strangers. They often lie unconsciously and then remember their lies with deep remorse. If they knew all other writers were liars too, it would cheer them up. . . Lying when drinking is a good exercise for their powers of invention and is very helpful in the making up of a story. It is no more wicked or reprehensible in a writer than it is to have strange and marvellous [sic] experiences in his dreams. Lying to themselves is harmful but this is cleansed away by the writing of a true [sic] book which in its invention is truer than any true thing that ever happened.*

The varied wording of the passage does cast part of what Hemingway suggests in a slightly different light; and he makes a fair point that alcohol – and presumably other drugs – can spark a writer's imagination. But he is again wholly disingenuous, not to say downright facile, by equating lying, by implication, with writing and creating of fiction. Both 'lying' and 'creating fiction' certainly involve 'invention' and – depending upon what a writer is attempting – might even include 'deception' in one form or another. [viii] But there the similarity ends. Central to the concept of 'lying' and telling a lie is not just that the 'liar' is fully aware of telling an untruth, but that his or her essential intention is to deceive; and it is usually for his or her own benefit, although there might well be circumstances where a lie is told for acceptable reasons. [1] Are Hemingway champions content to accept a bargain-basement analysis of the nature and art of 'writing' and 'creating fiction' that both can be equated with 'lying'? Might not a 'great writer' be expected to produce a more intellectually sophisticated, not to say more intellectually coherent, account of what she or he does? As for Hemingway's quasi-religious and distinctly odd claim that, in a sense, a writer's soul can be shriven

> *by the writing of a true book which in its invention is truer than any true thing that ever happened*

we might care to remind ourselves of the well-established, though disconcerting, truth that 'one man's profound insight is another man's sentimental twaddle'.

We don't know the circumstances of when, where or why the excerpt quoted by Tavernier-Courbin was written, [ix] but it does sound as though Hemingway, aware of his incessant fibbing and the danger that at any point each fib might be revealed, was attempting to ease himself off a hook and trying to justify why he told his lies. But it will not wash: those telling lies are certainly creating fiction, but those creating fiction are not 'lying' in any sense in which the word is customarily used; and crucially Hemingway was certainly bright enough to know the difference and that it was nonsense. Furthermore, by making his claim, he was, ironically, being dishonest.

. . .

Modesty, humility and, frankly, honesty, were never Hemingway traits, despite his pious pronouncement in 1942 in his preface to Men At War, an anthology of 'war writing' he edited. In the introduction he insisted that it was

> *A writer's job is to tell the truth. His standard of fidelity to the truth should be so high that his invention, out of his experience, should produce a truer account than anything factual can be. For facts can be observed badly; but when a good writer is creating something, he has time and scope to make of it an absolute truth.* [2]

Here Hemingway does touch upon a quirk of art: that a skilful writer's portrayal 'of

---

1 A captured soldier lying to his captors about his unit's location, for example, to thwart them, to save lives and to deny the enemy an advantage might be an 'admirable reason' for lying.

2 Facts can also 'be observed well', and however much 'time and scope' a writer has, that is no guarantee of the worth of the 'absolute truth' he or she believes they are expressing.

reality' seems sometimes able to transcend the 'worldly reality' it is portraying: what in our day-to-day existence is distressingly mundane can with the application of a writer's alchemy gain in colour, excitement and 'meaning', such that 'reality' seems somehow to be heightened. However, 'seems' is here the operative – and the crucial – word: the heightened 'reality' is illusory and an ephemeral impression; and why does Hemingway drag in the notion of 'absolute truth', and what does he mean by it? What is an 'absolute truth'?

. . .

As I point out above, some might argue that the 'truth' to which Hemingway alludes and insists it is a writer's duty to tell is 'artistic truth'; that the 'truths' a writer attempts to convey are intended to get to the 'essence of reality' (and, I don't doubt, 'describe the human condition'). [x] Such an explanation is plausible and many would insist they thus 'understand' what Hemingway means by 'absolute truth'; but it is distinctly and unhelpfully murky. Just how clear the notion is and how well it is 'understood' would soon become apparent if those who insisted that they did 'understand' it were asked to elucidate for the rest of us who are still in the dark. It might then become obvious that we are dealing with something more akin to woolly sentiment than intellect, with a jejeune airiness which would be more at home in a long-winded, early 19th-century German Romantic treatise on art, philosophy and poetry; and when you start dealing in such, inconveniently vague, metaphysical notions – though many delight in doing so – you are certainly in danger of slipping into talking blank nonsense. [1] In one respect, the essential problem is that many will continue to insist that they do 'understand' that blank nonsense. [xi]

. . .

Put aside for a moment any investigation into what 'truth' might be: perhaps we should ask the obvious question, one which seems never to be asked: why is it 'a writer's job to tell the truth'? The question might then swiftly – and brutally – be followed by 'and says who? Who is it laying down the law on the matter, and how is he or she qualified to

---

1   . . . as I have discovered repeatedly when reading commentaries, interpretations and analyses of Hemingway's work.

'Truth' in Hemingway

do so?' [1] Does 'a writer' even have 'a job', a specific purpose and particular obligations and duties? [xii]

If – as we might possibly interpret Aristotle in his Nicomachean Ethics – a 'brave man' is only 'brave' if he does 'brave' things, there would seem to be just one sole obligation 'a writer' has, just one thing he or she must do to qualify as 'a writer': write. No writing, no writer. It doesn't even matter what she or he writes, or how 'well' or 'badly' she or he writes it, how engaging or interesting or stimulating the work is; and it would seem that apart from doing 'the writing' – getting it down on paper [2] – there are no other rules. In fact, frankly, even that is not 'a rule'; there are no 'rules' – a writer is free to write about what she or he likes and in whatever manner or style she or he chooses. Whether or not our writer would find readers interested in, and engaged by, what she or he has written is another, but entirely unrelated, matter. Thus Hemingway had a very narrow view indeed of what 'a writer should do' and what might constitute 'good writing' and 'literature'. [xiii] And for him to pronounce on writing (as he does notably in Death In The Afternoon and Green Hills Of Africa) after having published just two novels and two collections of short stories is unashamed arrogance. [3] We can all have views on what we believe are 'good writing' and 'literature', but Hemingway went far beyond 'having a view', and he was more than happy to 'lay down the law' *de haut en bas*.

Yet the tricky question of what constitutes 'the truth' will not go way.

. . .

'The truth' is another of those slippery notions that we all think we understand until we examine our 'understanding' of it and are reduced to conceding that it is not quite straightforward. 'Understanding' the 'truth' and what could be meant by 'truth' becomes more like staring into thick fog than admiring the view on a sunny day. For example,

---

1   If the response is '*Hemingway, that's who! And as he was one of our greatest writers, we can accept he knew what he was talking about!*' we have already trapped ourselves in the circular argument I deal with in a later chapter. Essentially, that argument boils down to '*Ernest Hemingway was a great writer because he wrote this*' and '*this is a great piece of literature because it was written by Ernest Hemingway*' and so on.

2   . . . and completing it! Arguably a mediocre but completed work deserves more praise than an unfinished 'potential masterpiece'. We might appreciate the work done so far, but – well, it wasn't finished.

3   It would have helped if Hemingway had been a little more self-critical: reviewing Death In The Afternoon for the New York Times, R.L. Duffus wrote: '*In this book Mr Hemingway is guilty of the grievous sin of writing sentences which have to be read two or three times before the meaning is clear. He enters, indeed, into a stylistic phase which corresponds, for his method, to the later stages of Henry James.*' The comparison with James was not intended as a compliment.

what are we to make of the distinction between 'subjective truth' and 'objective truth'? Hemingway might certainly have been aware of that distinction, as the philosophical debate on the difference had long been underway when he began his writing career. The Danish philosopher Søren Kierkegaard insisted that some truths – 'subjective truths' – were personal, but no less 'true' for that. So what was the 'truth' Hemingway was talking about? One suspects it cannot be 'subjective truth': it is difficult to see how such a 'subjective' or a 'personal' truth could be 'shared', except in the limited sense of the writer telling the reader 'this is what I think' or 'this is what I have experienced'; but that is not what we here might understand by 'sharing'. Hemingway regards the 'truths' he is dealing with as 'universal' and true for all, and thus what Kierkegaard might have regarded as 'objective truth'; the idea of a writer sharing his universal 'truths' with his reader seems central to what Hemingway insisted was a 'writer's job'. In fact, Hemingway, the lifelong and self-appointed didact would have had it no other way. Yet implicit in the notion of subjective truth is that it is unique to me, that 'this is my view, my truth': it might well also be 'your view, your truth' and we might find ourselves subscribing to the same 'subjective truth'. But each of us 'having' the same 'subjective truth' means no more than that: it has no bearing at all on the particular 'truth' being discussed, and it certainly does not make that truth 'universal' – true for all of us – or 'objective' as I suspect Hemingway would have liked it. There also the question of why Hemingway was so convinced that his 'truth' was preferable – he might even couch it as 'truer' however silly that sounds – to the 'truths' of others? Would Swift's Gulliver's Travels, Lewis Carroll's Alice In Wonderland, H.G. Wells' The Time Machine and George Orwell's Animal Farm be considered 'true writing' by Hemingway?[1] They might pass muster with those who insist on 'artistic truth', but frankly who knows? One could argue that the 'truths' of some 'fantasies' (such as those works by Swift, Carroll, Wells and Orwell) 'ring true' because we recognise in them the kind of human behaviour we encounter in our own lives.

In fact, I'm now the one being disingenuous: the question is irrelevant, because – in my view – Hemingway's strictures on 'truth' are themselves irrelevant. What matters is what a writer produces: if it 'works', it 'works', if it doesn't, it doesn't, whether or not she or he has observed contemporary conventions or instead tried something very different. Unhelpfully, of course, what 'works' for one reader might well not 'work' for another; and what 'worked' 50 years ago might not really 'work' today – but it might well again

---

[1] I have chosen novels which many might in 2023 accept as 'classics'. There could be many other choices. All four novels might certainly be thought as trying to convey 'the truth' about human behaviour, but frankly the debate about whether this or that novel is 'true' and would pass the 'Hemingway Test' is uncomfortably close to arguing how many angels might fit on a pinhead.

'Truth' in Hemingway

'work' when a writer is 're-discovered' and back in fashion. [1] Yes, it's all that simple. And throughout the above I have taken care to try to side-step the intellectual snobbery of those who choose to rule on what 'is literature' and what 'is not literature', and for whom what 'is not literature' is not even worth considering in any serious sense.

We might, in fact, be bending over too far backwards to accommodate Hemingway's 'thought' and those who champion him as 'a great writer'. If we invoke Occam's Razor – or Occam's Law or Principle of Parsimony, which could be summed up as *in doubt the simplest explanation is probably the most likely* – when we discuss the 'problems' Hemingway's writing throws up, it might just boil down to concluding that Hemingway and his thinking and dicta on 'truth' and 'true writing' are not 'problematic' at all, but simply not a little muddled. [xiv] I suspect that intellectually Hemingway never progressed much beyond the thoughts and insights of that lad who was banging away on his typewriter in a rented room in Petoskey in northern Michigan in 1919. When he suggested that

> *All good books are alike in that they are truer than if they had really happened and after you are finished reading one you will feel that all that happened to you and afterwards it all belongs to you: the good and the bad, the ecstasy, the remorse and sorrow, the people and the places and how the weather was.* [2]

he's right that 'the best' writing does move us and can remain with us for many years; but it is hard not to hear the adolescent blathering of a lad in the romantic throes of young ambition. Hemingway might also have cared to comment upon why decades later sometimes re-reading a 'good book' which once so moved us often disconcertingly fails to live up to the magic in our memory. [xv]

Many might insist that 'they know what Hemingway is talking about', but their certainties would swiftly dissipate when they are asked to explain it for the benefit of those of us who are not quite as confident. As for 'truth', two hoary but useful examples will illuminate why the notion is anything but as straightforward as Hemingway seems to believe and imply: when is a 'noble freedom fighter' nothing but a 'filthy terrorist'?

---

1   Ironically, after J.S. Bach died in 1750 and in view the style of what younger composers were producing, for several years his work was regarded as a little old hat. It wasn't until the early 19th century that his work came to be performed again.

2   I hope I am not being too prissy when I suggest that this might have been expressed with rather more clarity – '. . . *after you are finished reading [a good book] you will feel that all that happened to you and afterwards it all belongs to you . . .*' does not strike me as being written by anyone at the top of his or her game. An additional comma here and there might have helped.

Is it 'true' that 'capitalism consists of nothing but a gang of uncaring, greedy bastards feathering their nests' or, conversely, is it 'true' that 'if it were not for capitalism, the global economy would grind to a halt and many would starve'? Discuss (though preferably once I've made myself scarce and found something more interesting to do than listen to the ensuing discussion).

So what is Hemingway's 'truth'? What is the 'truth' it is a writer's job to tell? In *A Moveable Feast*, Hemingway told us that he overcame a bout of writer's block by reminding himself that all he had to do was to *'write one true sentence. Write the truest sentence that you know'*. Here again we are back in the realm of sentiment and not of intellect [xvi]. As practical advice what Hemingway advocates is hardly useful; [1] as a cosy thought with which young would-be famous writers might console themselves, it might at least do the trick.

---

1   Far more helpful advice would be simply *'write something – anything – it doesn't matter what. What is important is to get started and do the work!'* Less welcome advice would be the hard 'truth' that *'if you can't even get started, you've got even less of a chance of finishing'* (to which one might add the even more useful, but certainly even less welcome, advice *'so stop fooling yourself'*).

Subjectivity: is objective judgment possible?

'[Critics] have neither wigs nor outriders. They differ in no way from other people if one sees them in the flesh. Yet these insignificant fellow creatures have only to shut themselves up in a room, dip a pen in the ink, and call themselves 'we', for the rest of us to believe that they are somehow exalted, inspired, infallible.

**Virginia Woolf, from An Essay In Criticism,
New York Herald Tribune, Oct 9, 1927.**

'[Critics are] lice who crawl on literature.'

Hemingway in Green Hills Of Africa, 1935.

WHEN discussing how Hemingway came to be regarded as a 'great writer', it would be useful to consider the credentials of those who were responsible for elevating him to that status. That elevation was, of course, a gradual process and not one without its reverses, though for many the decision of the Nobel Prize Committee to award him their Prize for Literature in 1954 will have helped to settle the matter. Initially it was 'the critics' who hoisted Hemingway to high status, and once they had lost faith, 'the academics' took over and sanctified 'Papa'.

Hemingway seems early on, after the success of his first two novels, to have regarded himself as a 'good writer', possibly a 'great writer'; but despite the public celebrity he had achieved by 1930, by the middle of the decade many of the critics, increasingly unimpressed with the new work he had been publishing, were becoming ever more sceptical about the bright young writer they had once cheered. [1] Until the late 1940s, it was their word that counted in 'literary circles', and crucially academia, which later played such the vital role in his elevation, was not yet involved; but when it eventually was, the game changed substantially: with the blessing of the academics – and the plethora of studies and papers they began to publish – Hemingway crossed the threshold into the sanctum of 'the greats'. [2]

I have already conceded – and I expect those who disagree with me to be as honest and to do the same – that my opinion of Hemingway's work is subjective; but then so is that of the critics and, no less, that of the academics. However, as Virginia Woolf points out in An Essay In Criticism, the 'ordinary' reader has on oddly dog-in-the-manger attitude to 'the critics' (and, although Woolf doesn't say so, by extension to the academics). In her essay, which was part of her review for the New York Herald Tribune [3] of Hemingway's second volume of short stories, Men Without Women, she is scathing about both 'the critics' and the rather credulous reader. Some commentators believe that in what Woolf writes she intended to highlight a difficulty perpetually faced by literary critics. Their difficulty, they suggest, is that whereas the ordinary reader has all the time in the world to reach a judgment of the 'worth' of a new novel or a volume of short stories, the critic – 'pity the poor critic' they claim Woolf implies – must make up his or her mind more or less immediately and then announce their conclusion to the public. This is surely a wilful misreading of what Woolf writes – she is very clear on the matter. Her essay begins:

> *Human credulity* [4] *is indeed wonderful. There may be good reasons for believing in a King or a Judge or a Lord Mayor. When we see them go sweeping by in their robes and their wigs, with their heralds and their outriders, our knees begin to shake and our looks to falter. But what reason there is for believing in critics it is impossible to say. They have neither wigs nor outriders. They differ*

---

1   Reviewing To Have And Have Not (published in 1937) J. Donald Adams of the New York Times declared simply that '*Mr Hemingway's record as a creative writer would be stronger if it had never been published*'.

2   What is notable is that even the two novels which the critics thought were awful – To Have And Have Not and Across The River And Into The Trees – sold very well. What had persuaded the 'ordinary' readers to buy a copy of those novels cannot realistically be established: was it word of mouth, was it because each was 'the new novel by the famous Ernest Hemingway', was it simply 'to keep up with the Joneses'? We don't know.

3   It appeared on October 9, 1927,

4   Credulity is not the most admirable of human traits – Woolf is not patting the reader on the back.

Subjectivity: is objective judgment possible?

> *in no way from other people if one sees them in the flesh. Yet these insignificant fellow creatures have only to shut themselves up in a room, dip a pen in the ink, and call themselves 'we', for the rest of us to believe that they are somehow exalted, inspired, infallible. Wigs grow on their heads. Robes cover their limbs. No greater miracle was ever performed by the power of human credulity. And, like most miracles, this one, too, has had a weakening effect upon the mind of the believer. He begins to think that critics, because they call themselves so, must be right. He begins to suppose that something actually happens to a book when it has been praised or denounced in print. He begins to doubt and conceal his own sensitive, hesitating apprehensions when they conflict with the critics' decrees.* [1]

If not entirely letting the critics off the hook, Woolf could, perhaps, be understood as explaining why later, more considered, readings of a work by other critics have shown earlier judgments to have been all at sea. 'In the heat of the moment,' a critic might plead, 'under pressure and faced with a deadline, we can't always be expected to get it right.' That explanation is certainly plausible, but it doesn't quite match the tone of what else Woolf has to say: mocking the critics as 'somehow exalted, inspired, infallible' does not speak of Woolf respecting them much and charitably cutting them a little slack. That explanation also implies that there is a 'correct' judgment, one that most competent critics would, if given enough time, independently reach. But if, as I contend, all judgments are subjective, it is from the outset nonsense to talk of a 'right' and 'wrong' reading or judgment. [i]

In fact, what Woolf writes can be interpreted in a very different way, one far less flattering to the critics and their senior cousins, the school and college English department academics who – tacitly – choose to lay down the law on the worth of this or that writer. And Woolf is equally unimpressed by the general reader who, she implies, is too willing meekly to set aside his or her own judgment and accept that of the critics, as well as the critics' own estimation of themselves as 'exalted, inspired and infallible'.

. . .

However one chooses to read Woolf, given the often divergent verdicts of critics,

---

1   Woolf's essay can be found in an appendix at the end of this book.

it would seem impossible that an 'objective' evaluation of a literary work is feasible: against what might it be measured except other works? And what would qualify those other works – or just one of them – to be 'the norm/the yardstick'? No doubt those unwilling to concede the contention that objectivity is a chimera will engage in all kinds of intellectual gymnastics – for example, coming up with various definition of what we can mean by 'objective' – to 'prove' that 'objective judgment' is indeed possible. Yet, the inconvenient fact is that there is no yardstick, no Archimedean fixed point, which would allow us to evaluate works objectively. [ii] Thus on the back foot, some might argue that, in a sense, 'objectivity' – or something that might be accepted as 'a kind of objectivity' – is still possible: that the – 'admittedly subjective' – judgments and opinions of some deserve to be 'taken more seriously' than those of others and that they should 'carry more weight'. Such advocates might point out that in the literary world, critics, academics, publishers' editors and writers themselves will be better – as in more widely – read and should thus be regarded as having a broader literary hinterland; this broader literary knowledge enables them, they might argue, to evaluate the scores and flaws of different works, and because of that wider experience, those critics, academics, publishers' editors and writers would be more likely to recognise the qualities of 'good writing' sooner than might we ordinary joes. Well, to quote Hemingway, 'isn't it pretty to think so'. As arguments go, it's respectable enough, but it fails immediately: their judgments would still be subjective. As with the 'is/ought gap' in moral philosophy highlighted by David Hume, there is no – simply because there cannot be – convenient bridge from 'subjective' to 'objective' judgment, one which allows the first to transmute into the second and where 'an opinion' can thus become 'a fact'. Even if one thousand critics agree with one another on the worth of a work, all we know – and all we *can* know – is that one thousand critics have agreed: the instance of 'a consensus' means – no less and certainly no more – than that 'there is a consensus'; it might persuade more to read a book, but it most certainly does not and cannot mean that a work of art universally regarded as 'excellent' is thus per se 'excellent'. [iii] To argue thus is simply to misunderstand the notions of 'subjective' and 'objective'. [iv]

. . .

We should bear in mind that what this year or in this decade or in this era is deemed by 'the critics' to be 'good writing' and 'good literature' might by a future generation of critics and readers be valued a great deal less: future generations might regard today's 'good literature' as stilted, archaic, verbose, artless and certainly not to 'modern tastes' in whatever respects those 'modern tastes' are 'modern'. Writing of the past can always be valued 'today' as an 'historical example', even if writing of its kind is no longer in vogue – the somewhat rotund style of the 19th century would, I suspect, not be taken seriously in the third decade of the 21st century if it were adopted by a contemporary writer except, perhaps, as a specific artistic device of some kind. In fact, our fickleness, our readiness to abandon yesterday's generation of literary heroes and rally around newer, younger ones is welcomed by publishers: 'new' always sells – if the marketing is to right. The past is littered with 'up-and-coming writers' whose heyday has long passed: who today still champions Hugh Walpole, Thomas Wolfe, Norman Mailer, Jack Kerouac and, more recently, Brett Easton Ellis and Martin Amis? [v] We might still read their work, but we do not approach it or them as we did when they were 'this year's bright new writer'. Hemingway might have become a notable exception, but why he became a notable exception is precisely what interests me and lies at the heart of the 'Hemingway enigma'.

In fact, it is – ironically – one of life's constants that today's younger generation delights in debunking the values of the previous generation, presumably as did each 'younger generation' throughout history. It's how they can define themselves more clearly and put clear blue water between themselves and the 'older generation' they are destined to replace. It was precisely this which benefited Hemingway when first he offered his short stories and subsequently his novel The Sun Also Rises for publication: whatever else his writing was, it most certainly was not 'boring old' Henry James, John Galsworthy, Arnold Bennett, George Gissing or Edith Wharton, writers whose work the bright young things of Hemingway's generation began to regard as stilted, archaic and verbose. As the New York Times put it when it reviewed The Sun Also Rises in October 1926, Hemingway was writing 'lean, hard and athletic narrative prose'.

. . .

There's a further dilemma for those who might insist that 'objective' judgments are possible: critics regularly disagree with each other on just 'how good' a new novel is – so what do we do when the verdict of one set of well-read critics and academics is wholly contradicted by the verdict of other equally well-read and well-informed critics and academics? Even opting to agree with one verdict rather than another is itself a subjective decision: on what might our preference be based? Here's an extreme example: reviewing The Sun Also Rises when it appeared in October 1926, the New York Times breathlessly recorded

> *No amount of analysis can convey the quality of the Sun Also Rises. It is a truly gripping story, told in a lean, hard and athletic narrative prose that puts more literary English to shame* [1] *... It is magnificent writing, filled with that organic action which gives a compelling picture of character. This novel is unquestionably one of the events of an unusually rich year in literature.*

On the other hand whoever reviewed the novel for The Dial [vi] three months later was notably less impressed and wrote

> *[Hemingway's] characters are as shallow as the sources in which they stack their daily emotions, and instead of interpreting his material – or even challenging — he has been content merely to make a carbon copy of a not particularly significant service of life in Paris.*

Then there's the polarity of opinion two decades later in reviews of Hemingway's post-war novel Across The River And Into The Trees. The general critical consensus was that it was not very good at all. [vii] In the New York Times [2] J. Donald Adams was unambiguous and admitted

> *To me, Across the River And Into the Trees is one of the saddest books I have ever read; not because I am moved to compassion by the conjunction of love and death in the Colonel's life, but because a great talent has come, whether for now or forever, to such a dead end.*

In a New Yorker review Alfred Kazin confessed

> *It is hard to say what one feels most in reading this book – pity, embarrassment that so fine and honest a writer can make such a travesty of himself, or amazement that a man can render so*

---

1   Quite of what 'more literary English' should be ashamed is not clear. In fact, this piece of hyperbole from the reviewer can be excused as we might charitably excuse a cat that has tracked down and murdered a sparrow on the lawn. Both are in the nature of cats and critics. 'Gripping', 'magnificent', 'compelling', 'unquestionably' would certainly awe most common or garden readers and, with luck, open their wallets to buy the book in question. My favourite piece of reviewers' hype is when we are assured a new novel is 'important'.

2   On September 24, 1950.

Subjectivity: is objective judgment possible?

marvellously the beauty of the natural world and yet be so vulgar.

In The Saturday Review of Literature Maxwell Geismar wrote

> *This is an unfortunate novel and unpleasant to review for anyone who respects Hemingway's talent and achievement. It is not only Hemingway's worst novel; it is a synthesis of everything that is bad in his previous work and throws a doubtful light on the future.*

Yet in his review for the New York Times that appeared two weeks before Adams' piece was published, the journalist and writer John O'Hara unequivocally declared

> *The most important author living today, the outstanding author since the death of Shakespeare, has brought out a new novel. The title of the novel is Across The River And Into the Trees. The author, of course, is Ernest Hemingway, the most important, the outstanding author out of the millions of writers who have lived since 1616.* (viii)

So who is 'right'? Adams, Kazin and Geismar? Or O'Hara? And given such fundamental disagreement, how does the reader who often lazily looks to 'the critics' for his or her opinions – and earns Virginia Woolf's scorn for doing so – decide whose judgment carries more weight? I suspect he or she would go with 'the majority view' – but would even that be justified?

It gets trickier: what if we 'non-expert' readers disagree with a consensus view of the critics? What weight – if any – do our dissenting judgments and opinions carry? Can the judgment of a 'non-expert' ever be regarded as just as credible as that of the 'professional', especially if it contradicts an orthodox and hitherto well-received view?[1] Many might be tempted to concede 'of course it can't' – just as we defer in medical matters to qualified physicians, we assume it is best in literary matters to defer to 'the professionals': the critics and the academics 'who know what they are talking about'. But having given in to the temptation of acknowledging that there is a hierarchy of judgment, the inconvenient question still remains unanswered: why exactly should that 'expert' judgment be given more credence? It is pertinent at this point to repeat Virginia Woolf's observation that

---

1   This book and its scepticism might be a case in point: how seriously should my view that Hemingway was certainly not a 'great writer' be taken when, it seems, it is at odds with what most everyone else seems to believe, not least the Nobel Prize committee in 1954?

> *'[critics] have only to shut themselves up in a room, dip a pen in the ink, and call themselves 'we', for the rest of us to believe that they are somehow exalted, inspired, infallible.'*

So: why *do* we doff our caps?

...

Hemingway, whose own subjective judgment of his writing abilities was that he was extraordinarily good, most certainly did not doff his cap to the critics. Early on he developed a contempt for critics, although quite why does not seem to have been established; in time that dislike evolved into an outright hatred, and he persuaded himself there was some conspiracy among the critics to do him down.[1] Even before he had been commercially published and was still a hopeful rather than an established writer, he expressed very trenchant views on literary critics. In a letter to Sherwood Anderson[2] in May 1925 – this was before he turned on Anderson in what biographers suggest was part of a strategy to free himself of his contract with Boni & Liveright to join Scribner's – he wrote:

> *God knows people who are paid to have attitudes toward things, professional critics, make me sick; camp-following eunuchs of literature. They won't even whore. They're all virtuous and sterile. And how well-meaning and high-minded. But they are all camp followers.*

Hemingway's contempt is ironic given that it was precisely the enthusiastic reactions of most critics to his book of short stories, In Our Time, and then to his 'first' novel, The Sun Also Rises, that were the major factor in establishing him on the literary scene and launching his career. The critics also played a crucial role in helping to create the figure of 'Hemingway the genius', and their initial consensus was that Hemingway was 'the real deal'. Yet his opinion of critics did not improve over the next 36 years, and that is not surprising: after his early success, his subsequent literary output met with ever less

---

1   This might, at a pinch, be cited as a symptom of a possible inferiority complex and probably his tendency to paranoia which found full expression in the last two years of his life.

2   Anderson was in his early forties when he met Hemingway in Chicago. He had been an advertising copywriter and eventually started his own business, but suffered a nervous breakdown when he was 36, although accounts of what happened, including his own, varied in the telling. He left his first wife and three children and became a full-time writer, eventually finding success with his short stories and novels. He was a well-known author when Hemingway met him, but his later work was not as successful as his early fiction. He died of peritonitis in 1941 in Panama after swallowing a toothpick.

critical enthusiasm. His bullfighting book Death In The Afternoon and Green Hills Of Africa came to be scrutinised more keenly and judged more harshly, and gave him ever reason to dislike 'the critics'.

. . .

Most readers, however, do not share Hemingway's callow scorn and, as Virginia Woolf noted, are more than ready to bow to the judgment of 'the critics'. Their obeisance might be suspect, but why complicate life: the critics are paid to 'have opinions' and such opinions prove useful in deciding what to read next. Yet some of us, having read a novel we are assured is 'acclaimed' by the critics, might find ourselves wondering just why it is 'acclaimed'. We might even be bold enough to venture the shy admission that 'to be honest, I didn't really enjoy it all that much', or, more cautiously, 'it wasn't quite my kind of thing'. Yet rather than risk looking foolish by disagreeing with the accepted opinion of the great and good – the accepted opinion of Woolf's 'exalted, inspired and infallible' critics – we probably opt to keep our scepticism to ourselves and concede – at least publicly – that we don't doubt this or that novel or poem is 'great' even though we ourselves don't quite see why.

Often a reader might not even have read a work but will acknowledge, in deference to the critics, that it is 'a masterpiece'; how many of those, for example, who have talked of Cervantes 'great novel' Don Quixote ('The Ingenious Gentleman Don Quixote of La Mancha'), Herman Melville's 'masterpiece' Moby-Dick, George Eliot's 'superb' Middlemarch or Chaucer's 'delightful' Canterbury Tales have actually read those works? How many of those who have read Hemingway's The Sun Also Rises or A Farewell To Arms and think privately 'well, it's really nothing special', but continue to declare publicly that it is 'a masterpiece' and its author 'a writer of genius'? If they do so, it is because that is the orthodox and hitherto received view (and, anyway, it says so on the back cover of their paperback edition). Privately they might console themselves for their lack of enthusiasm by conceding 'well, I'm probably missing something'.

. . .

A common practice – and this seems especially to have been, and still to be, the case with Hemingway – is to proclaim all of the work as superior simply because 'one of America's greatest writers' had written it. Matthew Bruccoli sums it up well in his book Scott And Ernest, The Authority Of Failure And The Authority Of Success:

Hemingway did not progress from strength to strength. His best work was done before he was thirty, and he produced only one major novel – For Whom the Bell Tolls – after 1929. Nonetheless, he spoke with the confidence of success. Everything he did, everything he wrote, became important because he was Ernest Hemingway.

There are several pertinent points in what Bruccoli writes on which it might be useful to dwell: that Hemingway's writing tailed off and did not recover after he had published his first two novels and his first two collections of short stories, even though his career was just four years old; that his work increasingly sold well simply because he was 'Ernest Hemingway'; and that he describes For Whom The Bell Tolls merely as a 'major novel' – whether by design or not Bruccoli, chose not to praise it and merely conceded that it was more than a 'minor work'. [ix]

Although Matthew Bruccoli was primarily a scholar who dealt with the life and work of F. Scott Fitzgerald, he was by no means hostile to Hemingway. But like many writing about Hemingway in the decades after his suicide in July 1961, a list that includes Michael Reynolds, James R. Mellow, Kenneth Lynn and Scott Donaldson, his eye was cooler and more sceptical than that of earlier, somewhat hagiographic, biographers and memoirists (Charles Fenton, John Atkins and, most notably, A.E. Hotchner, [1] who were all keen, for one reason or another, to fan the Hemingway flame).

In Bruccoli's introduction to Hemingway And The Mechanism Of Fame he makes his view clear that

Ernest Hemingway was famous for being famous

and he continues that in his view Hemingway pursued fame as a goal in itself:

He assiduously cultivated different and sometimes divergent personae – sportsman, soldier, aesthetician, patriot, drinker, womanizer, intellectual, anti-intellectual, sage, brawler, world traveller, war correspondent, big-game hunter, and even author – each chosen to foster his place in the American cultural consciousness and support the sales of his books. In every role he projected the insider's air of authority and expertise that was presumed credible, even when not wholly deserved. His success in these self-legendising efforts to couple non-literary celebrity with literary stature is evident in his continued fame among those

---

1   It is difficult not to be cynical about Hotchner for whom in many ways Hemingway and his association with the writer was something of a meal ticket.

> *familiar and unfamiliar with his books.*

A consequence of the assumption that 'this is by Hemingway, so it must be good' was that over the years everything he wrote has been analysed and interpreted, in which process objectivity be damned. Hemingway kept pretty much every scrap of paper on which he had written, [1] and in addition to the manuscripts of his novels and published short stories, each sketch, every discarded half-written short story and all the many scraps he was simply loath to throw away are now in the Hemingway Collection of Boston's John F. Kennedy Library And Museum. That in itself, by the same self-validating process outlined above, will be accepted by many as tacit 'proof' that 'Hemingway was a great writer': their argument will run that 'the John F. Kennedy Library wouldn't keep all that crap if Hemingway had not been great'. Well, frankly, they did and still do.

. . .

The suspicion of subjectivity masquerading as something a little more substantial also taints the conclusions made about 'meaning' and 'significance'. At best we can only make assumptions when analysing Hemingway's fiction (or, for that matter that of any other writer) for meaning and significance. Yet the received – and 'respected' – views of what this or that story 'means' gain ever greater heft as they are repeated and adopted by new generations. As Kelli A. Larson points out in Lies, Damned Lies, And Hemingway Criticism

> *Since scholars write about what they know well . . . such familiarity . . . leads to increased critical attention as scholars share their ideas with others via publication. Thus the cycle of critical debate begins anew with the opening of each semester and attests most clearly to Hemingway's 're-readability' down through the years.*

Given the status of being a 'great writer' Hemingway acquired when the academics became involved after 1950, they subsequently went into analytic overdrive to find 'meaning' and 'significance' in everything he wrote. Even where quite possibly none existed, [2] they summoned up that useful standby 'the subconscious' and suggested that although this or that allusion was perhaps not 'consciously' intended and that

---

1 The suggestion has been made that he was so convinced of his own genius that he kept them 'for posterity'.

2 See Caveat lector – The Rorschach effect, p.230ff.

Hemingway might even not have realised the resonance of this or that phrase, paragraph or scene, nevertheless . . . This line of argument is especially effective in that it is almost impossible to counter; but it is a claim that is difficult to square with how a writer can be praised for his or her artistry and skill if he or she was in part, or perhaps even wholly, unaware of what they were doing.

As Larson points out, one consequence of this cycle of critical debate is that the same interpretations are repeated again and again until, almost unobtrusively, they come to be regarded as 'fact'. Thus the 'subjective' has quietly and unobtrusively transmuted into the 'objective' even though it is nothing of the kind. A good example is the orthodox view – which now has the status of doctrine – that in his novel The Sun Also Rises Hemingway was portraying – indeed it is often suggested that he intended to portray – the despair of a 'lost generation'. Not only was the claim news to Hemingway who repeatedly denied he had intended anything of the kind, but oddly and tellingly it was not at all apparent to many of those critics who reviewed the novel, almost all enthusiastically, when it was published. In The Immediate Critical Reception Of Ernest Hemingway, Frank L. Ryan observes

> *No single factor was as illustrative of the failure of* The Sun Also Rises *to convince the critics that Hemingway was a great writer than its failure to convince them that it was the record of a generation and that its author was the spokesman for that generation. A year and a half after its publication, Richard Barrett spoke of the impressions which the novel was having on the younger people about him, of the young men and women who spoke so reverently of it, marked passages in it, and kept it by their beds, apparently for solace in the dark hours. But one searches in vain for this response from the reviewers who did not hear in it the mournful sounds of a lost generation.*

This begs several questions: if the 'despair' of a 'lost generation' was – as we are now instructed – a major, if not the major, theme of Hemingway's novel, why did few, if any, of its contemporary reviewers pick up on it? If the 'portrayal of a 'lost generation' is 'a fact' about the novel, there would be 'evidence' and 'proof'? Yet neither 'evidence' nor 'proof' is available because there can be none: neither 'evidence' nor 'proof' play any part in what we choose to believe, and the 'lost generation' interpretation is, at best, a

Subjectivity: is objective judgment possible?

matter of opinion [1] and subjective; and although one can have 'reasons' for holding an opinion and believing something to be the case, reasons cannot and never will amount to 'evidence' or 'proof': the notions of 'evidence' and 'proof' belong firmly in the 'objective' world of facts and 'knowledge'. Opinions are part of the 'subjective' world of 'belief' and 'faith'. [2]

Those who still insist that the orthodox 'lost generation' reading of the novel is the 'correct' one should explain the following: the *Sun*'s protagonists all drink too much, supposedly to cope with their despair over the meaningless of their lives. But what group of twentysomethings on a summer holiday in the sun doesn't drink a great deal, often to excess? As for that lack of meaning to their lives, leading to Jake and his friends' alleged despair, where is that despair? How does it manifest itself in the novel? There is also the inconvenience that insisting *The Sun Also Rises* is about a 'lost generation in despair' is directly contradicted by the quotation from Ecclesiastes Hemingway uses as one of his epigraph (and which provided him with the title of his novel): it is essentially optimistic and affirming. His epigraph could easily be summed up by Scarlett O'Hara's hopeful, though wistful, last line in the film Gone With The Wind as *'after all, tomorrow is another day'*. [x]

It must be conceded, however, that until kingdom come and beyond, on this matter as on the 'worth' of Hemingway's work overall and on the worth of thousands of other literary works, many of us are habitually more inclined to trust the judgments of 'the experts' than not. Even those who agree that those judgments are no more 'objective' than their own might have a niggling feeling that if they do contradict 'the experts', they will achieve nothing but look foolish. And we don't want that, do we? So why risk it?

---

1   The stark contrast between different and often contradictory interpretations is particularly well demonstrated by the several explanations of what Hemingway's story God Rest Ye Merry, Gentlemen is 'about'. See p.226ff.

2   In his or her first year at college, every student of philosophy will be asked to write an essay about 'knowledge' and 'belief', and with luck they will soon be able to understand how they are distinct and why the one is certainly not the other and, crucially, never can be.

What was it to be – 'artist' or 'celebrity'?

He has become the legendary Hemingway. He appears to have turned into a composite of all those photographs he has been sending for years: sunburned from snows, on skis; in fishing get-up, burned dark from the hot Caribbean; the handsome, stalwart hunter crouched smiling over the carcass of some dead beast. Such a man could not have written Hemingway's early books . . . It is hard not to wonder whether he has not, hunting, brought down an even greater victim.

John Peale Bishop, Homage To Hemingway, The New Republic, November 1936.

[Hemingway] had a literary reputation among ex-patriate writers before he had published a word of fiction.

Jeffrey Meyers, Virginia Quarterly Review, Autumn 1984.

Mediated ideology persists to such an extent that the myth becomes absorbed as legend, and thus the realism behind the figures becomes distorted. This is particularly evident in the case of American author Ernest Hemingway, whose celebrity image eclipsed the man and thereby created a culturally fruitful myth.

Siobhan Lyons, Remembering Hemingway: The Endurance of the Hemingway Myth.

What was it to be – 'artist' or 'celebrity?

> *To the hunters [would-be biographers and academics wanting to write about his work] closing in on their prey Hemingway resembled Lawrence of Arabia in seeming to back into the limelight. Why did he, for instance, avoid them and yet befriend gossip columnists, of all people, and bartenders?*
>
> **Denis Brian, The True Gen.**

> *. . . he radiated personality and cultivated publicity even as he pretended to scorn it. In his first letter to Perkins he mentioned – not wholly facetiously – that it would be 'worthwhile to get into Who's Who'. In short he wanted fame in both the Renaissance and the contemporary sense.*
>
> **Leonard Leff, Hemingway and his Conspirators.**

> *Far from being either the unwitting or unwilling recipient of this personal attention as he liked to intimate he was, Hemingway was the architect of his public reputation. Early in his career, he began to shape a public personality which quickly became one of his most famous creations, during his lifetime perhaps the most famous one.*
>
> **John Raeburn, Fame Became Him.**

> *Almost thirty-five years old, Ernest Hemingway was a newsworthy figure whose every public act was grist for the media: his broad shoulders and his round moustached face with its pronounced widow's peak becoming as widely recognised as some movie stars. Where once his fiction drew attention to his active life, now that life drew attention to his writing.*
>
> **Michael Reynolds, Hemingway: The 1930s.**

THE 'Hemingway enigma' is simple to define: he was neither 'a genius' and nor were his works 'masterpieces' (and furthermore the quality of his work was notably patchy), yet to this day that is the view of many around the world, and Hemingway is still routinely described as 'one of America's greatest writer' and 'a leading modernist'. So the question is: how were 'the facts' of his 'genius' and his 'masterpieces' so comprehensively established and why were they so widely accepted? How did he achieve a global literary and public prominence that was, especially for a writer, extraordinary?

It was essentially a concatenation of disparate forces, of which not the least were Hemingway's overweening, ruthless ambition, his bulldozing personality and his unstinting efforts to publicise himself. Arguably these traits and skills exceeded his writing talent and without them it is very unlikely anyone would today have heard of 'the writer Ernest Hemingway'. He worked hard to become famous, that work paid off, and eventually his literary reputation and his status as a celebrity were one and the same. In a piece that biographer Jeffrey Meyers wrote for the Virginia Quarterly Review two decades after Hemingway's death, he sums it up succinctly:

> *The boy who boasted in infancy that he was " 'fraid a nothing", that he had once caught a runaway horse, began to establish his public persona while on the editorial board of his high school newspaper. He was not a great athlete or scholar but constantly reported his own minor exploits in the Oak Park Trapeze. He inflated his genuine heroism in war through newspaper interviews and public speeches while he was still in his teens.* [1] *As a foreign correspondent, he learned how to create a romantic image and generate publicity. He had a literary reputation among ex-patriate writers before he had published a word of fiction.*

As Meyers suggests the irony is that in a sense Hemingway's 'fame' – narrow though it initially was – came before he was even a published author. Hemingway talked a very good game indeed, so well, in fact, that the reputation he was making for himself[2] among the ex-patriates in Montparnasse had soon crossed the Atlantic and persuaded Max Perkins at Scribner's in New York to ask F. Scott Fitzgerald (one of his authors, who was then living in Paris) to report back on who this new writer was. Perkins had somehow acquired a copy of *in our time* [sic], the slim 30-page volume of very short stories Hemingway had written [i], and became interested in Hemingway. Whether it was the volume's artistic merits or – more likely – the sales potential of unusual and 'exciting new' work which enthused him would now be impossible to establish. [ii]

---

1   I'm not sure what acts of 'genuine heroism' occurred in the four weeks of Hemingway's active Red Cross service from June 7 to July 8.

2   He was initially accepted as 'a great writer' simply because he told people he was. The practice worked for him throughout his life.

What was it to be – 'artist' or 'celebrity?

...

Hemingway had been trying his hand at writing fiction since his late teens. What of that work has survived, mainly pieces he composed for his Oak Park High School English literature class, is deemed imitative of his favourite authors, including Ring Lardner, and not in the least remarkable. He was one of the several editors of, and contributors to, the school's newspaper The Trapeze and its literary magazine Tabula, but in that respect, as well as in his literary ambitions, Hemingway was indistinguishable from thousands of other young men and women on the cusp of adult life. [1] Once he had returned from 'his war' in Europe in 1919 and had overcome his heartbreak over being jilted by Agnes von Kurowsky (his nurse at the Red Cross hospital in Milan, of whom more later), he remained in northern Michigan after the annual family summer break at their cottage Windemere [iii] had ended and rented a room in nearby Petoskey. There he spent hours on end at a typewriter composing stories which he then submitted to magazines, including the Saturday Evening Post. None was accepted. The first words he wrote that actually made it into print appeared in the Toronto Weekly Star in early 1920. These demonstrate that Hemingway, who so far regarded himself as a humourist, [2] had an often neat turn of phrase and shared the tendency of many late adolescents to adopt a pseudo-satirical, flippant take on 'life'. [iv]

Before joining the Red Cross in May 1918, Hemingway had spent just over seven months as a trainee reporter on the Kansas City Star, apparently then as now one of the most respected training grounds for newspaper journalism. None of the brief news stories he will have filed has been identified, mainly because a trainee reporter phoning in filler paragraphs and short police reports would never be given a by-line. And as the paper operated a system of 'rewrite men' who actually composed the stories which appeared in the paper, Hemingway will only have phoned in 'the facts'. [3] Even when he did write a story – there are reports from those who worked beside him in Kansas City of the enthusiastic young lad hammering away at a typewriter – what will have appeared in print will have been the work of the paper's copy editors (in Britain sub-editors).

In the early summer of 1920, back from his time in Toronto working as a companion to the son of Ralph Connable, Hemingway settled in again with his family at Windemere.

---

1   Inevitably, the fiction and journalism he wrote while at school were published, in 1993, as Hemingway At Oak Park High: The High School Writings Of Ernest Hemingway, 1916-1917, proving yet again that no barrel is too deep to be scraped.

2   Bizarrely, early while writing The Sun Also Rises, he described it to friends as 'very funny'.

3   In Britain on the bigger down-market ('tabloid') and middle-market newspapers the re-writing of news stories is done by its sub-editors.

He did not look for paid work, but simply lazed about with a friend who was staying and certainly did not attend to the various tasks his mother repeatedly asked the two to undertake. Whether he was also writing fiction has not been recorded. Finally, his time at Windemere was concluded when his mother had had enough of his laziness and back-chat, and – with her husband's wholehearted approval – threw him out of the house. Hemingway then took himself off to Chicago where he found a job with a publication called the Cooperative Commonwealth. [v] He later claimed he had been the journal's 'managing editor', [1] but whatever title he had – if indeed he even had one – he was de facto a jack of all trades, writing a great deal of the journal's copy and seeing it through production. While in Chicago, he lodged with Yenlaw Kenley Smith (known as Y.K.), the older brother of his Michigan friends Bill and Katie Smith. It was in Chicago that he met Hadley Richardson, one of Katie Smith's college friends, who had arrived from St Louis for a visit, and the writer Sherwood Anderson, a friend and former ad agency colleague of Y.K. Smith's.

...

When – between the few months he was writing in that rented room in Petoskey in the late summer of 1919 and his year in Chicago – Hemingway had been writing fiction is not at all clear. But he must have been doing some writing because he was able to show work to both Richardson and Anderson. However, none has survived. Possibly what was composed in those early years was in the valise stolen (or mislaid by a porter) from a train in Paris's Gare de Lyon in early December 1922 when his wife went off to buy a bottle of water or 'something to read' – accounts vary – and left it unattended [2]. Pertinently, any writing he will have shown Anderson was done before he met Ezra Pound and Gertrude Stein who, we are told, had such an important influence on his style; what the work consisted of, what he was writing about and what style he had chosen are unknown. Presumably it had now progressed beyond the 'derivative' and 'imitative' style of his very early work because Anderson declared himself enthusiastic

---

1   One can't help suspecting this was another piece of Hemingway's gratuitous hyperbole.
2   Hadley Richardson was off to join Hemingway in Lausanne and had packed almost all the work he had hitherto produced – as well as the carbon copies – because a fellow journalist had, it seemed, expressed interest in his fiction and she thought it might help to show him the work.

What was it to be – 'artist' or 'celebrity?

about what Hemingway was producing.[1] We might speculate that by late 1920/1921 he had already written his story Up In Michigan which seems to describe the – though non-violent – rape of an innocent young woman by the drunk man for whom she had conceived a passion and which Gertrude Stein deemed to be 'unpublishable' when she read it.[vi]

In his later years Hemingway ostentatiously abjured all and any talk of art and literature, although if he was more amenable to such discussions in private we don't know but we have no record of such occasions. Both during his months working for the Star in Kansas City and later in Chicago, though, he did take part in lively debates about such matters. Anderson was sufficiently impressed by Hemingway's pronouncements on writing and literature, and what he had read of his work to give him – after persuading him to go to Paris rather than Naples as Hemingway and Hadley had originally planned – letters of introduction, including one each to Pound and Stein.

Richardson, too, was a staunch supporter of Hemingway's intention to 'become a writer', and she thought his work was marvellous. We know about her enthusiasm from the letters she sent him from St Louis, and it is not unfair to suggest that a woman in love – especially one who had found a future partner comparatively late in life – might not be the sternest judge of 'her man's talents. We might thus, perhaps, query her judgment a little and wonder whether she had not – like others later in Paris – also succumbed to Hemingway's persistence in declaring how good a writer he was. Certainly, her encouragement – in her letters – does seem to echo what he might have informed her he planned to do as a writer, especially how she 'agrees' that he has a marvellous literary future ahead of him.[vii]

...

When Hadley and Hemingway met in December 1920, he was just 21, but at 29 she was almost eight years older and at the time women at her age were usually married. In some ways she had until then had an increasingly miserable life: after she fell out of a window as a child, her domineering mother treated her as an invalid. When she was 12, her father killed himself. A few years later, an older sister to whom she was close died in a fire, and Richardson reportedly then became very shy and more reclusive. It did not

---

1   Given that Hemingway 'went on to become a great writer', the conventional take on Anderson's praise is that it was the enthusiasm of an experienced writer for the abilities of a junior practitioner. Yet for all we know Anderson might simply have been encouraging a young man in his ambitions as it is kind to encourage all young people, whatever they hope to achieve.

help that another older sister shared her mother's domineering ways, and for several years Richardson had no life to speak of. When she was in her late twenties, however, her mother died, Richardson inherited a large trust fund and suddenly her life was her own. That is when she met Hemingway, and he reportedly became infatuated with her. According to her biographers Bernice Kert and Gioia Diliberto, Richardson, who had very few male admirers, [1] thought him very handsome and came under the Hemingway spell. Their courtship was overwhelmingly by letter, and they did not actually see much of each other in the nine months between first meeting and marrying at the beginning of September 1921. She and her new husband had at first planned to live in Y.K. Smith's apartment once they were married, but when Hemingway tactlessly condemned an affair Y.K.'s wife 'Doodles' was having, they were asked to leave. [viii] They moved into a pokey apartment in Chicago, but that didn't matter: by Christmas they were in Paris, Hemingway to begin life as one of the world's coming great writers – at least in his own estimation – and Hadley to begin life as the wife of one of the world's coming great writers.

. . .

Once in Paris, Hemingway almost immediately began submitting short features to the Weekly Toronto Star. In one of his first, possibly his very first, he wrote of his and Richardson's arrival in Spain from the US on their way to Paris. In a subsequent, 600-word piece, he described in detail how the favourable dollar/franc exchange rate made it exceptionally cheap indeed for a Canadian to live in Paris. [2] In another piece he already began establishing himself as 'Ernest Hemingway, the serious writer' by describing the many young Americans and British who swanned around Montparnasse posing as artists, but who never did any real work and who were certainly not 'serious'. The implication was that he was certainly not one of them, although his readers back in Canada would have had no notion of his literary ambitions. In this piece Hemingway was being disingenuous: arguably he was himself not shy of posing. He has been described as sitting alone in a corner of a café nursing just the one coffee or drink for hours as he composed a short story. The implication was that one coffee or alcoholic drink was

---

1   Though not strikingly beautiful, Richardson was said to have been personally and physically attractive, but it seems her mother and older sister had actively discouraged young men from showing any interest in her.

2   He was a US citizen, but he was, after all, writing for Canadian readers.

all he could afford [1], and he claimed that he resorted to thus writing in public because the cafés were warm. He has also been described shadow-boxing – as he walked down the streets of Montparnasse and later, once he had discovered bullfighting, parrying imaginary bulls; this would surely have drawn attention. This kind of showing off was and is certainly not unusual in young men, but he was being a little hypocritical criticising his peers for doing the same thing.

Reading the short pieces he wrote for the Weekly Star, there is no denying that Hemingway had a facility with words; but that facility was no greater than, or even as great as, that of many other writers – and journalists – past and present. What is notable – for this reader at least – is how that facility often seemed to fail him when he composed his early fiction. When later he was again producing the journalism he purported to despise – in his pieces for Esquire (his 'Letters', for which he was very well paid), for the short-lived political magazine, Ken, and in the few dispatches he sent to Collier's in World War II – his way with words was fully intact. It is not unlikely that when in his early twenties he came under the tutelage and influence of Gertrude Stein and Ezra Pound, he was so keen to be 'a good student' and learn what they believed they had to teach him that he abandoned all of his own ideas about writing [ix].

. . .

It was already at this point early on that the 'public' Hemingway and the 'real' Hemingway began two separate existences. In Our Time, his first commercially published book of short stories, had attracted interest because of its – for the age – 'shocking' content and distinctive style, and laid the foundations for his later public fame. The 'real' Hemingway did not subsequently develop in any significant way as a writer; on the other hand the 'public' Hemingway, the man concerned with building a reputation for himself, now set about that task with zeal. It helped to define him as 'out of the ordinary' that the work he had just published was for its time certainly 'different' [2]. In New York's The Sun, Herbert Seligman's commented – and demonstrated just how distressingly

---

1 Despite Hemingway's claims in his memoir A Moveable Feast that he and Richardson often went hungry in those early Paris years – claims certainly contradicted by his Weekly Star piece about how cheap it was for a Canadian or an American to live in Paris in the early 1920s. When Hemingway returned to Paris in January 1924 after resigning his Star staff job in Toronto, problems with Richardson's trust fund income meant occasionally the couple were short of cash, but this was only ever temporary, and the claims in his memoir were only intended to burnish his reputation as 'an artist who had been prepared to starve for his art'.

2 It was, though, not quite as original as he thought he was, and Hemingway was always irritated by suggestions that he owed a great deal to the style of his one-time mentor, Sherwood Anderson.

airy and arcane many book reviews can be – that the

> *flat even banal declarations in the paragraphs alternating with Mr Hemingway's longer sketches are a criticism of the conventional dishonesty of literature. Here is neither literary inflation nor elevation, but a passionately bare telling of what happened.* [1]

The New York Times enthused that Hemingway's

> *language is fibrous and athletic, colloquial and fresh, hard and clean . . . his very prose seems to have an organic being of its own.*

Like Mr Seligman, the New York Herald Tribune reviewer was also not shy of indulging in unashamed hyperbole. He wrote

> *I know no American writer with a more startling ear for colloquial conversation, or a more poetic sensitiveness for the woods and hills. In Our Time has perhaps not enough energy to be a great book, but Ernest Hemingway has promises of genius.*

. . .

When Hemingway was an unknown trying to make his mark, his advance in the world of literature proceeded gradually but steadily. He certainly impressed many, could be very charming and talked a good game. Essential, possibly more so than what writing talent he did have, was his talent for what we would now call 'networking'. In Hemingway: The Paris Years, Michael Reynolds hits the nail on the head:

> *As Hemingway was obviously learning, writing well was only half the game; making sure that influential people knew you were writing well was the other half. Before another year was out his game would be impeccable, the two complementing each other perfectly.*

As for his 'networking', F. Scott Fitzgerald, who was close to Hemingway in the mid-1920s and had actively promoted his new friend before he found success, later remarked that

---

1   Quite why we are invited to admire paragraphs with 'banal declarations' is not clear, and Mr Seligman's contribution does rather beg the question as to why stout-hearted book lovers such as he seem hitherto to have tolerated literature's 'conventional dishonesty'. It would also help if we knew just how that 'conventional dishonesty' had been expressing itself.

> *Ernest would always give a helping hand to a man on a ledge a little higher up.*

That Hemingway's career took off was also partly because he was the right man in right place. World War I (or the Great War as it was then known) had been a watershed in many ways, not least culturally and technologically. In the 1920s silent films evolved into 'talkies'; jazz was developing and gaining an audience, and the sales of records were soaring; radio stations were being established throughout the United States; [1] Prohibition and illegal drinking in speakeasies made life exciting for the young and, growing in self-consciousness, they were demanding a new kind of celebrity. According to Leonard J. Leff in Hemingway And His Conspirators, the young writer benefited from the demands of an age that was ripe for novelty of all and every kind:

> *The 1920s, the decade of the ascent of Ernest Hemingway, the decade of In Our Time, The Sun Also Rises and A Farewell To Arms, was also the era of modern advertising – bold and noisy and professionalised. Anything could be sold, even books, if only they were marketed well.*

Hemingway was fortunate to have Scribner's as his publisher – with Fitzgerald's connivance, he had jumped ship from Boni & Liveright – because it was going through its own, revitalising, changes. Boni & Liveright was a livelier, more *avant-garde*, but less respected house: Scribner's was well-established and eminently respectable. This, as biographers point out, will have been an attraction for the young writer from middle-class Oak Park, who despite his reputed *avant garde* 'modernist' style and the 'shocking' content of his work was essentially conservative. [2] By the 1920s, Scribner's, which had initially concentrated on publishing religious tracts when it was founded in 1846, was under increasing pressure from its younger staff, notably Max Perkins to attract younger readers by sloughing off its fusty and old-fashioned image. The 'shocking' nature of Hemingway's early work fitted the bill and he was thus their man. Scribner's

---

1   In 1922 there were only 30 stations broadcasting in the whole US. Eight years later there were almost 700. In 1923, just one per cent of U.S. households owned at least one radio receiver, while by 1931 a majority did. Until after World War II radio was the only broadcast medium – in 1947, less than ten thousand US households had a television set and TV didn't really develop until the early 1950s.

2   The complaint by Pauline Pfeiffer, Hemingway's second wife after he had ditched her and married Martha Gellhorn might indicate just how little of a bohemian 'free spirit' Ernest was: '*I don't mind Ernest falling in love, but why does he always have to marry the girl when he does it?*' He kept a strict and detailed account of his income and expenditure all his life and was punctilious about paying his taxes, although not averse to benefiting from every – legal – deduction the IRS allowed.

marketing campaign for The Sun Also Rises, emphasising Hemingway the hard-boiled 'action man' who boxed, fought bulls and was a sportsman, also worked well. To repeat the observation by Carlos Baker in the first full-length biography of Hemingway on the impact The Sun Also Rises had

> *Hundreds of bright young men from the Middle West were trying to be Hemingway heroes, talking in tough understatements from the one the side of their mouths.*

That Hemingway's fame carried on growing in the 1930s, despite his increasingly disappointing literary output, was down to that fierce ambition and uncompromising personality: in the introduction to his book Conversations With Ernest Hemingway, Matthew J. Bruccoli gives us a good insight into what went on:

> *He was a dedicated careerist who skilfully nurtured an heroic public image until the vainglorious role took over the man and it became necessary for him to live up to it.*

It wasn't even that simple: Hemingway, in fact, also came to adopt two, quite distinct roles. The first was that of the dedicated writer as artist who cared nothing for fame and was purely interested in his art, the pure artist who scorned publicity and would as soon write for nothing as long as he was able to carry on writing; and although he carried on playing the role of the 'pure artist' until he died, it became ever more ludicrous and dishonest. But he also revelled in 'being Ernest Hemingway': even as he was peddling the notion of 'the pure artist' at the beginning of his career, he subscribed to press cuttings services and asked for regular updates from Max Perkins on sales figures and how much money he was making; and although he still liked to be seen as 'a man of the people', he enjoyed hobnobbing with the rich, often the very rich. None of this is in itself reprehensible, but it is wholly at odds with the role of 'pure artist' Hemingway also chose to play. Leonard Leff sums it up well

> *In his first letter to Perkins he mentioned – not wholly facetiously – that it would be 'worthwhile to get into Who's Who'. In short he wanted fame in both the Renaissance and the contemporary sense.*

It would be wrong, though, to accuse Hemingway of plain hypocrisy. Both roles – the private artist who just wanted to be left along to get on with his writing, and 'Papa' Hemingway, the roistering, hard-drinking, all-action man who would fight anyone and would gladly have a drink with you – were certainly mutually exclusive, but such was the

What was it to be – 'artist' or 'celebrity?

complexity of his personality he seems sincerely to have convinced himself he was both.

. . .

The accepted view is that the prominence Ernest Hemingway acquired as 'a great writer' did not just endure but grew during his lifetime because of his work. But as John Raeburn makes clear in his book Fame Became Him, that was not the case – until the enormous success of For Whom The Bell Tolls, his literary reputation slowly declined in the 1930s. Crucially, Raeburn distinguishes between Hemingway's literary reputation and his status as what can only be described as 'a celebrity'. Furthermore, his literary reputation, if gauged – possibly contentiously – by his standing with the critics (as opposed to growing academic interest) did not rally significantly before his suicide in Ketchum, Wyoming, in July 1961, three weeks short of his 62nd birthday. However much the commercial success of For Whom The Bells Toll in 1940 and The Old Man And The Sea in 1952 and being awarded a Nobel Prize in 1954 raised his public profile, the books did little to boost Hemingway's critical reputation. Furthermore, Raeburn points out that increasingly many of those who lapped up the latest gossip about Hemingway – and 'gossip' is the only possible word – had quite possibly not read a word of his fiction. They knew all about 'the famous writer Ernest Hemingway' from the mid-market magazines they read; increasingly when Hemingway featured in them, quite often in photo-spreads in which the pictures far outnumbered any text, there was little, if any, mention of his literary work: by the last two decades of his life Hemingway was mainly famous for being famous.

Raeburn writes that America had a long tradition of honouring 'public writers', men and women such as Poe, Emerson, Thoreau, Hawthorne, Beecher Stowe, Longfellow, Whittier, Lowell, Wendell Holmes, Whitman, Dickinson and Mark Twain; but these poets and writers were known for their work, not for their private lives. Even among Hemingway's contemporaries and – as he saw them – 'rivals', there were similar 'public writers': Edith Wharton, Robert Frost, William Faulkner, Theodore Dreiser and Hemingway's erstwhile friend John Dos Passos. But there was one important distinction between them and Hemingway: their lives were private. Hemingway's was not.

. . .

After A Farewell To Arms appeared in 1929 and sold magnificently, Scribner's and Max Perkins were expecting more fiction from the man who was becoming one of their star writers. They did not expect Death In The Afternoon, although more or less from his first dealings with Scribner's Hemingway had made it clear that an English guide to bullfighting was to be a future project. The book's arcane subject matter – arcane for an English-speaking audience – did not promise much commercially, and the house cannot have been surprised that it did not sell well: the public were simply not interested in learning all about bullfighting, and the critics were also unenthusiastic. Many of them were particularly baffled that in his new book Hemingway, who had hitherto been celebrated for his terse, punchy, hard style and who was by now convinced he was a master of writing prose, could write such woolly, at times incomprehensible, English. In its review the New York Times noted that

> *It may be said flatly that the famous Hemingway style is neither so clear nor so forceful in most passages of Death In The Afternoon as it is in his novels and short stories. In this book Mr Hemingway is guilty of the grievous sin of writing sentences which have to be read two or three times before the meaning is clear*

and the Honolulu Star-Bulletin wrote

> *In his enthusiasm for the art of tauromachy, Mr Hemingway has departed, sadly, in places from his usually clear and forceful style. His earnestness in trying to put over his idea apparently has caused him to neglect pruning. The result is a surprising loss of conciseness, and occasionally a deplorably cluttered syntax.*

What had happened? Well, 'celebrity' happened: as both Raeburn and biographer Kenneth S. Lynn note, 'Hemingway the 'celebrity' was steadily gaining the upper hand at the expense of the 'Hemingway the artist'. Lynn says that Death In The Afternoon testified

> *. . . to the invasion of Hemingway's serious writing by his myth. The hero of the book is not a haunted Nick Adams, or a crippled Jake Barnes, or a hollowed-out Frederic Henry, but an overbearing know-it-all named Ernest Hemingway.*

It is Raeburn's contention that Hemingway putting himself centre-stage in Death In The Afternoon (and in Green Hills Of Africa three years later) was deliberate. He was consciously building up his public image, and Raeburn suggests this had been going on even before Hemingway was first published. Many of the pieces he filed when he was freelancing for the Toronto Star were about how he, Hemingway, saw the world. Raeburn also notes that even before he had published any work, the few editorial pieces he wrote for Ford Madox Ford's *transatlantic review* [sic] were a case in point and contributed to what we might today call a 'PR campaign'.

> *The transatlantic review articles are trivial in terms of Hemingway's literary career, but they are significant in terms of his career as public writer. They revealed that his public personality was incipient at the outset of his professional life, and that he was willing to use it for self-aggrandisement. They were a preview of the self-advertisements that would spread his fame in the next decade beyond the limited audience provided by an intellectual elite; and they foreshadowed that in his non-fiction his great subject was to be himself.*

. . .

Raeburn identifies in Death In The Afternoon nine different aspects to the persona Hemingway offered for public consumption: there were 'the sportsman, the manly man, the exposer of sham, the arbiter of taste, the world traveller, the bon vivant, the insider, the stoic and battle-scarred veteran and the heroic artist'. And to this day, even 60 years Hemingway's death, it is accepted by many that he was all of these things. The irony is that we have only Hemingway's insistence that he was any of them.

Hemingway's campaign of 'self-advertisement' took off in earnest when he was hired by Arnold Gingrich to write for Gingrich's newly founded men's magazine Esquire. Hemingway had an open brief to write 'Letters' about anything he liked. So in the more than two dozen, often monthly, 'Letters' he submitted, he wrote about hunting, fishing, fine dining, good wine, travelling and whatever else took his fancy, and on each subject he presented himself as the expert, passing on his knowledge of the subject. Hemingway also wrote for other magazines along the same lines and, says Raeburn, he was always centre-stage. So there is substantial irony in the censorious tone he adopted for his Esquire Letter of December 1934 – Old Newsman Writes [1] – when he attacks the 'I, me, my' school of frivolous personal columnists. He writes

> *But personal columnists, and this is getting to read a little like a column, are jackals and no jackal has been known to live on grass*

---

1 This title is another piece of myth-making: the 'old newsman' was not, as implied, a grizzled veteran with several decades' print experience, but a 35-year-old who had ended his journalistic career twelve years earlier when he resigned his job on the Toronto Star at just 23 after just three months having been demoted to the Toronto Star Weekly after falling out with his boss.

> *once he had learned about meat – no matter who killed the meat for him. [Walter] Winchell kills his own meat and so do a few others. But they have news in their columns and are the most working of working newspaper men. So let us return to the ex-favourite who projects his personality rather than goes for the facts.*

Even the pieces he filed for Collier's from Europe in 1944 about the war described 'Hemingway's experiences' and 'Hemingway's activities' rather than what was actually going on. And some of what he wrote was pure fiction: he did not take part in the Normandy landings as he obliquely intimated – he and other journalists never left the landing craft they were in – and he did not, as he described it to an acquaintance, take charge of a situation during the landings which had grown chaotic. [x]

. . .

Raeburn suggests there were many reasons why Hemingway chose to construct a public persona. For one thing, a high profile boosted the sales of his work: even To Have And Have Not which was not well-received by the critics, found favour with the book-buying public and earned him money (and while most of America languished in the Great Depression, the lifestyle he enjoyed was not cheap). But facilitating making more money was just one of many reasons. Raeburn also notes that

> *[Hemingway's] distrust of critics, his long-standing suspicion – to become a conviction – that they were out to get him, is consistent with his seeking a public esteem independent of the literary establishment. This general audience would not be so susceptible as the intellectuals to critical opinion, and thus it could insulate the writer's reputation from critical disfavour. His stature as a champion would be confirmed not by a few critics by a large heterogeneous audience which felt a personal loyalty to him.*

Also fuelling Hemingway's self-promotion was his lifelong competitive streak: he had to win and be seen to win, to be the best and acknowledged as the best. Thus, it might seem obvious that he also wanted to be regarded as the most famous of all his contemporary professional writers. Yet at the end of the day it is not possible to establish quite why Hemingway apparently put such a lot of effort into building himself up in the eyes of the public. We can only accept that he seems to have done so. [1]

---

1   See p.241ff for an account of a possible lifelong inferiority complex.

What was it to be – 'artist' or 'celebrity?

It was in the last two decades of Hemingway's life, but especially in his last ten years, that his celebrity as opposed to his literary reputation became global. He became a perennial staple not only of Life and Time magazines, but in time the other middle-market publications, available at every supermarket checkout, took to featuring him: Hemingway was great copy and Hemingway sold. And the point must be repeated: it was because he was 'Ernest Hemingway, the famous writer' that he was of interest to the readers of True (which ironically had carried his fictional account of taking part in the D Day landings), of Look, of Fisherman, of Parade, of This Week, of Picture Week, of Focus, of See and all the other magazines. It was not because of the quality of his writing or his take on life or the advice he could dispense.

In each of these Life, Time and middle-market magazine pieces the usual anecdotes, most of them fiction and originated by Hemingway himself, were trotted out – that he 'was a war hero' and a 'veteran of the Italian army's prestigious Arditi regiment' (and 'its youngest commissioned officer' no less), that he had bedded Mata Hari (who had, in fact, been executed the year before he arrived in Europe for his first visit), that he had seduced the girlfriend of the notorious gangster Legs Diamond, that he had led US troops ashore on D Day – continual repetition promoted all these fanciful anecdotes to the status of 'fact'.[xi] Ironically, in 1933, the Key West Citizen had written about the man who was by then the town's best-known inhabitant

> *Most modest of all American writers is Ernest Hemingway whose half-dozen published books have set a new style in contemporary literature, but who, nevertheless, shuns personal publicity as an owl shuns daylight. Hemingway does not even care to have any biographical material about himself made public . . . Though hundreds of thousands of persons know his works, however, very few know anything about the man himself. With what amounts almost to a mania, he avoids personal publicity of every kind.*

Many years later, Mario Menocal Jr, the son of one of Hemingway's Cuban friends who also knew the writer well, told one of his biographers

> *No one was more conscious than Ernest of the figure and image he possessed in the minds of the American press and reading public. He felt (I am sure) that this was an important matter to him in terms of dollars and cents in book sales or fees for articles. He deliberately set out to keep the legend and image alive in the form he wanted it.*

As several biographers have noted, 'Ernest Hemingway' was most certainly Hemingway's most famous and best creation. Even though old friends insisted that the private Hemingway they knew was nothing like that public Hemingway, their private Hemingway has been forgotten: it's the public Hemingway everyone 'knows' the man who is routinely revered as 'one of America's greatest writers'. There can be no denying that a man disciplined enough to stick to a daily writing regime for most of his life, even when he was not in good health, certainly took his work seriously, however mediocre the writing became; yet had he somehow been obliged to choose, one suspects that for factors buried deep in his psyche, his celebrity status eventually became rather more important to him than his reputation as a writer.

Personality, mental and physical health

He was good-tempered, high-spirited, ambitious, confident and courageous. He awoke each morning eager to face life. He invariably saw the humorous side of things and made fun of himself and others, displaying a talent for repartee. In conversation he held listeners spellbound with a dazzling mix of puns, expletives, flights of fancy, foreign phrases, snatches and songs and bursts of laughter. At his arrogant, aggressive worst he went around spoiling for a fight. He bragged outrageously, refused to concede he was ever wrong, ridiculed others – often with a searing wit – and believed he deserved special attention and recognition. When opposed he became irritable, even violent, threatening with the law those who thwarted his plans.

Denis Brian, The True Gen.

Killing cleanly and in a way which gives you aesthetic pleasure and pride has always been one of the greatest enjoyments of a part of the human race.

Ernest Hemingway, Death In The Afternoon.

Hemingway's anxiety and depression stemmed in large part from his failure to actualize his idealized self. Two factors were important in this failure: the image was so extreme that superhuman forces would have been required to satisfy it; secondly, a number of counterforces limited his available degree of adaptability... Throughout his life Hemingway attempted to abolish the discrepancy between his real and idealized selves. No alterations could be made upon the idealized self... All the work had to be done upon his real self; he pushed himself to face more intense danger, to attempt physical feats which exceeded his capabilities, while at the same time he pruned and streamlined himself. All traces of traits not fitting his idealized image had to be eliminated or squelched. The softer feminine side, the fearful parts, the dependent cravings – all had to go.

Psychiatrist Irvin D. Yalom and his wife Marilyn, the Archives of General Psychiatry, June 1971.

Few men can stand the strain of relaxing with him over an extended period.

Damon Runyon on Hemingway.

DESCRIBING Hemingway as a 'complex man' would be like describing Josef Stalin as 'a bit of a rogue'. He was a mass of contradictions: for every friend and acquaintance who reported what a charming and lovable friend and man he was, what good company, how courteous, considerate, down-to-earth, chivalrous and very funny 'Papa' was, there will be someone who was appalled by his rudeness, his boasting, his unacceptable behaviour, his unwarranted vindictiveness and his outright brutality. [1] He was very funny about other people, often cruelly so, but was hypersensitive if he thought he was the butt of the joke. Many admirers, for example the Canadian playwright and novelist Morley Callaghan who got to know Hemingway in Toronto and later in Paris, will admit they had heard the 'horror stories', but as far as they were concerned he was always a pleasant and delightful companion. Others will confirm they had heard what a fine chap Hemingway was but they themselves just couldn't see it, couldn't warm to him and did not like him. A great many men and women, past and present were, are and certainly in the future will be, just as complex, of course, yet few have achieved or will achieve the

---

1   In Denis Brian's book True Gen in which he interviews many men and women who knew Hemingway, it is remarkable who many of his fellow war correspondents between May 1944 and March 1943 rated him as a friend and colleague. There were one or two dissenters, but very few. Yet some who met him again after the war noted that he had changed and the more negative aspects of his character had come to the fore. Hemingway's biographers all remark how happy and contented he was during those ten months in Europe.

Personality, mental and physical health

global fame Hemingway's enjoyed; and it was largely the complexity of that personality rather than any great writing talent that was the major factor in Hemingway achieving his status as 'one of the 20th century's greatest writers'.

Without doubt Ernest Hemingway was by far the most important person in Ernest Hemingway's life; and despite his persistent denials, a great deal of his fiction is about Ernest Hemingway.[1] His central characters – notably Nick Adams in his short stories, but also Jake Barnes, Frederic Henry, Francis Macomber, Harry Walden, Harry Morgan, Robert Jordan, Richard Cantwell, Thomas Hudson, David Bourne and even the old Cuban fisherman Santiago – are arguably all, though often idealised, versions of Ernest Hemingway. In their own way they all behave heroically, stoically battling, although not necessarily overcoming, overwhelming difficulties.

Pertinently in The Snows Of Kilimanjaro – one of his 'better' short stories[2] – Hemingway even lends his main protagonist, the dying writer Harry Walden his own memories of his life in Paris a decade earlier. Harry's self-recrimination and guilt that he had allowed his wife's wealth and the good life it provided to corrupt his writing talent is exactly what in the mid-1930s Hemingway admitted he felt about the lifestyle Pauline Pfeiffer's money allowed him to enjoy. Mining one's self and one's life for material or inventing the kind of characters one would like to be is certainly not unusual among writers;[3] and doing so most certainly does not mean there is, or can be, no artistry at work. But Hemingway's insistent and his often angry denials that his work was in any way autobiographical are significant and add to the complexity: what would be so terrible if he had taken aspects of his life as his base material?[4]

There is little doubt that Hemingway was fundamentally egoistic, but his kindnesses and generosity indicate that he was not necessarily egocentric, although he did have a

---

1   This is according to psychiatrist Irvin D. Yalom and his wife Marilyn, a professor of literature, in their paper Ernest Hemingway – A Psychiatric View published in 1971. In his biography of Hemingway, Carlos Baker cites a conversation with author Irving Stone where Hemingway clearly said that his stories *'could be called biographical novels rather than pure fictional novels because they emerged out of lived experience'*. Arguably that is not quite the same as regarding them as autobiographical.

2   I've now twice used that phrase, despite my earlier scorn that 'good', 'bad', 'better' and 'worse' are, some contexts, useless descriptive words, so consider my wrists slapped.

3   Or so I understand – I have yet to have a novel or collections of short stories published, let alone produced a 'best-seller'.

4   It also reminds one of Queen Gertrude's astute observation in Hamlet that *'The lady doth protest too much, methinks'*.

lifelong, almost pathological, need to be the centre of attention.[1] Esquire proprietor Arnold Gingrich told author Denis Brian for his book The True Gen

> *As long as people around [Hemingway] were worshipping and adoring, why, they were great. The minute they weren't, there was a tendency to find others who were.* [i]

As psychiatrist Dr Christopher Martin and Swiss psychologist Sebastian Dieguez, who have both considered Hemingway's personality and mental make-up, point out, there was a distinctly narcissistic aspect to his character, and the central focus of Hemingway's life was certainly always 'Ernest Hemingway'. One even suggests that for Hemingway writing fiction was some kind of therapy. Biographer Jeffrey Meyers agrees. When Hemingway was asked to name his analyst, according to Meyers he replied: 'Portable Corona No 3'; and in a letter to the New Yorker writer Lillian Ross with whom Hemingway had struck up a friendship, he said his

> *analyst's name is Royal Portable (noiseless) the 3rd.*

Both remarks might well have been intended as nothing more than flip comments, but from what we know of Hemingway's life, it might well have gone a little deeper. Philip Young, one of the earliest academics to write about Hemingway (and who took a mainly psychological approach to examining Hemingway's fiction), cites Nick Adams explaining in the short story Fathers And Sons (in Winner Take Nothing, Hemingway's third collection)

> *If he [Nick Adams] wrote it he could get rid of it. He had gotten rid of many things by writing them.*

. . .

From what they contend, the American academics William Wimsatt and Monroe Beardsley and especially the French philosopher Roland Barthes might presumably advise us against resorting to examining 'Hemingway, the man' and all aspects of his life when interpreting and evaluating his fiction; but no such stricture is in place when considering his ambition and domineering personality, both of which played such a significant role in his rise to literary prominence and eventual celebrity status.

---

1 Although Hemingway hated being alone, some friends and acquaintances claim that it wasn't necessarily true that he always had to be the centre of attention and that he could be a good and attentive listener.

Personality, mental and physical health

Hemingway's life has been exhaustively examined by biographers, yet it is still oddly difficult to establish the essence of his personality. Hemingway, the hard-drinking, pugilistic braggart is well-known, but how do we square that man with the Hemingway some friends insist was essentially shy, sensitive and quite gentle, and who could be spontaneously generous? As Dr Martin notes

> *[Biographer Carlos] Baker pointed out that Hemingway was a man of many contradictions who was capable of alternately appearing shy or conceited, sensitive or aggressive, warm and generous, or ruthless and overbearing. It may have been that certain borderline personality traits caused him to appear erratic and dramatic.*

Perhaps to attempt to get a better comprehension of that personality, we could emulate how the Tao suggests a hole might be described: it is essentially defined by what delimits it. And two aspects of Hemingway's life which most certainly came to define him were his physical and mental health. One should, though, tread carefully.

Physicians sometimes joke that 'there's no such thing as a healthy person: there are only those who have been insufficiently investigated'. That observation might also be made of our mental health. How would any of us fare if we were subjected to rigorous, in-depth psychiatric examination? What is 'normal'? Who is 'normal'? To behave 'normally' merely indicates that our behaviour is close to 'a norm', yet that 'norm' is nothing but an 'average'. Despite the popular use of the word, to behave 'normally' means nothing more than that we are adhering to the standards of behaviour accepted, prescribed and tolerated in any given culture. Even if behaviour veers too far from 'the norm', it is often still tolerated, as eccentricity [1] perhaps, although when such 'eccentric' or 'abnormal' behaviour begins to affect and impact on the lives of others, it is increasingly frowned upon. Furthermore, it would be misleading to try to set up some kind of equivalence between an individual's mental state and his or her personality. We simply don't know how 'mental health' and 'personality' correlate, or whether they even do correlate at all or to any significant degree. Someone with a 'less usual' personality, one which stands out, can certainly not be equated with that person having 'bad mental health'.

Mental health can vary over a lifetime and, as with Hemingway, worsen (or, indeed, improve); and although different aspects of an individual's personality might be exhibited at different times, in different circumstances and in different company, the broad strokes of that personality might be expected to remain more or less constant,

---

1   The word is derived from the Greek '*ekkentros*' – 'out of the centre', away from the norm.

though over time aspects of it might evolve and vary, possibly considerably. In that respect each individual would surely be unique.

The fluctuations in Hemingway's mental health had a definite impact on him – he suffered from regular, often severe, bouts of depression all his life and went through a particularly deep depression in the mid-1930s. It would seem that his mental health began to deteriorate earlier in his life than is hitherto accepted. His excessive drinking from an early age might partly have been a form of self-medication: initially alcohol has a euphoric effect and will mask any 'low' we feel. Then it itself becomes a depressive, so we drink more to counteract that depression. It is assumed that both Hemingway and Ed, his father (who also shot himself),[1] were what is now called 'bi-polar', a condition once referred to as 'manic-depressive'. We might thus speculate that the various instances of his odd behaviour had possibly less to do with his distinct personality and were more the result of him experiencing a manic phase.[2] Anyone familiar with the details of Hemingway's life will be aware of his sometime odd behaviour: his unbridled enthusiasms and certainly his forceful insistence that everyone else should also engage in whatever he was enthusiastic about seem to be typical manic behaviour. Yet we are on shaky ground when analysing, especially at a distance, which behaviour is simply 'unusual' and which might be thought 'abnormal'. We are apt to celebrate 'unusual' individuals and their achievements, but are less inclined to favour 'abnormal' individuals. It wasn't until the year before his death in 1961 when Hemingway began to exhibit clinical symptoms of psychosis and paranoia that we can safely refer to his 'abnormal' behaviour;[3] yet throughout his life and as he got older in his dealings with others, he increasingly behaved in what might charitably he described as a 'singular' manner.

Despite his history of depressions, it seems likely Hemingway's mental health took a distinct turn for the worse seven years before his suicide after he was involved in two plane crashes in as many days in January 1954 while on his second African safari. They certainly took a toll on his already increasingly declining physical health. But those crashes, although the most serious instances since he was blown up by an Austrian mortar in July 1918, were only two in a number of major and minor accidents he suffered throughout his life, most of which caused head injuries. In 1928 in his Paris

---

1   In December 1928. Hemingway's sister Ursula and brother Leicester also killed themselves.

2   Biographer Mary Dearborn suggests that Hemingway was in a prolonged manic phase when he wrote Across The River And Into The Trees, which led to his delusion that it was 'the best' book he had ever written and then his consternation that no one else thought it was any good at all.

3   Finally, in 1961, a few months short of his eventual suicide, he was twice admitted to the Mayo Clinic in Rochester, Minnesota.

apartment bathroom, in the early hours (and probably while still drunk) he mistook the skylight chain for the lavatory cistern chain and, yanking it, brought a defective skylight crashing down on his head. Two years later, in a car crash near Billings, Montana, he almost lost his right arm and spent two months in hospital. Five years later while out fishing, Hemingway shot himself in the leg – he was trying to shoot a shark, and again he was probably drunk. He suffered another serious concussion in May 1944, in London. Returning to his hotel in the wartime blackout after yet another late-night party, the car in which he was travelling crashed headlong into a parked water tanker, and Hemingway was thrown through the windscreen. A head wound needed almost 60 stitches, but despite doctors insisting he should spend some time recuperating, he discharged himself from hospital after just three days (and had spent those three days knocking back bottles of champagne and spirits with well-wishers who dropped in). [1] He was concussed three months later in Normandy when he leapt from the pillion of a motorcycle into a ditch to avoid enemy gunfire and hit his head on a large rock. A year later, there was another car crash, in Cuba, in which Mary Welsh, his fourth wife, was thrown through the windscreen. In 1950 he injured his head when, again while drunk, he slipped on his boat. Then, in January 1954, came the two plane crashes East Africa. Hemingway's poor physical health was not, though, entirely the result of these accidents. At different times in his life he suffered from jaundice, malaria, kidney and liver problems, pneumonia, amoebic dysentery, an intestinal prolapse, hypertension, erysipelas, nephritis, hepatitis, diabetes and arteriosclerosis.

His taste for drinking developed when he left teetotal Oak Park in Chicago and was sent to Italy by the Red Cross, but from his mid-twenties on he was drinking a great deal and around the time his marriage to Hadley was disintegrating, he began to drink even more. By his forties he was an alcoholic who, his third son Gregory claimed, would drink a quart of whisky – almost a litre and more than a UK pint and a half – a day.

. . .

On the matter of Hemingway's mental health, Dr Martin and Dieguez have both compiled profiles which make interesting reading. The Mayo clinic in Rochester, Minnesota, has observed its undertaking never to release Hemingway's medical notes, but both Martin and Dieguez say they worked from information they found in biographies, memoirs and letters, and, of course, what they thought they might deduce from his published work. Both men cover much the same ground, although Martin

---

1   He also knew an allied invasion of Nazi-occupied Europe was imminent and he didn't want to miss witnessing and reporting on it.

focuses on Hemingway's suicide, while Dieguez considers the course of Hemingway's life after he was blown up on the Italian front in July 1918, just 13 days short of his 19th birthday.

In the Winter, 2006, issue of Psychiatry, Martin writes (in part)

> *Significant evidence exists to support the diagnoses of bi-polar disorder, alcohol dependence, traumatic brain injury, and probable borderline and narcissistic personality traits. Late in life, Hemingway also developed symptoms of psychosis likely related to his underlying affective illness and superimposed alcoholism and traumatic brain injury. Hemingway utilized a variety of defense mechanisms, including self-medication with alcohol, a lifestyle of aggressive, risk-taking sportsmanship, and writing, in order to cope with the suffering caused by the complex co-morbidity of his interrelated psychiatric disorders. Ultimately, Hemingway's defense mechanisms failed, overwhelmed by the burden of his complex co-morbid illness, resulting in his suicide.*

In Frontiers Of Neurology And Neuroscience in April, 2010, Dieguez discusses the trauma Hemingway suffered when he was blown up and the possibility that he might have undergone a possible 'near-death experience' (NDE). He cautions on the difficulty of analysing such NDEs because accounts are always subjective and that it is impossible, not least ethically, to construct controlled experiments to investigate them; but he suggests that

> *It is incontrovertible that Hemingway's war wound, if not his 'NDE', occupied a central part of his work and his outlook on life. In this respect, Hemingway seems comparable to other subjects who survived a life-threatening event and who sometimes report a new outlook on life, feelings of immortality and invincibility, a sense of personal importance and a loss of the fear of death.*

Dieguez then adds the pertinent warning

> *Nevertheless, both the 'NDE' and the [post-traumatic stress disorder] approach, though probably correctly underlying major themes of Hemingway's works (including some explicit references to war and wounds), should be more accurately perceived as additional factors to a pre-existing personality pattern. Such a*

Personality, mental and physical health

> *pre-existing temperament might underlie both the selected literary topics and the very near-death experience.*

Dieguez pointedly suggests that whatever effect being blown-up had on the development of Hemingway's personality (and thus his behaviour in later years)

> *. . . it was certainly no happenstance that Hemingway would find himself on a battlefield in the first place.*

In one sense Hemingway had only himself to blame for almost being killed in Italy: he had knowingly put himself in harm's way. When the US joined the war, he is thought to have volunteered, in turn, to serve in the US army, the marines and the navy but was turned down by all three because of his defective left eye.[1] Hearing that the Red Cross was recruiting ambulance drivers and that its physical requirements were lower, he applied and was accepted.[ii] How, though, did he progress from being employed to drive an ambulance several miles behind the front to being blown up on the Italian front line? Once in Italy, the Red Cross volunteers were sent to different ambulance stations, but Hemingway found driving too mundane and volunteered to run one of the rest stations located behind the front where cigarettes, coffee and chocolate were dispensed to Italian soldiers. Yet even that wasn't exciting enough, so he began – wholly unofficially – cycling to the front and delivering the cigarettes and chocolates to the men in the trenches. Shortly before midnight on July 8 he was blown up when an Austrian mortar shell landed nearby. Perhaps that behaviour demonstrates a young man's unwise craving for excitement; yet whatever incidents and influences then and later shaped his character and personality, both had been defined long before he was blown up in Italy. Although some dispute that Hemingway was bi-polar, both Martin and Dieguez certainly subscribe to the notion. In one account of a manic episode quoted by Martin

> *Hemingway's first wife, Hadley, found her husband 'sky-high, emotionally intense, and ready to explode'. His company was so difficult to tolerate that she sent him off on a trip alone. The episodic irritability that drove his father away from his own family was also manifested in the son.*

The mammoth writing sessions of which Hemingway often boasted are seen as episodes of his manic phases. He claimed that once while in Madrid he wrote three short stories

---

1   There is, in fact, disagreement on whether he did volunteer and was turned down or didn't bother to volunteer in the first place because he suspected he would be deemed unfit for service.

quick succession. [1]

Dieguez also writes about Hemingway's haemochromatosis, a genetic condition which prevents the body from ridding itself of the iron it accumulates from food and drink. In time that accumulation can lead to kidney and liver damage, diabetes, joint pain, depression and high blood pressure, and Hemingway suffered from all these conditions. Haemochromatosis is treatable, but unfortunately the conditions it causes are usually diagnosed and treated first, thus masking the fact that haemochromatosis is their root cause, so it can go untreated until it is too late.

. . .

A different account of Hemingway's health problems is given by psychiatrist Dr Andrew Farah in his book Hemingway's Brain, and he is one of those who dispute that Hemingway was bi-polar. According to Dr Farah, of the University of North Carolina, Hemingway's mental problems were the result of the nine head injuries he suffered in the course of his life, causing concussions that were left untreated. Dr Farah also suggests that although the electro-convulsive therapy (ECT) Hemingway was given at the Mayo Clinic benefits nine out of ten patients, in his case it did not. In fact, he says, as a result of the untreated concussions over the years, Hemingway suffered from undiagnosed chronic traumatic encephalopathy – brain damage – and the ECT sessions compounded the damage.

. . .

Psychiatrist Irvin D. Yalom and his wife Marilyn, who worked as a literature professor, also analysed Hemingway's personality, and in June 1971 published a paper outlining their conclusions in the Archives of General Psychiatry. Unlike Martin, who takes a narrow clinical approach, and Dieguez whose investigation is even narrower, concentrating on 'Hemingway's near-death experience' when he was blown up, the Yaloms' conclusions seem rounder. They say they were attempting

> *to illuminate the underlying forces which shaped the content and structure of his work*

and wanted to consider

> *the major psycho-dynamic conflicts, apparent in his lifestyle and*

---

1   If true, quite how Hemingway might square this with another claim he often made – that he found writing to be 'hard work' and that he wrote very slowly, continually re-writing what he was producing – is not clear.

fiction, which led to that event.

The balance between Irvin Yalom's work in psychiatry and his wife's in literature gells well, and their conclusions might well elucidate some of the startling contradictions in Hemingway's personality. Adopting some of the ideas of the German-American psychoanalyst Karen Horney, especially those in her book Neurosis And Human Growth, the Yaloms postulate that the central conflict in Hemingway was between his 'idealised self' and his 'real self', and that the conflict was never resolved. They write that according to Horney a

> *child suffers from basic anxiety, an extremely dysphoric state of being, if he has parents whose own neurotic conflicts prevent them from providing the basic acceptance necessary for the development of the child's autonomous being. During early life when the child regards the parents as omniscient and omnipotent, he can only conclude, in the face of parental disapproval and rejection, that there is something dreadfully wrong with him. To dispel basic anxiety, to obtain the acceptance, approval and love he requires for survival, the child perceives he must become something else; he channels his energies away from the realization of his real self, from his own personal potential, and develops a construct of an idealized image – a way he must become in order to survive and to avoid basic anxiety. The idealized image may take many forms, all of which are designed to cope with a primitive sense of badness, inadequacy or unlovability.*

They add that

> *Hemingway's idealized image crystallized around a search for mastery, for a vindictive triumph which would lift him above others.*

As I point out elsewhere, none of this can be accepted as copper-bottomed fact, merely as informed speculation. But what the Yaloms suggest would account for Hemingway's almost neurotic competitiveness to be the best at everything – not least that he was America's best writer – and the inferiority complex from which his wife Hadley Richardson and his schoolboy crush Frances Coates believe he suffered. The Yaloms add

> *Both publicly and privately Hemingway invested inordinate*

> *psychic energy into fulfilling his idealized image. The investment was not primarily a conscious, deliberate one, for many of Hemingway's life activities were overdetermined; he acted often not through free choice but because he was driven by some dimly understood internal pressure whose murky persuasiveness only shammed choice.*

They suggest that

> *Hemingway's anxiety and depression stemmed in large part from his failure to actualize his idealized self. Two factors were important in this failure: the image was so extreme that superhuman forces would have been required to satisfy it; secondly, a number of counterforces limited his available degree of adaptability. These secondary counterforces, e.g. dependency cravings and oedipal conflicts, were sources of anxiety in their own right and hampered the actualization of the idealized self.*

Interpreting his lifelong courtship of danger they write that

> *Throughout his life Hemingway attempted to abolish the discrepancy between his real and idealized selves. No alterations could be made upon the idealized self; there is no evidence that Hemingway ever compromised or attenuated his self-demands. All the work had to be done upon his real self; he pushed himself to face more intense danger, to attempt physical feats which exceed his capabilities, while at the same time he pruned and streamlined himself. All traces of traits not fitting his idealized image had to be eliminated or squelched. The softer feminine side, the fearful parts, the dependent cravings – all had to go.*

. . .

Hemingway was renown throughout his life for his ostentatious demonstrations of hyper-masculinity and machismo. His macho posturing, it is suggested, betrayed self-doubt about his sexual identity, and much is made of his mother, Grace, dressing him in girls' clothes when he was very young. In fact, some social commentators assure us that it was not unusual in the late 19th century for very young boys to be dressed in more feminine clothes. Furthermore, depending on what he and his sister were up to, both Ernest and Marcelline were also dressed in boys' clothes; yet that does not necessarily indicate that Hemingway was not affected. His mother even chose to treat Hemingway and Marcelline as though they were twins and is reported to have kept Marcelline back from starting school for a year so Ernest and his sister would be in the same class 'as twins'. It would not be too much of a stretch to suggest all this might have had an effect on his feelings of self-worth and impacted on the process each young child's goes through of establishing his or her own identity; the bravado, the showing off and the desire to be best at everything might well have betrayed an atavistic and certainly a subliminal impulse to prove his individuality, that he was not his sister. It might also have contributed to creating the inferiority complex I suggest Hemingway might have suffered throughout his life. In her book The Hemingway Women, author Bernice Kert writes

> *James Joyce once remarked that the two men [Ernest Hemingway and Robert McAlmon, an acquaintance in the Paris years who published Hemingway's first book] were confused about each other. 'Hemingway posing as tough and McAlmon as sensitive should swap poses and be true to life.' Joyce was noticing what Hadley and others had observed – that much of Ernest's swagger was a protective cover for a deeply anxious nature.*

The suggestion is that Hemingway was somehow ashamed of his sensitivity and tried to hide it. But however interesting and possibly informative such speculation about Hemingway's psychological state might be, [1] one should be wary of treading the path of what has become known as 'psycho-biography'. As for the oft-made suggestion that Hemingway was a closet homosexual, one can only retort that despite such claims from Scott Fitzgerald's wife Zelda – she and Hemingway disliked each other intensely – and the bi-sexual Robert McAlmon – nothing has ever come to light which might substantiate them. [iii] Those who engage in 'psycho-biography' usually resort to digging up this or that 'fact' about their subject and making large assumptions based on the kind of bargain-basement psychology found in Saturday and Sunday newspaper supplements. But such 'psycho-biographies' have a lot less to say – simply because they cannot know – what character and personality traits the subject might have inherited. In fact, the whole area of 'character' and 'personality' is so woolly that reducing it more or less to a

---

1 Speculation of this kind might well be regarded as no more than 'informed guessing', but in that respect the Yaloms, Martin and Dieguez are, perhaps, better qualified to speculate than others.

series of psychological traits is itself questionable. So when one considers Hemingway's character and personality, it might be best – or, at least, safest – to restrict oneself to reports from family, schoolmates, friends, colleagues and acquaintances of his habitual behaviour in their interactions with him.

...

Hemingway grew up in a god-fearing, church-going, teetotal household, the son of a strict father who often punished him physically, and notably he did not show any outright rebellious behaviour until he had returned from Italy. There is, though, the curious story of how as a teenager when staying at the family summer cottage at Walloon Lake, Michigan, he deliberately shot and killed a blue heron, a bird he knew to be a protected species; and he did so – it is claimed – precisely because it was a protected species. He then, briefly, went on the run – or, perhaps better, made himself scarce, apparently on his mother's advice – when the local game warden called at the cottage to investigate. In later years and true to form Hemingway exaggerated the incident and claimed he had been 'lying low' for a while. Yet he was only 16 at the time, and the incident cannot really be spun into anything more significant than an extreme form of teenage devilment.

Hemingway was variously said by those who knew him at school and later when he was in his early twenties to be friendly and funny, and shy and sensitive; but he was also described by school friends as sometimes being a vindictive bully. He was known for his charm and his wit, and was regarded by many as very good company; yet he also had a sharp and hurtful tongue, and could turn on someone in an instant if he felt slighted, bested or somehow put out, an aspect of his personality which governed his behaviour ever more as he grew older (and drank more). Some friends in later life described Hemingway as 'an intellectual', yet he did not like being thought one, and with increasingly boorish behaviour, to those friends' consternation, he liked to prove them wrong. We can certainly wonder why.

From an early age he was known as a braggart who told tall stories. When he was five, he insisted to his grandfather that single-handed he had stopped a runaway horse. Such hyperbole is quite common among very young and imaginative children, and is not unusual among teenage boys, but Hemingway's proclivity for telling such stories did not diminish as he matured. Such was the force of his personality and the conviction with which he made his claims that many accepted without question everything he said. He could be irascible and had a ferocious temper, traits which also became far more pronounced as he got older and drank more; he was regarded by some as a generous and loyal friend, yet by the time he died, he had fallen out with all his friends from his Paris years, except James Joyce and Ezra Pound.[1] He could be very generous, but oddly, according to one biographer, his generosity was usually extended just to his friends – he is said once to have sold stock so he could give John Dos Passos, who had been admitted to hospital with rheumatic fever, $1,000 (the equivalent of about $23,000 in 2023) to pay for his bills, and he made it clear to Dos Passos that he did not expect to be repaid. On the other hand he is said rarely to have given any presents to his wives and immediate family. Martha Gellhorn, his third wife, reports that in all the time they were together, Hemingway gave her just two gifts: just as they were about to embark on a hunting trip to the West, he handed her a pair of long johns and a shotgun – because he knew she would need both.

. . .

One core element of Hemingway's personality which certainly does help to explain his quite sudden rise to fame as a writer was his extraordinary competitiveness. In the foreword to his biography of Hemingway, Carlos Baker describes

> . . . *the immensely ambitious young man, unfailingly competitive, driven by an urge to excel in whatever he undertook, to be admired and looked up to, to assert his superiority by repeated example, to display for the benefit of others his strength and his endurance.*

Being 'driven by an urge to excel' is one thing and is not at all rare; but also being driven by an urge 'to be admired' – admittedly that is Baker's description – adds a curious dimension. As for Baker's claim that Hemingway was also driven by an urge to be 'looked up to' and 'to assert his superiority', it does more than hint at a possible underlying feeling of inadequacy and an inferiority complex. Baker's take on the conflicting aspects of Hemingway's character is also succinct. He speaks of

> . . . *the man of many contradictions: the shy diffident and the incredible braggart; the sentimentalist quick to tears and the bully who used his anger like a club; the warm and generous friend and the ruthless and overbearing enemy; the man who stayed loyal to some of his oldest friends while picking quarrels with others because he feared that they were beginning to assume a proprietary interest over him.*

---

1   Notably, he didn't see either man again after he left Paris, more or less after he married Pauline Pfeiffer in 1927. Joyce died in January 1941, and Pound in November 1972,

Although, as I point out above, one should be alert to the danger of conflating 'mental health' and 'personality', given the marked discrepancies in behaviour and attitudes Baker describes, we might still wonder just how much the bi-polar condition from which Martin and Dieguez believe Hemingway suffered did influence the expression of the different aspects of his personality. Even as a child Hemingway was extremely, almost neurotically, competitive: he had to be the best at everything, whether it was fishing, hunting, boxing, playing tennis and, later in life, at being able to drink vast quantities of alcohol. In his memoir, Hemingway's Bitterness, Harold Loeb recalls Hemingway on the tennis court:

> *He was no tennis player; a bad eye, damaged in a street brawl, [sic] and a weak leg injured by shrapnel, hampered his control. His back-court drives were erratic and his net game non-existent. Nevertheless, he put so much gusto into the play and got so much pleasure out of his good shots and such misery from his misses, that the games in which he participated were never lackadaisical. Also, we usually played doubles, and by assigning the best player to Hem, a close match could sometimes be achieved.* [iv]

Biographers report that if Hemingway met someone who knew about a subject of which he knew little, he quizzed them incessantly until he had extracted from them everything there might be to know about the topic until he, too, was 'an expert'. He liked to portray himself as very knowledgeable on most topics – another aspect of his competitiveness – and once he believed himself to be an authority on a subject, whether fishing, hunting, sports, gambling, writing, food, wine and the 'good life' and travelling, he would then lecture those around him. He prided himself as always having the 'inside gen' and being in the loop, and liked to be seen as 'insider'. If he developed a frenetic enthusiasm for an activity – which he often did – he cajoled everyone to join in the activity and took a dim view of anyone who tried to opt out. It comes as no surprise to hear that the journalist and writer Damon Runyon quipped that

> *Few men can stand the strain of relaxing with [Hemingway] over an extended period.*

Such enthusiasms and the occasions when he had, as he described it, the 'juice' might well have been a manifestation of the manic phase of his assumed bi-polar condition. The Torrents Of Spring (though it was only 30,000 words long) was written in just ten days, and he later told the journalist Lillian Ross in her celebrated 1950 New Yorker

Personality, mental and physical health

profile of him that he

> '. . . wrote The Sun when I was twenty-seven, and I wrote it in six weeks, starting on my birthday, July 21, in Valencia, and finishing it September 6, in Paris. But it was really lousy and the rewriting took nearly five months.'

His competitiveness extended to comparing writing to a contest, and even dead writers were regarded as rivals. Talking about his writing career in the same profile – and adopting the metaphor of boxing – he told Ross

> I started out very quiet and I beat Mr Turgenev. Then I trained hard and I beat Mr de Maupassant. I've fought two draws with Mr Stendhal, and I think I had an edge in the last one. But nobody's going to get me in any ring with Mr Tolstoy unless I'm crazy or I keep getting better.

After the profile was published and many commented that it made Hemingway – who had inexplicably also adopted a faux native-American way of speaking in all his conversations with Ross – look silly, he remarked that he had often been joking and had assumed Ross would have realised. [v] That might well have been true, but whether or not the accent and his comments were intended as light-hearted, it was not the only time when he described writers as being in competition with each other. Two of his contemporaries whose achievements were always to be trumped were F. Scott Fitzgerald and William Faulkner. Faulkner was, though, equally as prickly and competitive, and said of Hemingway

> He has never been known to use a word that might send a reader to the dictionary

to which Hemingway responded

> Poor Faulkner. Does he really think big emotions come from big words?

The writer, journalist, 'insider' and expert

Prose is architecture, not interior decoration, and the Baroque is over.

Ernest Hemingway.

There wasn't room in his head for cops and robbers, a six-day week, and serious writing. Even to his journalism he brought standards that were personally exacting. 'Don't talk about it before you write it,' he warned Mary Lowry [a fellow reporter] once, as they walked back to the Star after a provocative interview with the survivors of a Japanese earthquake. 'You mustn't talk about it,' Hemingway insisted. 'You'll spoil it.'

Charles A. Fenton, The Apprenticeship Of Ernest Hemingway: The Early Years.

In 1923, under the energetic leadership of [Harry C.] Hindmarsh's father-in-law, the late Joseph E. Atkinson, the Star was emerging as the colossus of Canadian journalism. Sensational headlines, red type, comic strips, eyewitness and flamboyant reportage, basic English and many photographs were the fundamental tools. In the bible-belt atmosphere of southern Ontario the Star's management also uncovered in religion an appeal which Hearst, for example, although he frequently attempted it, was never able to exploit fully in the United States. Atkinson's nickname in the trade was an indication of the pious hypocrisy his contemporaries felt they

> *detected in the contradictory components of his papers. They called him 'Holy Joe'.*
>
> **Charles A. Fenton, The Apprenticeship Of Ernest Hemingway: The Early Years.**

LIKE many writers, Hemingway began working with words as a journalist, and many young journalists shared and share his ambition to 'become a writer'. A few make it, many more do not. Although he later insisted that his journalism was ruining his writing and he ended his first stint of working as a journalist when he returned to Paris in January 1924, he resumed journalism in the early 1930s when he was invited to contribute 'Letters' to the then new magazine Esquire. He carried on turning out pieces for magazines intermittently for the next 15 years, although his months – over four visits – in Spain to report on the civil war and later his ten months in Europe in 1944 and 1945 on World War II filing features for Collier's magazine would see him most active as a journalist. [1] Despite his advice to young writers to give up journalism, many novelists have successfully pursued a career as both a writer and a journalist with neither activity apparently ruining the other. It doesn't help, of course, that the notions of 'journalism' and 'journalist' are unhelpfully vague: someone editing copy and writing headlines and captions for an angling or arts and crafts magazine is as much 'a journalist' as the 'hard news' man or woman reporting from a war zone, sniffing out skullduggery in high places and lunching with 'captains of industry'. [i]

When Hemingway decided 'to become a writer' is not recorded, but his literary ambitions were and are certainly not unusual among men and women in their late teens and early 20s, although most fall by the wayside. Cyril Connolly observed that

> *There is no more sombre enemy of good art than the pram in the hall*

but he might well have said the same about 'early ambitions' being at the mercy of that pram. That after the birth of his first child, John, in October 1923, Hemingway was – once back living in Paris – able to ignore domestic distractions and persevere with his writing was down to his ruthless single-mindedness and marked self-centredness as

---

1   The claim that he was 'working as journalist' in World War II Europe should be qualified; it was strictly true, but in ten month he filed just six pieces of about 5,500 words each. His output did not impress Collier's, especially given the very generous amounts the magazine was paying him. The magazine also objected to the substantial sum in expenses Hemingway tried to claim.

much as his then wife Hadley's staunch support – and her trust fund income. [1]

...

Hemingway's progress as a writer, from turning out the juvenilia he submitted to the Saturday Evening Post and other magazines to the triumph of his early published works a few years later, has been detailed by the former Duke University English professor, Charles A. Fenton. In his book The Apprenticeship Of Ernest Hemingway, he outlines Hemingway's development as a writer, from his first acquaintance with English literature at Oak Park High and the stories he wrote for class, to his, albeit short, training as a reporter on the Kansas City Star and his association with the Toronto Star Weekly and its sister morning paper, the Toronto Star. In the course of his research, Fenton remained undeterred by Hemingway's warnings, issued when 'Papa' got wind of his project in 1950, not to approach his family and those who had known him. Hemingway's attitude was, however, remarkably ambiguous. His claim in several letters to Fenton demanding that he abandon his research because it was 'an invasion of privacy' is odd for a man who also assiduously sought the limelight. [2] The irony might not even have struck him. His apparent reluctance to have his life examined is also somewhat contradicted by his continual self-promotion over the previous 20 years in his journalism for Esquire and other magazines, and his later whole-hearted willingness to feature in mid-market magazine photo-spreads. Biographer James Mellow tellingly points out that even while Hemingway said he did not want any kind of biographical work written about him, he was already passing on 'facts' to Fenton about his early life. Mellow notes that

> *When Fenton also began querying his sister Marcelline and his outlawed sister Carol (she had married her college boyfriend John Gardner in 1933, against Hemingway's wishes and he vowed never to see her again), Hemingway gave him a 'cease and desist' order [and] the correspondence developed into angry exchanges. Yet, with each angry response, Hemingway, by way of correcting errors, also began feeding out more tempting bait . . . it was to Fenton that*

---

1   Biographers report that in the early Paris days he informed Hadley that she should not talk at breakfast because he was 'already writing' and needed silence. Some might take this as proof of his dedication as an artist; some might simply conclude he was a bit of a pretentious soul.

2   Robert McAlmon, a nominal friend in Paris who published Hemingway's first work, Three Stories And Ten Poems, in 1923, was one of the first to comment on Hemingway's self-promotion. Hemingway, he said was *'the original Limelight Kid, just you watch him for a few months . . . Wherever the limelight is, you'll find Ernest with his big lovable boyish grin, making hay . . . He's going places, he's got a natural talent for the public eye, has that boy'*.

> *he gratuitously offered the dubious information that he had to get the hell out of Petoskey because of troubles with four or five girls.*

Some later biographers list by name the three or four girls Hemingway dallied with in northern Michigan, but none reports what would have been a most interesting 'fact' that, presumably as some kind of local Don Juan, Hemingway was forced to skip town. [1] It is more likely that despite ostensibly 'correcting' factual errors, Hemingway was again trying to contribute to the legend he had created for himself, this time stressing that he had been a womaniser even at an early age. One question which again demands to be asked is: was Hemingway even aware of what he was doing?

. . .

In tracing Hemingway's development as a writer, Fenton interviewed Oak Park High contemporaries and staff, fellow reporters and executives at the Kansas City Star who were there in 1917 and 1918, executives and colleagues on the Toronto Star and Star Weekly, and friends, acquaintances and fellow journalists in Paris. Fenton tells us – unremarkably given the overall tone of his account – that all who knew Hemingway as a young man were sure he would go on to achieve 'great things'. [ii] Certainly by the early 1950s, it was natural for Fenton to treat Hemingway as 'a great writer' as that was the public status he had by then achieved; yet the apparently almost universal intuition 30 years earlier about young Hemingway's future – notably, though, reported in hindsight once he was famous – makes Fenton's account read rather too much like those 'lives of the saints' written for young children in which the saint in question is shown to have been preternaturally virtuous as a child and an eventual canonization was inevitable. Fenton is also sometimes at odds with later biographers on some of the facts of Hemingway's life, although it is impossible to discover whether he or they were at fault. As evidence of Hemingway's literary gift, Fenton cites that the stories he produced for his Oak Park High English classes were read out as examples for his classmates to emulate. Context is always useful, and it would help if we knew whether any of his fellow students were similarly asked to read out their work to the class. It is more likely than not that it would have been, even of those who went on to become accountants, public servants, engineers, teachers or 'home-makers'.

Once Hemingway had arrived in Kansas City in October 1917 to train as a reporter on the Star, he was said to have been enthusiastic, eager to learn, that he volunteered for extra

---

1 While on honeymoon in northern Michigan with Hadley after they had married in Horton Bay, Hemingway rather oddly decided to introduce her to several of his previous girlfriends, to Hadley's distress and the girls' discomfort.

duties and talked incessantly about journalism and writing. Yet again there is perhaps rather less to this than meets the eye: assuming that working for a newspaper was the long-held ambition of a 17-year-old who found he was able to 'break into journalism' [1], which of them isn't eager and enthusiastic? Given that reputedly many journalists also intend in the long run to 'become a writer', Hemingway and his ambitions were not in the least unusual.

When he joined the Kansas City Star, Hemingway was, like all cub reporters, given a copy of the paper's style sheet which outlined all the rules the paper wanted its news staff to observe. It began

> *Use short sentences. Use short first paragraphs. Use vigorous English*

and Hemingway later declared they were the

> *best rules I ever learned for the business of writing.*

Certainly in his first two volumes of short stories and his first two novels [2] Hemingway observed those rules strictly, and in one review of In Our Time, his first volume, he earned plaudits for using short sentences, short first paragraphs vigorous English'. Oddly Hemingway seems to have forgotten those Kansas City Star strictures entirely when just seven years after his first volume of short stories appeared and six years after his first novel he published Death In The Afternoon which was, ironically, in part his guide to 'good' writing. In a review in September 1932 of Death In The Afternoon the New York Times observed that

> *In this book Mr. Hemingway is guilty of the grievous sin of writing sentences which have to be read two or three times before the meaning is clear. He enters, indeed, into a stylistic phase which corresponds, for his method, to the later stages of Henry James.*

It got no better three years later with Green Hills Of Africa which, again ironically, included his considered dicta on literature and writing. In 1939, the critic Edmund Wilson, who a decade earlier had been a staunch Hemingway champion, but who had since revised his views with each new book the writer published, noted that

---

1   It's odd how no one seems to 'break into banking' or 'break into engineering' or 'break into teaching' or even 'break into plumbing'.

2   The Kansas City Star was itself also impressed by The Sun Also Rises and observed in its review that their former cub reporter wrote with a *'swinging, effortless precision that puts him in the first flight of American stylists'*.

> [Hemingway] has produced what must be one of the only books ever written which make Africa and it's animals seem dull.

As Hemingway would – or, at least, should – have known, 'being dull' is a cardinal sin in journalism, but 'dull' is certainly an apt description of large passages of both non-fiction books. As for the prose in Green Hills Of Africa, Hemingway again comprehensively ignored 'the best rules [he] ever learned for the business of writing' laid out in the Kansas City style sheet rules. Edmund Wilson also records that in the book

> He delivers a self-confident lecture on the high possibilities of prose writing, with the implication that he himself, Hemingway, has realized or hopes to realize these possibilities; and then writes what are certainly, from the point of view of prose, the very worst pages of his life. There is one passage which is hardly even intelligible – the most serious possible fault for a writer who is always insisting on the supreme importance of lucidity.

In a contemporary review of Green Hills Of Africa for The Saturday Review of Literature, Bernard de Voto also concerns himself with the lack of lucidity in Hemingway's prose and writes

> The prize sentence in the book runs [to] forty-six lines. The one I should like to quote as typical . . . [and] though less than half that long, is still too long, and a comparatively straightforward one must serve. 'Going downhill steeply made these Spanish shooting boots short in the toe and there was an old argument, about this length of boot and whether the boot-maker, whose part I had taken, unwittingly, first, only as interpreter, and finally embraced his theory patriotically as a whole and, I believed, by logic, had overcome it by adding onto the heel.' This is simpler than most, but it shows the new phase . . . But, however earnest the intention, the result is a kind of etymological gas that is just bad writing.

A Hemingway champion might protest that Hemingway is celebrated mainly for his fiction not his non-fiction, but that would be news to 'Papa': by the early 1930s he regarded himself as fully-fledged, time-served 'man of letters', as his many pronouncements on what constituted 'good writing' made clear. If Hemingway did re-read what he had written, would not the flaws that bothered the critics have been so apparent to a purported 'great writer' that he might have revised many passages? If he did not re-read what he had written – which is frankly inconceivable – why not? Why did he think the *'kind of etymological gas that is just bad writing'* that bothered de Voto could pass muster? [1] In 1936 in one of his Esquire 'Letters', Hemingway advised would-be writers

> *The best way is to read [what you have previously written] all every day from the start, correcting as you go along, then go on from where you stopped the day before. When it gets so long that you can't do this every day[,] read back two or three chapters each day; then each week read it all from the start. That's how you make it all of one piece.*

That is good advice, and had he re-read the passage and others quoted by de Voto, he would have realised they were in need of re-writing. All-in-all in Death In The Afternoon and Green Hills Of Africa Hemingway seems to have forgotten his own dictum that

> *Prose is architecture, not interior decoration, and the Baroque is over.*

. . .

At the end of April 1918, Hemingway left the Star after just seven months to start his Red Cross service in Italy and was back in the US by mid-January. After spending the summer with his family at their holiday cottage on Walloon Lake in northern Michigan, he remained in the area when the cottage was shut for the season and began writing in earnest. In his rented room in Petoskey he produce more fiction to try to sell to magazines (and, according to his 'revelation' to Fenton, getting local girls into trouble). When he moved to Toronto for several month at the beginning of 1920 (not, as Fenton reports, by the end of 1919), it was through his employer Ralph Connable that he made contact with the Toronto Star Weekly. Shortly, its editor, Herbert Cranston, agreed to consider for publication any features he submitted. Yet the Toronto Star and its sister paper, the Star Weekly, and the Kansas City Star, their styles, their journalism and their standards were as chalk and cheese. Fenton writes:

---

1   Where was Max Perkins, Hemingway's editor at Scribner's, in all this? Biographers have established that he disliked confrontation and was apt to give way to Hemingway, one of Scribner's 'best earners'. Surely the awfulness of many of the passages in Death In The Afternoon and Green Hills Of Africa so obvious to critics were also apparent to him? Yet he seemed to have allowed it to slip past without a murmur. And given the poor reviews Death received, would Perkins not have been more alert to ensuring Green Hills was more up to scratch? Apparently he wasn't.

The writer, journalist, 'insider' and expert   113

> *In Kansas City Hemingway had worked under conscientious editors who took with the greatest seriousness their responsibilities to the profession in general and to young reporters in particular . . . Hemingway had been indoctrinated in the necessities of accuracy, in the obligations of vigorous prose, and the requirements of forceful narrative. It had been a school with high, harsh standards, rigidly enforced. Few such standards existed on either of the Toronto papers owned by the late Joseph E. Atkinson . . . The Star Weekly was in particular dedicated largely to the indiscriminate entertainment of its subscribers.*

The Star's imperative to entertain rather than to inform its readers was reflected in the paper's layout and visual impact. Fenton adds that

> *Sensational headlines, red type, comic strips, eyewitness and flamboyant reportage, basic English and many photographs were [its] fundamental tools.*

The Star needed a lot of copy week-in, week-out and, says Fenton,

> *More important, from Hemingway's point of view, the Star Weekly emphasized feature material on a virtually limitless range of topics . . . and bought most of its material, in 1920, from freelance writers.*

Any and all writing, irrespective of its purpose, which demands a certain discipline is good training for a would-be writer,[1] whether he or she hopes eventually to produce high art, low art or even, as Hemingway boasted of The Sun Also Rises, something which would engage both highbrows and lowbrows. It increases a familiarity with words, their varied use, their sound, their meanings and what might be described as their 'import'. So whether Hemingway was producing short, accurate and succinct news reports for the Kansas City Star – though inevitably re-written by a copy/sub-editor – or fluffy and disposable colour copy the Star required was neither here nor there: he was writing.

None Hemingway's Kansas City Star output seems to have survived, but some of the short colour pieces Hemingway produced in Toronto (and later in Paris) for the Star

---

1   It is far more of a challenge to edit 600 words of copy down to a snappy five-paragraph tabloid news story – about 80 words – than to edit them for a broadsheet which will be quite happy to use all 600 words.

Weekly have been, and they can be read on a Toronto Star website dedicated to the paper's connection with the writer. [1] Although some of the pieces Hemingway produced were quite good, much else was workaday. That last description, though, should not be regarded as criticism: Hemingway was not paid by the Star to produce literature, but to turn out the reams of copy it needed to fill the pages of the morning paper and its weekly stablemate. Those short pieces demonstrate that Hemingway had a neat turn of phrase, a colourful style and a facile gift – the phrase is not being used in a pejorative sense – for producing such fluff, though such a facility is not unusual among working journalists. What also stands out is a certain sardonic take Hemingway had on most things, although that, too, is not unusual in a young man in his late teens.

. . .

After Hemingway returned to northern Michigan for the summer, but was booted out of the house later that year and moved to Chicago, he found himself writing again, this time for the monthly newspaper Cooperative Commonwealth. For Hemingway the discipline of churning out copy by the yard was also good training. Sherwood Anderson, then riding high in literary circles and who had just returned from Paris, persuaded Hemingway to move to France and promised to supply him with letters of introduction to Gertrude Stein and Ezra Pound (though it is not recorded whether or not at the time Hemingway even knew who Stein and Pound were). Once he was in Paris by late-December, within days Hemingway was filing copy to the Star. It was more fluff: his first impressions of Europe (he and Hadley had travelled to Paris via Spain), the life of a freelance, his impressions of the 'bohemians' who were making Paris their home – it was exactly the kind of timeless, inconsequential, entertaining colour copy the Star Weekly wanted. But it, too, was journalism.

. . .

When Hemingway is spoken of, almost in awe and certainly with respect, as 'the youngest foreign correspondent in Paris at the time', it adds to the Hemingway legend: upon hearing this for the first time, the conclusion of many will be 'look, even as a young man Papa Hemingway was special!' Yet his arrangement with the Star Weekly – and, in time, with the Daily Star – was on the same freelance basis it had been in Toronto; he was paid for the copy that was published. Eventually, Hemingway was asked by the Toronto Star to undertake certain jobs, but even when, in April 1922, he was asked to attend the

---

1   They can be found at *https://ehto.thestar.com*.

The writer, journalist, 'insider' and expert

Genoa economic conference (and later that year the Lausanne peace conference), the Star wanted his usual chatty colour pieces not news reports – these they obtained from the wire services. As it turned out, Hemingway was partly providing those wire reports, too, although illegally: on his Genoa assignment he began 'moonlighting', contravening his arrangement with the Toronto Star, by privately supplying the Paris representative of the US International News Service with news copy under the name John Hadley. [iii] This was eventually spotted by John Bone, the Toronto Star's managing editor, when hard news copy the paper was buying from the INS was remarkably similar to copy Hemingway was filing. [iv] Hadley Richardson, who had been told of the arrangement before Hemingway left for Genoa, did not approve of his duplicity at all and told him so.

The trip to Constantinople, Smyrna and Thrace in the autumn of 1922 in the wake of the Greco-Turkish war had been Hemingway's suggestion, not his editor's. It was the excitement of war he craved, though working trips away from Paris paid better freelance rates, as well as $75 in expenses. [1] Herbert Cranston and later John Bone, were pleased with the copy he provided and, in the way of newspapers, eventually began to trail and hype up 'new reports' from 'their man in Europe'. But again there is rather less to this than meets the eye: it was and is a standard newspaper practice to build up a writer or reporter by name to try to persuade readers that they are getting extra value for the few cents their copy of the paper cost them. [2]

As a gregarious man Hemingway was soon socialising with other Paris-based journalists from whom he picked up a great deal, not least snippets of political analysis which he was able to use in the pieces he filed for the Star. One useful and common journalistic skill he soon mastered and employed in those pieces was to appear 'well-informed'. The role of 'the insider', of the man 'who knows', the man who had – in his own later phrase – 'the gen', was one he espoused with enthusiasm, and he played the role for the rest of his life. A decade later he developed this skill for the 'Letters' he wrote for Arnold Gingrich's Esquire, and very soon readers accepted him as an 'expert' in all kinds of areas: fishing, hunting, wine, fine dining and where to eat, etiquette, travelling, art and, of course, writing. It was a persona that, as John Raeburn demonstrates, contributed greatly to the 'public Ernest Hemingway'. When in Spain covering the civil war, Hemingway was apparently taken into the confidence of one Mikhail Koltsov,

---

1   Hemingway mentions this in one of the short pieces he submitted to the Weekly Star.

2   It is a ploy that works, too. When readers are offered, usually in large type with a big by-line photograph, 'the Elmer Fudd/Caspar Milquetoast/Walter Mitty interview',despite their habitual scepticism about the Press, they will invariably think to themselves 'my, oh my, this Elmer Fudd/Caspar Milquetoast/Walter Mitty *must* be shit-hot to get his own interview!' No, not really. As Jean François Paul de Gondi, Archbishop of Paris, noted in the mid-16th century *The most mistrustful are often the greatest dupes.*

nominally the Pravda correspondent but, in fact, an NKVD agent who is thought to have been reporting directly to Stalin. Koltsov had recognised Hemingway's vanity in wanting to be seen as the 'insider' who had 'the gen' and fed him all kinds of 'facts' that the Soviets wanted to have disseminated in the West. The character of Karkov in For Whom The Bell Tolls was based on Koltsov.

In Hemingway's first 22 months in Paris, the Star had asked him to go on several trips for them, but as his heart was not in journalism – and Hadley's trust fund income as well as the excellent dollar/franc exchange rate meant they didn't really need the money – he often turned down assignments. That would have been impossible for a staff man. When Hadley discovered she was pregnant, however, and Hemingway faced the prospect of providing for a family, he finally took up the daily Star's offer of a staff job in Toronto made earlier in the year, and he and his wife sailed to Canada in September 1923.

Hemingway was ridden hard in Toronto and got none of his own writing done. Harry C. Hindmarsh, the deputy managing editor, who happened to be married to the daughter of the Star group's owner, Joseph Atkinson, thought he was a cocky show-off and set about taking him down a peg or two. Most recent biographers agree that Hemingway did overdo the 'veteran journalist' who had 'covered wars' and who was to boot 'a published author' – that claim was made on the basis of his two slim volumes of poetry and short stories that had been privately published earlier in the year. [v] It didn't help that Hindmarsh was also at odds with his immediate boss, managing editor John Bone who was better inclined towards Hemingway. Within two months Hemingway had fallen out with Hindmarsh and was de facto demoted to working full-time on the Weekly Star. By Christmas he'd had enough and handed in his resignation, and that was the end of his association with the Toronto Star papers and regular journalism. Before the end of January he, Hadley and their new-born son, John, were back in Paris where Hemingway now intended to dedicate himself to writing full-time.

Now without an income of his own from Star freelance work, Hemingway, Hadley and their young son relied on Hadley's trust fund money. Money was a little tighter than it had been before the brief sojourn in Toronto, but Hemingway did not look for paid employment. At Ezra Pound's suggestion he began to work part-time on Ford Madox Ford's short-lived literary magazine *transatlantic review* and Ernest Walsh's This Quarter. At a pinch this might be regarded as journalism, but he was not paid a cent by either men (which eventually lead to bad blood between Hemingway and Walsh); at least he could now dedicate himself to writing fiction with no distractions.

In Paris, Hemingway was continually assuring friends how 'hard' he was engaged on 'difficult' work and that he was writing every day whenever possible, whether in cafés, at home or in a hotel garret room he later claimed he had rented nearby. But a frank assessment of how much work he produced between the beginning of December, 1922, when the valise went missing at the Gare de Lyon until October, 1924, when he dispatched the manuscript for his first commercially published work, In Our Time, to his New York publisher, Boni & Liveright makes it clear it was not a great deal. That manuscript included the three stories and the 18 very brief vignettes (which he called chapters) that had already appeared in his first two privately published works and 13 new stories. Of these, the two-part story Big Two-Hearted River, at just over 8,000 words, was by far the longest. The others were between 500 and 2,500 words long.

Although In Our Time attracted attention and impressed many in literary circles, it did not sell well. It had an initial print run of just 1,300 copies, and Hemingway, who now already regarded himself as an 'expert on publishing', told Boni & Liveright they should have printed at least 20,000 copies, and he claimed the poor sales were down to inadequate advertising. But at least Hemingway could now claim to be a professional writer: he was no longer a hack hired to supply reams of inconsequential copy, but an established and increasingly famous author. There was a world of difference.

'Rules on writing' and the 'Theory of Omission'

It wasn't by accident that the Gettysburg address was so short. The laws of prose writing are as immutable as those of flight, of mathematics, of physics.

Ernest Hemingway in a letter to Max Perkins, 1945.

The prize sentence in the book runs to forty-six lines . . . This is simpler than most, but it shows the new phase. Usually the material is not so factual as this and we are supposed to get, besides the sense, some muscular effort or some effect of colour or movement that is latent in pace and rhythm rather than in words. But, however earnest the intention, the result is a kind of etymological gas that is just bad writing.

**Bernard de Voto, Green Hills Of Africa,
Saturday Review Of Literature, October 26, 1935.**

QUITE soon in his career and after publishing just two volumes of short stories, a novella and two novels, Hemingway came to regard himself as an authority on writing. Death In The Afternoon, his third substantial work, was something of an oddity: intended as a guide for English speakers to bullfighting, its history, practice and lore and other matters Spanish, he also pontificated on writing and literature (and, to my mind rather tenuously, compared writers to matadors). Ironically, given the earlier praise in a New York Times review in 1926 of The Sun Also Rises for his 'lean, hard and athletic narrative prose that 'puts more literary English to shame', six years later a reviewer in the same paper noted that in his new book Hemingway was

> *guilty of the grievous sin of writing sentences which have to be read two or three times before the meaning is clear. He enters, indeed, into a stylistic phase which corresponds, for his method, to the later stages of Henry James.*

That must have hurt.

Hemingway again laid down the law on what constituted 'good writing' when, in 1934, F. Scott Fitzgerald, by then only nominally a 'close friend', asked for his comments on his newly-published fourth novel, Tender Is The Night (which had taken him eight years to write). Hemingway was now the mentor where once he had taken Fitzgerald's advice: when he had shown Fitzgerald the manuscript for The Sun Also Rise, Fitzgerald advised him that the opening two chapters were unnecessary and detracted from the novel, and he advised Hemingway to ditch them. Hemingway ditched them. [i] Eight years later, he was no longer the aspiring writer asking for advice from an established colleague, and he was unsparing in what he had to say about the new novel. [1] In his letter to Fitzgerald, he again reveals his oddly narrow view of what writers 'should' be doing; and certainly many of his criticism are contentious. [ii]

. . .

Hemingway was, though, by no means the first writer to hand out advice on how to 'write', and he will certainly not be the last. A brief internet search for 'rules on writing' will gather so much advice from so many authors that one gets the impression no self-respecting writer feels she or he dare not hand it out: Stephen King, Anne Enright, Neil Gaiman, A. L. Kennedy, V. J. Naipaul, Henry Miller, Jack Kerouac, Jonathan Franzen, Diane Athill, Roddy Doyle, Denis Lehane and Mark Twain are just a very few among a host of authors who have added their two ha'porth worth. The various 'rules' they lay down range from the very practical and sensible to the arcane and precious. What Hemingway would have made of some of the advice offered is anyone's guess.

Stephen King, a successful writer by any standard – the sniffier critics and academics might choose to argue his work 'is not literature', but he is certainly 'a writer' – advises writers 'to avoid distraction', 'write for yourself', 'write one word at a time' and to 'read, read, read'. On a technical note he advises 'avoid adverbs'. Anne Enright is equally practical and encourages would-be authors simply to 'have fun'. She also strikes a down-to-earth note when she insists – and notably splits an infinitive as she does so,

---

1   In later years he did warm to Tender Is The Night and admitted to Max Perkins, who had also been Fitzgerald's editor, that it was better than he had at first thought.

although these days only bores and dullards are bothered by that kind of thing – that

> *the way to write a book is to actually write a book. A pen is useful, typing is also good. Keep putting words on paper.*

Neil Gaiman and A.L. Kennedy similarly advise would-be writers simply to 'write', and Ms Kennedy adds with disarming, though for many hopeful writers possibly unwelcome, honesty that might well be above their heads

> *No amount of self-inflicted misery, altered states, black pullovers or being publicly obnoxious will ever add up to your being a writer. Writers write. On you go.*

V. J. Naipaul's 'rules on writing' are puzzling. Naipaul, who like Hemingway reputedly had a high opinion of himself, informs would-be writers that they should 'not write long sentences'. A sentence 'should not have more than ten or 12 words', and he adds that

> *each sentence should make a clear statement. It should add to the statement that went before. A good paragraph is a series of clear, linked statements.*

What then, one wonders, did Naipaul make of the work of, for example, Jane Austen, Anthony Trollope, George Eliot, George Gissing or Henry James? All are acknowledged as fine writers (and all reward focused reading); but none of whom was known for writing short sentences 'of no more than ten or 12 words'?[1] As for Naipaul's insistence that 'each sentence should make a clear statement', that would rule offside any writer who, for one reason or another, specifically does not want to make 'a clear statement', someone who by 'not making a statement' might instead be striving for a certain effect. So if a 'clear statement' is Naipaul's ideal, I should imagine he must have been less than impressed by Jack Kerouac's debut opus On The Road (waspishly described by Truman Capote – although several others are also said to have made the gibe – as 'that's not writing, it's typing').

Kerouac himself, one of the Fifties' beat generation's darlings, made rather more opaque contributions with his 'rules on writing'. He advised would-be writers to

> *be in love with your life*

and

---

1   This point might be countered by the observation that they were writing in a different era and Naipaul was addressing a 'more modern' audience. Discuss.

'Rules on writing' and the 'Theory of Omission'

> *accept loss forever*

and to

> *keep track of every day the date emblazoned in your morning.*

That last rule would certainly not have satisfied Naipaul's dictum that writers should 'make a clear statement': you think you understand what Kerouac is saying, but it's a struggle to discern anything at all. Even if Kerouac's rules sound suitably cool and hip to some, it is difficult to see how they actually relate to writing. I'm even more baffled by Jonathan Franzen's insistence that

> *You have to love before you can be relentless.*

That's another statement that would surely fail the Naipaul Test. Then [sic] there's Franzen's rule that only

> *lazy and tone-deaf writers use 'then' when they should use 'and'*

and that

> *Fiction that isn't an author's personal adventure into the frightening or the unknown isn't worth writing for anything but money.*

What does that mean? What can it mean? It is strictly without the scope of this book to mention it, but I do take exception to the implication that 'literature' which isn't composed from the purest of motives – to create 'art', say, or, apparently a staple of late 20th and early 21st century British literary creation, to 'investigate the human condition' – is somehow 'second-rate'. As for daring to write with an eye on possibly making a bob or two [1] from your work, if not a living – good Lord, the cheek of it! Those bloody hack Charles Dickens, Arnold Bennett certainly had something to answer for!

Scott Fitzgerald also added his thoughts and advice on writing, and like King, Enright, Gaiman and Kennedy what he offers is essentially practical. He advises writers to

> *begin by making notes. You may have to make notes for years . . . When you think of something, when you recall something, put it where it belongs. Put it down when you think of it. You may never recapture it quite as vividly the second time.*

---

1   Or a dollar or two.

He also advises

> *You ought never to use an unfamiliar word unless you've had to search for it to express a delicate shade – where in effect you have recreated it.*

In his own rules Hemingway, like Franzen and Kerouac, also takes a line more quasi-metaphysical than practical. As I point out above, he advises that to get started

> *all you need to do is write one true sentence. Write the truest sentence that you know*

leaving wide open the question of what a 'true sentence' might be. As with Kerouac and Franzen's advice, the moment you persuade yourself *'yes! Of course, of course! And Hemingway is so right!'* is invariably followed by growing confusion: the more you think about it, the less there is to it. Equally unhelpful is Hemingway's admonition

> *Don't describe an emotion – make it.*

To be fair, that would seem to be just a variation on the perpetual advice to writers to 'show, don't tell'; but what seems at first straightforward becomes ever less so: how do you 'make [create] emotion' on the page? For one thing, appreciation of a piece of prose or poetry is subjective; and for another how can the writer ever be sure that the emotion he or she is creating in the reader – or hopes he or she is creating – is the emotion she or he intends to create? We might recall Oscar Wilde's observation on Dickens' The Old Curiosity Shop that

> *One must have a heart of stone to read the death of little Nell without laughing.*

Dickens certainly created an emotion in Wilde's heart, but it is unlikely to have been the emotion he was hoping to create. Wilde's observation also reminds us that for many – and not just in Victorian Britain but increasingly as the 21st century proceeds – 'emotion' was and is often little more than cloying and superficial 'sentiment'.[1] Some writers certainly manage to create emotion, though for me Hemingway – whose prose is often flatter than a pancake – has never come anywhere close.

. . .

At the end of the day 'rules on writing' are neither here nor there, especially as this

---

1   Wilde nailed it when he observed that *'sentimentality is merely the bank holiday of cynicism'*.

year's new style will certainly be old hat at some point in the future. [1] When Scribner's published Hemingway's 'lean, hard and athletic' prose in 1925, it is likely to have hoped the reading public would lose its taste for the formal styles of James, Galsworthy and Wharton. Certainly advice and guidance handed out by published, experienced and successful authors – that is women and men who might be thought to know what they are talking about – is worth attending to; but it does beg the question as to what kind of work – what kind of 'literature' – a would-be writer wants to produce and, with that in mind, whether some of the advice handed out is appropriate, relevant or useful. If you intend to write thrillers or romances or science fiction – and hope to sell your work – does Hemingway's advice to 'write the truest sentence that you know' make much sense? Elmore Leonard advises 'don't go into great detail describing places and things' – but some readers of thrillers and romances and science fiction might well want exactly such detail and, furthermore, lots and lots of it. Hemingway certainly provides a great deal of detail, especially in For Whom The Bell Tolls.

'But,' I hear you sniff, 'we're talking *serious literature* here, not thrillers or romantic and science fiction and that kind of thing!' Well, if that is your point, it begs another question: what is 'serious literature'? Are you insisting that there is some kind a literary hierarchy which has 'serious literature' at its apex and 'lesser' forms of writing – those, for example, produced 'for money' – at descending tiers depending upon their assigned literary worth? If there really is such a hierarchy – and I don't believe there is – I suggest Hemingway's 'masterpiece' The Sun Also Rises comes nowhere near the top and that many passages in For Whom The Bell Tolls would be perfectly at home in modern chick-lit. [2] Are those two novels 'serious literature'? We are stretching the definition of 'serious literature' to breaking point if we include Hemingway's work: both A Farewell To Arms and For Whom The Bell Tolls are essentially Boy's Own adventure tales with an unconvincing 'love story' tacked on. I am here, perhaps, guilty of setting up my own Aunt Sally simply to knock it down again. Despite the claims that The Sun Also Rises was 'important' because it chronicled 'a generation in despair', it was Hemingway's new prose style which for some marked – and allegedly still marks – him out as a 'great writer'. That, at least, might be one justification to include Hemingway's work in a putative canon of 'serious literature': it is because of 'his place in literary history', the argument could run, that his novels still deserve our respect. To that the only honest response is that the matter is certainly worth discussing – as I do here – but the jury is still out

---

1 Publishers would, though, sagely point out *'we're not selling the new style at some point in the future, matey – we're selling the new style now'* (and you can almost hear the cry *'so grab it while stocks last!'*)

2 And frankly they might well have been turned down by the editors at Mills & Boon.

as to how well Hemingway's work compares with other works of 'serious literature'. Hemingway's assumed place in 'literary history', allotted to him because of his, for its time original, prose style, doesn't in itself improve the novels. Would that argument also apply to To Have And Have Not and Across The River And Into The Trees? In one sense, the Victorian Scottish poet William McGonagall also has 'his place in literary history', and for many his name is as well-known as those of the poets Donne, Shelley, Dickinson, Yeats, Eliot, Frost and Heaney. But what are we to make of his poetry? Read it and make up your own mind. [iii] If nothing else, 'historical status' has no bearing at all on how interesting and engaging a writer's work is.

. . .

Rather more perplexing than Hemingway's take on 'rules on writing' is his 'theory of omission', also known as his 'iceberg theory'. This is often given great prominence in many discussions about Hemingway and his place in literary history, but the irony is that Hemingway ostentatiously derided 'literary talk' as a matter of course. His 'theory' is also notable for standing very much alone as a piece of Hemingway literary theorising. This is how he sums up the essence of his theory in Death In The Afternoon:

> *If a writer of prose knows enough about what he is writing about he may omit things that he knows and the reader, if the writer is writing truly enough. will have a feeling of those things as strongly as though the writer had stated them. The dignity of movement of an iceberg is due to only one-eighth of it being above water. A good writer does not need to reveal every detail of a character or action.*

The rather foggy meaning of Hemingway's opening sentence apart – might we not expect a 'great writer' to be able to communicate his thoughts more clearly? – he is right that a writer need not necessarily reveal every aspect of a character or action. If a character is skilfully outlined and brought to life, the reader might well – probably unwittingly – use his or her imagination to flesh out in more 'detail' what the writer has provided. Such added details would, though, be personal to each reader, and each reader might add very different 'details'; but the writer wouldn't mind. Getting the reader to do some of the work is part of her or his art.

The passage from Death In The Afternoon quoted above can be offered as another instance where 'muddled writing betrays muddled thought': it is not at all clear what Hemingway is trying to say. Is he claiming – in a process it would not be facetious to describe as quasi-mystical – not just that 'truths' the writer 'knows' can be conveyed,

'Rules on writing' and the 'Theory of Omission'

but that 'facts' can similarly be conveyed? What he writes could well be taken to say just that. In fact, although in an opaque [1] manner, he is simply describing what has been accepted for many years: that a skilful writer – a 'good' writer – can convey over and above what is apparently there 'in the words on the page'. But why did Hemingway persuade himself he had discovered a 'new way of writing'; and what, one wonders, did he think other writers had been and were doing?

In a monograph examining Hemingway's 'theory of omission', the Hemingway scholar Paul Smith, of Trinity College, Hartford, Connecticut, summed up the dilemma of establishing what it was Hemingway was trying to say:

> *The theory [of omission] may well have been new to Hemingway.*
> *But most of his literary friends in Paris in the 1920s, like Ezra*
> *Pound, would have seen it as a version of the commonplace that the*
> *structures of literature, like the sentences of the language, imply*
> *more than they state and make us feel more than we know.*

In the first half of his monograph, Smith traces the evolution of Hemingway's theory and makes it clear that Hemingway was, in fact, convinced he was coming up with something new and was not simply redefining a traditional writing practice. But Smith also observes that Hemingway generally had little time for literary critics and theories. According to Hemingway's friend the poet Archibald MacLeish, he actively avoided taking part in any kind of literary discussion; [2] Developing a literary theory of his own, his 'theory of omission', was thus certainly unusual.

All that notwithstanding, over the years Hemingway seems to have taken 'his theory' increasingly seriously. He had first alluded to it, almost in passing, in a letter to Scott Fitzgerald in late 1925. From that letter it is clear that in the atmosphere of the self-conscious modernism of his peers in Paris and ensconced as he was in his self-image as a 'serious' young writer, Hemingway did think his theory had substance. Furthermore, from his letter to Fitzgerald he certainly appears to believe his theory was an original one. It makes its second, more definite, appearance seven years later in his paean to bullfighting Death In The Afternoon in which he also observes that

> *Anything you can omit that you know you still have in the writing*

---

1   Perhaps a kinder word than 'muddled'.

2   So surprisingly did James Joyce, according to George Plimpton, who co-founded and edited the Paris Review, though he was quoting Hemingway.

> *and its quality will show.*

The possibility notwithstanding that I am a little dense, the above is also unclear and decidedly badly written; and what does Hemingway mean when he goes on to write

> *When a writer omits things he does not know, they show like holes in his writing'?*

I can't even begin to imagine what he is trying to say. It might be overly pedantic to point out that if a writer 'doesn't know' something, she or he is in no position to omit it – 'omitting' presupposes you are consciously leaving something out. Similarly if a reader did detect 'holes' in a piece of writing, she or he would certainly be conscious of an absence, that something was missing; but they would have little idea what that 'missing something' might be. As with some of Hemingway's 'rules on writing', you begin to think you know what he might be getting at, but then you realise you are not even close. The most likely explanation is that Hemingway simply did not think through what he was trying to say; and you certainly understand why the anonymous New York Times writer reviewing Death In The Afternoon complained that in the book Hemingway was

> *guilty of the grievous sin of writing sentences which have to be read two or three times before the meaning is clear.*

. . .

Hemingway's 'theory of omission' had to wait for more than 20 years before it had its next airing. This came in an 'interview' with George Plimpton which appeared in the Paris Review. In his monograph, Paul Smith suggests that the Paris interview was not, as one might assume, a face-to-face encounter, but was largely written up and published – in 1958, several years after an initial meeting in Spain – from a series of questions submitted by Plimpton to which Hemingway provided written answers. However, the interview does read as though it had taken place face-to-face. Curiously when Hemingway briefly refers to his 'theory of omission' and his 'iceberg theory', he does not expound on it at all, and what he says in the printed version of Plimpton's interview is word for word what he had written in Death In The Afternoon 26 years earlier.

Hemingway's final comments on his 'theory of omission' were in his posthumously published memoir of his early Paris years, A Moveable Feast, and in an essay he wrote on The Art Of The Short Story. [1] The essay was intended as a preface to a new collection of some of his short stories for school students. Later, it was decided the collection should be for adult readers. The suggestion for publishing a new collection had come from Scribner's, but when Hemingway eventually submitted his preface, Scribner's read it, didn't like if and changed its mind; miffed, Hemingway called off the whole project and the collection never appeared. The preface – that is his essay The Art Of The Short Story – makes very odd reading indeed, though in Hemingway's defence we might remember that his health, both physical and mental, was breaking down at some pace and his judgment might well have been awry. [2] He informs us that he wrote his essay as though he were giving a lecture and speaking off-the-cuff, and that might explain why it seems either to have been dashed off in a hurry [3] or that Hemingway was drunk when he wrote it. It certainly gives the impression that it was ever revised – or even re-read – by Hemingway, however unlikely that might be – he had lambasted his one-time mentor Gertrude Stein for never revising her work (though Stein apparently did so 'on principle'). But that would not be the first time I have suspected Hemingway did a lot less revising and 'rewriting' than he claimed.

Dealing with Hemingway's The Art Of The Short Story, Smith is kind: he writes of the essay that

> *The diction is colloquial, the syntax casual, and the attitude at times defensive, at times belligerent . . .*

But Smith's gloss does beg the question as to why a published and well-known author with more than 30 years experience, a Noble Laureate and a man by then regarded by many as 'a writer of genius' should be content to release for intended publication an 'essay' which in part reads as though it had been written by a fifth-form or tenth-grade student. It's not surprising Scribner's rejected it.

. . .

In his essay, Hemingway makes a number of unusual claims which echo what he had to say about his 'theory of omission'. For example, he claims that

---

1   See the appendix to this book for the full text.
2   Mary Welsh was given excerpts to read as Hemingway was composing it, and she made several suggestions for changes. She feared readers might feel as though they were being condescended to. Hemingway accepted some of her suggestions, but not all of them.
3   It wasn't.

> *If you leave out important things or events that you know about, the story is strengthened. If you leave or skip something because you do not know it, the story will be worthless.*

This is essentially just a re-wording of his pronouncement in Death In The Afternoon and is just as muddled. How does leaving out 'important things or events' strengthen the story? Hemingway – or, now that he is dead, his champions – are obliged to make that clearer if he and they want us to take his 'theory of omission' seriously. [1] Hemingway also repeats his claim that

> *The test of any story is how very good the stuff is that you, not your editors, omit.*

Once again, is it facetious to ask just how a reader could even know what has been left out? I think I might know what Hemingway was trying to get at – Phillip Young would remind us this is simply a restatement of a writer allowing her or his readers to 'read between the lines' – but surely to goodness a competent journalist let alone a 'great writer' could try to express himself with a deal more clarity? We might ask, though frankly merely rhetorically: does the reader slowly aggregate, by some kind of mysterious osmosis, 'knowledge' of what has been left out because the writer has been 'writing truly' and is thus able to judge that a story is better than it might otherwise have been? That seems to be what Hemingway is suggesting. It is all very unconvincing, though suitably portentous and at one with Hemingway's self-image as an 'important writer'; and this is from a man who not only regarded himself as an authority on writing, but who had trained as a journalist and should have been aware of the imperative of clarity in communication. I suspect Hemingway is unclear simply because he hasn't thought through what he wants to say and so, crucially, he doesn't even understand it himself.

---

1   Elsewhere I make the point, but it is also worth making it here, that school or college students who might as yet be less confident in their own judgment will almost certainly blame themselves for not quite understanding 'what Hemingway is saying'. And it is more than likely they will try even harder to 'understand' the 'great writer'.

The Sun Also Rises and the 'lost generation'

It was an age of miracles, it was an age of art, it was an age of excess, and it was an age of satire.

F. Scott Fitzgerald in Tales Of The Jazz Age.

No single factor was as illustrative of the failure of The Sun Also Rises to convince the critics that Hemingway was a great writer than its failure to convince them that it was the record of a generation and that its author was the spokesman for that generation.

Frank L. Ryan The Immediate Critical Reception of Ernest Hemingway.

A new generation does not appear every thirty years . . . or 'about three times in the century' to quote Fitzgerald; it appears when writers of the same age join in common revolt against the fathers and when in the process of adapting a new lifestyle they find their own models and spokesmen.

Malcolm Cowley, A Second Flowering.

Instead of being the epic of the sun also rising on a lost generation, [The Sun Also Rises is] strikes me as a cock and bull story about a lot of summer tourists getting drunk and making fools of themselves at a picturesque Iberian folk-festival. It's heartbreaking. If the generation is going to lose itself, for God's sake let it show more fight . . . When a superbly written description of the fiesta of San Fermin in Pamplona . . . reminds you of a travel book . . . it's time to hold an inquest.

John Dos Passos, reviewing The Sun Also Rises for New Masses, Dec 1926.

THERE'S a cynical observation that if you ask ten economists to define 'economics', you'll get 20 definitions. Something similar is true when talk turns to Hemingway's so-called 'lost generation': depending upon who is asked, that supposed 'lost generation' will refer to any number of different groups of men and women. Whoever and whatever they are, though, it is an article of faith that Ernest Hemingway's novel The Sun Also Rises portrays and – more to the point – that Hemingway intended it to portray a 'lost generation of men and women in despair', such despair, in fact, that they had reduced themselves to leading aimless lives of drunkenness and promiscuity. Does it? Over the years that claim has evolved to become what Norman Mailer called 'a factoid' – he defined it as *'a fact which [has] no existence before appearing in a magazine or newspaper'*. Everyone 'knows' it is true, but it isn't, as even Hemingway himself tells us, in several letters to Max Perkins and to others.[1] Jake Barnes and his group certainly do a lot of drinking, and Brett Ashley spends an 'illicit' week in bed with Robert Cohn and not a few weeks later begins an affair with a nineteen-year-old matador; but that is the sum total of 'promiscuity' in the novel. As a rule, young people need no excuse to drink to excess and, when possible, to have sex, even in the pre-Pill days when women had to take care not to fall pregnant (which, of course, many still did). More relevant is that the now orthodox reading of the novel – that the generation was 'in despair' – was arrived at decidedly post hoc. Furthermore, those who repeat that orthodoxy are simply parroting what they were taught in class: the novel itself doesn't convey it at all. Furthermore, the orthodox reading didn't gain broad currency for some years after the

---

1   In an essay for the Hemingway Review in its Spring 2018 edition, Donald A. Daiker spells it out: *It's time, then, that we accept Hemingway's word that The Sun Also Rises does not portray members of a lost generation wandering aimlessly across France and Spain. The marketing folks at Scribner and at Houghton Mifflin Harcourt may have persuaded themselves that Stein's lost generation tag helps sell their books, but careful Hemingway readers . . . understand that Jake Barnes – representative of the generation of Americans who came of age during World War I – has over the post-war years recognized, like Solomon, recurring patterns that have enabled him to develop a practical definition of morality and a working philosophy of life. As the novel concludes, Jake is in no sense lost . . .*

The Sun Also Rises and the 'lost generation'

novel was published and was certainly not current at the time. Fifty-four years later, in 1980, by which time the canonisation of Ernest Hemingway as 'one of our greatest writers' was being more keenly scrutinised, Frank L. Ryan observed in The Immediate Critical Reception of Ernest Hemingway

> *A year and a half after its publication, Richard Barrett spoke of the impressions which the novel was having on the younger people about him, of the young men and women who spoke so reverently of it, marked passages in it, and kept it by their beds, apparently for solace in the dark hours. But one searches in vain for this response from the reviewers who did not hear in it the mournful sounds of a lost generation.*

In fact, Ryan is not quite on the button: several reviews at the time did comment on how 'degraded' the characters in Hemingway's novel were – one wonders what those 1920s reviewers would make of the behaviour of young folk in the third decade of the 21st century – and some chose to interpret the 'vanities' mentioned by the preacher in the quotation from Ecclesiastes as 'futilities'.[1] But as soon as Hemingway became aware that reviewers were picking up on a supposed 'lost generation' angle, he insisted he intended the, notably upbeat, biblical quotation from Ecclesiastes to contradict and discredit Gertrude Stein's dismissive – and second-hand – observation about him and his friends that 'You are all a lost generation'. The relevant message was in the biblical quotation, he insisted – *'One generation passeth away, and another generation cometh: but the earth abideth for ever'*. So the question is: how did the interpretation that the young men and women in The Sun Also Rises were 'in despair' even come about and, crucially, why is it now almost universally accepted?

. . .

Hemingway had, in fact, at one point thought of proclaiming that his novel was a portrait of 'his generation' – although not one 'in despair' – and considered calling it 'The Lost Generation'. This is apparent from the text of a foreword he wrote; but he

---

[1] The full quotation of the first six verses of Book 1 from Ecclesiastes in the King James version is: *The words of the Preacher, the son of David, king in Jerusalem. / Vanity of vanities, saith the Preacher, vanity of vanities; all is vanity. / What profit hath a man of all his labour which he taketh under the sun? / One generation passeth away, and another generation cometh: but the earth abideth for ever. / The sun also ariseth, and the sun goeth down, and hasteth to his place where he arose. / The wind goeth toward the south, and turneth about unto the north; it whirleth about continually, and the wind returneth again according to his circuits.*

changed his mind and decided not to use that title within days of completing its first draft. In that – though confused and confusing – foreword he merely indicated that he believed his generation was somehow 'searching' for something. [i]

Poet and literary critic Malcolm Cowley suggests that a better, more accurate, name for the so-called 'lost generation' would be the 'World War I generation of writers'. He identifies them as idealists born in the last decade of the 19th century, a generation which became disillusioned with their fathers' values and who, coming of age, had high hopes for change; but once the war was over, they soon realised it was business as usual.

Other commentators, more vaguely, choose to use the term the 'lost generation' to encompass all the writers who came to prominence in the 1920s (at least in the anglophone world). Still others claim it was specifically the group of ex-patriates who, like Hemingway, congregated in Montparnasse in the 1920s. Frankly, at the end of the day you pays your money and you makes your choice; yet whatever or whoever that 'lost generation' might be, Hemingway's novel is now firmly wedded to the idea that it is all about a 'lost generation in despair': never underestimate the potency of a 'factoid'.

. . .

Cowley makes his case well: in A Second Flowering, he examines the works of eight poets and writers born between 1894 and 1899 who might be thought to belong to that putative 'lost generation'. Some enlisted and fought in the war; some, like Scott Fitzgerald, joined up but never made it to the front; others, including the novelist John Dos Passos, the poet e.e. cummings and Hemingway himself served in a theatre-of-war ambulance service. [ii] All, says Cowley, were scornful of the older generation. He writes

> The war . . . gave them the feeling of having lived in two eras, almost on two different planets. The second era seemed tawdrier in many ways, but still it had become their own world or century

and he quotes Dos Passos from a letter the novelist wrote to a classmate

---

1 Pertinently many young people find themselves undertaking such a search before 'life' calls a premature, though, temporary halt to it all and insists they might better spend their time ensuring their taxes are paid and finding a larger home for their growing family. A line from The Eagles song Bitter Creek (from their second album Desperado, released in 1973) sums up nicely the confusion of a young man on the cusp of adulthood ill at ease with himself – '*Tried every ill to find the cur*e'. It would be very unusual for many of a new generation not somehow so be at sixes and sevens with 'life'. The exception might have been young Britons and Americans who took part in the June 6, 1944, Normandy landing and the invasion of Nazi Germany. They had little time to worry about 'their role in life', and in the next eleven months many of them lost that life. Not a great deal of worrying goes on in graves.

The Sun Also Rises and the 'lost generation'

> *If we only governed the world instead of the swagbellied old fogies that do . . . Down with the middle-aged!*

Cowley describes how

> *For a few months after the Armistice – only a few – young American writers were full of hope for themselves and the world. The democracies were triumphant, all the great tyrannies were overthrown, and perhaps young men could play their part in an old American dream, that of building a new order of the age . . . The hope faded in 1919. Among the events of that disastrous year in American history were the Treaty of Versailles, which the Senate would refuse to ratify for the wrong reasons; the May Day riots of servicemen against Socialists; the general strike in Seattle, followed by strikes in major industries . . . the Volstead Act, passed over the veto of a crippled President; the rescinding by Congress of all the progressive measures adopted during the war. Together those events . . . affirmed the moral dictatorship of congressmen from rural districts and left political power in the hands of businessmen with narrow aims: they wanted profits and very soon would have bigger profits than ever before, at an exorbitant cost to the world.*

One should, though, acknowledge that the scorn for, and disgust with, their fathers' generation Cowley attributes to the post-World War group of writers is hardly different to that of every younger generation, which, ironically, eventually becomes a new 'fathers' generation'. Two generations later, the young men who served in World War II – and who saw friends and fellow soldiers killed – were understandably upset and perhaps baffled that they and their values were rejected by their sons and daughters, the 1960s 'hippies'; then, of course, those same feckless 'hippies', now grown older, fatter, grey and respectable to become the 'boomer' generation, were scorned by 'Gen X' which in turn was disparaged by 'millennials'; we don't yet know the name by which the generation sired by those 'millennials' will be known, but we can be certain they, too, till turn on their parents with a vengeance.

. . .

Cowley's analysis of his World War I generation is reasoned, solid and useful, and the debilitation that generation's disillusionment caused might be demonstrated by an example: the life of Harold Stearns. Stearns makes an appearance in The Sun Also Rises as the drunken cadger Harvey Stone and was one of many real-life men and women Hemingway used, thinly disguised, to populate his novel. In fact, except for the character of Bill Gorton, who was an amalgam based on Hemingway's childhood friend Bill Smith and the writer Donald Ogden Stewart, almost every character in the novel had a direct real-life counterpart,[1] and none was too pleased by how they were depicted. In her account of the genesis of the novel, Lesley M.M. Blume notes

> *When The Sun Also Rises was released . . . those who had been translated onto its pages were incredulous that it was being marketed as fiction. 'When I first read it I couldn't see what everyone was getting so excited about,' recalled Donald Ogden Stewart . . . Hemingway repurposed him into the book's comic foil Bill Gorton. In his [Stewart's] eyes The Sun Also Rises was 'nothing but a report of what happened. This is journalism'.*

As a young man, Stearns was the very soul of enlightened liberalism. His father died before he was born, and he had a peripatetic childhood; but by the age of 16 he was earning money writing theatre reviews and was able to pay his way through Harvard with his journalism. When he graduated in 1913, he moved to New York and was eventually hired as a staff writer on The New Republic, founded in 1914 as a left-liberal progressive newspaper. Later, he edited the political and literary magazine The Dial for a year. He made his name with two books: the first, published in 1919, was Liberalism In America in which he juxtaposed President Woodrow Wilson's purported idealism with how in practice that liberalism was failing; then, in 1921, he published America And The Young Intellectual in which he accused the US of crushing its young 'free spirits'. A year later, he edited a collection of essays by leading prominent writers called Civilization In The United States. In it, according to the New York Times, America was depicted as a land of greed and puritanism where none of the finer things in life had a chance to flower. Stearns then declared himself disgusted with the US and moved to Paris; but there he began 13 years of increasing dissolution, eating very little and drinking a great deal.

Despite the favourable exchange rate that made Paris cheap for Americans in the 1920s, Stearns had very little money. He had intended to earn his living from writing, but he wrote nothing and soon existed by borrowing money. He largely kept himself to himself, though he existed on the periphery of that Montparnasse circle of ex-patriates of which Hemingway was a part. After several years of increasing poverty and desolation, a

---

1 Notably, Hemingway's wife Hadley who was also part of the group on the trip to Pamplona in 1925 on which the novel is based is not represented. But everyone else who was on that trip features in the novel.

well-wisher helped him land a job as a racing tipster for the Paris edition of the Chicago Tribune under the name 'Peter Pickem'. He later transferred to the Paris edition of Britain's Daily Mail, but was eventually sacked. Finally, after spending several months more or less living in the gutter, his teeth rotting and losing his sight, he was repatriated to the US by an American charity.

In short, Stearns was the very embodiment of a purported 'lost generation' in despair at the state of the world who took 'refuge' in drinking themselves to death. It would, though, be completely misleading to cite his life as in any way typical of his peers. Stearn's demons were personal – his mother was hopeless with money, and as a child Stearns lived a unsettled existence, never living at the same address for long – and he was an extreme example of 'the disillusioned liberal'. Others who could be regarded and are often cited as belonging to that 'lost generation' in Paris did not lead such dissolute lives: drinking to excess and indulging in all kinds of sexual activity, whether covertly or not, has been a consistent feature of all societies. Pertinently, the alleged 'bad' behaviour of the American ex-patriates was being viewed and condemned by a nation buttoned up by Prohibition and by – an often distinctly hypocritical – puritanism. Unhelpfully, when comparing Paris of the 1920s to the three *fin de siecle* decades leading up to World War I, most accounts judge the city as comparatively 'sober' and far less dissolute than it had been two and three decades earlier.

. . .

If one accepts Cowley's account of the gradual disillusion of young writers with their country and what they regarded as its venal values, there certainly was a 'lost generation', albeit a small one; more to point: were the characters as portrayed in Hemingway's The Sun Also Rises even part of a despairing 'lost generation' as is now almost universally claimed? At best one might respond: if they were, it is not at all obvious; and at worst the answer is a stark and definite: no, they were not. In his review for the Marxist magazine New Masses, Hemingway's then friend and confidant John Dos Passos quite possibly nails it when he scathingly wrote

> *Instead of being the epic of the sun also rising on a lost generation, [The Sun Also Rises is] strikes me as a cock and bull story about a lot of summer tourists getting drunk and making fools of themselves at a picturesque Iberian folk-festival. It's heartbreaking. If the generation is going to lose itself, for God's sake let it show more fight.*

Dos Passos [1] was acknowledging that there was some talk about a 'lost generation', presumably caused by Hemingway's use of the Gertrude Stein quotation (though, as noted, he put the lid on that interpretation). Pertinently, Dos Passos was as much telling *New Masses*' left-wing readers what they wanted to hear as giving his honest opinion of the novel; [ii] his analysis rings truer of the men and woman as described by Hemingway than the claims subsequently made that they were lost souls 'in despair'.

When considering the antics of Jake Barnes and his party, it is counter-intuitive to accept there must be a philosophical dimension to their behaviour, though as they are 'characters in a novel', many who believe that the work is 'serious literature' will be tempted to do so. [2] Yes, the Barnes' party do drink a great deal in Pamplona, but then so did the Spanish townsfolk and others attending the festival: presumably they were not part of a 'lost generation in despair'. One character – Brett Ashley – was easy with her favours and might by some be thought of as promiscuous (in the course of the novel she had three lovers: Robert Cohn, the young bullfighter Romero and, presumably, her fiancé Mike Campbell). [iii] But to assume *prima facie* that, in the parlance of the day, she was 'loose' and slept around because she was 'in despair' over the state of the world, of her and others' lives and the future of her generation is certainly not warranted by the text of the novel: such an assumption is fatuous. Of the other characters, Bill Gorton is, in fact, remorselessly upbeat and cheerful throughout, and Robert Cohn is essentially nothing but a spoiled rich kid mooning like a love-struck adolescent for the woman who has rejected him. Mike Campbell, the only main character apart from Jake Barnes who had fought in the war, might qualify as a member of a putative 'lost generation in despair'; yet although the war is briefly mentioned, nothing Campbell says or does in the novel would or could allow the reader to believe he is 'in despair'. [3] The only character who might have reason to be 'in despair' was Barnes himself: he had lost his penis during the war – though the exact nature of his wound is never spelled out – and he was

---

1   Dos Passos is likely to have picked up on the reference to a 'lost generation' from the remark Gertrude Stein made to Hemingway, which he used as one of his novel's epigraphs. Dos Passos had been part of Hemingway's party to Pamplona a year earlier.

2   I examine the oddities of 'literary interpretation' and liken them to a 'Rorschach effect' later. Essentially, we see and read what we want to see and read. Pertinently, by the mid-1950s when Hemingway's status as a 'great writer and artist' had been established, many academics reading the novel were keen find in it 'evidence of his artistry'. So, of course, inevitably they did find such evidence whenever possible, pretty much at every turn.

3   He was always short of money, didn't have the resources to pay his share of the costs, had been made bankrupt and might have felt a little low about it, but the novel makes no mention of Campbell being in low spirits; and that is not quite the existentialist despair Hemingway's novel is purported to describe.

no longer able to function sexually. [1] The novel makes clear that he is unhappy, yet his unhappiness relates to his personal situation: at no point is there a suggestion that it is 'the state of the world' that is making him unhappy. Count Mippipopolous, a secondary character, was badly wounded in 'four wars and seven revolutions', and might also have had cause to be 'in despair'. Unfortunately, as written by Hemingway, the count is also remarkably sanguine despite showing off his war wounds. Those who do insist on taking the line that the count was also part of a 'generation in despair' might, perhaps, justify his *joie de vivre* by arguing that the guiding principle of his life was *carpe diem quam minimum credula postero* (very loosely 'eat, drink and be merry, for tomorrow we die'). If so, nice try but no cigar.

. . .

It is difficult to establish just when or how the view that The Sun Also Rises portrayed 'a lost generation in despair' gained currency. Although the suggestion that Hemingway intended to portray a 'lost generation' could possibly be substantiated, to claim that generation was 'in despair' is more than a stretch. Frank L. Ryan's observation points out that even if the contemporary critics were aware of the novel's supposed theme, they made no mention of it in their reviews; and though absence of evidence is never evidence of absence, had the critics detected that theme, it is unusual that none thought it worth mentioning. Hemingway himself poured cold water on it: as Bertram D. Sarason writes in Hemingway And The Sun Set.

> *. . . Hemingway could not stop the legend that he was depicting the Lost Generation. He protested that Earth and not Jake Barnes, not even the matador, Pedro Romero, was the hero. Few critics believe Hemingway even today.*

Hemingway repeated his objections in several letters to Max Perkins at Scribner's; and in a letter to Paul Romaine, a second-hand books dealer, he wrote he was not

> *depressed at the prospect of being forgotten if I do not cease to*

---

1   Given the marked academic tendency when dealing with Hemingway (and other writers) to read significance into everything whenever possible, I'm surprised none has yet interpreted Jake Barnes' emasculation and related it to Hemingway's own situation at that year's Pamplona break. Biographers suggest Hemingway as well as Harold Loeb was infatuated with Duff Twysden / Brett Ashley: this, they write, was the basis of Hemingway's growing antipathy to Loeb and why he chose to make him look such a fool in his novel. Unfortunately, Mrs Hemingway – Hadley Richardson – was also present on the trip and that very much queered Hemingway's pitch if he wanted to attempt a roll in the hay with Twysden. That's emasculation in most men's book.

> write about 'Lost generations and bulls.' I wrote, in six weeks, one book [The Sun Also Rises] about a few drunks and to show the superiority of the earlier Hebrew writers over the later quoted Ecclesiastes versus G. Stein. (1)

...

In 1922, F. Scott Fitzgerald published his second novel, The Beautiful And The Damned, and shortly afterwards his collection of short stories, Tales From The Jazz Age. His heroes and heroines were also in rebellion against their parents' generation: they were flighty, unconventional, frivolous, thumbed their noses at acceptable behaviour, embraced sexual freedoms and generally upset older folk. In America's cities, many of the young were quick to follow new fashions and emulate the lifestyle of Fitzgerald's hedonists – although up to a point; and one wonders just how much such emulation took place in the smaller towns and communities in the backwaters of the United States, whose city population in the early 1920s was only just beginning to outstrip that of rural America. (2) Four years later came Hemingway's The Sun Also Rises, and young folk were presented with a new fashion to embrace: so out went light-headed Jazz Age frivolity and hedonism, and in came hard-drinking cynicism. As Carlos Bakers puts it in his biography of Hemingway

> Malcolm [Cowley] discovered that winter [of 1926 when The Sun Also Rises was published] that Hemingway's 'influence' was spreading far beyond the circle of those who had known him in Paris. Girls from Smith College, coming to New York, 'were modeling [sic] themselves after Lady Brett . . . Hundreds of bright young men from the Middle West were trying to be Hemingway heroes, talking in tough understatements from the one side of their mouths'.

Note, though, that although Cowley came across young folk imitating Hemingway's protagonists, he did not report meeting any who were or declared themselves to be

---

1   Hemingway's mention of 'a few drunk' ironically echoes Dos Passos' scathing comment in his New Masses review.

2   Broadly, the distinction between the US urban and rural populations at the time, sometimes unkindly described as 'the Slicks v the Hicks', had the 'slicks' – again very broadly – as of an enlightened, liberal outlook opposed to Prohibition and more tolerant of the US non-white citizens, and the 'hicks' at the opposite, 'God-fearing', 'reactionary' extreme. I doubt anyone is startled by those descriptions.

'in despair'. For a great many Americans true despair did come, three years later after the Wall Street crash and in the subsequent decade-long Great Depression which at its depths saw one-in-four men and women out of work: the illegal drinking and hard-edged cynicism were nothing but the latest fashion – there was no intellectual or existentialist dimension to their behaviour; and if there was, no one seems to have noticed or bothered to comment on it.

...

Quite telling is Hemingway's possible, or even probable, motivation for writing The Sun Also Rises. His comments in conversation and in letters – notably to his Scribner's editor, Max Perkins – before and after its publication indicate that it was anything but the work of a pure artist whose sole concern was for 'his art' and to whom everything else was irrelevant; on the contrary it seems to have been wholly calculated. Hemingway was desperate to have a literary career, and he knew that the recent publication of his first volume of short stories was not sufficient to establish one: he knew he had to write and publish a successful novel, but, to be frank, he had few ideas for one. Conscious of that imperative, just a month before he and his wife Hadley had set out for Pamplona at the beginning of July 1925, he had started writing a novel. He was calling it Along With Youth, but work petered out after he had written just 27 manuscript pages. Then came the trip to Pamplona in 1925, the drunken disharmony among his group presented him with 'a plot', and he immediately set about getting it down on paper. That 'plot', however, changed shape at least twice, and despite Hemingway's claim several years later in a letter to Max Perkins that

> *95 per cent of The Sun Also [Rises] was pure imagination. I took real people in that one and I controlled what they did. I made it all up*

that was largely untrue. Donald Ogden-Stewart was astonished when he read that The Sun Also Rises was being presented as fiction. According to Carlos Baker

> *Don Stewart was mildly amused at [sic] the caricature of himself in the figure of Bill Gorton. He recognised a few of his own quips in the talk between Bill and Jake, but the whole book struck him as a little more than a very clever reportorial tour de force.*

Here one must try to be fair: in a Spring 2018 piece for the Hemingway Review, Donald

Daiker [1] does make a case for the Sun Also Rises having a philosophical dimension, and he quotes several parts of it to try to substantiate his claim. The dilemma is that, viz what I regard as a 'Rorschach effect' [2], we simply cannot know how much this is simply what Daiker 'sees' or whether this really was that Hemingway intended. Unfortunately for Daiker, in their various analyses, rather too many fellow academics suggest contradictory interpretations of Hemingway's work, and that would seem to advise us to treat claims such as his with care. Notably, if Daiker is right and Hemingway did put a lot of thought into giving his novel a philosophical framework, the obvious question is: why did he not attempt to do so in his subsequent six novels? Given the ostensible social theme of To Have And Have Not, that novel would certainly have benefited, even in part, from such a philosophical approach; but there is nothing of the kind in the two adventure stories which make up the first two-thirds of the novel, and if it is present in the third part, it is undetectable.

. . .

Although Hemingway completed the first draft of The Sun Also Rises in nine weeks, it did not resemble the novel that was eventually published. Comparisons between the different drafts now stored in the Hemingway Archives of Boston's John F. Kennedy Library show it did not take shape until the work was extensively revised, and in letters to friends Hemingway variously described his novel in progress as 'tragic' and 'funny'. His preferred method of composition was to sit down and write on spec to see where his story would take him; he didn't draft an outline of The Sun Also Rises until he had written several thousand words. Thus what began as a short story became a long story and only became a novel when it dawned on Hemingway that it might be the work he knew he needed. Its focus also continually changed. The Sun Also Rises began its existence as a tale about a Spanish bullfighter, then Duff Twysden – the characters all retained their real names in the first drafts [3] – became the central character; she, in turn, made way for Jake Barnes – Hemingway's idealised alter ego – to take centre stage.

On a trip to Chartres on his own towards the end of September 1925, within days of completing his first draft, Hemingway considered various titles for his novel and cast about for ways to give the work a little more intellectual clout: he wanted to make his name as the writer of 'serious literature' and had previously indicated that the work

1 King Solomon, Gertrude Stein, and Hemingway's 'Lost Generation'
2 See p.226ff.
3 That in itself rather gives the lie to Hemingway's claim to Max Perkins that '95 per cent of it was pure imagination'.

The Sun Also Rises and the 'lost generation'

would appeal both to 'highbrows and lowbrows'. In Chartres, he wrote a brief foreword, given here in full (including Hemingway's spelling, punctuation and deletions):

> *One day last summer Gertrude Stein stopped in a garage in a small town in the Department of Ain to have a valve fixed in her Ford car. The young mechanic who fixed it was very good and quick and skilful. There were three other mechanics all about the same age in the garage.*
>
> *'Where do you get the boys to work like this?' Miss Stein asked the owner of the garage. 'I thought you couldn't get boys to work any more.'*
>
> *'Oh yes,' the garage owner said. 'You can get very good boys now. I've taken all these and trained them myself. It is the ones between twenty-two and thirty that are no good. C'est un generation perdu [sic]. No one wants them. They are no good. They were spoiled. The young ones, the new ones are all right again.'*
>
> *'But what becomes of the others?'*
>
> *'Nothing. They know they are no good. C'est un generation perdu [sic]. A little hard on them,' he added.*
>
> *I did not hear this story until after I had written this book. I had thought of calling it Fiesta but did not want to use a foreign word. Perdu loses a little something by being translated into lost. There is something much more final about perdu.* [1] *There is only this to say that this generation that is lost has nothing to do with any Younger Generation about whose outcome much literary speculation occurred in past times. This is not a question of what kind of mothers will flappers make or where is bobbed hair leading us. This is about something that is already finished. For whatever is going to happen to the generation of which I am a part has already happened.*
>
> *There will be more entanglements, there will be more complications, there will be successes and failures.* ~~There may be~~

---

1   This kind of seemingly authoritative pronouncement highlights the standard Hemingway tack of wanting to be regarded as something of an expert, in this case a more or less fluent French speaker with a real feel for the language. In French, *génération* is feminine, so it should be '*une génération perdue*'. In fact, both his French and his Spanish were said not to have progressed beyond the conversational stage. Whether or not *perdu / perdue* is more 'final' I can't say. See p.248ff.

> *other wars. A few will learn to live perhaps one or two may learn to write or paint.*
>
> *But the things that are given to people to happen to them have already happened. There will be many new salvations brought forward. My generation in France for example in two years sought salvation in first the Catholic church, 2nd communism Dadaism, third the movies, fourth Royalism, fifth the Catholic church again. There may be another and better war. But none of it will matter particularly to this generation because to them the things that are given to people to happen have already happened.*

Stein, Hemingway told us, pronounced his generation 'lost'; but in what sense was it 'lost'? Her garage owner was unhelpfully vague about the *'generation perdu'* [sic] he bemoans and simply informed Stein that they were 'spoiled' and 'no good'; but with nothing else to go on, we have no idea what had spoiled them, how it had spoiled them and in what way they were 'no good'. That they were between 22 and 30 tells us some will have fought in the war a decade earlier; the younger ones who had not fought might well – like many others in France – have experienced wartime deprivation. But would that really have 'spoiled' them and account for the lack of backbone which irritated the garage owner? We are reduced to guesswork. The garage owner might well simply have been a disgruntled employer in a bad mood on the day he spoke to Stein, sounding off just as many of my father's generation – who had seen friends and comrades killed in World War II – were apt to complain and write off my generation as 'long-haired layabouts'.

As for the 'lost generation' of which Hemingway was a part according to Stein, who seems to have been endorsing the garage owner's scorn, we also have no idea what she meant by that description, nor what led to her making her claim or the circumstances in which it was made to Hemingway. Notably, she says nothing about 'despair'; Hemingway might subsequently have reflected upon what she told him and independently decided that not only was his generation 'lost' but was also 'in despair'. Given the institutions and ideologies he lists in which that generation had purportedly 'sought salvation' – the 'Catholic church, communism, Dadaism, the movies and Royalism' – the suggestion might have substance. Unfortunately, he doesn't tell us or even indicate from what his generation might have been seeking 'salvation'; and he and his peers would certainly not have been the first young generation to cast about for 'answers' and 'the meaning of Life' before resigning themselves to a humdrum existence of marriage and mortgages, two-point-four children and taxes.

The Sun Also Rises and the 'lost generation' 143

To muddy already cloudy waters, Stein later gave a completely different account of how she first heard of a 'lost generation'. In the second part of her 1937 autobiography, Everybody's Autobiography (regarded as a follow-up to her 1933 work The Autobiography Of Alice B. Toklas) she wrote

> *It was this hotel keeper who said what it is said I said [sic] that the war generation was a lost generation. And he said it in this way. He said that every man becomes civilized between the ages of eighteen and twenty-five. If he does not go through a civilizing experience at that time in his life he will not be a civilized man. And the men who went to the war at eighteen missed the period of civilizing, and they could never be civilized. They were a lost generation. Naturally if they are at war they do not have the influences of women or parents and of preparation.*

This is entirely at odds with Hemingway's explanation, and not only do we have no other account of what he informs us Stein told him – though it is entirely possible that in the course of her life she was retailing both versions and he heard only one – Stein's second account refers only to the 'civilising of young men'; there is no suggestion at all that living through the war had somehow led them to despair.

. . .

In the event, one suspects Hemingway found it hard to convince even himself about the claims he was making for 'his generation'; crucially none of this agonising is conveyed or even touched upon in the The Sun Also Rises, overly or covertly. That he did not use the foreword he had drafted in Chartres hints, perhaps, that he realised it added nothing to his new work, was confused and confusing, and thus redundant; and what was he trying to say? His line that there

> *may be another and better war*

is odd and demands the question: what in God's name might a 'better' war be? His pronouncement that

> *. . . none of it will matter particularly to this generation because to them the things that are given to people to happen have already happened*

does speak of dispiriting early experiences – presumably in the war – which have somehow scarred, and it might be a profound observation. Others, though, might be more inclined to regard it as a young man's portentous and half-baked thought, poorly expressed; so which is it? The same thought earlier in his foreword runs

> *For whatever is going to happen to the generation of which I am a part has already happened*

and in that wording it is not just poorly expressed, but meaningless. Hemingway might be excused on the grounds that he presumably intended later to edit his foreword; but it does indicate that 'confused writing betrays confused thought' and that Hemingway was simply busking (and rather badly at that). As for his observation that

> *There will be more entanglements, there will be more complications, there will be successes and failures*

there is a great deal less to what he says than he might have hoped: well yes, Ernest, there certainly will be. And in the years to come there will also be many more love affairs, bank statements, months with 'r' in their name, divorces, births, recessions, family quarrels, dinner parties, bankruptcies and Christmas puppies abandoned in the second week of January. At what point are we supposed to nod sagely and murmur *'you know, Hemingway is quite right'*? Frankly, the foreword drifts from banal confusion to outright gobbledegook. What he is trying to say – though he fails – would make a little more sense if, charitably, we consider what I have already suggested: the ambitious 26-year-old was hoping to give his novel intellectual clout, a little more 'bottom', and thus pitch himself into the league of those who produced 'serious literature'.

...

Even though Hemingway abandoned the foreword in which he attempted to establish that his generation was indeed 'lost', that claim eventually became the orthodoxy 'that was what The Sun Also Rises is about'; but it is hard to square that claim with what we know of the novel's genesis: first a short story, then a longer story, then a novel, in different drafts about a young Spanish matador, then about a titled British barfly in Paris, then about disharmony at a Spanish summer festival. Finally, once Hemingway had completed his final draft and, one assumes, had 'shaped' the work and its themes to his satisfaction, he took Scott Fitzgerald's last-minute advice and binned the novel's first 3,600 words as, in Fitzgerald's view, 'irrelevant'. That might well be thought to have affected the novel's original 'shape' and the artistic expression of its theme. Did it? Presumably not, but that begs the question: did Hemingway not himself realise that his novel would be improved by deleting those opening chapters?[1] Here it is again worth recalling that The Sun Also Rises and its successor A Farewell To Arms are generally spoken of as the 'great writer's best work (as in 'the rest of it isn't as good').

Admittedly, the theme of the 'lost generation' need not necessarily have been present in the novel's early drafts. During revision, and recalling Stein's anecdote, Hemingway might have realised his novel could portray a 'lost generation' in despair and reshaped his story accordingly (which might be why 'given the novel's theme' Fitzgerald thought the opening chapters were superfluous). That, at least, is how one might reason; yet something is very much amiss when we are obliged to twist this way and that and strain to shoehorn the 'facts' into place to square them with the 'theory'.[2]

As for the despair of a 'generation' that 'became' lost because of the 'Great War', the obvious question is: who had greater reason to be 'in despair'? Would it be one of the 23 million casualties on all sides who survived the conflict, but who did so perhaps without a limb or two and for the rest of their lives suffered from debilitating poor physical and mental health? Would it be those who had lost a father, a husband, a brother or a son? Would it be those who returned to a soulless existence of being employed in a menial job or who could not even find work? Or would it be the people identified by John Dos Passos as

> *summer tourists getting drunk and making fools of themselves at a picturesque Iberian folk-festival?*

What about Jake Barnes, you ask, who 'lost his penis' in the war? Surely he had good reason to be in despair? Well, yes, he did and he was not happy: he cried at night, suffered because others thought his wound was akin to a joke and that he could not physically express the love he felt for Brett Ashley. But the 'lost generation' interpretation of The Sun Also Rises is not about Jake Barnes and his personal predicament. Others in his group – the successful novelist Bill Gorton, the very wealthy Jew Robert Cohn, the rather self-centred femme fatale Brett Ashley and the drunken bankrupt Mike Campbell – are not in despair, or not in the way those who champion Hemingway would have us accept. Robert Cohn's possible 'despair' is simply that Brett Ashley had first taken him into her bed and had then discarded him. Mike Campbell's despair, presumably, is that he is always short of money and has been declared bankrupt. Bill Gorton isn't in despair

---

1   Hemingway later claimed binning the novel's opening chapters was his idea. It wasn't.
2   There is, though, a great deal of this practice in academic work on Hemingway and his writing, and at times it becomes beyond parody – see the later chapters advising *caveat lector*.

at all and is a remorselessly cheerful soul. Brett Ashley might be said to be in 'despair' because the man she professes to love can't perform with her; but that would seem a pretty trivial kind of 'despair': compared to those 23 million casualties of the war, the alleged 'despair' of this group is pretty small beer.

A Hemingway aficionado might still insist that the Chartres foreword is evidence that 'the despair of a lost generation' was the central theme of Hemingway's novel; but to accept that claim, we are obliged to indulge in a great deal of intellectual origami. We would instead be better to heed William of Occam who advised that

> *The explanation requiring the fewest assumptions is most likely to be correct.*

After Hemingway discarded his foreword, he opted instead simply to use the two epigraphs which now precede the novel. The first was the remark Gertrude Stein had recently made: 'You are all a lost generation' examined above. The second was a biblical quotation, Ecclesiastes 1: 4-7. This runs (there are various versions)

> *Generations come and generations go,*
> *but the earth remains forever.*
> *The sun rises and the sun sets,*
> *and hurries back to where it rises.*
> *The wind blows to the south*
> *and turns to the north*
> *round and round it goes, ever returning on its course.*
> *All streams flow into the sea,*
> *yet the sea is never full.*
> *To the place the streams come from,*
> *there they return again.*

This is arguably an odd choice if the orthodox line that Hemingway intended his novel to portray 'lost generation in despair' is to hold. Whereas Stein's remark might – though vaguely – sound pessimistically in keeping with a novel purporting to portray a despairing generation, the quote from Ecclesiastes Hemingway uses is essentially upbeat and at odds with Stein's comment. It could well be paraphrased as Scarlett O'Hara's final line in the film Gone With The Wind that *'after all, tomorrow is another day'*. Hemingway was certainly aware that the subtext of the quotation he chose is 'despite all life goes on', and if Hemingway was aware of the intrinsic optimism of the quote, why do Hemingway scholars still insist on the orthodox reading that the novel's protagonists (and many

The Sun Also Rises and the 'lost generation'

others of their generation) were 'in despair'? Verses 1-3 of Ecclesiastes immediately preceding the quotation used might have been more appropriate to the mood of a group of such despairing people

> *'Meaningless! Meaningless!' says the Teacher.*
> *'Utterly meaningless! Everything is meaningless.*
> *'What do people gain from all their labours*
> *at which they toil under the sun?'*

Hemingway would surely have read those lines when he went looking for a significant quotation to use as an epigraph, and they sum up far better the mood of a 'lost generation' that allegedly opted to drink and fornicate themselves to death. The Sun Also Rises 'portrays a lost generation in despair'? Yet again one might quote Evelyn Waugh's Mr Salter: 'Up to a point, Lord Copper'.

A modernist writer?

There was some justice to Gertrude Stein's biting remark that Hemingway "looks like a modernist and he smells of the museums".

James R. Mellow in Hemingway: A Life Without Consequences.

Modernism is less a style than a search for a style in a highly individualistic sense; indeed the style of one work is no guarantee for the next.

Malcolm Bradbury and James McFarlane, The Name And Nature Of Modernism.

It will be well to make a little more certain of these matters by reading first Mr. Hemingway's earlier book, The Sun Also Rises, and it soon becomes clear from this that, if Mr. Hemingway is 'advanced', it is not in the way that is to us most interesting . . .

Virginia Woolf, from An Essay In Criticism.

WHO when practising in 'the arts' was a 'modernist' and what constituted 'modernism' and 'modernist' works is these days unhelpfully vague. In many ways Hemingway might well have been a 'modernist writer' as is accepted by many even today; but if so, 'his modernism' was not deep-rooted and was, in a sense, more a matter of appearance, for which read superficial. He initially looked like a modernist to his contemporaries, and so they accepted him as one; but it would be distinctly hopeful to claim that any of the work he produced after the appearance in 1925 of In Our Time, his first volume of short stories – not even The Sun Also Rises – was notably modernist. Even that work, in hindsight and side-by-side with other literary works regarded as modernist, [1] doesn't make the cut, despite its then 'shocking' and thus 'modern' subject matter, and its unusual and thus 'modern' syncopated style. The Sun Also Rises, the novel much anticipated after the impact of In Our Time, disappointed more than a few critics and other writers, and they said so in their reviews. Typical of the reviews which gave just two cheers to the full-length debut by the 'exciting new writer' Ernest Hemingway was Time's observation on Nov 1, 1926, that

> *A lot of people expected a big novel from burly young author Hemingway. His short work [In Our Time] bit deeply into life. He said things naturally, calmly, tersely, accurately . . . Now his first novel is published and while his writing has acquired only a few affectations, his interests appear to have grown soggy with much sitting around sloppy café tables in . . . Paris. He has chosen to immortalise the semi-humorous love tragedy of an insatiable young English war widow and an unmanned US soldier . . . The ironic witticisms are amusing, for a few chapters. There is considerable emotion, consciously restrained, quite subtle . . . But the reader is very much inclined to echo a remark that is one of Jake's favorites, and presumably, author Hemingway's, too, 'Oh, what the hell'.*

Such rather downbeat assessments are, though, swept aside by the Hemingway champions who seem determined their man should be flawless.

Hemingway's second volume of short stories, Men Without Women, and his follow-up novel, A Farewell To Arms, were even more conventional; and when he published Death In The Afternoon and Green Hills Of Africa – although admittedly neither was a work of fiction – he was firmly back in a traditional, often rather bad and, ironically, very prolix mode of writing. [2] In her Essay In Criticism, which was nominally a review for the

---

1 The Good Soldier by Ford Madox Ford, Hemingway's supposed friend and colleague in 1920s Paris, published in 1915 would serve as a better example, as would Mrs Dalloway by Virginia Woolf. Woolf published it in the same year as Hemingway's first volume of short stories appeared (1925), and living in Paris amid a supposed 'literary set', he might well have heard of it, if not actually have read it. The supposed modernism of The Sun Also Rises also contrasts sharply with James Joyce's Ulysses and several years later the work of William Faulkner.

2 In a letter to Max Perkins in 1945, obviously not at all aware of the irony, Hemingway declared '*It wasn't by accident that the Gettysburg address was so short. The laws of prose writing are as immutable as those of flight, of mathematics, of physics.*'

New York Times of Men Without Women, Virginia Woolf nails Hemingway's supposed modernism succinctly

> ... Mr. Hemingway is not modern in the sense given; and it would appear from his first novel that this rumour of modernity must have sprung from his subject matter and from his treatment of it rather than from any fundamental novelty in his conception of the art of fiction.

Pertinent here is Woolf's mention of a 'conception of fiction'. One notable aspect of modernism and modernist artists was the thinking which underpinned their work and artistic aims; and although Hemingway often repeated that his aim when writing was to create a reality that was – to paraphrase him somewhat – 'truer than true' or 'more real than real', his notional modernism certainly had no philosophical or intellectual basis. Why should it, you ask? Well, the work of other modernist artists, writers and composers did, and this might be what Woolf was indicating when she described Hemingway as 'modern in manner but not in vision'.

Throughout his life and especially as a young man, Hemingway made a point of ostensibly and vociferously disparaging all talk of 'art', although colleagues on the Kansas Star and, later, his room-mates in Chicago report that he took part in discussions on writing, fiction and 'literature'. Quite why he stood apart from addressing what might be regarded as the more philosophical aspects of modernism is anyone's guess, because he was never reticent about commenting on what constituted 'good writing' and 'literature'. One explanation for his stance might lie in the many, often stark, contradictions in his character: 'Hemingway the intellectual' was not an image he wanted the world to have of him – he seems desperate to be regarded as a down-to-earth action man who had no time for all that airy-fairy talk about art. In fact, when his publishers Scribner's advertised and marketed The Sun Also Rises, they firmly side-lined the notion of the effete writer as 'an artist sequestered in his garret' – with the implication 'like all the other writers' – and chose to sell Hemingway as a 'masculine' action man who happened to write well.

...

To help formulate a working definition of modernism, certain general observations might help. Although many today equate modernism with the stark, jagged, sometimes brutal works of the post-World War I painters and composers, by the time much of these were produced, modernism was already well-established. Modernism is broadly thought to have begun to evolve in the last two decades of the 19th century and had firmly

A modernist writer?

established itself in the first decade of the 20th century. The then younger generation of writers, philosophers, artists and architects, and composers throughout Europe were reacting against the traditions and conventions of their parents' and grandparents' (as younger generations usually do), and whereas 'realism' had been the aim for the previous generation of writers, modernist writers increasingly wanted to get beyond and beneath that 'surface' realism and examine the inner life of the individual.

In the 20-odd years leading up to the outbreak of World War I, the modernist movement was generally driven by optimism and positivity. Encouraged by developments in the sciences, philosophy, mathematics, psychology, new production techniques and the growing popularity of left-wing political theory, and alarmed by what were regarded as the dehumanising effects of growing industrialisation, modernists were keen to apply these innovations to how society might be reformed for the better. They reflected that aim in their art. But the optimism and positivity came to a halt in the first few months of the war which broke out in 1914 and was then destroyed by the subsequent four years of horror, destruction and misery. Arguably, the fragmentation and often self-conscious ugliness of those stark, jagged, brutal works produced in the 1920s and 1930s with which 'modernism' is now popularly associated were partly more a reaction to that horror, destruction and misery than anything modernist ideas, hopes and notions might have suggested and inspired. Equally as influential as modernism matured were the theories of the mathematician and theoretical physicist Albert Einstein and his notion of relativity. In 1905, he published his paper on 'special relativity', and over the next few years he developed his theories to cover 'general relativity'; and it was the notion of relativity, that 'nothing is fixed', which interested the modernists. In the arts that interest was expressed in, for example, the cubism developed by, among others, Pablo Picasso, and in the work of the expressionist painters. In literature many writers examined the conventional notions of time passing and subjective points of view. Although there was certainly no imperative for Hemingway to do the same, his fiction was, in the light of that new idea, decidedly two-dimensional. In his work, narration is always linear, and the 'point of view' is notably all too often that of the central protagonist, a Hemingway alter ego sitting squarely at the centre of it all. The essentially solipsistic nature of his writing might have been what led Gertrude Stain to gibe that

> *Hemingway looks like a modernist and he smells of the museum.*

. . .

One useful way of viewing modernism [1] is that it

> *was an attempt to find new ways of capturing experience and identity, ways that would prioritise the individual and the interior mind, and push the boundaries of language and form to its limits. The focus was on experimentation and newness, and abandonment of the fixed point of view, driven by a restlessness with regard to the traditional structures of 19th-century realism.*

With this description in mind, the young Hemingway might perhaps be regarded as a modernist in aim and intention, though in 'prioritising the individual' it should be noted that 'the individual' portrayed in his work was all too often the Hemingway proxy; and it was solely that proxy's inner life which interested him. As for finding 'new ways of capturing experience and identity', 'pushing the boundaries of language and form', focusing 'on experimentation and newness', and abandoning 'the fixed point of view' and 'traditional structures of 19th-century realism' – any claims that he did any of that are wishful thinking.[i] Ostensibly and superficially Hemingway briefly seems to have stepped out in that direction, but he did not stray too far from the straight and narrow of the Oak Park conservatism in which he was raised. Compared to the conventional style of what many of his contemporaries were producing, Hemingway's prose style was initially 'new' and striking, but he did not take off in that direction for long and soon turned back. Whatever was 'experimental' about his writing was limited, almost two-dimensional, which is perhaps why Gertrude Stein, once a mentor and friend, later a bitter enemy, made her observation.

The narrative routes of his three famous novels are linear, with a conventional beginning, middle and an end, and the only 'inner lives' with which Hemingway concerns himself are those of each work's central character, his proxy: Nick Adams, Jake Barnes, Frederic Henry, Harry Morgan, Robert Jordan, Richard Cantwell, Thomas Hudson, David Bourne and his Spanish fisherman Santiago.[ii] In The Sun Also Rises, for example, we get to know some of Jake Barnes' inner life (and possibly even a glimpse of the 'private' Lady Brett Ashley), and Frederic Henry in A Farewell To Arms does reveal some of his inner self, although we never discover just why he is telling his story

---

1 For which description I must credit and thank Suzanne Lynch of the Irish Times in a piece published on May 5, 2015.

A modernist writer?

and felt compelled to do so – a common failing of many 'first-person' narratives [1] – and throughout Hemingway's fiction the depths of the other characters remain wholly unplumbed. Despite the attempts by some academics and critics to dignify Henry's 'love interest' Catherine Barkley with 'depth', she and the supposed passion she and Henry feel for the other remain decidedly flat, adolescent and distressingly insipid. The irony is that something psychologically complex must have been going on in Catherine: apparently close to despair after losing the man she regarded as the love of her life in the war, she rapidly replaces that man with Henry after just one meeting. Such a *coup de foudre* would not be unprecedented, and a psychologist – and a better writer – might chose to analyse why Catherine selected Henry as a substitute: a truly modernist writer might well have examined the complex 'why' of her behaviour. Hemingway does none of this: at the end of the day Hemingway was simply not interested and concerns himself solely with his proxy, Frederic Henry. As for the novel's other characters, despite heroic attempts by some academics and critics to invest them with significance, they serve only as a foil to Henry.

In the story The Snows Of Kilimanjaro, Hemingway's hero, the writer Harry Morgan ruminates on his past in what could be described as a 'stream of consciousness' as he lies dying of gangrene. Harry's death-bed ruminations – his self-reproach for living off his wealthy wife's money echo Hemingway's own guilt at the time about doing the same – are made up almost exclusively of Hemingway's own memories. Other 'modernist' writers played with the passage and nature of time, with alternative, often conflicting, narratives. They examined the contradictions of differing perceptions of the same events and utilised a variety of styles. [iii] Hemingway essayed no such experiments. At times it seems the extent of his 'modernism' was, in keeping with the instruction from his 'mentors' Ezra Pound and Gertrude Stein, merely trying to ensure his prose was simple and unadorned; and in that regard, in the work he produced after 1930 and even as he increasingly saw himself as 'a great writer', he became less successful at doing so.

Hemingway once stated that his aim was to try

> *in all my stories to get the feeling of the actual life across – not to just depict life – or criticize it – but to actually make it alive. So that when you have read something by me, you actually experience the thing.*

---

1   It is also very puzzling how a 'first-person' narrator such as Robert Jordan, who – we are led to believe – is shot dead at the end of his story, manages to tell his story. This might not trouble a reader looking for a rattlin' good adventure story, but readers hoping for a novel from 'one of our greatest writers' with a minimum of 'thought' might wonder. In fact, a 'modernist' might well somehow have made something of the fact that a story is being told 'from beyond the grave'.

The obvious question is: was this not what many other writers were also trying to achieve, including those who are not regarded as 'modernist'? Was Victor Hugo not trying, in his novel Les Miserables, to get his readers to 'feel' what it was like to take part in the June 1832 revolution? Was Dickens not trying to convey the misery of the dangers and squalor many were forced to endure? Certainly readers do report that a writer has made an experience come 'alive' for them; unhelpfully, though, each such 'felt' experience is unique and subjective. [1] Another obvious question is (and it has no possible answer): am I experiencing what Hemingway is trying to make me experience? How can I be sure? Are you and I sharing the same experience when reading the same piece of Hemingway's fiction? That would be a reliable indicator that he had succeeded, but who knows? I can never know what you are experiencing and you can never know my experience. The point it there is and can be no way of knowing.

. . .

When writing the stories for In Our Time (and those which had previously appeared in the privately published volumes Three Stories And Ten Poems and *in our time*), Hemingway was certainly self-consciously trying something new. Under the tutelage of Pound and Stein, he wanted to discard ornamentation in his prose: out went most adjectives and all adverbs; but his style was not unique and reminded many – much to Hemingway's annoyance – of the work of his mentor Sherwood Anderson. It was also reminiscent of the style of Ring Lardner, a writer Hemingway admired and which a few years earlier he had consciously imitated. Responding to that technique, the prose in that first commercially published volume, was variously described by reviewers as

> *fibrous and athletic, colloquial and fresh, hard and clean*

and

> *terse, precise and aggressively fresh.*

Hemingway's subject matter was equally unconventional. The critics, thus, had high hopes for the young writer's debut novel, but when it appeared, its reception was mixed. Typical of the enthusiasts was the view of an early Hemingway champion, the then literary young Turk Edmund Wilson. He wrote

> *The barbarity of the world is also the theme of . . . The Sun Also*

---

1   It would here be useful to remind ourselves again of Oscar Wilde's reaction to the death of Dickens' Little Nell.

A modernist writer?

> *Rises . . . [its] whole interest lies in the attempts of the hero and heroine to disengage themselves from this world, or rather to arrive at some method of living honorably. The real story there is the story of their attempts to do this – attempts by which, in such a world, they are always bound to lose in everything except honor.* [1]

The New York Sun commented

> *There is no one writing whose prose has more of the force and vibrancy of good, direct, natural, colloquial speech. . . It seems to me that Hemingway is highly successful in presenting the effect that a sensual love for the same woman might have on the temperaments of three men who are utterly different in this position and training*

and the New York Herald Tribune gushed

> *The dialogue is brilliant. If there is better dialogue being written today I do not know where to find it. It is alive with the rhythms and idioms, the pauses and suspensions and innuendos and short-hands, of living speech. It is in the dialogue almost entirely Mr Hemingway tells his story and makes the people live and act.*

Others reviewing The Sun Also Rises, though, were less enchanted and impressed. The review by Time magazine (founded three years earlier and in later years notable for being a Hemingway stalwart as he became a public figure) is quoted above. In Nation & Athaeneum Edwin Muir writes that

> *Hemingway tells us a great deal about those people, but he tells us nothing of importance about human life.*

In Britain the Observer was even more direct

> *Mr Hemingway began brilliantly, with a set of short stories called In Our Time. But Fiesta [as The Sun Also Rises was known in Britain] gives us neither people nor atmosphere, the maudlin,*

---

1   Some readers might agree with me that Wilson was being fanciful and over-egging his pudding to an alarming degree. I can find little trace of 'barbarity' in The Sun Also Rises except in the choreographed slaughter of innocent bulls. As for '*the attempts of the hero and heroine . . . to arrive as some method of living honorably*' that strikes me as the usual reviewers' literary hyperbole rather than anything more respectable.

> *staccato conversations – evidently meant to be realistic in their brokenness and boringness – convey no impression of reality; and the characters, both men and women, in Paris and in Spain, are so consistently soaking themselves with alcohol as to lose all human interest . . . Why does Mr Hemingway, who can draw flesh-and-blood, waste his time on the bibulous shadows?*

Worse was the scathing New Masses' review by John Dos Passos,[1] although, as I've noted, he was writing for an avowedly left-wing publication and his scorn for the antics of decidedly 'bourgeois' protagonists getting drunk at a Spanish fiesta might be filed under 'predictable'; but his observation is spot-on and still valid. Overall, reviews were favourable and the novel sold – and continues to sell – steadily; but what is pertinent is that none of the reviews seemed to regard The Sun Also Rises as a 'modernist' novel, and if they did, they neglected to mention it.

. . .

The Sun Also Rises was certainly 'modern', but 'modern' does not equate with 'modernist'; and as unfortunately 'modern' tends to age all too rapidly and can soon become 'old hat', there is nothing in the novel that 'shocked' in the 1920s that would today dismay any reader or possibly even any reader ten years after it was published. However, in uptight, teetotal, God-fearing Oak Park just outside Chicago where Hemingway grew up, not yet a city suburb and once described as 'where the bars end and the churches begin', it disgusted his parents Ed and Grace Hemingway. In a letter to her son, his mother described his novel as

> *one of the filthiest books of the year . . . surely you have other words in your vocabulary besides "damn" and "bitch" – every page fills me with a sick loathing'.*

The city 'slicks' might have welcomed the novel, but his parents' outrage was shared with thousands of like-minded folk elsewhere in the country. Just why the novel caused such a stir among the rural 'hicks' can be gauged from the following observation of Middle America by Michael Reynolds in his biography Hemingway: The Paris Years:

---

1   In later life Dos Passos drifted firmly from left-wingery into neo-conservatism, a conversion which began gradually in Spain during the Civil War and carried on until he died in 1970. His disillusion with the Left was such that in the 1960s he campaigned for the Republicans Barry Goldwater and later for Richard Nixon.

A modernist writer?

> *Those were the days when Billy Sunday and Aimee Semple MacPherson led Bible thumpers down the fundamentalist trail that Americans periodically seemed compelled to travel. We remember the Scopes monkey trial in Tennessee, but forget that the school teacher lost, that the law forbidding Darwin's presence in the classroom was upheld. We forget about the Anti-Saloon league and the Clean Books Bill. We forget that the Little Review lost its case in the first Ulysses trial and that the meanest sort of reactionary spirit resulted in a resurgent Ku Klux Klan. American voters filled their presidency with conservative men determined to keep America isolated from the world, pretending that an inflated dollar was good for business. We all remember Lindbergh's daring 1927 flight across the Atlantic, but forget that he later admired Hitler's well-oiled military machine.*

In other words, Hemingway might have gained the enthusiastic admiration of a minority – the narrow literary world of New York and other major cities – and that of it's acolytes, the 'open-minded' and 'enlightened' folk in various parts of the country; but the majority of that country were less than pleased by the appearance of a novel in which – shamelessly! – words such as 'damn' and 'bitch' were prominent. Yet outrage can often be very useful as press agents and promoters know well; and given how much the novel alienated many, they might well have been prepared to accept Hemingway as 'a modernist'.

Max Perkins certainly rated him as a writer, but he had to overcome initial in-house resistance to publishing The Sun Also Rises. He and Scribner's younger editors were aware that competition in publishing was growing and that Scribner's was regarded as more than a touch fusty. The younger editors feared that Scribner's was in danger of being regarded by younger readers as too staid, and they hoped to rejuvenate it by publishing work such as Hemingway's 'modern' novel and a few years earlier had persuaded the reluctant senior Scribner's board members to publish F. Scott Fitzgerald's debut novel This Side Of Paradise and its follow-up, The Beautiful And The Damned.[1] But to repeat: 'modern' is certainly not necessarily 'modernist'. To strengthen his case with the board and overcome its resistance, Perkins had persuaded Hemingway to moderate his text: for example, a reference to a bull's 'balls' was changed to the bull's 'horns', and other language considered 'unacceptable' was toned down. Bona fide modernists

---

1 Perhaps to demonstrate quite how loosely the label modernist was and is used, F. Scott Fitzgerald has also been described by some as 'a modernist writer'.

in rather less buttoned-up Europe might have been more than a little bemused at such trifling objections – they would have been more impressed – or, better, depressed – by the publication ban imposed in the US in 1922 on James Joyce's truly modernist work Ulysses and not lifted until 1934.

The moderations to which Hemingway agreed did manage to blunt the board's reluctance, but did little to assuage the outrage of Middle America which also thoroughly disapproved of the novel's casual attitude to sex and adultery. It wasn't, though, the approval of Middle America Perkins wanted and, ironically, every instance of public outrage and disapproval was welcome. Perkins had begun his publishing career in Scribner's advertising department and knew such outrage was good publicity and great for sales: as much as older folk hated the novel, younger folk would love it. Reviewing Hemingway's short memoir, A Moveable Feast, many years later, The New Republic's then film critic, Stanley Kauffman recalled the extraordinary impact Hemingway's first two novels and first two collections of short stories had on him and his 1920s contemporaries. He wrote:

> To younger readers, those who came to Hemingway after
> World War II, he could not possibly look the same as to previous
> generations because the later group saw him in a different context
> . . . Those who began to read him in the mid-20s, or soon after,
> experienced a small epiphany, saw a powerful and incredibly
> timely writer appear, almost as a saviour bringing curt truth to a
> windy and shaken society.

Here the relevant word is 'context', and it is perhaps not surprising that as the 1920s became the 1930s, then the 1940s, then the 1950s, and as the 'context' changed and each new 'young generation' demanded its own heroes, what had startled and excited young readers when Hemingway burst onto the scene and made him 'modern' and nominally 'a modernist' became not just far less startling and exciting, but not in the least startling and exciting. That is a truism, of course, but it is a truism those who still champion Hemingway's fiction and style seem to ignore or forget.

. . .

'Context' is also relevant when one considers 'Hemingway the modernist' and whether he was one. Certainly, a reading public in the mid-1920s more accustomed to the polite and elegant prose of John Galsworthy and Edith Wharton will have been willing to accept that he was 'a modernist' (as the critics implied at the time – then

A modernist writer? 159

as today it seems few readers dare not hold an opinion until it has the imprimatur of 'a respected critic'). It is easy to accept why in its day In Our Time might be regarded as 'modernist', though a review of that volume in the Times Literary Supplement had noted – rather tartly – that

> *Mr Ernest Hemingway, a young American writer living in Paris, is definitely of the moderns. It is not merely a deliberate taste for writing ungrammatically now and again which points the way to Mr Hemingway's literary camp; it is rather his own concern for the conventional features of good writing. The short stories in the volume entitled In Our Time . . . achieve their affect by normal and rather puzzling means . . . Only one story in the book – Indian Camp, the first – has anything like a straightforward appeal, and even here the actual method is as elusive as in the rest of the tales.*

In the New Yorker shortly after the publication of The Sun Also Rises, Dorothy Parker also had her doubts that Hemingway was fulfilling his promise. She wrote

> *Now, The Sun Also Rises was as "starkly" written as Mr. Hemingway's short stories; it dealt with subjects as "unpleasant". Mr. Hemingway's style, this prose stripped to its firm young bones, is far more effective, far more moving, in the short story than in the novel. He is, to me, the greatest living writer of short stories; he is, also to me, not the greatest living novelist.*

One might raise an eyebrow about the first part of her claim given that at the time Hemingway had published just 16, often very short, stories;[iv] but the point is that she was one of several critics who seemed to feel The Sun Also Rises fell short of the 'modernism' apparently promised by the earlier work. The Times Literary Supplement was also underwhelmed by of the 'debut' novel and was quite candid in its view:

> *Now comes Fiesta [as The Sun Also Rises was published in Britain] . . . more obviously an experiment in story-making [than In Our Time], and in which he abandons his vivid impressionism for something less interesting. There are moments of sudden illumination in the story, and throughout it displays a determined reticence; but it is frankly tedious after one has read the first hundred pages and ceased to hope for something different . . . The Spanish scenes give us something of the quality of Mr*

> Hemingway's earlier book, but they hardly qualify the general impression of an unsuccessful experiment.

What contemporary critics and reviewers would and could not have known is that, as I suggest, Hemingway's prime motivation for writing the novel was not based on a modernist idealism of any kind or to examine the lives of a putative 'lost generation', but to build a career for himself as a writer.[1] Had they been aware of Hemingway's less idealistic ambitions, one does wonder what other modernist writers, artists and composers, many of whom were inclined to left-of-centre views and who were at odds with the established capitalist ethos, would have made of them.

. . .

The use of the phrase 'banal declarations' by the New York City Sun's Herbert Seligman in his review of In Our Time to describe in part Hemingway's style is both interesting and telling. Consider this paragraph:

> In the morning it was bright and they were sprinkling the streets of the town, and we all had breakfast in a café. Bayonne is a nice town. It is like a very clean Spanish town and it is on a big river. Already, so early in the morning, it was very hot on the bridge across the river. We walked out on the bridge and then took a walk through the town.

If you do not recognise the passage and if I told you it is a short excerpt from the travel diary of one Lewis Monroe, of Rockbridge, Illinois, written during his trip to Europe in his graduation summer in 1954, you might well accept what I'm saying without question. But it isn't – it is the opening paragraph of chapter 10 of The Sun Also Rises. It is, admittedly, an excerpt specifically chosen to make a point, but it is a crucial point: could this prose really be described as 'fibrous and athletic' and 'aggressively fresh'? 'Modernist' or not, it is utterly banal, and it is puzzling to be assured by academics and critics even today that Hemingway's prose was top-notch writing.[2] It would be interesting to know what today's Hemingway champions make of the turgid and often barely comprehen-

---

1   Just how determined Hemingway was to convey 'his philosophy' is a moot point. We really can't be sure that conveying what subsequent academic analysis has identified as 'Hemingway's themes' was his prime reason for writing.

2   If, however, one accepts the contention that The Sun Also Rises was primarily written so Hemingway could get a novel under his belt, this uninspiring passage, as padding, does serve a purpose.

A modernist writer?

sible prose in Death In The Afternoon and Green Hills Of Africa that was soon to come.

It is, of course, possible that Hemingway, in 'modernist' mode, specifically intended the tone of the paragraph quoted – the novel is written in the first person – to sound thoroughly banal (*'Bayonne is a nice town. It is like a very clean Spanish town and it is on a big river.'*). He might, for example, have wanted to give the reader an insight into his main protagonist's mindset. Yet if that was his intention – and I doubt it was – it would be wholly at odds with how Jake Barnes, a journalist and the novel's cynical, worldly-wise 'first-person' narrator is portrayed elsewhere in the novel.

One similarly wonders about other passages in the novel. Once Jake Barnes and his pal Bill Gorton have travelled south from Paris but before they meet the friends who will be joining them for the fiesta, they take off in a charabanc for several days fishing in the hills north of Pamplona. Describing their journey to Burguete near where they plan to fish, Hemingway treats us to long passages of how the charabanc is loaded and boarded by its passengers and of its journey into the hills. Academics now choose to interpret that blissful interlude – the journey and the few days spent fishing [v] – as a contrast with the supposed despair of those in Pamplona; but it is not surprising that in his review for the New Masses of Dos Passos insists that the novel reminds him of a travel book. Dos Passos' impression is worth bearing in mind when one considers the 224-word description of the bus journey to Burguete:

> *The bus climbed steadily up the road. The country was barren and rocks stuck up through the clay. There was no grass beside the road. Looking back we could see the country spread out below. Far back the fields were squares of green and brown on the hillsides. Making the horizon were the brown mountains. They were strangely shaped. As we climbed higher the horizon kept changing. As the bus ground slowly up the road, we could see other mountains coming up in the south. Then the road came over the crest, flattened out and went into a forest. It was a forest of cork oaks, and the sun came through the trees in patches, and there were cattle grazing back in the trees. We went through the forest and the road came out and turned along a rise of land, and out ahead of us was a rolling green plain, with dark mountains beyond it. They were not like the brown, heat-baked mountains we had left behind. They were wooded and there were clouds coming down from them. The green plain stretched off. It was cut by fences and the white house of Burguete ahead strung out on the plain, and away off on the shoulder of*

> *the first dark mountain was the gray metal-sheathed roof of the monastery of Roncesvalles.*

Hemingway's biographers tell us that Cezanne was one of Hemingway's favourite painters and that he said he wanted to write as Cezanne painted; and in the above one can see how he might be attempting to do so. But if one heeds and accepts W.K. Wimsatt and Monroe Beardsley's view (in their 1946 paper The Intentional Fallacy which I touch upon elsewhere [1]) that a work can and should only be judged on and in itself, the passage becomes more than a little deflated. It would not be at all out-of-place as part of an anodyne feature in an airline's in-flight magazine. A reader unaware of Hemingway's fondness for Cezanne's work and his ambition to 'write as Cezanne painted' might be far more inclined to accept he or she was reading another excerpt from the travel diary of Rockbridge's Lewis Monroe (or, for that matter, any travel book about Spain – you can see what Dos Passos was getting at). More to the point, whether or not you like the flat, veering on banal, style of the two passages quoted, it is difficult to see how they and other passages might have come from the pen of a 'modernist' writer attempting to push the boundaries of prose writing.

...

These and other passages are also notable in that they ignore one of the rules Hemingway laid down for writers. When Fitzgerald asked Hemingway for his candid opinion of his newly published novel Tender Is The Night in 1934, Hemingway was highly critical; but one particular stricture he accused Fitzgerald of not observing is relevant to his own work. First, consider the following (from the opening of chapter 5 of The Sun Also Rises which I give in full):

> *In the morning I walked down the Boulevard to the Rue Soufflot for coffee and a brioche. It was a fine morning. The horse-chestnut trees in the Luxembourg gardens were in bloom. There was the pleasant early-morning feeling of a hot day. I read the papers with a coffee then smoked a cigarette. The flower-women were coming up from the market and arranging their daily stock. Students went by going to the law school, or down to the Sorbonne. The boulevard was busy with trams and people going to work. I got on the S bus and rode down to the Madeleine, standing on the back platform.*

---

[1] They were discussing verse, but arguably their thesis can be extrapolated to prose.

A modernist writer?

> *From the Madeleine I walked along the Boulevard des Capucines to the Opera, and up to my office. I passed the man with the jumping frogs and the man with the boxer toys. I stepped aside to avoid walking into the thread with which his girl assistant manipulated the boxers. She was standing looking away, the thread in her folded hands. She was urging two tourists to buy. Three more tourists had stopped and were watching. I walked on behind a man who was pushing a roller that printed the name CINZANO on the sidewalk in damp letters. All along people were going to work. It felt pleasant to be going to work. I walked across the avenue and turned in to my office. Upstairs in the office I read the French morning papers, smoked, and then sat at the typewriter and got off a good morning's work. At eleven o'clock I went to the Quai d'Orsay in a taxi and went in and sat with about a dozen correspondents, while the foreign-office mouthpiece, a young Novell-Revue-Francaise diplomat in horn-rimmed spectacles, talked and answered questions for half an hour. The President of the Council was in Lyons making a speech, or, rather he was on his way back. Several people asked questions to hear themselves talk and there were a couple of questions by news servicemen who wanted to know the answers. There was no news. I shared a taxi back from the Quai d'Orsay with Woolsey and Krum.*

Now consider the above passage in light of what Hemingway had to say in his letter to Fitzgerald: he wags a finger at him and advises

> *. . . don't think anything is of any importance because it happens to you or anyone belonging to you.*

That 'rule' might well be summed up as 'leave out the irrelevant bits'. So what are we to make of the long paragraph above in the context of the novel as a whole? What purpose does it serve? Is it 'relevant' in some way – in any way, in fact? The style is not quite as flat – for which one might again read 'banal' – as that of Lewis Monroe's travel diary, but it is fair to ask quite what a modernist novel which purports to deal with the lives, spiritual disillusionment and despair of a mooted 'lost generation' is aiming to achieve with the above description of a mundane journey to work and which then details what the chap did when he got there.

As it happens, in this paragraph as elsewhere in the novel, there is a great deal of scope for supposedly profound and important exegesis and analysis by true believers. [vi] After all, they might assure us, Hemingway, almost universally acknowledged as 'a writer of genius', will have known what he was doing; so though we might not immediately understand the purpose and function of those paragraphs, there is certainly something deeper going on. Hemingway is setting the scene, they might suggest: the apparent banal mundanity of it all (*'I read the papers with a coffee then smoked a cigarette', 'I got on the S bus and rode down to the Madeleine, standing on the back platform'*) is intended – ironically perhaps? – to throw into relief the inner turmoil of the man, a man rendered impotent and very unhappy by a war wound, no less.

I don't doubt there might be other, equally plausible, interpretations. But again to apply the principle of Occam's Razor, we might conclude that this passage is also little more than padding. A true 'writer of genius' might well have boiled down the above 363 words to far shorter, but more telling – and more interesting and engaging – paragraphs. If there are some hidden significances in those paragraphs, they are certainly elusive. As for any alleged 'modernism', there isn't a whisper of it.

These are not isolated examples: early on in the novel there are several other instances where, apparently for no reason at all, Hemingway describes his passage through various streets of the Left Bank. Once he and his characters have arrived in Pamplona and the reader is treated to other such descriptions, it might be argued that those passages serve as a *mise en scene*; but that explanation would hold no water for the Paris descriptions, not least given how they are written. In a novel famous for purportedly portraying the lives and despair of a 'lost generation', they seem more than oddly superfluous. And note: I am simply holding Hemingway to his own rule – *'don't think anything is of any importance because it happens to you or anyone belonging to you'*. In fact, the 'padding' was necessary, though not for artistic reasons: had Hemingway 'left out' all the 'irrelevant bits' as he insisted Fitzgerald should have done, would the work have been long enough to be submitted as the novel he knew he had to write to consolidate his incipient career?

...

Guided by Ezra Pound and Gertrude Stein in the early 1920s, Hemingway initially developed a style which might superficially have resembled modernism, but that style did not survive for long. He did keep his sentences brief, eschewed adverbs and kept adjectives to a minimum; and he adhered to his stated intention simply to describe

A modernist writer?

without passing judgment. That the prose of In Our Time is in keeping with these principles might well be seen by some as 'modernist', although set side-by-side with what other 'modernist' writers had produced and were attempting, it is less than remarkable. Yet even in the stories of Men Without Women, his second collection, published a year after The Sun Also Rises, his style had already embraced the conventional, and Hemingway again continues to ignore his own strictures. In The Undefeated, the central character, the washed-up bullfighter Manuel (who is looking to be hired), says something 'hopefully', then something else 'reproachfully'. Later, the picador Zurito, a second character in the story, reads a newspaper 'laboriously'. How well does that sit with the imperative to eschew adverbs? Cannot Hemingway convey Manuel's hopes and reproaches with a little more skill? What happened to 'show, don't tell'? It gets worse: in Che Ti Dice La Patria, included in the second volume of short stories and lazily re-worked from a feature Hemingway had written and published in The New Republic, the young Fascist who demands a lift 'looked annoyedly' [1] when the car's radiator begins to boil. The obvious question is: was Hemingway even aware of these adverbs, which would not have been out of place in the juvenilia he had been producing during those months in Petoskey when he was 19? For a man who insisted he 'worked hard' on his writing and, he claimed, who revised and rewrote obsessively, we are obliged to take him at his word and conclude he must have been aware of them. So why on earth did he let them through? Or did he, perhaps, not revise quite as diligently as he insisted he did? [2]

...

Was Hemingway a 'modernist writer'? I'm certainly not persuaded, but much like 'beauty', 'modernism', what it 'is' and what 'qualifies' as modernism are very much in the eye of the beholder. Others will disagree and insist Hemingway was 'a modernist', though if they accept my contention that – given the genesis of 'modernism' – there was usually some kind of 'intellectual' and possibly philosophical dimension to attempting to produce modernist work, Hemingway – in my view – doesn't even start to make the cut. Yet I suspect the orthodoxy – that he was a modernist writer – will hold sway for some time yet simply because it gels neatly with his equally orthodox status as 'one of the greatest writers of the 20th century' (and we do prefer neatness in our thinking and so dislike loose ends). Frankly, to date Hemingway almost always gets a pass when such

---

1   A particularly egregious use of an adverb.
2   How carefully Hemingway revised his work, contrary to what he claimed, is looked at when I consider the so-called 'insoluble problem' presented by a later short story. See p.183ff

matters are raised because, as Matthew Bruccoli astutely observed – and bearing in mind the theology of Hemingway's existence as a writer –

> *Everything he did, everything he wrote, became important because he was Ernest Hemingway.*

Hemingway theology –
Round and round

Indeed, in New York a profile by Dorothy Parker on November 30, 1929, may be said to have marked the point at which Hemingway passed beyond mere fame into living legend.

Kenneth S. Lynn, in his biography Hemingway.

I know no American writer with a more startling ear for colloquial conversation, or a more poetic sensitiveness for the woods and hills. In Our Time has perhaps not enough energy to be a great book, but Ernest Hemingway has promises of genius.

New York Herald Tribune review of In Our Time, February 14, 1926.

Mediated ideology persists to such an extent that the myth becomes absorbed as legend, and thus the realism behind the figures becomes distorted. This is particularly evident in the case of American author Ernest Hemingway, whose celebrity image eclipsed the man and thereby created a culturally fruitful myth.

Siobhan Lyons, Remembering Hemingway: The Endurance of the Hemingway Myth.

He delivers a self-confident lecture on the high possibilities of prose writing, with the implication that he himself, Hemingway, has realized or hopes to realize these possibilities; and then writes what are certainly, from the point of view of prose, the very worst pages of his life. There is one passage which is hardly even intelligible – the most serious possible fault for a writer who is always insisting on the supreme importance of lucidity. He inveighs with much scorn against the literary life and against the professional literary man of the cities; and then manages to give the impression that he himself is a professional literary man of the most touchy and self-conscious kind.

Edmund Wilson, review of Green Hills Of Africa in The New Republic, 1935.

IT IS instructive to debate with Hemingway enthusiasts. In spirit, many are far more like football club supporters for whom their side can do no wrong than women or men who will discuss soberly why the work of this or that poet or writer is or is not exceptional. In brief: beware zealots. Their attitude is also remarkably similar to that of many 'people of faith' when they discuss the 'existence of God'.

In all monotheistic theologies, of whatever faith, two immutable facts are that 'God exists' and that 'God is always right and without fault'. These facts are, if you are a believer, the *sine qua non* of faith and, naturally, of every theological debate. Indeed they must be: what would be the point, for example, of basing the imperatives of a moral system on the 'word of God' and debating the various arcana of 'His' existence and 'His' laws if God, too, were flawed and imperfect and no better than us mortals? [1]

Given 'His' unimpeachability and perfection compared to mankind's pitiful corruptibility, it is axiomatic that if there are some aspects of God, of 'His' existence', of 'His laws' and of 'His word' we do not yet comprehend, it is necessarily our fault and we must try harder to understand what 'He' means and is telling us. To account for the apparent incomprehensibility of some aspects of 'God', such as the Catholic doctrine of the Trinity – 'three persons in one God' – these are legitimised and rationalised as being 'mysteries' which we sinful folk cannot be expected to understand (although we are assured that with 'His' grace we might do so in time). Furthermore, the concept of an unimpeachable, all-powerful and all-knowing God often results in a distressing circularity when it comes to debating or attempting to 'prove' 'His' existence to a non-believer. One 'proof' often offered is that 'I know He exists because I feel it in my heart'. Such 'proof' might satisfy

---

1   The many gods of so-called 'pagan' systems are in this respect far more interesting. They share a great many flaws with us humans.

Hemingway theology – Round and round

fellow believers who also feel 'His existence' in their heart, but it does not take anyone – an agnostic, say – much further down the lane. It is just another subjective truth of the kind described earlier: your 'knowledge' that 'God exists' is an utterly personal matter of sentiment; and although no one is doubting or downplaying how strongly you 'feel' that 'God exists', it is 'personal knowledge' and can never be the kind of empirical objective 'fact' which could be offered as 'proof' of 'His' existence. A similar attempt to 'prove' the existence of 'God' is offered by those who cite what they call and regard as 'intelligent design'. Because I suggest the 'proof' it claims to provide is wholly spurious, I might not be the best authority to describe what the proponents of 'intelligent design' believe; but one definition I have come across from a source that does subscribe to the notion is that

> *The theory of intelligent design holds that certain features of the universe and of living things are best explained by an intelligent cause, not an undirected process such as natural selection.* [1]

Here is not the place to debate 'intelligent design', but one might point out that its rationale does essentially depend on us seeing what we want to see and, tacitly, only admitting 'evidence' which suits us and rejecting what does not. I have no idea how proponents would respond to that observation, but it is clear – to me, at least – that once one has crossed over to become one of the group of 'believers' – whether it is that 'God' exists and 'He' created the world or that 'Ernest Hemingway was one of the 20th century's greatest writers' – everything else falls ever so neatly into place. Thus the question 'How do we know He is the one true God?' [2] will invariably get the response 'Because He tells us he is'; and if the next question is 'How do we know we can accept His assurance?' the answer is 'because He is God, and because He is God, He is always right'. 'How do we know God is always right?' 'Because He's God and He is perfect'. 'Why should we accept His word and obey Him without question?' 'Because he tells us we must'. 'And why must we accept that imperative?' 'Because he's God' – and on and on and round and round it goes.

I don't doubt believers will condemn what I have written as a shameless parody of their justifications of faith; [3] but the point is that a similar circularity seems long to have plagued many academics, post-graduate students writing a thesis or dissertation and

---

1   This sceptic would also point out that a belief in and the arguments for 'intelligent design' are intellectually no improvement on the line fed to many young children that *'only God could have created a world as beautiful as this'*.

2   I am capping up the H in 'He' and 'His' out of courtesy.

3   Not so many centuries ago I could be put to death for voicing such views which were 'blasphemies' in the language of the day and still are in some parts of the Islamic world.

all manner of scholars; it permeates their work when they discuss, examine, analyse, interpret and comment on the works of Ernest Hemingway, essentially 'proving' that he was one of our greatest writers' (although the more circumspect of their number might prudently take care in how they express themselves). Indeed, there is something quasi-theological about many such analyses and exegeses: it is more or less a given that Hemingway was a great writer. And the 'proof'? 'Well,' they might declare, 'we wouldn't bother dealing with him and his work in the first place if he wasn't, would we?' [1]

. . .

The essence of the, though usually unwitting, circularity – and it doesn't matter at which point on the circle you start – is that 'Ernest Hemingway is one of our greatest writers because he wrote stories like this' and 'this story is great because it is by Ernest Hemingway'. Then the answer to the question 'why is Ernest Hemingway great?' is 'because he wrote stories like this'; and because the 'fact' of Hemingway's status as 'one of our greatest writers' is passed on from one generation to the next, academics, scholars and post-graduate students writing a thesis are apt to tie themselves in knots interpreting his work rather than to concede that some of it doesn't always cut the mustard.

The blurb on the back of my paperback edition of The Sun Also Rises had proclaimed that Hemingway was 'a genius' and that the novel is 'a masterpiece'; and although when a publisher proclaims such 'facts', they can be regarded as little more than commercial hyperbole – no publisher ever undersells one of its authors. But these 'facts' were and still are accepted, by many without question, and repeated. So we might ask: exactly how were the 'facts' established that Hemingway was a 'genius' as a writer [i] – or more modestly 'a great writer' – and that his debut novel is 'a masterpiece'? How did what became the orthodox view of Hemingway's 'greatness' acquire – for some – the status not just of doctrine but of dogma, such that scholars will resort to spouting blank nonsense when discussing his work rather than consider that, like everyone else, Hemingway might occasionally have had feet of clay? [2]

. . .

Within not many years of Hemingway's suicide in July 1961, his reputation already

---

1   Collapse of stout party.

2   Even such obvious stinkers like Across The River And Into The Trees, Islands In The Stream and The Garden Of Eden are loyally defended by many Hemingway champions, who go to great lengths to discover traces of wheat amongst the chaff.

began to be re-evaluated. Writing in the New York Times in November 1985, reviewing Peter Griffin's and Jeffrey Meyers' new biographies of Hemingway, the writer Raymond Carver noted that

> *In the years since 1961, Hemingway's reputation as 'the outstanding author since the death of Shakespeare' (John O'Hara's wildly extravagant assessment in praise of Across The River And Into The Trees) shrank to the extent that many critics, as well as some fellow writers, felt obliged to go on record that they, and the literary world at large, had been bamboozled somehow: Hemingway was not nearly as good as had been originally thought. They agreed that at least one, maybe two, of the novels . . . might make it into the 21st century, along with a handful, five or six, perhaps, of his short stories. Death had finally removed the author from center stage, and deadly 'reappraisals' began taking place.*

One should immediately concede that a 'shrinking reputation' has no bearing either way on the 'worth' of a body of work: 'worth' – in this context – is nothing but a subjective assessment; and a 'shrinking reputation' conveys merely that a growing number have downgraded the 'worth' – but that is all it tells us. Furthermore, Carver's claim is ambiguous: did the critics and fellow writers confess they might have been 'bamboozled' because they had come to believe Hemingway's work was not as good as they had once thought? Or did they 'go on record' – did they 'feel obliged' to say – that they, too, had been 'bamboozled' because they sensed the literary mood was changing and they preferred to run with the pack? Or had they, in fact, privately never much rated Hemingway, but were previously disinclined to risk their peers' scorn by doubting the excellence of a man everyone else spoke of as 'one of the greatest writers of the 20th century'? Carver himself did rate Hemingway and still felt that 'with each passing year [his work becomes] more durable'. His description of the reappraisals as 'deadly' as well as the quotation marks around the word 'reappraisals' do hint that he, too, tacitly believed Hemingway was somehow 'great', if not unimpeachable. He certainly did not much like Meyers' biography and sniffily wrote that

> *Adulation is not a requirement for biographers, but Mr Meyers' fairly bristles with disapproval of its subject.*

Carver was also put out by Meyers' 'strong belief' that

> *like his heroes, Twain and Kipling [Hemingway] never fully*

matured as a writer.

Yet that view is not uncommon among some sceptics on the matter of Hemingway's 'greatness' and is certainly alluded to by Vladimir Nabokov in Strong Opinions, his collection of essays and interviews. When he was asked whether he had indeed described Hemingway (and Joseph Conrad) as 'writers of books for boys', he agreed that he had and added that

> *in neither [Ernest Hemingway and Joseph Conrad] can I find anything that I would care to have written myself. In mentality and emotion, they are hopelessly juvenile . . .*

A similar point about the appeal of Hemingway's work to the adolescent in us [1] was made as recently as July 2018 by N. J. McGarrigle in the Irish Times when he observed that

> *Your attitude to Hemingway depends on how early you reach him on your reading map.*

As for 'disapproving' Mr Meyers, who wrote his biography more than 20 years after Hemingway's death, he did certainly get off his knees, and his attitude was a welcome change from the earlier, quasi-hagiographic accounts of the writer by Malcolm Cowley, Charles Fenton, Philip Young, John Atkins and Carlos Baker, all written when Hemingway was still alive. A similarly more sceptical account of Hemingway and his work came from Kenneth S. Lynn whose biography appeared two years later, in 1987.

. . .

One difficulty in evaluating a writer's work is that it is not – and can never be – a simple question of aping the scientific, causal 'if this, then that', despite an unconscious tendency by many to do so. [2] There are no definitive answers to the worth of any writer's output – or even to the 'meaning' of her or his work – as there certainly are definitive answers to questions such as 'what is two plus two?' or 'what is sixty divided by twelve?' Insisting on absolutes and assuming there are 'correct' – and thus, of course, 'incorrect' – conclusions when judging the work of a writer is as fatuous as it would be to 'have an opinion' on whether or not 'two plus two equals four'. Yet this is precisely the habit many

---

1   Well, in some of us – I plead for exemption.
2   The varying and often contradictory interpretations of Hemingway's fiction should surely alert interpreters that they might somehow be barking up the wrong tree. They can't all be 'right'.

Hemingway theology – Round and round

Hemingway scholars – and no doubt scholars involved in the work of other writers – fall into. It is never overt, but the habit most certainly exists and is never far beneath the surface.

One example of such a mechanistic and ostensibly objective approach to analysis and appreciation is from Joan Didion, the novelist, essayist and journalist. [ii] In a piece about Hemingway in the New Yorker in October 1998, she quotes the first paragraph of his novel A Farewell To Arms and writes

> *. . . four deceptively simple sentences, one hundred and twenty-six words, the arrangement of which remains as mysterious and thrilling to me now as it did when I first read them, at twelve or thirteen . . .* [1]

So far that is nothing but the standard waffle which kicks off many a journalistic feature piece; but Didion then examines those four sentences and notes

> *Only one of the words has three syllables. Twenty-two have two. The other hundred and three have one. Twenty-four of the words are 'the', fifteen are 'and'. There are four commas. The liturgical [sic] cadence of the paragraph derives in part from the placement of the commas (their presence in the second and fourth sentences, their absence in the first and third),* [iii] *but also from that repetition of 'the' and of 'and', creating a rhythm so pronounced that the omission of 'the' before the word 'leaves' in the fourth sentence ('and we saw the troops marching along the road and the dust rising and leaves, stirred by the breeze, falling') casts exactly what it was meant to cast, a chill, a premonition, a foreshadowing of the story to come, the awareness that the author has already shifted his attention from late summer to a darker season. The power of the paragraph, offering as it does the illusion but not the fact of specificity, derives precisely from this kind of deliberate omission, from the tension of withheld information. In the late summer of what year? What river, what mountain, what troops?*

Here Didion has become more than faintly ridiculous as she attempts to pin down what moved her in the paragraph by listing the particular number and arrangement of

---

1   This might be pertinent – see, above, Vladimir Nabokov's reservations about Hemingway.

syllables, sentences and commas and how often the words 'the' and 'and' are used. Her approach reminds one of William Wordsworth's observation in The Tables Turned that

> *Our meddling intellect / Mis-shapes the beauteous forms*
> *of things / We murder to dissect.*

Quite apart from how effective or not a well-placed comma is, [1] each and every reaction to that paragraph will be unique and, far more to the point, utterly subjective. Didion says she was 'thrilled' by it, though she was still a young girl and not yet a woman when she first read it. Another reader might agree that first paragraph is lyrical – or even moving – but might not be as 'thrilled' by it as Didion, despite being confronted by the same number and arrangement of syllables, sentences and commas. [2] A third reader might enjoy the passage, but not find it in any sense outstanding or remarkable. So who is 'right' and who is 'wrong'?

The real difficulty with a great deal of literary interpretation is that although we might ostensibly not disagree that 'each reaction is subjective' and that thus, strictly, there can be no 'right' or 'wrong' interpretation, we all too often seem to believe that so-and-so is 'an academic' and 'a scholar' and thus 'a professional' in these matters, and, ergo, her or his opinion must surely 'carry a little more weight'. From there it becomes all too easy to slip into regarding the opinions of the 'professionals' as 'objective' and definitive and thus preferable. Earlier [3] I examined the contrast between 'the objective' and the 'subjective' and how – to Virginia Woolf's bafflement – 'lay people' might feel inclined that it is 'wisest' to bow to the 'better, more informed' judgment of 'the professionals'. But the point is worth repeating: evaluation – at least in artistic matters – is always subjective. Such judgments, whoever makes them, are as much a matter of opinion – and often fashion – as whether United are a better side than City [4] Carver obliquely acknowledged the role of literary fashion in his New York Times review when he noted that as Hemingway's reputation shrank, it was

> *not entirely coincidental, either, that soon after his death a*
> *particular kind of writing began to appear in [the US], writing that*

---

1   Given how cavalier Hemingway was with punctuation in his other writing – for example, where judicious punctuation would have made many a sentence rather more comprehensible – it is a little presumptuous for Didion to claim significance in his use of commas in this short passage. It might well have been as haphazard as it was elsewhere.

2   The tone of what Didion writes does inform us that she was very much 'a believer' for whom Hemingway and his work were unimpeachable.

3   See above p.59ff

4   Or the Yankees better than the Mets (though I confess I had to look that up).

> *stressed the irrational and fabulous, the anti-realist against the realist tradition. In this context it might be worthwhile to remind ourselves what Hemingway believed good writing should do. He felt fiction must be based on actual experience.*

Carver makes a fair point when highlighting what he regards as a sequence of cause and effect, although his underlying assumption seems to be that the new 'anti-realist' kind of writing was somehow inferior to what Hemingway was doing in his fiction: if that is what he did believe, it is simply yet another subjective value judgment. Arguably, Hemingway had a distressingly narrow – even simplistic – notion of fiction and its 'purpose', and, ever 'the expert', grandly condemned contemporary writers who did not observe his dicta on what was 'good writing' and how they should be writing. [1]

. . .

What might be described as Hemingway's 'canonisation' (or his 'sanctification' or even his 'deification' – they all amount to the same thing) was a gradual process which certainly did not proceed smoothly. When we trace Hemingway's rise from the ambitious and unknown young writer of the early 1920s to 'Papa', the grand old man of literature honoured with the Nobel Prize for Literature in 1954 and apparently revered by all, we should note that although his public status grew from the 1930s on, his standing in literary circles slowly declined. In 1954 even Hemingway himself ruefully acknowledged that the Nobel Prize for Literature he had been awarded tacitly marked a writer's past achievements and to make sure an ageing writer was honoured before he or she died. It irritated him; and by 1954 – when Didion was just 20 – and despite the Nobel Prize and the remarkable sales success of The Old Man And The Sea, [2] Hemingway's name certainly no longer had the same cachet among the critics as it had in the very early years of his writing career in the late 1920s. Yet by then the critics he so despised no longer mattered: by 1954 academic interest in Hemingway and his work was growing remarkably, sparked ten years earlier by Malcolm Cowley in his introduction to The Portable Hemingway. Thus by the mid-1950s there were, broadly, three constituencies shaping the future 'Hemingway, the [or one of the] greatest American writers of the 20th century' [iv]: the fickle literary critics, the public – many of whom, ironically, might

---

1   Should someone find themselves thinking '*well, why shouldn't he? After all, he was one of our greatest writers*', I suspect that so far they have very much missed the point of this chapter.

2   That 30,000-word work, sometimes called 'a novel' but 'novella' would be a more suitable description, was not universally applauded, and some biographers commented that some reviewers praised it because they were relieved it was not as awful as Across The River And Into The Trees.

have read little of this work but knew him as 'a celebrity' – and, crucially, academia.

. . .

Cowley had known Hemingway in Paris in the early 1920s, although more as an acquaintance than as a friend (he spent only a year in France on a study grant, and he and his wife did not live in Montparnasse, but in a town on the outskirts of Paris). The two had kept loosely in touch, although Hemingway was rather dismissive of Cowley, especially when Cowley became editor of the left-wing The New Republic; and he mocked him in his story The Snows Of Kilimanjaro: when the dying writer is reminiscing about his younger days in Paris – for which read Hemingway reminiscing about his younger days in Paris – Cowley appears briefly as

> *that American poet with a pile of saucers in front of him and a stupid look on his potato face talking about the Dada movement.*

In the first versions of the story, Cowley was referred to by name; under pressure from Max Perkins Hemingway agreed to amend it to 'that American poet'. Cowley, who was and remained a staunch Hemingway champion, knew none of this and once innocently asked a mutual acquaintance whether it had been Ezra Pound who Hemingway had been mocking in the story. The acquaintance knew the truth, but assured him that, no, he didn't think so, and he did not choose to enlighten Cowley further. [1]

. . .

The evolution of when, how and why Hemingway came to be accepted by some as 'a genius' and, less grandiosely, as 'one of our greatest writers' by many took place over a number of years, and it is impossible to establish when the tipping point occurred. His own insistence, even as an unknown, to anyone of any consequence that he was 'a great writer' will have helped. The word 'genius' in connection with Hemingway was used quite early on as his career was taking off, in a New York Herald Tribune review of In Our Time in February 1926, although the paper was, in fact, simply praising his potential. It wrote that the collection of short stories did not perhaps have

> *enough energy to be a great book, but [that] Ernest Hemingway [had] promises of genius.*

---

1   Although I came across this claim in several biographies, sadly I don't know who the 'mutual acquaintance' was, so sticklers reading this are welcome to treat it as nothing more than hearsay.

Hemingway theology – Round and round

As with the publisher's blurb on the back of my paperback, this can be marked down as exuberant hyperbole of the kind newspapers often adopt, but it does indicate the extraordinary impression In Our Time and its markedly different style and content made when the collection was published. Thirty-seven years later, the biographer and critic Maxwell Geismar wrote in the New York Times that

> *A re-reading of his first collection of stories, In Our Time, . . . makes it easy to understand the impact upon the post-World War I period of a new style and a singular vision of contemporary experience.*

Then, before the decade was over, came The Sun Also Rises, Men Without Women and A Farewell To Arms, and all seemed to confirm to the literary world that among its contemporary writers Hemingway was special. Kenneth S. Lynn notes

> *Superlatively favourable reviews in American channels by Malcolm Cowley, Clifton Fadiman, Henry Seidel and T.S. Matthews among many others plus equally enthusiastic comments in England by Arnold Bennett, J.B. Priestley and the anonymous reviewers for the Times Literary Supplement helped to create a demand for [A Farewell To Arms] and to spread the author's fame more widely than ever before. Indeed, in New York a profile by Dorothy Parker on November 30, 1929, may be said to have marked the point at which Hemingway passed beyond mere fame into living legend.*

In hindsight it was at this point – in late 1929 when Hemingway had just turned 30 and it was not yet five years since he first came to notice – that among his peers, the critics and intellectuals, Hemingway was at the zenith of his career. Then, with each new book published, the critics gradually began to lose faith and the professional decline started. [v] The success that marked For Whom The Bells Tolls eleven years later and The Old Man And The Sea, 24 years on was wholly untypical; by the mid-1940s Hemingway's reputation was essentially based on public adoration not literary admiration, yet it was sufficient to help set in train his canonisation, though the process did not begin for another 15-odd years; and had it not been for those two successful and best-selling works [vi] and had posterity only the work of the 1930s with which to evaluate Hemingway's literary standing, he might arguably have become a footnote as just another writer who 'did not live up to his promise'.

Winner Take Nothing in 1933 was not as highly regarded as his two earlier short story collections. More damaging to his literary standing had been the publication a year earlier of Death In The Afternoon, his rambling, comprehensive, exhaustive and – rather too many critics thought – badly-written guide to bullfighting and 'good writing'. That the book was nominally treated as 'important' was because it was 'by Ernest Hemingway', somewhat foreshadowing the logic which later underpinned what I describe as 'the theology of Ernest Hemingway'. In 1932 when it was published, he was the well-known best-selling author of two novels and two collections of short stories and still commanded respect. Yet the decade-long slide from grace was beginning and he was then far from unimpeachable: his path towards literary divinity was still to be long and stony. In 1934, he published Green Hills Of Africa in which he again pontificated on 'good writing', and reviewing the book in The New Republic, Edmund Wilson wrote that Hemingway had delivered

> *a self-confident lecture on the high possibilities of prose writing, with the implication that he himself, Hemingway, has realized or hopes to realize these possibilities; and then writes what are certainly, from the point of view of prose, the very worst pages of his life. There is one passage which is hardly even intelligible – the most serious possible fault for a writer who is always insisting on the supreme importance of lucidity.*

Wilson added

> *[Hemingway] inveighs with much scorn against the literary life and against the professional literary man of the cities; and then manages to give the impression that he himself is a professional literary man of the most touchy and self-conscious kind.* [1]

It got worse: as though to add insult to injury, in 1937 came To Have And Have Not which Wilfrid Mellers – though it was in his review of For Whom The Bell Tolls in the literary quarterly Scrutiny a few years later – described as

> *such a wickedly bad book that one began to despair of Mr Hemingway's reputation. It was chaotic and it was insincere*

At this point – when Hemingway's literary career was still just over ten years old – none of these and other critics would have agreed that he was – or even ever likely to

---

1   Revisiting the book four years later, again in The New Republic, Wilson was even less charitable, declaring that Hemingway '*has produced what must be one of the only books ever written which makes Africa and it's animals seem dull. Almost the only thing we learned about the animals is that Hemingway wants to kill them. And as for the natives . . . the principal impression we get of them is that they were simple an inferior people who enormously admired Hemingway*'.

be acclaimed as – 'one of the greatest writers of the 20th century' and a 'master stylist'. What on Earth, they might have asked anyone suggesting that would happen, makes you think that? In fact, in professional terms, except for his journalistic work for Esquire and in other publications, a decade after Hemingway had burst onto the literary scene his future looked bleak.

. . .

Yet it all turned around, and that turnaround is part of 'the enigma' that is Ernest Hemingway and the global standing he acquired. What was going on? The public fame certainly counterbalanced the increasing critical lack of enthusiasm, and, according to John Raeburn, much of the growth in that public standing was down to Hemingway himself. Hemingway was more than adept at self-promotion, says Raeburn, and he took a subtle but active part in raising his profile, a practice that had begun even when he was unpublished and an unknown working as Ford Madox Ford's deputy on the *transatlantic review* [sic]. The articles he wrote for that journal, says Raeburn, were

> *trivial in terms of [his] literary career, but they are significant in terms of his career as public writer. They revealed that his public personality was incipient at the outset of his professional life, and that he was willing to use it for self-aggrandisement. They were a preview of the self-advertisements that would spread his fame in the next decade beyond the limited audience provided by an intellectual elite; and they foreshadowed that in his non-fiction his great subject was to be himself.*

The self-promotion was also the essence of the 'Letters' Hemingway was hired to write for the new and popular lifestyle magazine Esquire. It was launched in 1933 as an upmarket lifestyle guide for men, and Arnold Gingrich, a founder and its editor, was keen to sign up Hemingway not because of his supposed literary standing but precisely because of his growing celebrity and public profile, and because he believed hiring Hemingway would attract other 'names'. Hemingway knew very well how much that was worth to Gingrich and insisted on being well paid: he demanded and received twice as much for each Letter than any other contributor could command for their work, and his fee rose by the year. Furthermore, Hemingway was free to write on whatever subject he chose, though, as Raeburn observes,

> *for the rest of his career [Hemingway] advertised his public*

personality in his considerable body of non-fiction, for whatever his nominal subject, he real subject was himself.

His profile rose even higher when from mid-1937 he visited Spain four times, both to help with filming a documentary about the country's civil war [1] and as a war correspondent, hired by the North American Newspaper Alliance. [2] In keeping with his by now public prominence, his departure for Spain was 'news' and duly reported in the papers. His celebrity was already such that in November 1937 the New York Times informed its readers that 'Hemingway Writes Play In Shell-Rocked Madrid'. [vii] At the end of May 1938 and realising that the Spanish Loyalists' cause was lost, he returned to the US, and this was also 'news'. Interviewed by the New York Times, he informed its readers that he was a little jaded with active reporting on the war front and wanted to write some short stories and a novel, though, he added, he might return to Spain 'if things get warm over there'. That novel became For Whom The Bell Tolls, and one might cite its publication in 1940 as the point when Hemingway crossed a threshold and began his literary redemption, and was assigned the role he so willingly assumed as 'one of America's greatest writers'.

The new novel's reception and sales were spectacular, and it substantially revived Hemingway's career among the critics. Almost all of them praised the novel as a return to form, although even then one or two remarked that they were unconvinced by the romance between Robert Jordan and Maria which struck them as artificial and superfluous. One notable dissident from the overall critical acclaim was the Spanish writer and journalist Arturo Barea, and he was especially scathing. Though his view of the novel is not without its own critics, many reading or re-reading the novel 80 years on might agree with his scepticism about how 'great' the novel was. Barea had lived alongside Hemingway and Martha Gellhorn at the Hotel Florida before the city was evacuated, and he and the writer were well-acquainted, not least because Barea was running the Loyalist government censor's office in Madrid which had to pass all correspondent's copy before it could be dispatched (by the same office). Reviewing For Whom The Bell Tolls for Horizon in May, 1941, Barea praised parts of it, but declared that

as a novel about Spaniards and their war it is unreal and, in the

---

1   It became The Spanish Earth for which he also wrote and spoke the commentary after an attempt by Orson Welles was thought too 'theatrical'.

2   Ironically, while in Spain Hemingway was rebuked by the North American Newspaper Alliance who asked him to write more about the war and what was happening and less about himself and his experiences.

> *last analysis, deeply untruthful, though practically all the critics claim the contrary, whatever their objections to other aspects of the book.*

This will not be happy reading for Hemingway champions who like to think Hemingway as something of an expert on Spain.[1] Barea added that a foreign reader [of the novel] would

> *come to understand some aspects of Spanish character and life, but [would] misunderstand more, and more important ones at that.*

Barea was also unimpressed by Hemingway's account of the three-day love affair between Jordan and Maria and dismissed it, remarking that a

> *Spanish girl of the rural middle class is steeped in a tradition in which influences from the Moorish harem and the Catholic convent mix [and] could not ask a stranger, a foreigner, to let her come into his bed the very first night after they had met . . .*

He declared that Hemingway's depiction of the Jordan and Maria's short liaison was 'pure romancing', a verdict that was echoed 20 years later by Maxwell Geismar in the New York Times who noted that For Whom The Bell Tolls

> *sometimes called Hemingway's best novel . . . is a curious mixture of good and bad, of marvellous scenes and chapters which are balanced off by improbable or sentimental or melodramatic passages of adolescent fantasy development.*

Yet Barea's view was a distinct outlier and did not reflect the mainstream critical opinion, and the remarkable success of For Whom The Bell Tolls – bolstered by the film of the novel starring Gary Cooper and Ingrid Bergman released three years later – meant Hemingway need no longer care about the critics and their opinions: the public loved it, and its sales were astonishing. According to biographer Jeffrey Meyers, For Whom The Bell Tolls sold half-a-million copies in the first six months, and its runaway

---

1 See p.248ff for an account suggesting Hemingway had a rather narrower knowledge of the country and its people than he imagined and that he was certainly no expert.

success was boosted when it was chosen as a Book of the Month. [1] More to the point his literary career was back on track and his status with the public as 'one of America's greatest writers' was well on its way to being assured. One irony of the novel's success was that whereas Hemingway once saw himself as primarily an artist who wrote 'serious literature', For Whom The Bell Tolls placed him firmly in the ranks of the popular, middle-brow novelists, a development underlined by the novel's – lucrative – Book of the Month status. Because many readers were – and are – inclined to equate public fame with ability, they were more than ready to accept Hemingway's purported status as a 'great writer'. His elevation had not yet had an official seal of approval, but that was now a matter of time as, gradually, academia also became involved. [2]

. . .

From 1940 until his suicide 21 years later in July 1961, Hemingway published just two more works of original fiction – the best-selling, but critically panned, Across The River And Into The Trees and best-selling and generally critically praised The Old Man And The Sea – and the contrasting reception of both highlighted in their own ways the ever-widening divide between his literary reputation and his public standing. As far as the public were concerned, if Ernest Hemingway was not 'one of the country's greatest living writers' – well, who was? Then came the academics, the third constituency determining Hemingway's unimpeachable status as a 'great writer'. Their entry into the debate – though frankly there was no debate as the extraordinary sales of all three novels [3] trumped the journeyman opinions of literary hacks – cleared the way for Hemingway's literary divinity to be confirmed.

---

1   This was another irony: as an unknown 'promising writer' of the 1920s, Hemingway had proudly purported to care nothing for material success and claimed to despise writers whose work succeeded because it was chosen by the Book of the Month club. By 1940 he had overcome his distaste, and his change of heart ensured he was a wealthy man for the rest of his life.

2   The Pulitzer Prize for Fiction had eluded him in 1940, but even so it indicated that the long and stony path to divinity was becoming far less irksome.

3   The Old Man And The Sea is more of a novella, but it also sold extraordinarily well, as did Across The River And Into The Trees which the critics treated as a poor joke in bad taste.

Hemingway theology – The tyranny of 'meaning'

Literature is that neuter ... the trap where all identity is lost, beginning with the very identity of the body that writes.

Roland Barthes, The Death Of The Author.

As to Hemingway, I read him for the first time in the early 'forties, something about bells, balls and bulls, and loathed it.

Vladimir Nabokov.

How is [the critic] to find out what the poet tried to do? If the poet succeeded in doing it, then the poem itself shows what he was trying to do. The simplest explanation is usually the most likely one.

W.K. Wimsatt and Monroe Beardsley, The Intentional Fallacy.

IN THE past and often still today literary theory has, to a greater or lesser extent, been influenced by, in turn, the tenets of formalism, new criticism, phenomenology, structuralism, post-structuralism and deconstruction. Literary works have also been examined through the prisms of psychoanalysis, feminism, gender and queer theory, new historicism, Marxism, post-colonial theory and cultural materialism – and the list is not exclusive. Yet however much each doctrine was championed when it came into fashion, none is 'right' or 'wrong' in its conclusions: broadly, each simply provides us with a different, sometimes fresh and often unusual, perspective on what we are examining. Some specifically choose to view a work and its 'meaning' from the reader's point of view, and notably some even argued that once a work had come into existence, the role of the author was no longer of consequence and that the role and reactions of the reader were central. [1] Yet whatever the literary practice to which an academic, post-grad student and any of the other assorted scholars subscribe when they interpret and analyse Hemingway's fiction and pronounce on 'underlying meanings', it does not seem to have been formalism.

Formalism would, for example, give short shrift to the, now conventional and accepted, doctrine that The Sun Also Rises portrayed a 'lost generation' of young people in despair. Formalism stresses the primacy of 'what is in the text' and as Frank L. Ryan (quoted above) unhelpfully pointed out, that interpretation was not obvious to anyone when the novel was published. As for the now orthodox reading of Big Two-Hearted River, the longer-than-usual two-part story which concluded Hemingway's first volume of short stories (and which he had at first intended to conclude with his thoughts on 'writing'), Kenneth S. Lynn, equally unhelpfully for those who revere Hemingway, noted in his biography of the writer that

> *the war-wound interpretation of the story was established not by textual evidence, but by what the critics knew about the author's life – or rather what they thought they knew about his life. After he was dead, they eagerly seized on his posthumously published comment in A Moveable Feast that Big Two-Hearted River was about 'coming back from the war', but there was no mention of the war in it as clinching proof that they were right. They would have been better advised to wonder if a master manipulator was not making fools of them from beyond the grave, as he so often had in life.*

Unabashed, many academics – and thus their students – still substantiate the claim that the story did indeed depict a young, shell-shocked vet returning from war. They might, for example do so by citing 'the town of Seney being destroyed by fire', the burnt landscape and Hemingway's allusion to 'the sinister' and the 'swamp'. Yet these claims are decidedly post-hoc and were made once the now orthodox 'meaning' of the story had been established. The town of Seney and its surrounding countryside had certainly been damaged by a wildfire, but wildfires were – and still are – a regular occurrence

---

1 Although a number of Hemingway's friends insist that beneath the braggadocio, he was essentially an intellectual man, equally on record is his blunt dismissals of talk on 'art' as airy-fairy nonsense, so one wonders how Hemingway, who was usually in some way central in most of his work, might have reacted to that suggestion.

in upper Michigan (and there have been two such fires in 2023 alone); any symbolic correlation with horrors of 'the Great War' (as it was then known) is not unlikely but is, at best, wishful and certainly obscure. It is, of course, quite possible that Hemingway did intend the burned devastation of one such wildfire to symbolise the devastation of the 'Great War'. The problem is that such an interpretation is not presented in the story, although true believers might here evoke Hemingway's 'iceberg theory' and claim his 'true writing' allowed him to 'omit' reference to WWI but the war is – somehow – present in the story. They might – and do – cite the concentration of detail: that Nick walking to the river, preparing a night shelter, then the fishing itself describe a 'shell-shocked' young man finding therapeutic equanimity in these simple and mundane activities. But does he? Do they? Who knows? As I repeatedly say, you pays your money and you makes your choice, though that suggestion is not very attractive to a mindset which craves the certainty of 'knowing' what a story 'means'. Until A Moveable Feast was published posthumously in 1964, 40 years after Hemingway's short story appeared, no one 'understood' that it was 'essentially to be an account of a young man recovering from his bad experiences in World War I'. The story was praised for its detailed and lyrical descriptions of nature – such descriptions were one of Hemingway's strengths as a writer – but the, now orthodox, interpretation wasn't adopted until Hemingway finally informed the world 'what the story was about'. Hemingway champions might again counter that he was a staunch advocate of 'less is more'[1] and that because he was writing 'truly', the reader should – they might insist would – have had 'a feeling of those things as strongly as though [he] had stated them'. But for one Kenneth S. Lynn didn't, nor did I and, oddly, neither did any number of other readers until – almost 40 years later – Hemingway 'revealed' the story's meaning. Then, of course, the champions chorused: '*Well yes, it's obvious! How did we miss it! Marvellous piece of writing, marvellous!*' But miss it they did. Would it be churlish to suggest that a better, more skilful, more artistically capable writer, perhaps 'one of the greatest writers of the 20th century', should have been able to convey successfully what he intended to convey so that a reasonably intelligent and alert reader, one with

sympathy and a few degrees of heightened emotional awareness [2]

did not have to wait until the story's meaning was finally 'revealed'? It all gets uncom-

---

1   Hemingway certainly did not adhere to a 'less is more' philosophy in Death In The Afternoon and Green Hills Of Africa, however, not by a country mile, but the champions might choose to point out that those works were non-fiction.

2   Carlos Baker's stipulation when intending to interpret Hemingway's work. See p.196ff.

fortably close to a situation where we pitiful sinners were unable to comprehend Hemingway's mysteries until in his love and wisdom and with his grace he finally granted us the ability to do so (with the high priests of academia acting as midwives).

. . .

As argued previously, there are no definitive interpretations of any of Hemingway's works of fiction because quite simply there cannot be: just how is one to gauge which interpretation is 'right' and which is 'wrong' (or, better, misguided)? Furthermore, a 'formalistic', 'new critical' or any other approach to interpreting and analysing works of literature is neither the 'correct' nor 'incorrect' approach to take: they are all just one of the many methodologies available for undertaking that task, and each might, at best, be expected to give the reader a new perspective. Yet insisting that a text – whether of prose or poetry – should be sovereign and should primarily be interpreted wholly in itself is an attractive analytical method, if only because it limits the scope for woolly speculation (of which there has been a great deal when it came to interpreting Hemingway's work). In their essay The Intentional Fallacy which appeared in the Sewanee Review in 1946, W.K. Wimsatt and Monroe Beardsley ask

> *How is [the critic] to find out what the poet tried to do? If the poet succeeded in doing it, then the poem itself shows what he was trying to do. And if the poet did not succeed, then the poem is not adequate evidence and the critic must go outside the poem for evidence of intention that did not become effective in the poem.*

Wimsatt and Beardsley were, admittedly, discussing poetry, and their take on literary analysis will for many now be old hat (and possibly regarded by more modern practitioners as simplistic and academically infra dig); but whether dated or not, there is no reason to assume that the principle which drives their approach is now invalid and cannot also be applied to prose fiction, here specifically to Hemingway's fiction. So: how 'great' is a writer who is obliged to 'explain' his work? If it is all there in the text – and a text can contain a great deal of information, much of it possibly conveyed obliquely which, we are assured by Hemingway and his champions, was his gift – it is fair to assume that, sooner or later, comprehension will come. At this point there might already be a chorus of objections; yet such protests would do little but echo the circular – the theological – argument which is intended to 'prove' Hemingway's celebrated literary stature: that 'because Hemingway is a great writer, it is up to us to understand what he is saying' and 'these stories and their themes demonstrate just what a great writer Hemingway was'. To which one might again quote Evelyn Waugh's Mr Salter: 'Up to a point, Lord Copper'.

. . .

For some the attraction of restricting oneself to the text of a story, novel or poem when analysing and interpreting is the rigour it imposes. If a publisher is sent a manuscript to be considered for publication and is told and knows nothing about the author or the work, she or he can do little else but evaluate it solely on what is presented within its two covers. [1] It might certainly be illuminating – later, perhaps – to acquire additional information about a writer and, say, the circumstances of a work's genesis; but in strikes me as wisest, in the first instance, to evaluate a work in and of itself.

In his 1967 essay The Death Of The Author, the French literary theorist Roland Barthes might be thought – by implication – to be reinforcing the suggestion by Wimsatt and Beardsley that a piece of literature must stand or fall on its own terms. He certainly insisted that each work is sovereign and that the author's ownership of it ceases as soon as its composition is complete. He suggests

> *literature is that neuter . . . the trap where all identity is lost,*
> *beginning with the very identity of the body that writes.*

From this one might proceed to the suggestion that the biography and life experiences of 'the author' – and what she or he declares is the 'meaning' of a story, novel or poem – are neither here nor there when attempting to 'understand' a story, novel or poem.

Again, neither Wimsatt and Beardsley nor Barthes are 'right' or 'wrong' in this matter. How one wants to interpret a work of literature is optional, and scholars are free to do as they please: over the past five or six decades, works of literature have been viewed through many lenses; but it is still legitimate to ask why, when they were first published, no one realised The Sun Also Rises was about a 'lost generation in despair' and that Big Two-Hearted River was about a young man returning home broken by war? Were the critics and readers and, latterly, the academics, scholars and post-grad students not reading the works attentively enough? And what are we to make of Kenneth Lynn's dig at Hemingway that the writer eventually offering us his 'explanation' of what was 'really' taking place in Big Two-Hearted River was simply another instance of a 'master

---

1   This is, of course, a wholly theoretical situation. It is unlikely a manuscript will turn up at a publisher's without a covering letter, either from the hopeful writer or from the writer's agent. But I hope the point stands.

manipulator' at work? With Lynn's claim in mind, it is equally legitimate to inquire why a man almost addicted to self-promotion and who, if the mood took him, would lie about and fabricate his past sooner than breathe, would – exceptionally – decide to play with a straight bat in matters of his work and 'literature'?

Although Hemingway had been something of a romantic fantasist from an early age, the fabulous inventions of his last 20-odd years were of a different order: pertinently, it was at this point in his life that he supplied his own interpretations for some of his stories, interpretations which had hitherto eluded others. When considering those interpretations, we are, of course, obliged to concede that they might well be 'true'; but we should also be more than mindful of trying to balance 'possibility' against 'probability'. The faithful might protest that whatever else he was, Hemingway was a conscientious artist of integrity; but if they do so plead, they would wilfully be ignoring that the claim is solely based on what Hemingway informed us about himself, his conscientiousness and his integrity. They would also thus re-enter the circular logic of Hemingway's literary divinity: their argument might run 'Hemingway was a conscientious artist and a conscientious artist wouldn't lie' and 'because Hemingway wouldn't lie, we must believe him when he tells us that he was a conscientious artist'. They might then insist that when he chose to elucidate aspects of his work – such as in revealing the 'meaning' of Big, Two-Hearted River – we must take him at his word because 'as a conscientious artist he wouldn't lie'.

...

By the last decade of his life, Hemingway's status as 'a great writer' came to rest on the two pillars: the widespread public esteem – unprecedented for a 'serious writer' – and the attention his work began to get from scholars and academia. Of the two, the academic attention was by far the most crucial.

Despite being wary of the approaches from Carlos Baker, Philip Young, John Atkins and Charles Fenton, Hemingway was also flattered. By the time he was awarded his Nobel Prize, Malcolm Cowley's insistence that there were hidden depths to Hemingway's work had become very much the orthodoxy and for many 'a fact' –and surely, those many might add, being awarded the Nobel Prize was 'proof' that his work was exceptional. Soon, in the wake of those early academic studies, ever more learned papers, PhD and Masters' dissertations and contributions to literary journals about aspects of Hemingway's were published. To this day, for example, 60 years after Hemingway's death, about a dozen articles of one kind or another, research papers on Hemingway's work and life, and reviews of books about the writer appear in each issue of the twice-yearly Hemingway

Review. Still ongoing is work on a projected seventeen-volume collection of Hemingway's letters from Cambridge University Press, of which so far only five volumes have been published. More recently, the well-known filmmakers Ken Burns and Lynn Novick released a three-part, six-hour documentary on Hemingway's life. The central, more or less irrefutable, belief driving all this work was and is that 'Hemingway was one of the greatest writers of the 20th century'. The tone of much of the work underway leads one to suspect that – this is only a slight exaggeration – Ernest Hemingway is tacitly and unwittingly regarded as unimpeachable; so as with 'God' and his 'mysteries', if some of his work is puzzling or apparently flawed, we must accept that it *most certainly is not* and that we must redouble our efforts to understand what it was the 'great writer' intended.

This stubborn act of faith has led to some curious claims when Hemingway's work is interpreted and some odd contortions by scholars when they attempt to justify various apparent anomalies, oddities and inconsistencies in his work. A very good example of the tendency for academics to tie themselves in knots rather than consider that Hemingway was not always literary perfection made flesh is what has been called the 'insoluble problem' in his short story A Clean, Well-Lighted Place. Tracing the history of commentary on it and 'solutions' offered to solve 'the problem' is certainly informative.

...

A Clean, Well-Lighted Place first appeared in Scribner's Magazine in March 1933 and was included in Hemingway's third volume of original short stories which appeared later that year. It concerns two waiters in a cafe ready to shut up for the night and their only customer, an old man who is lingering, despite the late hour, presumably because he is lonely and doesn't want to go home. The two waiters discuss the old man: one waiter, younger, is impatient for him to leave so he can join his wife in bed; the other, older, is more sympathetic, because, as the reader comes to understand, he shares the old man's loneliness. We discover that a week earlier the lonely old man had tried to hang himself, but was saved from death by his niece. The story's problem – in view of the differing views on the matter and how various commentators deal with it I'm obliged to write its 'apparent' problem – stems from what appear to be inconsistencies in what the two waiters say in dialogue.

Although initially Hemingway does not identify either waiter, they are soon referred to as 'the young waiter' and 'the old waiter'; and once we know which man is which, we can track back to what each is saying about the old man. This is where the alleged inconsistency occurs: from what one waiter says, he 'knows' a detail about the old man's suicide attempt and comments on what he 'knows'. Yet if the to and fro of conversation as detailed by Hemingway is conventional, this waiter cannot have 'known' what he apparently 'knows'. It should have been the other waiter who 'knew' the relevant detail because of what he says at other points in their exchange.

This inconsistency apparently went unnoticed for 26 years until the American literary critic and poet Judson Jerome did notice and wrote to Hemingway in 1956 pointing it out; Hemingway responded that he had re-read the story and, he claimed, it made sense to him.

Three years later, two English literature professors – independently – each published a paper in the February 1959 edition of College English, the journal of the American National Council of English Teachers, discussing the inconsistency. Crucially, the two academics – F.P. Kroeger, who described it as an 'insoluble problem' (by which name it is now generally known), and William E. Colburn, did not agree on the nature of the inconsistency. Kroeger attributes the error to 'Hemingway, or someone [being] careless'. Over the following few years, more academics joined in the debate, and eventually Hemingway's publishers, Scribner's, acknowledged that something was amiss and decided to emend the text for a new version of the story. This appeared in 1965, and that was when the trouble started.

Here again Occam's Razor might have proved useful if all those academics had resorted to applying it: the problem occurred because, as Kroeger suggested, 'Hemingway or someone' had been careless. It could have been a typist transcribing Hemingway's manuscript or a printer setting the story in type. In fact, evidence based on the original manuscript suggests Hemingway himself had been at fault: it would seem he hadn't kept track of details in his story and hadn't noticed the discrepancy when it crept in. That explanation does, though, make puzzling his, somewhat ambiguous, response to Jerome that he had re-read the story and it made sense to him. Yet the discrepancy was certainly present. If Hemingway simply missed it, one unavoidable conclusion is that despite his persistent claims throughout his life that he re-wrote and revised his stories many times over, he wasn't always as punctilious as he liked the world to believe. Furthermore, examination of the manuscript indicates to one commentator that A Clean, Well-Lighted Place was written in one sitting – at under 1,500 words it is not long – and revised, probably just a day later, just once.

After Kroeger and Colburn published their thoughts in College English, many other academics decided to add their two ha'porth worth, especially in view of Scribner's controversial 'emendation' in 1965: a few commentators did agree that Hemingway was probably at fault; but many – tacitly resorting to the same theistic logic which seems to underpin the orthodox attitude to the writer – reasoned along the lines that 'as one of the greatest writers of the 20th century, Hemingway will have known what he was doing, so this was not an error!' They then contorted themselves severely to substantiate their article of faith.

. . .

Arguably one of the most double-edged aspects to literary commentary (or commentary of any kind, for that matter) is 'plausibility'. If an explanation or a piece of analysis is thought 'plausible', it seems oddly, quietly and unobtrusively, to gain a spurious validity; and in the minds of some that very plausibility might stealthily grant it the status of 'being true'. In fact, that an analysis or theory is 'plausible' means nothing more and nothing less than that it is 'plausible' – 'it could be the case but we don't as yet know'; and it would again be useful to remind ourselves of the distinction between 'possibility' and 'probability' – what 'might be possible' and what 'is more probable'?

As for possibility, Professor Otto Reinert argued that Kroeger's 'insoluble problem' was not a problem at all; that although the convention when writing dialogue was usually to start a new indented line for each fictional speaker, it was after all only a 'convention' and need not necessarily be observed. Reinert suggested that Hemingway had, in fact, in this instance decided to break the convention because he wanted to indicate a 'reflective pause' by one of the waiters when speaking. That is certainly 'plausible'; but how 'probable' is it? [i]

Another attempt to account for the discrepancy in A Clean, Well-Lighted Place is by of Joseph F. Gabriel in the Logic of Confusion, which appeared in College English two years after Kroeger and Colburn published. Advocates of Gabriel's explanation might certainly claim it is 'plausible', but quite how probable is another matter. Gabriel argued that the apparent 'problem' was intentional: it was certainly not carelessness by a typist, a typesetter or even Hemingway that led to the 'error'; and nor was it a break with the conventions of writing dialogue as Reinert suggested. In fact, says Gabriel, there was no 'error' at all: Hemingway wanted the dialogue to confuse the reader in order to make an existential point, one which was, moreover, the essence of his short story. The reader's confusion, Gabriel claimed, reflected the confusion and chaos of life which had driven an old man to attempt suicide and which one of the waiters also experienced. This is how Gabriel puts it:

> *The dialogue is so constructed that the reader, in his attempt to impose order upon the chaos of inconsistency and ambiguity, is stripped of his dependence on the objective. In so far as the dialogue*

> *fails to conform to the norms of logic, the reader himself is, like the older waiter, plunged into the existential predicament and made to confront the absurd.*

Gabriel notes that when one waiter – at this point not yet identified – asked the other what had led the old man to try to hang himself, the reply is

> *'He was in despair.'*
> *'What about?' the first asks.*
> *'Nothing,' says the second.*
> *'How do you know it was about nothing?' asks the first.*
> *'He has plenty of money,' says the second.*

Gabriel suggests that in this exchange Hemingway uses the word 'nothing' ambiguously: the one waiter understands it to mean the old man tried to hang himself *'for no reason'*, but the other – who Gabriel then identifies as the 'older waiter' – takes 'nothing' to signify *'the meaningless of existence'*: the old man had tried to kill himself because for him life no longer had a purpose. Later in the story that same, older, waiter is shown to be similarly lonely and despondent – he parodies the Lord's Prayer, repeating the Spanish for 'nothing' (*'nada'*) – and 'nothing' in the sense of 'the meaningless of existence' is what the story is about.

What, you might ask, does this have to do with the 'anomaly' in the story, Kroeger's 'insoluble problem'? Well, Gabriel writes, there *isn't* one, and the story was, in fact, 'artfully contrived'. The alleged 'inconsistency' in the dialogue was *intended* by Hemingway and thus there is no 'inconsistency'. He writes

> *Thus, in addition to the two major meanings already assigned to the word nada in the story, there is a third: nothingness is synonymous with man's radical subjectivity, with his total freedom. Indeed, man may be defined as the being who is forced to announce the idea of finding a guarantee for his existence outside himself. It is this third meaning of nothingness which partially escapes the older waiter. He is, after all, no philosopher. And he does not fully understand what he feels. In the end he wonders whether it isn't only insomnia from which he suffers. Nevertheless, despite the limitations in the older waiter's understanding of his predicament, Hemingway manages with consummate skill to incorporate this third meaning of nothing into the texture of the story.*

Gabriel argues that

> *In his attempt to make sense out of the story, the reader, too, is forced to assume contingency, is forced to deal with values and meanings which cannot be given objective justification, and is even brought finally to a recognition of his own radical subjectivity.*

Gabriel's explanation is certainly 'plausible', but as suggested above, that isn't saying a great deal; and one wonders what William of Occam would have made of his analysis. William might agree that Hemingway's story is about loneliness and, with increasing age, a growing despair that the loneliness will never end; but he might also agree that the story is slight one, and the profundity attributed to it – not just by Gabriel, but by many other commentators – over-eggs the pudding to an alarming extent. [1]

Unfortunately for Gabriel and Reinert, in January 1979 Warren Bennett published his paper, The Manuscript And The Dialogue Of A Clean, Well-Lighted Place, in American Literature and takes issue with their and others' hi-falutin' claims. His explanation is equally 'plausible' and, bearing in mind the crucial and often necessary distinction between 'possibility' and 'probability', arguably more 'probable' than some. Since 1972, Mary Welsh, Hemingway's widow had been donating her husband's manuscripts to the John F. Kennedy Library in Boston, and among these was the original handwritten manuscript of A Clean, Well-Lighted Place. Bennett examined it. The manuscript was written in pencil and, Bennett deduced, Hemingway made slight revisions as he was writing the story, further small revisions a little later that same day, and then a few more a day or two later. Bennett justifies his suggestions by claiming that one can distinguish between the original body of the text and the subsequent slight revisions by the varying thickness of the pencil (or pencils) used at different times, the space between the lines on the manuscript, the size of Hemingway's handwriting and the number of lines on the 11-page manuscript.

Comparing this manuscript and its changes with the story as originally published, Bennett concluded that a typist or a typesetter was certainly responsible for one error, but that Hemingway was responsible for the main inconsistency. Further, Bennett sanctioned the emendation made to the published text by Scribner's in 1965 because it did resolve one of the problems; but then Bennett pulled his punches. Perhaps subconsciously acknowledging Hemingway's status, he lets the 'great writer' off the hook: although he tacitly acknowledged that in writing and revising A Clean, Well-Lighted

---

1 It would also be fair to suggest that even if Gabriel is 'right', Hemingway might have conveyed the 'meaning' of his story with a little more skill.

Place, Hemingway – who always stressed the immense care he took in his writing and how he weighed every word – had indeed been careless, he absolved him because the matter of the 'insoluble problem'

> *pictures Hemingway not as the slow perfectionist, hovering over every word and detail, but an artist 'fired up', and writing at considerable speed in producing what must be regarded, in spite of the flaw in the dialogue, as classic Hemingway: expressing much by showing little.*

With this nifty – and frankly not quite respectable – piece of footwork Bennett was able to insist there still was a God. Yet his explanation does beg a pertinent question: there's nothing wrong with being 'fired up' and 'writing at considerable speed' – but what was stopping Hemingway, the putative and self-declared perfectionist, then taking as much time as he needed and wanted to revise the piece and ensure it was exactly as he felt it should be? Why the rush? Was he writing to a deadline? Did he simply forget about the story until he dug it out to send to the publishers? Did he re-read it a few days or weeks or months after it was composed before delivering it to Scribner's? When he was alerted by Judson that something might be amiss with his story and gave his assurance that it made sense to him, had he even read it again? And if he had read it again – after Judson had, presumably, outlined what he thought was amiss – why did he dismiss Judson's concerns?

Bennett's conclusion would, of course, rule out Gabriel's conviction that Hemingway, in existentialist mode, was intentionally confusing the reader. Those who subscribe to Gabriel's thesis could well protest that as a consummate artist, Hemingway would certainly have revised the story with his usual painstaking care, and he would thus have noticed the 'inconsistency' in the dialogue. But then realising it might add to the story's artistic impact, he decided to allow the 'inconsistency' to remain to highlight the reader's own 'existential dilemma'. This is 'the solution' suggested by Ken Ryan in his paper The Contentious Emendation Of Hemingway's A Clean, Well-Lighted Place that appeared in the September 1998 edition of The Hemingway Review.

Ryan's findings would also be 'plausible' and would also help to elucidate Hemingway's response to Jerome that the story made sense to him. Yet after Bennett had allowed a little daylight to illuminate the whole 'debate', Ryan returned to square one: his view is underpinned solidly by the theological article of faith that 'Hemingway was a great writer who knew what he was doing [all the time] and he did not make mistakes'.

Equally 'plausible', of course, would be that Hemingway had written the story in one sitting, fired up in with artistic passion, revised it a little but missed the inconsistency, had not re-read as he had assured Jerome and simply brushed him off. Who knows? I doubt, though, that the our planet will stop spinning until we find out. Yet again and as all too often in such a debate, you pays your money and you makes your choice.

At the end of the day, of course, as with evangelical Christians, radical Islamists, life-long Communists, MAGA stalwarts and zealots of all stripes, there is no choice to be made: *they* are 'right' and *you* are 'wrong' – there the matter ends and dissenters be damned to Hell! So to this day more than 100 years after Hemingway was born and more than 60 since he blew off his head, the onus is still on us, the reader, to try even harder to 'understand' what Hemingway was telling us if it is not at first apparent: after all, we are reminded, he was 'a great writer'.

Caveat lector – Enter academia

It is on Hemingway as artist that Carlos Baker has concentrated, writing with fervent piety as if he must make up for all the injustices that have ever been done his subject . . . Mr Baker, almost as reverential toward Hemingway as [George Lyman] Kittredge was toward Shakespeare, also proves a rewarding commentator. His comments on the major works are often illuminating and his is particularly helpful in talking about some of the minor ones.

Granville Hicks, New York Times, October 12, 1952.

Academia is to knowledge what prostitution is to love.

Nassim Nicholas Taleb, author of The Black Swan, mathematical statistician and 'risk analyst'.

THIS collection of essays is subtitled 'How did a middling writer achieve such global literary fame', and although other related topics are considered, examining that question is its central purpose. Whether or not Hemingway was 'a great writer' or merely 'a middling writer' is, of course, a matter of opinion, and there are still more than enough cheerleaders for 'Papa' to ensure the sceptic rabble are rarely heard and can be ignored. What is indisputable, whether he was a 'great' or merely a 'middling' writer, is just how famous he became in the last 20 years of his life; so the question is: how did he become so famous when other writers remained relatively unknown?

In this, the third decade of the 21st century, those under 60 might well have heard of Hemingway, but will personally be less familiar with the phenomenon of his global fame; they must simply accept that he was extremely famous. His standing in some hypothetical Top Twenty of Famous People will have fallen over the years as the world and its media acquired new 'heroes' to celebrate; but he still stands out: he was not famous as a sportsman, a politician, a rock star, a TV or film star or royalty but as a writer, and that was distinctly unusual. Furthermore and pertinently, he was not seen as a 'popular novelist' whose work sold well, but who was regarded as distinctly infra dig by the literary world: Hemingway was – and by a great many still is – accepted as 'a serious writer' – his Nobel honouring was surely 'proof' that he was. His global fame was extraordinary, and although his novels and short stories are now out of fashion as set texts in school and college classes, there are to this day more than distinct echoes of that fame. [i]

Hemingway was, though, not unique: a contemporary and comparably 'globally famous writer' was William Somerset Maugham, although Maugham was born in 1874, 25 years before Hemingway, and outlived him by four years. They had one or two things in common: both were debilitated by declining mental health at the end of their lives – Maugham's increasingly odd and unpleasant behaviour in the years before he died is thought to have been caused by ever-worsening dementia, then – 60 years ago – a disease that was not very well understood; [1] both had wanted 'to be a writer' since they were young; both served with the Red Cross in World War I, although Maugham, who was a qualified doctor, served for far longer than Hemingway; but the two men were otherwise as unalike as chalk and cheese. Maugham did not pontificate on what was and was not 'good writing', and he did not preen himself and was inclined to downplay his, not inconsiderable, achievements. [ii] Such modesty played no part in Hemingway's character, and he considered himself to be 'a great writer' all his life, although several biographers have suggested that 'being Papa Hemingway' for the world to revere became an ever-greater strain and might well have helped to hasten the mental decline of his last 15 years. As biographer Jeffrey Meyers pointed out

> *In the last decades of his life, the Papa legend undermined the literary reputation and exposed the underlying fissure between the two Hemingways: the private artist and the public spectacle.*

One notable distinction between the two writers is that Maugham did not attract the widespread academic scrutiny of his work that Hemingway received. That scrutiny took off in the last decade of Hemingway's life and was the icing on the cake for a man who was not only supremely ambitious and competitive but who was, according to two

---

1   Medicine has advanced a little over the years: at the time a diagnosis of lung cancer was pretty much a death sentence, though contemporary medical advice to heavy smokers was to 'try to cut back on the cigarettes'.

psychologists who have written on the matter, essentially a narcissist. [1]

...

By 1950 when Hemingway published Across The River And Into The Trees the gulf between his public status and fame and his standing with 'the critics' had become very wide indeed. He had published nothing since the best-selling For Whom The Bell Tolls ten years earlier and much was riding on the new novel; but it was universally deemed to be a turkey – the critic Dwight Macdonald later described it as

> *an unconscious self-parody of almost unbelievable fatuity.*

Yet in the US it became that year's third best-selling novel, and for many such success will have substantiated and justified the public's reverence. Now, in addition, the increasing interest and attention academia began to show was tantamount to Hemingway's canonisation as 'a serious artist'. The critics? Those awful critics who were 'lice who crawled on literature' and who hated him? Once the academics were involved, who needed the critics? Certainly not 'Papa' Hemingway: the academics, the intellectual heavyweights – they were the real deal. Furthermore, now that the academics had sanctioned Hemingway's writing and elevated it to be worthy of their study and analysis (and continue to do so), you and your judgment risked being wholly dismissed if you did not sign up to the creed. The boot was on the other foot: it was now up to the doubters and sceptics to 'prove' Hemingway was not a great writer – the interest and attention of academia demonstrated that it was a given. An irony was, though, that Hemingway, who prided himself on his 'built-in bullshit detector', had long had – or possibly had feigned to have – a distaste for academia.

As a best-selling and apparently iconoclastic author when he first published in the 1920s, Hemingway was profiled in the more serious publications throughout the 1930s and 1940s. For example, his new 'socially engaged' attitude in To Have And Have Not – reluctantly adopted, it has to be said, after pressure from 'the left' at the height of the Great Depression – was scrutinised and contrasted with that of his peer John Dos Passos, then still avowedly left-wing. But however worthy the publications in which these profiles appeared, such journalistic scrutiny was not the same as being written about by the college men (and later women). In 1952, possibly rallying to Malcolm Cowley's clarion call [2] that Hemingway should be taken far more seriously 'as an artist',

---

1   See p.89ff.

2   Cowley wrote this in the preface to The Portable Hemingway, which he had edited and which appeared in 1944. It was one of a series of such anthologies published by Viking Press.

several American academics and a British writer, poet and playwright published books examining with Ernest Hemingway's work. They were by Carlos Baker, Philip Young, John Atkins and Charles A. Fenton. Baker, who was later nominated by Hemingway to be his official biographer (on the curious grounds, according to his fourth wife, Mary Welsh, that he and Baker had never met), published Ernest Hemingway: The Writer As Artist; John Atkins published The Art Of Ernest Hemingway; and Philip Young — though only eventually as for over a year Hemingway refused his publisher permission to quote from his work — came out with Ernest Hemingway. [1] All three books were closely argued works and more than 'plausible' enough to persuade even the most sceptical just how special the academics — and as, by implication, should the 'serious reader' — thought Hemingway's fiction was. Two years later, in 1954, Charles Fenton published The Apprenticeship Of Ernest Hemingway. Hemingway had become eminently respectable for academic attention, and to this day an ever greater number of books, learned articles, theses, essays and dissertations have flowed from academic pens. The imprimatur was final: Hemingway was now officially 'a great writer' (with the unspoken and for many clinching sub-text that *and we academics wouldn't, of course, waste our time on him if he were not*'). [2]

. . .

Earlier, I drew attention to Virginia Woolf's scorn that we, the reading public, are all too eager to doff our caps and bow to the superior judgment of 'the critics'. [iii] The same seems to be even truer of academia. The lay reader is more than ready — to put it crassly — to bow low before the conclusions of 'academic opinion', and the academics are more than happy to bask in such reverence. Even if we choose to adopt a superficial scepticism about them and their work, especially when faced with a book or a paper with some convoluted title we barely understand, not a few of us will be intimidated. We are less than confident that our own threadbare intellectual clobber can match the robes and wigs academia seems to wear. We decide it's best not to mix it with those we tacitly regard as 'the experts' and risk looking very silly: thus any 'debate' is over before it might even begin — the lay reader gives in and accepts academic pronouncements without question. Now consider in particular the young men or women studying

---

1 It was revised and re-published in 1966, five years after Hemingway's death, as Ernest Hemingway: A Reconsideration.

2 It is also very unlikely that the imprimatur would be withdrawn. Academic interest in Hemingway might wane, but the waning would be unobtrusive, and all we might be aware of would be a radio silence. It is very unlikely that, whether justified or not, academia would turn around and confess '*look, about Hemingway — we might have got it wrong after all*'.

English literature at school and college, keen to do well. As part of their studies, they will encounter the analyses and judgments of the academics, some of whom might even be their teachers and tutors; and it would seem natural, when you are in your late teens and early twenties, to regard these men and women as 'exalted, inspired, infallible', as the 'experts'. Young folk, still less sure of themselves than they might be, would well deem it wisest to conceal whatever 'sensitive, hesitating apprehensions' they harbour about a writer and his or her work. The best and safest policy will be to repeat in seminars, in your essays and in exams the orthodox views you have heard, especially if you hope to achieve good grades. Then, having thus imbibed what was decreed to be the case, several of those students might after graduation take up high school and college teaching as a career; thus the orthodoxies are perpetuated. Admittedly, in recent decades there has been an ostentatious encouragement for students to 'think for themselves', and they are often urged to 'think outside the box' and 'think the unthinkable'; but to some extent that is little more than liberal window dressing in keeping with the times rather than a sincere invitation to upset the apple cart.

A further dilemma faces those, especially young students, who want to examine and discuss the academics' interest in Hemingway and his work: it might well amount to commenting on, and at times even criticising, the practices and intellectual habits of academics in general (at least those engaged in 'the arts' subjects rather than the sciences). Yet again the risk of looking – or being made to look – stupid is immense. A withering retort from academia along the lines of *'We think you'll find it's a little more complex than that'* would be enough to convince most of those intimidated by the virtual wigs, robes and outriders that the doubter in question really is something of a dolt and should best be ignored. It would, admittedly, be both foolish and wrong to indulge in wild, iconoclastic philistinism [1] as a matter of course and to dismiss the academics and some of their conclusions out of hand; but it is equally foolish and wrong slavishly to accept their every word. Yet such is the power of those virtual wigs, robes and outriders that many do just that without a second thought.

...

When we consider the putative expertise and the conclusions and pronouncements of the academics working in 'the arts', it is important to remember that their thinking is not – and, by the nature of what it deals with, can never be – in the same class of thinking

---

1   This is, though, certainly not unknown: many a professional contrarian has forged a good career by being the perpetual iconoclast, often with assistance from the various print and broadcasting media for whom he or she is 'good copy' and 'marvellous radio/television'.

as that involved in mathematics and the sciences;[1] yet what seems to be obvious is largely ignored, if not entirely forgotten. As I pointed out earlier, in mathematics you can't 'have an opinion' on whether or not two and two really do equal four as you can agree or disagree on whether – as Philip Young hypothesises – Hemingway's fiction was informed and sustained by the various 'wounds' big and small he suffered while growing up. Nor can Young be 'right' or 'wrong', however interesting and plausible his suggestions are: it would, though, be 'wrong' to deny that adding two and two gives you four. Put aside for now the complication that atomic physics tells us an electron is at one and the same time – or better behaves – both as 'a wave' and 'a particle' [an object with mass], at a macro level there are in mathematics and the sciences demonstrable 'facts': adding an acid to an alkali results in a chemical reaction which produces a salt and water. Time and again this has been found to be so, and we are confident it will always be so. Similarly, there are one or two 'facts' which might be cited when dealing with an author and her or his work, but they are far more limited in scope. There will be biographical and other, possibly indisputable, 'facts': publication dates and how many editions of a work were published, whether and when it was translated into this or that language, where it was written, and so on. There will, for example, be the 'facts' that several of Charles Dickens' novels are set in London and that Shakespeare wrote his plays to be performed by the theatre company he co-owned. As far as Hemingway is concerned, it is also a 'fact' that For Whom The Bell Tolls takes place over three days during the Spanish civil war, and that Across The River And Into The Trees describes the brief love affair between a fifty-something army colonel with a heart condition and a Venetian woman just short of her 19th birthday. But interpretations, conclusions reached by 'close reading' and analysis, are never as copper-bottomed: that parts of The Sun Also Rises take place in Paris, Pamplona, Burguete and Madrid are 'facts' about the novel; that it portrays a 'lost generation in despair' and that it is 'a tragedy' are opinions, suggestions, conclusions, speculation – call them what you will – but they are not 'facts'. Furthermore, as opinions, suggestions, conclusions and speculation they are subjective (of which we become particularly aware when different interpretations contradict each other as all too often they do). Yet time and again academia will, possibly unwittingly, present its 'conclusions' as though they were 'facts', whether they are dealing with the work of Hemingway or any other writer. For each individual academic, her or his take on a novel, story or poem might well 'be a fact'; for the rest of us, matters should not necessarily be quite as certain. But such is 'the power of credulity' observed by Woolf

---

1   It is probably not a point Hemingway would have endorsed: in a letter to Max Perkins at Scribner's in 1945 he announced '*The laws of prose writing are as immutable as those of flight, of mathematics, of physics*'. Evelyn Waugh's Mr Salter would have disagreed. As do I.

and the 'exalted, inspired, infallible' status many of us accord the critics – and, I suggest, the academics – that these findings might also be accepted as 'fact' by many, whether student or lay reader. Thus, at some point – a point no doubt already reached by many reading these chapters – not only does it sound odd for sceptics to disagree with the academics, de facto it is thought the onus is on the sceptics to prove the academics are – or even simply could be – 'wrong'. So Woolf's advice to the students and lay readers is worth repeating: ignore those imaginary wigs, robes and outriders, whether worn by critic or academic, and pay rather more attention to your own judgment (and, I shall add, always keep an open mind).

. . .

As I suggest, when one considers, analyses and 'interprets' the work of any writer, it might initially be desirable, as formalist theories suggest, to judge that work in isolation. In practice that is almost impossible. That Hemingway was reputedly sometimes a bully, a belligerent drunkard and a know-all, or, as his sons attested, a loving and kind father and, as some friends insisted, something of an intellectual should have no bearing on how we evaluate his work or judge it to have succeeded. We now know that the English sculptor Eric Gill was an incestuous paedophile, as revealed in a biography in 1989. [1] That knowledge might bear on whether or not, and where and how, his work should be exhibited; but should it influence our various aesthetic conclusions about that work? Do those works engage and interest us any the less, is his craftsmanship any the less impressive once we know what he got up to with his sisters and daughters? If, as many appear to believe, 'works of art' have an intrinsic, almost metaphysical, quality of 'being art' – and I don't – did that quality in Gill's work vanish from one moment to the next as soon as his vices were revealed? [iv] Or was it perhaps never present in the first place and we only realised our mistake when we were told of his incestuous behaviour?

In his essay The Death Of The Author, the French philosopher and literary theorist Roland Barthes observed that

> . . . *criticism still consists, most of the time, in saying that Baudelaire's work is the failure of the man Baudelaire, Van Gogh's work his madness, Tchaikovsky's his vice: the explanation of the work is always sought in the man who has produced it, as if, through the more or less transparent allegory of fiction, it was*

---

1   Although his predilections were known in his lifetime, there is no mention of them in an earlier biography.

> *always finally the voice of one and the same person, the author, which delivered his 'confidence'.*

Barthes was keen that works of art should be evaluated and judged in and of themselves, and insisted that once 'completed', these works become independent of 'the author' (and, one assumes, of the composer, painter or sculptor). This is, of course, not 'a fact', just another 'opinion', a 'point of view'; but it is one which, if accepted and adopted as a guiding principle, would severely stymie the work of those many academics who, when they interpret and evaluate Hemingway's work, delve deeply into his life and the letters he wrote and consider his own and others' memoirs when they interpret and evaluate.[1] For example, Philip Young's thesis that 'the wounds' Hemingway suffered in his early life, not least when he was blown up in the Italian front in 1918, largely informed his work would be rendered redundant if one accepted what Barthes says. It would also give rise to an irony: Hemingway always himself insisted that his work was not autobiographical and that he had taken 'what he knew from his own experience' and somehow transmuted it; that would chime in with what Barthes is suggesting. So who do we believe: Hemingway or Young?

What Barthes and the formalists insist is, of course, wholly theoretical: de facto it is impossible to ignore what we know of a writer when we consider the work. Yet even if we decide to reject Barthes' view and concede that referring to a writer's biography is useful, the matter is still not straightforward – now the sticking point will be: which biography, which account of her or his life, which 'facts' should we consider? That difficulty is highlighted by Debra Moddelmog in New Essays On Hemingway's Fiction (and Young take note). She writes

> *The identity of Hemingway – or of any other biographical subject including ourselves – is thus a process of articulating into being. Because this articulation takes the form of narrative, the biographer always tells a story, but the story does not come out of nowhere, nor is it implicit in the 'facts' of the author's life. Rather, the biographer chooses a story from among the many*

---

1   As I point out above, Cambridge University Press is still only five volumes into a project to publish an eventual seventeen-volume collection of Hemingway's letters. There are said to be more than 6,000 letters of which so far only 15 per cent have been published. Whether or not it (or someone else) also has plans to compile a definitive collection of 'Papa's' shopping and laundry lists, I don't know and can't say. That comment might strike some as facile and fatuous, but frankly from my reading of Hemingway's work, the Cambridge undertaking is equally facile and fatuous, although I don't doubt that for many it is further 'proof' that Hemingway was 'a great writer'. *'Why else would they bother?'* they might ask.

that his or her culture makes available and selects the facts that will make the story cohere. Thus the biographer's biography – like the historian's history – always tells two stories. The first is in the text itself and is a story of inclusion: the text includes not only the plot that the biographer selects out of many, but also those particular experiences that enable this plot to come together. The other story exists only in the negative, the absent, for it is a story of exclusion: the numerous plots that the biographer rejects and those experiences that must be censored of omitted for the sake of narrative unity and ideological consistency.

Moddelmog might also agree that the text of the biography itself, the language used and the descriptive words and phrases chosen by a biographer or commentator also add to and inform the biographer's 'story'. Words are subtle and they are not 'neutral', and they convey more than just their meaning. Thus I cannot exclude myself from Moddelmog's observation, not just in what I record in the 'potted biographies' which follow later, but in what I have so far written. When, for example, I describe Hemingway as 'pontificating' on what is and what is not 'good writing', not only is the verb 'to pontificate' distinctly pejorative, but by using it, I reveal a great deal about my attitude to Hemingway. [1]

This is not just true of me, as I trust Moddelmog, a Hemingway admirer, would concede. The words and phrases Hemingway's biographers and, pertinently, the many men and women commentating on and analysing his work chose to use are equally subjective. In one sense, even the titles of Carlos Baker's book – Hemingway: The Writer As Artist – and that of John Atkins – The Art Of Ernest Hemingway – have already loaded the dice before we read a single word: they tell us full well where Baker and Atkins stand. [2] One might counter that the titles chosen by Baker and Atkins simply – that is merely – indicated 'what their books were about'. [v] That's true, of course; yet the titles tacitly do more: when presented with these books by two 'experts', the still inexperienced student and lay reader might already feel judgment has been passed; and she or he is more than likely to accept the observations and evaluation of both as 'correct' and 'fact' from the outset. Yet, what Baker, Young and Atkins have to say is certainly not copper-bottomed truth and is as contentious as any other point of view.

---

1   I did, in fact, chose to use the word specifically. I believe that 'pontificating' is, in context, the right one to employ: even close friends became fed up with Hemingway's insistence that he was an expert in most areas of life and remorselessly instructing those around him on all manner of matters. Hemingway pontificated to an alarming degree like the best bar stool bore.

2   The same is, of course, true of the title of this book, but that doesn't invalidate the point I make. On the contrary it highlights it and might be regarded as a good example.

Throughout his book Baker describes Hemingway as 'a true artist', and his insistence would certainly impress most young students and lay readers; but they would still be best advised to discount Baker's virtual robes and wigs, and keep an open mind: at the end of the day Baker's analyses, interpretations and claims are no more than opinions.

Perhaps to underline the point that it's wisest to stick to the thin line between not accepting wholesale but keeping an open mind, [1] even one or two of the details Baker provides about Hemingway's life are at odds with what more recent biographers have found (which reinforces Moddelmog's advice to be cautious of the narratives with which we are presented). For example, throughout all four editions of Baker's book (the fourth and most recent published nine years after Hemingway's death), he refers to Hemingway as a 'veteran' of the Great War; as I point out above, words are subtle and not neutral, and given how the word is, in this context, habitually employed, it implies that Hemingway saw active service as a fighting soldier, probably for some time. But he didn't: for the rest of his life he liked people to believe he had 'fought in the war', yet his 'war service' lasted for less than five months in total, and for only four weeks of those five months was Hemingway in any way 'active'. [vi] Notably, while researching and writing his book, Baker was in postal communication with Hemingway and says Hemingway corrected various of his 'errors'. Granted it has no bearing on the theme of his book, but Baker's claim is typical of the somewhat adulatory tone he adopts which, more pertinently, also infuses his insistence on Hemingway as 'the artist', a description which most of us great unwashed assume broadly obliges us to genuflect. Whoever reads his book should be aware of Baker's bias; and Baker's bias is severe.

. . .

Being blessed with the attention of academia might well be seen not just as the catalyst for the transformation of 'Ernest Hemingway, the famous writer' the public esteemed into 'Ernest Hemingway, the artist', but for his ascension to literary heaven as 'one of the 20th century's greatest writers'. To substantiate his view that Hemingway was certainly more than just another best-selling scribbler, Carlos Baker writes

> *[Hemingway's] short stories are deceptive somewhat in the manner of an iceberg [a reference to Hemingway's 'theory of omission']. The visible areas glint with the hard factual light of the naturalist. The supporting structure, submerged and mostly invisible except to the patient explorer, is built with a different kind of precision – that*

---

1   This is certainly not synonymous with 'sitting on the fence', and it is harder than one might assume.

of the poet-symbolist. Once the reader has become aware of what Hemingway is doing in those parts of his work which lie below the surface, he is likely to find symbols operating everywhere, and in a series of beautiful crystallizations, compact and buoyant enough to carry considerable weight. [1]

It is all convincing enough and has, no doubt, been accepted and repeated in many an essay and exam by students worldwide. This passage might serve as a very good example of the seductive potency of words: Baker speaks of the *'patient explorer'*, *'precision'*, *'the poet-symbolist'*, *'beautiful crystallizations'* and *'buoyant'*. Those words and descriptions all aim to convey the sense the Hemingway was very good at what he did and thus help to reinforce the notion that we should admire him. There is, of course, no reason why Baker shouldn't use these and other phrases if they describe what he believed: my point is that words and language are very rarely neutral and used skilfully – *ars est celare artem / the art is to conceal art* – can quietly achieve a great deal. Yet the passage falls short of its goal of distinguishing Hemingway 'the artist' from run-of-the-mill writers in that it begs one important question: if, as Baker claims, Hemingway 'built' his short stories with the 'precision' of 'the poet-symbolist', why did he not – and demonstrably he did not – apply the same 'poet-symbolist's precision' to the verse he wrote?[2] Surely the kind of 'precise artistry' which Baker says Hemingway made his own would be particularly suited to writing verse? In fact, Hemingway's verse is banal, superficial, adolescent and obvious,[3] and I have yet to come across any commentator who thinks – or has at least so declared publicly – that any of it is worth a candle.

Similarly, other 'facts' 'proving' Hemingway's artistry and which Baker presents as almost unassailable also don't quite stack up. He writes, somewhat airily,

> *If he had wished to follow the mythological method of Eliot's Waste Land [sic] or Joyce's Ulysses, Hemingway could obviously have done so. But his own esthetic [sic] opinions carried him away from the literary kind of myth-adaptation and over into that deeper area of psychological symbol-building which does not require special literary equipment to be interpreted. One needs only sympathy*

---

1   An irony is Baker's celebration of 'the symbols' in Hemingway's fiction: the man himself was decidedly ambiguous and carefully non-committal on the matter. See p.215.

2   I prefer to use the word 'verse' rather than 'poetry', as 'verse' is easily identifiable, whereas what is 'poetry' and what makes this piece of verse but not that piece 'poetry' is, even on a good day, as clear as mud (although an excellent excuse for sustained waffling).

3   Just 'an opinion', of course.

> *and a few degrees of heightened emotional awareness. The special virtue to this approach to the problem of literary communication is that it can be grasped by all men and women because they are human beings. None of the best writers are [sic] without it.*

Thus, Baker continues, in both The Sun Also Rises and A Farewell To Arms, Hemingway symbolically distinguishes between 'the mountains' and 'the plains'. The mountains are 'home' and 'natural' and thus – according to Baker – in Hemingway's aesthetic 'beautiful'. They are associated with dry-cold weather, peace and quiet, love, dignity, health and happiness. On the other hand 'the plains', which are 'not-home' and 'unnatural' and thus 'ugly', are associated with rain and fog, obscenity, indignity, disease, nervousness and war and death. In The Sun Also Rises, Jake Barnes and his friend Bill Gorton go trout fishing in the mountains – well, strictly in the hills – north of Pamplona and there they find peace and solace, whereas the plains – Montparnasse in Paris and Pamplona itself – are where all the drunkenness, discord, jealousy and ugliness reside. In A Farewell To Arms Frederic Henry ignores the priest's invitation to spend his winter furlough with the priest's family in the hilly Abruzzi region and instead goes drinking and whoring in a city; later Henry and his pregnant partner, Catherine Barkley, find sanctuary after escaping Italy in the Swiss mountains. The plains are where the troops are stationed and where the military police are executing officer deserters and which – says Baker – are 'sinister'.

Once again, this analysis is plausible enough – 'plausibility', I'll repeat, plays an important role when considering the evaluations, conclusions and verdicts of literary academia – and there is a neat symmetry to Baker's juxtaposition that might convince, and probably has convinced, many. Inconveniently, however, it doesn't work: 'the mountains' are also where the enemy is positioned and from where it will attack, where the fighting between the Italians and Austrians takes place and where Henry is blown up and might have been killed (as are many Italians). 'The plains' are where the retreating Italians head to find safety from death at the enemy's hand. One might even add – adopting Baker's method – that it is on the plains where Henry finds true love [1] and is thus eventually redeemed from his habitual cynicism and where he had found a good, loyal and true friend in the Italian officer Rinaldi. With those points in mind, it would seem Baker's neat analysis of Hemingway's apparent 'psychological symbol-breaking' breaks down (even for those lucky readers with sympathy and a few degrees of heightened emotional awareness).

In fact, it gets stickier and even less convincing: Baker seems to contradict his own

---

1 Milan and much of Lombardy are very flat – the plains. I once, briefly, lived in Milan.

findings when he writes about The First Forty-Five Stories. [vii] Examining one of those stories, Alpine Idyll (which appeared in Hemingway's collection Men Without Women), the 'psychological symbol-building' is turned on its head by Baker (and it is puzzling that he did not seem to realise what he had done in his analysis). The mountains, in The Sun Also Rises and A Farewell To Arms the 'beautiful' 'natural' place, now become the 'unnatural' place: up in the mountains (writes Baker) the Swiss peasant at the centre of the story had 'lived too long in an unnatural situation' and 'his sense of human dignity and decency [had] temporarily atrophied'. When

> *he gets down into the valley, where it is spring and the people are living naturally and wholesomely, he sees how far he has strayed from the natural and the wholesome, for spring has been established in the [narrator's] internal monologue as the 'natural' place. In the carefully wrought*[1] *terms of the story, the valley stands in opposition to the unnatural high mountain spring.*

So which is it: are the mountains 'natural' or 'unnatural'? Are the plains and the valleys 'home or 'not-home'? The Sun Also Rises and the later short story, Alpine Idyll, described by Baker as an 'apparently simple tale', are admittedly two separate works; and Hemingway was under no obligation to adopt and repeat the 'psychological symbol-building' of his first novel and apply the 'different kind of precision . . . of the poet-symbolist' (if that was what he was doing) when writing his short story. Yet Baker also makes the point that to truly comprehend what Hemingway was 'telling us', the stories should be read as one body of work; so it is not unreasonable to assume that any 'psychological symbol-building' by Hemingway might be consistent throughout that body of work. It is unusual, if Baker's analysis holds, that in the subsequent short story Hemingway should reverse the symbolism of the first novel, only to revert to the original symbolism when composing his second novel; and if he had purposely done so, as a 'poet-symbolist' who works 'precisely', we might assume that he would have had his reasons. If so what are they? What might they be? Baker doesn't attempt to say.

In fact, the suggestion is not that Hemingway was at fault, but that Baker was: once Baker had elevated Hemingway to the status of 'artist', one suspects he felt obliged to find significance, meaning and, above all, artistry in every corner and aspect of Hemingway's work; and he does so with the true believer's zeal, at the expense, it would seem, of

---

1   '*Carefully wrought*' is another useful phrase to convey Hemingway's purported excellence as a writer/artist.

consistency. [1] Thus he also detects – flatly contradicting his claim that Hemingway did not choose to follow Eliot's and Joyce's 'mythological method' – supposed correlations between elements in The Sun Also Rises and Homer's Odyssey and Greek and other myths. Mike Campbell quotes Robert Cohn comparing Brett Ashley to Circe (who turned men into swine), with Campbell adding 'I wish I were one of those literary chaps'. Baker comments

> *Was not Brett Ashley, on her low-lying island in the Seine, just such a fascinating peril as Circe on Aeaea? Did she not open her doors to all the modern Achaean chaps? When they drank her special potion of French applejack or Spanish wine, did they not become as swine, or in the modern idiom, wolves? Did not Jake Barnes, that wily Odysseus, resist the shameful doom which befell certain of his less wary comrades who became snarling beasts?*

Baker also chooses to detect echoes of Homer when a miserable Jake Barnes wakes at night and weeps a little over the impotence which denies him sexual union with Brett Ashley; and Baker hears echoes of Homer when Robert Cohn falls asleep among the casks in the back room of a Pamplona wine shop. All this is convincing enough for those who are determined to be convinced, and, proclaims Baker, it all adds up to Hemingway's artistry. He goes further: before the fiesta week has begun, Jake Barnes, a Roman Catholic, intends to make his confession and Brett Ashley wants to go with him to hear it; Barnes tells her that would not be possible, that it would not be as interesting as she thought it might be and it would be in a language she did not understand, which, says Baker, pursuing more possible 'significance', would not be Spanish or Latin, but 'the Christian language'. Later, as the image of San Fermin is taken from church to church and Brett and Jake go to follow it into one chapel, Brett is denied entrance

> *. . . ostensibly [writes Baker] because she has no hat. But for one sufficiently awake to ulterior meaning of the incident it strikingly resembles the attempt of a witch to gain entry into a Christian sanctum. Brett's witch-hood is immediately underscored. Back in the street she is encircled by the chanting pagan dancers who prevent her from joining their figure: 'They wanted her as an image to dance around.' When the song ends, she is rushed to a wine-shop*

---

1 In this respect, Baker reminds me, though obliquely, of the advice given to all young reporters (in Britain, Australia and New Zealand at least – perhaps fledgling American hacks are more principled and less corruptible): '*Don't let a couple of facts get in the way of a good story*'.

> *and seated on an up-ended wine-cask. The shop is dark and full of men singing – 'hard-voiced singing'.*

Baker continues

> *The intent of this episode is quite plain. Brett would not understand the language used in a Christian confessional. She is forbidden to follow the religious procession into the chapel. The dancers adopt her as a pagan image. She is perfectly at home on a wine-cask amidst the hard-voiced singing of the non-religious celebrants. Later in fiesta week, the point is re-emphasised. Jake and Brett enter the San Fermin chapel so that Brett can pray for Romero's success in the final bullfight of the celebration. 'After a little [says Jake] I felt Brett stiffen beside me and saw she was looking straight ahead.' Outside the chapel Brett explains what Jake had already guessed: 'I'm damned bad for religious atmosphere. I've got the wrong type of face.'*

Brett, says Baker,

> *in her own way is a lamia with a British accent, a Morgana le Fay of Paris and Pamplona, the reigning queen of a paganised wasteland with a wounded fisherman as her half-cynical squire [i.e. Jake Barnes].*

Well, perhaps – but there again perhaps not; and one should also note that despite the seeming plausibility and apparent neatness of Baker's analysis, those readers who are 'sufficiently awake to ulterior meaning of the incident' might also be alert enough to spot that Baker is decidedly sloppy: he conveniently chooses to gloss over that at her second attempt to enter a chapel, Brett – a quasi 'witch' and '*lamia* with a British accent' – is no longer denied entry and has no trouble getting into a 'Christian sanctum'. As for Baker's insights, for example when outlining a

> *reigning queen of a paganised wasteland with a wounded fisherman as her half-cynical squire*

is he onto something? Or is he, conversely, blandly over-egging his pudding? Far more fundamentally – and this is certainly a crucial point – had Hemingway 'the artist' actually intended to make any of the allusions that Baker – and the reader with 'sympathy and a few degrees of heightened emotional awareness' – detects? Twenty-five years later as a

Nobel Laureate, Hemingway might well have conceded that 'well, of course, certainly I did' and basked in the kudos of being a deep and skilful writer whose artistry was worthy of literary prizes; but the fact is that we don't and we cannot know because there is no way of knowing. Even if we had listened to Hemingway thirty years on thus acknowledging his own skill and classical learning, we might still care to keep more than one ear open to the caution biographer Kenneth S. Lynn urged about heeding the wiles of 'the master manipulator'.

The central point is to remind ourselves that although for some readers Baker's analysis might well add to their enjoyment and appreciation of Hemingway's novel, it is neither 'right' nor 'wrong' because there can be neither a 'right' nor a 'wrong' reading. Pertinently, though, and recalling Virginia Woolf's astonishment at the 'power of human credulity', many, perhaps most, might still be more inclined than not to accept the collected dicta of Carlos Baker; and from there it is an easy step to treat Baker's findings as established 'facts' – that he is 'right' in his analyses. After all, as a Princeton professor of English no less, Baker surely possessed more virtual wigs, robes and outriders than you or I could shake a stick at. We are, though, not just advised but obliged to tread carefully.

. . .

There is also the dilemma the reader faces when one analysis wholly contradicts another: both might be equally believable and convincing, but they can't both be 'right'. For example, Baker also makes a great deal of Bill Gorton, while up in the hills above Burguete on his fishing trip with Jake Barnes, castigating his Paris-based friend for 'being an ex-patriate' and thus turning his back on his home country and rejecting its values. The notion of 'the ex-patriate' is relevant here: after World War I and throughout the 1920s, an ever greater number of young Americans – in their tens of thousands, in fact – left uptight, puritan, Prohibition-era America to settle in Paris, attracted by an extremely favourable exchange rate as much as the promise of a more hedonistic, less constricted lifestyle. Their parents' generation did not approve at all, and it became an 'issue of the day': newspaper editorials and think-pieces in learned journals complained that their ex-patriate lifestyle was unwholesome and unnatural. They accused those young ex-patriates of betraying America and its values as much as, Baker suggests, Bill Gorton castigates Jake Barnes. Thus Baker finds tragic significance in Gorton's condemnation of Jake Barnes, and his analysis is plausible. Unfortunately and very unhelpfully for

Baker, several biographers read the scene – as well as when Gorton riffs on 'irony and pity' while on the fishing trip – as a light-hearted, tongue-in-cheek interlude. They have suggested that Hemingway, who prided himself on being able to write humorously, was satirising the outrage and preoccupations of contemporary America's more respectable men and women with 'ex-patriates'. Such an analysis is equally as plausible, but it is wholly at odds with Baker's take. So who is 'right': the biographers or Baker? In fact, yet again it doesn't matter: despite the impression academia, casting envious eyes on the sciences, likes to give – admittedly tacitly – of being conclusive and informed, no definitive analysis or interpretation – call it what you like – is available or even possible, simply because there cannot be.

Caveat lector – Erich von Däniken takes a bow

If you don't have the intellectual wherewithal to comprehend what we are saying, you can't blame us.

A hypothetical arts academic.

Too often the papers of academic experts are addressed only to their peers in a jargon that seeks to mimic the rigorous discourse of the sciences: such criticism is published only in the expensive volumes destined for purchase by libraries and not by the common reader.

Declan Kiberd, Ulysses And Us.

We think you'll find it's a little more complex than that!

Another hypothetical arts academic.

WHEN considering what Baker and some of his academic colleagues have to say, circumspection is always advisable despite their putative 'exalted, inspired, infallible' status: some academics appear to stray perilously close to the method of one Erich von Däniken and his many, equally intellectually dubious, imitators. [i] Von Däniken was a Swiss writer (and a convicted thief and fraudster) who made a great deal of money publishing a series of books positing that extra-terrestrial aliens had repeatedly visited Earth; while here, writes von Däniken, the aliens were responsible, among other things, for building the Egyptian pyramids, erecting England's Stonehenge and the Easter Islands statues, and constructing Peru's Nazca Lines. Von Däniken's method was simple: first, he asked questions and suggested ('*Is it possible that . . . ?*'); a little later he tacitly treated the 'possibilities' he had posited as 'probabilities' ('*As we know, it is not unlikely that . . .*'); finally, a little later still, those 'probabilities' were presented to the – gullible – reader as 'established facts' ('*As we've seen . . .*'). Academics would certainly recoil in horror and outrage at the suggestion that they might be thought to be adopting 'von Däniken's method', even unconsciously; but all too often it certainly looks as though they do. [ii]

Earlier, I highlighted the 'insoluble problem' presented in Hemingway's short story A Clean, Well-lighted Place in which what might simply be – and most probably was – just a piece of carelessness by Hemingway leads to confusion when reading the story. Yet obeying an imperative of the Hemingway theology, rather than concede that 'one of America's greatest writers' might be at fault, the 'apparent' confusion was rationalised this way and that in an ongoing debate between academics until one, a Joseph Gabriel, insisted it was, in fact, *deliberate*: that Hemingway, in existentialist mode, *intended* the confusion in the text to reflect the 'confusion of life' when a lonely old man who had attempted suicide and a sympathetic elderly waiter are confronted by 'nothingness' ('*nada*'). More to the point, Gabriel adopted von Däniken's method and began by suggesting his reading as a possibility and concluding by treating it as a conclusive explanation – a fact.

Baker does much the same when he spins quite ordinary events – Brett Ashley being refused entry into a place of Christian worship, being surrounded by boisterous revellers, Robert Cohn falling asleep in the back room of a wine shop, an insomniac Jake Barnes weeping at night over his impotence – into significance. Following the method of von Däniken and his imitators, he first asks questions and makes suggestions:

> *Was not Brett Ashley, on her low-lying island in the Seine, just such a fascinating peril as Circe on Aeaea? Did she not open her doors to all the modern Achaean chaps? When they drank her special potion of French applejack or Spanish wine, did they not become as swine, or in the modern idiom, wolves?* [1]

So far these are presented as 'possibilities'; but very soon the 'possibilities' evolve into 'probabilities' and then into 'facts': Baker writes

> *The intent of this episode is quite plain . . . [and] in her own way [Brett] is a lamia with a British accent, a Morgana le Fay of Paris and Pamplona, the reigning queen of a paganised wasteland with a*

---

1   Baker might plead that these were rhetorical questions, and he might well be right. But they would still be 'suggestions'.

> *wounded fisherman as her half-cynical squire.*

As far as Baker is concerned *quod erat demonstrandum* – it is 'quite plain', he insists – and readers will agree, especially those who pride themselves on having 'sympathy and a few degrees of heightened emotional awareness'. Yet however 'plausible' and convincing, at the end of the day such analyses are mere hi-falutin' speculation; time and again they are tacitly represented as quasi 'facts', which, crucially, are liable to be accepted as such wholesale by readers and students, and, of course, then perpetuated.

...

Carlos Baker discovers symbolism everywhere in Hemingway's fiction, though Hemingway himself was conveniently ambiguous on the matter. Was there symbolism in his work, were his stories as Baker insists 'built with a different kind of precision – that of the poet-symbolist'? If there was, Hemingway chose neither to confirm nor deny the suggestion. Seven years after Baker first published his book, Hemingway was 'interviewed' for the Paris Review by its co-founder and editor George Plimpton. Revisiting the matter of mooted symbolism in his work, Hemingway says

> *I suppose there are symbols since critics keep finding them . . . If five or six or more good explainers can keep going why should I interfere with them? Read anything I write for the pleasure of reading it. Whatever else you find will be the measure of what you brought to the reading.*

This was a clever response from the 'self-promoter' Hemingway – I use that description in keeping with the 'narrative unity and ideological consistency' of these chapters – and he seems to be playing both ends against the middle. He neither kills off the suggestion that his work contains symbolism and concedes there might well be, nor does he confirm that was what it habitually contained; thus he stokes the fire a little more, presumably to ensure he remained centre-stage.

A few years earlier, commenting on analyses and interpretations in some reviews of his 1953 novella The Old Man And The Sea in which many detected decidedly Christian symbolism, Hemingway observed, again ambiguously, that

> *No good book has ever been written that has in it symbols arrived at beforehand and stuck in. That kind of symbol sticks out like raisins in raisin bread. Raisin bread is all right, but plain bread is better.*

If we adopt the practice of 'close reading' advocated by Baker, there is, in fact, even less to what Hemingway says than meets the eye: he simply sets up his own Aunt Sally in order to knock it down again. It is certainly possible that a writer, while creating her or his fiction, might decide that including this or that symbol – or more probably this or that set of related symbols – could prove to be technically and artistically useful, though the how, why and when the symbols are introduced – if at all – would certainly vary from writer to writer and individual method and practice of composition.

In 1936, F. Scott Fitzgerald advised his fellow novelist John O'Hara (who was younger by nine years) to spend two months planning his new novel, establish where the novel reached its climax, then spend the next three months working backwards and forwards from that point to establish the story's various details. Finally O'Hara should work out the story's continuity and accordingly set a work schedule; some might assume that was how Fitzgerald went about writing his novels. [1] At the other extreme was Hemingway's practice: he tells us he simply wrote on spec to see where his story might take him. [2] Depending upon how a writer prefers to work, any symbols might be decided upon in the planning stage, and, according to Hemingway, they would certainly have been 'arrived at beforehand' (although to dismiss them as standing out like 'raisins in raisin bread' is prima facie unwarranted. How well they are incorporated into a body of work would be down to the skill of the writer). On the other hand, in the somewhat mysterious and poorly understood act of creation, the writer might gradually realise that certain 'elements' [3] in what has so far been written stand out, and she or he might decide to utilise them as 'symbols'. Though they came into existence ad hoc, during subsequent revision and editing the writer might choose subtly to highlight them in some way. It is even possible that a writer was unaware of any symbols in a work but which readers later believe they have detected. Bearing in mind that analysing the process of creation is anything but straightforward, the question of what might be symbolism and when and how it was introduced is nigh-on impossible to answer. Yet note, Hemingway is only commenting on 'symbols arrived at beforehand and stuck in'; and that, presumably, would distinguish them from 'symbols' created during the act of creation.

---

1   I am, though, not persuaded Fitzgerald was entirely serious and was, perhaps, having a little fun at O'Hara's expense. We'll never know.

2   Presumably Hemingway had a notion of where he might arrive – or where he wanted to end up – but judging from some of his work, that is not at all certain. Many of his stories give the impression of being written on the hoof and barely revised. That would, of course, sit badly with Baker's insistence that Hemingway worked with the 'precision' of 'the poet-symbolist'. Examples would be The Three-day Blow, Che Ti Dice La Patria? (taken almost word for word from a factual account of a trip he and a fellow journalist made to Fascist Italy in 1927) and The Capital Of The World.

3   It is impossible and could be misleading to try here to define what those 'elements' might be.

Caveat lector – Erich von Däniken takes a bow 217

. . .

Hemingway is, though, certainly right when he says that sometimes some symbols

stick[s] out like raisins in raisin bread

because the Christian symbolism he incorporates in The Old Man And The Sea does stick out noticeably, and his use of it is cack-handed in the extreme. Those who disagree might care to consider the all-to-obvious symbolism that after returning from his 'three-day' fishing trip – now where have we come across a significant 'three days' before? – the old man

unstepped the mast and furled the sail and tied it. Then he shouldered the mast and started to climb [up a hill]. It was then he knew the depth of his tiredness. He stopped for a moment . . . [then] started to climb again and at the top he fell and lay for some time with the mast across his shoulder. He tried to get up. But it was too difficult and he sat there with the mast on his shoulder and looked at the road.

Once he has reached his shack, he wants to do nothing but sleep so

He pulled the blanket over his shoulders and then over his back and legs and he slept face down on the newspapers with his arms out straight and the palms of his hands up. [1]

One should always be prepared for outright contradiction, but those passages do remind one – especially those adept at the 'close reading' Baker advocates – of Christ's journey to Golgotha, shouldering the cross on which he was to be crucified, falling – three times – along the way, and his eventual crucifixion with his palms nailed to his cross on outstretched arms. So one wonders at Hemingway's implicit denial in his observation that

raisin bread is all right, but plain bread is better.

It does beg the question – to adopt Hemingway's own metaphor – as to why he didn't stick to producing plain bread when he composed his novella? If the use of such Christian symbolism was intentional – and it is very unlikely it would just 'slip in' –

---

1   It must have been uncomfortable sleeping 'face down' but with his palms face up, but that is how, Hemingway tells us, the old man fell asleep.

a pertinent question is: why? Why did Hemingway include it? What purpose does it serve? It is still not clear how 'Christ's message of redeeming mankind by dying for us on the Cross' [1] has any relevance or can add any dimension to his story of the old man's fruitless fishing expedition. Would it be overly cynical to suggest that as with using the Ecclesiastes quotation that precedes The Sun Also Rises, Hemingway was hoping to give his, rather mawkish, tale a little more intellectual depth?

...

A related, often intractable, problem when dealing with academic interpretations is that it is sometimes impossible to understand what the interpreter is hoping to convey. Admittedly, this might be the reader's fault, but it would be unwise to assume that is always the case. For example, at one point Baker comes up with the following 'insight': he has just remarked that in writing both The Sun Also Rises and A Farewell To Arms, Hemingway had somehow 'purged' himself and, Baker adds,

> There was much more to [The Sun Also Rises and A Farewell To Arms], of course, than an act of personal exorcism, however complicated. For to destroy by embodying is also to create by arranging. The artist's special blessing exists in an impulse to destroy an aspect of the thing he creates, and to render permanent what for him, in another and internal dimension, must be permanently destroyed.

Some might insist they understand what Baker is saying; others will be more than confused by this passage and, perhaps, even – like me – entirely baffled. Individual phrases make a certain transient sense; and, at a pinch, the passage might have a superficial meaning and give the impression of being intellectually coherent to those who have 'sympathy and a few degrees of heightened emotional awareness'. Brought into sharper focus, there is more than a faint suspicion that it is essentially nothing but mellifluous waffle. As for Baker's claim that writing The Sun Also Rises was for Hemingway 'an act of personal exorcism', that is very much Baker's gloss, and I have yet to come across any biographer or other commentator making the same claim. What might Hemingway have been hoping to purge or exorcise? If it was his memories of being blown up outside Fossalta on the night of July 8, 1918, that claim might hold true for A Farewell To Arms, but it is a very bad fit for The Sun Also Rises. It would have helped had Baker given us

---

1   For further details and a fuller outline of Christ's message, this atheist advises you to look elsewhere.

his thoughts.

If we are charitable, the phrase 'to destroy by embodying' might just make the sense: Baker seems to suggest that Hemingway was 'destroying' what he wanted to exorcise from his life by 'embodying' it in his novel, thus making writing a distant cousin of 'talking therapy'. Biographer Jeffrey Meyers might have agreed – he suggests that for Hemingway writing was some kind of release, and Hemingway seems to confirm that. [1] But when the phrase is conjoined with 'to create by arranging' it all becomes oddly nonsensical: what does that mean? What can it mean?[2] As Baker expresses himself, the two would seem to be different sides of the same coin; but, unhelpfully, until we know what he is conveying – or, more truthfully, trying to convey – we are in no position to contradict him.

Even less clear is what might be going on when an artist's

> *special blessing exists in an impulse to destroy an aspect of the thing he creates*

thus rendering

> *permanent what for him, in another and internal dimension, must be permanently destroyed.*

The phrase 'special blessing'[3] adds a certain glitz to Baker's thoughts on 'the artist', but let's stay sober: this, too, is also little more than hi-falutin' waffle. And exactly how does 'destroying an aspect of the thing the artist creates' 'render [it] permanent'? Is the artist 'destroying' or 'creating'? What might 'the aspect' of the thing Hemingway is creating actually be? If you have – and presumably then act on – an impulse to 'destroy [permanently]', how would you then 'render it permanent'? 'To render' is the opposite of 'to destroy' and 'to render [something] permanent' speaks of long-term existence not of destruction. It seems that again 'confused thought' is leading to considerably 'confused writing'. Overall, Baker is far too obscure: however 'profound' his insights in this passage might be, there seems little point in trying to pass them on if in trying to do

---

1 In a letter to New Yorker journalist Lillian Ross with whom Hemingway had struck up a friendship, he told her his *'analyst's name is Royal Portable (noiseless) the 3rd'*, and he later he told actress Ava Gardner that the only psychiatrist he would ever submit to was his Corona #3.

2 In a sense, Baker's phrase is also tautologous: 'arranging' – whether it is words, sound, paint, elements of a script or whatever the 'creator' is working with – is surely the quintessence of 'creating'. And it is her or his skill at that 'arranging' – her or his 'artistic ability' – which distinguishes one creator from another.

3 'Special blessing' is another of those magic phrases designed to make 'the artist' –in this case Hemingway – stand out from the rest of us great unwashed.

so he makes them more or less incomprehensible. [1]

. . .

My brief analysis of the passage might strike some as little more than philistine carping, but it is not: I am – initially at least – allowing Baker the benefit of doubt. I am willing to agree that perhaps – somehow – it does all make sense and that if intellectually the reader goes the extra mile to trace the course of Baker's thinking, comprehension might come sooner or later. But for how long should we indulge in such polite contortion? At what point do we concede that what Baker writes is not a complex suggestion about the nature of Hemingway's work, but a muddled attempt to express a half-baked belief and, again, tantamount to 'mellifluous waffle'? When do we resolve that 'enough is enough'? The point is that if Baker wants to communicate his thoughts and conclusions to his reader, it would help if he – and thus the reader – had a clearer idea of what those thoughts and conclusions are. Some reading the passage might still keep the faith and decide to give Baker – a Princeton professor of English literature, no less, well-suited to the virtual wigs and robes in which we cloak him – a pass. Yielding to the power of human credulity identified by Virginia Woolf, they might feel if they don't quite 'get' what Baker is saying, they must try even harder to understand him. [2] Thus more so than with the critics, the benefit of doubt is invariably with 'the experts', the academics: if Baker, Young and Atkins tell us that Hemingway was 'an artist' – thus reinforcing his reputation as 'one of America's greatest writers' – many will conclude, given Baker, Young and Atkins' 'exalted, inspired, infallible' status, that they certainly know what they are talking about and it's best to ignore the sceptics and doubters. Academic attention certainly was the icing on the cake for Hemingway.

. . .

Academics would certainly disagree with the cutting observation by one Nassim Nicholas Taleb, a writer, statistician, mathematician, a former 'options trader' and 'risk analyst' that

Academia is to knowledge what prostitution is to love

---

1   It occurs to me that Baker might have been essaying a little 'intellectual impressionism': not making specific points exactly, but hoping to convey 'the feel' of what Hemingway was doing and trusting that those lucky souls with 'sympathy and a few degrees of heightened emotional awareness' would pick up on it. I wonder.

2   In this respect they would closely resemble those 'people of faith' who might not yet understand some aspect of 'God's word' and his 'mysteries' and who resolve to pray even harder for an understanding.

but those who have come across passages like the above from Baker and or who have tried to read article after essay after book after dissertation after analysis of what often appears to be incomprehensible verbiage might give Taleb's gibe a quiet cheer. We should again remind ourselves of the respect – which often unwittingly shades off into a quiet reverence – we accord academics; so we might again be wise to distinguish between academics active in the sciences and those working in the arts, particularly in the field of English literature. One fundamental distinction between the two is made clear by Declan Kiberd in his book on Joyce, Ulysses And Us when he writes

> *Too often the papers of academic experts are addressed only to their peers in a jargon that seeks to mimic the rigorous discourse of the sciences: such criticism is published only in the expensive volumes destined for purchase by libraries and not by the common reader.*

Certainly arts academics are, like city traders, IT technicians, nurses, lawyers and, I don't doubt, train drivers and traffic wardens, entitled to use their own 'jargon'; it will be a useful shorthand to adopt when dealing with colleagues, and there is per se nothing reprehensible in choosing to write papers which might ultimately prove intelligible only to the initiated. But although a shorthand would be expected to streamline communication, whether spoken or written, and to make it clearer, providing clarity does not seem to be a gift shared by too many academics; a cynic might even suggest that at times in the – reputedly competitive – world of academia a certain obscurantism is also in play, possibly in tandem with a little quiet showing-off. More innocently, there often seems something of a teen fan club feel about it all, one whose members eagerly exchange obscure and arcane details about their idol. Those points could be illuminated by the titles of pieces that have appeared in the Hemingway Review [1] over these past few years: The Elephant's Eye And The Maji-Maji War – A Non-Anthropocentric Reading of David's African Story In The Garden Of Eden; Hemingway's Dialectic With American Whiteness: Oak Park, Edward Said And The Location Of Authority; and Hemingway's 'Now I Lay Me', Prayer and The Fisher King. Less recherché but still in teen fan club spirit would be Behind The Scenes With Pauline Pfeiffer, Hemingway And Jane Kendall Mason. [2] Then there's a particularly telling, though admirably straightforward title, A Never-Before-Published Essay About Growing Up With Hemingway, Written By His

---

1   The Hemingway Review has been published, currently twice yearly, since 1981.

2   Mason was a rich young American living in Cuba with her husband with whom the Hemingway's socialised. Hemingway is believed to have had started an affair with her in the early 1930s after Pfeiffer, a devout Roman Catholic, would for medical reasons only consent to sex if Hemingway practised coitus interruptus.

Unrequited High School Crush. [1]

Those academics publishing less fluffy pieces might assume their 'readers' are most probably academic colleagues and fellow initiates, but the assumption does seem to promote a tendency to 'over-intellectualise', a practice that might well further intimidate many a lay person who comes across such pieces and is already in awe of the 'exalted, inspired, infallible' experts. [iii]

. . .

A good and telling example of this tendency to over-intellectualise which, I suggest, permeates a great deal of research on, and writing about, Hemingway – and, I don't doubt, other writers – is an analysis of the Hans Christian Andersen tale The Emperor's New Clothes by the academic Hollis Robbins, of the University of Utah, written for the publication New Literary History when she was still teaching at Princeton. In fact, describing her article, The Emperor's New Critique, as 'an analysis' of Andersen's tale is misleading: Robbins is not so much analysing the tale as commenting on a commentary by the French philosopher and 'deconstructionist' Jacques Derrida who was himself commenting on a commentary by Sigmund Freud on Andersen's tale. Ostensibly, and most probably, Andersen intended his tale as a satire: he was ridiculing the vanity of a ruler for whom clothes and dressing well are more important than taking care of matters of state; Andersen was also, according to Robbins, sending up the pusillanimity of Denmark's civil servants and their ilk in general. But, Robbins insists, there is far more to it than that: Andersen's tale, she assures us, is a

> critique of criticism . . . [a] tale, teller, interpreter and critical case study all in one . . . Yet if it is true that the tale's very transparency is a critique of the desire to critique – or rather, the exhibitionistic desire to unveil publicly – Derrida's privileging of the themes of analysis, truth, and unveiling in his (albeit brief) reading of The Emperor's New Clothes provides evidence that the awareness of this desire does not reduce its influence. The desire to read The Emperor's New Clothes as either a fantasy of critique or a new

---

1   The 'unrequited high school crush' was Frances Elizabeth Coates, and she was reluctant to talk about Hemingway with his first biographer, Carlos Baker. While Hemingway was wooing her, she was 'seeing' another guy while at high school and didn't take things further with Hemingway because she didn't want to complicate her life. But it seems she and Hemingway were corresponding intermittently until the mid-1930s, and he partially immortalised the girl by adopting her name for his heroine Liz Coates in Up In Michigan. See p.241ff for an account of Hemingway's 'crush' on Coates and her take on his character, notably what she believed was his deep inferiority complex.

literary history critique of the fantasy of critique is symptomatic of our assumptions about what it means to be a reader-analyst.

So there you have it [1]: it's plausible, and many an academic might comment 'well, of course!' – but, at the end of the day, what does it mean? No doubt Robbins intended her piece for an academic audience; the less academic reader might well understand individual phrases, in relation to one another, but overall they do challenge comprehension. Concerted reading is very necessary before you even approach having an inkling of what Robbins is trying to convey. As to whether she is 'right' or 'wrong' in her 'analysis', well, it would be easiest to toss a coin to decide. And I suspect, were they honest, most academics would also find themselves a little at sea trying to get a handle on the point Robbins is attempting to make.

It is perhaps unfair to quote an extract of what Robbins writes out of context, though supplying that context would not make the piece much more comprehensible. Yet Robbins and Derrida were certainly 'over-intellectualising' to an alarming degree. Many academics working in English literature departments, adopting the role of 'the expert' whose experience and qualifications seemingly allow them greater insight, might here protest '*sorry, but if you don't have the intellectual wherewithal to comprehend what we are saying, you can't blame us*'; but again, if only it were that simple. All such articles, essays and books do, initially at least, deserve the courtesy of slow, careful reading, and many might reward thoughtful attention and patient consideration; but such is their abstruse nature, it's never clear which might and which might not. It would also help if some English literature academics put a little more effort into trying to achieve simple clarity: even a complex thought should allow the reader a sporting chance of eventually being comprehended (and once again the observation that 'confused writing betrays confused thought' is appropriate). The whole point of 'setting down in writing' is to communicate – whether to introduce a new theory, a different interpretation, to refute a previous analysis or any other number of matters. If the reader is left floundering, still puzzled by what she or he has read – assuming the reader has given it her or his best shot – and is still all at sea, the attempt at communication has failed.

. . .

Given the nature of the subjects scientists deal with – and we might note that 'verifiability' is a cornerstone of scientific work and research – it is essentially straightforward for them to evaluate work by their peers, however complex the subject matter.

---

1   . . . or not as the case might be.

Attempting such 'verifiability' in literary studies is nigh-on impossible, as the variety of different, often contradictory 'readings' show. Furthermore, even slow, careful reading and thoughtful attention don't guarantee that what is being stated – or, better, what is being claimed – is 'true'. All too often what might be regarded as a 'Rorschach effect' occurs when academics read fiction and verse: they gaze intently at a passage and see what they want to see. [1] Debra Moddelmog might even concede that what they 'see' will be what best suits the 'narrative unity and ideological consistency' they favour. Thus Carlos Baker, who decided to regard Hemingway as a 'poet-symbolist', detects symbols everywhere in Hemingway's work; Philip Young insists that Hemingway's fiction reveals the impact the great and small childhood and teenage wounds had on him and might well interpret it all in terms of 'wounds'; John Atkins highlights how Hemingway made a point of distinguishing between the 'natural man' and the 'unnatural man', and the 'political' and the 'apolitical' man, and unsurprisingly can find 'obvious' examples of both. Yet there are no 'right' or 'wrong' answers in a Rorschach test: the very point of the test is for others to gain an insight into 'the psyche' of the subject being tested by noting what she or he 'sees'. Nothing is definitively or not 'shown' by the inkblots. At best the findings and claims of Baker, Young and Atkins might provide an added dimension to, and another point view of, a piece of fiction and might possibly enrich our reading. [2] But such analyses and interpretations are not – and cannot be – in the same class of thinking as work in scientific disciplines and mathematics.

Arguably, it can get even less convincing if at the heart of many analyses by academics is what I earlier described as the 'theology of evaluating Hemingway'. If thinking and writing about him and his work has fallen prey to the marked circularity of logic I outlined – that 'Hemingway was a great writer and a consummate artist, so this seemingly straightforward or possibly even this rather confusing passage must have a deeper meaning than is at first apparent' – whatever is concluded is already biased: once the analytic sleuthing is underway and the elusive 'deeper' meanings are eventually located – as of course they will because they must be – the logic can only dictate: 'Well! Here is even more proof of what a great and consummate artist Hemingway was!' It was in this manner – taking the useful route later blazed by Erich von Däniken of 'possibility, then probability, then fact' – that Baker 'established' and informed readers of his book that Brett Ashley was

the reigning queen of a paganised wasteland with a wounded

---

1   Please don't assume I am not aware that might also be true of me.
2   For some they might even suggest an insight into the personality of each of these three writers.

Caveat lector – Erich von Däniken takes a bow

fisherman as her half-cynical squire.

Although there is no way it might investigated, it would be interesting to know how many times Baker's 'fact' has been repeated over the years in essays, theses, dissertations and exams by students hoping to achieve high grades or otherwise impress. It would certainly add an unexpected dimension to Dos Passos take on

> *a cock and bull story about a lot of summer tourists getting drunk and making fools of themselves at a picturesque Iberian folk-festival.*

Caveat lector – The Rorschach effect

ALL of Hemingway's fiction has been subjected to concentrated textual analysis, but some of the novels and short stories more so than others. The common, central theme of all this work is the assumption that 'because Hemingway is a great writer, there is significance in every detail of a story'. Thus nothing is irrelevant, everything is meaningful, and if we don't at first understand what the great writer is saying, we must dig deeper! As part of the theistic approach to Hemingway I contend is operating, what might be described as a 'Rorschach effect' is apparent. As I have tried to show above when analysing Carlos Baker's readings of some of Hemingway's fiction, such analysis can get out of hand, and one story in Winner Take Nothing, Hemingway's third collection of original short fiction, demonstrates just how unwieldy – and, frankly, ludicrous – such analyses can become. Furthermore, the various and disparate readings of what Hemingway 'was trying to say' in that story underscore my point that they are all subjective and that none is or can be definitive and 'objective'.

. . .

God Rest You Merry, Gentlemen was first published in a standalone limited edition of 300 copies before it appeared in Winner Take Nothing, Hemingway's third collection of short stories, and initially received little attention. When that collection did appear, it did not find much favour – contemporary critics were less impressed by it than they had been with its two predecessors. Damning it with faint praise, in the New Yorker Clifton Fadiman [i] described its stories

> *as honest and uncompromising as anything [Hemingway had] done [but] somehow they were unsatisfactory. They contain strong echoes of earlier work [but] they mark time*

and he added that in Winner Take Nothing Hemingway wasn't 'giving his talents a fair show'. Equally underwhelmed was John Chamberlain who wrote in his New York Times review that Hemingway had

> *evidently reached a point in writing where the sterile, the hollow, the desiccated emotions of the post-war generation cannot make him feel disgusted; he is simply weary of contemplation. He feels sorry for himself, but he has lost something of the old urgency which impelled him to tell the world about it in good prose.*

As for the story God Rest You Merry, Gentlemen, Britain's Times Literary Supplement simply described it as

> *a really terrible story.*

Several decades on, a handful of academics analysed the story again, and although, by implication, they might have agreed with each other that in their view the Times Literary Supplement's judgment was wrong, that was all they might have agreed upon: their very different interpretations serve well to illustrate a 'Rorschach effect' at work. Each analysis also highlights that compulsion to detect meaning and significance in Hemingway's fiction, come what may.

. . .

Like One Reader Writes, another story in Winner Take Nothing, God Rest You Merry, Gentlemen had an unusual genesis. While briefly living in Kansas City in 1931 awaiting the birth of his third child, Hemingway had met and befriended a Dr Logan Clendening, who had written several popular books on medicine and wrote a regular medical advice column that was syndicated in more than 380 US newspapers. The two kept in touch, and at one point Dr Clendening passed on six of the hundreds of letters he received from readers seeking his advice. [1] Hemingway worked two of them up into short stories. One Reader Writes was based on a letter from a woman who discovers her husband had contracted syphilis while away for a year stationed as a soldier in China and wonders whether it is still safe for them to have sex (she describes it as 'being with him'). Apart from two brief paragraphs, one opening the story, the other concluding it, Hemingway quotes the woman's letter to Dr Clendening verbatim. [ii] The second letter Hemingway utilised was from a devout teenage boy distressed by his sexual urges which were leading

---

[1] Quite why he passed these on to Hemingway and whether it was at Hemingway's request does not seem to have been established.

him to masturbate and which made him feel guilty because he believed onanism was a 'sin against purity'. These circumstances were fictionalised by Hemingway to produce God Rest You Merry, Gentlemen.

The story is unusual in that despite being told by a first-person narrator (who appears to be recalling an incident that occurred when he was younger), unlike in many Hemingway stories, notably those featuring his alter ego Nick Adams, the narrator would seem to be of no relevance. Even the guilt-ridden teenager only appears in reference. Central to the story are two 'ambulance doctors' manning the reception room of a Kansas City hospital on Christmas Day. One is portrayed as competent, compassionate and Jewish, and the other as incompetent, dismissive of the teenager and his woes, and Christian. Briefly, the narrator, referred to as 'Horace' by one doctor – which appears to have been a jokey nickname – makes his way to the hospital. The standard assumption of most commentators is that he's a local newspaper reporter doing his calls for the following day's paper. His occupation is not stated in the published version, although according to one commentator, Horst Herman Kruse, it was mentioned in one of the two early drafts of the story, but Hemingway deleted it in his final draft. Kruse believes he did so because he did not want the story to be regarded as autobiographical.

After enjoying a free Christmas Day turkey lunch at a local saloon with his colleagues ('*confréres*'), then admiring a silver car in a showroom on his way, the narrator arrives at the hospital where he is reminded by the two doctors of the distressed teenager he had met the previous afternoon when the young lad turned up and asked to be castrated to rid him of his 'impure' urges. The boy had been sent packing by the Christian doctor, but the Jew had tried to comfort him by reassuring him that his 'urges' were wholly natural. Later, in the early hours, the boy had been re-admitted, now bleeding badly after mutilating his penis with a razor; he had almost died from loss of blood because the Christian doctor was too incompetent to treat him. The rest of the story, which at just under 1,350 words is not long, is taken up by the Jewish doctor teasing his colleague about his incompetence and his lack of compassion, particularly on Christmas Day.

...

Robert Paul Lamb, of Purdue University, La Fayette, Indiana, believes the key to the story is that all four protagonists – the narrator, the two doctors and the 16-year-old – 'misread' everything about the situation and each other. Lamb [1] begins by noting that at the time of composing his own analysis, the story had so far attracted scant attention.

---

1 In The Hemingway Short Story: A Study In Craft For Writers And Readers, Louisiana State University Press, 2013.

Caveat lector – The Rorschach effect

Listing three previous analyses, he records that

> *Peter Hays reads the story as a modern revision of the legend of the Fisher King; Julian Smith sees it as an analeptic tale told by Jake Barnes of The Sun Also Rises with the narrator's identity withheld; and George Monteiro believes that its main interest lies in the light it sheds on Hemingway's attitude toward Christianity and the medical profession but faults it for having an unnecessary and insubstantial first-person narrator who is not meaningfully connected to the plot.*

Lamb does not pass direct judgment on their conclusions, except obliquely when he describes their conclusions as 'speculative' and those of Smith is 'wildly speculative'; but he insists that all three miss the central point: that Hemingway's 'odd tale' is all about the problems of reading a text and the consequences of misreading. Hays, Smith and Monteiro are all on the wrong trail, he writes, because the story is specifically

> *about semiotic confusion, a confusion caused by the failure of signifiers to point to appropriate signifieds (not merely the subtle forms of slippage that concern deconstructionists, but the sorts of wholesale aberrations that would bother most folks), and about characters who employ the wrong inter-texts or misapply sign systems in their efforts to interpret signifiers.*

As far as Lamb is concerned the theme of 'semiotic confusion' was certainly intended by Hemingway who, he argues, begins his story

> *[by employing] a narrative strategy of presenting a description that describes nothing: 'In those days the distances were all very different, the dirt blew off the hills that have now been cut down, and Kansas City was very like Constantinople'. This sentence presents a non-map with which to locate the story by informing the reader that a present-day sense of spatial relations is unhelpful; that the one concrete image in the sentence no longer exists; and that Kansas City can best be imagined through an inter-text, Constantinople, which – even if the reader has seen it – would be of no use since the narrator does not say, aside from the dirt, how the two cities are alike. As if this were not frustrating enough, the reader is immediately told: 'You may not believe this. No one*

believes this; but it is true.'

Once the narrator arrives at the hospital and meets the two doctors

> *the theme of semiotic confusion is further advanced by the problematizing of cultural stereotypes. Fischer is Jewish, but has sand-blond hair and 'gambler's hands'; Wilcox is gentile, dark, and carries a book. The book, a medical guide, gives symptoms and treatment on any subject, and is also 'cross-indexed so that being consulted on symptoms it gave diagnoses'. The incompetent Wilcox is sensitive about the book but cannot get along without it. Fischer, who holds Wilcox in contempt, has sarcastically suggested that future editions of the book 'be further cross-indexed so that if consulted as to the treatments being given, it would reveal ailments and symptoms'. This would serve, he says, 'as an aid to memory'. Wilcox's dependence on the book reveals his inability to read the physical symptoms of the body on his own. Memory (competence within the sign system) enables Fischer to read these physical symptoms, but what if the illness is emotional and cultural rather than physical? This takes us into the heart of the tale.*

Lamb warms to his theme of 'semiotic confusion', with all involved misunderstanding everyone else, which, additionally, explains other 'oddities' in the story: the narrator on his way to the hospital after his free turkey dinner who spots a silver car in a showroom windows 'misreading' the sign *'Dans Argent'* ('in silver'). These are all (says Lamb)

> *the failure of signifiers to connect with proper signifieds, the faulty mastery of sign systems, the employment of inappropriate sign systems, and the triumph of a false sign system*

and

> *this answers the questions of those critics who have seen the story as scant and/or pointless.*

When the Jewish doctor Fischer asks the narrator for 'news along the Rialto', this is, for Lamb, merely

> *a jocular reference that further defamiliarizes the Kansas City street.*

So far so convincing for those who would like to be convinced (and, of course, who have, Carlos Baker might demand, 'sympathy and a few degrees of heightened emotional awareness'). But, bluntly, how 'right' or 'wrong' is Lamb? How 'speculative' or not is he himself? How much of what he contends is 'true'. All of it? None of it? Some of it? Does that question even make any sense? Well, no it does not. Lamb's insistence that Hays, Smith and Monteiro have missed the point suggests in plainer language – he is too diplomatic to say so – that as far as he is concerned they have 'got it wrong'. Yet at the end of the day debating which interpretation might be 'right' and which others are thus 'wrong' is futile: it has as little bearing, the argument could run, on how 'great' or not a writer Hemingway was as would the petty bickerings of assorted courtiers about the 'majesty of a monarch'. Lamb's and the subsequent readings I examine exist in a curious no-man's land of existence, in a limbo hovering between objectivity and subjectivity, even, if you like, between 'fact' and 'fiction'. The whole tone of Lamb's analysis confidently suggests that 'this is what Hemingway meant and was doing', and that Lamb's interpretation is more than a subjective reading and certainly more than just his opinion. Why else would he claim that Peter Hays, Julian Smith and George Monteiro were on the wrong track because their very different interpretations failed to realise that the story is all about 'semiotic confusion'? As for Lamb's claim that mention of the Rialto is a 'jocular reference that further defamiliarizes the Kansas City street', Horst Herman Kruse would turn the tables on him and suggest it is, in fact, Lamb who is 'wrong'. [1]

. . .

Kruse, then of the University of Münster, Germany, insists the reference to the Rialto is, in fact, an oblique reference to the put-upon Jew Shylock in the Merchant Of Venice. As for the loose ends in God Rest Ye Merry, Gentlemen listed by commentators, Kruse concedes that they

have nearly always induced scholars to call the story a failure

but, he tells us, there are no 'loose ends'. In fact, he believes he can show that

Shakespeare's The Merchant Of Venice and the New Testament thus would seem to combine – and ingeniously to complement each other – in Hemingway's effort to transform the 'raw stuff' of experience into a highly complex story in which an incident at the Kansas

---

1   Allusions To The Merchant Of Venice And the New Testament In God Rest You Merry, Gentlemen, Spring 2006 issue of the Hemingway Review.

> *City General Hospital carries the burden of an outright attack on puritanical attitudes in contemporary America.*

Kruse insists that not only can the alleged oddities be accounted for, but what some critics had found incongruous in the story in fact demonstrated Hemingway's artistry. He is convinced the story is essentially a religious tale, and he finds relevant – and necessary – allusions everywhere. He also believes he 'proves' that Hemingway was not the anti-Semite he was often charged with being.

Like Baker and other commentators, Kruse is determined to discover significance in every nook and cranny and, metaphorically, will not take no for an answer. In his analysis, he begins by attempting to show that the alleged 'loose ends' are nothing of the kind and that, on the contrary, the story is one

> *of challenging complexity with a well-developed allusive subtext that accounts for most of its seeming disparities.*

In view of that claim, it might be worth quoting the opening paragraph of God Rest Ye Merry, Gentlemen in full:

> *In those days the distances were all very different, the dirt blew off the hills that now have been cut down, and Kansas City was very like Constantinople. You may not believe this. No one believes this; but it is true. On this afternoon it was snowing and inside an automobile dealer's show window, lighted against the early dark, there was a racing motor car finished entirely in silver with Dans Argent lettered on the hood. This I believed to mean the silver dance or the silver dancer, and, slightly puzzled which it meant but happy in the sight of the car and pleased by my knowledge of a foreign language, I went along the street in the snow. I was walking from the Woolf Brothers' saloon where, on Christmas and Thanksgiving Day, a free turkey dinner was served, toward the city hospital which was on a high hill that overlooked the smoke, the buildings and the streets of the town.*

Usefully for the various academics analysing the story, Hemingway wrote several drafts[1] for its beginning before settling on the version which was published. In the first two drafts, Kansas City is compared with Constantinople in some detail, but in his

---
1   Now held by the JFK Library in Boston.

Caveat lector – The Rorschach effect

final version Hemingway cuts out almost all the references to the Turkish city. All that remains are the – in context cryptic – opening three sentences

> *In those days the distances were all very different, the dirt blew off the hills that now have been cut down, and Kansas City was very like Constantinople. You may not believe this. No one believes this; but it is true.*

There is no further reference to Constantinople or any explanation as to what relevance or purpose mentioning that city might have, but that does not bother Kruse at all. He tells us

> *The published story retains and highlights only those details that help to make up the allusive subtext with its critical thrust*

and he insists the lack of further references to Constantinople is not a 'loose end' but simply that it

> *represent the author's typical process of foreshortening along with a gradual sharpening of the story's focus.* [1]

Possibly; but given that the opening left rather a lot of other commentators, critics and readers wondering what Constantinople had to do with anything, Hemingway's 'focus' was perhaps not quite as 'sharpened' as it might have been.

The two original drafts indicate that the story could well have begun life as a quasi-autobiographical piece, with Hemingway – who had lived and worked in Kansas City for eight months – reminiscing about how the city had changed; then in the third draft, which appeared in print, he changed his mind, cut out such memories and left the reader with the three bald sentences quoted above. But Kruse knows better: these three sentences were intended, he says, to highlight allusions to the New Testament, though as Constantinople doesn't figure in the Bible at all, it is not clear how he thought the allusions were supposed to work. This doesn't delay Kruse, however, and he hastens on to add that the

> *sequence shows Hemingway moving towards a sentence that combines the formulaic opening of the Biblical Christmas story – 'Indiebus illis . . .' according to the Vulgate; 'In those days . . .'*

---

[1] Hemingway aficionados might here choose to suggest his 'theory of omission' was again in play.

> *according to the King James Version – with deliberate alliteration, carefully chosen words and fine cadences. By quietly evoking a foil that will grow in significance as the story moves along, the sentence, in both wording and tone, points to the legendary quality of what follows and, together with the quotation in the title, introduces the author's own contemporary version of the Christmas story.*

This is all plausible enough – though we might again reflect that there's often rather less to 'plausibility' than meets the eye – and especially so given the title of the story which indicates 'a Christmas theme'; but it would also serve as a good example of a putative Rorschach effect: why, apart from Kruse, have other academic analysts and commentators not picked up on that and the other allusions highlighted by Kruse? More fundamentally, given the essence of the Nativity story – for Christians an 'inspiring' and 'joyous' story of the birth of their 'Saviour' – what relevance might it have to an unhappy teenage boy mutilating himself and possibly dying from a loss of blood? Kruse offers no explanation, but is otherwise determined to interpret all aspects of the story as meaningful allusions to the New Testament or Shakespeare's Merchant Of Venice, and to demonstrate that Hemingway's tale has a religious dimension. Thus, for him the '*confrères*' with whom 'Horace' shared a free Christmas turkey lunch are not his colleagues and acquaintances (possibly on other local newspapers), but highlight a

> *parallel between doctors and Christian ministers. The doctors are called 'confrères,' and their sharing the dinner is described formally as 'partaking' in a meal.*

Kruse goes on to suggest that this

> *parallel is strengthened by Doctor Wilcox's carrying with him a conveniently cross-indexed volume called The Young Doctor's Friend And Guide, a booklet 'bound in limp leather' [Kruse's quote marks] that fits into his coat pocket and serves him as an indispensable vade mecum, just as a prayer book of similar appearance will serve a minister in his quotidian routine. After these suggestions, it emerges that Fischer's account of how the two doctors dealt with the case of the young boy and his presumed lust actually dramatizes the responses of two ministers with differing interpretations of their duties.*

Caveat lector – The Rorschach effect

He tells us that

> *Fischer's reference to [the incompetent and uncharitable] Wilcox as 'the good physician' would seem to point to the Good Samaritan of Luke 10:30-37, but Wilcox – in a typical inversion* [1] *of most of such references throughout the story – is the very opposite of a compassionate person and anything but generous or ready to help people in distress.*

This passage also demonstrates Kruse's zeal to parade instances of Hemingway's 'challenging complexity' and the 'story's artistry', and he resorts to insisting there is significance when – possibly even because – Hemingway 'inverts' conventions. Thus

> *Hemingway's description of Doc Fischer as 'thin, sand-blond, with a thin mouth, amused eyes and gambler's hands', for instance, breaks up a traditional stereotype. In fact, as the story progresses and the Jewish doctor is set up as its true moral center, the portrait of his perspicacity and humanity might be viewed as an attempt on Hemingway's part to atone for his former anti-Semitism.*

. . .

More recently, Shannon Whitlock Livitzke [2] contends that the story is about 'alienation'. She opts to confirm that scholars have exposed

> *the story's mythic substructure and [unearthed] its complex negotiation of religion, music and ethical engagement*

and returns to the story's opening that

> *In those days the distances were all very different, the dirt blew off the hills that have now been cut down, and Kansas City was very like Constantinople*

but Livitzke is unaware of any biblical allusions and Christian dimensions; instead she

---

1   How is this inversion 'typical'? And more to the point why would Hemingway, exceptionally, 'invert' a reference? If he had done so, presumably he had a reason, so what might that reason be? Kruse remains silent on the matter.

2   In Those Days The Distances Were All Very Different: Alienation In Ernest Hemingway's God Rest You Merry, Gentlemen. Autumn/Fall 2010 issue of the Hemingway Review.

suggests that the reference to distance is part of the story's theme of 'alienation'. She takes Robert Paul Lamb's lead about 'semiotic confusion' to work up her analysis that each of the story's four protagonists – the narrator, the two doctors and the teenage boy who mutilates himself – forever 'misunderstand' each other and don't 'hear' what they other three protagonists are saying. She says

> *That the boy's panic is rooted in a misguided moralism is less significant than the revelation that the characters are all walled off by private barriers that prohibit true communication, incapacitated by the great 'distances' that leave them isolated from one another.*

Warming to her purpose, she then works in the cryptic reference to Costantinople and writes – perhaps, like many of her peers, slipping into intellectual overkill – that

> *An increasing emphasis on alienation, evident in the Constantinople allusion and the reconfigurations of Kansas City's landscape, suggests that the tragedy is not solely the result of adolescent insecurities or medical malfeasance, but is, rather, symptomatic of a more universal despair.*

A sceptical reader might query that if 'alienation' is so 'evident', why had other commentators not picked up on it: Lamb had reminded us that Peter Hays read the story as a modern take on the Fisher King legend, Julian Smith saw it as an analeptic tale told by Jake Barnes of The Sun Also Rises, and George Monteiro believed it shed on Hemingway's attitude toward Christianity and the medical profession; but none appeared to have noticed the 'alienation'.

Warming to her theme, Livitzke also observes that

> *The story begins with a definitive declaration about the nature of space ('In those days the distances were all very different') and grammatically connects it to specific geographic locales ('Kansas City was very like Constantinople'), suggesting, on one level, a physical connection between the cities mentioned. The mileage between Kansas City and Constantinople has obviously remained unchanged from the time of the boy's tragedy, though, so the opening line also functions metaphorically as a commentary on the state of humanity, on the way people communicated with one another when the events took place... While the Kansas City-Constantinople pairing is admittedly unusual, it*

> *also encompasses East and West, youth and historicity. Given Hemingway's reworking of the introduction and knowledge of both places, it is likely that the cities serve as points of reference that indicate the distressing extent of modern despondency.*

She concludes that

> *The ultimate tragedy in God Rest You Merry, Gentlemen then, is not only that the doctors cannot save the youth from self-mutilation, but, more broadly, that the fundamental impossibility of human connection leaves one human unable to save another.*

Some might be convinced by Livitzke's reasoning; others less so.

. . .

So there you have it: several different and distinct interpretations of the same story, all of which are 'plausible'. Discussing and commenting on the above, I might be thought guilty of a gradgrindian insensitivity, not to say unforgivable philistinism; but we should remind ourselves that the central issue is: 'how great a writer was Ernest Hemingway?' Are we prepared to accept that when he wrote his story God Rest You Merry, Gentlemen he intended to convey all or some of the above? And given that the three interpretations I've examined, not to say the three analyses dismissed by Lamb, all seem to be mutually exclusive,[1] which best matches what Hemingway intended? Is any of them on the 'right' track? What would the man who was ostensibly and ostentatiously unimpressed by 'arty' talk and who prided himself on having a 'built-in bullshit detector' make of all the above? Would he, too, also have been guilty of gradgrindian insensitivity?

Elsewhere I have appealed to the advice of the 14th-century friar William of Occam that 'of all possible explanations, the simplest is the most likely'. It is a simple and useful rule of thumb, and does not preclude that the 'real' explanation could well be revealed as more complex than at first thought; but it might work as a useful departure point when trying to understand anything. Applying Occam's Razor to the various readings of Hemingway's story above would tell us that we can't, in fact, be sure of much at all, especially when one analysis so clearly contradicts another.

For example, Kruse confidently tells us that Doc Fischer's cheery greeting to Horace

---

1   The analyses of Robert Paul Lamb and Shannon Whitlock Livitzke might claim a certain vague kinship, but whether Lamb and Livitzke would be content for them to do so is quite another matter.

'What news along the Rialto?' is a deliberate allusion to Shakespeare's The Merchant Of Venice because Fischer is quoting from the play; Lamb, who is keen to demonstrate that the theme of the story is 'semiotic confusion', would disagree and tells us it is

> a jocular reference that further defamiliarizes the Kansas City street.

So which is it? Some might argue that it is feasible for Kruse's and Lamb's accounts to work on both levels and that Kruse and Lamb could both be 'right'. Friar William of Occam – and I – might opt for a simpler explanation and one that is more likely: the greeting by Doc Fischer ('What news along the Rialto?') is just an example of the common practice folk have of using one of the many phrases which originated with Shakespeare and have since passed into colloquial usage. Other examples might be (from Macbeth) 'Lay on, Macduff' (when encouraging someone to action), 'What's done is done', 'Come what [come] may'; (from Hamlet) 'Clothes make the man' and 'The lady doth protest too much'; (and from The Tempest) 'Fair play', 'In a pickle' and 'Such stuff as dreams are made on [of]', and there are many more. Doc Fischer might well have 'deliberately' been quoting Shylock, but Occam's Razor suggests we might initially consider the simplest explanation. William of Occam might also raise an eyebrow at Kruse's claim that

> whereas Shakespeare's Jew is characterized by his business acumen, his greed, his thirst for revenge, and his insistence on the principles of his religion, Hemingway's counterpart is the exact opposite: Fischer has never given his Jewishness 'its proper importance', as he himself remarks. All of Shylock's negative and supposedly Jewish traits are shown to be those of Fischer's Christian antagonists rather than his own.

This – another example of 'inversion' being supposedly and usefully adopted by Hemingway according to several analysts – might strike William of Occam as nothing but nifty legerdemain practised by Kruse to allow him to pursue his theme (according to what Debra Moddelmog might recognise as his 'ideological consistency'). Yet we are entitled to ask: why would Hemingway sometimes make a straight comparison, but at other times – and for no very obvious reason – make an 'inverted' comparison? A similar inconsistency is pointed out above where Carlos Baker insists that in The Sun Also Rises and A Farewell To Arms 'the mountains' symbolise what is 'beautiful and natural' and the valley and plains what is 'ugly' and 'unnatural', but then without explanation

Hemingway 'inverts' the symbolism in his short story Alpine Idyll. [1] Baker's and Kruse's accounts and those of many others come disconcertingly close to playing with a marked deck of cards.

. . .

Those who come across varied analyses such as the above can, of course, subscribe to whichever 'explanation' they like; but each faces the obvious questions: is this what Ernest Hemingway intended? And if the answer is 'yes', we can then inquire: how do we know? Those questions remind us why the sciences insist on 'verifiability'. In the presentation of each analysis, the affirmative response – 'yes, this is what Hemingway intended' – is implicit; why else has a particular analysis been put forward? So we might then ask: how do we verify it? At this point an English literature academic might finally lose patience and try to brush off the persistent questioner by invoking that useful escape clause *'We think you'll find it's a little more complex than that!'* To this there is, of course, no adequate response: in simpler language the sceptic is being told to stop being such a nuisance and to make her or himself scarce! In fact, the suspicion is the sceptic is perhaps getting uncomfortably close to revealing the circular logic implicit in many academic studies: that 'Hemingway was a great writer, so this is excellent writing' and 'this is excellent writing so Hemingway was a great writer'.

. . .

What might William of Occam have made of Hemingway's story God Rest You Merry, Gentlemen? He might suggest there is, in fact, less to it than the assortment of academic analysts have claimed. Basing his story on the account passed on by his friend Dr Clendening of a 16-year-old who mutilates himself, Hemingway, says William, composed a small, ironic tale of how on Christmas Day, a major festival which Christians celebrate as a day of goodwill to all, it was not the Christian doctor who behaved charitably and with compassion, but Doc Fischer, a member of the outcast Jewish race which does not even celebrate Christmas. William of Occam might even stick his neck out and suggests the irony is further underlined by the 'inversion' of stereotypes: the kind Jew is presented as a white, Anglo-Saxon – 'thin, sand-blond, with a thin mouth' – whereas the incompetent Doctor Wilcox is portrayed as a stereotypical Jew – 'short, dark'; and such a small, ironic tale would work and have nothing to be ashamed about.

---

1   See p.205ff.

As for other elements in the story – the reputed loose ends such as comparing Kansas City to Constantinople, the free turkey dinner with '*confréres*' at Woolf's saloon, the 'silver car' in the showroom, Doc Fischer referring to the narrator as Horace and so on – William of Occam might choose to remain silent. They are indeed loose ends for which there is no obvious explanation despite the disparate – I'm tempted to write 'desperate' – ingenuity of the assorted academics. If pressed a little on the point, William of Occam might give way a little and cite Hemingway's self-declared method of composition, starting a story without a plan to see where it might take him: that he wrote, then discarded, two openings before drastically cutting them and proceeding to the essence of his story. 'What about the comparison of Kansas City and Constantinople?' one might inquire of William. At first tactfully disinclined to comment, William might eventually be coaxed to give his view that Hemingway, now himself familiar with the genesis of his story, believed that, according to his 'theory of omission', the reader would pick up on whatever he, a writer writing 'truly', knew. William might then add – *sotto voce* – that it had not quite come off; oh, and that Hemingway had perhaps not proceeded with the care expected of a 'great writer'.

. . .

At the end of the day, whatever one makes of this or that interpretation and analysis by this or that academic is irrelevant. What is relevant is that by the time these three academics were writing (as well as the three academics dismissed by Lamb), academia had already nominated Hemingway as a writer worthy if its attention; that was an important – perhaps the most important – staging post in his progress from famous, best-selling author to his status as 'one of America's greatest writers'; and once academia had nominated Hemingway as a writer worthy if its attention, there really was no going back without considerable loss of face.

The suspected inferiority complex

A lot of his toughness was real, but a lot was put on to cover his sensitivity. Ernest was one of the most sensitive people I have ever heard of and easily hurt. Most people thought he was too sure of himself, but I believe he had a great inferiority complex which he didn't show.

Hadley (Richardson Hemingway) Mowrer, quoted by Denis Brian, The True Gen.

. . . a great, awkward boy falling over his long feet . . . in life, a disturbing person with very dark hair, very red lips. Very white teeth, very fair skin under which the blood seemed to race, emerging frequently in an all-enveloping blush. What a help his beard later was to be, protecting and covering this sensitivity . . . The inferiority complex remained to the end and with it came the braggadocio and the need to become somebody to himself . . . a quick and deadly jealousy of his own prestige and a constant . . . and consuming need for applause.

Frances Coates, on whom Hemingway had a high school crush, from an unpublished memoir.

THE FOCUS of this collection of essays is not on whether or not Ernest Hemingway was 'a great writer' or perhaps even 'one of the 20th century's greatest writers' – that, as I have suggested more than once, is just a matter of opinion. What is indisputable it the extraordinary global literary prominence he achieved; so for doubters not much impressed by his literary credentials the questions are: how and why did he come to be regarded by many as 'one of the 20th century's greatest writers'? Other writers were immensely popular in their lifetime – of those active in the 19th century writing in English one thinks of Sir Walter Scott, Frances Hodgson Burnett, Charles Dickens, Herman Melville, Wilkie Collins, Elizabeth Gaskell, Jane Austen, Anthony Trollope, George Eliot, Louisa May Alcott, Wilkie Collins, the Brontë sisters, [1] Washington Irving, Edgar Allan Poe, Robert Louis Stevenson, Nathaniel Hawthorne, James Fenimore Cooper and Ralph Waldo Emerson, and there were many more. The 19th century did not, though, have radio, television, streaming networks, online gaming, social or any other all-pervasive media, and reading for pleasure was still one of the main leisure-time activities.

Yet even with the establishment and growth of radio, then television and then the other modern pursuits favoured by many over reading, few writers in the past century achieved the level of celebrity in his or her lifetime that Hemingway did: his repute was truly global. Perhaps Somerset Maugham was as well-known while he was alive as Hemingway, but although acknowledging and admiring Maugham's output, few insist he was 'a great writer'. [2] Hemingway's contemporaries William Faulkner and John Steinbeck were also praised for their work and regarded by many as 'great writers' (and they produced far more work than Hemingway, including what was posthumously published). But although both were well-known, neither came close so achieving the global fame that Hemingway did. Hemingway seems to have carved out a niche of his own, and fifty years after his death his name will still resonate with many who might not even know why. But aside from his popular prominence, what is remarkable about Hemingway, and to some of us baffling, was that he was – and still is – not classed as a mere 'popular novelist and writer' – there were many of those, many now long-forgotten – but as one literature's 'greats'. Why might this have come about?

I have suggested that equally as effective and helpful as his mooted literary ability in the promotion of his career as a writer and as 'a celebrity' were the developments and innovations in advertising and marketing which arrived in the Western world almost in

---

1   The sisters' father was Patrick Brontë, an Anglican clergyman originally from County Down in the north of Ireland. Rev Brontë was born Patrick Brunty, and his surname is thought to have been, with the more common variation Prunty, the anglicisation of the Irish surname of the Ó Pronntaigh clan. This was said in earlier centuries to have been a family of scribes, although when Brunty / Brontë was born (on St Patrick's Day) in 1777 his father worked as a farm labourer. He was a bright boy and eventually won a scholarship to Cambridge and it was while there that he altered the spelling of his name. Quite why has not been established.

2   He was, though, to my mind a better writer than Hemingway. Maugham understood the psychology of his fellow man – his play The Letter which he reworked from his short story of the same name – is testament to that. Hemingway seems, at the end of the day, to have been interested in and intrigued by only Ernest Miller Hemingway.

The suspected inferiority complex

a rush after World War I. Then there was the 'Ernest Hemingway' who was transforming himself into 'Papa' Hemingway before he had even turned thirty: a larger-than-life character who certainly had a facility for relentless self-promotion. As John Raeburn puts it in Fame Became Him.

> *Early in his career, [Hemingway] began to shape a public personality which quickly became one of his most famous creations, during his lifetime perhaps the most famous one.*

Apart from his enjoying fame as a writer, he had come to be regarded by many as a top-notch hunter and fisherman, an expert on wines and writing, a womaniser, a fount of knowledge on everything from gambling to art to baseball and politics. Why? Well, mainly because he told everyone he was, although as Matthew J. Bruccoli reminds us in the introduction to Hemingway And The Mechanism Of Fame, the public played an important part in the process. Bruccoli writes

> *Hemingway got away with his braggadocio because his readers wanted to believe him. Why they wanted to believe him is unclear.*

In a sense, Hemingway's most useful asset was for many years 'Ernest Hemingway', but although biographers have made us aware of the expansive and often wholly contradictory personality which helped to drive his emergence as a global celebrity, there are still some aspects of his life and character none seems to have touched upon or has done so only lightly. Yet each aspect does to some degree illuminate the man and personality a little more and thus suggest how he acquired his celebrity.

. . .

Hemingway's first biographer, Carlos Baker, did much of the spadework digging up the facts of Hemingway's life upon which subsequent biographers based their work. Some of them undertook – or said they had undertaken – additional research, but once the basic details had been established, there was little variation – though often some contradiction – in what they had to report. All tell us that Hemingway was a popular figure at secondary school, Oak Park High (now Oak Park and River Forest High), but that was mainly with his male contemporaries and he was not known to have dated many girls. It seems he was rather shy, both when young and, as several good friends remarked upon, later in life. But we know of two girls with whom he became infatuated. One was an Annette Devoe, and for her Hemingway wrote a poem which began

I'd gladly walk thru Hell with you.

Nothing seems to have come of this infatuation, although Robert Elder, author of The Hidden Hemingway and writing in the Paris Review in May, 2017, tell us that Devoe kept a framed photograph of Hemingway all her life. How significant that was we don't and can't know. Another crush Hemingway had was on Frances Elizabeth Coates, a fellow classmate and a colleague on Tabula, the school magazine; and it is her recollections of Hemingway as a young man which allows us an interesting and illuminating glimpse into his character.

Hemingway fell for Coates badly. She was a friend of Hemingway's sister Marcelline and often confided in Marcelline about Ernest. For his part, although Marcelline teased him about his crush, Hemingway used Marcelline as a go-between to further his cause with Coates. Sadly for Hemingway, Coates was not as interested in him as he was in her and was herself smitten with another Oak Park High pupil, John Grace, whom she married in 1920. Yet while being courted by Grace, she did go on several dates with Hemingway – out to dinner, to the movies, canoeing, skating and even visiting the opera. When Hemingway was taken on by the Kansas City Star as a trainee reporter in October 1917, he and Coates wrote to one another. Although those letters have been lost, we know many details because later in life Coates told her granddaughter, Betsy Fermano, about Hemingway and wrote a short ten-page memoir of him which Fermano kept.

According to Elder, Marcelline blamed Coates for Hemingway's decision to sign up with the Red Cross ambulance service and take off to the war in Europe. However, that is merely Marcelline's claim, and what else we know of Hemingway while he worked in Kansas makes it less likely than not. He was a young man keen for adventure and to get to the 'war in Europe', and he only joined the Red Cross because the other armed services would not take him – or he realised they would not take him – because of his bad eyesight.[1] After Hemingway was blown up at Fossalta on the Piave river and was treated in the Red Cross hospital in Milan's via Manzoni – and even while he was also courting Agnes von Kurowsky whom he persuaded himself he would marry – he and Coates carried on writing to each other. In one letter to Coates he wrote

> *Dear Frances, you see, I can't break the old habit of writing you whenever I get a million miles away from Oak Park. Milan is so hot that the proverbial hinges of hell would be like the beads of ice on*

---

1   Before being taken on by the Kansas City Star, Hemingway had also conceived a plan to head for the West Coast, sign up as a ship's deckhand and seek his fortune to the East in Asia.

The suspected inferiority complex

> *the outside of a glass of Clicquot Club by comparison. However, it has a cathedral and a dead man, Leonardi [sic] Da Vinci and some very good-looking girls, and the best beer in the Allied countries.*

Elder notes that Hemingway seems to be

> *trying to make [Frances] jealous. He's trying to say 'look at all these beautiful women around me', and then he's bragging about trying beer, which would've been sort of the ultimate sign of rebellion, because he grew up in Oak Park, which was a town sort of founded on the temperance movement and was a dry town.*

Remarkably, Coates kept all his letters – the last exchange between them was as late as in 1927 after Hemingway and Hadley Richardson had separated – and according to Betsy Fermano, who has preserved the letters, Coates had a small gold-framed photo of Hemingway. She kept an envelope of newspaper clippings recording his successes, his marriages and divorces, and his suicide in 1961.

Pertinent to what we know about the man Hemingway became in his later years is Coates' description of the young Hemingway. She recalled that he was

> *a great, awkward boy falling over his long feet . . . in life, a disturbing person with very dark hair, very red lips. Very white teeth, very fair skin under which the blood seemed to race, emerging frequently in an all-enveloping blush. What a help his beard later was to be, protecting and covering this sensitivity. The whole of his face fell apart when he laughed.*

Particularly relevant is Coates' observation that

> *The inferiority complex [which one assumes Coates believed she had discerned in Hemingway] remained to the end and with it came the braggadocio and the need to become somebody to himself . . . a quick and deadly jealousy of his own prestige and a constant . . . and consuming need for applause.* [1]

---

1   As far as we know, Coates never met Hemingway again after he left Oak Park, and her claim that the 'inferiority complex remained to the end' can only be supposition based on what he wrote to her until 1927 and subsequently what she read and heard about him in the media.

Boasting, showing off and 'playing the big man' is, of course, common among males on the cusp of adulthood, and Hemingway was far from unique; yet in his case it was a habit which never left him and seemed even to have evolved as he got older. Rather fewer have a 'consuming need for applause', but this was a facet of Hemingway's character for the rest of his life and likely to have been a central driver of his self-promotion. Certainly, her reacted badly when that applause was not forthcoming. [i]

Coates' reference to an inferiority complex is echoed by Hadley Richardson. By then long divorced from Hemingway and married to Paul Mowrer, Hadley and Hemingway's friend in Paris, she is quoted by Denis Brian in The True Gen that

> *A lot of [Hemingway's] toughness was real, but a lot was put on to cover his sensitivity. Ernest was one of the most sensitive people I have ever heard of and easily hurt. Most people thought he was too sure of himself, but I believe he had a great inferiority complex which he didn't show.*

Hemingway's sensitivity – which very often manifested itself as an over-sensitivity – has been noted by all biographers, but none seems to have suggested he might have been rooted in an inferiority complex, either when he was young or throughout his life. If it was – and both Coates and Hadley believe it was – it might illuminate quite a lot about his behaviour. That sensitivity would explain that although he was critical and judgmental of others, often quite viciously, Hemingway could never abide himself or his work being criticized, and he hated being teased. Family and friends say than when he was the butt of a joke, his otherwise keen sense of humour failed completely. An inferiority complex might also explain why as he grew older he liked to seek out the company and acquaintance of the rich and powerful, despite ostentatiously disapproving of them. It might also illuminate why he increasingly demanded almost absolute devotion from friends and acquaintances, and dropped those who did not offer it. Esquire editor Arnold Gingrich, who was close to Hemingway for several years in the 1930s and often spent time with him in Key West, noted that

> *As long as people around [Hemingway] were worshipping and adoring, why, they were great. The minute they weren't, there was a tendency to find others who were.*

An underlying and unresolved inferiority complex would also explain Hemingway's frantic competitiveness, his often almost comical machismo (not least his silly

The suspected inferiority complex

adolescent boast in his middle age about 'we bad boys'), his insistence on being – and being acknowledged as – an expert on everything; and his tendency, as the British say, of 'getting his retaliation in first'.

This mooted inferiority complex would, of course, only have a bearing on his writing in as far as his personality played a role in his writing; but it is a possible aspect of the man that seems not to have been much discussed, and it would help us to understand his relentless self-promotion, proving to himself as much as the world that he wasn't the man he feared he might be. The husband and wife team, psychiatrist Irvin and historian Marilyn Yalom, have suggested that a crucial part of Hemingway's personality and possibly one cause of his chronic depressives episodes was his attempts and his continual failure – at least in his own eyes – to reconcile the man he 'feared' he was with the man he would ideally have liked to be. This caused perpetual psychic conflict, they suggest, and it would be of a piece with a mooted life-long inferiority complex and Hemingway's continual over-sensitivity. [1]

---

1 For more detail on the Yaloms' analysis of Hemingway, see p.89ff.

The linguist

Perhaps the most compelling of [Juanito] Quintana's memories concerns Hemingway as a person: 'Hemingway was strange, very strange. He was a strange man.'

**Jeffrey Herlihy-Mera, University of Puerto Rico,
Hemingway Review, Spring 2011.**

While Hemingway remained devoted to things Spanish throughout a life that could be considered an experiment in trans-nationalization, Spaniards at times ridiculed him for his pretensions of insider status with bullfighting circles and for what some perceived as his poor ability to speak Spanish. According to José Castillo-Puche, Hemingway's friend and biographer, by the end of his life 'Ernesto was no longer a fascinating figure to people in Spain; he had become a sort of joke, in fact'.

**Jeffrey Herlihy-Mera, University of Puerto Rico,
Hemingway Review, Spring 2011.**

IN KEEPING with the image Hemingway liked the world to have of him as a knowledgeable man-of-the-world, an expert on everything and someone who was inevitably privy to inside knowledge was to be regarded as fluent in French and Spanish, and Italian and German are often added to the list of foreign languages he was said to have spoken well. He also liked to be thought of as an expert not just on bullfighting but on Spain and Spanish life and its culture in general. Yet at the very least those claims are all questionable. When Hemingway and Hadley arrived in Paris in December 1920, he did not speak a word of French. Hadley had learnt some at school and is said to have become

The linguist

fluent, but Hemingway did not, and he is reported of have relied upon her heavily. It is not unlikely that over the following ten years he did learn conversational French, although whether it was simply an ability to make himself comfortably understood or whether he was able to hold involved conversations and express himself clearly and succinctly in French is unclear: standards in what passes for fluency vary a great deal, and almost one hundred years later it is impossible to establish how great his command of the language was. Notably, although he did have some French acquaintances, his habitual social circle – which included Gertrude Stein, Ezra Pound, Ford Madox Ford, Archibald MacLeish, Evan Shipman, F. Scott Fitzgerald, Bill Bird, Robert McAlmon and Ernest Walsh – was composed largely of American and British English speakers. The received consensus is that despite his claims, he never bothered to become fluent in French. It is thus unlikely that he read French authors in their native language, and so it is debatable whether he – or anyone else who does not have an almost native command of a foreign language – was able to pick up on a foreign language work's nuances, its subtleties and the hidden allusions intended by the writer, conveyed by the use of, say, a particular idiom, a style of writing and a certain phrase or a colloquialism.[i] Given the circumstances and comparative brevity of his visits to Italy, Austria and Germany, Hemingway's command of Italian and German was also more likely than not to have been rudimentary. It would have allowed him to order a meal in a restaurant or a drink in a bar and possibly to hold a general conversation, but, as many have discovered, being able to ask questions and make simple statements in a foreign language lags far behind understanding clearly and comprehensively what is being said. Hemingway might have persuaded himself that he 'spoke Italian and German', but a distinct doubt must remain.

To some extent the same is true of Hemingway's facility in Spanish, although he consistently claimed and certainly believed he was bi-lingual. In a letter to William Faulkner he wrote

> *Difference with us guys is I always lived out of country . . . Found good country outside, learned language as well as I know English . . . Dos [Passos] always came as a tourist . . .*

but that was countered by Spaniards who knew him. During the Spanish Civil War, the Spanish writer and journalist Arturo Barea ran the Republic's censorship office in a telecommunications building near the Hotel Florida in Madrid where Hemingway and many other correspondents were based. When journalists wanted their reports and features cabled to head office, they could only do so through Barea's bureau, and Barea met Hemingway regularly. Reviewing Hemingway's Civil War work For Whom The Bell Tolls, he writes that in his novel Hemingway

> *commits a series of grave linguistic-psychological mistakes . . . such, indeed, as I have heard him commit when he joked with the orderlies in my Madrid office. Then, we grinned at his solecisms because we liked him.*

In his review, Barea is also critical of Hemingway's claim to 'know Spain'. He does get some details right, Barea wrote, but he also gets a lot more wrong. He notes

> *Reading For Whom The Bell Tolls, you will indeed come to understand some aspects of Spanish character and life, but you will misunderstand more, and more important ones at that. Ernest Hemingway does know 'his Spain'. But it is precisely his intimate knowledge of this narrow section of Spain which has blinded him to a wider and deeper understanding, and made it difficult for him to 'write the war we have been fighting'.*

Writing in the Hemingway Review in 2011, Jeffrey Herlihy-Mera of Puerto Rico University, concurs with Barea and questions how well Hemingway did know Spain. He notes that

> *Hemingway spent [a total of] roughly forty days in Spain during 1923, 1924, and 1925. His prolonged absences between these brief initial encounters with the country are important to understanding his initial perceptions. Each time the author returned to Spain after an average absence of about eleven months, he would have re-lived a 'honeymoon period,' wherein language and cultural barriers remained more stimulating than annoying.*

Quoting other researchers, Herlihy-Mera notes that each visit by Hemingway to Spain could well have been marked by

> *euphoria, enchantment, fascination and enthusiasm during which visitors are still innocent of negativity about the realities of life in the new place*

and that

> *Visitors are open and curious, ready to accept whatever comes. They do not judge anything and suppress minor irritations. They concentrate on nice things . . . such as the food, landscape, people,*

The linguist

> *and country.*

Herlihy-Mera adds that

> *Because each of Hemingway's first seventeen trips to Spain was short – [in total] less than three months long – we might argue that he left each time before he could experience 'culture shock', [a] process of acculturation [that] allowed Hemingway to imagine Spain as a perpetual paradise.*

Herlihy-Mera also argues that in Hemingway's enthusiasm for bullfighting

> *seems to have centered his transformative quest for Spanishness on the example of specific social demographics – male, upper middle-class toreros, aficionados, and their affiliates, figures who often represent conservative sectors of Spanish society ... Concentration on this subgroup exposed Hemingway to certain social, political, linguistic, and cultural realities and lessened his exposure to other – no less typically 'Spanish' – arenas.*

He adds that

> *Throughout his life, [Hemingway] would emphasize his preference for certain wines (Rioja and Valdepeñas, not Cava or Malvasia) and foods (jamón serrano or suckling pig, not butifarra or vieiras), and he adopted particular ways of speaking Spanish (with occasional distinción of c and z, mixed in with seseo), all of which derive from contact with northern regions. We might argue, then, that Hemingway's Spanish mimicry was specific to the taurine subgroup and its regional particularities.*

In short, Hemingway's Spain was a rather narrow view of Spain. As for Hemingway's command of Spanish, Herlihy-Mera quotes the bullfighter Luis Dominguín who said that

> *It was difficult to converse with him ... because his Spanish was extremely poor, even childlike*

but Herlihy-Mera attempts to even the keel and adds

> *Such rejection – from Spaniards in particular – must be qualified.*

> *For centuries, Spanish grammarians have written prescriptive texts that recognized only peninsular versions of the language. The Real Academia Española did not officially recognize Latin American Spanish until 2009 – a remarkable circumstance, as speakers of peninsular Spanish currently comprise less than 10% of the Spanish-speaking world.*

Hemingway, writes Herlihy-Mera

> *lived in Cuba longer than any other place (the United States included), and we might surmise that by 1954 [when he first met Domínguín] his exposure to Latin American dialects of Spanish exceeded his exposure to peninsular speech . . . However, a significant amount of colloquial Cuban language, including variations in spelling, pronunciation, word order, pronoun placement, use of the perfect tense and diacritics – would have been considered 'incorrect' by peninsular standards in Hemingway's lifetime, especially coming from a native speaker of English.*

It should also be noted that at some point Luis Domínguín took against Hemingway after he came to believe the writer was biased towards the skill and abilities of his fellow bullfighter and brother-in-law Antonio Ordóñez. Hemingway biographer Jeffrey Meyers quotes Domínguín as saying that he when he first met Hemingway in a Madrid bar, he was not aware of his reputation as a writer. Dominguin goes on

> *Hemingway was a great personality, but I immediately knew he was an embustero – a liar – when he claimed he had killed water buffalo with a spear, like the Maasai. He had a gigantic ego. He pretended to knowledge he didn't have. I was a rebel, refused to call him Papa and used his proper name, Ernesto.*

Dominguin says that

> *it was difficult to converse with him, especially at his Finca in Havana [in September 1954] . . . because he worked in the mornings and because he began to drink heavily as soon as he stopped writing. There was only a brief period during the first few drinks when good talk was possible. Hemingway talked mainly about*

The linguist

> *women and bragged of his sexual conquests at the Floridita, a Havana bar with an upstairs bordello. He once said he had made love five times that morning. This was obviously absurd. It was naive of him to think that I would believe him, would be impressed by his claims and would agree that five times is better than four times, that quantity was better than quality.* [1]

Such personal antagonism aside, however, Herlihy-Mera also notes that

> *Spaniards at times ridiculed [Hemingway] for his pretensions of insider status with bullfighting circles and for what some perceived as his poor ability to speak Spanish. According to José Castillo-Puche, Hemingway's friend and biographer, by the end of his life, 'Ernesto was no longer a fascinating figure to people in Spain; he had become a sort of joke, in fact'.*

A man as sensitive as Hemingway might well on occasion have been aware of that attitude and, if so, it cannot have pleased him. Pertinently, although his reputed, supposed broad, knowledge of Spain, bullfighting and the country and its culture played and still play a large part in Hemingway's fame and reputation, it seems that they were not necessarily all they were cracked up to be.

---

1   Such bragging about alleged sexual conquests would be of a piece with Frances Coates and Hadley Richardson Mowrer's belief that Hemingway suffered from a bad inferiority complex and felt the need to prove himself. It also echoes the analysis by Irvin and Marilyn Yalom who concluded that throughout his life Hemingway was trying to live up to an unattainable ideal of his self. See p.89ff

The unknown lover and sex roles in bed

When Leopoldina died, Hemingway paid for and attended her funeral. 'A solitary man who accompanied her remains to the cemetery paid for her funeral. He was gray-haired and bearded, an American wearing a short-sleeved guayabera, large moccasins and a pair of very wide baggy pants'. Bulit [Leopoldina's niece] suggests that witnessing the senseless suffering of friends like Leopoldina and finally losing them may have contributed in part to Hemingway's own feelings of hopelessness and possibly his 1961 suicide.

Andrew Feldman, Hemingway Review, vol 31, Fall 2011.

I don't mind Ernest falling in love, but why does he always have to marry the girl when he does it?

Pauline Pfeiffer, the second Mrs Hemingway.

ALTHOUGH Hemingway liked the world to see him as a bit of a rogue, a 'Jack the lad' and a 'bad boy', he was essentially conservative in nature: as they might say, 'you can take the boy out of Oak Park, but you can't take Oak Park out of the man'. He was not a natural rebel. He always made sure his taxes were paid on time and in full, and when the lawyer who handled his tax payments once suggested a ruse to bring down his tax bill, Hemingway sternly told him that he would not tolerate anything unethical. He was as punctilious about his finances as his father, and as his father had insisted when he was still a young lad living at home, he kept detailed records of his spending. [1] Later, he kept similar records of his income and outgoings. Living in Cuba he did, though, make use of his non-domicile status to help to reduce his tax bill, which after the success of For Whom The Bell Tolls became remarkably high; but this was entirely legal. When he wasn't being exceptionally rude and unpleasant, he was polite, charming and chivalrous (and it is suggested this extreme dichotomy in his behaviour was the consequence of a then undiagnosed bi-polar disorder). He also liked the world to regard him as something of a Don Juan, but biographers agree the man from Oak Park did not sleep around and had been to bed with comparatively few women. These would, obviously, have included his four wives, but we know of only four affairs he had while married – with Pauline Pfeiffer, Jane Mason, Martha Gellhorn and Mary Welsh (although when he met Welsh his marriage to Gellhorn was de facto over) – and thus he married three of his mistresses. Furthermore, there is uncertainty about whether he even did have a sexual affair with Jane Mason, despite the heavy hints dropped by Hemingway. Some biographers claim he did have one and that the liaison lasted a year or two; others say it lasted for only a few months; and Mary Dearborn, Hemingway's most recent major biographer, [2] seems to imply there was no affair at all, although she is oddly reticent and uninformative on the matter. Dearborn argues that Mason and Pauline Pfeiffer were very good friends and got along well, and that Mason might have drawn the line at betraying that friendship by sleeping with Pfeiffer's husband. If true, this would echo the moral position taken by Lady Duff Twysden – the Sun's Lady Brett Ashley – who was a good friend of Hadley Richardson and who also drew the line at sleeping with her friends' husbands. Thus for Twysden the unmarried Harold Loeb was fair game to be taken to her bed, but Hadley's husband Ernest was not, apparently to Hemingway's annoyance, and that is thought by some biographers to account for the antagonism which led him to ridicule Loeb as Robert Cohen in The Sun Also Rises.

Hemingway was remarkably good-looking in his twenties and thirties, and once he had overcome his teenage awkwardness and blossomed, his looks, personality and enormous energy attracted both women and men; but in one way he seems not to have matured much at all. In a somewhat adolescent manner, Hemingway was forever falling in love, with the good-looking wives of friends, with Marlene Dietrich (whom he had met crossing the Atlantic and with whom he formed a lasting friendship) and later with two women young enough to be his daughters (Adriana Ivancich and Valerie Danby-Smith,

---

1   His father's strict rules on spending did chafe the teenage Hemingway a little and he often lumped items for which he couldn't or didn't want to account under 'miscellaneous'.

2   At the time of writing.

both under 20 when he met them). None fell in love with him. As for his sexual 'conquests', he claimed that in Michigan he had slept with a local Indian girl, Prudence Boulton, although it seems more likely that she, a girl reputed to have been free with her favours, had seduced the then shy and awkward teenager. [i] A year or two later, in 1918 and in New York waiting to ship out to Europe with the Red Cross, Hemingway told his family that he had become engaged to Mae Marsh, at the time a young, successful film starlet who had appeared in D.W. Griffith's controversial film Birth Of A Nation. His parents were horrified, and he quickly reassured them it wasn't true and that he had been joking (and as the young Hemingway was prankster, that might well have been true). Hemingway recounted another version of his engagement to Dale Wilson, a fellow Kansas City Star reporter. He said he asked Marsh to marry him, bought an engagement ring with money given him by his father and suggested the ceremony could take place in a small church 'around the corner' (in Kansas City). In this telling, Marsh knew that Hemingway was off to Europe with the Red Cross and had turned him down on the grounds that being a 'war widow' did not appeal to her. So where did 'the engagement' take place, in New York or Kansas City? Or was it just another Hemingway tall story? Oddly, in her biography, Mary Dearborn claims Hemingway had indeed known Marsh in Kansas City. She writes that Marsh was staying in the city and in the course of his Star duties – unspecified by Dearborn – Hemingway had met her. They socialised, says Dearborn, but there was no romance because Marsh was involved with another man It is possible she, then 23, might have enjoyed hanging out with the good-looking and engaging 18-year-old trainee reporter, but in fact both Hemingway's and Dearborn's versions are fiction. Almost 50 years later, it occurred to Dale Wilson to check whether the story Hemingway had told him was true and, he says, he tracked down and rang Marsh at her home in California two years before her death in 1968. Marsh told him, says Wilson, that not only was she never engaged to Hemingway, but she had never met him, although she would have liked to have done. Where Dearborn found her 'facts' is not clear.

Hemingway never actually claimed Marsh had been one of his 'conquest', but he did claim Kate Smith, the older sister of his Michigan friend Bill Smith, had been. Though this is also unlikely, we have no way of knowing the truth. Kate Smith was almost eight years older than Hemingway, an age difference more marked when the male involved is in his teenage years. Kate was also a friend of Hadley Richardson from when both attended Bryn Mawr College in Pennsylvania (though Hadley did not graduate), and it was through Kate, a Hemingway flatmate in Chicago, that he met Hadley when she came to visit Kate. Attempting to substantiate his image as a stud Hemingway also claimed – or, better, strongly hinted – that he had slept with the owner of a small pension in

Taormina, Sicily. She, he told friends, had hidden all his clothes and had obliged him to service her all week. Hemingway is thought to have concocted this account to conceal that in December 1919 he had, in fact, spent the week at a rented Taormina villa with his Red Cross superior, James Gamble, who was seventeen years older than him. He also claimed he and his hospital nurse Agnes von Kurowsky had been sexual lovers. She always denied it, although her letters show her interest in Hemingway was greater than she later cared to admit. As von Kurowsky was not short of admirers, and on the balance of probabilities, his claim is also doubtful. [1] When in Constantinople in 1922 covering the aftermath of the Greek-Turkish war for the Toronto Star, Hemingway says he spent a hot, sticky night with a big-breasted, Turkish whore. This claim is another which is dubious: Hemingway also tells us he was covered in lice and quite ill while in Constantinople, and one wonders whether in that state intercourse with a local prostitute seemed at all enticing. Twenty years later, now living at the Finca Vigia, he liked it to be thought he ('we bad boys') regularly slept with whores – his usual hangout, El Floridita in Old Havana, had a brothel on the floor above the bar. Perhaps he did. He most certainly brought one Havana whore, who he nicknamed Xenophobia, back to the Finca Vigia several times when his wife Mary Welsh was away. [2] One account has it that he arrived at the Finca Vigia with Xenophobia while Mary was at home and he was very drunk. Other accounts have it that he introduced the woman to Mary on Pilar, his fishing boat. [ii] But as Debra Moddelmog insists, when reading a biography caveat lector – there are inevitably many versions of 'the truth'.

In the last decade of his life, Hemingway regularly and openly boasted – often with Welsh present – about all the whores he was sleeping with, so perhaps, apart from these six women, there were several other 'lovers'. To that mooted number, however, one should add a seventh, one Leopoldina Rodriguez.

. . .

Rodriguez is notable in several ways, not least in that of all Hemingway's biographers only Carlos Baker mentions her in his work. Why the other major English-language biographies ignore her existence is unclear, although we might well guess; Andrew

---

1   Von Kurowsky also advised Hemingway to turn down Gamble's invitation for him to become his secretary and companion for a year in Europe, all expenses paid. She suspected the offer had a homosexual motive of which Hemingway then still only 19 and for all his assumed worldliness might have been unaware.

2   Welsh discovered the visits and was furious when she found photographs taken of Xenophobia at the Finca Vigia. That the woman had visited more than once was obvious because she was pictured wearing different dresses in different photos.

Feldman, writing in the autumn 2011 edition of the Hemingway Review, puts it down to the bad to almost non-existent relations between Cuba and the US after Fidel Castro took power which made research on the island difficult if not almost impossible. Thus, Feldman points out, Cuban and Russian biographies of Hemingway on the other hand are quite detailed about Leopoldina and her relationship with Hemingway. It seems he met her at the Floridita bar which he began visiting from 1940 on and where she was a regular visitor. She apparently did sell her body for sex, but it would be unfair to regard her as a common prostitute; and although Hemingway might well have had sex with Leopoldina, the two seemed to have formed a lasting friendship and this was an important one for Hemingway. As Feldman puts it

> *Leopoldina Rodríguez was neither a Floridita barfly nor Hemingway's would-be mistress, but a complex woman with her own history, experiences, and desires.*

Feldman is thought to have been the first North American scholar to be allowed access to the Finca Vigía Museum, and he interviewed many of Hemingway's Cuban friends as well as the Cuban journalist Ilse Bulit, Leopoldina's niece. Bulit was born in 1941 and lived with her aunt and grandmother while growing up and knew Hemingway. Pertinently she says Hemingway paid the rent on the flat where Leopoldina, Ilse and Leopoldina's mother lived and that later he paid all her hospital bills when she developed cancer, and he covered the cost of her funeral. Hemingway's Cuban friends and Bulit confirm that Leopoldina was close to Hemingway and, says Feldman, his portrayal of 'Honest Lil' in Islands In The Stream is a useful description of Leopoldina. She was of mixed African, Asian and white heritage and was born the daughter of a maid to upper-class Cubans. Like many young women like her, she became the mistress of a wealthy man and bore him a son, hoping that he would marry her. He didn't, but he did take her to Paris. There they parted ways and she became the mistress of a Falangist leader who was eventually executed by Franco's fascists in 1936, but who had given her money to return to Cuba.[1] It was enough to allow her to open her own dress shop, but the business did not flourish. Leopoldina was as well-educated as a woman in her position might be, was said always to dress elegantly and, like Honest Lil, abhorred 'unkind words and obscene actions'. She had many well-connected friends and acquaintances – the Floridita is said to have been frequented by many Cuban politicians, businessmen and journalists – and Feldman writes that for Hemingway she was a valuable source of information:

---

1   This was José Antonio Primo de Rivera whose father General Miguel Primo de Rivera had been the Spanish dictator from 1923 to 1930.

> *Throughout the writer's residence in Cuba, Leopoldina was a resource concerning all things Cuban. She appears to have influenced the writer's religious practices as well as helped him to understand and appreciate Santería (an Afro-Cuban religion combined with elements of Catholicism), popular folklore, and other elements of Cuban culture.*

From what Feldman writes and what he was told by those he spoke to in Cuba, it seems that the relationship Hemingway had with Leopoldina was very different to his relationship with three of his four wives and other women. Hadley, Pauline and Mary were accustomed always to bow to Hemingway's wishes and whims, but Leopoldina is reputed to have given Hemingway as good as she got and refused to play up to 'the great writer'. For example, she was especially dismissive of his novella The Old Man And The Sea. According to Feldman (quoting Bulit who overheard the conversation when Hemingway visited her aunt, by then dying of cancer):

> *Leopoldina was making fun of Hemingway and calling him a liar: 'That old man is as false as the perfumes sold at the Ten Cent on Galiano Street. He is just a hero you invented.'*
> *'He exists,' Hemingway repeated in broken Spanish, 'He exists.'*[1]
> *The more Leopoldina insisted that he did not exist, the angrier Hemingway became.*
> *'Both knew their weak points well. Leopoldina was completely exasperated when he yelled at her that she was stupid.*
> *'The women of our family were not raised to accept man-handling', reports Bulit, 'using a sharp tone that I still remember, Leopoldina said, "Let's see if you have the courage of your fisherman after you have your entrails ripped out of you or you are faced with a really desperate situation, as I am now". This retort apparently left the writer speechless.*

Leopoldina was thus her own woman, strong, proud and self-respectful, and although of Hemingway's four wives Martha Gellhorn was also strong-willed and proud, Leop-

---

1   Bulit's reference to Hemingway's 'broken Spanish' is interesting. A little earlier I report how Hemingway's command of the language was perhaps not as good as he claimed it was – he told Faulkner he was bi-lingual in English and Spanish. Bulit is writing of the time when Leopoldina was close to death in the early 1950s, and she would have had no ulterior motive to understate Hemingway's facility when speaking Spanish. There is only one way to interpret the phrase 'broken Spanish'.

oldina does not seem to have shared the self-regard in Gellhorn which irritated many who met her. [iii] Notably, Hemingway seems to have responded to Leopoldina's strength of character in a way which might otherwise seem alien to him. As Feldman writes in his conclusion

> *Their lasting relationship appears to have been one of meaningful confidences and sincere friendship as well as emotional and possibly physical affection.*

. . .

One aspect of Hemingway's personality and psychological make-up which has been touched upon but not much discussed by his biographers is his practice of sometimes taking 'the girl's role' in sexual encounters. He admits it in a comment he inserted in his fourth wife's diary, and it is one theme of his novel The Garden Of Eden. I suggest there is a simple and not at all 'shocking' explanation, and that those who might assume it was the expression of latent homosexuality or that Hemingway suffered from an, albeit mild, gender dysphoria would be wholly on the wrong track. With his youngest son Gregory, however, it was all more complex.

When Gregory was about eleven, Ernest came across him trying on some of Martha Gellhorn's stockings. Gregory went on to become a fully practising transvestite and eventually underwent reassignment surgery to become the transgender woman Gloria. We are always warned not to confuse transvestism with gender dysphoria, but in Gregory/Gloria's case the cross-dressing does seem to have masked an underlying gender dysphoria. Notably at one point Hemingway remarked that Gregory 'has the biggest dark side in the family, except me'. This seemingly revealing comment can be interpreted in different ways, and it is not at all clear what he regarded as his 'dark side', and he is not recorded as explaining what it was.

That the biographies don't much deal with Hemingway's enjoyment of sexual role reversal it is not surprising: it is only in comparatively recent years that sexual matters and less conventional sexual behaviour have been openly discussed. It is possible that an anxiety, perhaps beginning with puberty in the second decade of the 20th century about his apparently less conventional desires in part help to explain a determination to prove he was a 'real man'. The suggestion that Hemingway's ostentatious machismo was designed to hide a closet homosexuality can almost certainly be ruled out. If he was a secret gay, he does not seem to have engaged in any homosexual activity: given the prominence he achieved nationwide – and later worldwide – surely claims would be made by male partners, and it would have been impossible to keep it quiet. [iv]

An element of Hemingway life and a potentially telling influence on his later behaviour is his mother Grace dressing him up in girls' clothes until he was about five (and conversely dressing his sister Marcelline in boys' clothes). [1] But we can only speculate on how much and how – if at all – that was an impact on his sexuality.

As an adult Hemingway developed a hair fetish, and as early as his first marriage to Hadley Richardson he is thought to have engaged in sexual role reversal in bed. In his second novel A Farewell To Arms the hero Frederic Henry and the woman with whom he falls in love with hint at it: they liked to pretend that 'the one can become the other'. That theme is repeated in the brief sexual encounters of Robert Jordan and Maria in For Whom The Bell Tolls and far more explicitly in the posthumously published novel The Garden Of Eden. Most explicitly, Hemingway himself wrote in his fourth wife Mary Welsh's diary that he liked to be one of her 'girls' [sic] and she liked to be 'his boy' during their sexual activities.

Earlier, I posited that Hemingway adopted a full-on macho persona not because he was unsure of his sexuality, but partly because of an inferiority complex from which both his first wife Hadley Richardson and his high school crush Frances Elizabeth Coates believe he suffered. The suggestion by Irvin and Marilyn Yalom that there was a conflict between the 'real' Hemingway and the 'ideal' Hemingway could also be relevant. To extrapolate from their conclusions and the beliefs of Richardson and Coates, one might consider that Hemingway promoted the image of a macho 'Papa' Hemingway who always took charge to distract any attention from the 'real Ernest Hemingway' he feared would not be accepted. And note: it was the presence of 'fear' – whether justified or not – which would be pertinent and central: even a wholly unfounded fear can be debilitating.

A likely explanation for his enjoyment of 'role reversal' might be far more straightforward and sympathetic if we interpret adopting 'the girl's role' and being Mary Welsh's 'boy' as simply relinquishing the dominant role to his sexual partner. [2] Several biographers insist that as Hemingway became older and the heavy drinking and accidents ensured that his health was slowly giving way, the strain of 'being' macho 'Papa'

---

1   Although Marcelline was a year and a half older than Ernest, Grace liked to treat them as twins and even delayed part of Marcelline's schooling by one year to that both might be in the same class, notably dressed identically

2   Such sexual role reversal in which Hemingway might be thought, in traditional thinking, to take a 'submissive' role certainly does not suggest a sado-masochistic dimension: I have come across no suggestion that, despite his preoccupation with violence Hemingway was ever inclined to such behaviour. Given his high public profile from the age of 30 and the macho image he portrayed, gossip would surely have leaked out had there been any instance of sado-masochism.

Hemingway, living up to being image he had created became ever harder to sustain and took its toll. As biographer Jeffrey Meyers observed in the Virginia Quarterly Review [1],

> *The public wants to believe in the existence of a phenomenal human being who fights, hunts, loves, and writes so perfectly. This heroic image satisfies the needs of the public but is irrelevant to the real Hemingway; it tempted, corrupted, and finally helped to destroy him.*

It might thus be almost obvious that in the privacy of his bedroom and with a woman he loved and, crucially, trusted and with whom he felt comfortable, Hemingway found a kind of relief for once not being, or having to be, the dominating, always-in-charge, all-knowing 'Papa' Hemingway. Allowing himself, occasionally, to take a secondary, subservient – and in bed the nominal 'girl's role' – would have nothing to do with 'emasculation' or some kind of quasi-homosexual 'being the woman' quirk. There is nothing to suggest that Hemingway 'secretly wanted to be a woman', and nothing at all to suggest he ever 'wanted sex with men'. At the end of the day his apparent desire to take a backseat is, as it were, perfectly reasonable. [2]

---

1   Autumn/Fall 1984 edition.
2   We might also reflect on the futility of attempting to jam 'life' and its manifestations into our artificial but convenient pigeon-holes and instead put a little more effort in trying to comprehend its infinitely subtle nuances.

A lifetime's work

It may be said flatly that the famous Hemingway style is neither so clear nor so forceful in most passages of Death In The Afternoon as it is in his novels and short stories. In this book Mr Hemingway is guilty of the grievous sin of writing sentences which have to be read two or three times before the meaning is clear. He enters, indeed, into a stylistic phase which corresponds, for his method, to the later stages of Henry James.

R.L. Duffus, New York Times.

The problem was not only that Hemingway was sounding like himself in a manner that seemed synthetic. It was also that the self he sounded like was not the self he any longer was [sic]. Writing for him had apparently ceased to be an act of self-discovery and had become an act of self-resuscitation.

John Aldridge, University of Michigan, on The Old Man And The Sea.

HEMINGWAY certainly left his mark on literary history, but given that we also still recall the work of the Dundee poet William McGonagall, McGonagall did too; so is 'leaving a mark on literary history' enough to justify the appellation of 'a great writer' or even 'one of the 20th century's greatest writers'? What else did Hemingway have to offer? Not much, I suggest: the status he went on to achieve had far more to do with the circumstances of his debut in the books' market and his keen ambition. He did have a certain – as I put it – 'middling' gift, but it was essentially a journalistic gift, not a literary gift. As the very short – and inconsequential, workaday – feature pieces he sold to the Toronto Star as a freelance in 1919 and 1920, then his 'Letters' for Esquire for several years in the mid-1930s, the accounts he filed from Spain in the late 1930s, for the NANA (North American News Alliance) and later the pieces he filed from Europe to Collier's magazine in 1944 and 1945 show, Hemingway had a way with words and an often entertaining turn of phrase; but so did and do any number of print journalists. It's all very well, for example, for enthusiasts to cite the lyrical 126-word long opening paragraph of A Farewell To Arms, but that lyricism is not a sustained feature of the novel, and beyond that passage the novel becomes more or less a journeyman adventure yarn which evolves into, and is concluded by, an unconvincing love story. Enthusiasts draw attention to Hemingway's account of the Italian retreat after the Battle of Caporetto, but this is down to Hemingway's journalistic gifts, not any putative literary ability. Do we learn anything about human nature in that novel? Are there for those who insist that 'profound insight' is essential in the work of a 'great writer' any 'profound insights' in it? No, there are none. Did Hemingway create a list of memorable characters as did Charles Dickens, Mark Twain and others we honour as great writers? No, he did not: as in almost all his work and certainly in all his novels, 'Ernest Hemingway' always plays the central role, whether as Jake Barnes, Frederic Henry, Robert Jordan, Richard Cantwell, Santiago or, of course, Nick Adams. He does put some flesh on the bones of Brett Ashley and, in For Whom The Bell Tolls, Pilar and Pablo – who are both notable as Hemingway characters in being distinct and rounded – and, to a lesser extent, the men who make up Pablo's gang; but at the end of the day they all primarily serve merely as foils to the central character, Hemingway's alter ego, who is always 'in charge' and the one with the expertise and skills.

Once Hemingway had come under the tuition of Gertrude Stein and Ezra Pound, he self-consciously worked at creating a new prose style; yet as most of the work he had produced before moving to Paris was lost when a valise went missing in the Gare de Lyon, we can't compare the 'old' style with the 'new style'. Of the work which might have survived – Up In Michigan, perhaps – we have no way of knowing whether or not Hemingway rewrote it in light of how Stein and Pound were urging him to compose prose.[1] Nor do we know what work he had shown to Sherwood Anderson in Chicago which had impressed the established writer, and nor do we know whether Anderson thought it was 'good' or merely 'promising'. Then there's the matter that a new prose style is not per se interesting or effective: the interest it holds and its effectiveness are qualities over and above its novelty value; and whether or not Hemingway's new prose style was interesting and effective is, unavoidably, again a matter of opinion not fact.

---

1   Stein didn't like the story at all.

A lifetime's work

Furthermore, that prose style was simply not strong enough to survive for more than a few years, and we are obliged to ask 'so what happened as his career progressed?' The only response to that is: in literary terms not much at all to very little indeed. Matthew Bruccoli's observation that

> *Everything he did, everything he wrote, became important because he was Ernest Hemingway*

draws our attention to an odd aspect of Hemingway's rise to literary prominence: as absurd as it might sound, he essentially came to be acknowledged as 'a great writer' not because of the work he produced, but because he told people he was 'a great writer' and his assurance was accepted. As Jeffrey Meyers notes in the VQR (Virginia Quarterly Review) in autumn 1984

> *Hemingway had a literary reputation among ex-patriate writers before he had published a word of fiction.*

Quite why is left unexplained. We know that he showed some work to the journalist Lincoln Steffens while both were working in Lausanne in 1922 – this might well have been one or several of Hemingway's 'vignettes' – and Steffens was intrigued enough to want to see more (which is why Hadley Richardson packed up almost all of Hemingway's work in the valise which eventually went missing at the Gare de Lyons). But as to date there are no accounts by Hemingway's Paris contemporaries that he circulated his work for comment, the puzzle was, as Bruccoli sums it up, that

> *Hemingway got away with his braggadocio because his readers wanted to believe him.*

Crucially, Bruccoli adds,

> *Why they wanted to believe him is unclear.*

Other non-literary factors also helped to boost Hemingway's career and reputation, then and throughout his life: his talent for self-promotion as much as his – quite sincere – conviction that he was a great writer dovetailed neatly with the social and commercial changes underway in Twenties' America. Then there was, of course, the ever-present public demand, especially from the young public, for novelty: Hemingway benefited from all these. With the 1930s came very different social changes, and the course of Hemingway's career in that decade could be seen to parallel America's decline, although far less dramatically. [1] It did not help that the writer who had gained attention for his unusual fiction so soon decided to try his hand at non-fiction and thus rather confused the reading public. As biographer Michael Reynolds put it in a piece for the New York Times almost thirty years after Hemingway's death

> *In the 1930s, when Hemingway moved into non-fiction with Death In The Afternoon (1932) and Green Hills Of Africa (1935), neither his established audience nor the New York Times knew quite what to make of his new direction. His style, once so 'lean', was in Death In The Afternoon sometimes so complex that it was difficult to 'distinguish the subordinate verbs from the principal one,' according to the Times reviewer (who compared the style to Henry James) . . .*

Here, Reynolds' use of the word 'complex' should not, I suggest, be equated with 'intellectual' and 'deep thinking' as, I suspect, some might be prefer and it often is, and thus thought to be a reason to award Hemingway points. Some could be tempted to assume that's what Reynolds wanted to convey, but it's not: after reading Hemingway's non-fiction, it seems obvious that Reynolds' use of the word 'complex' makes it synonymous with 'tangled', 'muddled', 'confused'. This was certainly the view of many critics. In his New Yorker review of Death In The Afternoon Robert Coates wrote

> *To sum up, then: a strange book, childish, here and there, in its small-boy wickedness of vocabulary; bitter, and even morbid in its endless preoccupation with fatality. As far as momentary popularity goes, it seems almost a suicidal book in its deliberate flouting of reader and critic alike, and I feel sure that because of it Mr. Hemingway has let himself in for some hard panning from those who have been most hysterical in praise of him.*

Coates did though, perhaps counterintuitively, add

> *in spite of this, I think it contains some of the most honest and some*

---

1   At no point in Hemingway's life during the Depression did he feel the pinch, and his wife Pauline Pfeiffer's family money – as well as 'hand-outs' from her doting, childless uncle Gus – meant that unlike other writers, most of whom could not live on the money their fiction brought in, he needed no side gig to pay the bills. One wonders how well he, his career and his writing would have fared had he been obliged to 'clock on' like other ordinary joes. He did make money from journalism, but would certainly not have sustained his expensive lifestyle. He wasn't wealthy in his own right until the best-selling success in 1940 of For Whom The Bell Tolls.

> *of the best writing he has done since In Our Time.*

In the New York Times R.L. Duffus did not much agree with that praise when he wrote

> *It may be said flatly that the famous Hemingway style is neither so clear nor so forceful in most passages of Death In The Afternoon as it is in his novels and short stories. In this book Mr Hemingway is guilty of the grievous sin of writing sentences which have to be read two or three times before the meaning is clear. He enters, indeed, into a stylistic phase which corresponds, for his method, to the later stages of Henry James.*

The 'complex' prose of Green Hills Of Africa also reminded the New York Times' Charles Poore of Henry James. Poore observed

> *Some of his sentences . . . would make Henry James take a breath. There's one that starts on page 148, swings the length of 149 and lands on 150, forty lines or so from tip to tip. It's been a gradual development, but it shows at its best in this book* [1]

although he did add

> *The writing is the thing; that way he has of getting down with beautiful precision the exact way things look, smell, taste, feel, sound.*

'Complex'? Is that good or bad? Discuss.

. . .

Reynolds' use of the phrase 'new direction' might similarly be taken in two ways: a 'new direction' might well lead us into interesting and engaging territory; it might equally take us up a blind alley to a very dead end – a 'new direction' is in itself neither here nor there. As many reviewers pointed out at the time, the prose in both books of non-fiction was often not just bad, but sometimes almost incomprehensible; so just how useful was Hemingway's 'new direction', and I'll repeat the question: what happened after 1930? The third collection of short stories that appeared in 1933 was also deemed weaker than the first two; and although Hemingway's third novel did sell well, the critics

---

1   In context 'best' might seem to be an odd word, but that is what Poore wrote.

universally decided it wasn't a patch on his first two. [1] Of To Have And Have Not the English critic Wilfrid Mellers observed that it was

> *such a wickedly bad book that one began to despair of Mr Hemingway's reputation.*

So the obvious question is: was To Have And Have Not also the output of 'a great writer'?

Then came For Whom The Bell Tolls which, at the time, most critics praised, although biographers later pointed out that the reviewers' enthusiasm was as much relief that their erstwhile *Wunderkind* seemed finally to have made a comeback (and thus they no longer looked quite as silly for backing him years earlier as they had looked silly after To Have And Have Not appeared). Eighty years on, For Whom The Bell Tolls has also not survived the test of time. It is very much a curate's egg, as Maxwell Geismar pointed out in the New York Times on the first anniversary of Hemingway's death:

> *Sometimes called Hemingway's best novel, too, [For Whom The Bell Tolls] is a curious mixture of good and bad, of marvellous scenes and chapters which are balanced off by improbably or sentimental or melodramatic passages of adolescent fantasy development.*

Even at the time of publication, F. Scott Fitzgerald was unimpressed and wrote that the novel was

> *so to speak Ernest's Tale Of Two Cities though the comparison isn't apt. I mean it is a thoroughly superficial book which has all the profundity of Rebecca.*

Ten year later came the disastrous Across The River And Into The Trees before, in 1952, Hemingway achieved redemption of a kind with The Old Man And The Sea, although that work, too, divided opinion. But that was it – he published no more original work in the last nine years of his life.

. . .

We are familiar with the huzzahs which greeted Hemingway's work when he first published, and given Hemingway's conventional status that he was 'one of our greatest

---

1   After the poor literary and commercial performance of the two non-fiction books which preceded To Have And Have Not, it might again be apt to ask how much its sales were influenced by the desirability and assumed social cachet of having 'the latest Ernest Hemingway novel' on middle-class coffee tables.

A lifetime's work

writers', that literary cheering gets almost all the attention; the minority reports are rarely acknowledged, but even in the early years some reviewers did strike a less adulatory note. In its evaluation of the first collection of short stories, In Our Time, the Yorkshire Post and Leeds Intelligencer is not just less jubilatory than the cheerleaders in US, but manages to strike a good and fair balance. It wrote that

> *There is vigour, too, and a personal quality of observation in his stories and vignettes; but nothing that one wishes particularly to remember seems to us to emerge from them. The general atmosphere might be described as one of American adolescence – a hard, sterile, restlessness of mood conveyed in a hard, staccato sometimes brutal prose. Mr Hemingway uses his method very skilfully; we feel he is both sincere and successful in carrying out his purpose, but his purpose seems to us narrow and unfruitful – withered at the root.*

Pertinently the reviewer adds

> *[Hemingway] is a natural writer who has not yet found an environment worthy of him.*

Commenting on The Sun Also Rises (published as Fiesta in Britain), Edwin Muir, another British critic, who was writing in Nation & Athaeneum, was also rather less starstruck than his contemporary reviewers in the US. He acknowledged that

> *Mr Hemingway is a writer of quite unusual talent. His observation is so exact that it has the effect of imagination; it evokes scenes, conversations, characters. His dialogue is by turns extraordinarily natural and brilliant, and impossibly melodramatic; when he has to describe anything he has a sureness and economy which recall Maupassant; he neither turns away from unpleasant details, nor does he stress them.*

But Muir then notes that although

> *The original merits of the book are striking; its fault, equally apparent after one's first pleasure, is a lack of artistic significance. We see the lives of a group of people laid bare, and we feel that it does not matter to us. Mr Hemingway tells us a great deal about those people, but he tells us nothing of importance about human*

> life. He tells us nothing, indeed, which any of his characters might not tell us; he writes with honesty, but as a member of the group he describes; and, accordingly, his narrative lacks proportion, which is the same thing as significance.

However, Muir did end his review on the encouraging note that

> [Hemingway] is still a young writer; his gifts are original; and this first novel raises hopes of remarkable achievement.

...

Looking back almost one hundred years, I suggest most of the stories in Hemingway's first collection show promise; other pass muster, and some fail. I can appreciate the impact of Indian Camp, especially how a young lad comes face to face with death. Soldier's Home, The Battler and Cat In The Rain are also effective, but in some of the other stories – The Revolutionist and Out Of Season – something crucial seems to be missing. Other stories do nothing but make weight: to this day I'm baffled by Mr And Mrs Elliot.[i] Hemingway champions try to get him off the hook by claiming that the story was 'a satire'; but what Hemingway was satirising and, more to the point, why, is not at all clear. The Hemingway scholar Paul Smith, who worked at Connecticut's Trinity College and was a founder of the Hemingway Society, was, unlike me, not an sceptic, but he, too was also distinctly unimpressed by the story. He wrote that

> Mr and Mrs Elliot has been both more and less neglected that it deserves to be. One might wish that those biographers who found in it yet another instance of Hemingway's bad taste, callous contempt, and occasional stylistic infelicity had neglected the story altogether; while one might also wish for a larger company of critics who thought of it as, possibly, a short story. Never a story to attract much critical notice, once the object of the story's satire was revealed, there was little more to say except to regret its triviality.

Another tale which deserved no place in the collection – in any collection, in fact – was A Very Short Story. This was another instance of Hemingway being gratuitously unpleasant – this time to Agnes von Kurowsky, the nurse in Milan who had dumped him – and it shows him at his adolescent worst; one wonders how and why it even made the cut. Perhaps as a still inexperienced writer Hemingway was not aware of how

A lifetime's work

pointless, juvenile and dreadful it was; but his Scribner's editor Max Perkins would and should have been, and he should have said so and dropped it from the collection as he had insisted Up In Michigan should be dropped.

. . .

Although in hindsight Hemingway's first collection of short stories might now be seen as something of mixed bag, it was a literary sensation when it appeared in 1925, and his first novel was keenly anticipated. Yet, again in hindsight, one can argue – as I do – that there was less to that novel than met the eye. Parts of it entertain, some of it is padding, and there are some excessively flat and banal passages, although, I am obliged to concede, each to his own: my 'flat and banal' might well be your 'Hemingway's unique style'. Arguably, the work might have been cut and tightened up to become a rather better work; but thus edited, it would have become more of novella; and was keen young Ernest Hemingway even aware that some, perhaps much, of his story was superfluous? I suspect he thought it was all marvellous.

Men Without Women, the second collection of short stories, also demonstrated – for me, at least – why Hemingway was at best a middling writer and not a 'great' one. For example, The Killers is anthologised, much lauded and analysed, but it doesn't quite convince.[1] Half-shut your eyes and ignore – as contemporary reviewers, of course, could not – that it was by 'the exciting new writer Ernest Hemingway', and it reveals itself as a pale attempt to emulate the work of the hard-boiled pulp magazine writers. That nowadays the story receives more academic attention than does the work of those pulp magazine writers – although they sometimes do – has less to do with any literary quality it might be thought to possess than because it is by 'Ernest Hemingway'.[ii] Once Hemingway's work had somehow crossed the threshold into 'serious literature' and the literary world cast about for reasons to praise the story, it gained spurious marks, for example for 'reflecting' the stoicism of the Hemingway 'code hero'. Yet at a technical level it demonstrates artistic flaws, not least in how Hemingway handles, or rather mishandles, the passage of time; and there are niggling lacunae in the story which a more gifted writer might have dealt with.

---

1   Hollywood has filmed The Killers twice, first in 1946 starring Burt Lancaster and Ava Gardner and directed by Robert Siodmak; and in 1964, starring Lee Marvin, Angie Dickinson, Ronald Reagan and John Cassavetes, and directed by Don Siegel. The first film was based on Hemingway's short story but with an expanded plot; and the second has a wholly different storyline. A film version which is truest to the original was a short made as a college project in 1956 by the Russian directors Andrei Tarkovsky and Aleksandr Gordon.

The theme of stoicism in the 'code hero' also turns up in that volume's The Undefeated, a tale about an ageing bullfighter on the skids. It is a touching story, but it, too, is flawed: Hemingway gives far too much space to describing the bullfight itself, to the point where his enthusiastic, in context excessively detailed, blow-by-blow account of the encounter takes over and almost suffocates the story itself. The tale is about the ageing man's stoicism and fate, not his last bullfight, and better and more skilful writer – and certainly a more aware artist – might well have realised the imbalance and, with his readers in mind, curbed his own enthusiasm.

Another highly praised story in the second collection that also suffers from artistic flaws is Hills Like White Elephants. It deals with a young man and his partner – whether wife or lover we are not told – who are sitting on a station platform waiting for a train. Notably, the young man is – or is generally assumed to be – trying to persuade the young woman to abort the child she is carrying. This was distinctly shocking stuff for 1927 fiction to deal with and at the time was taken as another sign that Hemingway 'was modern' and thus in the eyes of many 'a modernist'. It is, superficially, a 'good read' and perhaps to an extent the subject matter shields the flaws; but they are certainly present. Again Hemingway fails to convey the passing of time convincingly and again there are odd, niggling lacunae in the story. The conversations between the two characters as the man insistently tries to persuade the woman to have an abortion are telling, yet the exchanges as presented by Hemingway would have been concluded in just a few minutes. Thus the couple either also talk of other matters – not recorded – or they sit in silence; and given the testy, uncomfortable atmosphere, their other chit-chat or possibly a silence would have been strained and arguably of potential dramatic interest; but it is left unexamined and ignored. The story also exhibits an occasional quirk in Hemingway's writing: when he seems at a loss as to what next to do with a character, he makes them 'have a drink'; so while waiting for their train, the man and the woman each has two glasses of beer and, in addition the man treats himself to an anisette. This is oddly out-of-kilter: the pair were waiting long enough for each to drink two glasses of beer which would not necessarily have been finished off in a matter of minutes. Were they drinking in silence, perhaps in an uncomfortable silence? If they were talking, what else were they discussing? Either way, I suggest, it would have been pertinent and Hemingway might have accounted for and incorporated that passing of time in his narrative. Quite how he could have dealt with it is not the reader's concern: it is a matter for the author to deal with in whatever way she or he feels fit. All we, the reader, know is that there is 'something missing'. Hemingway might have believed that his 'iceberg theory' was here in play and that if he was writing 'truly', it would all somehow

A lifetime's work

be conveyed to the reader. Well, here and in other stories, it is not: these lacunae ensure that overall the story doesn't quite gell; the story is too syncopated, and so it, too, doesn't fully convince.

...

Some stories in Men Without Women do work: Canary For One, A Simple Enquiry and – a rather odd but effective tale – A Pursuit Race; several are hit and miss. With its rather tacky humour revolving around a mountain dweller using the corpse of his newly-deceased wife, stiffened by the winter cold, as somewhere to hang his lantern An Alpine Idyll might appeal to adolescents, but yet again what is the point of the tale? Ever keen to 'prove' just how 'great' a writer Hemingway, the story has been interpreted this way and that to indicate 'significance'. Earlier, I outlined Carlos Baker's insistence that An Alpine Idyll exhibits the artistry of Hemingway's 'psychological symbol-building'; but as Baker's account of its supposed symbolism flatly contradicts another account he gives of the same symbolism elsewhere, there is a distinct impression of Baker trying just a little too hard.[1] Then there are other stories in the collection, for example A Banal Story and especially Today Is Friday, that fall flat very badly. Pertinently, these stories were written before 1929 and, according to Matthew Bruccoli, they were part of Hemingway's 'best' work; one reading of what Bruccoli says might certainly thus be that what Hemingway produced later was not up to the same standard.

One might argue that not everything can be pitch-perfect, yet whether fairly or not, a reasonably consistent pitch-perfection is what we are accustomed to expect in the work of those we choose to regard as 'great artists' – that is why we agree to rate them as 'great'. With other 'greats', in whatever field, their 'mediocre' work is often of a higher standard than the 'best work' of their less able peers; and it is with such 'great' men and women that we are expected to rank Hemingway

As part of Hemingway's pre-1929 'best work' Bruccoli also included his second novel, A Farewell To Arms, and it, too, could be said to stand proud with fiction of its kind: but there's the rub – what 'kind' would that be it? It would be more appropriate to class the novel as an 'adventure story' than as 'great literature'. The derring-do of its main protagonist – as usual Hemingway in fictional form – is entertaining enough and the story rattles along; but the novel's overwhelming flaw is its 'love story': it is quite

---

1   It betrays the circularity discussed in the theology of Ernest Hemingway earlier which to this day dictates that because he was 'a great writer', there has to be significance and artistic worth somewhere in the story: all we have to do is track it down. That the story might not be particularly good is never considered.

awful and, as one critic said of the even less convincing 'love story' in For Whom The Bell Tolls, it is 'adolescent fantasy'. Hemingway was hopeless at conveying love and romance. In The Sun Also Rises he more or less managed to persuade the reader that Jake Barnes and Brett Ashley were sweet on each other – though theirs is certainly no profound love – but he fails in his subsequent three novels. Catherine Barkley doesn't even make it into two dimensions, let alone three, and she is so drippy that you want to strangle her. Furthermore, although Frederic Henry's and Catherine's love affair begins in and evolves out of the war, the novel's two themes – love and war – lose each other entirely: in artistic terms neither has any bearing on the other and they become wholly independent; by the end of the novel the war is forgotten. So what is the novel's central theme? What is it about? War in its many manifestations? Or a love affair, tragic in that 'the girl' dies giving birth? Either way the novel sells the reader short: the war element is left hanging, and despite the tragic ending with the heroine's dying in childbirth, the love element is far too thin and unconvincing to sustain the novel. [1]

The lack of cohesion of the two themes did not just trouble Max Perkins – the novelist Owen Wister was also bemused by it. He had been asked by Perkins to supply an endorsement as part of Scribner's marketing campaign and submitted a piece of blurb that rang with praise for the novel; privately he was not as enthusiastic. As biographer Michael Reynolds records

> *In a separate statement to Perkins, Wister voiced his concerns about Hemingway's use of the first-person narrator and the novel's conclusion, suggesting that the nurse's death be softened and that the ending bring together the two themes of love and war. Perkins agrees completely. The book's flaw, he tells Wister, is that the war story and the love do not combine.*

On the basis of these two novels and two collections of short stories and their re-evaluation almost a century, a re-evaluation free of the razzmatazz they created when they were published, it would certainly not be unfair to describe Hemingway as merely a

---

1   Once Frederic and Catherine had reached the safety of Switzerland and established themselves in a small hotel or pension in the mountains, they would have waited for at least four or five months before Catherine came to term. Yet we get no account at all of what they got up to in this time. Would one be necessary? Perhaps not, but I for one would be curious to know how a couple who did not really know each other well rubbed along in comparative isolation. As her pregnancy progressed, Catherine might have become increasingly uncomfortable, cumbersome and possibly irritable, and Frederic might well have felt at a loose end. An outburst of short temper now and then would have been understandable, but with no details to go on, we can only assume there was no trouble in paradise and the two love-birds passed their time cooing sweet nothings to each other.

middling writer. But here's the problem: in Bruccoli's view these two novels and two short story collections were Hemingway's 'best'. So what might 'not Hemingway's best' look like? Well, he showed just that in the books what came next, Death In The Afternoon, Green Hills Of Africa and a third novel.

. . .

Max Perkins was reputedly not overly pleased when Hemingway announced that his next book would be a guide to bullfighting, although to be fair almost as soon as they met, Hemingway had made it clear to Perkins that writing such a guide was on his agenda; but the excellent sales of A Farewell To Arms had pitched Hemingway into a strong position, so Perkins went along with the plan. Although no such guide so far existed for the English reader, Hemingway imagined he was producing something greater than a mere guide: his new work was also intended to be his dicta on writing and literature. It is not just my view that Death In The Afternoon — which did not sell well and by some accounts barely broke even — is a tedious read. As several critics pointed out, for a 'great writer' Hemingway did not write at all well in Death In The Afternoon. The reviewer of the Honolulu Star-Bulletin noted that

> *In his enthusiasm for the art of tauromachy, Mr Hemingway has departed, sadly, in places from his usually clear and forceful style. His earnestness in trying to put over his idea apparently has caused him to neglect pruning. The result is a surprising loss of conciseness, and occasionally a deplorably cluttered syntax.*

Those who here might object that Hemingway's reputation as 'a great writer' rests on his fiction rather than his non-fiction should note that was certainly not what the man himself believed: by the early 1930s he considered himself to be an all-round 'man of letters'. That conviction was not just demonstrated in his confident pronouncements *de haut* on what 'good writing' was and should be, but what he told friends and acquaintances in letters. The literary establishment was far less persuaded. Less than six years after R. L. Duffus had praised Hemingway's 'terse, precise and aggressively fresh' prose, he complained in the New York Times that in Death In The Afternoon

> *Mr Hemingway is guilty of the grievous sin of writing sentences which have to be read two or three times before the meaning is clear.*

Duffus' criticism is especially pertinent given that as a former journalist Hemingway would – or at least should – have been aware of the imperative for clarity in such a work; so it is tempting again to ask whether he even re-read what he had written. That might seem to be an outrageous question, of course, and he should most certainly have read the galley proofs; but if he had, would he not have noticed how confusing some of his prose was? If he did not notice, why not? Aren't we assured that the mark of a 'great artist' is that he or she takes infinite pains? Even less successful than Death In The Afternoon was Green Hills Of Africa, Hemingway's second non-fiction work, an account of his East African safari. This was often equally badly written. Edmund Wilson noted his astonishment that

> *There is one passage which is hardly even intelligible – the most serious possible fault for a writer who is always insisting on the supreme importance of lucidity.*

Once again: what was going on? Do Hemingway stalwarts insist on counting these two books as 'the work of a great writer'?

. . .

Hemingway had published a third collection of original short stories two years before Green Hills Of Africa appeared. Its sales were more gratifying than those of Death In The Afternoon, but some critics were less impressed and rather underwhelmed by the collection, and some felt that success and the good life had rather blunted Hemingway's sensibilities.[1] Writing in Nation, William Troy did not pull his punches

> *It is among Mr Hemingway's admirers that the suspicion is being most strongly created that the champion is losing, if he has not already lost, his hold.*

Even Malcolm Cowley, a lifelong cheerleader, was disappointed. Reviewing the 1938 publication by Scribner's of Hemingway's play The Fifth Column and The First Forty-Nine Stories, he admitted the pieces of short fiction in Winner Take Nothing were

> *a rather meagre collection.*

Unlike the first two volumes of short stories, this third collection had more misses than hits, and even the more successful stories showed signs of laxity. For example, as the young Turk in Paris under the tutelage of Ezra Pound, Hemingway had made a great

---

1   Ironically, as Hemingway described in The Snows Of Kilimanjaro, a story he published two years later in Esquire magazine, that had increasingly also become his concern.

A lifetime's work

deal – following Pound's guidance – of ostentatiously and self-consciously eschewing adjectives and adverbs. This had been one feature of his prose which less than a decade earlier had moved a New York Times reviewer to laud it as

fibrous and athletic, colloquial and fresh, hard and clean . . .

Yet by 1933 when Winner Take Nothing appeared, his scorn for such linguistic shortcuts had vanished, and the stories contain some true horrors: in The Capital Of The World, we are presented with a young woman 'laughingly' refusing, priests being 'hurriedly' conscious and one waiter walking 'swingingly' away. There is nothing at all 'wrong' with these constructions – after all, as the liberal in me is obliged to insist, each to his own – but they do smack more of work produced in the first semester of a creative writing course than from the pen of 'one of America's greatest writers'. Even The Capital Of The World, one of the collection's better stories, has a notable flaw – it is oddly amorphous: what is it about? The story begins by reflecting its title in that we are presented with a cross-section of guests at a small Madrid lodging house as one might find at random in a capital city. The lives of several are described, and we wait to find out how the apparent theme will play out – but then the story goes off at a distinct tangent. Its focus becomes a young waiter with ambitions to become a matador, who bleeds to death when a piece of juvenile tomfoolery goes wrong: the story's other protagonists are forgotten and disappear, abandoned. In view of the story's tragic outcome, its title, The Capital Of The World, is oddly irrelevant. Would not a 'great writer' revisit a work once the first draft is concluded, reappraise and it revise and shape it to create a coherent and self-contained whole? There is, after all, no deadline, and the writer can take as long as he or she likes to produce whatever effect he or she wants. What effect was Hemingway trying to achieve in that story? It is impossible to know.

Hemingway was, I contend, by now well on the slide down from the apex he had once commanded. Despite his earlier boasts that he spent hours working 'hard' on his writing, searching for the right word and revising his work, one is often left with the impression that he had all too often taken to cutting corners. This is apparent in another of that third collection's more celebrated stories, A Clean, Well-Lighted Place, notable for its 'insoluble problem'. I have dealt with the 'problem' and the various 'solutions' earlier, but in view of Hemingway's pious claims, it is worth repeating that the several ingenious solutions offered are all flatly contradicted by the findings of one academic who simply did bit of basic groundwork. He examined the story's original draft and concluded that it was written in haste and that the few revisions Hemingway made were done on the same or the following day: this had led to an inconsistency in the work that had come to be labelled 'an insoluble problem'.

Nor did 'the great writer' redeem himself with his third novel To Have And Have Not. It was essentially just another tepid adventure tale a 'middling writer' could have written standing on his head. [1] Disjointed, neither fish nor fowl, the apparently socially relevant scenes of 'the rich haves' which Hemingway intended should contrast the life of Harry Morgan, one of 'the poor have nots', float around helplessly towards the end of the novel and are notably untethered to the 'adventure' elements in the story. Though the public liked the novel and bought it – after all, it was by the now famous Ernest Hemingway – the critics saw it as an embarrassing mess. [2] Typical of their dismay was the sentiment of J. Donald Adams in his New York Times review. He wrote that

> *Mr. Hemingway's record as a creative writer would be stronger if [To Have And Have Not] had never been published.*

The 'great' writer's already flagging career had taken yet another downturn – but then, *mirabile dictu*, came For Whom The Bell Tolls and that career was unexpectedly and, in sales terms at least, spectacularly revived.

...

Frankly, despite its reputation, For Whom The Bell Tolls comes nowhere close to being 'great literature' and must certainly it can also be regarded as the work of a 'middling writer': it is essentially just another, often rather flabby and overwritten, adventure yarn interlarded with a 'romance' that would have been risible in a bad chick-lit novel. Furthermore, in his new novel Hemingway, who had been noted for his 'command' of dialogue, quite simply forgot how to write dialogue. He had already been taken to task on that score in 1937 by Donald Adams who had previously written that the dialogue in To Have And Have Not was

> *false to life, cut to a purely mechanized formula. You cannot separate the speech of one character from another and tell who is speaking. They all talk alike.*

In For Whom The Bell Tolls Hemingway employed dialogue extensively, but it is often thoroughly banal and comes across as cheap padding. Many passages badly overstay

---

1   Despite that, Hemingway had trouble completing it: though it was cobbled together from two previously published short stories with a longer tail-piece, it took him two years to finish.

2   One might here again wonder how many copies of the novel were brought because it was 'the latest from Ernest Hemingway' and would grace a coffee table for a while, but would otherwise remain unread.

A lifetime's work

their welcome and become very dull. Hemingway also tried to convey the coarse, obscene language he wanted his characters continually to use without raising objections from his publisher; but the method he chose to do so falls flat and he simply produced oddly stilted language which jars every time. The same is true of his attempts to render idiomatic Spanish in English – it just sounds extraordinarily silly. Technically For Whom The Bell Tolls is also deeply conventional – the one-time supposed 'modernist' had long since left the building: what elements in For Whom The Bell Tolls might be thought 'modernist'? The novel is generally told in the first-person, and although Hemingway uses a technique of allowing others to narrate, notably Pilar when she describes the brutal massacre of Fascist sympathisers at the hand of Loyalists, [1] he also resorts to the point-of-view of an all-knowing narrator; it, too, jars. The alleged modernist again also employs – Ezra Pound and his careful tuition now be damned to Hell – a great many adverbs, those qualifiers all-too-often used as shorthand by lazy writers. Hemingway seems, too, to have forgotten his own strictures on writing, especially his condescending instruction to Scott Fitzgerald in the early 1930s when Scott's star was waning and his was waxing, that he should 'leave out the irrelevant stuff'. Sadly, there's a great deal of 'the irrelevant stuff' in For Whom The Bell Tolls. [2] One wonders what Ezra Pound thought of Hemingway's celebrated prose if by chance he ever got to read the novel. Although For Whom The Bell Toll restored Hemingway's reputation as a 'successful writer', he did not publish anything else for the next ten years until his fifth novel, Across The River And Into The Trees appeared. [3] After the runaway success of For Whom The Bell Tolls it was highly anticipated, but universally deemed a complete stinker; one of the kinder comments about Across The River And Into The Trees came from the British critic Cyril Connolly who observed that

> *It is not uncommon for a famous writer to produce one thoroughly bad book. . .* [4]

Yet while he was writing it, Hemingway was convinced it was his best work so far. Biographer Mary Dearborn believes that delusion came about because while he was writing

---

1   It is one of the novel's few successful elements and might have become one of Hemingway's better short stories.

2   What is and is not 'relevant' is certainly contentious, but just as Dos Passos compared the writing in The Sun Also Rises in part to a travel book, much of For Whom The Bell Tolls is simply descriptive – and dull – and does comes across as adding nothing to the novel.

3   One suggestion is that he was worried he could not repeat the success of For Whom The Bell Tolls, although we should also remember that in the first three years of the 1940s he was also involved in his 'spy network' and 'submarine hunting' and this took up much of his time.

4   I have not been able to discover which other famous writers Connolly had in mind.

the novel, Hemingway was in a distinct manic phase of a bi-polar cycle. The critical panning the work was given meant that once again the 'great' writer seemed to have lost his crown – only to stage second comeback two years later in 1952 with his novella The Old Man And The Sea. Given that it became a staple of high school English classes, not least because it was short and written in simple English, it is perhaps the Hemingway work with which most are familiar. This short account about an old and unlucky fisherman was both a public as well as a critical success at publication, though yet again there were the sceptics. [1] Writing in the Saturday Review nine years after Hemingway's suicide, the critic and English literature professor, John Aldridge, sums up The Old Man And The Sea rather well. The novella, he writes,

> *was, in short, a safe book in the sense that it was made up of the best of Hemingway's old market-tested materials, stylistic and dramatic effects which at one time had been arrived at with some real originality and risk through a vital engagement of life, but which were now merely postures and autographs of famous but dead emotions. The problem was not only that Hemingway was sounding like himself in a manner that seemed synthetic. It was also that the self he sounded like was not the self he any longer was. Writing for him had apparently ceased to be an act of self-discovery and had become an act of self-resuscitation.*

More to the point, as Hemingway did not publish any more work in the final nine years of his life, the success of The Old Man And The Sea ensured at least that he ended his active writing career on an up-note.

That last work was certainly an improvement on any fiction or non-fiction Hemingway had written since 1929, although it, too, is certainly not flawless. Like me, some might have a distinct distaste for the story's cloying sentimentality, and the Christian symbolism in it is not just unsubtle but curiously out-of-context. Reviewing the story in the Virginia Quarterly Review at the time, John Aldridge felt that

> *the prose [in The Old Man And The Sea] . . . has a fabricated quality, as if it had been shipped into the book by some manufacturer of standardized Hemingway parts.*

---

1   Some biographers have suggested that, as with the reception of For Whom The Bell Tolls, when the novella appeared after Across The River And Into The Trees had misfired so badly, many critics were relieved Hemingway had once again pulled his fat out of the fire.

A lifetime's work

Thirty years later writing in The Atlantic, James Atlas was remorselessly downbeat:

> *The end of Hemingway's career was a sad business. The last novels were self-parodies, none more so than The Old Man And The Sea. The internal monologues of Hemingway's crusty fisherman are unwittingly comical ('My head is not that clear. But I think the great DiMaggio would be proud of me today'); and the message, that fish are 'more noble and more able' than men, is fine if you're a seventh grader.*

That, in sum, was Hemingway's published output between 1925 and 1952: two for their time quasi-original novels and two collections of short stories, two rather odd tomes of non-fiction, a third, rather less impressive short story collection followed by two mediocre adventure novels, then a truly bad novel and finally a somewhat mawkish and sentimental novella. It is not a long list. William Faulkner, whom Hemingway considered a true rival, published twenty novels in a writing career that was only a year longer than Hemingway's. [iii] Was that output, or even just some of it, really the work of 'a great writer', 'one of the 20th century's greatest writer'?

Describing his career as 'starting at the top and working his way down' might be an unsubtle way of putting it, but it does seem to hit the nail on the head. It is, though, important to remind ourselves that this was the work he published before he died. After his death more was to come.

Work published posthumously

[Islands In The Stream] consists of material that the author during his lifetime did not see fit to publish; therefore it should not be held against him. That parts of it are good is entirely to his credit; that other parts are puerile and, in a pained way, aimless testifies to the odds against which Hemingway, in the last two decades of his life, brought anything to completion.

John Updike, on Islands In The Stream.

Now that it is possible to assess the banked fiction [i.e. Islands In The Stream and The Garden Of Eden], it is clear that Hemingway held it back because he knew that it wasn't good enough for him.

Los Angeles Times review of The Garden Of Eden.

So that whirling sound we hear during this 100th-anniversary month of his birth is Papa Hemingway rotating in his grave over the antics of his son Patrick and the corporate juggernaut that's selling off what he never meant to have people read.

Frederick Zackel review of The Dangerous Summer, January Magazine.

The famous style occasionally flares into fineness, but is really no more than a pretender to its former royalty. Sentences are either casually functional or busily functional; in the latter category are many sentences that are completely uninteresting except that they carry on as if they were very interesting, as if they were little lozenges of lyricism when in fact they only leak information.

James Wood review of The Dangerous Summer, New York Times.

As a novel, however, its merits are dubious: the writing – which dates from roughly the same period as such lesser works as Islands In The Stream, The Old Man And The Sea and The Dangerous Summer – is frequently synthetic and contrived; the characters, sketchily defined; the storyline, by turns static and abruptly melodramatic.

Michiko Kakutani reviewing The Garden Of Eden in the New York Times.

The work was wildly uneven, and much of it was embarrassingly weak, though portions had sustained strength and suggested a new sort of Hemingway, one whom E. L. Doctorow would characterize in his review of the book as reaching for a fuller, more thoughtful, emotional range with a hint of feminine understanding.

Tom Jenks, who edited The Garden Of Eden, on his first impressions of the novel, 2010.

What strikes one, in reading these flaccid and rather ugly pages, is how painful it is that the great master of narrative pacing . . . must hang on to an incident for pages of chatter simply because he doesn't quite know what to do next.

Irving Howe, reviewing Islands In The Stream for Harper's

HEMINGWAY began writing again soon after he had returned to the Finca Vigia in Cuba from his ten-month stint in Europe at the end of World War II. When he was writing, he worked steadily every morning as was his disciplined wont, but a large part of what he wrote was not published until after his death. One fair estimate would be that from the summer of 1945 until his death 16 years later in 1961 he wrote almost half-a-million words, more than he had produced before he died. [1] The only work he published in those 16 years was the novel Across The River And Into The Trees and the novella The Old Man And The Sea, both written in the late 1940s and early 1950s; why he did not publish any of the other work while he was alive is unclear. Hemingway himself offered no explanation, and it is assumed that perhaps he was not satisfied with it and intended to re-write it. In time all the posthumous work was published by Scribner's: it consisted of two more novels, an expanded version of a feature about going on safari in Africa written for Life magazine and presented as – Hemingway's description – a 'fictional memoir', and two versions of a bona fide memoir, A Moveable Feast.

That memoir, the last work he 'completed', [2] was the first to be published posthumously. [3] Hemingway wrote the sketches of which it consists, then tinkered with them and their sequence, over the last five years of his life. Whether he left a definitive version of that memoir is still debated, but today it exists in two editions: the first, which appeared in 1964, was edited by Mary Welsh, his fourth wife; forty-five years later, in 2009, Hemingway's grandson Sean re-edited the memoir, re-ordering the sequence of chapters and re-instating parts Welsh had deleted. Of all the posthumous work, A Moveable Feast garnered the most respect: critics thought that 35 years on, reminiscing about the times in Paris with his first wife, Hadley Richardson, Hemingway's writing had recaptured some of his early lyricism; but many were also a little put off by how he chose to disparage several of the friends and acquaintances who had helped him launch his career, notably F. Scott Fitzgerald. One critic also thought he detected a certain insincerity in the memoir. Writing in Encounter Tony Tanner noted that

> *The book is written with a good deal of arrogance: every episode is turned to leave Hemingway looking tougher, more talented, more honest, more dignified than anyone else. When he touches on his faults – and 'touches' is the word – they turn out to be those of the sportsman (gambling) or of the dedicated artist (bad temper).*

Ironically pre-empting the conclusions about Hemingway husband and wife Irving and Marilyn Yalom reached, [4] Tanner adds

---

1   Hemingway had by then apparently forgotten his own supercilious gibe that some writers *'never learned how to say no to a typewriter'*.

2   In context this is pertinent.

3   Oddly, Hemingway somewhat mysteriously suggested those reading it might also care to regard his memoir as fiction if they so chose.

4   See p.89ff

Work published posthumously

> *behind all the aggressive implications that Hemingway alone has the secret of the good life, one detects the over-assertiveness of a man troubled by anxiety and fear, a man whose tight tough confidence seems strained by wariness and suspicion, a man mythologising himself to avoid confronting himself.*

At one point, Hemingway seemed to have settled on a version of the manuscript with which he seemed to be happy; but for most of 1959 Hemingway spent many months criss-crossing Spain with an entourage, attending a series of bullfights, and the manuscript never made its way to Scribner's. When it was eventually published, it became a best-seller and is still popular.[i] Despite the constant re-writing of the memoir and the re-arranging of chapters, production of A Moveable Feast was comparatively straightforward. Publication of the rest of the posthumous work, however, presented quite a few problems and divided critical opinion, largely not in Hemingway's favour.[1]

. . .

Back at the Finca in 1945 after 'his war' in Europe and not having written a word of fiction for five years, Hemingway had announced to Max Perkins that he planned to write a 'land, air and sea book' about the recently ended war; this he sometimes referred to as his 'big book'. He began the task by continuing work on a short story he had started in the late 1930s about the Bahamian island of Bimini, but in the event 'the big book' was never written. Instead it evolved into three individual volumes – the 1950 novel Across The River And Into The Trees, the 1952 novella The Old Man And The Sea and the novel, Islands In The Stream. In tandem with his work on 'the big book', Hemingway was also writing another novel, published in 1986 as The Garden Of Eden.[2] Except for his stoic fisherman novella, all the works feature – one is tempted to write 'as usual' – a fictional version of Hemingway, and the two novels had to undergo substantial and controversial editing before they were thought fit to be published. Both novels had champions, but even they admitted to the works' curious curate's egg nature. In their reviews there was often a dutiful and unconvincing note to the rather thin praise some critics allowed themselves, and what some had to say was often harsh. The first posthumous work to appear after A Moveable Feast was published, in 1970, was Islands In The Stream, and reviews were mixed. In the Saturday Review, John Aldridge wrote that despite hoping

---

1   For further details on A Moveable Feast, see p.482ff.
2   The biographers are at odds on when Hemingway started writing what became The Garden Of Eden. Some say it was written in tandem with work on 'the big book'. Others that he didn't not start work on it until the late 1940s or even the early 1950s.

to be surprised by the book, honesty compelled him to admit that it was

> neither very good nor very bad, but that it is both, in some places downright wonderful, in others as sad and embarrassingly self-indulgent as the work of any sophomore.

Aldridge added that in some respects Islands In The Stream resembled For Whom The Bell Tolls and that the two novels were most strikingly similar in the way each brought together in a single narrative – at times within the space of a single page – some of the best and worst features of Hemingway's writing. His view was echoed by Christopher Ricks in the New York Times who declared, using a line spoken by the novel's chief protagonist, that Islands In The Stream is

> is not straight or simple or good.

The novelist John Updike was kinder and noted that

> [Islands In The Stream] consists of material that the author during his lifetime did not see fit to publish; therefore it should not be held against him. That parts of it are good is entirely to his credit; that other parts are puerile and, in a pained way, aimless testifies to the odds against which Hemingway, in the last two decades of his life, brought anything to completion.

Updike, writing in the New Statesman, blamed Scribner's that

> a gallant wreck of a novel is paraded as the real thing, as if the public are such fools as to imagine a great writer's ghost is handing down books intact from Heaven.

In Harper's, Irving Howe was a good deal less gentle than Updike and remarked

> What strikes one, in reading these flaccid and rather ugly pages, is how painful it is that the great master of narrative pacing, the Hemingway who could make tightness of phrase into a moral virtue, should now write so slackly, as if he must hang on to an incident for pages of chatter simply because he doesn't quite know what to do next.

. . .

Work published posthumously

Fifteen years later, in 1985, Scribner's published The Dangerous Summer, an expanded book version of Hemingway's three-part feature on bullfighting that had appeared in Life magazine. Both the feature and the book had a chequered history and – the Life feature had appeared twenty-five years earlier in 1960 – it is not clear why the expanded version was published. One might, however, suggest a plausible reason: by the early 1980s, Scribner's fortunes were declining. Its mid-century best-selling authors – John Galsworthy, Edith Wharton, Owen Wister, Thomas Wolfe, [1] S.S. Van Dine, Ring Lardner and F. Scott Fitzgerald – were long dead and Hemingway had died 25 years earlier. James Jones had died in 1977, and two still living 'names' on its books, Erskine Caldwell and Alan Paton, were in their dotage and had not written much of consequence for years. Scribner's had no younger popular authors and was treading water, and needed more commercial success. In 1978, as a 'medium-sized' publishing house, it and Atheneum Books, another such 'medium-sized' house, had agreed to merge and they formed The Scribner Book Company. Jointly, they hoped, they would be strong and resilient enough to fight off any attempted takeover. Although both houses remained independent, they agreed to share some of their facilities to keep costs down. However, the manoeuvre was fruitless, and in 1984 Macmillan acquired both houses, mainly to get hold of Scribner's list of reference books and its back list of famous titles, including the work of Hemingway and F. Scott Fitzgerald. [ii] Going through the list of Scribner's properties it now owned, Macmillan might have decided to publish the expanded version of The Dangerous Summer under the Scribner's imprint to help to make its new acquisition pay off and recoup some of its money. The book did sell reasonably well, but it did Hemingway's reputation no favours.

The Dangerous Summer [2] had started life as an addendum to a suggested new edition of Hemingway's 1932 bullfighting book, Death In The Afternoon, and at the invitation of Nathan 'Bill' Davis, a rich, sometime acquaintance who lived on his estate in Malaga, Hemingway and his wife Mary Welsh took off to Spain to spend the summer touring bullfights. [3] When Life heard of the trip, it contracted Hemingway to write a 10,000-word feature; but when he began writing it, Hemingway found he could not stop, and eventually he produced 108,000 words. This was far too long for Life, who told him so, and with the assistance of his confidant and occasional amanuensis A.E.

---

1   Wolfe had, though, left Scribner's in a huff, reportedly unhappy with how Max Perkins had drastically cut his second novel, and in 1934 he had signed up with Harpers & Brothers.

2   The title betrays the silly hyperbole which in the 20th century was insinuating its way into many aspects of life: what might have been 'dangerous' about that summer?

3   Davis was a somewhat vague acquaintance who, according to different accounts, either first met Hemingway in Havana in the mid-1930s or in the early 1940s. They were not close, but the very wealthy Davis has a reputation for 'collecting celebrities', and among others he had entertained Noel Coward, Lauren Bacall, Ava Gardner, Beverly Bentley and Laurence Olivier at his estate.

Hotchner, Hemingway boiled his work down to 30,000 words. This was still more than Life wanted, but the magazine agreed to publish the feature in three instalments (and also to pay him more). [1] In the event the new edition of Death In The Afternoon never appeared. For the book version of the Life feature, Scribner's – that is its then new owners Macmillan who were calling the shots – edited the original body of work down to 70,000 words. It might have seemed obvious to reviewers that the publisher was simply trading on the Hemingway name, but either way it meant little to them, and they were, anyway, largely underwhelmed by the work. In the New York Times, William Kennedy admitted he had tried to read all three parts of Hemingway's Life feature when they appeared but they

> *had resuscitated all the boredom I'd felt in reading The Green Hills [Of Africa]*

and he did not remember finishing any of them. He then went on to declare of the book version that although he had

> *lived remote from bullfighting all [his] life, [and had] next to no personal interest in it and tend[ed] to identify with the bulls . . The Dangerous Summer [was] one of the best sports books I [had] ever read.*

That is all fine and dandy, but The Dangerous Summer could not have made quite the impression on Kennedy as he suggested given that almost nothing else in his 3,285-word review deals with the book he is ostensibly reviewing; it's as though he can find little to say about the book itself, and he resorts to padding out his piece with generalities about Hemingway and his journalism, his life, his previous work and his complaints about other writers. What Kennedy actually thought about The Dangerous Summer might be inferred by his comment on the sheer volume of verbiage Hemingway had originally produced

> *And so here is Hemingway — who derided F. Scott Fitzgerald's 'gigantic, preposterous' outline for The Last Tycoon and wrote that Fitzgerald would never have finished the book — unable to finish his own runaway journalism. Here is Hemingway — calling Thomas*

---

1   Hotchner found it was not a simple task: by late 1959 and early 1960 Hemingway's mental health and equilibrium were in a very poor state, and at first he rejected all of Hotchner's suggested cuts, complaining they were ruining the 'nuance' of his work. After a week, the 108,000-word manuscript had been cut by a mere 300-odd words; but Hotchner persevered and eventually more than 78,000 words were deleted.

Work published posthumously

> Wolfe the 'over-bloated Lil Abner of literature' and saying that if Wolfe's editor (and his own), Maxwell Perkins of Scribner's, 'had not cut one-half million words out of Mr. Wolfe everybody would know how he was' — psychopathically viewing his own rampant verbosity as sacrosanct.

Hemingway, Kennedy said, was

> very cuttable, and the book is indeed wonderful; but the question remains: whose wonderfulness is it? Is it half Hemingway? Hemingway by thirds? Should the by-line read: 'Words Put In by Hemingway, Words Taken Out by Hotchner and [Michael Pietsch, a Scribner's editor]'?

The notoriously acerbic New York Times book critic Michiko Kakutani did not pull her punches and described The Dangerous Summer as a

> discursive, flaccid volume [that] offers the reader little else – except an unnecessary and unflattering portrait of Hemingway in decline, his masculine esthetic hardening into macho posturing...

She added that Hemingway's

> fine, spare use of language [had dwindled] into empty mannerism. What Hemingway did in the 1920s was to invent a new style of writing, a style whose austerity and precision implied a moral outlook, a way of looking at the postwar world, as much as a narrative strategy. Unfortunately, however, as the author's own confidences were shaken, as he became increasingly trapped within the armor of his public image . . . only an attitude and the outward remnants of a technique remained. As a result, the writing began to sound synthetic – Across the River And Into The Trees reads like a parody of the early Hemingway; and The Old Man And The Sea, while deftly controlled, has a reductive, vestigial feel to it, as though the author were just going through the motions of writing something remembered dimly from long ago.

In The Literary Review, Antony Beevor is also scathing, tellingly bemoaning that The

Dangerous Summer had not been written as fiction.[1] It is, he said,

> a compelling story, but the self-centred commentary draws attention to Hemingway in all his unloveliness – his paranoid egotism, mythomania and irresponsibility.

Beevor is somewhat bemused that

> when the sword goes into the bull at the moment of truth, the prose adopts bodice-ripper euphemisms for sexual intercourse and orgasm.

He adds that

> from the first page, Hemingway takes himself as seriously as ever. He half expects the brigada politico social to be waiting to seize the famous anti-fascist champion [at the border], but is waved through. The frontier guard had of course read all his books and admired them greatly. There was little to fear, and as this book shows, Hemingway hardly cared a fig for the Republic any more.

Hemingway, says Beevor,

> seems to forget how [the] bullrings had been used as concentration camps, or how a socialist deputy had been 'run' and put to death with flaming banderillas. The few references to the civil war are flat.

. . .

A year later, again possibly under orders from the new owner Macmillan, The Garden Of Eden, Hemingway's second posthumously published novel, appeared, 16 years after Islands In The Stream. After Hemingway had worked on the manuscript, on and off, for 15 years, he seems more or less to have abandoned it, and it needed quite drastic and controversial reconstruction before it could be published. Two editors, including Charles Scribner Jr (also known as Charles Scribner IV) himself tried their hand at getting Hemingway's sprawling manuscript into shape, but threw in the towel; then

---

1   Beevor published The Battle for Spain, his account of the Spanish Civil War in 2007.

Tom Jenks, a young Scribner's editor, was landed with the task.[1] He was handed two large paper shopping bags containing Hemingway's manuscript by Scribner and finally boiled down Hemingway's original 200,000 words to just under 70,000.[2] He also managed to fashion a 'story' from the welter of words Hemingway had written, though in the process he decided to delete two central protagonists and a whole 'sub-plot'. To forestall potential controversy, Charles Scribner disingenuously insisted in a publisher's note prefacing the novel that

> *In preparing the book for publication we have made some cuts in the manuscript and some routine copy editing corrections. Beyond a very small number of minor interpolations for clarity and consistency, nothing has been added. In every significant respect the work is all the author's.*

Given that Jenks rid the novel of almost 140,000 words, Scribner was working with a very broad definition of 'some cuts'; and his note did not prevent all controversy: some critics wondered just how much The Garden Of Eden was a 'Hemingway novel'. Several years later, Jenks admitted that to shape a coherent story from Hemingway's outpouring and to compensate for the deletion of the two protagonists, in his salvaging operation he was obliged to rewrite some scenes; but, he insisted, he had added nothing new and that all the words and passages in the novel were what Hemingway had written; he had simply 'recycled' [my word, not Jenks'] passages he had deleted elsewhere and patched them in where necessary. As for what considerations he had given to the decisions he made, Jenks gave the rather woolly assurance that he was guided by what he believed Hemingway had 'intended'. One does thus wonder, as many did and still do, how much of an 'original work' the novel was: is The Garden Of Eden an 'Ernest Hemingway novel' or not? As the novelist John Updike noted in his New Yorker review

> *The propriety of publishing, as a commercial endeavor, what a dead writer declined to see into print is, of course, dubious. The previous forays into the Hemingway trove have unfortunately tended to heighten our appreciation not of his talent but of his psychopathology; even the charming and airy A Moveable Feast, the first and most finished of the posthumous publications (1964), had its ugly flashes of malice and ingenuous self-serving. Islands In*

---

1   He refused to undertake the task twice, before finally agreeing.
2   The 200,000-odd word 'manuscript', in fact, contained several versions of the story – it seemed Hemingway had tried to write it several times.

> *The Stream (1970) was a thoroughly ugly book, brutal and messy and starring a painter-sailor whose humanity was almost entirely dissolved in bar-room jabber and Hollywood heroics.*

Yet Updike did find some elements of the novel resurrected by Scribner's and Jenks he could admire and suggested that under the circumstances of its writing and subsequent editing, the published novel was better than it might have been:

> *There is every reason – its hackneyed title, Baker's scorn, the forty years of murky fiddling that have passed since its conception – to distrust The Garden Of Eden; yet the book, as finally presented, is something of a miracle, a fresh slant on the old magic, and falls just short of the satisfaction that a fully intended and achieved work gives us. The miracle, it should be added,*
> *does not seem to be Hemingway's alone but is shared with workers unnamed in the prefatory note, which blandly admits to 'some cuts in the manuscript and some routine copy-editing corrections. Some cuts.* [1]

The novelist E.L. Doctorow also gave the novel an encouraging review – headlined by the New York Times as 'Braver than we thought' – in which he described Hemingway as

> *unquestionably a genius*

but he added the puzzling and not very clear qualification

> *of the kind that advertises its limits.*

As for the novel he wrote

> *For there are clear signs here of something exciting going on, the enlargement of a writer's mind toward compassion, toward a less defensive construal of reality.*

He added

> *There are enough clues [in the novel] to suggest the unmistakable*

---

1   Updike notes that in Carlos Baker's official biography of Hemingway, he had described the novel as an experimental compound of past and present, filled with astonishing ineptitudes. But, Updike, adds Baker had, of course, only seen the welter of copy, some handwritten, some typed that Hemingway had eventually locked away at his Havana bank.

> *signs of a recycling of Hemingway's first materials toward less romance and less literary bigotry and greater truth. That is exciting because it gives evidence, despite his celebrity, despite his Nobel, despite the torments of his own physical self-punishment, of a writer still developing.*

Doctorow would seem to be talking about the work's subject matter which was certainly a departure for Hemingway; and it is suggested that the nature of that subject matter, which involved lesbianism and sexual role reversal, might have persuaded Hemingway not to publish his novel. In it, its two main protagonists – as noted two other central character were culled by Jenks – swap sexual roles in bed, with the woman becoming a boy called Peter and the man, David Bourne – Hemingway's alter ego – becoming her female lover, Catherine. Hemingway also writes of David giving Catherine the nickname 'Devil' and subjecting him to devilish sexual practices in which he is 'the girl'. Some commentators speculated that this might have involved sodomy (known today as 'pegging'), but nowhere in the novel is Hemingway specific. We know from Hemingway's fourth wife, Mary Welsh, that she and Hemingway did the same in bed, and although there is little evidence, it is not unlikely that Hadley Richardson and Pauline Pfeiffer also agreed to do the same with Hemingway. Both certainly indulged Hemingway in his hair fetish. The pertinent point is that Hemingway was writing and revising the novel in the 1940s and 1950s, and it is possible that he came to suspect it revealed too much of his psyche publicly. That there were several versions of the work in the long manuscript handed to Jenks might indicate that despite several attempts, he felt unable to produce what he hoped to produce.

Other reviewers were not as enthusiastic as Updike and Doctorow, and the Los Angeles Times also doubted whether the work might even be regarded as a bona fide 'Ernest Hemingway' novel. It commented

> *The words are Hemingway's, but the book is not*

before noting that

> *The best way – certainly the most generous way – to regard this work is as Hemingway's warm-up exercise [because much of it was written before he wrote Across The River And Into The Trees] to get back into his old writing habits after the five-year lay-off following For Whom the Bell Tolls.*

The LA Times concluded that

> *Now that it is possible to assess the banked fiction [i.e. Islands In The Stream and The Garden Of Eden], it is clear that Hemingway held it back because he knew that it wasn't good enough for him.*

In her customary acerbic manner, the New York Times' reviewer, Michiko Kakutani was decidedly unimpressed with the new novel. She wrote

> *Instead of describing bullfighting or big game hunting or fishing, Hemingway spends most of his time in this book writing about eating, love-making and sunbathing. And instead of writing about a man of action or even a wounded man of emotion like Jake Barnes, he's chosen, as his protagonist, a wimp – a frustrated writer, who's so passive in his dealings with women that he makes even the tongue-lashed Robert Cohn look like a self-assured, stand-up sort of guy. For these reasons – as well as the simple fact that it is a 'new' work by Ernest Hemingway – The Garden of Eden will no doubt be widely read. As a novel, however, its merits are dubious: the writing – which dates from roughly the same period as such lesser works as Islands In The Stream, The Old Man And The Sea and The Dangerous Summer – is frequently synthetic and contrived; the characters, sketchily defined; the story-line, by turns static and abruptly melodramatic.*

Kakutani does, however, generously add that

> *Given its history, however, it is impossible to say just how much responsibility Hemingway, himself, bears for the novel as it currently appears.*

She concludes that

> *Sometimes Hemingway sounds as though he were parodying an earlier self ('All your father found he found for you too, he thought, the good, the wonderful, the bad, the very bad, the really very bad, the truly bad and then the much worse'). And sometimes, he sounds as though he were parodying Norman Mailer ('He treated evil like an old entrusted friend, David thought, and evil, when she poxed him, never knew she'd scored'). In the end, though, the flaccid writing alone is not what makes The Garden of Eden*

> *such a flimsy, disposable book. What makes us most impatient is Hemingway's simple failure to turn his characters into sympathetic or recognizably complex human beings.*

Finally, it is also worth pondering on Scribner/Macmillan's motives for publishing a novel that needed such a large amount of work to get it into shape. If it is suggested the publishers felt a moral duty to examine all the 'great writer's' work, why had they waited 25 years after that great writer's death to do so? Arguably more telling, indicating that 'making more money' was the prime motivation, is that several deals were struck pre-publication: one to make The Garden Of Eden a Book Of The Month, and with various magazines – including, oddly, Sports Illustrated – to publish excerpts.

. . .

The final piece of Hemingway's writing to be salvaged, whether in the interests of literature or simply to bank a little more moolah while enough readers were alive with whom the name 'Ernest Hemingway' still resonated, appeared in 1999. This was True At First Light, his 'fictional memoir' of his second safari in East Africa; ostensibly or actually – who knows and how could we tell? – it was published to celebrate the centenary of Hemingway's birth on July 21, 1899. He seems to have regarded the work as 'a novel', and although much of what takes place mirrors the actual safari, biographers agree that other elements were clearly invented. He had started writing it in the autumn of 1954 after he had more or less recovered from almost dying in the second of two plane crashes in East Africa, and he worked on it for the next two years. He had written around 200,000 words before the filming of his novella The Old Man And The Sea and then illness which kept him bed-bound for more than a month brought work to a halt. By then, he confessed, he was also having trouble remembering what had happened, and he finally abandoned work in October 1956, depositing his manuscript in his Havana bank vault. It is unclear what he later intended to do with it.

Reviewing the work for the January Magazine, the novelist Frederick Zackel recalled Hemingway's own conviction that

> *the first draft of anything is shit*

and that True At First Light was a first draft he never intended to publish. Zackel added

> *that whirling sound we hear during this 100th-anniversary month of his birth is Papa Hemingway rotating in his grave over the antics of his son Patrick and the corporate juggernaut that's selling off*

what he never meant to have people read.

Between them, Patrick Hemingway – who had been living in East Africa in the early 1950s and was sometimes part of the safari group – and the publisher's editors had cut the manuscript down by half. Patrick Hemingway came up with the work's title from a passage his father had written

> *In Africa a thing is true at first light and a lie by noon and you have no more respect for it than for the lovely, perfect weed fringed lake you see across the sun baked salt plain. You have walked across that plain in the morning and you know that no such lake is there. But now it is there absolutely true, beautiful and believable.*

Zackel gives the 'fictional memoir' or 'novel' a pass on the grounds that Hemingway himself did not himself edit his manuscript and was thus unable to complete it; the implication is that 'Papa' would have smoothed the rough edges. But given that Hemingway locked the manuscript away several years before his death, the obvious question is how might Zackel have been so sure? Hemingway's admission that he was beginning to have trouble remembering details (and had previously boasted of his excellent memory and that he never took notes) suggests he simply lost interest.

Other reviewers, however, were not as understanding as Zackel. James Wood, writing in the New York Times, was underwhelmed by Hemingway's 'novel' and writes

> *The famous style occasionally flares into fineness, but is really no more than a pretender to its former royalty. Sentences are either casually functional or busily functional; in the latter category are many sentences that are completely uninteresting except that they carry on as if they were very interesting, as if they were little lozenges of lyricism when in fact they only leak information.*

True At First Light, he notes,

> *contains all that is most easily imitated of Hemingway's style, reminding us again that after about 1935 [!] the author franchised himself in increasingly despairing outlets. The book's failings are ones that have passed into contemporary currency in American writing. There is much sloshing male sentimentality, in that now characteristic form in which masculinity is taken to be inherently*

Work published posthumously

> *metaphysical (to hunt game is to quest, to be sexually needy is to confront 'the loneliness').*

Wood's colleague on the Times, Michiko Kakutani, was also less than impressed by the last original work by Hemingway to be published. She sums up what she thought of it in a parody of Hemingway's style with which she begins her review.

> *Africa was a fine subject, and he had written about it well and truly in the past, but the old days were gone now, and he was old and weary and ailing, and what he wrote this time was not good and it was not true. The writer was a proud man and he took pride in his writing, and when the writing of the Africa book did not go well, he put it away. Long ago, he said that there was nothing worse for a writer than for his writing 'which has been rewritten and altered to be published without permission as his own,' and he believed this as he believed few things. Later, when he was gone, others would forget his pride and his love of words, and they would publish his Africa book and other books he had put aside. They would publish the books because the writer was a famous writer and he had many readers, but they would do damage to his name.*

Kakutani also makes it clear that if the work was not up to snuff, Scribner's – that is Macmillan – were as much, if not more, to blame than the writer himself. After all Hemingway had decided not to publish the work, although we cannot second-guess him and his motive for not doing so. She castigates the publisher

> *No one has given such critics more ammunition than his estate and publishers, who have brought out a succession of posthumously published books consisting of writing that Hemingway himself chose not to publish – books that show Hemingway in the worst of all possible lights, his prose a near-parody of his earlier style; his self-portraits exercises in self-aggrandizing bravado. The latest of these volumes is True at First Light, a so-called 'fictional memoir,' laboriously extracted by Hemingway's son Patrick from a 200,000-word, untitled manuscript.*

. . .

These two novels, the two version of the memoir and the expanded Life feature were not the only Hemingway work to be posthumously published; but they were the only original work. Rather obviously displaying what might all too easily be mistaken – no doubt erroneously – for corporate venality, in the past 62 years, the various owners of the rights to Hemingway's work have released The Snows Of Kilimanjaro And Other Stories, The Fifth Column and Four Stories of the Spanish Civil War, The Nick Adams Stories, 88 Poems and Complete Poems, [1] The Short Stories Of Ernest Hemingway, The Complete Short Stories Of Ernest Hemingway. The collections are all the same fifty-odd short stories. Then there are Hemingway On Writing, Hemingway On Fishing, Hemingway On Hunting, Hemingway On War and, most recently in 2008 – Hemingway On Paris. Each to his or her own, of course.

Still to come are the final nine volumes of the projected 16-volume collection of Hemingway's letters, the most recent volume of which, the fifth, was published in 2020. Whether or not some enthusiastic literary body is compiling the definitive collection of Papa's laundry lists I cannot say, but I wouldn't be in the least surprised; and nor would I be surprised that in the nether regions of academic departments worldwide there is an insatiable desire to read and study them.

---

1   Though no one has ever praised Hemingway's verse or, to my knowledge, ever remarked upon how interesting it is.

In sum: chacun à son goût

The discrepancy between eloquence and maudlin self-indulgence was often visible on a single page; I never knew when he would soar and when he would lapse into the fabled macho pose that has proved so irresistible to parody.

James Atlas, associate editor The Atlantic, Oct 1983, on re-reading Hemingway's novels.

. . . we sometimes forgot that this was a writer who had in his time made the English language new, changed the rhythms of the way both his own and the next few generations would speak and write and think.

Joan Didion, The New Yorker, October 25, 1998.

. . . the most pernicious danger of Hemingway's celebrity lay in the overpowering temptation to assess the writing in terms of the writer's life and legend.

Scott Donaldson.

Even people who rarely read novels are driven by curiosity to investigate a story supposedly based on real people and events. When such a novel is additionally acclaimed by the critics and widely hailed as the Bible of a whole generation, the furore increases geometrically. Over a period of years information purported to be 'the truth' about the novel and its prototypes multiply and are synthesized, resulting in a confusing array of

> *legends which not infrequently contradict each other. Thus has it been with Ernest Hemingway's The Sun Also Rises.*
>
> **Bertram D. Sarason, Hemingway And The Sun Set: About The Sun Also Rises.**

A POINT repeatedly made in these pages is that we should always distinguish between 'subjective judgment' and 'objective judgment': the one is not the other and, crucially, it never can be. Those who disagree and insist objective judgment of a work of art is possible should, for the benefit of sceptics, go ahead and prove that they are right, that such objectivity is possible and that we sceptics are wrong. If both sides can agree on nothing else, they can at least agree that if such proof does exist, it would be demonstrable. I shan't, though, be holding my breath in anticipation. Whether Ernest Hemingway was 'a great writer' and perhaps 'one of the best in the 20th century' or whether he was a 'middling writer' who essentially 'struck lucky' are no more than points of view: both are simply opinions. Neither statement is 'right' or 'wrong', and neither describes 'a fact'. Yet even if Hemingway had been 'a great' rather than merely 'a middling' writer, the public fame he achieved worldwide would still be unusual; so examining how he achieved that fame might still be warranted. If, on the other hand, his talent and output were – at best – no more than 'middling', his global literary reputation and status, and how he acquired both would certainly be 'an enigma'.

While acknowledging the distinction between 'subjective' and 'objective' judgment, we might also examine the qualifications of those who declare Hemingway to be 'a great writer' and ask what sanctions them to make their ruling. While doing so, we might also – in the interests of clarity – remind ourselves of the differences between scientific investigation and the academic 'research' of those working in 'the arts', specifically in English literature departments: we should be clear that what can be 'known' in science is quintessentially different to the 'knowledge' acquired by 'arts' academics. As I pointed out earlier, it would be fatuous to 'have an opinion' on whether or not two and two add up to four; yet when it comes to discussing the worth or otherwise of the work of this or that writer and 'how great' he or she is, 'an opinion' is all we can allow ourselves – 'facts', 'evidence' and 'proof' don't come into it. Those points are worth repeating because too often, though tacitly, literary knowledge is paraded as having as much academic worth as scientific knowledge; and as Virginia Woolf alerts us in her Essay On Criticism, we timid ones, we great unwashed, are apt meekly to accept the academics on their own

In sum: chacun à son goût

terms. [1] As the Irish writer Declan Kiberd has pointed out in his book Ulysses And Us (although he was primarily commenting on academic output not academic method)

> *Too often the papers of academic experts are addressed only to their peers in a jargon that seeks to mimic the rigorous discourse of the sciences.*

If arts academics come across Kiberd's complaint and perhaps suspect they will look silly if they don't object, they might insist that they do no such thing; yet Hemingway himself seemed to have believed there was an intellectual equivalence between the rigorous methods of 'the sciences' and the rather woolly findings of those academically involved in 'the arts'. [2] In a letter to Max Perkins in 1945 he wrote

> *It wasn't by accident that the Gettysburg address was so short. The laws of prose writing are as immutable as those of flight, of mathematics, of physics.* [3]

If Kiberd is right, one wonders why arts academics do attempt 'to mimic the rigorous discourse' of the sciences; and the answer is, perhaps, quite straightforward: they believe it gives their work and their findings, their 'research', their claims and their 'facts' – that, for example, 'Ernest Hemingway was a modernist and one of the 20th century's great writers' – more credibility; and such credibility is important: it is as though they are aware of the insurmountable distinction between 'fact' and 'opinion', between 'knowledge' and 'belief', but are determined to surmount it anyway. Would the Nobel Prize for Literature awarded to Hemingway in 1954 really be convincing 'proof' that he was 'one of our greatest writer' if it simply reflected the consensus of subjective opinion among the members of the prize committee? At this point the Hemingway champions in academia and elsewhere might indulge in a kind of pretzel logic that is reminiscent of the circularity I outlined when describing 'the theology' of Hemingway and his work

---

1   Woolf was writing about 'the critics', yet I suggest her strictures apply equally to the men and women who strut their stuff in the 'groves of academe' (Mary McCarthy). She wrote: '*Yet these insignificant fellow creatures have only to shut themselves up in a room, dip a pen in the ink, and call themselves "we", for the rest of us to believe that they are somehow exalted, inspired, infallible.*'

2   We might, for example, remind ourselves of the confident though frankly fanciful conclusions of Carlos Baker, Philip Young, John Atkins, the several academics suggesting 'solutions' to the 'insoluble problem' presented by All Clean, Well-Lighted Place and the distinctly varied interpretations of the story God Rest Ye Merry, Gentlemen.

3   This is a wholly fatuous claim, but if you agree with Hemingway and disagree with me, I suspect you will long ago in disgust have thrown this book into a corner and will certainly not be reading this footnote.

– that 'Hemingway was a great writer because he wrote this' and 'this is great writing because it is by Hemingway'. Here that pretzel logic would dictate that 'the Nobel Prize for Literature was awarded to Ernest Hemingway because the nominating committee agreed that he was a great writer', with the clinching subtext 'and the Nobel Prize for Literature would not have agreed and awarded the Prize to Ernest Hemingway had he not been a great writer'. Thus, courtesy of the Nobel Prize committee, the statement that 'Hemingway was a great writer' evolves from being a mere 'opinion' among many into a 'fact': the distinction has apparently been successfully surmounted.

Accounts of Hemingway, his personality and his behaviour from family, friends and acquaintances are so varied and contradictory that they might be of two different men; and so the 'Hemingway enigma' extends even further. We can tie ourselves in knots trying to 'understand' the man, but it might be sanest to conclude that attempting to do so is not just futile but unfair to Hemingway. Rather than subject him to the kind of lightweight psycho-analytical scrutiny popular with the more respectable Saturday and Sunday newspapers and trying to shoehorn him into one of our convenient pigeon-holes, it would be simpler – and certainly more honest – to concede that many men and women often are very complex. More to the point, none of it – not the contradictory behaviour, the shyness, the bragging, the boozing, the fantastical claims and lying – has any bearing at all on the work upon which his reputation as a supposed 'great writer' rests. Again, some will disagree and insist that 'the man (or woman) is the work and the two cannot be distinguished'. I don't: that claim is just another point of view and it is not mine. I am more persuaded that the work of any author should – perhaps must – ideally be read and evaluated on its own terms and hermetically, and stand on its own.[1] The many details we have about a writer might interest us and might help to illuminate some aspect or other of his or her work; but ultimately such details have no bearing on the degree and success of the writer's artistry, thought and the purported aesthetic 'value' of an individual piece: in that respect they are irrelevant. Roland Barthes suggested that once a piece of writing – and, I suppose, once the creation of any work of art – is deemed by its creator to have been concluded and the work is then presented for the attention of

---

1   This is also the view of Tom Jenks, the Scribner's editor who was tasked with knocking Hemingway's huge and unwieldy manuscript for The Garden Of Eden into the novel that was eventually published. Addressing the Modern Language Convention in New York just after The Garden Of Eden went on sale he said '*Today I continue to hold that the work – any writer's work – should speak for itself. Editing is a mediumistic occupation, and an editor's place is offstage.*' He then, however, qualified that view as regards The Garden Of Eden by adding '*It's unseemly and maladroit for an editor to step in front of an author, but The Garden of Eden is exceptional in its genesis and in its representation of its author . . .*' For more on the drastic editing that novel needed before it could be published – for which read 'put on sale to the public' – see p.282ff

In sum: chacun à son goût

others, it takes on an existence which – crucially – is independent of its creator. Thus, in that sense the creator is of no consequence. The notion that a work should stand or fall 'in itself' is also essentially what Wimsatt and Beardsley suggest in their paper The Intentional Fallacy. That suggestion is not, of course, an ontological 'fact'; it is merely a convenient way of considering how we might evaluate 'works of art' and try to do so with a clear head. But it is a useful one.

Usefully, that approach clarifies the distinction between 'a work' and 'the creator', and stresses that no knowledge of 'the creator' is necessary for evaluation of the work. Would those who read Hamlet's soliloquy rate or enjoy it, its poetry and its thought less if they did not know it was written by William Shakespeare or even had no idea who this 'William Shakespeare' was? Can we evaluate an anonymous poem, short story or novel if we know nothing of its author? Of course we can and, more to the point, we do. We have no idea who wrote Beowulf [1] or who 'Homer' was or even whether 'Homer' was just one person or, as has been suggested, a name we now give to a collection of otherwise unknown poets; [i] yet the poems Beowulf and the Odyssey and the Iliad are in no way thus diminished. Not knowing who wrote a poem, a short story or a novel would – and should – not bother us at all if the writing is obliged to stand on its own. If we believe a work is interesting, engaging, well-written or otherwise laudable, would – or should – it make any difference to our judgment if we were subsequently told the piece had been written by a rapist? Our new knowledge might influence our decisions on how we treat the work – refusing to include it in an anthology, perhaps – but it can and would have no bearing on how we evaluate it artistically. [ii] Earlier, I cited the dilemma faced by museum and exhibition curators when in 1989 a biography of the British sculptor Eric Gill revealed that he had been an incestuous paedophile. I suggested that although that fact might impact on whether or not to exhibit Gill's work (particularly his drawings of the daughter he abused), I asked: did it have any bearing on our reaction to, and appreciation and evaluation of, his art and sculptures? Would it have been reasonable, or even made sense, to suggest that henceforth graphic artists and printers should stop using Gill Sans or any of the other typefaces he designed? Some might argue that Gill's works should still be exhibited, though informing the visitors of Gill's sexual behaviour; some might conclude that 'we still think Gill's work succeeds artistically, but it is now inappropriate to exhibit it'; others might argue that Gill's incestuous paedophilia somehow diminishes the work artistically. Given differing views, a committee might

---

1   Perhaps we should consider that the 'Beowolf poet' might not actually have composed the poem, but had simply recorded on parchment his (or her) version of a ballad that was until then only known from oral performances.

then be convened to discuss the matter and after long debate reach a consensus on whether or not to exhibit his work; but their decision would have nothing at all to say on the 'artistic worth' of any piece of Gill's work. [1]

That we might ignore extraneous matters and treat a work hermetically when evaluating it is, of course, purely 'the theory' – 'the practice' is muddier: try as we might, it would prove to be impossible to discount everything except the work itself. Dealing with a first work by an unknown writer, the publisher's marketing department, with both eyes on maximising sales, might tell the world about 'an exciting new talent', [iii] as Scribner's did when it published The Sun Also Rises: the advertising and marketing campaign proclaimed that the then unknown Ernest Hemingway was not the effete kind mouldering away in a cold garret: he was different, he was a 'man of action' who was also an artist dedicated to writing. Ironically, twenty-three years later Scribner's imperatives had changed and the situation was reversed: when Hemingway's fifth novel, Across The River And Into The Trees, was published in 1950, 'the name' and 'the man' mattered far more than the book's literary qualities; and despite the public scorn of 'the critics'. 'Papa' Hemingway's new novel was a huge success, topping the New York Times best-sellers' list in October and November 1950 (and doubtless also becoming a fixture of many a coffee table).

Knowing about a writer and her or his life and previous work might for some add to their engagement in, and enjoyment of, a new work; but it does again stress the necessary distinction between 'the subjective' and 'the objective'. If evaluation and judgment are thus personal – if what you enjoy and rate as 'good' is not what I enjoy and rate as 'good' – they are a matter of opinion and thus subjective. So I shall repeat: the orthodox insistence that 'Hemingway was a great writer' – with its list of corollaries – is just another subjective judgment, even though Hemingway champions might far prefer his 'greatness' to be a copper-bottomed 'fact' rather than a mere 'opinion'.

. . .

Related and equally as sticky are the questions: what makes *this* writer 'great' but not *that* writer? What do we expect of 'a great writer'? Does 'greatness' transcend popularity? [iv] Is 'greatness' eternal – or at least lasting – or just occasional? Could a writer be 'great' for 50 years, then deemed 'not so great' for another 50, then reinstated among the greats? That last question might sound fatuous, but frankly so is our modern

---

1   Gill's 1931 sculpture of Prospero And Ariel which graces the BBC's Broadcasting House in London was defaced by protesters in 2022. Restoration worked began in May 2023.

In sum: chacun à son goût

insistence on 'grading' or 'ranking' our artists – 'the Ten Best Novelists of the 19th century' – though doing so is almost certainly simply a publishing industry sales ploy with which the unwitting readers play ball. Faced with the question of what makes a writer 'great', we might be better off trying to agree on the length of the average piece of string. Poets, playwrights and writers from previous centuries are still acknowledged and honoured because there is a consensus that the essential qualities we admire in their work have survived over the decades and centuries, and are still apparent. Since the late 16th century when William Shakespeare was writing, the meaning and pronunciation of many words he used have changed, and some of his rhymes, puns, allusions and jokes no longer immediately work for a 21st-century reader and listener; sometimes his work is even a little obscure to modern ears. Yet quite apart from the pleasure we still get in hearing and reading his plays and verse and considering his thought, his ability succinctly to convey insights into human behaviour have not aged at all and are still appreciated. [v] Although Henry Fielding, Jane Austen and George Eliot were writing more recently and their more rotund, less modern style is noticeably from a different era, what we appreciate in their work has also transcended time.

Can the same be said of Hemingway sixty years after his death? Will the same be said 200 years after his death? Is the modern reader who comes across the short, one-paragraph vignettes in In Our Time as impressed by them as they impressed many critics when that volume was published almost 100 years ago? A 21st-century high school or college student reading them and that volume's longer stories might well be at a loss to understand why they were praised and should still be regarded as 'great'. [1] Do they still have an intrinsic 'artistic worth' or are they today notable merely because they were part of Hemingway's first collection of short stories and – the student is still assured – 'Ernest Hemingway was a great writer'? [vi] Is their significance perhaps now no longer literary but simply historic? Arguably, Shakespeare's sonnets and the novels of Fielding, Austen and Eliot still have an intrinsic literary appeal over and above their historic significance which is still apparent to, and appreciated by, a modern reader. On the other hand 'to get' Hemingway, a student might now need to be told how his fiction compared with other fiction being written at the time, in both style and content. [2] Is The Three-Day Blow still a significant story or now just – as it strikes me – a somewhat thin and rushed

---

1   As far as the vignettes are concerned, I suspect the contemporary context of their publication would be vital for a reader fresh to them to start 'appreciating' why they are supposedly 'better' than any short newspaper filler paragraph chosen at random.

2   This is certainly true of many other writers of the past. And when we 'modern' folk read the work of those who wrote 200, 300 and 400 years ago, it does often help to have 'notes' illuminating this or that allusion or joke which otherwise might puzzle us.

account of two lads in their late teens getting a little drunk and then deciding to go out? Does the prose stand out in anyway? Is The Killers still notable as a 'modernist work' or is it now – as it seems to me – seen as just a pale attempt at writing pulp fiction? If it had not been 'by that new writer Ernest Hemingway', might it perhaps more likely have been greeted with a polite 'thanks, but no thanks' if submitted to a publisher? Frankly, without the necessary context, very little of the early work Hemingway wrote now leaves much of an impression: would anyone really choose to break a lance for, say, Mr And Mrs Elliot and A Very Short Story?

...

As with our gaggle of ten economists asked to define 'economics' who come up with 20 different definitions or our Hemingway enthusiasts when asked to describe what the 'lost generation' was, I suspect most academics would be hard-pushed to agree on a list of attributes that make a writer and her or his work 'great'; and if they did manage to settle on a list, they would certainly disagree on the status and importance of each quality suggested. Implicit, of course, is the snobbish distinction between 'serious literature' and – well, what might one call work what is not 'serious literature'? [vii] Given that each age has its own preoccupations, some might insist that 'serious literature' and great writing should reflect the concerns of its age. [1] Others might demand 'profound insights' into 'what makes us human' (or, alternatively, 'the human condition'). A writer's degree of 'artistry' might also feature, although what could be regarded as 'artistically successful' would be yet another debating point dividing opinion. 'Style' might come lower on the list than expected: Truman Capote distinguished between 'stylists', 'styleless stylists' and 'nonstylists', [2] though even the concept of 'style' becomes uncomfortably vague when you examine it – what some might regard as 'poor writing' is often defended by others as 'the writer's unique style'; one reader's enthusiasm for a 'unique style' might be another's impatience with 'unreadable nonsense'. One wonders how high on the list of what makes a writer 'great' would be that he or she told 'a rattling good story'. Might a writer working in a genre otherwise regarded as infra dig gain points because he or she is 'better' than their peers? Several of those who care to arbitrate on these matters might scoff at the notion that Rafael Sabatini was a 'great writer'; yet he certainly understood human nature and how it expressed itself as well as many regarded as producing 'serious literature'. [viii] What

---

1   A current popular go-to theme is 'the climate crisis', but I don't doubt that will be replaced at some point by a newer, sexier 'concern'. As I write (or better as I revise) it is already giving way to 'examining the dangers or AI'.

2   I would prefer the spellings 'style-less' and 'non-stylists'.

In sum: chacun à son goût

are we to make of the work by writers who regularly garner 'serious' literary awards and other 'honours', but which is, frankly, often turgid, dull and sometimes pretentious?[1] In fact, the process by which *this* writer has come to be regarded as 'great' but not *that* writer is as nebulous as the election of a new Roman Catholic Pope. Devout RCs like to believe that the 'Holy Spirit' takes an active part in the proceedings, yet it is far more probable that a great deal of negotiating – the polite word for 'horse trading' – takes place between different power blocs in the College of Cardinals in conclave to determine which 'candidate' upsets the majority of them the least. Nothing as venal or organised will have taken place to facilitate the rise of Hemingway to the status of 'one of our greatest writers', but the process was equally nebulous. One crucial difference is that the good cardinals proceed in private and have no need of the support of that body of readers whose credulity, Virginia Woolf reminds us, sanctions and legitimises the 'exalted, inspired [and] infallible' judgments of the literary great and good.

. . .

The more I have discovered about Hemingway and his work, the more I am inclined, though reluctantly, to agree with Gore Vidal when he wondered how the United States – and by implication the rest of the world –

could have produced someone like Hemingway and not seen the joke?

I also have to agree with Vladimir Nabokov's scorn that Hemingway was 'a writer for boys'. But why reluctantly? Well, my reluctance is easily explained and not what you might assume: 'Papa' Hemingway and his work might no longer be the buzz of literary salons around the world, but just as we are still picking up background radiation from the Big Bang 13.8 billion years ago, at the back of many minds is still the 'knowledge' that Ernest Hemingway was a 'great writer'; and those many minds might wonder: who is this ridiculous fool – that would be me – who is telling us it's nonsense that Papa was a great writer and he was nothing of the kind? The fact is that few of us care to be regarded as 'ridiculous fools': hence my reluctance; yet unfortunately, from whatever angle I consider 'Papa' Hemingway and his work, I find it impossible to see anything but, at best, a decidedly 'middling' writer and one who, quite frankly, struck it very lucky.

I am familiar with the many claims made about him and his writing; yet to each claim I can't help but respond: so what? It is said that 'Hemingway broke down the wall between journalism and literature'? So what? Carlos Baker assured us that Hemingway

---

1   Here I have two contemporary English language novelists in mind who are often spoken of as 'important' – but no names, no pack drill.

wrote with 'the kind of precision of the poet-symbolist'. Well, that's as maybe – and I think Baker's claim is more than a little overwrought – but once again: so what? Did Baker – or does anyone – really think that the prose of Hemingway's two 1930s non-fiction books which was stodgy and sometimes poor to borderline incomprehensible, was the work of 'a great writer'? Even Matthew J. Bruccoli, a Hemingway admirer – of sorts – confessed that Hemingway 'did not progress from strength to strength', that 'his best work was done before he was thirty', and that 'he produced only one major novel — For Whom the Bell Tolls — after 1929'. Bruccoli adds that

> *Nonetheless, he spoke with the confidence of success. Everything he did, everything he wrote, became important because he was Ernest Hemingway.*

That is, admittedly, just 'another opinion'. One might reason that the phrase 'his best work' means just that: perhaps, Hemingway apologists would assure us, what came later was not 'quite as good and no longer comparable to his best', but 'it was still good'. But was it? Your answer will depend on your baseline; and if, as I have claimed throughout, The Sun Also Rises was essentially little more than a sour, romantic pot-boiler and A Farewell To Arms nothing more startling than a Boy's Own tale which meanders its way to become a tepid love story, the bar has already been set quite low. [1]

Earlier, I insisted that the two words 'good' and 'bad' are worse than useless: they tell us nothing, and they do little except, again obliquely, indicate personal preference; so it's best to avoid those words. Setting aside Death In The Afternoon and Green Hills Of Africa because they are non-fiction, what do we make of the last three novels? Are they in any way outstanding, to such an extent that they can be regarded as the work of a 'great writer'? To Have And Have Not, frankly, is a shambles, at its best mediocre and at worst downright embarrassing. [2] What of For Whom The Bell Tolls: can we really ignore the trite, adolescent 'romantic' elements in the novel because the rest of it the

---

1   Certainly, grand claims have been made for The Sun Also Rises, that, for example, parts of it act obliquely as a moral commentary. For example, it has been pointed out that Jake Barnes will sometimes dwell on 'the price to be paid' for certain behaviour and that he often seems concerned with the cost of items. Superficially, this might makes sense and impress; but unfortunately I suspect here, too, the Rorschach effect is again at play and that commentators espy significance where they would like it to exist. We would be wise to remember that significance, like beauty (and the '*precision of the poet-symbolist*' detected by Baker), is all too often in the eye of the beholder. We might also ask why, if this was indeed the kind of technique Hemingway had partly adopted in his first novel, he did not bother with any similar moral commentary in his subsequent work.

2   The first two parts might pass muster as short adventure tales, but the orthodoxy is that Hemingway wrote 'serious literature' and was certainly not a mere scribbler of such fare. The third part is nothing but a muddled mess.

In sum: chacun à son goût

work is somehow 'excellent'; and if the rest of that novel is not 'excellent' – which in my view it most certainly is not – why do we still talk of it as 'Hemingway's best'? As for Across The River And Into The Trees, it sold well – as I suggest elsewhere of other work, probably because 'it's by Hemingway' – but it garnered no respect at all. The Old Man And The Sea? It's a simple tale that has delighted many adolescents, but it does sink rather too often into very sticky mawk and syrup; and as was pointed out by several reviewers, it does come uncomfortably close to 'Hemingway by numbers'.

Yet the process goes on: at almost every turn, on every topic Hemingway gets a pass because, the theology insists, he was 'a great writer': we continue to choose to claim that the writing in The Sun Also Rises is 'lean, hard and athletic' when, in fact, swathes of it are flat, dull, banal and jejeune. Hemingway's literary achievements are defended and qualified until there might is little left to defend and qualify, and it all begins to look rather too much like salvage operation (as the two posthumous novels were salvaged [1]). Yet still legions of academics and faithful true believers, like the emperor's courtiers and the emperor's subjects, insist that the literary clothes the noticeably stark-naked Hemingway is wearing are quite simply the finest, the richest, the most sophisticated and most exquisite they have ever seen! They are not: almost from the off Ernest Hemingway has stood before us in nothing but his birthday suit, yet the world opts to ignore the obvious. The real enigma is not just that to this day a decidedly middling writer is so universally lauded, but that everyone is – still – prepared to play the game, to admire the non-existent clothes. To repeat Bruccoli's observation

> *Everything he did, everything he wrote, became important because he was Ernest Hemingway.*

Quite. If you disagree, re-read your Hemingway, with what I have written in mind.

---

1   See p.282ff.

THE LIFE

THE following biographical essays are no more than a précis of various biographies of Hemingway and other related accounts of the man. They are intended to provide those who so far know little about him or who do but who are familiar only with the standard tales told about 'Papa' with a more rounded view of the man and writer: they might help to illuminate Hemingway's personality and, perhaps, clarify his behaviour, his ambition, his success and – what I regard as – the enigma of his literary standing.

Earlier, I quoted Debra Moddelmog of the University of Nevada about biography, but it is worth repeating the advice she gives in New Essays On Hemingway's Fiction to beware that

> *the biographer always tells a story, but the story does not come out of nowhere, nor it is implicit in the 'facts' of the author's life. Rather, the biographer chooses a story from among the many that his or her culture makes available and selects the facts that will make the story cohere.*

I read Moddelmog as warning readers that no biographer can ever establish 'the truth' about her or his subject. The biographer's view is inevitably subjective, much as I suggest all evaluations of Hemingway's work and all the interpretations and analyses of his fiction are subjective. Even in what follows, my decisions – whether conscious or and subconscious – on what to include or leave out and how to phrase what I write will be equally subjective, although I hope it will be accepted that any bias is unintentional and is certainly not calculated, despite my view that Hemingway was never more than a 'middling writer'.[1] In several respects because Hemingway's various biographers and commentators on his work disagree in what they write, it is impossible to establish who is 'right' and who is 'wrong'. Was Hemingway fluent in French and Spanish, or was that just his wishful thinking? Was his 'spy network' and 'submarine hunting' in Cuba in the early 1940s useful to the war effort or it just more Hemingway self-importance and part of his desire to be regarded as a man of consequence 'on the inside'? Who knows? But it does help that a reader is aware that there are discrepancies in the several biographies, some of which are notable. Thus once again: caveat lector.[2]

One of the first quotations I used to kick off this book was from the 1962 John Ford Western, the Man who shot Liberty Valance. Maxwell Scott, the man I quote, is one of the film's minor characters, a newspaper reporter who wants to write about how, as a young man, a now respected US senator shot the notorious outlaw Liberty Valance. Once Scott realises it never happened and it is all a myth, he tears up his notes and announces:

This is the West, sir. When the legend becomes fact, print the legend.

In other words when the truth is too dull, promote the fiction: people don't want the truth, they want the razzmatazz, the hype, the legend: people want the Hemingway who could drink the world under the table, the expert on writing, the purported lover of many women, the expert on deep-sea fishing, hunting, bullfighting, the brawler and boxer who could and did take on any man and win – but the man who could also write like an angel. It is that quirk of human nature – a quirk beloved and long appreciated by 'the yellow press' and the 'red tops' – to prefer the fiction to the fact which goes some way to explaining how Ernest Hemingway, a 'middling writer' with a narrow talent became 'a leading modernist' and 'one of America's greatest writers' – not because of but despite the work he produced.

---

1   As Hemingway was by all accounts a 'larger and than life' character, he seems to me, at least, to prove that the phrase 'larger than life' is code for 'complete pain in the arse' (US 'ass').

2   My quote marks when describing Hemingway's activities in Cuba at the beginning of World War II are a case in point and indicate what I believe to have been the case.

1899-1921 – The early years

OAK PARK where Hemingway was born and grew up was then not yet the Chicago suburb it is now, but an independent township. It was a well-off and middle-class community that was exclusively white and overwhelmingly Protestant, and was once described as 'where the bars end and the churches begin'. In 1899, the year of Hemingway's birth, the ethos of Oak Park was firmly late-Victorian and conservative, and both his parents, Clarence – known as Ed – and Grace were strict, teetotal and God-fearing folk, and his father did not flinch from inflicting physical punishment on his children. Ed was a physician who worked from a surgery at home; Grace had trained as an opera singer, but had given up a potential career on stage when she married. It has been suggested that she agreed to marry Ed only when she realised that for health reasons she wouldn't have a career in stage. Grace was by all accounts the dominant force in the family; she gave private singing and music lessons, and acquired her own large custom-built music room after she inherited money when her father died, building a new family home. Her professional income was many times over greater than that of her husband, Ed.

In later life Hemingway claimed that at some point, possibly when he was in his early teens, 'the family fell apart', that Grace had ruined his father's life and that he hated her; but it is unclear what he is talking about, although no one can know the dynamics of any family. On the face of it, he does not seem to have had an unhappy childhood and adolescence, although as an adult he customarily referred to his mother as a 'that bitch'. When Ed shot himself in 1928, worried about money and his declining health, Hemingway insisted that his mother had driven his father to suicide. Biographers agree that Hemingway inherited Grace's domineering personality and that he became hostile to her from his teenage years on because, it is said, she and his third wife Martha Gellhorn were the only two women who would stand up to him.

The family had a summer cottage, Windemere Cottage, on the edge of Walloon Lake in rural north Michigan, and Ed, a keen hunter and fisherman, loved the outdoors and passed on his enthusiasms to his son. For her part Grace ensured that all of her children were educated in the arts, and she regularly took them to concerts and exhibitions in Chicago. All in all Hemingway seems to have had a steady and settled upbringing. He did well at school, regularly had his work highlighted in English classes, did not get into trouble [1] and was never happier than when out in the fresh air fishing and hunting. He never elaborated on what it was that had made the family 'fall apart' – if, in fact, anything had – although one notable hiccup in Ed and Grace's marriage was Grace's relationship with a singing pupil.

Some biographers and writers suggest it might have been a lesbian attachment, but there is very little evidence for that, if any. When Grace was 36 (and Ernest was eight), she took on as both a singing pupil and as a live-in mother's helper a Ruth Arnold, who was then just 13. Grace had four more children after Ernest was born and his sister, Madelaine, was only four when Ruth moved in. Ruth had a rather troubled family background and became part of the family, and she came to address Grace in letters she sent her as 'Muv'. Ernest and his siblings referred to her as a 'nursemaid'. Ruth lived with the Hemingways for many years until one day when she returned to Oak Park from Walloon Lake, where in the meantime Grace had built herself her own cottage and where she and Ruth stayed with the younger children, Ed told her she was no longer welcome. Ed, it seems, had come to believe local gossip that there was indeed a romantic relationship between Grace and Ruth, as, some biographers believe, eventually did Ernest. Grace wrote Ed a letter reassuring him on the matter, but Ruth had to move out and did not call on Grace unless Ed was not at home. It is equally, and quite possibly far more, likely that Ruth simply came to regard Grace as a mother figure (as suggested by the 'Muv' of her letters). Whatever the truth, after Ed's death she moved back into Grace's household and shared her home until Grace died.

. . .

After graduating from high school in the summer of 1917, Hemingway spent the next few months mooching about and hunting small game and fishing while staying at the family summer cottage on Walloon Lake. It was about this time that he began to imagine having a career as a writer. He had been one of the stalwarts of, and had contributed reports to, his high school paper, Trapeze, and several of his short stories were published in Tabula, the school's literary magazine. To Ed's disappointment – he

---

1   Except once: in his mid-teens he shot a blue heron, a protected species, supposedly out of devilment and was eventually fined.

wanted his son to follow his footsteps into practising medicine – Hemingway began to consider a career in journalism instead of attending college. His later claim that he was unable to go to college because Grace had frittered away money intended to fund his college years on building her own Walloon Lake summer cottage is generally dismissed by his biographers as another piece of his customary invention.

In October 1917, Hemingway was taken on as a trainee reporter by the Kansas City Star – his uncle Alfred Tyler Hemingway had been a classmate of the Star's chief editorial writer and had secured an introduction to the paper. The Star had a good reputation nationally, not least for the rigour with which it trained its apprentice reporters, and Hemingway always maintained he learned a lot about writing by diligently observing what was laid down in the paper's stylebook. He was by all accounts an industrious, popular and ambitious reporter, and was always prepared to take on extra work when asked; but he was not with the paper for very long.

Just over six months after Hemingway had joined the Star, he and two young colleagues volunteered to serve as Red Cross ambulance drivers in Europe and resigned at the end of April. He later claimed he had, in turn, already applied to serve in the US army, the US navy and the US marines and had been rejected by all three on the grounds of his poor eyesight. Other accounts have Hemingway not even trying to enlist in those services because he suspected his eyesight would see him marked unfit and had opted to volunteer for the Red Cross because the physical standards it demanded of recruits were lower. As often with Hemingway no definitive evidence to corroborate that claim has been found. There is even an intriguing claim, based on a letter Hemingway's sister Marcelline wrote to her schoolfriend Frances Coates, [1] that Hemingway signed up 'to go to war' – albeit with the Red Cross – because of his unrequited love for Coates. This is thought to have been wholly unlikely.

Hemingway was told to travel to New York to report for induction and training, and on May 23, now commissioned with the rank of a Red Cross second lieutenant, he and his batch of fellow volunteers sailed for Europe. After passing through and spending a few days in Paris on their way to Italy, they arrived in Milan in the first week of June 1918 and were immediately put to work collecting corpses and body parts after a large explosion the day before in a munitions factory ten miles north of the city. Although they were non-combatants, it was a kind of baptism of fire. They were then assigned to their various stations, some of which were busier than others; but soon Hemingway felt his station wasn't busy enough, that he wasn't seeing as much action as he wanted, and he volunteered to serve even closer to the Italian/Austrian front-line. There his duties

---

1   See p.241ff.

1899-1921 – The early years

were to run a canteen, which was some distance behind lines, where troops could relax; yet that wasn't exciting enough for him, and off his own bat he began cycling to the front to deliver coffee and cigarettes to the Italian soldiers. Late one night on one of his trips to the front, 12 days short of his 19th birthday and after being in Italy for just four weeks, Hemingway was badly wounded when an Austrian mortar landed near him. He was lucky to survive – an Italian soldier who had been standing next to him was killed and another had both legs blown off. After first-aid treatment, he was taken to a field hospital and several days later transferred to the Red Cross hospital in Milan on the Via Manzoni, just down the road from La Scala. It was there that he met and fell in love with one of his nurses, Agnes von Kurowsky (who served as the model for Catherine Barkley, the heroine of his novel A Farewell To Arms).

. . .

What had actually happened just before midnight on July 8 at the front on the banks of the river Piave has never been clear. There are several accounts which all contradict each other. One has Hemingway first being knocked unconscious, then, once he had regained his senses, insisting that others should be carried to safety before his wounds were attended to. Another, more heroic, account has him carrying a badly injured Italian soldier from the front-line to safety[1] despite being hit in both knees by machine gun fire as he did so. Another account has him being shot in the thigh and yet another being shot in the foot. Uncharacteristically, Hemingway insisted he had no memory at all of what had happened, but he never denied it might well have been the case that he carried the soldier to safety. Sceptics then and since have pointed out that if he was also hit by machine-gun fire and that both his knees were badly damaged, it is unlikely he would have been able to carry another man even a few feet. The claim is now generally accepted to be just another piece of Hemingway myth-making.

As he grew older, the claims he made about his 'wartime experiences' became ever more extravagant. Just a few months later, after he had undergone several operations and was recuperating, he visited an officers' club in Milan where he was asked about his 'war wound stripes': he claimed they were for injuries he had been sustained in action. He said he had been serving with – and commissioned into – an elite Italian corps, the Arditi, and had led a battalion into battle as its youngest officer. This was outright fiction. His sole 'front-line' experience in World War I was the four weeks when, first, he drove a Red Cross ambulance and then began delivering cigarettes and coffee to the troops. Hemingway never fought or 'saw action'.

---

1   The distance from the front to 'safety' is never specified

When he was finally discharged from the hospital in Milan after three months of treatment, Hemingway was again posted to the front, but within days he was struck down by jaundice and readmitted. By then von Kurowsky had been posted to Florence to care for 'flu victims and the two saw far less of each other. She was back in Milan by the beginning of November, but nine days later she was again sent off, this time to Treviso. In the last two and a half months of their five-month romance, Hemingway and von Kurowsky saw each other just twice (or possibly three times – biographer James Mellow believes they also saw each other on New Year's Eve, five days before Hemingway sailed back to the United States.)

In the nine days they had together in November, he and Agnes had apparently made plans to get married; although in later life Agnes played down their romance and denied she and Hemingway had ever been physical lovers, Hemingway insisted they did have sex, though that claim, like the many he made throughout his life, might best be taken with more than a pinch of salt: Agnes' colleagues in Milan say that although some nurses were known to be 'free with their favours', it was never said of Agnes Although she and Hemingway wrote almost every day while they were not together and her letters were as passionate as his, there is a strong suggestion she was already having second thoughts. She was a popular and attractive woman with many suitors and was beginning to re-consider marriage to someone so young. He was still only 19 and at 26 she was more than seven years older – and, she discovered, he was still quite immature. She later claimed in an interview that she had tried to convey her doubts about their relationship to Hemingway on one of the last times they were together (on a train from Padua to Milan), but had given up when Hemingway became upset and they had quarrelled.

...

While recovering from his jaundice, Hemingway was visited by Captain Jim Gamble, his Red Cross CO, a wealthy man and a keen artist who became a friend and confidant, and who is thought by some biographers to have been in love with Hemingway (who was said to have been remarkably good-looking). Hemingway first met Gamble several months earlier, when Gamble, the Red Cross' 'Inspector of Rolling Canteens', arrived at where the ambulance drivers were billeted and asked for volunteers to run one of the stations handing out cigarettes and coffee to Italian troops on the front. Hemingway, his friend Bill Horne and a third driver agreed. This was on July 1, and exactly a week later, just before midnight, Hemingway was blown up by an Austrian mortar. When Gamble later asked Hemingway to be his secretary and companion for a year in Europe with all expenses paid, Agnes urged him to turn the offer down and to return to the

United States. Biographers suggest that by then not only was she keen to cool things with Hemingway and get him out of Europe, but she might also have believed that there was a homosexual angle to Gamble's offer of which the still unworldly 19-year-old Hemingway was unaware. He did, though, spend a week with Gamble at a rented villa in Taormina, Sicily, over Christmas, though when he returned to Milan he did not tell Agnes that he had spent the time with Gamble. In fact, in conversation with his new friend 'Chink' Dorman-Smith, who knew he had gone to Sicily, he spun an odd story that he had not been able to see anything of Sicily because the woman who ran the pension in which he had stayed had hidden his clothes to prevent him leaving and had kept him as some kind of sex slave. That might have been intended as an obscure joke, but that does not explain why he seemed to want to keep quiet about his time with Gamble in Sicily. How he explained it to Agnes is not recorded. [i]

Several months later (when he was back in the US) — and two weeks before Agnes wrote to him in Oak Park ending their romance — Hemingway had written to Gamble in Europe asking whether his offer was still open. By then Gamble was, in fact, also back in the US, but when the letter finally reached him in April, he invited Hemingway to stay with him in the upscale summer and winter resort of Eagles Mere, Pennsylvania. Hemingway did not go, but a few years later, now living in Chicago and courting Hadley Richardson, he again considered contacting Gamble with a view to taking up the offer. This time it was Hadley who persuaded him not to do so.

. . .

Decommissioned, Hemingway sailed from Genoa on January 4 and arrived in New York two weeks later to a hero's welcome and to be interviewed on the quayside by the New York Sun as 'the first American to return home from the war in Europe'. From Oak Park, he wrote to Agnes almost daily, but her letters to him became less and less frequent. Finally, at the beginning of March Hemingway received her letter (which he admitted to a friend he had already been dreading) calling off the marriage. The tone of that 'Dear John' letter — she addressed him as 'Ernest, dear boy' and told him she was now engaged to an Italian officer — is cited by biographers as a good indication that she had never taken him or his marriage proposal as seriously as he did. Biographer Scott Donaldson even suggests that Agnes had accepted Hemingway's marriage proposal both to keep him away from Jim Gamble and to get him off to the US sooner rather than later as already by November 1918 she wanted to cool the relationship. According to Donaldson, however, Agnes' claim later in life that she had merely been very fond of Hemingway and had at the time been as fond of a number of other men doesn't square with the passionate nature of her early letters to him.

Agnes' rejection hit Hemingway badly, but what rejection hasn't badly hit many an adolescent boy or girl (of all ages)? He spent three days in bed and then simply lounged around at home, not getting up until noon. In and around Oak Park he was celebrated as a war hero, and the Chicago Italian community organised two parties in his honour, which were held at the Hemingway house. [1] When out and about in Oak Park, he played up to the role of the returning hero, flamboyantly and incongruously wearing an Italian army uniform and a black cape, and doing nothing to correct the impression gained by many that he had actually fought on the Italian front.

An invitation from a former teacher at Oak Park High to give a talk about his experiences in Italy to the school debating society led to invitations for more such talks, and over the summer and autumn of 1919 Hemingway gave a series of public lectures in Oak Park and in communities around Walloon Lake, Michigan. At these lectures he exhibited the blood-stained trousers, complete with shrapnel holes, he had been wearing when he was blown up, as well as the medal he had been awarded by the Italian government. Some accounts claim he was awarded as many as four medals, but it has never been clear whether he did receive four or just two – the medal given to all Americans who had helped the Italian war effort and one for being wounded. None, as later claimed and not denied by Hemingway, was presented to him by the king of Italy.

In September 1919, his parents shut up the Windemere Cottage at Walloon Lake for the winter and returned to Oak Park, but Hemingway remained in North Michigan and lodged with a local family. When they, too, shut up their cottage, he rented a room in nearby Petoskey where he set about writing fiction on a borrowed typewriter and sending off stories to various magazines. None was accepted.

It was after one of his 'my war' lectures in north Michigan that Hemingway was approached by a Mrs Harriet Connable, one of his mother's local acquaintances, and hired by her and her husband Ralph (who ran the F. W. Woolworth chain in Canada) to act as a live-in paid companion and mentor for their disabled teenage son while they were in Florida on vacation. In January 1920, he moved into their Toronto mansion, and before the Connables had left for their Florida break, he had persuaded Ralph Connable, who knew various executives on the Toronto Star, to get him an introduction. He then took to hanging around the Star offices 'hoping to be given an assignment' [2] and was eventually introduced to the Weekly Star's editor, J. Herbert Cranston, who agreed to

---

1   Ed and Grace Hemingway were none too keen that parties where wine was to be drunk would be held in their strictly teetotal household.

2   I confess I am unable here to sneer at Hemingway's naivety on the grounds that those who live in glass house are best advised not to three stones.

consider for publication any freelance features he submitted. In the six months he was in Toronto, he sold several short, chatty pieces to the paper and, crucially, Cranston like his work and took a shine to him.

. . .

When the Connables came home from Florida, they invited Hemingway to stay on as their house guest, and he didn't return to Windemere Cottage at Walloon Lake until the beginning of June. He now felt he was entitled to relax, spend time with his friends and go fishing; but his parents had other ideas. From letters they sent him throughout the summer, it is clear there were arguments with his parents in which he became quite belligerent. Eventually, he and a friend moved into the guest annex at Windemere Cottage, but he still refused to find paid work, didn't do the small tasks about the cottages he was assigned (including at the cottage his mother had built on the other side of the lake) and simply continued his life of leisure, hunting and fishing. Throughout June and July things went from bad to worse, and finally, his parents, individually, asked him and his friend to leave the property and told their son not to return until he was invited back. He had just turned 21.

Where Hemingway stayed for the following few months has not been recorded, but by the beginning of October, he had finally found a job: he had answered a small ad in the Chicago Tribune and was taken on by a publication called the Cooperative Commonwealth. This described itself as 'The Weekly Magazine Of Mutual Help' and was published by the Cooperative Society of America. Hemingway claimed he was the magazine's 'managing editor', but in fact he was just one of a number of young men churning out the necessary copy to give the magazine substance and seeing the publication through production. Both the magazine and society were founded by one Harrison M. Parker and were part of an elaborate scam to part suckers from their money. Hemingway later claimed he had suspected as much by the following spring and resigned, but at least one biographer writes that despite realising what was going on, he had stayed in his job until June when the magazine was wound up and Parker was taken to court. By then Parker had filched $15 million of the society's money. [1] In Chicago, Hemingway soon began lodging in the Chicago apartment of Y.K. Smith, the older brother of his North Michigan friends Bill and Katie Smith. Katie was also living there and in time he met her schoolfriend Elizabeth Hadley Richardson (known as Hadley) when she came to visit Katie for three

---

1   Accounting for inflation that would be $228 million in 2023. To cover his tracks, Parker kept the money in a bank account in his wife's name. She was named as the Cooperative Society of America's 'secretary'.

weeks after the recent death of her mother (her father had shot himself 16 years earlier). Hadley and Hemingway hit it off from the start.

...

Their courtship until they married 11 months later was overwhelmingly conducted by letter – in that time Hemingway and Hadley might only have seen each other three times: when they first met in Chicago, when he spent a few days in St Louis, her hometown, and in March 1921 when he took her to Oak Park to introduce her to his parents. [1] But it seems they had decided to marry soon after they met. By June 1921 they began making practical plans for their wedding, but Hemingway then fell into a depression about it all and even – quite bizarrely – spoke of killing himself. [2] At the turn of the year, Jim Gamble had been back in touch and had repeated his invitation to Hemingway to spend a year with him, all expenses paid. Hemingway again turned down the offer, and by then he and Hadley were considering moving to Naples so he could do 'his writing'. They changed their plans and settled on moving to Paris at the recommendation of the writer Sherwood Anderson, a former ad man and a friend of Y.K. Smith's who was accustomed to drop in. Enthusiastic about the short stories Hemingway showed him, [3] Anderson insisted that Paris was where it was all happening in the arts and that is where the couple should move, not Italy as they planned. Hemingway and Hadley were married in the Methodist church in Horton Bay on September 3, 1921 – one biographer writes that for some reason Ed Hemingway was under the impression his son did not want him to attend the ceremony and had to be reassured by Hemingway that he did – and spent their two-week honeymoon at the Walloon Lake cottage. Oddly, during their honeymoon in North Michigan, Hemingway decided to introduce Hadley to all his previous girlfriends. She and none of the girls were impressed. [4]

Y.K. Smith had initially agreed that the couple could live in his flat once they were

---

1   Hadley later commented that she and Grace 'were not made to be friends'.

2   The same happened several years later after Hadley and he had parted, and he was on the point of marrying Pauline Pfeiffer, but added pressure then was that he was living alone and feeling very guilty about leaving Richardson. Whether this first depression in Chicago amounted to what now might be called 'clinical depression' or whether he simply got cold feet is not recorded. As a rule 'clinical depression' is not transitory, and a young man's cold feet might well have been at play.

3   As I have earlier remarked, whether Anderson thought Hemingway had an unusual literary gift or whether – which is to my mind more likely – he was simply encouraging a young man in his ambitions as many an established writer might we cannot now know.

4   I have earlier suggested that, in part, fundamental to Hemingway's personality was a deep inferiority complex. Tactlessly introducing his bride to young women he had previously squired might well be thought as symptomatic, as though he felt he had something to prove to Hadley.

1899-1921 – The early years

married, but there had been a falling out after Hemingway informed Y.K. that his wife, 'Doodles', was sleeping with another of the lodgers. It turned out Y.K. knew and didn't care as he and his wife had an 'open' marriage and he was also having affairs, and when the falling-out worsened, Y.K. rescinded his offer. Instead the newly married couple found a small apartment in Chicago where they lived for a few months and eventually set sail for Europe in mid-December, 1921. To help Hemingway on his way, Sherwood Anderson provided him with letters of introduction to several friends and acquaintances in Paris, informing them that the young man would be calling on them and who he was.

1921-1924 – Paris and life are sweet

WHEN Hemingway arrived in Paris, he was just another literary wannabe, one of many who washed up in Montparnasse, though ironically by the early 1920s the quarter's heyday was over and its reputation as a bohemian hotspot was waning. Just under five years later he was a commercially published author, although it would not be for several more years before he achieved his other ambition of earning his living solely from his writing; yet that did not matter: for the next twenty years and until his second wife, Pauline Pfeiffer, divorced him in November 1940, Hemingway was largely sustained by the money of his first two wives, both of whom had independent means. In addition Pauline had a very wealthy uncle who doted on her and indulged her and her eventual husband Ernest. [1]

Because of his subsequent fame, it is often assumed that when Hemingway began working in Paris as 'a foreign correspondent' at just 22, it was because he was such a talented journalist. That over-eggs the pudding badly: he was never on staff in Paris, and the claim on a Toronto Star website dedicated to the writer that he was 'the paper's European correspondent', though strictly true, is ambiguous (and perhaps, given Hemingway's later global fame, intentionally so). By the time Hemingway and Hadley arrived in Paris in late December 1921, his journalistic experience was not extensive: it consisted of just six months working as a trainee reporter on the Kansas City Star, five months in Toronto as a freelance selling short (and inconsequential) pieces to the Weekly Toronto Star and his months helping to produce the Cooperative Commonwealth in Chicago. But he had a lively and entertaining journalistic style, though one more suited to writing colour pieces than news stories. He was also adept at giving the impression

---

1   Had he chosen a more modest lifestyle. he might well have been able to exist on the royalties from the work he published and what he earned from his journalism. But after meeting Pfeiffer (and a little later very wealthy Gerald and Sara Murphy), he found he liked living a rather grand life.

he knew what he was talking about, a skill reporters always find useful and are wise to acquire. He was a good and attentive listener and, for example, while later covering conferences in Genoa and Lausanne, he picked up a lot from his more experienced colleagues, political and economic insights he passed on as his own in an authoritative manner to Toronto Star's readers.

The deal he reached with the Toronto Star before he moved to Paris was straightforward: he would write short pieces for the weekly Star and it would pay him for what it chose to print. If the paper sent him anywhere on assignment, which in time it did, he would, in addition, be paid his expenses. Yet had Hemingway not tried to be a little too clever by half, according to William Burrill, a former Toronto Star writer, columnist and editor, he might have landed himself a far better deal.

In his book Hemingway, The Toronto Years, Burrill says that the freelance features Hemingway produced for the Weekly Star edited by Herbert Cranston came to the attention of John Bone, the Star's managing editor, and Bone kept his eye on Hemingway, but for a very specific reason. It seems, says Burrill, that Bone was engaged in a little skulduggery to make some money on the side: he sold his writers' copy to other publications under his own by-line and pocketed the payments. His dilemma was that if he passed off the copy of his better-known writers as his own, his double-dealing might be discovered; so he restricted himself to passing off the copy by the less-known staff. Bone was impressed with Hemingway's work and reasoned that if he could get Hemingway to Paris as the paper's staff correspondent, he might be a source of good copy and stories he could then sell. So in the spring of 1921, Bone contacted Hemingway in Chicago and offered to hire him to go to Paris. Hemingway declared he was interested, but countered that he liked his job in Chicago which was paying him $75 a week – in fact he was being paid just $40; he told Bone he would not accept the job for less than $85 a week (a rather nice $1,118 in 2023). That was too much for Bone and the offer was withdrawn, so when Hemingway arrived in Paris was as just another stringer on rather poorer terms.

At first Hemingway submitted general colour pieces about whatever caught his fancy, but eventually John Bone began asking him to cover particular events. Yet the arrangement was still that Hemingway was paid only for what he produced. [1] It is also pertinent that his freelance status allowed him to refuse assignments if he wanted to, with no comeback. He had done so when the Star asked him to go to Russia. Hadley, by then pregnant, put her foot down as she did not want to be left alone in Paris and told him he couldn't go. No staff correspondent would or could do that if they wanted to

---

1   We know this because in one piece he sent to Toronto, he described that he preferred getting out-of-town assignments because they paid better – lineage and expense rates were higher.

keep their job. His freelance status also meant he and Hadley could take off on vacation whenever they chose.

...

Hemingway and Hadley were just two of an increasing number of Americans and British who moved to Paris throughout the 1920s, partly because the dollar's exchange rate with the French franc was so attractive, and they were able to live comfortably in the city on a sum that at home would have been a pittance. Biographer Michael Reynolds reports that by January 1924 when the Hemingway's returned from Toronto and arrived in Paris for the second time, there were '32,000 permanent American residents and twice as many British' living in the city.[1] The income from Hadley's trust fund, a respectable amount even in the US, was more than enough to sustain the newly married couple – the rent on the apartment they moved into in January 1922 was the equivalent of just $18 a month. The trust fund had been set up after Hadley's mother died in late 1920. In early 1922 it paid around $3,600 a year or about $300 a month/$70 a week. Taking inflation into account, those sums, in 2023, are the equivalent of $55,000 a year and $4,500 a month. Hemingway's later claims in his memoir A Moveable Feast that he and Hadley existed in penury are just another piece of his habitual myth-making, though after they returned from Toronto in January 1924 and his association with the Toronto Star had ended and Hemingway was earning next to nothing, they had to rely solely Hadley's trust fund. Money could get tight if her quarterly cheque from the fund was late.

They had left the US in mid-December 1921, arrived in Paris, via Spain, a few days before Christmas and moved into a hotel where Sherwood Anderson had previously stayed and where he had booked them a room. It was there that their first contact in France, Lewis Galantière,[2] looked them up two days after Christmas. It was to be the occasion of very odd, but typical, Hemingway behaviour which is almost inexplicable. Galantière, an acquaintance of Anderson's who was just five years older than Hemingway, had been asked by Anderson to take Hemingway and Hadley under his wing. When he received the letter of introduction written by Anderson, he called on the young couple and took them out to dinner. Afterwards he was invited back to their hotel room for a glass of cognac. There Hemingway handed him a pair of boxing gloves

---

1 I have no idea where he go his figures from, however.
2 Despite his name, Lewis Galantière was not French but an American born in Chicago, though he did learn to speak excellent French and partly made his living as a translator.

and invited him to spar. [1] Though slightly built, short-sighted and at least a foot shorter than Hemingway – and perhaps a little bemused by the unusual challenge – Galantière gamely agreed and was astonished when, thinking the sparring was over and he was already taking off his boxing gloves, Hemingway punched him hard and knocked him to the floor. No explanation was offered, though one biographer has suggested that Hemingway was irritated and jealous because he felt Galantière had been paying Hadley too much attention at dinner. Yet despite being floored (and his glasses being smashed), Galantière honoured Anderson's request and spent the following days showing the couple the sights of Paris and helping them find an apartment. In fact, Hemingway's friendship with Galantière continued for several years, but eventually cooled after Hemingway, in another inexplicable incident, insulted Galantière's fiancé.

The dynamics of Hemingway and Hadley's relationship meant that he took all the decisions, and he finally settled on renting a dismal two-room apartment for them four floors up in the rue de Cardinal Lemoine. It had no bathroom, a tiny annexe with a two-ring gas burner for a kitchen and the lavatory was the old-fashioned 'hole-in-the-ground' kind on the landing, shared by everyone else living on the same floor. Quite why Hemingway chose to live there was a mystery to friends who visited them and who knew Hadley's trust fund income would have allowed them to rent somewhere far nicer. Some biographers suggest that Hemingway, who kept a tight record of his spending all his life, was concerned that he and Hadley should live within their means and he erred on the side of caution. Yet money was certainly not tight: the day after they moved into their new flat, Hemingway and Hadley left Paris for a three-week skiing trip to Chambry in Switzerland, their first vacation in 1922.

. . .

In late February and March, Hemingway followed up his other letters of introduction from Anderson and called on Ezra Pound and Gertrude Stein and on Sylvia Beach, who ran the well-known bookshop Shakespeare And Company and had been the first to publish James Joyce's Ulysses.

The first Hemingway and Hadley called on was Pound (though other accounts have Hemingway meeting Pound by chance in Beach's bookshop) and over the following months he showed Pound the stories and poems he had so far written. Pound, who had a solid background discovering and fostering talent, liked what he read, but considered

---

1 One must wonder why Hemingway had with him two pairs of boxing gloves, but apparently he did.

Hemingway to be raw material that needed to be worked on. [1] The pieces he was shown consisted of the very conventional and derivative short fiction Hemingway had been unsuccessfully submitting to magazines for the past three years. Pound began his instruction by telling Hemingway to avoid adjectives and adverbs in his writing, and gave him a long list of texts and books to read. According to Michael Reynolds in his book Hemingway's Reading, the list included 'Homer, Ovid, Catullus, Propertius, Dante, Villon, Voltaire, Stendhal, Flaubert, the Goncourts, Corbiere and Rimbaud'. Whether or not Hemingway did read his way through that – rather daunting – list is uncertain; but still the modest and eager pupil and not yet in the role of the wise, experienced writer he had cast himself in by the end of the decade, he diligently practised what Pound preached.

Next he and Hadley called on Stein. Stein had a very high opinion of herself and her talent: she sincerely regarded herself as a genius and once stated that

> *the Jews have produced only three originative geniuses: Christ, Spinoza and myself.* [2]

She also once declared

> *Nobody has done anything to develop the English language since Shakespeare, except myself and Henry James perhaps a little.* [3]

Stein indulged in what has been described as 'cubist writing' which was 'based on rhythm, rhyme and repetition rather than on a sense-making plot', and she urged Hemingway to do the same. She also encouraged him to practise 'automatic writing', a technique of simply writing down what comes into your head without consciously thinking about it. But as Stein, oddly for a genius, was averse to editing and re-writing her work, the product of her 'automatic writing' was and is considered by many to be unreadable (and perhaps some editing and re-writing would not have gone amiss). She does have her few champions among academics, but sales of her work that has been commercially published have been slow to non-existent.

...

---

1   This was presumably the work Hemingway had shown Sherwood Anderson which had impressed the older man and which was lost in the Gare de Lyon the following year.

2   There does not seem to be any suggestion that her tongue was in her cheek, although it have been. Nevertheless, Stein did regard herself as exceptionally talented.

3   Ditto.

1921-1924 – Paris and life are sweet

Hemingway had been submitting short, colour pieces of his impressions of Paris to the Toronto Star almost from the day he arrived, but towards the end of March, 1922, he was asked to cover the upcoming economic conference in Genoa. As luck would have it, travelling there by train at the beginning of April, he fell in with a group of far more experienced journalists who proved to be very helpful, filling him in on background and who remained friendly colleagues for the following few years.

Once the conference had ended, he and Hadley were off again [1] to ski in Switzerland, and from there they embarked a sentimental trip to north-east Italy for Hemingway to show Hadley the sights of his – it has to be said extremely short – 'war'. That trip down memory lane was not a success. Since the end of the war just three and half years earlier in 1918, the countryside had already healed itself of its battle scars and Hemingway couldn't even work out where the trench in which he had almost died was.

That summer, Bill Bird, one of the journalists who had befriended him on the train, acquired an ancient hand-printing press and founded the Three Mountains Press. He decided to produce a series of limited editions, a project which evolved into 'an inquest into the state of contemporary English prose' with Ezra Pound as editor, and Hemingway was asked to contribute work. In August he and Hadley were off on vacation again – the third of that year – taking a hiking trip in Germany's Black Forest with Bird and his wife and Galantière and his fiancé (to whom Hemingway took one of his instant dislikes, a dislike which eventually led to him insulting her and Galantière deciding he didn't want Hemingway as a friend any more).

In September the Star finally agreed – some accounts have it that it was at Hemingway's suggestion [2] – to send him off to Constantinople to report on what was left of the conflict between Greece and Turkey. Hadley did not want him to go – she was still not quite confident speaking French and did not like being left alone in Paris where she knew few people. The couple rowed, the first serious disagreement of their marriage, and did not speak to each other for three days before Hemingway departed. The row with Hadley, however, was also over another matter: a second reporting deal Hemingway had struck. Apart from providing the Star with features and reports, he quietly agreed to provide two Hearst news agencies with copy through their Paris office. His agreement with the Star was exclusive, though, and Hadley had strongly disapproved. Hemingway's double-dealing might have remained undetected had he not eventually become a lazy and resorted simply to sending the agencies duplicates of his Star copy. John Bone was

---

1 Their second vacation in 1922

2 The belief is that 23-year-old Hemingway suggested the assignment because he thought it would be exciting 'to cover a war'.

angry when reports identical to the ones it was getting from Hemingway appeared in US papers, though under the by-line 'John Hadley'. Hemingway tried to blame the Hearst agency point man in Paris who had hired him, claiming he had stolen his Star copy and passed it off as his own. Bone did not buy it. [1]

By the time Hemingway arrived in Turkey the actual fighting was over and there was not much to write about. To add to his disappointment, the conditions were uncomfortable: his hotel bed was full of bugs, he became covered in lice and developed a fever, possibly malaria, and eventually sought treatment at a British hospital. When the Turks had taken Smyrna, agreed an armistice and gave the Greeks in Thrace 15 days to evacuate the city, Hemingway and his fellow hacks took off to Thrace to cover the evacuation, and he wrote and filed a report about the long line of refugees fleeing the city. This account was later reworked into one of the short 'chapters' or 'vignettes' which appeared in *in our time* and later in In Our Time. His later claim that he had spent the night before leaving for Thrace with a voluptuous, big-breasted Turkish whore is, in view of his lice-riddled, feverish condition almost certainly just another Hemingway tall tale.

...

In December he was off again, this time to cover the 1922 Lausanne peace conference. Possibly to keep Hadley sweet and agree to his attending, he arranged for her to join him in Lausanne before they made their way to Chambry for Christmas. But a bad bout of the 'flu delayed her departure, and when she did finally leave Paris, a small valise into which she had packed almost all the work Hemingway had so far completed – including his carbon copies – went missing from her train compartment in the Gare de Lyon. [2] When she arrived in Lausanne and informed Hemingway, he was said to have been devastated. One biographer suggests the loss might have caused the first fissure in their marriage (still just over a year old) and eventually lead to his split from Hadley several years later.

Hemingway's reaction to the loss of his early work, like much else in his life, is a

---

1   This is ironic given Bone's own scam selling on his writers' copy as his own. But such double-dealing is not at all uncommon even among executives. I once worked for a large provincial evening paper – in the days when even provincial papers were selling well – which sacked its foreign editor when it discovered he 'employed' a host of fictional correspondents around the world and was pocketing the money he was 'paying them'.

2   Another journalist in Lausanne had shown interest in Hemingway's work and she thought it would please her husband to be able to show him more of it. Quite what Hemingway had shown the journalist is unknown.

little obscure. For many years the accepted story – for which Hemingway' memoir A Moveable Feast written almost 40 later is the only source – has him organising cover for his Lausanne duties and catching an overnight train to Paris to check that his manuscripts hadn't after all been left in the flat. Such a swift reaction would be in keeping with the image of 'the artist dedicated to his work' he was keen to establish in the memoir. Eventually – like many facts of Hemingway's life – that account came under scrutiny. One biographer, Michael Reynolds – in Hemingway: The Paris Years published in 1989 – accepts that Hemingway did chase off to Paris, but points out that he could not, as he claimed, have had lunch with Gertrude Stein and Alice Toklas the following day and was consoled by them simply because Stein and Toklas weren't in Paris at the time. By checking dates in letters and diary, Reynolds established that the couple had already taken off to their Provencal retreat for Christmas and were not back in Paris until the beginning of February.

Three years later, biographer James R. Mellow – in Hemingway: A Life Without Consequence – goes further with his scepticism: he writes that Hemingway invented his account in A Moveable Feast and that he had not chased off to Paris as he claimed; once the Lausanne conference was over, he and Hadley carried on to Chambry in Switzerland as planned, and they did not get back to Paris until mid-January. Only then was Hemingway able to confirm that Hadley had also lost his carbon copies. Mellow bases his conclusions on the contents of a letter Hemingway wrote to Ezra Pound dated January 23, a week after he had returned from Chambry.

. . .

Hemingway's ambitions to establish himself as a writer were certainly not hampered by the grubby necessity of earning a living. Within weeks of returning from Chambry in mid-January, he and Hadley were off yet again, this time to Rapallo to where Ezra Pound and his wife Dorothy had moved. While there, he met an Edward O'Brien who was also visiting the area. O'Brien edited an annual volume of short stories and after reading My Old Man (one of only three stories that had survived the Gare de Lyon loss) he asked Hemingway to contribute to the next issue. Hemingway also met another friend of Pound's, Henry 'Mike' Strater, who completed two portraits of him and told him all about bullfighting; another new acquaintance – he never became a friend – was Robert McAlmon, a habitué of Montparnasse who had also dropped by. McAlmon and his wife had a lavender marriage – she was lesbian and McAlmon was gay – and courtesy of her family's money, McAlmon had decided to start a small publishing house in Paris to handle his own and others' fiction. [1] He, too, asked Hemingway to submit work.

At the beginning of April after almost a month in Rapallo and a short walking tour with Pound, he and Hadley were off for more skiing, this time in Cortina in the Italian Dolomites. Halfway through their stay, Hemingway broke off to undertake a Star assignment to the industrial German Ruhrgebiet. He had suggested to the Star that he should make the trip while still in Rapallo after the French occupation forces had invaded the Ruhr a few weeks earlier, but the Star's John Bone had not agreed until the end of March. Bone wanted him to spend a month in Germany, but Hemingway gave him just ten days [2] and then rejoined Hadley in Cortina. While in Cortina and enthused by O'Brien's request, he began some serious writing, and though the work he produced was slim – just six brief 'vignettes', each a paragraph long – their new style boosted his confidence. By the beginning of May and back in Paris, and Hemingway turned his attention to producing more short work for Bird's project to add to his six 'vignettes'. In June a tour of bullfights in Spain with Bill Bird and Robert McAlmon sparked Hemingway's lifelong obsession with bullfighting. Through Stein and Toklas he heard about the San Fermin festival in Pamplona and in July, he made his first trip to the Basque town, with Hadley. By then, though, Hadley's pregnancy, first discovered in March 1923 in Rapallo, was very evident.

. . .

The pregnancy had not been planned and certainly cast a shadow over Hemingway's carefree existence – he complained to Gertrude Stein that he was 'too young' to be a father and there are even suggestions that he urged Hadley to abort her unborn child. [3] Their son John's birth, in October 1923, certainly put the couple's relationship under some strain and changed its dynamic, and it might have marked the second step towards their eventual divorce. Most biographers report that Hemingway's move to Toronto in September 1923 to join the Star staff came about because Hadley didn't trust French doctors and wanted her child do be born on American soil. Yet that begs the question of why they moved to Canada and not America. On the other hand, biographer Michael Reynolds believes he found evidence in letters that Hemingway had, in fact, been offered a staff job in Toronto a year earlier by John Bone. Hemingway, still intent on becoming

---

1   His wife's father Sir John Ellerman was an investor who also owned a shipping line and was very wealthy indeed.

2   Once again this such cavalier behaviour would not have been possible for a staff man.

3   I don't much care for speculation, but those who do might care to wonder whether Hemingway's story Hills Like White Elephants in his second collection of short stories had its genesis in a conversation he had with Hadley along the lines of her aborting the foetus.

a full-time writer – though, admittedly, he had still not produced much work – had turned down the offer and only decided to accept it when he realized that as a family man he would need a more regular income.

Hemingway's career on the Star staff was miserable and brief. Though Bone had been impressed by his work, his deputy, Harry Hindmarsh, the Star's city editor who was Hemingway's immediate boss (and who had married the daughter of the paper's proprietor, Joe Atkinson) regarded Hemingway as a cocky upstart.[1] Accounts by Toronto Star contemporaries confirm that when he arrived in Toronto, a swaggering Hemingway chose to play up the 'experienced newsman' who had been reporting on important events in Europe.[1] Hindmarsh – who didn't get on with Bone and disliked what he regarded as Bone's protégés – decided to take him down a peg or two. According to Hemingway, he was assigned what he regarded as puff pieces and dispatched to various parts of the country to cover stories he believed were trivial. Given that one story he was asked to investigate – a possible million-dollar mining fraud by a dodgy company – was anything but a 'puff piece' suggests his objections were more petulant than justified.[2] His first big row with Hindmarsh occurred just over a month in the job when Hemingway returned from New York where he had been covering the visit of the former British Prime Minister, David Lloyd-George. While in New York, he decided not to file a story about the deputy mayor somehow 'belittling Britain' because he did not think it was important enough. This was unfortunate because both Hindmarsh and Atkinson did think the story was important, given that a great many of the Star's readers were of British descent. While Hemingway was still on the train back to Toronto, Hadley gave birth, and alerted by friends, Hemingway went straight to the hospital from the station. Hindmarsh was furious that on top of missing the 'deputy mayor' story, he had not first checked in at the office, and when he appeared in the office, Hemingway was hauled in for a dressing down. According to the Toronto Star website 'celebrating' their former employee, during a row that followed, Hemingway told Hindmarsh that henceforth any work he would from then on be required to do would be done 'with the most utter contempt and hatred'. From there on relations with Hindmarsh went from bad to worse, and Hemingway was soon reassigned to work on the Weekly Toronto Star,

---

1   In his book Hemingway, The Toronto Years, William Burrill reports that apart from playing the seasoned foreign correspondent, Hemingway also chose to arrive at the Star offices dressed in a rather bohemian fashion. That also did not go down well with Hindmarsh. Burrill's claim that Hemingway's boots were often covered in mud is, though, disputed.

2   According to the Toronto Star his first job as a staff reporter when he began work in September 1924 was to cover a prison break. That does not sound much like a mere 'puff piece', either. On the other hand, like all the other reporters, Hemingway was also required to take part in cheesy advertising stunts, which he hated.

a demotion in all but name.

The account of how Hemingway resigned from his Star job has also been transmuted into an heroic myth: he is said in a furious outburst to have typed pages of vitriol attacking Hindmarsh, glued them together into one long screed and posted it on the newsroom wall. [1] In fact, after returning from a brief one-day visit home to Oak Park, he wrote a short letter to John Bone tending his resignation which, he said, would take effect from January 1, 1924. [2] He and Hadley left Toronto by train for New York on January 12, and set sail a week later. They were in Paris by the end of the month

Hemingway's resignation was not as spontaneous as it might appear. It is clear from a letter dated November 11, 1923, that Hemingway – and presumably Hadley – had by then already decided to cut short their time in Toronto and move back to Paris. Writing to the literary critic Edmund Wilson with a copy of Three Stories And Ten Poems which had appeared the previous August

> *I hope you like the book. If you are interested could you send me the names of four or five people to send it to get it reviewed? It would be terribly good of you. This address [in Toronto] will be good until January when we will be going back to Paris.*

---

1   In later years some of Hemingway's colleagues at the Star in 1924 said they distinctly remembered the many pages Hemingway had pasted together and pinned up trailing down the wall and on to the floor. Other colleagues can remember nothing of the kind and insist they would have done so had it been true.

2   One of the final straws appears to have been Hindmarsh carelessly throwing away the only copies of important papers with which Hemingway had been entrusted by a contact.

1924-1925 – Learning to be a success

. . . the jazz age in microcosm, with all its extremes of hysteria and cynicism, of carpe diem, of decadent thriftlessness . . . To recapture its atmosphere one would not, like Proust, dip a madeleine into a cup of tea, but a canapé into bathtub gin.

Novelist Edith Stern describing Hemingway's first publishers Boni & Liveright when she worked there as a reader and later as an office manager.

ONCE Hemingway was back in Paris in January 1924 and relations with the Star had been sundered, there was no more freelance work to help meet the bills, and he and Hadley had to rely solely on her trust fund income to pay their way. Furthermore, the cheques from the fund were often late, which sometimes caused problems; in time the amount paid was further diminished after the family friend who had taken over managing the fund on Hadley's behalf either made a poor investment or – and this was certainly Hemingway's view and more recent biographers subscribe to it – had embezzled some of her money. Yet despite his domestic responsibilities Hemingway still did not look for paid work (and perhaps he and Hadley believed her trust fund cheques were more than enough for them to live on: what he contributed to the household budget from the money the Star had paid him as a freelance was negligible compared to her income). At Ezra Pound's suggestion the British novelist, poet and critic Ford Madox Ford, who had just launched the literary journal the *transatlantic review* [sic] in January 1924, took on Hemingway as his deputy, but the work was unpaid. Yet Hemingway's later oft-repeated claims that he spent the next two years living in penury are typically wide of the mark. He and Hadley sometimes had to borrow money from friends to see them through until the next trust fund cheque arrived, but they were never on their uppers. [i] Certainly, they watched their spending and when they went off on vacation, they covered their costs by sub-letting their apartment, but life was still inexpensive. In fact, when they spent a full three months in a hotel in Schruns, Austria, from December 1924 to early March 1925, the cheap Austrian schilling allowed them to live on even less than in Paris. To boot, Hemingway had an oddly cavalier attitude to money and spending it: he never stinted himself, but didn't mind that Hadley's clothes were almost falling off her – the wives and girlfriends in the couple's social circle often took pity on her and passed on their clothes, wondering why Hadley acquiesced so meekly to what looked like Hemingway's selfishness – it was after all her trust fund money that paid the bills.

. . .

In his ambition to earn his living as a writer, let alone make his name for himself, by early 1924 Hemingway was still barely off the starting block. So far he had only two slim volumes to his name, both privately published: 300 copies of Three Stories And Ten Poems produced by Robert McAlmon's Contact Publishing Company and 170 copies – part of the intended 300 edition hand-printed run had been damaged – of *in our time*, published by Bill Bird's Three Mountain Press. As no commercial imperative underpinned either undertaking, both McAlmon and Bird might best be regarded as 'gentlemen publishers' and Hemingway was paid nothing for his work. McAlmon funded his publishing with his wife's money, and Bird co-owned a press agency, and for him printing and publishing were a labour of love which he undertook in his spare time. Both men had standing in the Paris ex-patriate literary community, but their enterprises were very small-scale indeed, and Hemingway, unsurprisingly, craved the kind of recognition that publication by a bona-fide commercial house would give him.

His November 11, 1923, letter to Edmund Wilson from Toronto was one of his first moves to try to attract wider attention to his work. Wilson had given him encouragement of sorts: he told Hemingway that in his view some of Three Stories and Ten Poems was good, but then he qualified his praise. He said he did not much like Up In Michigan and My Old Man reminded him of Sherwood Anderson's work; and, Wilson added, he thought the stories were better than the poems. (Everyone thought Hemingway's stories were better than the poems – his poetry has never been acclaimed.) All in all, one might sum up Wilson's reaction to Three Stories And Ten Poems as 'promising so keep it up'. But this did not disillusion Hemingway: he thanked Wilson for his interest, although he objected to the comparison with Anderson's work. The astute, not so say, calculating side of Hemingway's character might be gauged from a part of his letter in which he had disingenuously and blatantly flattered Wilson. He wrote

> *Yours is the only critical opinion in the States I have any respect for.*

In Hemingway: The Paris Years, the second volume of his biography, Michael Reynolds points out that

> *As Hemingway was obviously learning, writing well was only half the game; making sure that influential people knew you were writing well was the other half. Before another year was out his game would be impeccable, the two complementing each other perfectly.*

. . .

Ford Madox Ford had a solid existence and reputation in the literary world, and had long championed young writers. He had been impressed with Hemingway's writing as soon as he read it. Hemingway, however, took an immediate and irrational dislike to the novelist as soon as they met: Ford was corpulent, wheezed (as the result of being gassed in World War I), [ii] was much given to bragging about his literary connections, was apt to tells fibs and had a high opinion of himself. Hemingway became increasingly and publicly insulting, but the older, more experienced writer never wavered in his admiration for Hemingway's work. Reynolds observes that

> *Ford never understood Hemingway's animosity, and Ernest never understood the walrus-like Ford of the wheezing voice. The man could never tell the truth, Ernest said. Perhaps he saw something of himself in Ford, something he did not like but could not control any more than could Ford.*

In addition, Hemingway disagreed with Ford's editorial policy for the *transatlantic review*; he felt the choice of content was not *avant garde* enough and that Ford was still beholden to the pre-war world of literature. His animosity became embarrassing later in the summer of 1924 when Ford went off to the US to try to drum up more financial backing for the magazine and Hemingway was left in charge. Putting together the July issue, Hemingway more or less sabotaged what Ford was trying to do. [iii] Yet despite this rather ungracious disloyalty, Ford gave Three Stories And Ten Poems a good review in the *transatlantic review* and published the early short story Indian Camp.

Although Hemingway's career as a writer was still taking off, he was making some progress: in the small coterie of Left Bank ex-patriates his name became well-known as that of a promising writer; and bit by bit word also got back to literary folk in the US – well, to the literary folk in New York – that a young American in Paris was producing interesting work. One man who began to pass on the word was F. Scott Fitzgerald, the bright new thing of American letters who had found fame in 1920 with his debut novel This Side Of Paradise and its follow-up The Beautiful And The Damned. He alerted Max Perkins, his editor at his publisher, Scribner's, and at Perkins' bidding obtained a copy of *in our time*. Perkins liked what he read, yet none of the magazines in the US to whom Hemingway was submitting his stories were as enthusiastic and none choose to publish them. The commercial magazines didn't think his stories were what their readers wanted and the literary magazines were simply not impressed.

Undaunted, the ambitious networker in Hemingway began to hit his stride. In the spring he had met and made friends with John Dos Passos and Donald Ogden Stewart, both established and published writers, and Harold Loeb who was about to have his first novel published; he enlisted the help of all three in finding a commercial publisher. Ogden Stewart was signed up to the New York house Boni & Liveright, who had recently acquired Sherwood Anderson, Hemingway's first benefactor, and the house was also due to publish Loeb's novel. When Dos Passos and Ogden Stewart returned to New York later in 1924, Hemingway gave Dos Passos a copy of the In Our Time manuscript so he and Ogden Stewart could hawk it around the publishers. The manuscript eventually made its way to Boni & Liveright.

At the time Boni & Liveright had asked Leon Fleischman to take over as its representative and scout in Europe (from the writer Harold Stearns who had become an unreliable drunk),[1] and Loeb, who knew Fleischman, suggested he consider recommending Hemingway's work to his employer. One evening in early autumn, Loeb and his girlfriend Kitty Cannell took Hemingway to Fleischman's apartment for an initial meeting. According to Loeb, writing in his memoir The Way It Was 35 years later, Fleischman immediately agreed to forward Hemingway's name to Boni & Liveright – Loeb suggests Fleischman was already familiar with Hemingway's work from the two previously privately published volumes – but the meeting at Fleischman's apartment marked another example of very odd behaviour from Hemingway. During the evening, he reportedly became ever more subdued and said very little; but once the evening had ended and he, Loeb and Cannell were back out in the street, he launched into an obscene anti-Semitic rant about Fleischman. Loeb, himself Jewish, later brushed off the outburst

---

1   See p.133ff.

as merely the kind of 'locker room talk' in which men indulged; but Cannell – who was not Jewish – was shocked. In his memoir Loeb speculates that Hemingway was angry because he felt Fleischman had been patronising him; yet whatever the reason for the nasty outburst, Hemingway nevertheless dropped off another copy of his In Our Time manuscript at Fleischman's apartment a few days later.

When in mid-December, Hemingway and Hadley went off to spend Christmas in Schruns, they invited Loeb to join them and others, but Loeb decided to return to New York to oversee the publication of his novel. This was a stroke of luck for Hemingway: when Loeb dropped in at the Boni & Liveright office after Christmas, the head of the firm's editorial department told him that none of Liveright's readers had liked Hemingway's stories and the In Our Time manuscript was about to be returned. Loeb insisted Hemingway was a talented writer and urged her to reconsider the decision. Then, by chance, Sherwood Anderson rang Liveright, and when he was told of the readers' views, he also urged the firm to publish the work. So Boni & Liveright changed its mind and cabled Hemingway that it was accepting his collection of stories, although with one exception – Up In Michigan was thought too coarse, and later the house also insisted the story Mr And Mrs Smith, which became Mrs And Mrs Elliot, should be re-written.

This was perhaps the moment when Hemingway's career as a writer finally sparked into life. He immediately cabled his agreement to the three-book deal Boni & Liveright were offering and signed and returned the contract it had sent by the end of March: he was finally about to become a bona-fide published writer. As it turned out, matters would not be quite as straightforward.

On the strength of reading *in our time*, the slim volume brought to his attention by F. Scott Fitzgerald, Max Perkins at Scribner's had already written to Hemingway in Paris early in February asking whether he had any more work he might like to submit to the house. However, Perkins' letter was misaddressed and became lost in the post. Once alerted to this mishap and given the correct address, he wrote again, but by the time Hemingway received the second letter, he had signed up with Boni & Liveright. He informed Perkins he would gladly have submitted his work to Scribner's, but was now contracted to Boni & Liveright. Notably, in view of how he managed to wriggle out of his contract and switch to Scribner's a year later, he made a point of stressing that under his arrangement with Liveright his contract would lapse if the house did not accept within 60 days a manuscript submitted for publication. And, tellingly, he promised Perkins that if his deal with Boni & Liveright did end, Scribner's would have first refusal on his work.

...

Finding a publisher in March 1925 was a turning point for Hemingway in more than one way: more changes were to come. Within 19 months, by the end of 1926, he had discarded one set of friends and acquired a new set, separated from his first wife and was about to marry his second, and – most notably – his 'debut' novel was published to wide acclaim. 'Hemingway, the promising young writer' was soon to become 'Papa' Hemingway, 'one of our greatest writers'.

During 1925, his growing prospects began to reveal aspects of his personality with which his friends and social circle were already acquainted, but which became ever more pronounced. For one thing, he now felt qualified to pontificate on what constituted 'good writing', a habit he kept for the rest of his life. What constituted 'good writing' was not, though, the only topic on which Hemingway came to regard himself as an expert, and over the years he became something of an all-round know-all. More immediately, he now thought he also knew all about publishing, and writing to Boni & Liveright with his strict instructions that no changes should be made to his work without his explicit approval, he also informed the house how many copies his volume of short stories would sell. Boni & Liveright did not share his confidence: the initial print run for Sherwood Anderson's latest novel was 20,000, but only 1,335 copies were printed in the first run of In Our Time (and it took two years for all of them to sell).

It is now obvious that very soon after signing his contract with Boni & Liveright Hemingway became disillusioned with the house, though on the face of it, quite why is less obvious. In Hemingway: The Paris Years Michael Reynolds suggest Hemingway could simply have cancelled the contract, but the well brought-up, middle-class Oak Part boy felt he had given his word. Compared with Scribner's, established in 1846 to publish religious tracts, Boni & Liveright, established in 1917, less than eight years earlier, was by far the livelier and more *avant garde* house. Its roster of authors included Eugene O'Neill, Sigmund Freud, William Faulkner, Ezra Pound, e.e. cummings, Hart Crane and Djuna Barnes. Scribner's on the other hand was seen as ultra-conservative, fusty and old-fashioned, and it counted established authors such as Frances Hodgson Burnett, Robert Louis Stevenson, Henry James, John Galsworthy and Edith Wharton among its writers, [iv] and its royalties were generally thought to be decidedly stingy.

As a young woman, the novelist Edith Stern had worked as a reader and later office manager at Boni & Liveright's; she described Boni & Liveright as

> *the jazz age in microcosm, with all its extremes of hysteria and cynicism, of carpe diem, of decadent thriftlessness ... To recapture*

> *its atmosphere one would not, like Proust, dip a madeleine into a cup of tea, but a canapé into bathtub gin*

so one might assume being contracted to Boni & Liveright would be welcomed by a literary young Turk keen to make his name as a modernist writer. But there were other crucial distinctions between the two houses. Biographer Jeffrey Meyers suggests Hemingway reasoned that if he jumped ship and signed up with Scribner's, he

> *would then obtain the benefits of a more commercially successful firm, an influential editor in Max Perkins, and a profitable outlet for his stories in Scribner's Magazine.*

Michael Reynolds believes Hemingway soon convinced himself that Boni & Liveright were not sufficiently interested in him and his work. Hemingway also complained that once it had published In Our Time, the house had not bothered to market it. In addition, with Perkins' interest in him and his work established, the siren voice of F. Scott Fitzgerald urging him to jump ship and, Reynolds suggests, Hemingway's innate conservatism guiding him, ditching Scribner's became more and more attractive.

In Hemingway And His Conspirators: Hollywood, Scribner's, And The Making Of American Celebrity Culture, academic and film writer Leonard Leff agrees that the writer's intrinsically conservative nature played a part in his eventually ditching Boni & Liveright for Scribner's; but he suggests Hemingway's anti-Semitism was also a factor. In a letter to his childhood friend Bill Smith discussing possible New York publishers he might approach and three months before receiving Boni & Liveright's offer to publish In Our Time, Hemingway had announced he was

> *all for keeping out of the manuals of the Semites as long as possible.*

He noted that at Boni & Liveright Leon Fleischman, who had been employed in New York before moving to Paris, the house's public relations manager Isodore Schneider, Edith Stern, Richard Simon (who went on to found Simon & Schuster) who worked in its sales department, and the house's owner Horace Liveright were all Jewish. Unaware of Scribner's interest, pragmatism had prevailed when Boni & Liveright had made its offer and nothing else was on offer; but once Hemingway realized that signing up with Scribner's was possible, Leff observes that the god-fearing, cautious – and anti-Semitic – Oak Park which had raised Hemingway held sway. Hemingway, he also notes, was less modern than what he wrote. Scribner's was respected, sober, financially sound and had a good name. Boni & Liveright, whose owner Horace Liveright flew by the seat of his pants (and, for example, used profits from publishing to subsidise a string of unsuccessful theatrical productions) was not and did not. [v] By 1927, two years after In Our Time was published, Liveright, an alcoholic, lost control of the house he had helped found. By 1933, a few months short of his 50th birthday he was dead.

. . .

Another aspect of Hemingway's personality which began to come to the fore in 1925 was his unsavoury practice of turning on the friends who had helped him and discarding them in favour of those who might prove to be more useful. Fitzgerald summed it up neatly several years later when he observed that

> *Ernest would always give a helping hand to a man on a ledge a little higher up.*

In his biography of Carlos Baker notes that Hemingway's

> *capacity for contempt, already shown in dozens of other ways, was also apparent in his habit of accepting favours from people whom he then maligned behind their backs. He re-paid a dinner invitation from Louis and Mary Bromfield by surreptitiously speaking of his host as 'Bloomfield', impugning his gifts as a writer, criticising the quality of the wine he served and commenting satirically on Mary's pet cats, which he said swarmed over the dining table stealing 'what little fish there was' and then defecating in odd corners of the room.* [vi]

Michael Reynolds writes

> *At 26, he had become the writer he set out to be, but the seven-year apprenticeship had changed him. Old friends saw it clearly. He was harder now, less simple, his moods deeper, their shifts more sudden.*

Then there was his shabby treatment of Sherwood Anderson. Anderson, who he had persuaded the ambitious young man he met in Chicago to move to Paris not Naples as Hemingway had planned, had provided him with letters of introduction to Gertrude Stein, Ezra Pound, Sylvia Beach and Lewis Galantière, and who had championed him at Boni & Liveright, was to become a victim of Hemingway's shifting loyalties. Harold Loeb who regarded himself as one of Hemingway's closest friends became another. One might even suggest, contentiously, that Hadley was yet another victim. [vii]

Hadley Richardson had supported Hemingway, not least financially, completely and unselfishly in his years as an unknown. She had put up with his emotional volatility (now seen as the manifestation of a bi-polar condition he is thought to have suffered) and his self-centred demands – there was to be no talk at breakfast, he had told her, if he would be spending the day writing. She had not complained when he developed his crush on Duff Twysden – Brett Ashley in The Sun Also Rises – and later began his affair with Pauline Pfeiffer. But Hadley's loyalty counted for nothing. Hemingway even disingenuously blamed her for the separation: by daring to confront him on whether anything was going on with Pfeiffer, he said, she had ended their marriage.

Michael Reynolds has noted that after Hemingway returned from Toronto, by now the father of a young child, and had buckled down to write the stories which appeared in In Our Time, the underlying theme of many of them was – as Hemingway saw it – the corrosive effect of marriage on a man and a man's freedom. Some stories, for example Cross Country Run, portray a man who feels he is being entrapped by his impending marriage and others present a rather sour view of marriage. Reynolds suggests that this reflected Hemingway's feelings about his union with Hadley. In a letter to Sherwood Anderson in May 1925 thanking him for helping getting Boni & Liveright interested, Hemingway rather unenthusiastically remarks that he and Hadley were

as fond of each other as ever and get along well.

At that point his marriage was still just three and a half years old, and for a union that young, Hemingway's comment might be thought odd. After giving birth to their son in October 1923, Hadley had not lost the weight she had gained during pregnancy and, never close to having the thin and boyish physique of young women fashionable in the 1920s, [1] she was, at almost 33, said to have looked 'matronly'. She had come to see another side to Hemingway in July 1924 when she, Hemingway and several friends – the party included John Dos Passos and a girlfriend, Ogden Stewart, McAlmon and Bill Bird and his wife – decamped to Burguete for a week after a second visit to Pamplona. There, according to Hemingway's calculations – he kept an almost Teutonic record of these matters – her period should have begun; but she was late, and for several days Hemingway, already feeling fatherhood encroaching on his freedom and fearing she was pregnant with a second child, sank into a foul mood and treated her very badly, so badly that eventually Bill Bird's wife, Sally, lost patience with him and gave him a good talking to. When her period did finally come, Hemingway was contrite, but the episode

---

1   Pauline Pfeiffer did, though.

shook Hadley. As Michael Reynolds puts it

> *No longer feeling guilty [that she might be pregnant again], she looked at Ernest in a new light. He had made her feel like a worthless drag on his life. It was not a nice revelation, nor did the space between them immediately close.*

It was another step towards the disintegration of their marriage.

1925-1926 – Finally on the literary map

95 per cent of The Sun Also Rises was pure imagination. I took real people in that one and I controlled what they did. I made it all up.

Ernest Hemingway, letter to Max Perkins, Nov 1933.

Don Stewart was mildly amused at the caricature of himself in the figure of Bill Gorton [in The Sun Also Rises]. He recognised a few of his own quips in the talk between Bill and Jake, but the whole book struck him as a little more than a very clever reportorial tour-de-force.

Carlos Baker, Ernest Hemingway, A Life Story

THE new friends Hemingway made in the spring of 1925 were all to prove significant. Thereced Pauline Pfeiffer, who was to break up his marriage to Hadley and become his second wife; Lady Duff Twysden, upon whom he based the character of Lady Brett Ashley in The Sun Also Rises; and, most significantly, F. Scott Fitzgerald.

Hemingway was introduced to Pfeiffer at a party given by Kitty Cannell, Harold Loeb's then girlfriend. The attraction was not immediate, but Pfeiffer – like Hadley several years older than Hemingway – soon took a shine to him. She was already 30 and thought by some in Paris to be 'looking for a husband', although Hemingway biographer Michael Reynolds suggests she had moved to Paris from New York as much to escape being married off to a wealthy cousin as for the prestigious job with Vogue she had been offered. That suggestion notwithstanding, before meeting Hemingway, she had previously considered other men as potential partners, including Harold Loeb, and Hemingway, already married and a father, was not an obvious choice. Pfeiffer was unimpressed when she and her sister Jinny called on Hemingway and Hadley after meeting the couple at Cannell's and were ignored by an unshaven Hemingway in the next room, lounging on his bed and reading.

In his memoir A Moveable Feast, Hemingway later claims that Pfeiffer had somehow wheedled her way into his affections by subterfuge, using 'the oldest trick in the book' by making his wife 'a best friend' and then stealing that friend's husband. Reynolds refutes this: he suggests that without strong and quite definite encouragement from Hemingway – for whom marriage to Hadley seemed to be paling and who already had hopes of acquiring a mistress available for inconsequential sex – Pfeiffer would have held back. [1] Reynolds suggests that as a strict, practising Roman Catholic whose church insisted on the 'sanctity of the sacrament of marriage', Pfeiffer would never have considered having an affair with Hemingway unless it was to lead somewhere. That she and he were eventually able to be married in a Roman Catholic ceremony after Hemingway and Hadley were divorced was simple: as Hemingway and Hadley had been wed in a Methodist ceremony, their marriage was not a 'real' marriage in Roman Catholic eyes and thus Hemingway could not be 'divorced'. Similar legerdemain was adopted when Hemingway was required to prove he had been received into the RC church and was eligible to marry an RC woman: he claimed that soon after being blown up in July 1918 in Italy, he had been 'baptised' by an Italian army chaplain because he had received the sacrament of 'extreme unction'. Not only was this claim unsound (and it was a wonder the RC church accepted it), but no baptismal certificate or proof of any kind was ever produced or has since turned up. In the event, though, no more questions were asked. [i]

. . .

Although Hemingway soon fell for Pfeiffer – and, some suggest, her trust fund income, substantially larger than Hadley's, added to her attraction – in 1925 he had first developed a crush on the twice-divorced Lady Duff Twysden. Born Dorothy (or possibly Mary) Smurthwaite, the daughter of a Yorkshire wine merchant, Twysden had acquired her title through her second marriage. She was not yet divorced when she met Hemingway, but she had lost custody of her son. In Paris, she and her supposed fiancé, her cousin Pat Guthrie – who became Mike Campbell in The Sun Also Rises and was thought by some to be gay – were two impecunious and hard-drinking spongers

---

1   Some biographers report that in the kind of male locker-room talk men enjoy, he had several times discussed with friends that he would like to follow what he assumed was the French practice of a married man also having a mistress.

and fixtures in the Montparnasse ex-patriate community. They existed on irregular maintenance cheques which arrived from Guthrie's rich mother. Although Twysden was said not to have been particularly beautiful, many found her attractive, and Hemingway was only one of many men who fell for her. Harold Loeb was another, and Loeb was more successful in his pursuit.

Hadley was well aware of Hemingway's feelings for Twysden, which he made no attempt to hide, and many years later she admitted she had 'suffered' during the summer of 1925; but she did so in silence, believing his infatuation would blow over. She later told biographer Michael Reynolds she did not think Hemingway and Twysden had a physical affair, and Twysden is believed always to have drawn the line at sleeping with married men. Loeb, in the other hand, was no longer married and she did sleep with him: while Guthrie was in London, Loeb took Twysden off to St-Jean-de-Luz, south-west of Biarritz, for a week-long tryst. Hemingway didn't find out until later, but when he did, he was furious and his jealousy led to the bad blood in Pamplona that July that became the basis for the story of The Sun Also Rises.

. . .

In April Hemingway had met F. Scott Fitzgerald and as often with Hemingway there are various accounts of how it came about. [1] According to A Moveable Feast, he was out drinking with Twysden and Guthrie in the Dingo Bar, a favourite ex-pat haunt, when Fitzgerald either introduced himself or Hemingway introduced himself to Fitzgerald. Sometimes it was said not to have been in the Dingo Bar but in another of Montparnasse's bars. To confuse matters, in his memoir, Hemingway writes that Fitzgerald was in the company of a Dunc Chaplin, a baseball player; but Chaplin later declared that no only did he not meet Hemingway, but he wasn't even in France at the time. Like much about Hemingway's life and its 'facts', it all gets a confusing.

Fitzgerald was just three years older than Hemingway; yet where Hemingway had been struggling for recognition as a writer, let alone making a living from his work, Fitzgerald had already published two novels, was earning very good money indeed selling 'jazz age' and 'flapper' stories to magazines and had just published The Great Gatsby, his third novel. (His earnings in 1925 were $18,333 – around $317,331 in 2023 – and $25,686 – $444,606 – the following year.) He and his wife Zelda had been living in the South of France and had recently moved to Paris; he began to spend a lot of time with Hemingway, taking the budding author under his wing, alerting Max Perkins to

---

1   All too often when dealing with the facts of Hemingway's life, 'various' means 'conflicting' or 'contradictory'.

Hemingway and his new style, and giving him advice on getting published and even on writing. Fitzgerald's advice and connections paid off, but ironically as Hemingway's star now began to wax, Fitzgerald's began to wane, and in just a few years Hemingway, enjoying the role of the 'established professional writer' he had by then assumed, was handing out advice to Fitzgerald.

Biographers of the two writers have commented that Fitzgerald spent more time promoting Hemingway's career than his own and that his attitude to his new best friend was akin to hero worship. His wife Zelda did not share his admiration, though: she and Hemingway disliked each other on sight. Zelda later told Hadley she'd noticed that the Hemingway family always did what Ernest wanted. The remark irritated Hemingway, but according to Reynolds, Hadley later agreed on just how perceptive Zelda had been. Zelda's suggestion that Hemingway and Scott were having a gay affair, though, is almost certainly nothing but malice.

. . .

Hemingway knew that the short stories he was producing and their imminent publication would not be enough to help him make his name as a writer: he needed to produce a novel. Publishers made very little money from selling short story collections and would usually only consider publishing such a collection by an already established author. If it sold, it was only likely to sell on the back of one or more successful novels. Hemingway's problem was that he had very little confidence in his ability to produce a long piece of work – his longest work so far, the story Big Two-Hearted River, was at around 12,000 words by some stretch longer than any of his other stories. Nor did Hemingway have any ideas for a novel. [ii] He had recently attempted to write one, but the project petered out after just over two dozen pages.

The visit to Pamplona's San Fermin festival in 1925 finally presented Hemingway with material for the novel he was looking for. That year's party consisted of himself and Hadley, Duff Twysden and Pat Guthrie, Donald Ogden Stewart, his childhood friend Bill Smith and Harold Loeb. It wasn't until everyone had congregated in Pamplona that Hemingway, still in the throes of his crush on Twysden, found out about Loeb's recent tryst with her in St-Jean-de-Luz. Despite the presence of both his wife and Guthrie, Hemingway is reported to have behaved as though Twysden were 'his woman' and he was furious. Pat Guthrie was also less than pleased and continually sniped at Loeb, and the atmosphere in Pamplona was awful. At one point it almost led to a fist fight between Hemingway and Loeb.

Hemingway began writing the first draft of what was to become The Sun Also Rises in mid-July as soon as he and Hadley had left Pamplona for Madrid for a month-long tour of Spain. His routine was to write in the late mornings and early afternoons, then spend the rest of the day watching bullfighting. After four weeks he and Hadley moved to Hendaye, a small French fishing village on the Atlantic coast south of Biarritz. A day later, Hadley left for Paris to pick up their young son John, known as Bumby, from the family which had been looking after him, and Hemingway spent another week alone in Hendaye carrying on with his novel before also returning to Paris. He had completed his first draft by mid-September. When it was published in the autumn of the following year, Ogden Stewart, who with Bill Smith was amalgamated into the character Bill Gorton, was unimpressed, declared the novel had no artistic merit and described it as close to a bald account of what had happened in Pamplona as dammit. Loeb was mortified by, and angry about, the portrayal of him as the ineffectual Robert Cohn. On the other hand, Duff Twysden, who comes across as a loose woman, appeared to shrug off the notoriety it brought her, although later in life did admit the novel had upset her. (She died young, in 1938). But theirs were minority opinions. Others, not least Scribner's, insisted the novel was an extraordinary work, and that is certainly the line its publishers – unsurprisingly – and many in the literary world have taken to this day.

. . .

Quite apart from Hemingway's joy at finding a commercial publisher fading when he realised Boni & Liveright was staffed almost entirely by Jews, his antagonism grew when Harold Loeb told him about the changes Boni & Liveright were making to his, Loeb's, first novel: in an attempt to appear 'modern', Loeb had removed all definite and indefinite articles – 'the' and 'a' – from his text; without consulting him, Boni & Liveright had simply reinstated them. Hemingway sternly informed the house that no changes could be made to his stories without his explicit approval. He was also irritated when he eventually discovered that Boni & Liveright had initially rejected the manuscript of In Our Time and had only changed its mind after lobbying on his behalf by Loeb and Sherwood Anderson. He professed to despise authors who succeeded because of 'who they knew' and not because of the quality of their work, and he did not want to be classed as one. He was also angry that Boni & Liveright refused to include his story Up In Michigan in the collection; and after In Our Time was published in the first week of October 1925, he blamed subsequent low sales on poor marketing. Yet at what point he finally decided to sever his link with Boni & Liveright and jump ship is not clear.

It was plain, at least to Michael Reynolds, that Hemingway became determined to leave Boni & Liveright as soon as he realised that not only were Scribner's interested in him and his work, but that so, too, were other publishers; the decision to break his contract was made well before In Our Time was published. At some point in August, Jane Heap, editor of the literary magazine The Little Review, had asked Hemingway how happy he was with Boni & Liveright and told him she had heard from a publisher who would consider taking him on. Responding, Hemingway again noted – as he had previously told Perkins – that although under his contract the house had agreed to publish two more books (after In Our Time), should Horace Liveright refuse to publish either, its options on his future work would lapse. He added that although he could not yet talk business with another publisher, he would like to meet them because 'you can't ever tell what might happen'.

Michael Reynolds suspects that despite Hemingway's later insistent denials, he had by then already made up his mind to break his contract, and Reynolds notes

> *What might happen was perfectly obvious . . . In Our Time was only six weeks from being released and Hemingway was thinking seriously of ways to break his contract. . . Horace Liveright's letters were full of business but no stroking of his fragile ego. He wanted to get letters from someone like Max Perkins who knew how to make a writer feel secure. Perkins offered him a contract on the basis of his work, not the people he knew. Sure, Scott [Fitzgerald had] got his name in the door, but Max liked his stuff.*

Reynolds points out a significant oddity of Hemingway's letter to Heap: he had torn off the bottom half of a page in which he had informed her exactly how Liveright's option might lapse: Reynolds suspects Hemingway had already come up with a strategy to force Boni & Liveright to end his contract and was about to reveal it to Heap, but then had second thoughts and removed any reference to it from the letter.

. . .

In Our Time was published in the first week of October, 1925, and generally met with acclaim from the US critics, but the reading public's response was muted and sales were very slow. Writing in the New Yorker a year later and after the publication of The Sun Also Rises, Dorothy Parker observed that the publication of In Our Time

> *caused about as much stir in literary circles as an incompleted dogfight on upper Riverside Drive.*

Despite low sales, most contemporary reviews of In Our Time will, at least, have encouraged Hemingway. The review in Time magazine (which had been founded only two years earlier) set the tone:

> *[Hemingway] is that rare bird, an intelligent man who is not introspective on paper . . . Make no mistake, Ernest Hemingway is somebody; a new, honest, un-'literary' transcriber of life – a writer*

and the New York Herald Tribune joined in the praise:

> *I know no American writer with a more startling ear for colloquial conversation, or a more poetic sensitiveness for the woods and hills. In Our Time has perhaps not enough energy to be a great book, but Ernest Hemingway has promises of genius.*

For the New York Times

> *[Hemingway's] language is fibrous and athletic, colloquial and fresh, hard and clean . . . his very prose seems to have an organic being of its own*

and the New York City Sun declared that

> *The flat even banal declarations in the paragraphs alternating with Mr Hemingway's longer sketches are a criticism of the conventional dishonesty of literature. Here is neither literary inflation nor elevation, but a passionately bare telling of what happened.'*

Britain's Yorkshire Post and Leeds Intelligencer took a more balanced view. It wrote

> *The general atmosphere might be described as one of American adolescence – a hard, sterile, restlessness of mood conveyed in a hard, staccato sometimes brutal prose. Mr Hemingway uses his method very skilfully; we feel he is both sincere and successful in carrying out his purpose . . .*

but it concluded on the sober note that

> *. . . his purpose seems to us narrow and unfruitful – withered at the root. . . [Hemingway] is a natural writer who has not yet found an environment worthy of him.'*

The Times Literary Supplement (though reviewing the volume over a year later) noted that

> *Mr Ernest Hemingway, a young American writer living in Paris, is definitely of the moderns. It is not merely a deliberate taste for writing ungrammatically now and again which points the way to Mr Hemingway's literary camp; it is rather his own concern for the conventional features of good writing. The short stories in the volume entitled In Our Time . . . achieve their affect by normal and rather puzzling means . . . Only one story in the book – Indian Camp, the first – has anything like a straightforward appeal, and even here the actual method is as elusive as in the rest of the tales.*

Although Hemingway had begun subscribing to a cuttings service, it is unlikely that at this very early point in his career he would have come across the British reviews quoted; and although the US review were sure to have pleased him, he had already developed his life-long distaste 'literary critics'. In a letter to Sherwood Anderson – five months before In Our Time was published – he described them as

> *camp-following eunuchs of literature [who wouldn't] even whore.* [1]

. . .

In early 1926, Hemingway was to spend a few months re-drafting and re-writing the manuscript for The Sun Also Rises, but before that, in late 1925, he set about freeing himself from his contract with Boni & Liveright. Beginning in the fourth week of November and completing it in just ten days, he wrote a 30,000-word long novella sending up Dark Laughter, the latest novel by his friend and benefactor Sherwood Anderson's. About the subsequent upset he caused, he later pleaded innocence and claimed, rather pretentiously and pompously, that his send-up, which he called The Torrents Of Spring, was merely a call to order to Anderson: his latest work, he insisted, was sub-standard and that 'as a fellow writer it was his duty to tell Anderson'. [2] All the circumstantial evidence suggests otherwise, and Michael Reynolds spells out quite

---

1   His loathing grew and grew not many years later when he was no longer the golden boy and the critics stopped singing his praises and began taking him to task.

2   This attitude is notable for highlighting the rapid shift which had taken place in Hemingway's self-appraisal and his growing self-regard. Where just a few short years earlier he had been the apprentice, the willing student, the novice and men like Anderson and Pound were his mentors, he now assumed the role of one of their equals. Yet at the time he had only a volume of short stories to his name and his debut novel was still a year away from being published.

1925-1926 – Finally on the literary map

clearly that

> *The point was to write a short book that Liveright could not possibly accept and simultaneously make it clear to critics that Sherwood Anderson was no longer his literary role model. With Anderson so recently signed to a contract and selling well, Liveright could not afford to offend him with Hemingway's slapstick, Ernest was counting on their choosing Sherwood and setting himself free to find another publisher.*

When his wife Hadley and friend John Dos Passos read the manuscript, both were shocked that he should chose to ridicule Anderson in such a manner and urged him not to submit it for publication. But Scott Fitzgerald, for whom getting Hemingway to join him at Scribner's had become a serious project, and Hemingway's soon-to-be mistress Pauline Pfeiffer egged him on. His scheme worked: the manuscript for The Torrents Of Spring was typed up and mailed off to Boni & Liveright in New York by the beginning of the second week of December. Three weeks later, by now in Schruns, Austria, where he was spending Christmas with his family, Hemingway received a telegram from Horace Liveright rejecting the novella and telling him he was looking forward to receiving the manuscript for his other novel. Hemingway immediately wrote an odd and ambiguous letter to Scott Fitzgerald that both confirmed and denied that submitting The Torrents Of Spring manuscript was just a ploy to get him out of his contract. He told Fitzgerald

> *I have known all along that they could and would not be able to publish it. I did not, however, have that in mind in any way when I wrote it . . . So I am loose.*

Writing to Liveright, he presented him with an ultimatum he knew would be rejected: either publish the manuscript he had submitted – and which he had submitted in good faith, he insisted – or he would consider himself free to go to another publisher. The fact that he knew that other publishers, especially Scribner's, were interested in signing him will have boosted his bravado, yet he wasn't quite as confident as he sounded. Rather than let the matter drag on for weeks or even months as letters made their way to and fro across the Atlantic, he decided to resolve the matter in person. He left Europe for New York on February 3 (after five-day stopover in Paris to visit and go to bed with Pauline Pfeiffer), and the day after he arrived on February 9, he met Horace Liveright, who simply threw in the towel: Hemingway was free. He then made his way to the Scribner's office where despite not having seen a word of the new novel, Perkins offered him a contract. Perkins also agreed to publish The Torrents Of Spring – from a legal point of view his agreement to do so was apparently crucial – and he asked Hemingway to return the following Tuesday to sign the contract and view the dust jacket for The Torrents Of Spring which would by then have been designed. The Hemingway legend was about to be launched.

1926-1927 – Out with the old, in with the new

So long as he published with 'little' or literary magazines like The Quarter or transatlantic review or with Left Bank publishers of limited editions like Robert McAlmon, Hemingway was one of a crowd, a piece of the Montparnasse firmament, fitting comfortably into his niche . . . Hemingway's move to Boni & Liveright with In Our Time raised him only slightly among his peers. However, when he signed the Charles Scribner's Sons contract, Hemingway moved into the major league. That the shift took place at the same time that he was ridding himself of Hadley and moving to a more sophisticated woman seems to have been coincidental, but it was all of a piece with his life.

Michael Reynolds, Hemingway: The Homecoming

HEMINGWAY'S infatuation with Duff Twysden had faded once he and Hadley had left Pamplona, and it had been replaced by a growing friendship with Pauline Pfeiffer that within months developed into a full affair. Initially, Pfeiffer made the running, but by Christmas she and Hemingway were close enough for him to invite her to join him and his family on their holiday in Schruns, Austria. With Hadley in bed nursing a bad cold for part of the holiday, Pfeiffer and Hemingway spent a great deal of time together.

For a while Pfeiffer and Hemingway – and even Hadley – maintained the fiction that all three were simply very good, close friends who were fond of each other, and biographers remark that Hadley's apparent passivity might to Hemingway have seemed to be an unspoken acquiescence. Many years later Hadley told Michael Reynolds that because her husband had been so good-looking, many women threw themselves at him, and he often openly flirted with them; but she had persuaded herself almost to the last that like all his other infatuations, his feelings for Pfeiffer would blow over. In Hemingway: The Homecoming, the third volume of his biography, Reynolds observes

> *In Schruns, when she first saw the pattern forming, she could have challenged her husband's fascination with Pauline, but that was not her way . . . When he came in from moonlight walks with Pauline, she had made light of it.*

Whether or not Hemingway and Pfeiffer first slept together in Schruns as has been suggested or it wasn't until he stayed with her in Paris on his way to New York at the end of January is not known; but in the first edition of his memoir A Moveable Feast, edited by his widow Mary Welsh from the various manuscripts he had worked on and which was published in 1964, he chose to portray himself as an innocent led astray by predatory rich folk and the guile of a young woman. In that version of how it all happened, Hemingway recalls he felt terrible that, once back in Europe from his New York trip in February 1926, he did not immediately return to his family in Schruns but had spent a few more days with Pfeiffer. He says his heart broke when he was met by Hadley and his young son at Schruns rail station. How much of that version was down to how Mary Welsh wanted the story to be recalled might be pertinent, although we cannot know. Forty-five years later, in 2009 in a new edition of A Moveable Feast, re-edited from the same collection of manuscripts by his grandson Sean, Hemingway tells a different story: he acknowledges that because he had encouraged Pfeiffer in her pursuit, irrespective of the pain it was causing Hadley, he was equally to blame for the break-up of his marriage.

. . .

Once Pfeiffer had left Schruns to return to Paris in mid-January, Hemingway and Hadley were joined by John Dos Passos and Gerald and Sara Murphy, a very wealthy American couple who now lived in Juan Le Pins near Cap d'Antibes in the South of France and were friends with both Dos Passos and Pfeiffer. In his memoir Hemingway describes Dos Passos as the 'pilot fish' which guided the 'predatory rich folk', the Murphys: they were an integral part of the new and wealthier social world Hemingway was entering in which, it became ever clearer, Hadley had no part. The Murphys, especially Gerald, who, according to Michael Reynolds, almost hero-worshipped Hemingway, had joined the Hemingway fan club and were already persuaded that he had a great literary future; they believed chic and sophisticated Pfeiffer would make a far more suitable wife for a writer than down-to-earth but dowdy Hadley. Hadley's days as the first Mrs Ernest Hemingway were numbered.

The crisis in her marriage to Hemingway's came to a head after Hadley was invited by Pauline Pfeiffer to join her and her sister, Jinny, on a short break, a road trip through the Loire valley. It was an odd few days. During the trip, Pfeiffer was by turns friendly and snappy with Hadley, who finally asked Jinny whether she thought Pauline was in love with her husband. Jinny's vague and unhelpful, though telling, response was to admit that Pauline and Hemingway were 'rather fond' of each other. Reynolds reports:

> *Back in Paris [Hadley] asked her husband straight out what it was between himself and Pauline ... He could not help it, he claimed. It happened, it was happening, and there was nothing he could do about it. If Hadley had not brought it out in the open, it would not have become a problem. Somehow it was Hadley's fault.*

The marriage was to last for only another few months.

...

In April Hemingway finished revising and re-writing the manuscript for his novel, and towards the end of the month he sent it off to Max Perkins at Scribner's. Another trip to the San Fermin festival in Pamplona was scheduled for July, but first Hemingway planned to go to Madrid for several weeks to attend the San Isodro festival, to write and to watch some bullfights. Hadley and their young son Bumby travelled to the South of France to stay with the Murphys where Hemingway was to join them. The lad had a persistent cough, however, that was diagnosed by a local doctor as whooping cough; the Murphys became fearful for their own children's health and thought it best that Bumby and Hadley should be quarantined. Scott Fitzgerald and Zelda offered her the use of the villa they were renting nearby until the lease expired in the middle of June as they had decided to move to another, larger villa.

While he was in Madrid, Hemingway sent Hadley a series of letters reproaching her for not joining him, and she became increasingly angry that he did not consider the strain she was under: she was taking care of their ill son, she told him, and she was broke and was relying on the food the Murphys were supplying. Finally, at the end of May – on the day The Torrents Of Spring was published – Hemingway joined them all from Madrid. Pfeiffer had already arrived from Paris and had gone to stay with Hadley (she explained that she'd had whooping cough as a child and was in no danger). When in mid-June the lease on the Fitzgerald villa ran out, Pfeiffer, the Hemingways, their son and their Paris cook cum housekeeper Marie Rohrbach (who had arrived from Paris to nurse Bumby) all moved to a small hotel. And there the pretence that Hemingway, Pfeiffer and Hadley were just very good, very close friends who doted on each other was continued, with Pfeiffer even joining Hemingway and Hadley for breakfast in bed.

At the beginning of July, Bumby was taken back to Paris by Rohrbach, and Hemingway, Hadley, Pfeiffer and the Murphys travelled to Spain to spend two weeks in Pamplona and enjoy that year's San Fermin festival in their second week. For the Murphys those two weeks were a new and extraordinary experience – the 'most intense moments of their lives' – and in a letter Gerald sent Hemingway and Hadley within days of the festival ending, he described the bullfighters as living

> ... in a region all their own – and alone each, somewhere between art and life – and eclipsing at times each of them – make you feel that you are as you find other people – half-alive. They are a religion for which I could have been trained. This knocked at my heart all the time I was at Pamplona.

One wonders how the younger Hemingway, the new arrival in Paris who purported to despise 'the phoneys' he encountered in Montparnasse or the man who later proclaimed that the

> most essential gift for a good writer is a built-in, shockproof, shit detector

reacted to such vacuous gush? Perhaps the Hemingway who read that letter and who was in the process of re-inventing himself as a serious and successful writer and who rather liked being friends with the rich Murphy's had become rather more tolerant.

When the festival ended, the party took off from Pamplona to San Sebastian on Spain's northern coast, from where Hemingway and Hadley set off for a small tour of bullfights. The Murphys and Pfeiffer carried on to Bayonne for a train to Cap d'Antibes and Paris respectively. Writing a postcard from the Bayonne station buffet, Sara Murphy anticipated her husband's flowery rhapsody with a dose of her own. She wrote

> As for you two children: You grace the earth. You're so right, because you're so close to what's elemental. Your values are hitched up to the universe. We're proud to know you. Yours are the things that count. They're a gift to those who see them too.

1926-1927 – Out with the old, in with the new

It was a distinctly different tone to the one she would adopt eight weeks later in a note to Hemingway once he and Hadley had separated.

...

It was in Spain, apparently in a number of heated arguments, one caused by a letter from Pfeiffer (now back in Paris) that stated, between the lines although quite unmistakeably, that she would 'get' Hemingway – she wrote 'I get everything I want' – that he and Hadley decided to end their marriage. One their way back to Paris they called in at Juan-le-Pins, where Hemingway picked up the galley proofs for The Sun Also Rises which Scribner's Max Perkins had sent to the Murphy's home, and it was their train journey back to Paris which became the basis for the short story A Canary For One,[1] written in the weeks after the break-up.

Neither returned to their flat in rue Notre Dame des Champs: Hadley moved into a small hotel and Hemingway had been given the use of the studio Gerald Murphy had worked in when he was still painting in Paris a few years earlier. Hadley was still persuading herself that Hemingway's affair with Pfeiffer was just another passing infatuation, and she thought that if she gave Hemingway time and space, he would tire of Pfeiffer and their affair would blow over as had his infatuation with Duff Twsyden. Hemingway and Pfeiffer, though, had other ideas and planned to marry as soon as Hemingway was free of Hadley.

For the first few weeks after their separation Hadley and Hemingway continued to meet up, but all too often these occasions ended in acrimony and bitter rows. Reynolds says the rowing was usually about money: Hadley had it, although she was soon obliged to pay rent on both a new apartment on the rue de Fleurus near Gertrude Stein into which she had moved and the dingy flat in the rue de Notre Dames des Champs. Hemingway had very little: the cost of their extended summer break in Antibes, Pamplona and Spain had eaten up most of the advance Scribner's had given him for The Sun Also Rises. Realising his predicament, Gerald Murphy had, unbidden, deposited $400 (about $6,858 in 2023) in his bank account to tide him over. Unsurprisingly, Gerald and Sara Murphy took Hemingway's side in the split with Hadley, although 34 years later they, as 'the predatory rich folk' and his, by then nominal, friend John Dos Passos as the 'pilot fish' were squarely blamed for causing the breakdown. Gerald had long convinced himself that Hemingway was a writer of genius to whom Hadley was unable to give

---

1 In my view one of Hemingway's better short stories.

the kind of support a genius would need. When he and Sara heard Hemingway and Hadley had separated, and concerned about how Hemingway might be coping, they travelled up to Paris from the South of France at the end of August and had supper with Hemingway and Hadley. Later Sara, in stark contrast to the sentimental and pretentious description of the couple in her postcard from Bayonne station two months earlier, wrote to Hemingway about his desire to leave Hadley and, giving the separation her blessing, told him

> *In the end you will probably save us all by refusing (among other things) to accept second-rate things, places, ideas or human nature. Bless you & and don't budge.*

To biographer Michael Reynolds it is clear that Sara regarded Hadley as 'second-rate', and it is hard to disagree with Reynolds' view. For his part Gerald was more concerned that Hemingway's resolve to leave Hadley might slowly weaken, and he wrote to him about his fear, declaring that Hemingway might be deterred from 'acting cleanly'. Reynolds suggests this was Gerald Murphy's unambiguous advice to press ahead with his plans to divorce Hadley.

By mid-September Hadley, weary of the arguments which invariably reduced her to tears, decided it would be best for both her and Hemingway if they no longer met. She still hoped for an eventual reconciliation, but informed Hemingway at a dinner with their friends Paul and Winifred Mowrer that if he and Pfeiffer did not see each other for 100 days but still wanted to be together once the time was up, she would give him the divorce he wanted. Hadley hoped that absence would not make the heart grow fonder and that Hemingway and Pfeiffer's affair would peter out. They accepted her terms, but feared they would be unable to stay apart for three months if both lived near each other in Paris; so Pfeiffer, who had anyway been planning to return to her family home in Piggott, Arkansas, for Christmas, left France a week later to spend those 100 days in the US.

. . .

The following months were not pleasant for Hemingway: he now had neither Hadley nor Pfeiffer for company. He had already corrected the galley proofs for The Sun Also Rises and sent them back to Scribner's at the end of August. He spent his time writing short stories for a second collection, but though he dined out with a few friends, he was largely left to his own devices in Gerald Murphy's large, cold studio, and he did not like it at all. In mid-October he and his friend Archibald MacLeish took off to Zaragoza for a few days to attend a festival, but once back in Paris he was again thrown back onto his own company, and, his biographers stress, he always hated being alone. Since he and Hadley had separated, he had avoided his old Montparnasse haunts and his cafe acquaintances because he did not want repeatedly to explain the circumstances of their separation. Although he and Pfeiffer had promised to write to each other every day, her letters arrived irregularly, and Hemingway sank deeper and deeper into depression. At one point he became so low that he wrote Pfeiffer a histrionic letter telling her that if the matter of a divorce from Hadley was not settled by Christmas, he would kill himself. Ironically, he had made the same threat to end his life in the weeks before his marriage to Hadley.

. . .

While married to Hemingway, Hadley had consciously played 'the dutiful, supporting wife' despite Gerald Murphy's belief that the Hemingway marriage had failed precisely because Hadley had not given him the support he needed as a writer and could not give it; but over the years she had suffered under his emotional ups and downs. On the dynamic of Hemingway and Hadley's relationship which Zelda Fitzgerald had remarked always worked to Hemingway's advantage, Reynolds adds that after Hadley had split from Hemingway, she seemed to blossom and come out of herself more and more. He observes

> *The five years of her marriage to Hemingway had toughened her up more than she had realised. Now, for the first time in her life, she was free to live as she pleased and how she pleased, answering to no one. . . Despite the ache of loss, Hadley discovered a new wholeness to herself . . . no longer tied to Ernest's emotional roller-coaster. Perhaps her highs would no longer reach the peaks they had with him, but then neither would she have to face his suicidal lows.*

As Hadley's new self-confidence grew, she increasingly felt able to move on with her life and finally decided that the 100-day separation she had imposed on Hemingway and Pfeiffer could be called off. By the mid-1920s, Hadley's friends Paul and Winifred Mowrer had grown apart and had amicably agreed to separate. Winifred, who had noticed the increasing fondness of Hadley and her husband for each other encouraged them to get more involved. (Paul and Hadley eventually married). She and Hadley had decided to spend ten days in Chartres at the beginning of November to see the sights, and away from Paris and all its pressures and concerns, Hadley had her change of heart. The day before she returned to Paris from Chartres, she wrote to Hemingway informing him he could have his divorce, although she insisted that he had to divorce her and must foot all the legal bills incurred by the proceedings. Hemingway readily agreed. Although Hemingway would not be free to marry Pfeiffer for another six months until after the divorce was finalised, he perked up immediately. He wired Pfeiffer in Arkansas to return to Paris. She wired back informing him that she had just been offered a staff job with Vogue in New York, but Hemingway made it plain she should not accept the job but join him in Paris; in an echo of Zelda Fitzgerald's gibe that the Hemingway family always did what Ernest wanted, she turned the job down. Hemingway found a lawyer to deal with his divorce, and proceedings were initiated by the first week of December.

. . .

In the weeks before Christmas Hemingway was made aware that Sherwood Anderson was visiting Paris, but he did not make contact for ten days until, unable to avoid a meeting, he and Anderson met for a drink on Christmas Eve. It was the first time they had seen each other after Hemingway's novella The Torrents Of Spring lampooning Anderson had been published. Hemingway claimed the meeting was pleasant and friendly, and that the two of them had several drinks together before parting amicably. Anderson tells a different story. He says the occasion was stilted, that Hemingway was very uncomfortable and once they had a quick drink, he had soon departed.

The following day, December 25, Hemingway left for Gstaad where he spent Christmas with Pfeiffer's sister Jinny and Archibald and Ada MacLeish. Hadley and the Mowrers had travelled to Schruns, the Hemingways' old haunt in Austria, and according to Reynolds in Gstaad the transformation Hemingway was undergoing became more apparent: in Schruns, he and Hadley had led an easy-going life and in the two months they usually stayed, Hemingway let his hair grow unchecked and acquired a beard. Now in the more genteel and upper-class Gstaad he habitually wore a tweed suit – which Pfeiffer had bought him – and his facial hair was restricted to a neatly clipped moustache. The metamorphosis of Hemingway from semi-bohemian iconoclast into the respected author of was well underway. Five days after Christmas, Pfeiffer sailed from New York for Europe, and nine days later Hemingway travelled to Cherbourg to meet her and bring her to Gstaad.

Towards the end of January the proceedings divorcing Hemingway from Hadley passed their first stage, although they would not be finalised for another three months.

Yet even once the divorce was complete, he and Pfeiffer still had to wait a few weeks before they could marry. Halfway through March Hemingway took a last bachelor trip, joining his journalist friend Guy Hickok on ten-day jaunt to and around fascist northern Italy. [i] He and Pfeiffer were finally married on May 10.

1927-1929 – Fame and a comfortable life

All April [1927] he stayed away from Montparnasse where sidewalk cafés were crowded noon and midnight with American tourists, some looking for a glimpse of characters out of [The Sun Also Rises], others behaving as if they were auditioning for the parts.

Michael Reynolds, Hemingway: The Homecoming

Now, in the warm streets of summer, Paris was less lovely for Ernest than she had ever been in winter rain. Five years earlier, he and Hadley, unknown and in love, delighted in discovering the city . . . When the franc was at twelve to the dollar, they were tourists; as it rose to eighteen, they became old hands in the neighbourhood, recognised at the Dôme by painters and writers. Now [in 1927] with the franc at twenty-five, Hadley was in California and he, having become legendary along Montparnasse, took no joy on the boulevard.

Michael Reynolds, Hemingway: The Homecoming.

SINCE returning from Gstaad in March 1927, Pauline Pfeiffer, her sister, Jinny and Ada MacLeish had between them found and started organising an apartment for Pauline and her husband-to-be. Although the new Paris apartment at 6 rue Ferou was bigger, smarter and quieter than the down-at-heel walk-up with a communal lavatory on the landing in rue Notre Dames des Champs, Hemingway and Hadley's home since early 1924, it was barely more expensive. By now, of course, Hemingway's life had moved on and he no longer saw himself as the dedicated writer prepared to starve for his art in a garret: now he was the established and published author, a serious man of letters. Yet although he was no longer 'starving' — although, of course, he never was despite his romantic claims later in life, notably in his memoirs A Moveable Feast — he still wasn't earning his living from his writing as he had set out to do when, five years earlier, he arrived in Paris. More to the point, he was still obliged to live off a wife's income; and that irked him.

Despite being different in many ways — for example, Hadley was tall and matronly whereas Pfeiffer was short and petite — the two women had much in common and both benefited from a generous trust fund income. Pfeiffer's fund paid her $3,600 a year (about $55,770 in 2020), and given the still advantageous exchange rate — you got FF25 to the dollar in 1927 — Pfeiffer had an annual income of FF90,000. It was more than enough to sustain her and Hemingway — for example, the annual rent on their new apartment was just FF9,000. Furthermore, when Pfeiffer and Hemingway married on May 10, her extended family showered the couple with gifts of cash — cheques for $1,000 ($15,000 in 2023) were not unusual — and according to biographer Michael Reynolds the couple would have been able to live off the money for a year. Then there was the largesse of Pfeiffer's very wealthy uncle Gus Pfeiffer. Uncle Gus had no children of his own and doted on his nieces Pauline and Jinny, and he was extraordinarily generous to them. So when Hemingway and Pfeiffer took on the apartment in rue Ferou, Uncle Gus paid the many bills involved in sub-leasing it — three month's rent in advance and the equivalent of a year's rent to the leaseholder, three month's back taxes owed by the leaseholder and deposits for various utility services.

As for Hemingway's ambition to become a professional writer earning his living from his pen, it would be quite a few more years yet before he realised it, but he did begin earning money from his fiction. On the back of the success of The Sun Also Rises, Hemingway's short stories were now being accepted by various magazine, although none was attracting anywhere near the fabulous sums his friend Scott Fitzgerald was being paid for his short fiction. [i] Nor did Hemingway benefit from the success of his novel: in his zeal to rid himself of Hadley and marry Pauline Pfeiffer, he had impulsively signed over to her all royalties, current and future, from the sales of The Sun Also Rises (and it was a decision he later regretted and about which he complained bitterly). Within two days of the divorce coming through in mid-April, Hadley and her young son had sailed for New York, and — she told Hemingway — $5,000 ($76,477 in 2023) in royalty payments were waiting in her bank account: so much for Hemingway earning his living from his writing. As one of his better short stories, The Snows Of Kilimanjaro, in which a dying writer reproaches himself for living off his wife's income, made clear, it rankled a great deal.

With his second marriage, the Paris years, which saw Hemingway establish himself and, arguably, when he produced his better work, [1] were drawing to a close. He was no longer enjoying and living in the city as once he had. When he and Hadley arrived in December 1921, the young couple had toured Paris looking at the sights, but since the publication and success of his novel The Sun Also Rises, Hemingway was now himself 'one of the sights'. Americans flocked to Paris – the cheap franc made it very affordable for most – and they haunted 'the Latin Quarter' bars and cafés hoping to catch a glimpse of the writer himself. In Hemingway: The Homecoming, biographer Michael Reynolds spells out that

> *Between those newly resident intellectuals and the burgeoning tourists, the Left Bank was losing its charm [for Hemingway]. Evenings in the cafe with the light beginning to fail and saucers piling up, those evenings were becoming impossible . . . Wherever he looked pretentiousness abounded. The latest guidebook to Paris 'with the lid lifted' assured its readers that at Deux Magots one could hear 'more dirty stories and advice as to where to buy "adorable dresses" all in English than anywhere else in Paris'. The Select, one read, was filled with 'gentlemen with long, wavy hair and long painted fingernails and other gentlemen who, when they walk, walk "Falsetto", toss their hips and lift their brows".*

By 1927 'the city of light' was for Hemingway not what it had been and, ironically, he and his successful novel were two of the causes. Although he was nominally a resident of Paris for another three and a half years, between May 10, 1927 – when he and Pauline Pfeiffer were married, first in a civil ceremony in the town hall of Montrouge, then in a Roman Catholic ceremony in St Honoré d'Eylau – until the couple and their young son, Patrick, finally settled in Key West, Florida, 55 months later December 1931, in all he spent less than eight months in the city.

After an almost month-long honeymoon in the South of France (where the perpetually accident-prone Hemingway cut his foot and was infected with anthrax, and where he continued work on his second collection of short stories), he and Pfeiffer returned home to Paris; but just three weeks later, they were off again, this time to Pamplona for the annual trip to the San Fermin festival, followed by another leisurely trawl through Spain. They finally began domestic married life at their new rue F apartment at the beginning

---

1   Some might claim his only halfway decent work.

of September, and within days Hemingway (who now had his own room in which to work) began work on a new novel.

. . .

    Hemingway knew that he needed to publish a second novel to consolidate his career and status as a coming writer lauded by all the critics and – in Malcolm Cowley's later flattering judgment – 'a master at 26'. That second novel, which at first he called A New Slain Knight, was intended to chronicle life on the road for a 'professional revolutionist' [1] and his 14-year old son, and the lad's education by his father in the ways of the world. Work went very well to begin with, and a week after Hemingway's new short story collection Men Without Women was published on October 14, he was telling friends that he had already written 30,000 words.

    Michael Reynolds suggests that Hemingway's preferred method of composition – to write on spec, not knowing where his work would take him – was based on his conviction that it would keep a story vibrant and fresh. It was how he had written The Sun Also Rises and it had worked then; but this time his method did not pay off. Although he conscientiously carried on working on the novel every morning throughout the autumn of 1927, he slowly dried up. He tried to correct what might be wrong by switching from a first-person narrative to a third-person narrative. At one point he gave the 'professional revolutionist' a new name, but nothing could get his story moving again. In November he and Pfeiffer spent ten days in Berlin, and once back in Paris he re-read what he had so far written and – as he told one correspondent – the novel was 'all right part of the time' and that at other times it was 'horse manure'.

    In mid-December Hemingway, Pauline, Jinny and his son Bumby travelled to Gstaad for a two-month Christmas and New Year break, and work on the novel was interrupted when he developed 'flu, piles and toothache. Then Bumby accidentally cut the pupil of Hemingway's – good – right eye with his little finger, rendering him comparatively sightless for a few days. Back in Paris by mid-February, the writing was still no easier, and Hemingway finally gave up on the novel in mid-March. (His manuscript is now in the Hemingway section of the JFK Library in Boston with his other 'manuscripts, typescripts, drafts, notes, and galleys for Hemingway's published and unpublished writings'.) Michael Reynolds suggests that it wasn't just Hemingway's aimless method of composition that was causing him problems: after his second collection of short stories, Men Without Women, was published four months earlier in October, his self-confidence was shaken by a few of the reviews it had received. Ironically, many reviews had praised

---

1   Whatever he thought that was. I have no idea.

the work – The New Yorker recorded that the collection was

> ... a truly magnificent work ... [the reviewer did] not know where a greater collection of stories can be found ... Hemingway has an unerring sense of selection ... His is, as any reader knows, a dangerous influence. The simple thing he does looks so easy to do. But look at the boys who try to do it.

But Hemingway paid attention only to those reviewers who were less impressed with his collection: in a letter to Scott Fitzgerald he complained that

> ... these goddam reviews are sent to me by my 'friends', any review saying the stuff is a pile of shit I get at least 2,000 copies of.

He had previously been irritated by suggestions that The Sun Also Rises was – in the words of Douglas Ogden Stewart – not a novel, but a 'skilfully produced travelogue'; so Percy Hutchisson's New York Times review of Men Without Women will have hurt, despite the praise. Hutchisson commented

> Hemingway's is the art of the reporter carried to the highest degree ... His facts may be from experience, and they may be compounded solely of imagination; but he so presents them that they stand out with all the clearness and sharpness (and also the coldness) of pinnacles of ice in clear, frosty air. To sum up in a figure, Hemingway's is a stark naked style.

In The Saturday Review Lee Wilson Dodd handed out brickbats as well as bouquets. He admitted that

> ... the present critic ... is amazed and genuinely admires the lean virtuosity of Mr Hemingway

but he added

> the second most astonishing thing about him is the narrowness of his selective range.

Dodd concluded that

> In the callous little world of Mr Hemingway I feel cribbed, cabined, confined; I lack air – just as I do in the cruel world of Guy de Maupassant – just as I do, though not so desperately, so gaspingly,

> *in the placid stuffy little world of Jane Austen. But there is room to breathe in Shakespeare, in Tolstoy. And – yes – it makes all the difference.*

Virginia Woolf was also less than impressed. She conceded that

> *Mr Hemingway, then, is courageous; he is candid; he is highly skilled; he plants words precisely where he wishes*

but she concluded that

> *he is modern in manner but not in vision; he is self-consciously virile; his talent has contracted rather than expanded; compared with his novel, his stories are a little dry and sterile.'*

Wyndham Lewis was also ambivalent about Hemingway's new collection. Although he described Hemingway in his review of Men Without Women (which he had himself forwarded to Hemingway in Gstaad) as

> *. . . easily the ablest of the wild band of Americans in Europe*

he added, rather tactlessly given Hemingway's growing high opinion of his own literary abilities, that he

> *. . . . is obviously capable of a great deal of development before his work reaches maturity.*

Hemingway had a thin skin, and it was not quite what he wanted: in essence Lewis was telling readers that 'Hemingway can do better and has some way to go yet'. None of this was what Hemingway wanted to read. Reynolds records

> *Hemingway wrote Fitzgerald that he had seen the reviews of Burton Rascoe and [Virginia] Woolf and a couple of others . . . 'Am thinking of quitting publishing any stuff for the next 10 to 15 years.' The reviews, he said, were ruining his writing.*

Quite apart from those less than enthusiastic reviews and that his inspiration was dissipating as he wrote his new novel, Hemingway's mood had surely not been improved when the week before he finally abandoned his work in mid-March, he suffered another accident. At around 2am one morning – and, as biographer Kenneth Lynn suggests, probably while drunk (Pfeiffer was already concerned about how much he was drinking) – he mistook the skylight chain for the lavatory cistern chain, gave it one strong yank and brought the skylight down on his head. It cut his forehead badly and the wound needed six stitches, and the accident left him with a prominent scar on the left side of his forehead.

. . .

By chance, Bill Horne, his old buddy from the Red Cross days in Italy, had written to Hemingway out of the blue the previous November, and Horne's letter possibly revived memories of Italy. Hemingway might have known little about revolutions and 'professional revolutionists', but his – albeit rather short – time serving with the Red Cross in northern Italy meant he had seen war and knew a little about life on the front. Reynolds suggests that being contacted by Horne as well as being 'wounded' by the falling skylight were catalysts that prompted Hemingway to abandon A New Slain Knight. Instead, he started writing A Farewell To Arms to offer the world as his 'second novel', although like The Sun Also Rises it, too, began life as a short story and then evolved. The novel's protagonist, Frederic Henry, was – like Hemingway – an American serving as an ambulance driver with the Italian army, and Catherine Barkley, the novel's rather two-dimensional second protagonist, was – like Agnes von Kurowsky, the woman who broke the young Hemingway's heart – a Red Cross nurse. The other notable details of the novel, Italy's ignominious retreat after the Battle of Caporetto, Hemingway had garnered from war histories and maps – the battle and retreat had taken place seven to eight months before Hemingway first set foot in Europe.

. . .

At some point during the family winter holiday in Gstaad, Pfeiffer realised she was expecting her first child, and preparations for giving birth, due at the end of June, now dictated all of the Hemingways' plans. Pfeiffer wanted her baby to be born in America (Hadley had, too, but she gave birth to Bumby in Canada because Hemingway had started his staff job on the Star). Accordingly, the Hemingways left France for the US via Havana in mid-March, a week after Hemingway had abandoned work on his novel. They had decided to visit Key West on the recommendation of Hemingway's John Dos Passos, who had been much taken with the island, and then to travel north to Piggott, Pfeiffer's family home. They sailed from Le Havre for Havana and caught a ferry to Key West, 90 miles north of Cuba. [ii]

. . .

1927-1929 – Fame and a comfortable life

For the public, the name 'Hemingway' is still inextricably linked with Key West (and later Cuba), but it was happenstance that he made the island his home for the next ten years. When he and Pfeiffer arrived and discovered that the new car Uncle Gus had bought them had been delayed on the Florida mainland, Hemingway and Pfeiffer were forced to wait for its arrival in Key West and rented a small apartment. [1] Over the following weeks they explored the small island and met and became friends with one of Key West's wealthiest couples, Charles and Lorine Thompson. Hemingway had already tried his hand at fishing from the quayside – he spent every morning writing what was to become A Farewell To Arms and every afternoon fishing – but Charles, whose family owned many of the island's businesses, introduced Hemingway to deep-sea fishing. The Thompsons and the Hemingways got on well, and Pauline later admitted that she would not have agreed to settle in Key West as Hemingway was suggesting – because of his new enthusiasm for deep-sea fishing – had it not been for the prospect of Lorine's company.

What with the writing going well and the deep-sea fishing, Hemingway was in no rush to leave Key West even though Pfeiffer was getting ever closer to term, and finally, her father, Paul Pfeiffer, arrived to speed up matters. Pfeiffer left Key West by train, and Hemingway drove to Piggott in the company of his father-in-law which in those days was a three-day journey, often travelling on unsurfaced dirt roads.

From Piggott, Hemingway and Pfeiffer carried on to a hospital in Kansas City for the birth of their first child, Patrick, and the child was delivered by caesarean section at the end of June. Pfeiffer spent several weeks recuperating in Kansas City before Hemingway took her and the baby back to Piggott, then returned to Kansas City to meet up with Bill Horne to go hunting in to Wyoming. Within weeks, they were joined by Pfeiffer, who had left her baby son in the care of her sister Jinny. [2] By the end of September, Hemingway and Pfeiffer were back in Piggott, but soon on the road again. On his own, Hemingway made a rare visit to see his family in Oak Park before moving a few miles east to Chicago to drink and reminisce with friends. There he was joined by Pfeiffer, and they carried to Massachusetts and New York to see friends, a trip which included a memorable reunion with Scott Fitzgerald and his wife Zelda when Fitzgerald again got hopelessly drunk and again disgraced himself.

. . .

---

1   Yet gain the 'facts' vary: other accounts have the car – supposedly a yellow Ford coupé – waiting for Hemingway and Pfeiffer on the quayside. Who knows? Would they have remained in Key West if it had been and they didn't have to wait?

2   Pauline Pfeiffer later confessed she 'had never had a maternal instinct' and was uninterested in children until they were at least six years old.

One of the most significant events of Hemingway's life, perhaps as significant as his near-death experience in July 1918 at the front near the Piave river, was the suicide of his father Ed Hemingway. As a boy Hemingway had enjoyed his father's company and cherished the times they spent together, hunting and fishing near the family summer cottage at Walloon Lake, Michigan; but when Hemingway was barely in his teens, Ed increasingly withdrew into himself and away from the family. He had long suffered from depression, but in the late 1920s he had also developed diabetes, suffered from angina attacks and was worried about some investments he had made in real estate in Florida. Just before lunch on December 6, 1928, he had returned home from the hospital where he had been working that morning, gone upstairs to his bedroom, put an antique pistol to his head just behind his right ear and ended his life.

Hemingway was told of the death — although not yet how his father had died — by telegram on a train back to Key West from New York where he had picked up his son Bumby who had arrived from Europe. He put his son in the care of the train's conductor and changed trains at Philadelphia for Chicago, and it was only when he was collected from Chicago Union Station that he was told how his father had died.

For the rest of his life Hemingway uncharitably regarded Ed's suicide as an unforgivable weakness; but more than that he believed his mother Grace had driven Ed to take his own life, and from then on he told everyone how much he hated her. Yet one of the many oddities about Hemingway is that despite his antagonism, as he sorted out his father's affairs in the months following Ed's death not only did he treat his mother generously, but a year or two later he established a trust fund for her benefit that doubled her monthly income; and he supported her financially until she died just under 23 years later.

...

Hemingway and Pfeiffer had intended to return to Paris in November 1928, but at some point during their Wyoming fishing and hunting trip they decided instead to spend the winter months in Key West. Their new friend Lorine Thompson found them a house to rent short-term — one big enough to accommodate not just Hemingway and Pfeiffer, but their new son, Patrick, Pfeiffer's sister Jinny, who would help look after the baby, and Hemingway's sister Madelaine, known as Sunny, who had agreed to type up the manuscript for A Farewell To Arms that Hemingway had just finished.

The household was settled in the weeks before Christmas, and Pfeiffer and Sunny typed up what was to become A Farewell To Arms, completing the task towards the end of January, 1929. With work on his second novel out of the way, Hemingway entertained friends in Key West for the next few months, including Max Perkins, his Scribner's editor. Hemingway was keen to introduce everyone to his new enthusiasm deep-sea fishing and even the otherwise rather staid Perkins was roped in, encouraged by Hemingway's light-hearted threat that unless he collected the new manuscript in person, he wouldn't get it. [iii]

Hemingway's new novel was due for September publication, but he had also agreed for it to be serialised in Scribner's Magazine, and the first instalment appeared in May , although to Hemingway's great annoyance words and phrase deemed by the magazine to be offensive and unacceptable had been edited out. [1] He and Pfeiffer finally set sail for Europe from Cuba at the beginning of April (with, according to Michael Reynolds, a second new Ford given them by the ever-generous Uncle Gus stowed away in the ship's hold), and by September they and Patrick were back in Paris. With a view to possibly returning to Key West, however, they had left some belongings on the island.

---

1   Some tend to regard the past, in this case that of a century ago, as more 'innocent'. If only. In fact, Scribner's Magazine's prissy attitude was simply a hangover from America's 'Victorian' age. It is also worth noting that such prissiness, in Europe as well as the US, always goes hand in hand with outright hypocrisy.

1929-1934 – Becoming the legend

A man is essentially what he hides. The real and most important of the many Hemingway was the reflective man who wrote the books and concealed his innate sensitivity under the mask of a man of action. Though he liked to rage against aesthetic posturing – 'Artist, art, artistic! Can't we ever hear the last of that stuff' – he was, as James Thurber remarked, 'gentle, understanding, sympathetic, compassionate.' Yet Hemingway rejected this side of his character. Max Eastman said that in Death In The Afternoon Hemingway deliberately turned 'himself into a blustering roughneck crying for more killing and largely dedicated to demonstrating his ability to take any quantity of carnage in his powerful stride'. . . The transformation from private to public man, spurred by wealth and fame, began to take place in the early 1930s. It helped to explain the gradual decline of his work after A Farewell To Arms and the sharp descent after For Whom The Bell Tolls.

Jeffrey Meyers, Hemingway: A Biography.

The break with Dos Passos was an important turning point in Hemingway's life. He had quarrelled with Anderson, Stein, Ford, Lewis, Fitzgerald and MacLeish; with Robert McAlmon, Ernest Walsh, Harold Loeb, Don Stewart, Dorothy Parker, Morley Callaghan and Max Eastman. He was still on good terms with Pound and Joyce, but they lived in Europe and had taken different paths, into the Cantos and Finnegans Wake. After 1937, Hemingway had no close writer-friends: jealousy, bitterness,

1929-1934 – Becoming the legend

> *arrogance, ambition, pride, and politics knocked them all out of his life. In the 1940s and 1950s he knew soldiers, sportsmen, cronies, millionaires, hangers-on, actors and parasites – but he had no friends who were artists. Their absence coincided with the emergence of Papa Hemingway, his last public persona.*
>
> **Jeffrey Meyers, Hemingway: A Biography.**

THE FOURTH decade of the 20th century saw Hemingway's fame steadily grow, but after just four years in the literary vanguard, it also saw his reputation as a writer begin a slow decline. Although he wrote steadily throughout the 1930s, much of what he produced was journalism, which paid him well, but journalism is not on what his accepted status as 'a great writer' is based. His industry also produced two works of non-fiction, a third collection of short stories and a novel, yet the stir he had created early in his career was not to be repeated until he produced For Whom The Bell Tolls. For many in the 1930s it was becoming clear that the promise Hemingway had shown as a young, iconoclastic Turk in Paris might not be vindicated.

For the sake of convenience, one might consider there to have been four separate stages in Hemingway's life, each stage correlating to one of his marriages. The first saw him, with Hadley Richardson as his first wife, living in Paris and intent of making his way as a writer, fathering his first son and learning to network. It concluded with the success of his first collection of short stories, the almost overnight success of his novel The Sun Also Rises, his divorce from Richardson after five and a half years of marriage, and his second marriage, to Pauline Pfeiffer.

When the second stage began, he was riding high: he had made a name for himself as an up-and-coming young writer and was completing what was to become a second best-seller. He fathered two more sons and published several more books, and, partly because of his second wife's money, Hemingway was now able to live the life of a wealthy man. [1] But just a few years into his second marriage, he began an affair with a woman who was 14 years younger than Pfeiffer, and although Michael Reynolds doubts that this affair took place, other biographers insist it did; but it did not break up his marriage. It was a second affair, with the woman who was to become his third wife, that did that, and Hemingway's divorce from Pfeiffer and marriage to Martha Gellhorn in November 1940 concluded what might be seen as the second stage of his life. The third stage saw

---

1   The 1929 stock crash which led to the 'great depression' of the 1930s and saw millions of Americans suffer exceptional misery left Hemingway financially wholly unscathed.

Hemingway publish just one work, For Whom The Bell Tolls, but it, too, was a best-seller. The third marriage disintegrated within just four years, in part due to Hemingway's insistence that Gellhorn should be the kind of doting wife Richardson and Pfeiffer had been and should put him at the centre of everything, including her life. Gellhorn, herself a published novelist and a working journalist and, not least, ambitious, was not that kind of woman. For a while she did try to live as 'the novelist Ernest Hemingway's wife' (and his three sons became fond of their new stepmother, though they are said to have regarded her more as an older sister); but she was unhappy and she soon sought and found journalistic assignments which took her away from home. By the time Hemingway acknowledged that his third marriage had failed and, in 1945, agreed to give Gellhorn the divorce she wanted, he had already started a relationship with the journalist Mary Welsh. Despite Welsh's profound misgivings, both from the start of her relationship with Hemingway and throughout their marriage, in 1946 she became his fourth and last wife, and a nominal fourth stage of his life began.

...

Even though Scribner's Magazine started serialising A Farewell To Arms in May 1929, the work was not yet wholly complete. Hemingway was dissatisfied with the novel's ending and so – he claimed [1] – he wrote a few dozen more, trying to find the right way to conclude his story. He had worked on that ending while crossing from Havana to Europe in the spring of 1929 and when back in France he continued trying to find the right one. Once he was back, though, he immediately took off to Hendaye when his son Patrick, not yet 12 months old, was hospitalised with influenza. It didn't matter that, in addition, his wife Pauline had to undergo surgery to clear her sinuses. Hemingway, according to Reynolds, had a 'mortal fear of 'flu' and thought it best to remove himself from the danger of contracting it from his baby son. Several years earlier he had written the last few pages of The Sun Also Rises in Hendaye; now he was back there to find that satisfactory but elusive conclusion to A Farewell To Arms. In the event he did not and only came up with the ending to the novel as we now know it when he had returned to Paris by the middle of May.

In July Hemingway was in Pamplona for the bullfighting, this time with Uncle Gus, Pauline's sister Jinny and his journalist friend Guy Hickok. Pauline had remained in Paris, but joined him after the fiesta had ended (with her hair dyed blonde to surprise him), but their subsequent extended tour of Spain for more bullfights and a return to

---

1   This is usually a necessary proviso whenever Hemingway tells us something, so much so it would be simplest to regard it as a perpetual understood.

1929-1934 – Becoming the legend

Santiago de Compostela was not a complete success: Hemingway and Pfeiffer argued so much that Hemingway even made a note in his diary of the days when they did not argue. For one thing, Pfeiffer was becoming ever more concerned about how much Hemingway was drinking, but Reynolds gives a different reason. He suggests that the volatile moods and outbursts of temper which were spoiling the trip were also because now Hemingway had finally finished his novel, he felt 'empty'. Hemingway himself pronounced, rather pretentiously, though in keeping with his growing conviction that he was a 'great writer', [1] that

> *within the writer there was his death, and that death was the book.* [2]

The writer might physically survive any number of books, Hemingway informs us, but

> *each [book] would kill off a part of him, a piece of what he knew, leaving the book with a life of its own.* [i]

Another possible reason for the arguments between the couple might have been Pfeiffer's opposition to artificial contraception and the effect it had on Hemingway's sex life. After her problems when giving birth to her second son – Patrick was eventually delivered by caesarean section after a very long labour – Pfeiffer was told by her doctor that she should not consider having another child for three years. Various biographers have established that Pfeiffer – then still a devout Roman Catholic – refused to use any artificial form of contraception and would only consider practising *coitus interruptus*.

. . .

Although Hemingway and Pfeiffer carried on renting their flat in the rue Ferou, they did not settle there and spent the next few years commuting between Paris and Key West and travelling to Spain and Wyoming. After their two-month tour of Spain, they returned to Paris, and A Farewell To Arms was published towards the end of October 1929. Sales were spectacular, and on the back of the fame-cum-notoriety Hemingway had achieved with The Sun Also Rises, the novel consolidated his position as a writer on whom to keep a keen eye. The first 30,000 copies of the new novel were sold out within three weeks, and in quick succession two more print runs of 10,000 each were ordered. His fame and new position as a writer of consequence also had a bearing on

---

1   The scrap of paper from which this is taken is, like all the other scraps of paper Hemingway could not bring himself to throw away, in the JFK Library in Boston.

2   I don't know what this means, but that might well be my fault.

his lifestyle. For several years Hemingway and Hadley had enjoyed spending Christmas in cosy, comfortable and – for Americans with dollars to exchange for local currency – exceptionally cheap Schruns in Austria. Christmas 1929 was spent in Switzerland in a much grander style, with various wealthy friends, including Gerald and Sara Murphy, Scott and Zelda Fitzgerald, and with John Dos Passos and Katie Smith (who had recently married, but who were certainly not as wealthy as the Murphys and Fitzgerald).[1] This, too, was part of the transformation of 'Ernest Hemingway, the aspiring young writer' into Ernest Hemingway, the 'successful new writer'.

Hemingway and Pfeiffer did not see in New Year 1930 in Switzerland, and just over a week after returning to Paris, they set sail back to Key West. Later in the year, Hemingway took off with his family for his first trip to spend several months hunting and fishing in the American West, and it became his practice to spend the late summer and early autumn of each year in Wyoming, later in Montana and later still in Idaho. He had already started work on his 'bullfighting and writing' book Death In The Afternoon earlier in the year in Key West while Max Perkins had been staying and carried on writing it over the following months.

...

The ostensible reason for returning to Key West had been for Hemingway to have somewhere quiet to write; he was, in fact, quite happy settling down to write wherever he was, whether in Key West or the Rockies, following his usual routine of writing in the morning and hunting or fishing in the afternoon. Then, in the November, came the car crash in Wyoming in which he was badly injured and which forced him to abandon work on his 'bullfighting' book for several months. Driving with Dos Passos as a passenger, he had been dazzled by the lights of an oncoming truck, swerved and rolled the car. The accident saw him break his right arm severely between his elbow and shoulder, and writing became impossible. Holed up in hospital in Billings for many weeks did not improve his mood. Archibald MacLeish, at the time still a close friend from their Paris days, spent 48 hours travelling all the way from the east coast to visit Hemingway, only to be accused by him, bizarrely, of coming to see him die.[2] When he was eventually discharged just before Christmas 1930, he spent the holiday in Piggott with his wife's

---

1   Katie Smith who had more or less introduced Hemingway to Hadley was also, coincidentally, a friend and roommate of Pfeiffer's at Bryn Mawr College.

2   In time Hemingway's friendship with MacLeish also has some bad fallings out and for several years they were not on speaking terms. Eventually, after World War II, Hemingway wrote to MacLeish apologising for some insulting comments he had made and the friendship was resumed.

family but was still able to do little with his right arm.

After living in Key West rentals for almost two years, in the spring of 1931 Hemingway and Pfeiffer bought a house in Whitehead Street, or rather good old generous Uncle Gus bought it for them. The house was 80 years old and by then somewhat dilapidated, but it had once been one of the smartest houses on what was then still an island; over the following years Pfeiffer renovated and extended it. It was a distinct improvement on the pokey tenement flats with a communal lavatory in the hallway Hemingway had chosen to live in Paris; thus the transformation of Hemingway, the 'writer who had starved for his art' of his early years into Hemingway 'the wealthy and well-known novelist' continued apace.

A Farewell To Arms did ensure he was, more or less, now earning his living from his pen: when passing through New York on his way from Paris to Key West at the end of January, he was informed that in just three months the novel had already sold 80,000 copies. According to Michael Reynolds, Hemingway's accounts for 1929 showed that he had earned $18,416 (the equivalent of $325,464 in 2023). With the addition of Pfeiffer's annual trust fund income of $6,000 ($106,070 in 2023) Hemingway was now able to live a very good life. That said, the lifestyle he and Pfeiffer chose for themselves was not at all cheap.

His right arm took some time to heal, but once it was finally functional and Hemingway was able to work again, he and Pfeiffer sailed back to Europe, Hemingway to Madrid to undertake research for Death In The Afternoon and Pfeiffer back to Paris. She eventually joined him in Spain, and in July it was back at the Pamplona festival, then another extended tour of Spain began. By September – despite the warnings from her doctor – Pfeiffer was seven months pregnant, and she and Hemingway sailed back to the US. It was on that voyage that Hemingway met Jane Kendall Mason with whom he went on to have his first affair [1] while married to Pfeiffer.

. . .

The startling success of his early years had come to a halt by the early 1930s. He had completed Death In The Afternoon, his curious amalgam of an extensive guide to bullfighting, its history, practices and lore, as well as his pronouncements on writing and literature, by the end of January 1932; it was published the following September. In 1935 came Green Hills Of Africa, his semi-fictional book about his two-month safari

---

1   As I point out above, biographers disagree on how long it lasted or even if there was an affair. I'm assuming there was one as that is what most biographers suggest, but note what Debra Moddelmog has to say about writing biography.

in East Africa of the year before (which, like the cars and the house in Key West and its renovation, was also funded by Uncle Gus). This book was another curious amalgam, this time his account of big-game hunting, its practices and the African people with whom he came into contact; and in it, too, Hemingway pronounced – pontificated would be a better word – on writing, literature and the work of several of his fellow writers. By then, still only in his mid-thirties Hemingway regarded himself as some kind of literary sage and believed he was qualified to lay down the law on what constituted 'good writing'. Neither his bullfighting book nor his safari book sold well, and both had a mixed and unenthusiastic critical reception. Reviewing the book in The New Republic, the influential critic, literary theorist and, notably, a one-time Hemingway champion Edmund Wilson wrote

> *[Hemingway] delivers a self-confident lecture on the high possibilities of prose writing, with the implication that he himself, Hemingway, has realized or hopes to realize these possibilities; and then writes what are certainly, from the point of view of prose, the very worst pages of his life. There is one passage which is hardly even intelligible – the most serious possible fault for a writer who is always insisting on the supreme importance of lucidity.*

The criticism was quite specific, especially in Wilson's concern about a lack of lucidity in the prose which, as far as he was concerned, verged on unintelligibility. A wiser writer might have taken note, but Hemingway was too convinced he was one of America's finest writers and took no heed (or perhaps only seems not to have done – it is possible he was simply blind to his shortcomings). Revisiting the book several years later – and still unimpressed – Wilson added

> *[Hemingway] has produced what must be one of the only books ever written which make Africa and its animals seem dull. Almost the only thing we learned about the animals is that Hemingway wants to kill them. And as for the natives . . . the principal impression we get of them is that they were simple and inferior people who enormously admired Hemingway.*

Writing in the New York Times, Charles Poore was not as dismissive and noted

> *The writing is the thing; that way he has of getting down with beautiful precision the exact way things look, smell, taste, feel,*

sound.

But this praise is more than tempered by his astonishment that

> *Some of his sentences in Green Hills Of Africa would make Henry James take a breath. There's one that starts on page 148, swings the length of 149 and lands on 150, forty lines or so from tip to tip.*

Again: what was Hemingway, the advocate of 'the importance of lucidity', thinking? Did the writer who insisted – boasted would be truer – that he re-wrote and revised his work obsessively even bother to read over what he had produced? It's hard to believe he had done so. A sentence which

> *starts on page 148, swings the length of 149 and lands on 150, forty lines or so from tip to tip*

might well have benefited from revision, especially if parts of the book, according to Wilson, were 'hardly even intelligible'. Perhaps Wilson, Poore and the other critics who were less than enchanted by Hemingway's new book were also rather put off by his – now very well-known and somewhat tactless – description of them in Green Hills Of Africa as

> *lice who crawl on literature.*

. . .

Two years earlier, in 1933, Hemingway had published Winner Take Nothing [sic], his third volume of short stories, and it, too, had failed to set the reading public alight. It has been suggested that in Depression-era America the downbeat title of the collection did its sales no favours; its lukewarm reception by the critics did not cheer up Hemingway, who demanded unalloyed admiration. That was one point satirically made in The Artist's Reward, a profile of Hemingway Dorothy Parker had written for the New Yorker four years earlier just after A Farewell To Arms had been published. She observed:

> *As I wrote this, the reviews of A Farewell To Arms had not yet reached Ernest Hemingway in Paris. All those by what are called the big critics may be laudatory, serious and understanding; but it is safe to say that if there be included among them one tiny clipping announcing that Miss Harriet McBlease, who does 'Book-Looks'*

> *for the Middletown Observer-Companion, does not find the new Hemingway book to her taste, that will be the one Our Hero will select to brood over . . .'*

Overall, the 1930s did see Hemingway at his industrious best, and his time was certainly not all spent marlin fishing and hunting in Wyoming and Montana. He produced several short stories, following his established routine of getting down to write in the early morning, then, four or five hours of work done, relaxing in the afternoons. Apart from his fiction, he also produced light, journalistic pieces, particularly for the men's lifestyle magazine, Esquire, and later for Ken, a left-leaning political magazine, which were both co-founded by Arnold Gingrich.

Ken first appeared in April 1938, but lasted for just over a year, falling foul of the dislike potential advertisers had for it's political position even though this had been toned down before its launch specifically to keep them on-board. The 'Letters' Hemingway wrote for Esquire were mainly – although not exclusively – articles on hunting and fishing, and he had licence to write on whatever topic he liked. As Raeburn demonstrates in Fame Became Him, Hemingway was invariably always centre-stage in these pieces, subtly establishing his credentials as an expert or authority on pretty much everything. The arrangement – and Hemingway later admitted that he could hardly believe his luck in landing it – came about because of the high public profile he was enjoying from 1930 on. Arnold Gingrich, who had launched Esquire in 1933 as a fashion magazine for men along the lines of Vogue, calculated that having Hemingway's by-line would give his new magazine cachet and attract male readers. Gingrich had bumped into him in a New York bookshop several months before the magazine appeared and on the spot asked him whether he would write for Esquire. According to Adrienne Westenfeld, Esquire's books and fiction editor, writing in 2021 about the friendship between Gingrich and Hemingway, there was a second reason why Gingrich wanted to hire Hemingway: the magazine was to be distributed in gentlemen's clothes stores and haberdashers, and Gingrich was worried it might mainly attract a gay readership which, he feared could, discourage heterosexual readers. His solution – which might now make us laugh [1] – was, writes Westenfeld,

> *to publish supposedly 'manly' stories about sports and outdoor pursuits. He set his sights on Hemingway, an ascendant celebrity novelist and prolific journalist with two acclaimed novels under*

---

1   Anyone who in 2023 still thinks homosexual mean are simpering effeminate darlings with a penchant for pink frills, show tunes and expensive scent has not met many homosexual men.

> *his belt (The Sun Also Rises and A Farewell To Arms), but also an avid outdoorsman as famed for his hyper-masculine pastimes as for his literature.*

Gingrich was an astute businessman, but Hemingway was also astute and knew his worth: the contract he signed saw him – eventually – being paid twice as much as any other contributor. For the first issue, however, Hemingway had, uncharacteristically, agreed to a comparatively modest $250 ($5,862 in 2023) for each piece he wrote when Gingrich told him that was all his magazine could afford; but, says Westenfeld, Hemingway swore Gingrich to secrecy: he feared it would damage his reputation if word got out that he, the great writer, had settled for such a 'pittance'. When the first issue in October 1933 sold far better than expected and Gingrich decided the second and future issues should also be available on news-stands, Hemingway immediately demanded $500 for each 'Letter' (and his fee later reached $1,000). In a letter to Gingrich, Hemingway, says Westenfeld, outlined that his philosophy was

> *[to] make all comercial [sic] magazines pay the top rate they have ever paid anybody. This makes them love and appreciate your stuff and realize what a fine writer you are.*

Gingrich, who regarded hiring Hemingway as something of a coup and later in life confessed he had seen Hemingway as the magazine's 'principal asset', also agreed to allow Hemingway's work to remain unedited and appear as it was submitted. A bonus of Hemingway's involvement was, for Gingrich, that it had also encouraged other 'name' writers such as Theodore Dreiser, Scott Fitzgerald, John Dos Passos, Dashiell Hammett and Ring Lardner to contribute to his new magazine.

1934-1936 – Poor sales and growing depression

In spite of its frequent strength as narrative writing, To Have And Have Not is a novel distinctly inferior to A Farewell to Arms . . . Mr. Hemingway's record as a creative writer would be stronger if it had never been published.

J. Donald Adams, the New York Times.

BY THE mid-1930s, Hemingway was under increasing pressure from Scribner's to produce a follow-up novel to A Farewell To Arms. The publisher was disappointed with the sales of the non-fiction books, Death In The Afternoon and Green Hills Of Africa, which some accounts suggest only just broke even, and Hemingway's third collection of short stories, Winner Take Nothing, had not sold as well as hoped and expected. To Hemingway's immense irritation, he was also under pressure from a largely left-of-centre literary world still in thrall to its sanitised view of Soviet Russia to write more politically engaged fiction – the US was in the middle of its Great Depression. Hemingway had long resisted such political engagement and insisted that a writer's job was to write, not to indulge himself in politics. As early as 1932 he had written to the Chicago bookseller, Paul Romaine, who was consistently urging him to become more politically engaged

> *There is no left or right in writing. There is only good writing and bad writing.*

He did, though, make a notable exception to this stance after hundreds of Great War veterans working on a government project in the Florida Keys died in the worst hurricane

1934-1936 – Poor sales and growing depression

to hit the area in many years on Labor Day, September 2, 1935.

...

The veterans were based on Upper and Lower Matecumbe Keys just 80 miles west-north-west towards the mainland from Key West and had been employed, at $30 a month ($703.50 in 2023) plus free bed and board, on a Federal Emergency Relief Administration (F.E.R.A.) scheme to build bridges and roads to link the Florida Keys. In 1934, Monroe County, to which Key West, the county seat, belonged, had declared bankruptcy, and unemployment had risen by 80% after the naval base and many factories and businesses on its islands closed down. When Franklin D. Roosevelt became president, his government planned to revitalise the county into an attractive tourist destination, and to do that it needed to improve access.

By 1933, just under four years after the Wall Street crash, one in four American citizens able to work, many of them Great War vets, was unemployed, but the then President, Republican Herbert Hoover, stubbornly refused to spend government money on social welfare schemes. He insisted that in time the US economy would sort itself out, and for him the war veterans were an embarrassment. The vets were angry; in 1924 they had been promised a war service bonus, but it was not due to be paid until 1945; so in 1932, 17,000 unemployed veterans – calling themselves the 'Bonus Expeditionary Force' – petitioned the government to pay them their bonus early. They gathered in Washington and were joined by another 27,000 hungry men, women and children, settling in shanty camps in and around the capital. Hoover's government simply dismissed the vets' request and told them to return home. When the protesters ignored the order and police were sent in to evict them from any government property they had occupied, a riot developed and two of them where shot dead. Hoover then ordered the army at gunpoint to drive all 44,000 protesters out of Washington. Unsurprisingly, the following November in a landslide Democrat victory, he was voted out of office, and Roosevelt, once inaugurated in March 1933, set about trying to get the US economy going again. F.E.R.A. was created as one of his measures.

...

Hurricanes were a seasonal hazard in the Florida Keys, but the September 2, 1935, Labor Day hurricane was particularly strong. Its force was badly underestimated and its position was not well-known by the then US Weather Bureau, which had initially warned of a 'rainy windstorm'. By the time the full danger from the storm was apparent and it was thought wise to evacuate the veterans, it was far too late. The evacuation plan involved a train being sent south from the mainland, but first it had to be assembled – because of a misunderstanding the deputy administrator on duty thought it was already on standby and summoned it far too late – and it didn't leave Miami until mid-afternoon on September 2 when the storm was well underway. The train was then delayed after a steel cable had been blown across its track in the high winds, and this had to be cleared. When it finally arrived in Upper Matecumbe, the whole train except the heavier locomotive was then blown over and derailed.

The vets had been housed, despite warnings from locals when the vets and their families had arrived, in flimsy wooden shacks on the Matecumbe Keys beaches and had no protection whatsoever. Even many of the solid brick houses in which the locals lived which usually withstood the hurricane winds were demolished. The vets had no chance. They were blown out to sea, struck by flying debris, drowned in towering waves, and many bodies were washed into the trees where in the hot sun they decomposed over the following days. Figures on how many veterans and locals died in the hurricane vary from between 300 to more than 1,000.

Hemingway visited the scene a few days later, and the appalling death and devastation the hurricane had caused moved him to write and publish in the left-wing journal New Masses – in response to a request from the journal, a point that is rarely made – a polemical piece taking the authorities to task for sending the veterans to the Keys during hurricane season.[1] Hemingway entitled his piece Who Killed These Men? but to his immense irritation and without his permission, the New Masses editor changed the title to Who Murdered The Vets? It began by asking

> *Whom did [the veterans] annoy and to whom was their possible presence a political danger? Who sent them down to the Florida Keys and left them there in hurricane months? Who is responsible for their deaths?*

He continued

> *[The writer of this article] does know that wealthy people, yachtsmen, fishermen such as President Hoover and President Roosevelt, do not come to the Florida Keys in hurricane months. Hurricane months are August, September and October, and in*

---

[1] I shall again contend that Hemingway's true gift was for journalism, not literature.

> *those months you see no yachts along the Keys. You do not see them because yacht owners know there would be great danger, inescapable danger, to their property if a storm should come . . . But veterans, especially the bonus-marching variety of veterans are not property, they are only human beings; unsuccessful human beings, and all they have is to lose their lives.*

Describing the scene and the dead vets he saw, he wrote

> *. . . you found [the vets' bodies] high in the trees where the water had swept them. You found them everywhere and in the sun all of them were beginning to be far too big for their blues jeans and jackets that they could never fill when they were on the bum and hungry.*

It was an effective piece, but a distinct rarity among his writing. Hemingway, who strongly believed in 'small government' and the least possible official involvement, had previously been very sniffy about F.E.R.A. and its activities, and in Green Hills Of Africa had described it as some

> *. . . sort of YMCA show. Starry-eyed bastards spending money that somebody will have to pay. Everybody in our town quit work to go on relief. Fishermen all turned carpenters. Reverse of the Bible.* [i]

Pertinently, though, the piece for New Masses was journalism not fiction, and Hemingway still believed writers should steer clear of politics. He made that clear a few years later in his introduction Men At War, his selection of 'war writings'. He insisted

> *The hardest thing in the world to do is to write straight honest prose on human beings. First you have to know the subject; then you have to know how to write. Both take a lifetime to learn, and anybody is cheating who takes politics as a way out. It's too easy. All the outs are too easy, and the thing itself is too hard to do.*

Quite apart from his views about writers and politics, this observation is typical of Hemingway (as John Raeburn might have pointed out): yet again he implies – almost underlines it without directly saying so – that he is the 'expert' and the one with the 'real gen', the 'insider': his sub-text is clearly *'but I, Ernest Hemingway, unlike many, am not only able to do the hardest thing in the world, but I both know about human beings and how to write'.* An irony is that Hemingway was still in his early forties when he wrote the above and had published just four novels and three collections of short stories: his boast that *'writing takes a lifetime to learn'* would make a little more sense – and be less self-regarding more acceptable – from a writer who had at least come close to completing his three score and ten and had rather more published work to his name.

...

Halfway through the 1930s Hemingway suffered a severe and prolonged bout of depression, but it seems to have become particularly acute in 1936. Although he had experienced depressions throughout his life, this episode was worse than anything he had suffered for some time. Whether or not this latest deep bout was the mooted bi-polar cycle at its lowest ebb, or whether there were definite causes would be impossible to establish; but after enjoying success for several years, Hemingway was now having to accept that a great deal was no longer going his way. After the triumphant reception of his first two novels and his first two collections of short stories, the largely negative reaction, both critical and public, to his recently published works of non-fiction upset him far more than he cared to admit. At first the critics and the public had not known what to make of that non-fiction. In the Pull Of Politics, Milton Cohen observes

> *The reviews of Death In The Afternoon were more puzzled than disrespectful; this was, after all, Hemingway's first book after his acclaimed A Farewell To Arms, and in 1932 his reputation was still riding that wave of critical adulation.*

Then came his third volume of original short stories, and Hemingway was disappointed by its rather pale sales performance and the critics' response. Cohen writes

> *The collection of stories that followed in 1933, Winner Take Nothing, also received mixed reviews. Some were now edged with impatience since it was clear from the stories that Hemingway's indifference to the times in Death In The Afternoon was not an anomaly and that the author had not at all changed his theme and focus from the 1920s – themes such as existential despair that did not speak to the Depression 1930s. Since the short story was a Hemingway specialty, the mixed reviews stung even more than those of the bullfight book, suggesting either that something was amiss with the fundamentals of Hemingway's writing, or, as he*

preferred to believe, that the critics were just out to get him for not conforming to the times.

In The Nation William Troy's scathing dismissal was simply that

It is among Mr Hemingway's admirers that the suspicion is being most strongly created that the champion is losing, if he has not already lost, his hold.

Troy's own view of the collection of stories was that it was

... the poorest and least interesting writing [Hemingway] has ever placed in public view.

When Green Hills Of Africa, the work that followed his volume of stories, was also dismissed, quite brutally by some critics, Hemingway was finally convinced that the critics hated him, and he made his view plain. Statements such as this from Granville Hicks in the left-wing New Masses in which he candidly queried whether Hemingway had simply lost it will not have helped at all:

He is very bitter about the critics and very bold in asserting his independence of them, so bitter and so bold that one detects signs of a bad conscience ... Would Hemingway write better books if he wrote on different themes? 'Who Murdered The Vets?' suggests he would ... In six years Hemingway has not produced a book even remotely worthy of his talents.

Hicks' left-handed concession – that Hemingway still had 'talents' – will have done little to soften the blow. And though publicly Hemingway's attitude was stout-hearted defiance, privately, it seems, he became ever more depressed. He is also likely to have read the sober assessment of his recent work by the poet John Peale Bishop, published towards the end of 1936 in The New Republic. Bishop had known Hemingway well in the Paris years, from the time when he was still unpublished until after A Farewell To Arms appeared, but they had then lost touch. In his piece, entitled Homage To Hemingway, Bishop had nothing but praise for the unknown young writer he had met in Paris in 1922. The Hemingway he then knew, he wrote,

had many of the faults of the artist, some, such as vanity, to an exaggerated degree ... [but these] were compensated for by extraordinary literary virtues.

He added that Hemingway

> *was instinctively intelligent, disinterested, and not given to talking nonsense. Toward his craft he was humble, and had, moreover, the most completely literary integrity it has ever been my lot to encounter.*

This was high praise indeed, so Hemingway, in the depths of his depression and now, he believed, assailed on all sides must have been disheartened then to read Bishop's observation that by 1936

> *he has become the legendary Hemingway. He appears to have turned into a composite of all those photographs he has been sending out for years: sunburned from snows, on skis; in fishing get-up, burned dark from the hot Caribbean; the handsome, stalwart hunter crouched smiling over the carcass of some dead beast. Such a man could have written most of Green Hills Of Africa.*

Like the other critics, Bishop was unimpressed by Green Hills Of Africa, which he described as 'hard-boiled'. He goes on to elaborate:

> *If that word is to mean anything, it must mean indifference to suffering and, since we are what we are, can but signify a callousness to others' pain. When I say that the young Hemingway was among the tenderest of mortals, I do not speak out of private knowledge, but from the evidence of his writings. He could be, as any artist must in this world, if he is to get his work done, ruthless. He wrote courageously, but out of pity; having been hurt, and badly hurt, he could understand the pain of others. His heart was worn, as was the fashion of the times, up his sleeve and not on it. It was always there and his best tricks were won with it. Now, according to the little preface to Green Hills Of Africa, he seems to think that having discarded that half-concealed card, he plays more honestly. He does not. For with the heart the innate honesty of the artist is gone. And he loses the game.*

Hemingway always took an interest in what was said about him publicly, and he is more

1934-1936 – Poor sales and growing depression

likely than not to have been aware of Bishop's concerns and disappointment. It will not have been easy reading for him.

Milton Cohen alludes to another worry which might have been darkening Hemingway's spirits – that less than ten years on from the 'shocking' impact of his novel The Sun Also Rises and the subsequent hi-falutin' claims that it described the 'despair' of the younger generation, Hemingway was now out of touch. The world had moved on and so had he, but in a different direction. Cohen writes that in the negative reviews of his works of non-fiction

> *one senses not merely disapproval but exasperation with Hemingway's assumptions that the American public of 1935 – still staggering under a worldwide economic depression, and now confronting the rise of Nazism and the aggression of Italian fashion fascism – would thrill to the expensive adventures of the sportsman in a far-off land and eagerly devour his most casually delivered pontifications on American literature and letters. To the economic and issues of the day the book is serenely indifferent – except to the leftist critics who have dared to criticize the author.*

So the penny finally dropped, and despite Hemingway's consistent misgivings and his long-held conviction that writers should not be political, he capitulated to the pressure from his left-wing literary peers. They had been impressed by his polemic Who Murdered The Vets? in New Masses and were convinced he could be persuaded to throw in his lot with them? Fine, he would write the 'socially-engaged', political work they were demanding!

. . .

After the lack of success of Hemingway's last three works – more a comparative lack in the case of his third short story collection – further pressure, which he could no longer ignore, came from his editor Scribner's Max Perkins who increasingly urged him to produce new fiction. Perkins, who always indulged Hemingway a great deal [1] and had agreed to publish Death In The Afternoon against his better judgment, had been dismayed by the poor sales of Hemingway's non-fiction books and kept up urging him to write another novel. To do as he was bidden as well as to assuage the literary left,

---
1   Perhaps to Hemingway's detriment – it was said of Perkins that he disliked confrontation.

Hemingway conceived of To Have And Have Not; and although he did not settle on that title until after the writing was well underway, it succinctly expressed what he hoped was the work's 'left-wing theme'. But writing the novel took several years and was not easy; and his confused motivations, his method and his intentions might explain the literary hotch-potch he eventually delivered to Scribner's.

There was possibly also another source of pressure on Hemingway to write the novel, but it was pressure he imposed on himself: Hemingway is said to have confided in Hollywood director Howard Hawks that he wrote To Have And Have Not because he 'needed money'. On the face of it that is an odd admission. In Depression-era 1930s America the Hemingway Key West household income was stable and enviably high; and although Hemingway spent a great deal, he would not have been short of money. The problem was more personal: his contribution to the household from what his pen earned him was rather smaller than what Pfeiffer contributed from her trust fund: he felt he was living off his wife, and this irked him a great deal, especially in his depressed state in 1936.

In the spring and summer he had written two of his better known – and better – short stories, The Snows Of Kilimanjaro (which appeared in Esquire in August) and The Short Happy Life Of Francis Macomber (which Cosmopolitan published in September). Both were an oblique, probably unconscious, commentary on his marriage to Pfeiffer. [1] Both the stories' protagonists – Harry, a writer dying of gangrene who feels he has squandered his talent, and Francis Macomber, a coward who redeems himself – resent their wives (who are thought to have been based jointly on Pfeiffer and Jane Mason with whom his affair had ended badly). Harry feels that by opting for the soft, good life his rich wife's money paid for, he had betrayed his talent. Rich Francis Macomber knows that his wife, described by Hemingway as 'an all-American bitch', just wants him for his money. He despises himself because he kowtows to her and tolerates her infidelity, and he, too, feels he has been corrupted. From letters to, and in conversation with, friends, Hemingway also revealed he felt he had sold out to Pfeiffer's money. The claim that Hemingway told Hawks he wrote his novel because he 'needed money' was made in In Who The Devil Made It by the Hollywood director Peter Bogdanovich in which he records conversations he had with several notable directors of the 1940s and 1950s. He reports how Hawks recalled the genesis of his film version of To Have And Have Not and told Bogdanovich that

---

1 In this respect they would remind us that Hemingway did something similar in several short stories written in last years of his marriage to Hadley Richardson.

> *[when] I told Hemingway I could make a picture out of his worst book, he said, rather grumpily, 'What's my worst book?' I said, 'That bunch of junk called 'To Have and Have Not'.'*

Hemingway then justified writing 'that bunch of junk' because he 'needed money' according to Hawks. [1]

. . .

Perhaps how Hemingway came to compose To Have And Have Not was an indication, not least to himself, that he was running out of steam. Had no new ideas for a novel occurred to him at all in the eight years since he had written A Farewell To Arms? It seems they had not, and to produce the novel Perkins was demanding, Hemingway decided to amalgamate – 'cannibalise' might sound cruel but would not be inappropriate – two previously published short stories. The first, One Trip Across, was about a hard-done-by jobbing boat owner and had appeared in Cosmopolitan; the second, The Tradesman's Return about the same boat owner, had appeared in Esquire. To conclude the novel, Hemingway planned to add a longer novella. A cynic might point out that proceeding in such a manner rather than producing original work suggested that Hemingway's imagination was barren. If so, that, too, would have weighed on his mind and darkened the moods that continued to plague him.

As usual in the autumn (when the hurricane season precluded deep-sea fishing) in 1936 Hemingway and his family travelled from Key West to spend several months on the L Bar T dude ranch near the Montana and Wyoming border. There he worked on his new novel in the morning and made good progress, but his depression did no lift. Tommy Shevlin, a young, wealthy fishing friend Hemingway had first met in Bimini (one of the islands that make up the Bahamas) and who had been invited to join the Hemingways at the L Bar T, later remembered of his time at the ranch

> *It's extraordinary the number of times [Hemingway] mentioned suicide.*

Michael Reynolds writes

---

1   It is, of course, possible that Hemingway was simply trying to save face when he told Hawks he had written To Have And Have Not because he 'needed the money'. He might also have been aware that the novel was, as Hawks described it, 'a bunch of junk', but rather than admit, even to himself, he wasn't as great a writer as he thought he was, he was possibly trying to persuade himself that he had 'needed the money'.

> *For a thirty-seven-year-old man at the height of his physical and mental powers, Hemingway was inordinately drawn to the contemplation of his own demise.*

He adds that

> *he had written to Pauline's mother that the Pfeiffer bloodline was what his children needed 'to try to breed some of the suicide streak' out of them.*

At about the same time Hemingway told his friend Archibald MacLeish

> *Me I like life very much. So much it will be a big disgust when I have to shoot myself.*

His talk of a family 'suicide streak' is rather lurid and overly dramatic, but arguably there was one: Hemingway's father, Ed, had killed himself in 1928, Hemingway blew off his head in 1961, his sister Ursula took her life five years after Hemingway's death, his brother Leicester killed himself 15 years later and his granddaughter Margaux took a barbiturate overdose in 1996.

. . .

Hemingway had planned to write a complex, multi-layered novel incorporating his main theme of contrasting the lives of the 'rich haves' and the 'poor have-nots' as well as examining how revolutions come about. What eventually appeared was nothing of the kind. [ii] Although his new work was intended to satisfy the demands from the literary left for a 'politically engaged' novel, once it was published in October 1937, many were bemused, not to say confused, by the values Hemingway had attributed to its hero. The nominal 'have-not' Harry Morgan was a man who stressed individuality and self-reliance – standard Hemingway themes and very much right-of-centre to right-wing views. So how might he be thought to celebrate the idea of a 'community' working together for 'the common good' – a standard left-of-centre to left-wing theme? It didn't add up. Nor did it help that Morgan not only turned to crime, but then became a cold-blooded murderer. Had Morgan, arguably, been forced to go outside the law by economic circumstance – a rich man, a 'have', does not pay Morgan what he is owed and that Morgan had not choice but to turn to crime – the left might have been assuaged; but Hemingway's 'hero' not only murders a man in cold blood but abandons a boatload of would-be immigrants without a second thought. Such a man was certainly not the paradigm of enlightened, brotherly and socialist behaviour the literary left hoped Hemingway would champion.

Such political quibbles aside, the novel was also deemed to be a mess. The various plots and sub-plots Hemingway planned to include but then abandoned, the shifts in narrative viewpoint (from first to third person, then back to first person), the often melodramatic descriptions and an overall narrative patchiness of a work arbitrarily shackled together added to confusion, and it did not win over the critics. There are occasional brave attempts to re-interpret the novel's muddled shape as 'innovation', but frankly that smacks of desperation. [iii] Biographers claim the novel also served to settle scores. One unpleasant character, the rich 'have' Helène Bradley, is believed to be intended to discredit Hemingway's former lover, Jane Mason (whose other supposed alter ego Margot Macomber was 'an all-American bitch'). Another less than admirable character, the left-wing, drunk, despised, cuckolded and impotent novelist Richard Gordon is taken to be a gratuitous attack on Hemingway's – by now nominal – 'close friend' John Dos Passos. Dos Passos and his wife Katie had, independently, both known Hemingway before he became the very well-known 'Papa' Hemingway, and they were more than inclined to tease him about his airs and graces. Biographer Carlos Baker reports

> *As old and easygoing friends Dos and Katie did their best to keep him "kidded down to size". In their eyes he had become a shade to conspicuously 'the famous author, the great sports-fisherman, the mighty African hunter'.*

Ever prickly and sensitive to criticism, it is unlikely that Hemingway took kindly to such ribbing and is thought to have taken his revenge. Thus, he wrote that the character he based on Katie Dos Passos, née Smith

> *likes to steal as much as a monkey does.*

As it was an open secret that Katie Smith suffered from kleptomania, Hemingway's Esquire editor Arnold Gingrich – with whom Hemingway also eventually fell out – was able to persuade him to delete or tone down other more libellous passages in the novel.

The publication of To Have And Have Not did little to halt the downward course Hemingway's literary reputation had taken. Sales began well – they reached a more than respectable 36,000 in the first few months, and Jeffrey Meyers suggests that a reading public that had waited eight years for a new 'Hemingway novel' were keen to buy it; but to Scribner's continuing disappointment sales then tailed off and did not match those of Hemingway's previous two novels. In fact, it is possible that Scribner's were pessimistic from the outset, and fearing low sales after the poor reception of Death In The Afternoon and Green Hills Of Africa, the house had ordered an initial print run for To Have And Have Not of just 10,000 copies – for A Farewell To Arms the initial print run was 30,000. [iv]

If the left-wing was unimpressed with Hemingway's new novel, the critics were also underwhelmed. One New York Times reviewer chose to look on the bright side and wrote that

> *Like an inventor without a patent, [Hemingway] has lived to see other men make more money out of the way of writing he developed. But no one else can use it with his integrity, force and precision.*

But the Times' man did note in the novel 'the disjointedness of an expanded short story'. Another New York Times reviewer, J. Donald Adams, commented that

> *The famous Hemingway dialogue reveals itself as never before in its true nature. It is false to life, cut to a purely mechanized formula. You cannot separate the speech of one character from another and tell who is speaking. They all talk alike.*

And pre-dating Bruccoli's later observation on the gradual decline in the quality of Hemingway's work, Adams also observed

> *[Hemingway] has moved steadily toward mastery of his technique, though that is by no means the perfect instrument it has been praised for being. Technique, however, is not enough to make a great writer, and that is what we have been asked to believe Mr Hemingway was in process of becoming. The indications of such a growth are absent from this book, as they have been absent from everything Mr. Hemingway has written since A Farewell to Arms. There is evidence of no mental growth whatever; there is no better understanding of life, no increase in his power to illuminate it or even to present it. Essentially, this new novel is an empty book.*

Adams concluded

> *In spite of its frequent strength as narrative writing,* To Have and Have Not *is a novel distinctly inferior to* A Farewell to Arms *... Mr. Hemingway's record as a creative writer would be stronger if it had never been published.*

...

Hemingway's affair with Martha Gellhorn began at some point after they first met in Sloppy Joe's Key West bar in December 1936. Gellhorn, her mother Edna and her brother Alfred had decided on a break off the beaten track after her father Dr George Gellhorn died, and somehow they ended up in Key West. Gellhorn meeting Hemingway is usually portrayed and accepted as a chance encounter, but one of Hemingway's more recent biographers, Mary Dearborn, has suggested it was engineered by Gellhorn because she wanted to meet the writer who was for her a literary hero. One does wonder why a respectable, newly-widowed upper-middle-class St Louis woman and her two adult children would choose to travel to a decidedly out-of-the-way and at the time down-at-heel island which was not yet a tourist destination and decide to have a drink in a scruffy bar such as Sloppy Joe's. In short, Dearborn might have a point. Gellhorn had long been a fan of Hemingway's writing and was then still an aspiring writer with a novel and a volume of short stories to her name (although it has rather cattily been claimed that her literary ambitions were greater than her talent). She will have known that Hemingway lived in Key West and might have heard that he drank at Sloppy Joe's, but whether she suggested visiting Key West in the hope of tracking him down or that meeting him really was just coincidental is also something that can now never be known.

The affair with Gellhorn was, though, not Hemingway's first since marrying Pauline Pfeiffer seven years earlier, although despite his juvenile macho boasting of 'whoring', he is unlikely to have had any others in the 1930s except with Jane Kendall Mason. [1]

Hemingway met Jane Mason when sailing back to the US from Europe in the autumn of 1931. He and Pfeiffer, heavily pregnant with their third son Gregory, came to know fellow passengers Grant Mason and his young, very good-looking and – Hemingway's later description – 'uninhibited' wife Jane. The Masons lived in Cuba, in a very grand style, and both were rich in their own right. Grant Mason had co-founded Pan American Airways four years earlier and ran its central American and Caribbean operations;

---

[1] I must repeat that whether Hemingway did have an affair with Mason or not and, if so, how long it lasted is still a matter of debate and disagreement.

his wife, just 22 when she met Hemingway, had modelled for a Pond's Cold Cream ad (though that was, it seems, the sum total of her modelling career). She was said, much to Hemingway's later appreciation, to have been an excellent shot, a marvellous fisherwoman, excelled at most sports and could certainly match Hemingway for hard drinking. She also partied hard, and the festivities the Masons organised at their mansion in Jaimanitas to the west of Havana were said sometimes to have lasted for over 24 hours.

Hemingway had first visited Cuba after he completed Death In The Afternoon in January 1932, and in April, alerted to the marlin that swam off the Cuban coast, he decided on a short trip to the island. The short trip was soon extended and eventually lasted several months, and until he moved to Cuba in 1939, he spent many months at a time in Cuba away from Key West, for the fishing and the bar-life. He and Pfeiffer, who regularly took the ferry from Key West to join her husband, became friends and socialised with the Masons. At first Jane Mason accompanied Hemingway fishing for marlin and pigeon shooting, but as some point their affair began, and they are believed to have met for sex in room 511 of the Ambos Mundos Hotel in Havana where Hemingway always stayed.

Biographers report that after the birth of Hemingway's third child, Gregory, in late 1931, Pfeiffer insisted that the only intercourse she would have with her husband should involve *coitus interruptus*; thus their sex life might well have ceased which helped to end their marriage. Many years later, divorced from Hemingway and having lost her strong Roman Catholic faith, this seems to have been confirmed by Pfeiffer who reportedly told a friend

> *If I hadn't been such a bloody fool practicing [US spelling] Catholic,*
> *I wouldn't have lost my husband.*

One of the many attractions Jane Mason is said to have held for Hemingway was that she was unable to conceive and there was no need to use contraception. (She and her husband adopted two boys, but their sons' upbringing was largely left to staff.) How long the affair between Hemingway and Mason lasted is uncertain. Jeffrey Meyers says it was on and off for four years. Another account describes it as just a short 'two-month' affair, and Michael Reynolds doubts there even was a liaison. He argues that Pfeiffer was often in Havana and continuing an affair would have been impossible. He doesn't, though, seem to have considered what Hemingway and Jane might have got up to when Pfeiffer was safely back in Key West 90 miles away. At one point Jane, who was said to have been emotionally unstable, jumped off a second-floor balcony at her Jaimanitas mansion in an apparent suicide attempt and broke her back. The incident came two days after the car she was driving, with Hemingway's sons Jack and Patrick and her son Anthony as passengers, was forced off the road and rolled down an embankment. No one was hurt, but whether jumping from the balcony had anything to do with her subsequent state of mind after the crash or the state of her affair with Hemingway (or possibly for some other reason) is not known. It did, though, lead Hemingway to make the tacky quip that Jane had literally 'fallen for him'. Some biographers have speculated that Hemingway was lining up Jane to be the third Mrs Hemingway, but that after she jumped from the balcony, he decided that she was too unstable. They also suggest he still wanted to father a daughter and Mason's infertility also had a bearing on his reluctance. In the wake of the incident, her husband had her treated for psychological problems and she had to spend a whole year in a brace.

Reynolds' doubts notwithstanding, Pfeiffer is thought eventually to have known about her husband's affair with Jane, as did Jane's husband Grant; but whereas Grant apparently did not care, Pfeiffer took the view that it would burn itself out, an ironic echo of what Hadley Richardson had decided when Pfeiffer was having her liaison with Hemingway in Paris. The affair did finally end, but it did so badly, although the details are obscure. Despite Hemingway's tacky joke, it would seem he was the keener party and had fallen for Mason. He most certainly could never abide rivals, but 'uninhibited' Jane refused to restrict herself to just one lover and began another affair with a white hunter she had met on safari in East Africa. When the man arrived in the US to see her, their sexual relationship continued, and Jane made no effort to conceal it from Hemingway, and the situation became too much for him and he called it a day. But never one to settle for being bested, he had his revenge: biographers agree that the femme fatale Margot Macomber, who shoots her husband in the back of the head – an accident or murder? – and the rich and nasty Hélène Bradley in his novel To Have And Have Not were vindictive portrayals of Jane Mason. Both are shown to be distinctly unpleasant women. Hemingway's description of Margot in The Short Happy Live Of Francis Macomber quite possibly reflects how he felt about Mason once their affair had ended: Margot was

enamelled [sic] in that American female cruelty.

According to biographer Kenneth Lynn, in Hemingway's essay The Art Of The Short Story written in 1959, but not published for another 22 years, he confirms that he chose Jane as his model for Margot Macomber, although he does not name her. Hemingway wrote

> *I invented her complete with handles from the worst bitch I knew (then) and when I first knew her she'd been lovely. Not my dish, not my pigeon, not my cup of tea, but lovely for what she was, and I was her all of the above, which is whatever you make of it.*

An irony is that despite Hemingway's subsequent disingenuous claim she was not his 'dish, pigeon or cup of tea', he, not Jane, did all the running in the affair; Jane knew she was very attractive and was never short of admirers, and it was undoubtedly she who added the anonymous, jokey and teasing entry into the log of his 35ft-cruiser Pilar that 'Ernest loves Jane'. As for Grant Mason, he is believed to have been Hemingway's model for Hélène Bradley's playboy husband Tommy. The two men did not get on, but did not fall out, either, and are said simply to have been indifferent one another.

1936-1940 – Cuba and a second divorce

Leaving Paris and dividing his time between Key West and Wyoming cut Hemingway off from Cosmopolitan culture and educated friends, and shifted his interest to marlin fishing and bear hunting. He had no intellectual equals in Florida and dominated friends who deferred to him as the local hero. He was a great listener before he moved to Key West and a great talker afterwards. The new atmosphere encouraged him to adopt coarse language, to indulge in heroics, to boast, to swagger, to suppress the sensitive side of his nature and to cultivate the public image. In Key West Hemingway was (and is) not only a living legend, but also the main tourist attraction.

Jeffrey Meyers, Hemingway: A Biography.

I don't mind Ernest falling in love, but why does he always have to marry the girl when he does?

Pauline Pfeiffer.

FOR Pfeiffer, Hemingway's affair with Martha Gellhorn was far more serious and threatening than his dalliance with Jane Mason, [1] and it eventually broke up her marriage, although unlike Hadley Richardson, Pfeiffer fought hard to keep her husband. After Gellhorn met Hemingway in Sloppy Joe's and later accompanied him home for supper (where guests had been waiting several hours for him to show up), she remained on

---

1   If there was one – as I point out two biographers don't think there was.

the island when her mother and her brother left. In a manner reminiscent of Pfeiffer's own tactic to snare Hemingway away from his first wife, Gellhorn was invited to stay with the Hemingways at their Whitehead Street home and did so for two weeks. When she returned to the mainland in early January, Hemingway followed her to New York, although their relationship was ostensibly – and perhaps then still was – that of two writer-journalists who had bonded because both were determined to get to Spain to cover the civil war. In New York Hemingway was hired by the North American Newspaper Alliance (NANA) to report on the war for them. NANA, which served more than 60 publications nationwide, agreed to pay him handsome fees, much to the later irritation of his fellow hacks in Spain when they found out how much: $500 for a cabled report ($10,558 in 2023) and double that – $1,000 ($21,156) – for a, presumably longer, report sent by mail. While in New York, Hemingway, John Dos Passos, the playwright Lillian Hellman and his friend Archibald MacLeish formed the company Contemporary Historians to fund and produce a documentary about the civil war that Joris Ivens, a young Dutch communist filmmaker, wanted to make. After a quick trip back to Key West (where Pfeiffer tried to talk him out of going to Spain, as much for his safety as realising he would be together with Gellhorn), he was off for Spain, via New York and Paris, and arrived in mid-March 1937 for the first of four visits.

Trouble gaining the credentials necessary to get into Spain delayed Gellhorn, and she did not arrive until a few weeks later. Still primarily a novelist and short story writer, she did not yet have much of a journalistic track record and landing a contract had proved impossible. Finally, she had persuaded Collier's magazine to 'sponsor' her and sign the papers she needed to obtain a visa. Soon, however, she picked up paid work, filing 'human' colour pieces about the conflict to publications back in the US. [1] Once in Madrid, she joined Hemingway at the Hotel Florida, where many of the reporters covering the war stayed, even though it was under constant bombardment from the Nationalist rebels – the front line was less than a mile away, and it was often hit by shells intended for the nearby telephone exchange, press bureau and censors' office building. Though it is unclear when Hemingway and Gellhorn began their sexual relationship, it had certainly started by the time they were holed up in the Hotel Florida. Although Gellhorn had her own room – and once, to her fury, was locked in there by Hemingway 'for her safety' during a bombardment – they shared his bed.

John Dos Passos had intended to help Joris Ivens with filming The Spanish Earth in practical ways – carrying equipment, scouting locations and generally assisting – but when he heard that his friend Jose Robles had disappeared and decided to find out

---

1   Gellhorn went on to make her name as a war correspondent rather than as a novelist.

what had happened to him, he stood down and suggested Hemingway should take over those duties. There can be no doubt that Hemingway often put himself in real danger in Spain, while helping with filming and reporting on some of the battles. He seemed to thrive on danger and was regarded as 'brave', but he did not fight in the civil war as he often claimed. Bizarrely, in later life Pfeiffer insisted that Hemingway had, in fact, been a soldier, commanding a Loyalist battalion, but had to do so secretly and that his journalism was just a necessary 'cover'. That claim could only have come from her husband and was just one of the list of tall stories Hemingway was telling. [1] Biographers agree that being in dangerous situations seemed to bring out the best in Hemingway: his mood improved and he became less irascible, he got on better with people, was good and amusing company, and liberally shared the food, wine and whisky his friend the 'Jewish matador' Sydney Franklin [2] always managed to scare up in Madrid where all were in short supply.

Franklin was born in Brooklyn, New York, as Sydney Frumkin, the son of a nasty NYPD cop who beat him badly as a child. He was gay – and according to at least one biographer a paedophile – but he was attached to, and admired by, Hemingway. Jeffrey Meyers says Franklin became jealous of Gellhorn the closer she got to Hemingway. He was not very politically aware: after he agreed to travel to Spain with Hemingway – he had lived and worked in Mexico and spoke Spanish – he disingenuously asked him 'whose side are we on, Ernie?' There have been suggestions that Hemingway's story The Mother Of A Queen was an attack on Franklin, but this is unlikely. That story was published in the collection Winner Take Nothing in 1933, and a year earlier in Death In The Afternoon, Hemingway had written a glowing description of Franklin's abilities as a matador. He might well have known about Franklin's homosexuality, but if he did, it did not affect the friendship he felt for him.

Hemingway was not universally popular in Madrid. Apart from the generous fees the NANA were paying him, his fellow journalists also envied the perks his fame and high profile brought him: courtesy of the Loyalist government, he was sometimes given the use of car, a driver and an allowance of gasoline, which was in short supply. Despite his apparent sincerity in wanting to fight fascism, Hemingway seems to have regarded the war as something of a spectator sport. In July 1936 after rebel army garrisons rose up against the Republican government and fighting broke out between Franco's Nationalist forces and Spanish Loyalists, he was determined to go to Spain, but was delayed by

---

1   He also claimed to have taken part in the mass execution in a basement of more than 100 Falangists. No evidence of that has ever come to light.

2   Franklin was reputedly known as *El Torero de la Torah* – the Bullfighter of the Torah.

having to finish writing and revising his novel To Have And Have Not. Describing his frustration in a letter to Max Perkins in September, he confessed he was worried the fighting would be over before he reached Spain, adding

> I hate to have missed this Spanish thing worse than anything in the world . . .

Two months later when he realised the war would not after all soon be over, he again wrote to Perkins

> I've got to get to Spain. But there's no great hurry. They'll be fighting for a long time and it's cold as hell around Madrid now!

One man who was less than impressed with Hemingway and his gung-ho attitude was an international brigade fighter in the British Battalion, Jason Gurney. In Crusade In Spain, his memoir of his time fighting for the Loyalists, Gurney describes meeting Hemingway when he visited the front who he said was

> full of hearty and bogus bonhomie. [1] He sat himself down behind the bullet-proof shield of a machine-gun and loosed off a whole belt of ammunition in the general direction of the enemy. This provoked a mortar bombardment for which he did not stay.

Biographers also note that despite believing he was political astute, Hemingway was rather naïve about the Loyalists and the ruthless control Stalin and the Soviets had over them. Kenneth Lynn sums it up

> If [Hemingway] was fatally susceptible to the temper of the times, it was mainly because of his lack of political sophistication. Only at rare moments in his life had he taken an interest in politics, yet he proposed to make his way through the Spanish labyrinth. The results were foreordained. Although he presented himself to the readers as an unfoolable 'Papa', he in fact was easily fooled and the Communists were well-served by him until the outcome of the war as in no doubt.

The Loyalist government was itself also naïve: at one point, Stalin persuaded them to hand over their gold for 'safe-keeping' in Russia. This they did, the gold was shipped to

---

1   This is reminiscent of the impression gained by John Pudney, an RAF PR man assigned to look after Hemingway when he arrived in Britain in May 1944.

the Soviet Union and never seen again. The Loyalists consisted of a bewildering number of disparate groups. They included anarchists, social democrats, Marxists, other Comintern communists, Trotskyists and syndicalists, and all were constantly falling out and feuding with each other. Also supporting the Loyalists were Spanish democrats of the centre, who simply wanted to protect their new republic. Finally, the Loyalists forces were joined by idealistic foreigners, who believed the neutrality espoused by the governments of the US, Britain and France was not an option. These young men, not just from all Europe but from as far off as the US, South Africa and Australia, wanted to fight the growing fascism in Europe. Of the Soviet-controlled Loyalists and the fascist Nationalists (backed by Germany's Adolf Hitler and Italy's Benito Mussolini) they considered the communists the lesser of two evils. Most important for them was that, with their own governments opting for neutrality, Stalin was the only force confronting fascism. Those foreigners fighting for the Loyalists who did not want to ally themselves with Stalin and the Comintern – such as George Orwell – aligned themselves with POUM, a Marxist and Trotskyist grouping. It didn't help the Loyalist cause that supporters of the Stalinist Comintern and POUM were bitter rivals.

Despite their idealism and honourable intentions, the Loyalists were something of a disorganised rabble. Many of the volunteers who enlisted in the International Brigades had too little or no military training and often appalling commanders. In his memoir, Jason Gurney is less than complimentary about the several leaders he served under. A few were gifted soldiers, he said, but others simply had no idea what they were supposed to be doing and how to go about doing it. He describes André Marty, the chief political commissar of the International Brigades who welcomed the foreign recruits when they arrived in Barcelona, as 'sinister and a ludicrous figure' who

> *always spoke in an hysterical roar, he suspected everyone of treason, or worse, listened to advice from nobody, ordered executions on little or no pretext – in short he was a real menace.*

Hemingway was also unimpressed by the 'murderous' Marty, one of several real-life civil war participants included in his novel For Whom The Bell Tolls; he portrays him as condoning the horrors committed by the communist Loyalists. Yet Hemingway himself often turned a blind eye to these horrors and, unlike John Dos Passos, also tacitly condoned what was going on. He almost certainly knew of the Loyalist purges and will also have heard reports of the Stalinist show trials and summary executions in Russia; but he chose to disregard them and work with the Stalinists because he felt they gave the disorganised Loyalists much-needed structure, 'discipline' and useful cohesion. Hemingway seems to have been something of a dupe and was played like a fiddle by

Mikhail Koltsov, publicly Pravda's correspondent in Spain covering the civil war, but privately an NKVD agent and thought to have been reporting directly to Stalin. Koltsov, who became Karkov in For Whom The Bell Tolls, worked on Hemingway's vanity as wanting to be seen as 'a man who had the inside gen' and fed him all kinds of stories about 'fascist collaborators' which Hemingway believed and repeated. Koltsov's aim was simply to ensure disharmony and distrust among the groups making up the Loyalists so that the Soviets could control them better. Being Stalin's man didn't much help Koltsov, however: at the end of 1937 he was recalled to Moscow and arrested for criticising the Russian purges and show trials, and shot just over two years later. Having an affair with the wife of his then NKVD boss didn't help, either him or her: She, too, was shot.

Hemingway's links to the Soviets didn't end there: after the collapse of the Soviet Union in 1991, a former KGB officer, Alexander Vassiliev, was going through old NKVD files and discovered that in 1941, when Hemingway was just about to start a tour of China with Martha Gellhorn, [1] he agreed to supply the Soviets with information. He was thus – though de facto just nominally – 'a NKVD agent' and given the codename 'Argo'. In the event he supplied the Soviets with very little, if any, information and nothing of value.

Hemingway's facility speaking Spanish is as questionable as his political astuteness. Some accounts, unsurprisingly including Hemingway's own, insist he eventually came to speak the language fluently. Others report that his command of Spanish – and for that matter French and Italian – was always flawed, notably grammatically. Arturo Barea, who ran the Loyalist press bureau and censor's office near the Hotel Florida where reporters had to have their stories cleared before they could be filed, recalls that he and other Spaniards were often amused by the infelicities and malapropisms of which Hemingway was guilty when he spoke Spanish. Later, in the 1950s when he visited Spain and had been living in Cuba for almost two decades, Spaniards were equally amused by the thick Cuban accent he had acquired. Like much in Hemingway's life the outlines of what was and was not the case are more than a little blurred. [2]

While in Madrid living with Gellhorn at the Hotel Florida, Hemingway wrote his only play, The Fifth Column. Like much of Hemingway's work, it was quasi-autobiographical, although any such suggestion always annoyed him and he insisted it wasn't true. The play's central character – yet again Hemingway's alter ego – was a cynical, hard-drinking, hard-living American and self-confessed 'third-rate' journalist in Madrid

---

1   See p.414ff.

2   I have touched on the question of how well Hemingway spoke foreign languages above. See p.248ff

1936-1940 – Cuba and a second divorce

ostensibly reporting on the Spanish Civil War as a cover for his work as a secret agent. The rather dumb blonde American who is in love with him and with whom he has an affair was a barely disguised Martha Gellhorn. By all accounts Hemingway's portrayal of her was said to be remarkably true to life, except that Gellhorn was certainly not stupid.

After each sojourn in Spain Hemingway returned to Key West and his wife and sons, but to an increasingly fraught atmosphere. Pfeiffer, under no illusions at all about what was going on with Gellhorn, was desperate to save her marriage. He didn't stay at home for long and was soon off to Bimini 50 miles east of Miami, which he had discovered a few years earlier when he was told there was excellent fishing. There he finished and corrected the gallery proofs of To Have And Have Not, but this task was interrupted by a trip to New York to make a speech at a writers' conference and to complete narration of The Spanish Earth. Before returning to Spain for his second trip to cover the civil war, he also visited the White House to attend a private viewing of the film for President Roosevelt and his wife Eleanor (who was a friend of Gellhorn's), and, with Pfeiffer, went to Hollywood to raise money for the Loyalists.

. . .

In mid-August 1937, Hemingway and Gellhorn headed back to Spain, though for appearances' sake they travelled separately. It was while he was in New York waiting to board the liner to take him to France the following day, that Hemingway had his silly 'fight' with Max Eastman in Max Perkins' fifth-floor Scribner's office on New York's Fifth Avenue when he unexpectedly dropped in on Perkins and found Eastman already present. Eastman's review of Death In The Afternoon a few years earlier, entitled Bull In The Afternoon, had enraged Hemingway. The review began by conceding

> *There are gorgeous pages in Ernest Hemingway's book about bullfights – big humour and reckless straight talk of what things are, genuinely heavy ferocity against prattle of what they are not. Hemingway is a full-sized man hewing his way with flying strokes of the poet's broad axe which I greatly admire.*

But very soon Eastman developed his theme, declaring that there was also

> *an unconscionable quantity of bull – to put it as decorously as possible – poured and plastered all over what he writes about bullfights. By bull I mean juvenile romantic gushing and sentimentalizing of simple facts.*

He ridiculed Hemingway's suggestion that bullfighting was 'art' and a 'tragedy' and – this was what really got to Hemingway – compared his literary style to

> *wearing false hair on the chest.*

Hemingway, always sensitive on the subject of his masculinity, had taken this to imply he was less than manly. So in Perkins' office, he pulled open his shirt to reveal a chest full of hair and persuaded Eastman to bare his, comparatively hairless, chest. Until that point it was all very light-hearted, but Hemingway's mood suddenly changed. Spotting the book in which Eastman's review had appeared on Perkins' desk, he picked it up and slapped it in Eastman's face. Accounts of how the subsequent – and very brief – 'fight' then developed vary, with both sides claiming 'victory'. Eastman reported that he had thrown Hemingway over Perkins' desk and stood him in the corner on his head. Hemingway later said he could have punched Eastman much harder, but held back because Eastman might have fallen out of the office window into Fifth Avenue. As it was Eastman landed on the window seat. Perkins' private account, in a letter to Scott Fitzgerald, is probably closest to the truth: concerned that Hemingway, a younger, then fitter and stronger man, might harm Eastman, he rushed around from behind his desk to try to separate the two. He found Eastman sitting on Hemingway's chest and Hemingway grinning broadly, his temper outburst over and his mood again light-hearted. The story made the New York Times three times, but publicly Scribner's would only confirm that 'the affair had taken place', adding only that

> *this is a personal matter between the two gentlemen in question.*

. . .

From Paris, Hemingway and Gellhorn carried on to Madrid and arrived by mid-September. To Have And Have Not was published a month later, and in December Pfeiffer, pining for Hemingway and without warning him, crossed the Atlantic for Paris and was reunited with him just after Christmas. Accounts suggest it was not a happy or peaceful holiday. She and Hemingway were back in Key West by the end of January, but relations between them, though polite, were cold. The marriage was ending, though at a slow pace. Six weeks later Hemingway was off to Spain again, and again he was joined Gellhorn. Back in the US by the end of May, he spent four weeks with Pfeiffer in Wyoming, then spent September and October with Gellhorn in Paris before returning to Spain where the Loyalist were on the brink of defeat. It civil war was soon over and by the beginning of

December Hemingway was back in Key West. After Christmas he rejoined Gellhorn in New York.

It was around then that he conceived the story that became his novel For Whom The Bell Tolls, and in mid-February 1939, he took the ferry from Key West for Havana where he started writing it, completing the first two chapters in a month. Back at home in Whitehead Street in Key West, the superficial harmony with Pfeiffer now gave way to continual rowing and anger. Finally, Hemingway sailed his boat, Pilar, to Havana where he was joined by Martha. They initially stayed at the Hotel Ambos Mundos, but moved to the Hotel Sevilla, although Hemingway had his mail forwarded to the Ambos Mundos to keep up the pretence that it was where he was living. Bar the divorce proceedings 20 months later, Hemingway's marriage to Pfeiffer was now over.

...

One early bone of contention between Hemingway and Gellhorn was his personal hygiene and the conditions in which he was content to live. Martha, who did not just prefer, but demanded cleanliness and order, soon got fed up living hand-to-mouth in the hotel with the untidy, unhygienic and often dirty Hemingway. She found and rented a rundown and overgrown farm, Finca Vigia, 15 miles from Havana and Hemingway joined her there, and she slowly brought the Finca Vigia back to life. After the anger and upset in Key West with Pfeiffer, Hemingway's romance with Gellhorn ironically did not go too well at all. It had thrived amid the drama of the Spanish civil war and in the context of an illicit affair; but in the supposed bliss and domesticity of the Finca Vigia it already began to come under strain. One fundamental problem was that Gellhorn, like Hemingway's mother, was a strong and independent woman who stood up for herself. Hemingway preferred compliant women, such as his first two wives, who would put him at the centre of everything, especially their lives. He was also possessive, and at the time friends who knew them both wondered why Gellhorn put up with his behaviour. She also quickly became bored with the domesticity and routine, and missed her life as a working journalist. Gellhorn was, though, smitten with Hemingway, as her letters to him at the time demonstrate, although some biographers claim she was as much smitten with being the partner of 'a great writer' as with the man himself. Although early in their affair she had boasted to friends about Hemingway's performance in bed, by her own admission the sexual side of their marriage was not important to her. It seems some physical aspect of her genitalia made intercourse difficult for her, although the problem seems finally to have been remedied by a visit to her physician. At first the strains on their relationship were not too bad, but comparatively soon she felt restless to be up and away and working as a journalist again. She wanted a little independence and, not least, money she had earned for herself; she was not content simply running Hemingway's household. He did not take well to that, and over time he became ever more fed-up with her attitude and, once she had taken off on assignment, with her prolonged absences. For the present, though, those incipient strains were ignored.

...

The Fifth Column was finally premiered on Broadway in March 6, 1940, by Lee Strasberg, but his production was not of the work Hemingway had written. What Strasberg staged was a left-of-centre anti-fascist piece; it was based on Hemingway's play but had been rewritten by the Hollywood screenwriter Benjamin Glazer, who had been hired as what today is called a script doctor. The play was not a success and ran for just 87 performances, closing on May 18. The New York Mint Theater Company claims its own production of The Fifth Column 68 years later, in March 2008 and the work's first revival, was the world premiere of the play Hemingway had actually written; but it, too, ran for less than ten weeks. In its review of that revival, the New York Times was less than complimentary, and it described the play as 'more a literary curiosity' which, it complained, was 'full of repetitions, extraneous scenes and lazy devices'. A review in New York's Theater Mania was even less kind: the piece, it said, had a central conundrum – 'a lack of mounting tension constructed from the series of vignettes that Hemingway thought constituted a play'. It concluded

> *When Hemingway was being lionized as America's foremost writer, it was often the clipped dialogue that won him praise. So when Max says, 'The bed is good,' he's speaking pure Hemingway. The same can't be said of the play, though. As Papa might have penned: 'It is not good.'*

A second revival of the play came in 2016 in London, and reviewing it, Britain's Guardian had some praise for the production, but overall was unimpressed and described the play itself as 'a rambling affair' and a 'minor work by a major writer'.

The Fifth Column had been published by Scribner's in the autumn of 1938 in a volume entitled The Fifth Column And The First Forty-Nine Stories. Consisting of the play and the first 49 stories Hemingway had written, it included four new and more recent short stories first published in Esquire and Cosmopolitan. But after the critical disappointment of To Have And Have Not and that novel's comparatively poor commercial performance, it still wasn't what Scribner's wanted from Hemingway; so

1936-1940 – Cuba and a second divorce

Max Perkins and the house were delighted that Hemingway's experiences in Spain were finally to help him to produce the novel they had been pressing him for.

. . .

Begun in Havana, the writing had carried on in Key West and then on hunting and fishing trips to the Rockies with Gellhorn (though now he was visiting Idaho instead of Wyoming). The new novel's huge success was a very welcome comeback for Hemingway and a relief for Scribner's. The career that little by little had been drifting nowhere for a decade was spectacularly back on track.

Contemporary reviews were wildly enthusiastic about For Whom The Bell Tolls. The New York Times described it as

> *a tremendous piece of work. It is the most moving document to date on the Spanish Civil War, and the first major novel of the Second World War. As a story, it is superb, packed with the matter of picaresque romance: blood, lust, adventure, vulgarity, comedy, tragedy.*

Other reviewers also unpacked their superlatives. Time magazine (which, with Life magazine, became a stalwart champion of Hemingway for the next 20 years as his fame and celebrity grew which made him excellent copy) wrote that after the work he had published in the 1930s

> *Even his admirers wondered where he was going to find another experience big enough to make him write another A Farewell To Arms. If ever he did, they thought, he would produce another great book. They misunderstood Hemingway's apparent obsession with killing, forgot that the dominant experience of this age is violent death. In 1936 Hemingway found the great experience – the Spanish Civil War. This week he published the great novel – For Whom The Bell Tolls . . . [it] is 1) a great Hemingway love story; 2) a tense story of adventure in war; 3) a grave and somber tragedy of Spanish peasants fighting for their lives. But above all it is about death . . . For Whom The Bell Tolls, unlike other novels of the Spanish Civil War, is told not in terms of the heroics and dubious politics of the International Brigade, but of a simple human struggle of the Spanish people.*

And Time warned that

> Leftists may claim the book, but they will not like realistic descriptions of the cynical G.P.U. agents ... However he may fancy himself as a leftist sympathizer, as great and sensitive artist Ernest Hemingway is well over of the Red rash. The bell in this book tolls for all mankind.

In a piece marking the 50th anniversary of the novel's publication, biographer Michael Reynolds writes

> Dorothy Parker wrote that it was 'beyond all comparison, Ernest Hemingway's finest book'. The Nation thought the book set 'a new standard for Hemingway in characterization, dialogue, suspense and compassion'. Clifton Fadiman in The New Yorker said it 'touches a deeper level than any sounded in the author's other books. It expresses and releases the adult Hemingway'. The Saturday Review of Literature [now Saturday Review] called it 'the finest and richest novel which Mr. Hemingway has written ... and it is probably one of the finest and richest novels of the last decade'. Edmund Wilson loved the novel: 'Hemingway the artist is with us again; and it is like having an old friend back'.

However, Reynolds also notes that

> Amidst such effusive praise, only John Chamberlain, of the major reviewers, had the reserve to question whether this was Hemingway's best novel or not. We would not know, he said, 'until the passions of the present epoch have subsided'.

Notable dissent from the majority view came from Arturo Barea, Hemingway's acquaintance in Madrid. As an active Loyalist he had escaped Nationalist vengeance by a whisker as the war ended. When all seemed lost, he had decided to surrender and be shot rather than face lynching by a Nationalist mob. But the Nationalist interrogator he faced turned out to be an old school friend who immediately declared that surrendering was nonsense, found him a set of clothes and quietly set him free. Barea finally found sanctuary in a British consulate whose consul managed to spirit him away on a boat

1936-1940 – Cuba and a second divorce

via Mallorca. [1] In a review that appeared in May 1941 in the British literary magazine Horizon, Barea declared that he was

> *fascinated by the book and felt it to be honest in so far as it renders Hemingway's real vision.*

Yet, he went on,

> *I find myself awkwardly alone in the conviction that, as a novel about Spaniards and their war, it is unreal and, in the last analysis, deeply untruthful, though practically all the critics claim the contrary, whatever their objections to other aspects of the book.*

Barea suggested that although Hemingway thought he knew Spain and the mentality of the people, he did not. [2] The people would never behave in the way he described and would never so brutally slaughter the Nationalists as Hemingway had portrayed. Pertinently for the 'love story of the novel', no self-respecting middle-class girl would jump into bed with a man on the very first night after meeting him. The mass rape of Maria was also too far-fetched: no Spaniard would care to have sex – even in rape – with a woman 'still moist' from a previous encounter. At the time, though, Barea's verdict was very much a minority view, although in the 80-odd years since the novel appeared judgment has certainly sobered and enthusiasm for it waned. A more balanced verdict might be that of Maxwell Geismar in 1962 in the New York Times:

> *Sometimes called Hemingway's best novel, too, [For Whom The Bell Tolls] is a curious mixture of good and bad, of marvellous scenes and chapters which are balanced off by improbably or sentimental or melodramatic passages of adolescent fantasy development.*

At the time F. Scott Fitzgerald, arguably a better writer than Hemingway even on a bad day, could only summon two cheers: For Whom The Bell Tolls, he said was

---

1   Barea had first looked for sanctuary at the US consulate, but the consul turned him away on the grounds that the US was neutral and didn't want trouble with the victorious fascists who would now be running the country.

2   The same point is made by Jeffrey Herlihy-Mera, University of Puerto Rico, who argues that Hemingway had a narrow knowledge of Spain, limited to the outlook and life of a certain kind of middle-class, bullfight aficionado mainly from northern Spain and certainly not typical of the Spanish as a whole. See p.248ff.

> *a thoroughly superficial book which has all the profundity of Rebecca.* [i]

For Whom The Bell Tolls was given an initial print run of 210,000 copies, an astonishing 200,000 more than To Have And Have Not, which might suggest Perkins and Scribner's had a great deal more faith in the commercial prospects of Hemingway's latest novel than they had had in To Have And Have Not. The film rights were immediately snapped up by Paramount for $110,000 ($2,383,480 in 2023). Within six months the novel had sold just short of half a million copies, not least because being a Book-Of-The-Month Club choice had prompted even greater public interest. This was an irony given the scorn Hemingway had earlier in his career expressed for novels chosen by the Book-Of-The-Month Club and those authors who benefited from the boost in sales.

With the publication of For Whom The Bells Tolls and a new wife, a second nominal stage of Hemingway's life was concluded. He had finished writing and revising the novel two weeks before his divorce from Pfeiffer. Two weeks after it was published he married Gellhorn.

. . .

As biographer Jeffrey Meyers points out, the invention of John Peale Bishop's 'legendary Hemingway' and the figure of 'Papa' the world came to know and to some extent revere had begun in the 1930s. Although that figure was based on the 'real' Ernest Hemingway, it was a certainly a self-conscious and thus an artificial contrivance. From 1940 on, the private man – the sensitive writer – and the public figure Hemingway sold to the world – the action-man celebrity – diverged ever more, and the public figure eventually swamped the private man. It is thought that from then and for the rest of his life Hemingway increasingly found it a strain to live up to the image of himself he had created. Many friends from his early days had testified to the thoughtful, intellectual, quite shy and kind man they had met in Hemingway; but this man was much at odds and came into total conflict with the action-man writer he seemed to want the world to accept: the 'hard man' who drank a great deal, was free with his fists and would take no bullshit from anyone. Little by little the 'old, private' Hemingway came to be buried and the 'new, public' Hemingway took over. Certainly, that conflict affected his work, the quality of which continued to tail off. Despite the excitable and incomprehensible claim by biographer Michael Reynolds that in his 1935 book Green Hills Of Africa,

Hemingway had taken writing 'into a fourth and fifth dimension', [1] he never recaptured the reputation for iconoclasm he had – to my mind and in hindsight spuriously – gained in the Paris years. Worse, over the next 20 years it became ever more apparent to Hemingway who, like his friend Scott Fitzgerald before him had been touted by some as 'the voice of a generation', that he was no longer in sync the new generation. The world had moved in but he had simply not escaped the immaturity of his early 20s. When Maxwell Geismar draws attention to the

> *improbable or sentimental or melodramatic passages of adolescent fantasy development*

in For Whom The Bell Tolls, his view chimes with the observation of the novelist Vladimir Nabokov that Hemingway 'was a writer for boys'.

---

1   I have no idea what that means or even what it might mean, and in my book it is just more of the intellectual waffle many literary commentators slip into. On a practical note, it is the kind of baffling statement which might unfairly intimidate a young reader who comes across it (presumably in her or his studies) and chip away at their self-confidence: '*Oh dear, I don't understand that – what's wrong with me?*' To which let me give the reassuring response is: nothing at all.

1940-1943 – Trying and failing to settle

On top of his dresser was the signed contract, dated July 15, calling for Hemingway's royalties to be 15% on the first 25,000 copies sold; thereafter they rose to 20%, higher rates than most authors received, but Hemingway in 1940 was not most authors. He may not have published a best-selling novel during the entire 1930s, but through his non-fiction, his Esquire articles, his Spanish Civil War journalism, and his personal exploits hunting in East Africa and marlin fishing in the Gulf Stream, he had become the most widely read male author in America.

Michael Reynolds, Hemingway: The Final Years.

Marty [Martha Gellhorn] said to me in 1997: 'I should have taken my mother's advice and never married him. The relationship was fine as long as we were lovers. Marriage was a disaster. My wise mother knew it and tried to warn me but I would not listen'.

Valerie Hemingway, neé Danby-Smith in her memoir Running With Bulls.

HEMINGWAY had already settled into the Finca Vigia with Gellhorn before he was divorced from Pauline Pfeiffer, and they were married on November 21, 1940, in Cheyenne, Wyoming, 17 days after the divorce came through. With that third marriage began another of what might be regarded as distinct stages in his life. If the first had seen remarkable literary success, the second comparative failure and a slow decline in his reputation, the third began with a spectacular revival of his standing with the

1940-1943 – Trying and failing to settle

publication of For Whom The Bell Tolls in 1940. Yet Hemingway was already growing unhappy and drinking even more, not least because his latest novel was such a success that he feared he could not and never would repeat it. He was also plagued by guilt about ditching Pauline Pfeiffer to marry Gellhorn (as he had been plagued when he ditched Hadley Richardson for Pfeiffer). There was also the uncomfortable fact that within a year of marrying, the strains in his and Martha's relationship were already showing, and he could not ignore them. Not least was the problem that he and Gellhorn had different ideas of what married life and their future together should look like.

When they married, Hemingway and Gellhorn had been together as a couple, illicitly and then openly, for more than three and a half years; and although, according to Bernice Kert in The Hemingway Women, some claimed that in the early days Gellhorn had done most of the running, it was Hemingway who was eventually pushing for their union to be solemnised. [i] Unkind friends – there are always one or two – also suggested that at heart Gellhorn was more interested in a relationship with Ernest Hemingway, the well-known writer, than Ernest Hemingway, the man. Yet given the, eventually desperate, tone of the letters she wrote to him from Britain in 1943 in which she repeatedly urged him to join her, she does seem to have loved him a great deal. While they had been conducting an affair, their partnership worked well, especially when they were together in Spain to cover the civil war, where it is said to have thrived on the 'excitement' of war and the supposed secrecy of their liaison. But unlike Hadley and Pauline, Gellhorn, who was already both a published novelist and a working journalist with some experience, was ambitious. She made it plain she would not be abandoning her career, and this did not sit well with Hemingway.

After Hemingway and Gellhorn's third trip to Spain, Collier's had asked her to report for them on the situation in Czecho-Slovakia, and Hemingway returned to the US alone, first to New York, then to Key West and then on to Montana. He was back in Paris at the end of August where Gellhorn joined him. On the last day of September 1939, the Munich Agreement was signed, [1] and ever eager to be in the fray, Gellhorn returned to Prague in November to cover the forced cession of the Sudetenland to Germany. Just over a year later while Hemingway was immersed in writing For Whom The Bell Tolls, Collier's again contacted Gellhorn, this time to enlist her to cover the invasion of Finland by Soviet Russia, and she was off again for two months. At the time Hemingway seemed to support her decision to accept the assignment, but he was not pleased (and told friends, half-seriously, 'what old Indian likes to lose his squaw with a hard winter

---

1   It is still known in the Czech Republic and Slovakia, more truthfully, as the 'Munich Diktat' and the 'Munich Betrayal'.

coming on?'). It was clear that however much she adored – her word – Hemingway, there was no way Gellhorn was going to give up her professional life to become the mothering housewife he had expected and increasingly now demanded. She was adamant that her career would always come first, and that became the prime fault line in their union. But, as she confessed to her mother Edna, she also carried on working because she both wanted and needed her own money – she always insisted on paying her way and sharing the Hemingway household expenses. As an independent woman of principle who had grown up the daughter of an active campaigner for women's rights, Gellhorn resented being assigned the role of 'Ernest Hemingway's wife' and later remarked that she had not wanted to be 'a footnote in someone else's life'. When The Heart Of Another, her collection of short stories, appeared in October 1941, Hemingway asked her to publish it under the name 'Martha Hemingway'. She refused, and in her book The Hemingway Women, Bernice Kert writes that the suggestion irritated her. Kert also reports that as marriage to Hemingway approached, Gellhorn began to feel trapped. She records that when Gellhorn wrote to her friend Clara Spiegel just before leaving for Finland to tell her she and Hemingway were soon to marry, Gellhorn had added that it

> *was perhaps simpler all round, but she herself thought 'living in sin' wonderful.*

Almost 20 years later, in a letter to her friend Leonard Bernstein, Gellhorn admitted

> *By the time I did marry [Hemingway] (driving home from Sun Valley) I did not want to, but it had gone too far in every way. I wept, secretly, silently, on the night before my wedding and my wedding night; I felt absolutely trapped.*

Nor did Gellhorn hide her doubts about marriage from Hemingway, and when she voiced them, he took it badly. Michael Reynolds writes

> *While submerged in the final corrections [to the proofs of For Whom The Bell Tolls], Ernest's emotional center took a heavy hit when Martha began questioning the wisdom of their marrying. At four in the morning Ernest wrote her a note, saying her news busted his heart and left him with a first-class headache. He knew that for the last eighteen months he had been 'no gift to live with', as she put it, but she must remember how he helped her with her book – The Heart Of Another. But if she was not going to marry him, she should tell him before he took the Pilar alone to Key West giving himself too*

> *much time to think, another veiled threat of suicide.*

The problem was, Reynolds adds,

> *not that Martha loved him too little but he loved her too much. To Rodrigo Diaz, his pigeon-shooting companion and sometime doctor, Ernest was always at risk in his relationship with Martha. Easily hurt, he was tremendously vulnerable beneath the tough exterior with which he faced the world.*

This was certainly not the first time Hemingway had used the threat of suicide as emotional blackmail. In the run-up to both his previous marriages he had also hinted darkly to his then brides-to-be that he might kill himself (and his reasoning on both occasions was less than clear).

According the Michael Reynolds, Gellhorn's mother, Edna, was also unhappy that her daughter had agreed to marry Hemingway. Edna had first met him in August 1940 in Miami and although she liked him, she advised Gellhorn against marriage. A few months later when Edna arrived for the wedding ceremony – biographer Kenneth S. Lynn claims 'unexpectedly', but it would have been natural for Martha to have invited her mother – she again tried to persuade her daughter to call off the wedding. Many years later, Gellhorn confirmed to Valerie Danby-Smith that her mother had had misgivings about the union. In 1959, Danby-Smith, who later married Hemingway's third son, Gregory, had spent five months as part of Hemingway's entourage in Spain where he was criss-crossing the country attending bullfights and another six months with the Hemingways in Cuba in 1960. In her memoir Running With Bulls she writes that Martha Gellhorn told her

> *I should have taken my mother's advice and never married him. The relationship was fine as long as we were lovers. Marriage was a disaster. My wise mother knew it and tried to warn me but I would not listen.*

But the wedding ceremony did go ahead, conducted by a justice of the peace – no more church weddings for Hemingway – in the dining room of the Union Pacific Railroad in Cheyenne, Wyoming. It was when the couple eventually settled down to the routine of domestic life at the Finca Vigia that the strains became ever more obvious.

. . .

Before they married and while out West, Gellhorn had suggested to Collier's that in view of increasing Japanese aggression, she should visit China and the Far East to report on the defences in the area and the influence Japan was having in the region. Japan had first invaded China in 1931, and a second Sino-Japanese war began six years later. Hemingway was against the trip, but he assumed that Collier's would agree to send Gellhorn and so he intended to tag along, as he told friends, to protect her from 'war, pestilence, carnage and adventure'. Without telling her, he arranged to supply the recently founded liberal daily PM newspaper with features on the situation in China. Privately he also agreed to report to the US government, which was supplying the Chinese nationalists with money and weapons to fight Japan. The US, which regarded the Communists as 'less corrupt' than the Nationalists, suspected that the Nationalist leader Chiang Kai-shek was using the funds they were supplying to wage a renewed civil war with the Communists and also pocketing some of the money.

In mid-January 1941, Hemingway and Gellhorn set off on their extended tour of the Far East, which they jokingly referred to as their 'crazy honeymoon', beginning in New York where they first had to complete various errands. While they were there, Gellhorn agreed to help the newspaper columnist Earl Wilson interview Hemingway at the hotel where they were staying, and the meeting was underway when she returned from a shopping trip. The central bone of contention between them again became apparent when Hemingway joked to Wilson that Gellhorn had agreed to report for Collier's on the Russian invasion of Finland simply to make money to allow him to go on writing his novel. This quip – one assumes Hemingway had meant it as a light-hearted comment – did not go down at all well with Gellhorn. Bernice Kert writes that

> *[Martha] was smiling and cordial until Ernest asked her whether he should tell the columnist how he was busted and she went to Finland to make some more money to he could go on writing his book. Her expression darkened and she said curtly not to believe him, that that was just one of his jokes. Wilson was puzzled and Martha did not elaborate. What irritated her was that Ernest interpreted everything in terms of himself. The simple fact that she supported herself, that journalism was her job, was not satisfactory to his ego. He preferred to believe that she was doing it for him.*

The trip to the Far East lasted for just over four months, and for Hemingway it began with four weeks in Hong Kong while Gellhorn flew off for a short tour of China. She then re-joined Hemingway in Hong Kong and together they embarked on a very miserable, very cold and very rainy tour of southern China, which involved travelling up-river by boat and several days of riding mean Mongolian ponies along muddy mountain paths. They met Chiang and – in a clandestine operation – the Communist leader Zhou Enlai, but neither enjoyed the tour at all. Then they parted, Hemingway slowly made his way back to the US while Gellhorn carried on to Burma, the Dutch East Indies and Singapore. There she was astonished by how disorganised British defences were whereas the Dutch, she reported, had been a paradigm of efficiency.

Although Hemingway had not been keen on the trip from the start, he was at least stoical about the conditions they encountered, but for Gellhorn it became a never-ending agony. Hemingway was notorious for his low standards of hygiene and dishevelled appearance, but Gellhorn was fastidious over cleanliness, both her own and those of her surroundings. She hated the filth and squalor she found in China, especially the ever-present smell of 'night soil', the euphemism for human shit. None of this bothered Hemingway, who enthusiastically took to Chinese cuisine and enjoyed the many boozing sessions with Chinese officials and the endless banquets held in their honour. Gellhorn did not.

Once back at the Finca Vigia in Cuba in mid-1941, life ran along the lines Hemingway envisaged but which began to challenge Gellhorn ever more. She did not enjoy having to run his household and organise staff. She disliked that it was always open house for Hemingway's drinking buddies from Havana, who would drop in at all times. When Hemingway's sons came to stay for the summer, she ensured they were always amused, but that encroached on time she would rather have spent writing. At first she gamely played along with Hemingway's ad hoc and disorganised living regime, although she did make her feelings known. Hemingway's sons were impressed that unlike Hadley Richardson and Pauline Pfeiffer, Gellhorn did not kowtow to their father, talked back and gave him as good as she got. That her strong personality was a match for Hemingway was demonstrated when her mother Edna came to stay and the three of them were due to meet for lunch in Havana. When Hemingway did not show up, a furious Gellhorn tracked him down to La Floridita where he was drinking with friends, bawled him out in front of them for being so rude to her mother then dragged him off.

. . .

On December 7, 1941, Japan attacked Pearl Harbor, and both Hemingway and Gellhorn's lives took a distinct new direction. Accounts of Hemingway's activities in Cuba over the following 27 months vary in detail, though the broad outlines are clear. As soon as the war in Europe had begun, Gellhorn could not understand why Hemingway didn't try to get himself hired as a war correspondent and head over there, and she increasingly nagged him to do so. But Hemingway was content to go fishing on his boat Pilar and drink with his Cuban buddies. Nor did he attempt any new writing except to edit Men At War, a selection of 'war writings' (in which he, not so modestly, included some of his own work) and to supply an introduction.

Quite how Hemingway acquired a reputation for being an 'authority on war' is a puzzle. He certainly read very widely on the subject, but although in later life he claimed he had 'gone to war' in World War I and, strictly, he had done so, it was certainly not in the sense understood by most as 'being under arms and fighting'. Hemingway later claimed that in Spain during 1937 and 1938, Republican commanders had sought his advice on tactics; and although Charles Collingwood, a fellow World War II fellow correspondent, conceded that Hemingway's wide reading on military matters was an advantage when being briefed by senior officers, that he was ever 'consulted on tactics' by them is almost certainly just another grandiose exaggeration, if not an outright invention.

By May 1942, though, after a few months of inactivity, he did come up with a project which might make him useful. Hemingway believed that among the many Spanish in Cuba were quite a few fascist sympathisers who might try to assist the Germans and their U-boat fleet. He approached Spruille Braden, the newly-appointed US ambassador, to suggest that he should set up a counter-intelligence network to monitor any possible sympathisers. Braden was enthusiastic, although when he published his memoirs, Diplomats And Demagogues, 30 years later, he claimed it was his idea to set up such surveillance. Braden wrote that he had enlisted Hemingway as a stop-gap until he could get additional FBI men to Cuba (a claim that still begs the question of why he would choose Hemingway for the role). The network, which Hemingway eventually nicknamed 'The Crook Factory' and whose headquarters were in a guest annexe to the Finca, was 26-strong and made up of six full-time agents and 20 part-timers. They were all Hemingway's Havana friends and acquaintances, high and low – drinking buddies, bartenders, fishermen, whores and even a Basque Roman Catholic priest, one of the few clergy in Spain who had not supported the Falangists and who had fled and washed up in Cuba. Hemingway's team of informants were instructed to pass on to him what they heard and saw, and he visited the US embassy once a week to deliver a summary of their information to Robert Joyce, the Havana embassy's second secretary. Very little information of any use was uncovered by the network, but (writes Jeffrey Meyers) Joyce, a friend of, and sympathetic to, Hemingway, explained why the Crook Factory's reports were tolerated at the embassy and in Washington. If the reports, says Meyers, were

> *sensational [The Crook Factory was] paid more – $20 instead of $10. [But] most of these reports were contradictory – less than*

1940-1943 – Trying and failing to settle

> *useful, as he caused confusion in Washington headquarters at the Pentagon – not to speak of the FBI at home and in Havana.*

But, Meyers adds,

> *a major-general who headed G-2 in the Pentagon in 1942, said Army intelligence was interested in and welcomed reports from military attaches on all matters . . .*

Whether useful and productive or not, the activities of Hemingway's 'spy network' did not suit the FBI, and there began a mild feud, perhaps more on the side of the FBI. The FBI agents stationed at the embassy under 'legal attaché' Raymond Leddy felt Hemingway was encroaching on their territory. They became particularly worried when Hemingway and his network began 'investigating' Cuba's head of police whom Hemingway suspected was corrupt. He most probably was, but the FBI did not want to fall out with a man on whose cooperation it relied. Leddy also became aggrieved after Hemingway once introduced him to friends as a member of 'the Gestapo' and later described the FBI as 'Franco's Bastard Irish' – Hemingway was convinced the FBI was run by Irish Roman Catholics who had instinctively supported the Fascist nationalists in Spain's Civil War. Soon a file was opened on Hemingway which caught the attention of the FBI's founder and boss, J. Edgar Hoover; but Hoover advised his men on the ground in Cuba to tread carefully as Hemingway seemed not only to have the ear of ambassador Braden, but, through Gellhorn, who was friends with Eleanor Roosevelt, that of US president Roosevelt. [ii]

Within weeks – biographer Kenneth Lynn suggests Hemingway soon grew bored with the 'counter-intelligence' – he had begun another undertaking which helped him convince himself – although certainly not Gellhorn, who ridiculed the Crook Factory as an excuse for Hemingway and his cronies to live it up – that he was contributing to the 'war effort'. After the shock of the Japanese attack on Pearl Harbor and the devastating success German U-boats were having sinking commercial ships, Frank Knox, the US Secretary of the Navy had appealed to all US boat owners on the east and south coasts to play a useful role, and Hemingway decided to volunteer his and Pilar's services. The U-boats had been particularly effective in the Caribbean and the Gulf of Mexico, attacking vessels carrying bauxite (needed to produce aluminium) and oil. In February 1942 the Germans had sunk nineteen ships, another nineteen in March, eleven in April and thirty-eight in May. In the eleven months after the attack on Pearl Harbor, 263 ships were sunk in the Caribbean Sea. Hemingway's plan was to sail the Pilar in waters off the Cuban coast to lure a German U-boat to the surface – there had been occasions when U-boats had stopped small private vessels to commandeer whatever fresh water, fish and vegetables might be on-board. Then, Hemingway hoped, he and his crew could gun down any German seamen on deck, lob grenades into the U-boat's conning tower, disable the vessel and capture it. [1] However unlikely it seemed, Hemingway's proposal found favour with ambassador Braden, and he agreed to allocate a supply of rationed gasoline, machine guns, grenades and bazookas to Hemingway and his crew. The Pilar was also equipped with a shortwave radio and US marine radio operator to monitor any broadcasts from U-boats and report nightly to the US navy Gulf force. (The flaw in that proposal was that no one on the Pilar, least of all the assigned marine radio operator, spoke or even understood German.)

At first Hemingway, who called this new wheeze that took over from his Crook Factory derring-do 'Operation Friendless', sailed the Pilar out of Havana and returned home to the Finca each night;. Soon he decided to expand his operations to monitor the many secluded bays and inlets along Cuba's long coastline where a German U-boat might berth unobtrusively and leave stocks of munitions and provisions. He stationed the Pilar on a small sandbank off the north-eastern coast of Cuba, and the missions began to last for several weeks at a time. In the event no German U-boats were captured – or blown up – and no secret stocks of munitions or provisions were discovered. Once when Hemingway thought the Pilar had spotted a large Spanish vessel towing why might have been a German U-boat, it was shown to be a false alarm. [2] Despite a conspicuous lack of success, Hemingway took his 'war effort' seriously, but another sceptic, one Mario Ramírez Delgado, a captain in the Cuban Navy who did actually sink a German U-boat – the U-176 on May 15, 1943 – described Hemingway as merely

a playboy who hunted submarines off the Cuban coast as a whim.

Gellhorn was as scornful of the scheme as she was of the counter-intelligence network. She believed it was nothing but a silly ruse to obtain gasoline so Hemingway could continue his marlin fishing. [3] The counter-intelligence operation ceased at the

---

1   Hemingway's scheme, which he was convinced could work, does remind one of Nabokov's gibe that he was 'a writer for boys'. When U.S. Marine Colonel John W. Thomason, who served with the US naval intelligence in the Caribbean, informed Hemingway no U-boat would come near the Pilar, he shrugged off the scepticism and began referring to the officer as 'doubting Thomason'.

2   The Pilar 'gave chase' but was soon outrun by the 'U-boat', which most certainly had not known a zealous American patriot and his crew had it in its sights and was determined to destroy it. Quite what kind of vessel the Pilar spotted has never been established.

3   None of the biographers report that Hemingway and his crew did any fishing, however, but they did sometimes lark about, on at least one occasion amusing themselves by lobbing grenades at buoys off the coast and machine-gunning them.

1940-1943 – Trying and failing to settle

end of April 1943, apparently as planned. Soon a number of necessary repairs kept the Pilar in dock and out of action, and Hemingway was left kicking his heels. Finally, in October 1943, and after waiting for more than five months for the renewal of US navy authorisation for the Pilar to continue her patrols, Hemingway was informed it would not be coming through. The British had cracked the Enigma coding machine which the German admiralty used to communicate with, and coordinate, its U-boat fleet, and the Allies had proceeded to decimate Germany's U-boat fleet. The Germans now no longer posed a threat to Allied shipping.

1943-1944 – Lonely and the third marriage ends

The loss of literary friends, remoteness from cultural life and lack of intellectual stimulation were increased by the move to Cuba, which put him out of touch with social and political reality in America. At the same time his estrangement from his family and separation from his children increased his sense of isolation. The dolce far niente life in the tropics made it more difficult for him to discipline himself. When Martha was away, he missed his immediate audience, became lonely and lacked the orderly household and attention to his needs that he had become accustomed to with Hadley and Pauline. When Martha was home, their domestic quarrels upset him. As his third marriage headed towards disaster, he found it more and more difficult to concentrate on his fiction.

Jeffrey Meyers, Hemingway: A Biography.

WHEN Hemingway's patrols began to last longer and he did not return to the Finca at night to live it up, Gellhorn had relished the peace and quiet, and tried to get on with writing a new novel (which was published in 1944 as Liana). The time was also a respite from the rows she had with Hemingway that occurred more and more – over her complaints that he was wasting his time, his boozing sessions and, biographer James R. Mellow reports, about their respective writing.[1] This was a topic on which Hemingway was particularly sensitive. While Gellhorn was progressing with her novel, he had written nothing, and certainly no fiction, since For Whom The Bells Tolls was published, and that

---

1   This is puzzling: no biographer, not even Meyers or Mellows, has recorded that Hemingway was writing any fiction at the time, and he did not start writing again until he was back from Europe in 1945. If he was, nothing has been identified.

1943-1944 – Lonely and the third marriage ends

work's success was intimidating him. [1] Their arguments could become vicious: Hemingway's youngest son, Gregory, recalls his father shouting at Gellhorn

> *I'll show you, you conceited bitch. They'll be reading my stuff long after the worms have finished with you.*

Yet Gellhorn also felt that she, too, should be doing more than just writing fiction. Finally, in mid-1942, she was hired by Collier's to undertake an extensive tour of various Caribbean islands and report on how they were being affected by the submarine war. She was away for two months, and as always when she was not with Hemingway, her heart beat faster for him and (according to Bernice Kert) she wrote him ardent love letters almost daily. She was back at the Finca at the end of October, but the day after Christmas she took off again, to visit her widowed mother in St Louis. Back at the Finca and when Hemingway was home from his 'Operation Friendless' sub-hunting trips, her nagging that he should get himself over to Europe to report on the war carried on throughout 1943, but still he refused. Then, in mid-summer, Gellhorn accepted another offer from Collier's, this time to become one of its war correspondents in Europe, and she left in September. [2] With the Pilar in dock for maintenance and the navy dragging its heels over whether it still required the vessel's services, Hemingway was high-and-dry: he was no longer sub-hunting, he could not go fishing, he was afraid to start writing again but, worst of all, he was left to his own company, and he hated being alone.

Writing to Hemingway, first from New York, where her departure had been delayed for several weeks, and then from London, Gellhorn still expressed her deep love for him and again repeatedly urged him to join her; but Hemingway was adamant that he would stay in Cuba, and no one is sure why. Jeffrey Meyers suggests that he

> *had risked is life in Spain and still suffered from the emotional effects of his break with Pauline, was exhausted by the strain of completing For Whom The Bell Tolls and discouraged by the extreme discomforts of his trip to China. After his experience in Spain and China, he believed that the lies, propaganda and*

---

1   Mary Dearborn reports that in 1943 Hemingway hinted to Max Perkins at Scribner's – who was always keen for new work he could publish – that he had written several short stories for a new collection. When several months later Perkins asked Hemingway directly how the work was going, Hemingway informed him he 'was working on two long stories'. This allowed Max (writes Dearborn) to believe that otherwise the 'collection' was almost complete. This was nonsense.

2   Presumably not to report from a front-line as apparently women were only allowed near the front-line to nurse wounded and none could work as a war correspondent. But whatever her role and duties, Gellhorn took off for Europe on behalf of Collier's.

> *censorship necessary in war made it almost impossible to be an honourable correspondent.*

But however plausible – and high-minded – such an explanation might sound, even Meyers seems to have his doubts: he also quotes Patrick Hemingway's take on his father's reluctance to travel to Europe to report on the war:

> *He felt that he was entitled to stay behind, living in a place that he liked and enjoying himself.*

That his son Patrick gave this as Hemingway's reasoning suggests it might even have been something his father had explicitly told him; or had Patrick inferred it from what his father had said? There is now no way of knowing, yet what is certain is that Hemingway was miserable. In the final volume of his five-part biography Michael Reynolds offers this explanation:

> *Martha misunderstood Ernest's lack of interest in going to another war as a journalist, but then she misunderstood the Pilar patrols also. Having spent six [sic] weeks as a Red Cross man in World War I and having covered the Greco-Turkish War (1922) as a reporter for the Toronto's Daily Star and the Spanish Civil War (1937-38) as a journalist for the NANA (North American News Alliance), Ernest was loath to repeat the frustrations of watching the action without being able to participate, and not since his brief experience as a reporter in Toronto (1923-24) had he written news stories. He was a feature writer whose personal perspective was always a key ingredient in the story.* [1]

Hemingway, Reynolds suggests, probably rightly

> *wanted to command troops in battle, but with the freedom that independent ventures like the Pilar patrols allowed. . . He did not want an honorary commission to feed the US propaganda machine, nor did he want to become a cog in some huge operation over which he had no control. In May 1942, he explained to Max Perkins that he was willing to go to the war, send his sons to the war, and give*

---

1   This line is, of course, at odds with Hemingway's brag at other times that he was 'a newsman'. For example, he adopted the role of the 'seasoned journalist' in his Esquire Letter of December 1934, headlined 'An Old Newsman Writes'. We can't know for sure, but it is not unlikely Hemingway himself suggested that headline.

> *his money to the war effort. The one thing he could not do was write propaganda.*

But Hemingway's attempts to 'go to war and fight' had so far never succeeded. Some accounts have him, at 18 while still working for the Kansas Star, in turn volunteering for the US army, the US navy and the US marines, but being turned down by each service because of the poor sight in his left eye. Other accounts say he did not even bother trying to enlist because he suspected his bad eye would fail him in his medical; instead he went straight to the Red Cross to get himself over to Europe.[1] On his four visits to Spain in 1937 and 1938 he had done no fighting or shot a weapon in combat despite the tall stories he told. According to both Reynolds and Dearborn, in early 1944 he was briefly considered for a role in the Office for Strategic Services (the OSS, which after the war evolved into the CIA). Apparently, the approach to the OSS did not initially come from Hemingway but was made – quite possibly at Gellhorn's instigation – by Robert Joyce who by early 1944 had himself joined the OSS.[i] Writing in Studies In Intelligence in 2012, Nicholas Reynolds confirms that an approach was made and adds

> *Joyce cabled OSS headquarters with the suggestion that OSS Director Donovan and Whitney Shepardson, the sophisticated international businessman who was head of Secret Intelligence (SI, the espionage branch of the OSS), to consider approaching Hemingway about working for SI. This message caused some head scratching as it worked its way around the OSS. Just what could Hemingway do for the OSS? wondered Lt Cdr Turner McWine, the chief intelligence officer for the OSS in the Middle East. The author's prominence and reputed temperament would make it hard for him to fit in.*

Nicholas Reynolds records that

> *The SI wasn't convinced Hemingway would be of any use to them and passed the matter on to Morale Operations (MO), the OSS black propaganda arm who it thought Hemingway might have more potential than for the work of SI. Hemingway's file duly made its way over to MO, whose leaders concluded a few days later*

---

1   There are even claims that once the US armed forces had turned him down, he volunteered to fight in Europe for Canada, but was also unsuccessful in enlisting. In view of these various contradictory claims, Debra Moddelmog's cautious advice about biographies and memoirs is always worth bearing in mind.

> that Hemingway was too much of an individualist even for their unconventional mission.

Thus the approach came to nothing, and Michael Reynolds quotes an OSS document dated May 1, 1944, explaining that it had decided

> in the negative about Hemingway. We may be wrong, but feel that, although, he undoubtedly has conspicuous abilities for this type of work, he would be too much of an individualist to work under military supervision.

Whether at any point Hemingway was aware of these views – though he might well have been informed by Joyce – does not seem to have been recorded.

...

After six months away in Europe, Gellhorn returned to the Finca in March 1944 and Hemingway's frustration and anger boiled over, and he took it out on her viciously. Kert, Meyers and Hemingway's other biographers report that he subjected her to a constant and vicious litany of complaints and insults, accusing her of vainglory and selfishness, and of madly putting herself in harm's way simply to seek thrills. [1] Gellhorn later told Kert that he would sometimes even wake her at night to continue his tirade. Hemingway's marriage was most certainly coming apart and was very soon to end. Michael Reynolds believes his vicious verbal assaults on Gellhorn were a symptom of his purported manic depression. But, he writes, as Gellhorn had never seen her husband behave in that manner

> even at several years remove [she] did not consider that Ernest might be suffering from something other than loneliness. The charges [he made against her] of being insane, of seeking out danger, or acting selfishly and irresponsibly applied as much to himself as to her. His son Gregory firmly believed that his father changed during the 1943-44 period into a different person. Hemingway's last wife, Mary Welsh, would experience the same sort of abuse that Martha reported. It was as if some inner, furious animal was set loose, an animal over which Hemingway had some

---

1   This sounds like a very good summing up of Hemingway's own behaviour and would explain how he came to get himself blown up in July 1918. It might substantiate the belief that we are apt to accuse others of our own failings.

control in public, but little at home. Anyone looking backwards from 1960-61 might say that his behavior was a manifestation of the depression that eventually destroyed him.

Shorter 'patrols' in the Pilar had resumed in the last months of 1943, but the final patrol ended in early January 1944. After that Hemingway spent his time brooding and drinking (and had spent Christmas 1943 without Martha). At some point in the new year, he had changed his mind about travelling to the 'war in Europe', but no biographer has suggested when or why. With a view to working as a correspondent, he contacted Collier's magazine (or was contacted by the magazine – again biographers differ) and by early March he had been hired. Bagging 'the famous writer Ernest Hemingway' must have been regarded as a coup by Collier's and the deal to which he agreed was very good indeed: $3,000 ($51,731 in 2023) for each feature of between 2,500 and 3,500 words. He was also promised that 'reasonable expenses' would be reimbursed, though once he was back in the US in 1945, that part of the deal caused him grief. When he submitted a three-page-long list of expenses, adding up to an extraordinary $13,436 ($231,668), Collier's informed him his expense claims were anything but 'reasonable'. The magazine's managing editor described them as 'out of all proportion to the enterprise' – in his ten months in Europe Hemingway had filed just six pieces – and the claims were rejected. Hemingway was furious, but eventually settled for 'just' $6,000 ($103,463).

. . .

The US Department of War would allow each publication to send only one front-line correspondent, and Gellhorn was demoted by Collier's. Some, not least Gellhorn, suggest that by approaching Collier's instead of any other publication – many would certainly have hired him – Hemingway was guilty of spite;[1] but Michael Reynolds points out that another Department of War regulation meant female correspondents were not allowed any closer to the front than women serving in the US army (usually as field hospital staff). Thus Gellhorn would not have been able to work on the front-line anyway. What was certainly spiteful, however, was Hemingway's refusal to negotiate a seat for Gellhorn on the RAF plane flying him to Britain. Ironically, she herself had helped him to secure a seat on the flight by putting him in touch with the children's author Roald Dahl. (Dahl was a British air attaché in Washington – part of Hemingway's

---

1   Or not – this point is also confusing. According to Mary Dearborn, it was Gellhorn who had suggested to Hemingway that he should get in touch with Collier's and offer to write a series of articles. Did she do that? If she did, did she or not realise her own position would then be in jeopardy given the 'only one front-line correspondent' rule for the print media?

Collier's brief was to profile the Royal Air Force); but when she asked her husband to secure a seat for her, too, he claimed that women were not allowed on the flight. In fact, they were — the actress Gertrude Lawrence and the singer and comedienne Beatrice Lillie were also on-board. Instead Gellhorn found herself a berth on a Norwegian ship carrying explosives to Europe and departed a day or two before he flew off. Her voyage lasted for more than two weeks and was made all the more uncomfortable because there was no alcohol on board, and Gellhorn, who usually smoked forty cigarettes a day, was also forced to abstain because of the ship's cargo.

. . .

Arriving in London on May 17, Hemingway settled into the Dorchester Hotel in Park Lane and began a round of socialising, re-connecting with journalist friends and, inevitably, heavy drinking. A week later, the photographer Robert Capa, who had known Hemingway in Madrid during the Civil War and had also stayed at the Hotel Florida, threw a welcome party for him on May 24 (and, according to his autobiography, managed to drum up ten bottles of Scotch, eight bottles of gin, a case of champagne and some brandy). At 4am the following morning, the car in which Hemingway was returning to the Dorchester, driven by another guest as drunk as he was, crashed head-on into a steel water tank in the blacked-out Lowndes Square. Hemingway was thrown head-first into the windscreen and his scalp was partly detached from his skull. He was at first reported dead, but the following day was said to have suffered only 'slight injuries'. In fact, he injuries were bad. He damaged both knees and was diagnosed with severe concussion, the first of several serious head injuries over the following months and years which are now believed to have affected his mental as well as his physical state. He was taken to hospital where his head wound required more than fifty stitches. Gellhorn, who had finally arrived at Liverpool on May 31, travelled to London immediately to visit him, only to find Hemingway with a circle of visiting cronies, living it up and drinking spirits and champagne, his head swathed in a bandage that looked to her like a turban. At the sight of him and much to Hemingway's irritation – he had been expecting sympathy – Gellhorn burst out laughing. She was also angry that though he was supposedly suffering from a serious head injury, he was still boozing, and she soon left. As Reynolds puts it

> *Having had plenty of time at sea to review their relationship, Martha entered the room half-sure their marriage was over; when she left she had no doubt. 'If he really had concussion, he could hardly have been drinking with his pals or even receiving them. He did not look in the least ill anyway.' The concussion*

> *was real enough, and drinking was a sure way to make it worse. Ernest, garrulous and full of male-bonding jokes . . . was [now] with Martha in the war zone she so fervently desired, but it was a husband she hardly recognised. . . Before the ground war began on the beaches of Normandy, the private war between Martha and Ernest was finished. There was no acknowledgement of defeat by either party, but that was only a formality.*

Hemingway was discharged just days later, still in his 'turban' and still with his 57 stitches in place. His concussion alone should have required several weeks of recuperation, and some biographers believe he discharged himself. He was also suffering from bad headaches and continued to do so for many months; but he and the other war correspondents knew that the long-planned invasion of Europe was imminent and he did not want to miss it.

The correspondents were rounded up on June 2 and driven to the south coast, and finally set out across the English Channel on the night of June 5. In the early hours of June 6, they were transferred to the various landing craft which carried the Allied troops to the Normandy beaches. There the men stormed the beaches – and many died – but the correspondents, including Hemingway, had to stay on their landing craft and were eventually taken back to the ships which had brought them over.

Once back at the Dorchester Hotel that night, Hemingway wrote his account of the invasion – or what he saw of it – in his first report for Collier's (although it did not appear in the US for another six weeks). It was a somewhat fanciful account and, typically, Hemingway takes centre stage. In it he hints, obliquely, but does not say so, that he had actually landed on Omaha Beach – he writes, ambiguously, 'the day we took Fox Green'; less obliquely he gives the impression that he had more or less been obliged to take over command of his landing craft from the inexperienced US army lieutenant in charge who had sought his advice. Several conversations between the two men are repeated verbatim, and that might have alerted sceptics, although at that point the reputation of the 'famous writer' as a 'man of action' was rarely doubted. (His new editor at Collier's later told Hemingway he thought the work he had filed from Europe was poor, but that the readers had liked it.) A week or two later, Hemingway's account of the D Day invasion grew into a wholly fictional description of what he had done 'once he was on the beach'. This account was given to a young naval lieutenant, William van Dusen, who he had met in mid-May on the RAF flight over from the US and with whom he had stayed in touch in London. Eighteen years later, in a piece entitled Hemingway's Longest Day and published by True magazine in February 1962, van Dusen recounted how Hemingway had 'taken charge and rescued a US combat team who were pinned down on the beach by enemy fire on'. [1] After leading the men to safety, van Dusen wrote, Hemingway had crawled all the way back across the beach to a command post to report on the situation and German positions. In his piece Van Dusen attributes the information to 'a source'; in fact, the only 'source' for this piece of fiction was Hemingway himself, and van Dusen had swallowed the tale whole.

---

1   Such an account of 'bravery' and 'heroism' was exactly the kind of copy True magazine liked. True was a distinctly down-market publication for men which was founded in 1937 and its contents were invariably laddish accounts of derring-do, laddish humour and other laddish writing. Hemingway and his activities featured regularly in the 1950s. It folded in 1974.

1944-1945 – Playing soldier and wooing again

Did he receive preferential treatment as a war correspondent? Yes, I'm sure he did. So did a great many others . . . But Hemingway's special privileges by no means depended on his literary renown. He had covered wars before and was, moreover, very much a military buff. He was an expert on strategy, tactics and military history. He spoke the same language as senior officers and many of them sought his company and conceived a great respect and personal affection for him.

Jeffrey Meyers, in Hemingway, a biography quoting fellow war correspondent Charles Collingwood.

The Tempest is a great, gaunt airplane. It is the fastest pursuit job in the world and is as tough as a mule. It has been reported with a speed of 400mph and should dive way ahead of its own noise. . . . You love a lot of things if you live around them, but there isn't any woman and there isn't any horse, nor any before nor any after, that is as lovely as a great airplane, and men who love them are faithful to them even though they leave them for others.

Ernest Hemingway, London Fights The Robots, Collier's, August 19, 1944.

WITHIN days of arriving in London in Mid-May and while Martha Gellhorn was still at sea on her way to Britain, Hemingway had already met, Mary Welsh, the woman who was to become his fourth wife, at Soho's White Tower restaurant where she was lunching with the novelist Irwin Shaw. He himself took her to lunch there a few days later, but that first date was apparently not memorable, and Welsh who was accustomed to male attention, says she thought nothing of it. But one night Hemingway called on her at her room in the Dorchester and when he left, he surprised her by informing her he intended to marry her. It would seem Hemingway, too, had decided – or realised – his marriage to Gellhorn was over. Between D Day on June 6 and finally arriving in France in mid-July, Hemingway spent much of his time with Welsh and toured RAF stations in England, inspecting the RAF's new Tempest aircraft and joining several bombing missions over France as an observer (which flights he loosely described in later life as 'serving with the RAF'). Many of those he met had read his work, and he was largely celebrated as 'the famous author Ernest Hemingway'; but he did not impress everyone. After he was introduced to several senior officers in the mess of one RAF station, he later wondered – in print – why they had not joined the more junior ranks on dangerous missions over Europe. The implication that they were keeping out of harm's way annoyed many – Hemingway did not know that because these officers were privy to the D Day plans, the War Office had grounded them in case they crashed in France, were captured and interrogated. Although Hemingway would not have been told why they were not flying, it was distinctly tactless of him to suggest they were cowards. Generally, there was a feeling that Hemingway, all high spirits and bonhomie, was trying too hard 'to be Ernest Hemingway'. In his biography, Carlos Baker quotes an RAF public relations officer, John Pudney, who found Hemingway's behaviour curiously offensive:

> 'To me,' said Pudney, 'he was a fellow obsessed with playing the part of the Ernest Hemingway and hamming it to boot, a sentimental 19th-century actor called upon to act the part of the 20th-century tough guy. Set beside . . . a crowd of young men who walked so modestly and stylishly with Death he seemed a bizarre cardboard figure.'

. . .

After a brief one-week visit to France in mid-July when Hemingway was attached to one of General George Patton's tank divisions, he returned to London complaining he did not understand tank warfare and was bored. He was soon back in Normandy, attaching himself to the 22nd regiment of General Raymond Barton's infantry division under Colonel Charles 'Buck' Lanham. For the next seven months, between late July 1944 and the end of December, what fighting Hemingway saw and occasionally took part in was in the company of Lanham and men. Hemingway idealised Lanham and he partly based Colonel Richard Cantwell, the central protagonist of his later novel Across The River And Into The Trees, on him. Jeffrey Reynolds sums it up well:

> *It would not be an exaggeration to say that Lanham, Hemingway's alter ego, was one of his greatest fictional creations. He was idealized to heroic proportions to match Hemingway's urgent need for a wartime comrade who would reflect, confirm, exalt and perpetuate his own martial expertise and daring adventures.*

Meyers quotes fellow correspondent Bill Walton, who was also attached to the 22nd regiment, who described Lanham as 'small, delicate and very neurotic' and, adds Meyers,

> *With his lean, gray look, [Lanham] bore a striking resemblance to Dashiell Hammett. Though a gallant soldier, he was also old-fashioned, straitlaced, thoroughly conventional, personally unimpressive and surprisingly dull. Gregory Hemingway [Hemingway's third son who met him later when Lanham visited Havana] characterized him – in a far-fetched but perfectly appropriate word – as 'nebbish'.*

According to Meyers, Lanham also seems to have idolised Hemingway. He writes that Lanham

> *like Mary [Welsh] accepted [Hemingway's] faults and adored him. Lanham, with some exaggeration (Hemingway never carried a canteen of vermouth and did not drink heavily in war) told the New York Times correspondent C L Sulzberger: 'Hemingway has the heart of the lion and is first-class in war, but horrible in peace. Hemingway used to wander around with two canteens strapped to his belt. One was filled with gin and the other with vermouth. Whenever there was a quiet moment, he would haul out a battered tin cup and suggest: 'Let's have a martini'. He was a good fighter with all weapons, although strictly speaking he was not permitted to bear arms . . . He is entirely fearless.*

Despite Hemingway's claims later in life, his experience of 'the war', both as a correspondent as well as at the front, was patchy. Just as a Cuban submarine commander had suggested Hemingway was merely 'a playboy' when he was supposedly hunting

German U-boats a year earlier (and fooling no one but himself), much the same might be claimed of his 'soldiering' in France after D Day, although he was certainly sometimes in danger and on one or two occasions could well have been killed. There are several accounts of Hemingway's *sang froid*, but his biographers cannot decide whether he was brave or simply reckless. Meyers writes

> *Under fire, Hemingway lost all fear of risking himself in war and all the tact and restraint that had characterised his behaviour in Spain. His deliberate exposure to danger was inspired by a number of complex factors: a fatalistic attitude, an ability to dismiss the possibility of death, a belief that he was lucky and therefore invulnerable, and a desire to make an impressive adolescent gesture – even at the risk of his life – which would prove his courage.*

Perhaps the pertinent word here is 'adolescent': notable are Hemingway's conduct and behaviour which might be regarded as essentially adolescent was his bragging about sex, hinting at all the 'broads' he had bedded and later embarrassing Lanham and other friends about how many times he and Mary Welsh were having intercourse; his almost neurotic competitiveness, and his constant need to be the best at, and an expert on, everything. Assuming his habitual no-nonsense, anti-intellectual tough-guy stance and playing down any notion that he might be in any way sensitive almost screams of teenage insecurity and does indicate immaturity. As for his apparent fearlessness, it is argued that he was, perhaps, simply no longer thinking straight. Barely two months after sustaining concussion in London in his early morning, blackout car crash, he was again concussed in France at the beginning of August. He banged his head on a large rock after leaping to safety from a motorcycle when he and photographer Robert Capa rounded a bend in the road and came face-to-face with a German anti-tank gun. For several weeks he suffered from constant ringing in his ears, his speech was slow and slurred, he had a continual headache and complained he could not think clearly. That mishap also exacerbated the impotence (as his letters to Welsh indicate) from which he began to suffer after the London crash and that lasted until well into November.

At one point Hemingway gave up all pretence of being a war correspondent when he 'took command' of a ragtag of French resistance fighters he had come across and who had adopted him as their leader and addressed him as 'captain' and 'colonel'. He and 'his men' made their headquarters in a hotel in Rambouillet, a town 30 miles south-west of Paris, and he sent them out on patrol to garner intelligence on German positions. In this instance Hemingway could well be accused of 'playing soldier' – he had removed his 'war correspondent' insignia from his uniform, acquired a large arsenal of rifles, pistols, ammunition and grenades in his hotel rooms, and interrogated German soldiers who had surrendered or been captured. [i] When four days later his fellow correspondents arrived with the US army – some of whom were not keen on Hemingway and his grandiosity – they felt his activities were putting their lives in danger: the Germans were entitled to execute as a spy any correspondent they came across in uniform but without credentials and they might decide that Hemingway's antics made all correspondents fair game. Several correspondents complained and at the beginning of October Hemingway was summoned to testify in a military investigation.

. . .

It wasn't just Hemingway's fellow correspondents who were irritated by his grandiose airs. The French general Jacques-Phillipe Leclerc had been nominated by General Charles de Gaulle to lead the French forces into a liberated Paris (which he did on August 25) and he had arrived at the Château de Rambouillet, the summer residence of the French presidents, in preparation for the French forces' triumphal entry. In the company of David Bruce, who headed the newly formed OSS in France, Hemingway had arrived at the chateau and announced he wanted to advise Leclerc on the best way to approach the city. In short order Leclerc told him to 'fuck off' and mind his own business. But a chastened Hemingway got his slight revenge: in a piece for Collier's which appeared on October 18 several weeks later, he wrote that he had been

> *informed that the general himself [Leclerc, though here not named by Hemingway] was just down the road and anxious to see us. Accompanied by one of the big shots of the resistance movement and Colonel B [David Bruce] . . . we advanced in some state toward the general. His greeting – unprintable – will live in my ears forever.*

It is improbable that Leclerc, who – as Hemingway admits – dismissed him out-of-hand, was in any way 'anxious' to see him or solicit his advice, and the incident bruised Hemingway's vanity to such an extent that for the rest of his life he referred to the general as 'that jerk Leclerc'. Later in his Collier's piece Hemingway – adopting his man-of-the-world persona of the insider who consorted and conferred with generals as a matter of course – wrote

> *In war, my experience has been that a rude general is a nervous general*

but if he hoped thereby to biff one back at Leclerc, it was a tad feeble. Given Leclerc's military experience – which dwarfed Hemingway's – and his courage and determination, nervousness was one fault of which he could not be accused.

Two weeks before the Collier's piece appeared, Hemingway had arrived in Nancy to give evidence at the investigation the US army had ordered into his conduct. For the first time in his life Hemingway played down his claims of derring-do (and, it is claimed, with a view to containing the matter as quickly as possible, he had been instructed by General George Patton's staff to perjure himself). Yes, he admitted to the investigating officer, information about German activities had come his way, but this had been passed on to brigade headquarters as was his 'duty as a loyal American'. Yes, he had carried arms, but he had never done so in the town and it was for his own safety. (In fact, most correspondents carried a weapon for their own safety even though they were not allowed to do so.) And, yes, if on occasion his insignia marking him out as a war correspondent were not visible, it was because they were attached to his jacket, and this he had often removed because of the hot weather. All in all, the army had felt obliged to follow up the correspondent's complaints if only to keep them happy, but it was not inclined to be seen to punish 'a loyal American' simply 'doing his duty'. Had Hemingway been found to have contravened the rules governing accredited correspondents, he would have been stripped of his accreditation and sent back to the US (and it would have done his reputation not good at all). But he was let off the hook, and some accounts even suggest the investigation was regarded as something of a joke by the army. One practical consequence of the hearing was that until he was back in Cuba Hemingway, made a point in letters and conversation of stressing that he was always 'going by the book'. He wasn't, of course.

. . .

Hemingway certainly sometimes shared the discomforts and tribulations of war with the officers and men (as did all front-line correspondents), especially during the disastrous and very nasty – and, as historians now argue, wholly unnecessary – Hürtigenwald campaign between mid-September and mid-December 1944. But all in all his eight months in France were certainly not uncomfortable. In his book Hemingway Goes To War, military historian Charles Whiting even suggests that the longest Hemingway was at the front at one stretch before he took off back to the comparative comfort of Paris was eighteen days. It must, though, be added that Whiting does not seem much to have liked Hemingway, and in his book he is guilty of at least one very bad howler: he writes that Hemingway's maternal grandfather was a 'Hadley' and that

1944-1945 – Playing soldier and wooing again 439

'Hadley' was Hemingway's middle name. Such an error does counsel caution. But other biographers confirm that after the liberation of Paris in mid-August Hemingway seems to have spent more time living it up in Ritz Hotel than reporting on 'the fighting'. In fact, after returning from Hürtigenwald in mid-December, he had rejoined Lanham's 22nd regiment on the Belgian border with Germany, but spent almost all of his time at Lanham's HQ, bed-ridden with pneumonia. Then after he and, by an ironic chance,[1] his estranged wife Martha spent Christmas and New Year with Charles Lanham, he returned to Paris and in the three months he remained in Europe, he never returned 'to the front'.

. . .

Between July 22 when Hemingway's first dispatch, Voyage To Victory, was published by Collier's and November 18 when his final report, War In [sic] The Siegfried Line, appeared, Hemingway had filed just six pieces. In view of what they were paying him, the Collier's was not at all happy, but that did not bother Hemingway. By his own admission he had travelled to 'the war in Europe' for material to turn into fiction. Jeffrey Meyers writes that after Roald Dahl had read several of the Collier's pieces, he was distinctly underwhelmed by Hemingway's performance as a war correspondent. In a letter to Meyers, Dahl admitted

> *I would rate [Hemingway] as very poor, but he didn't try to be good then. I remember him telling me about a wonderful episode concerning a man jumping out of a burning tank after his return from the invasion and when I said 'but you have to put that in your Collier's piece,' he answered, 'you don't think I'm going to give them that do you? I'm keeping it for a book.'*

Another anecdote also illustrates the quality of Hemingway's dispatches for Collier's. In early August 1944 when several correspondents were spending a long weekend at a hotel on Mount St Michel, Hemingway showed his then most recent piece to fellow scribe Charles Collingwood and asked for his comments. In a letter to Jeffrey Meyers, Collingwood recalls that

> *Being a brash youngster, I blurted out 'well, Papa, it sounds like a parody of Ernest Hemingway'. His face froze, and I forget whether*

---

1   She had been invited by a mutual friend who did not know she and Hemingway had ended their relationship.

> *he actually ushered me out or made it very clear I was to leave, which of course, I did – feeling like the most insensitive clown after so flattering a gesture on his part. He cut me dead for weeks . . . [But after the war, in Cuba] he asked me if I remembered the time in France when he had asked me for my opinion of a piece he had written for Collier's and I [had] said it sounded like a parody of Ernest Hemingway. 'You were right, of course,' he said.*

Collingwood confirmed that like many of the more famous figures who worked as correspondents, Hemingway did receive preferential treatment, but, he added

> *Hemingway's special privileges by no means depended upon his literary renown. He had covered wars before and was very much a military buff. He was an expert on strategy, tactics and military history.* [1] *He spoke the same language as senior officers and many of them sought his company and conceived a great respect and personal affection for him.*

Tellingly, none of his biographers gives any detail at all of what Hemingway was up to between the end of December, 1944, and mid-March, 1945, when he was back in Cuba. We know that he was ensconced at the Ritz Hotel where he had been joined by Mary Welsh and where he proceeded to cajole her into marrying him. But what he actually did, apart from drink and party, is not recorded. He certainly did not file any more copy to Collier's, and nor has there been any suggestion he did any other writing.

. . .

Just as whether or not Ernest Hemingway was one of the 20th century's great modernist writers is a matter of opinion, persuasion or prejudice, whether or not he was a brave, though, unofficial combatant for several months in World War II or essentially a martial dilettante is equally debatable. Knowing quite what to believe is almost impossible, and given Hemingway's propensity in later life for making extraordinary claims about his exploits, it is advisable initially to treat them all with extreme caution. He certainly did kill one or two Germans – that he gunned down one or two when the plywood cabin in Hürtigenwald that Col Lanham had made his headquarters came

---

1   This does, though, beg the question as to whether 'book learning' is as useful as 'real fighting experience'. And how was Collingwood to know how 'expert' Hemingway was on strategy, tactics and military history?

1944-1945 – Playing soldier and wooing again

under attack has been documented. But his tale of taking the lives of over one hundred Germans, a figure which grew ever larger in each subsequent telling, for example, is nonsense. In a letter he sent to his publisher Charles Scribner III after the war, he even claimed

> *One time I killed a very snotty SS kraut who, when I told him I would kill him unless he revealed what his escape route signs were said: 'You will not kill me, because you are afraid to and because you are a race of mongrel degenerates. Besides it is against the Geneva Convention.' What a mistake you made, brother, I told him and shot him three times in the belly fast and then, when he went down on his knees, shot him on the topside so his brains came out of his mouth or I guess it was his nose. The next SS I interrogated talked wonderfully.* [1]

Hemingway was certainly a soldier manqué. Although he read widely and deeply on military matters, he had never led men in battle – certainly not, as he always claimed, leading a command of Arditi as its youngest ever lieutenant in the Battle of Monte Grappa; but he was said – pertinently by others – to have been accepted by many professionals as having a good military brain. Yet to his eternal chagrin, and despite his later very tall stories, his few days in August 1944 freelancing with a gaggle of French resistance men in Rambouillet and the time he was present at the Hürtigenwald offensive with Lanham and his 22nd regiment were the sum total of the World War II 'fighting'.

---

1   It is difficult to accept that a man by then in his early fifties would expect such fantastical adolescent bluster to be taken at all seriously, but there is no reason to assume Hemingway did not. Nor can this gruesome account be dismissed with the suggestion that he liked to tell tall stories for amusement. On the other hand, according to biographer Mary Dearborn, Hemingway's cycle of manic highs and depressive lows was becoming ever faster in the 1950s when this letter was written, and being in a manic phase might explain such immature bragging.

1945-1954 – Fourth marriage and infatuations

[Hemingway's] pre-1946 depressions usually followed the completion of a book when he did not know what to write next. His post-1946 depressions were different. Because he was leaving work largely completed but not quite finished, one or more books for always begging for attention. As a result, he would move back and forth among them, even during his depressed periods, and unfinished work was always at the back of his mind.

Michael Reynolds, Hemingway: The Final Years.

The Old Man And The Sea is a short novel, only 27,000 words. It is much simpler and enormously better than Mr Hemingway's last book, Across The River And Into the Trees. No phony [sic] glamour girls and no bullying braggarts sentimentalized almost to parody distort its honest and elemental theme. No outbursts of spite or false theatricalism impede the smooth rush of its narrative. Within the sharp restrictions imposed by the very nature of his story Mr. Hemingway has written with sure skill. Here is the master technician once more at the top of his form, doing superbly what he can do better than anyone else.

Orville Prescott, New York Times, August 28, 1952.

Edmund Wilson, the most distinguished critic in America, wrote the most influential study of Hemingway. Wilson's 1939 essay, Hemingway: Gauge Of Morale, marked a turning point in the

1945-1954 – Fourth marriage and infatuations

history of Hemingway's critical reputation. Though Wilson had been a great admirer of Hemingway's early work, he now contrasted the successful art of the 1920s with the radical decline in the following decade and emphasized [Hemingway's] exhibitionism, his public personality, his lack of objectivity, craftsmanship, taste, style and sense.

Jeffrey Meyers, Hemingway: A Biography.

Despite his tough-guy image, Hemingway was a soft-hearted man. He was apparently persuaded to grant [Malcolm] Cowley's interview in Cuba after the critic pleaded that his son's education was at stake.

Jeffrey Meyers, Hemingway: A Biography on Malcolm Cowley's profile in Life.

THE nominally fourth and final stage of Hemingway's life lasted for 16 years. It began when he arrived back at his home at the Finca Vigia near Havana from 'his war in Europe' in mid-March 1945 and ended at around 7am on Sunday, July 2, 1961, at his home in Ketchum, Idaho, when he was able to end his life at his third attempt. Those final 16 years were marked by ever-worsening health, both mental and physical, a stormy fourth marriage, and two middle-aged *amour fou* for women who, at just 19, were several decades years younger than him. Notably for a man regarded by many, not least by himself, as one of America's greatest writers, those last years saw a scant published output. Yet, ironically, he actually wrote more fiction between 1945 and 1961 than he had in his first 16 years as a 'celebrated author'; but he published a fraction of it, just two works. These were a novel, Across The River And Into The Trees, and The Old Man And The Sea, a work that is sometimes called 'a novel' but at 27,000 words can better be regarded either as a novella or even a long short story.

Across The River And Into The Trees appeared in 1950 and was almost universally derided. The Old Man And The Sea, though, was celebrated and praised to high heaven, although a dissenting few gave it only two cheers. The remainder of the welter of words he produced in those final 16 years – and 'welter' seems to be the most appropriate word – was not published until several years after his death and then only after substantial pruning and editing. Those posthumous works consisted of a memoir, A Moveable Feast (first published in 1964), a novel, Islands In The Stream (1970), The Dangerous

Summer, a second 'bullfighting book' which began life as a feature he was contracted to write by Life magazine (1985), a second novel, The Garden Of Eden (1986) and True At First Light (1999), a 'fictional account' – Hemingway's own description – of his second African safari. Quite why Hemingway was reluctant to offer those works for publication is unclear. Some biographers suggest he suspected some of it was still not up to snuff and he intended to revise it until he believed it was. The Garden Of Eden dealt in part with sexual ambiguity and role reversal, and Hemingway is thought to have feared it could not be published in his lifetime. In the mid-1950s it would certainly have startled those middle-brow Americans who now made up his core readership.

As for publishing the posthumous work, it might not be too unkind to suggest that Scribner's (and later its owners) were more concerned with squeezing the last remaining dollars out of their property than adding to the body of 'world literature'. Doubtless the publisher would deny such a charge and insist the world had a right [1] to read all the work of an 'important writer'. Some academics have loyally claimed that some of the writing does have merit, but it is difficult to rid oneself of the suspicion that the occasional attention it is given is overwhelmingly because it is 'by Ernest Hemingway'. Substantiating the suggestion that Scribner's had more than one eye on the bottom line were the publication in 1964 of By-Line: Ernest Hemingway, a compendium of his journalism from throughout his career, and, in 1985, Dateline: Toronto, a collection of the freelances pieces he filed from Paris for the Toronto Star. [2] A Moveable Feast was re-edited by his grandson Sean Hemingway and re-published in 2009. Between Hemingway's death in 1961 and 2009, Scribner's or those publishers it had licensed to recycle the short stories released 'work' to keep the tills ringing. As I point out above, it seems no barrel is too deep to be scraped. [i]

. . .

When Hemingway returned to the Finca Vigia, he set about preparing it for the arrival of Mary Welsh whom he expected to join him and become his fourth wife. To make marriage to Welsh possible, he had visited Martha Gellhorn in the Dorchester Hotel in London (where she was laid up with influenza) while on his way home from Europe and finally agreed to the divorce she had demanded. Gellhorn was desperate to possess a passport which identified her under her maiden name. Yet, however keen Hemingway

---

1   Possibly even a 'moral duty'. Who knows?
2   Although in my view Hemingway's journalism was overall better than his fiction, there is nothing memorable in any of these pieces, and they are mainly of interest to those who would be ready to shell out thousands for a sliver of 'the True Cross' or the last pair of socks Elvis wore before he died.

was on taking another wife, unfortunately Welsh was not quite as sold on the idea. She had already been married twice, and when she informed her parents she was about to divorce her second husband, she told them only that she *might* be marrying Hemingway. Although Welsh had agreed to marry Hemingway in Paris in August 1944 – reportedly persuaded to do so by Marlene Dietrich who had first met Hemingway more then ten years earlier – she was certainly in two minds about the prospect. Between mid-May 1944 when Hemingway had met and started courting her and when he left for Cuba in March, 1945, she had already seen and fallen foul of his ugly, often vicious, side. By turns Hemingway could be very sweet and loving – as several mawkish love poems he had written for her testified – and very nasty, especially when he was drunk, which he often was. In those nine months he had been rude to and insulted her in public on several occasions, and had already hit her. Once – apparently on Valentine's Day 1945 – and again while steaming drunk, he had placed a framed photograph of Noel Monks, her second husband, in a Ritz Hotel lavatory bowl and blasted it with a set of German machine pistols with which his US army friend 'Buck' Lanham had just presented him as a gift. Furthermore, Welsh had never been short of admirers, which aroused Hemingway's jealousy, and he even accused her of sleeping with senior army officers to gain information. Monks himself was also jealous of what his wife was getting up to while he was away covering the war. He and Welsh had married on New Year's Day, 1939, in Chelsea, London, but when Welsh found out he was having an affair while he was based in Cairo she, too, began to play the field. In a letter to Welsh in February 1945, Monks' list of her lovers included 'a pip-speak general', 'a film unit guy' (which would have been the Irwin Shaw), a 'queer-looking guy' and 'pimply-faced [Michael] Foot' (who later became an unsuccessful leader of Britain's Labour Party). As for Hemingway, Monks declared she had thrown 'a sprat into the sea and caught [herself] a whale'. He and Welsh were divorced in Chicago on August 31, 1945.

Despite whatever misgivings she had, Welsh joined Hemingway in Cuba in May 1945, and once his divorce from Gellhorn was finalised in December 1945, she and Hemingway were married the following March. Yet her doubts continued: after a somewhat fraught two-part civil ceremony at a lawyer's office – it was all in Spanish and Welsh didn't understand a word – and several off-colour quips from Hemingway that upset her, then a pleasant wedding reception in a friend's apartment, he again turned nasty on the drive back to the Finca. That night (as we know from the diary she kept) she resolved to leave him. The following day she changed her mind. Those 24 hours were pretty much the template of their subsequent married life together. On many occasions Hemingway treated Welsh like dirt: once while entertaining friends to dinner he tipped the supper she had prepared onto the floor. On another occasion when he was due home for lunch with friends, he turned up with a young Cuban prostitute in tow. [1] Later, he would always be sweetness and light and attempt to soothe Welsh's anger with an expensive gift. To the astonishment of their friends who witnessed how Hemingway treated her, Welsh rolled with the punches, and though she often confided in her diary that she wanted to leave Hemingway, she never did. Part of the problem was that for many years she did not feel the Finca Vigia was her home: Martha Gellhorn had discovered, renovated and furnished it, and pictures of Martha were still everywhere. Unlike Hemingway's first three wives who had a well-off upbringing, Welsh came from a 'humble' [2] background (although her father, a riverboat captain, was unusually enlightened, listened to classical music and insisted his daughter should always stand up for herself). She felt she could not compete with the smart, often very attractive wives of Hemingway's friends, with whom he might flirt openly in front of her and with whom he often believed himself to be in love. Two of the ridiculous infatuations Hemingway developed in the following 16 years, one with a 19-year-old Venetian woman and, ten years later, with an Irish would-be journalist of the same age, humiliated her, but she clung on. Even after an excruciating extended visit to Spain in 1959 when she finally made firm plans to leave Hemingway and even bought an apartment in New York in which to live, she could still not make the break and was at his side in the final 18 months of his life when his mental health finally gave way and he blew his head off. [ii]

. . .

Despite Hemingway not submitting any work for publication in the ten years after the success of For Whom The Bell Tolls in 1940, Scribner's showed remarkable patience with the writer the house still regarded as one of its principal assets. Yet in 1947 Max Perkins, who had guided Hemingway's career for 20 years, had, according to biographer Kenneth Lynn, privately confided in his wife that 'Hemingway is through'. Then in 1950 came Across The River And Into The Trees. As had three of the four novels Hemingway had so far published, it began life as a short story and was based on the first of his middle-age infatuations. Lynn suggests Perkins would have been aware of the work's many weaknesses and would strongly have advised Hemingway not to publish it as a novel but as a short story; but Perkins had died suddenly a few months after voicing his misgiving about the writer's future and did not oversee the novel's publication or witness the critical mauling it received. However, the critics be damned: despite the

---

1   As usual, though, there are different versions of this anecdote.

2   This is the patronising word often used in this context, but as I dislike it, I offer it in quotation marks.

awful reviews it was given, Scribner's patience was rewarded: the novel sold very, very well, spent seven weeks in the best-selling lists and was serialised by – the decidedly middle-brow and mid-market – Cosmopolitan magazine. Even more gratifying were the sales of The Old Man And The Sea which appeared two years later.

Despite publishing just those two works in the final quarter of his life, Hemingway had been writing consistently, for several months at time, ever since he returned from Europe. Nominally he had attended World War II – an interlude he later always promoted to 'fighting in Europe' – as a war correspondent; but he was quite candid that his purpose was essentially to collect material for his fiction. Within months of his return to Cuba, he set about writing what he declared would be his 'big book', a 'war novel' that would cover the conflict at sea, on land and in the air. The 'sea' war story was to be based on his 'submarine hunting' off the Cuban coast, the 'land' war on the weeks he had spent with Col Lanham's infantry regiment in France, Belgium and Germany, and the 'air' war on his few flights with the RAF. Following his usual disciplined routine of rising early and working until about noon, he set to work in earnest in October 1945, initially continuing to work on a story based on Bimini he had begun before the war. In tandem he also began writing the novel that was eventually published – though drastically pruned and re-written, [1] with two central characters removed completely – as The Garden Of Eden. [2] This period of intensive writing carried on until 1948. By then he had abandoned his plan for an 'air' war novel, perhaps realising that his few flights with the RAF as an observer might not furnish him with enough material. Work on his 'big book' also stopped because his health increasingly deteriorated. Since returning to Cuba in 1945, he was drinking ever more heavily, had put on even more weight and his blood pressure was dangerously high. Some biographers suggest he was afraid he would die suddenly of an aneuryism, and following his doctor's orders, he managed – briefly – to lose weight and bring down his blood pressure. But he could not regain the impetus to carry on with his writing.

. . .

It was around this time that Hemingway attracted the attention of three journalists

---

1   'Edited' would be too kind a word to describe the process it needed to shape it into a work that could be published.

2   There is, in fact, irreconcilable disagreement among his biographers as to when Hemingway began writing the novel: Kenneth Lynn, James Mellow, Jeffrey Meyers and, most recently, Mary Dearborn contend work was begun in the mid-1940s, but Michael Reynolds suggests the novel wasn't started until the early 1950s.

and of several academics.[1] In 1948, Aaron Edward (A.E.) Hotchner, who was then working for Cosmopolitan, was asked to visit him in Cuba and sign him up to contribute to a series it planned on 'the future of literature'. Hemingway agreed, but as part of the contract, he stipulated that Cosmopolitan should publish two of his short stories (which he had not yet written) and serialise part of his 'war novel'. He wanted $15,000 (just over $189,515 in 2023) for the overall deal. He explained that sum might seem less than he would usually demand, but as a writer resident outside the US, the tax implications were favourable: he explained that tax-free those $15,000 were worth $75,000 ($947,476) before tax. The proposed series of articles was, in fact, abandoned after Cosmopolitan appointed a new editor, and nor were the two short stories ever written; but according to Michael Reynolds, Cosmopolitan still paid up and did serialise his next novel, though it was not the 'war book' both expected it to be. These dealings saw the start of Hemingway's relationship with Hotchner (who soon moved on from Cosmopolitan) and the two became friends and collaborators. Hotchner, who had studied law but was trying his hand at journalism, became something of an acolyte and confidant who was often in attendance and always on call until Hemingway killed himself. Eventually he and Hemingway formed a small company, H&H Enterprises, which produced radio and, later, TV drama of some of Hemingway's works. (The dramas were sponsored by Buick and featured in the Buick-Electra Playhouse. The initial series of four dramas screened was so popular that Buick wanted to commission a second series, to include The Sun Also Rises and A Farewell To Arms. However, one condition it stipulated was that the TV versions should be adapted to have a 'happy ending'. Unsurprisingly Hemingway passed.)

In that same year, Malcolm Cowley, his acquaintance from the early years in Paris, was commissioned by Life magazine to write a long profile of Hemingway. Over the years, Hemingway had generally been rather dismissive of the more left-wing Cowley, but his standing with Hemingway had risen with the introduction Cowley wrote to The Viking Portable Library volume of Hemingway's work that was published in 1944: in it he suggested Hemingway should be treated far more seriously as artist. Despite that plaudit, Hemingway was not immediately keen on granting Cowley an interview and having a profile published. Throughout his life Hemingway had a decidedly ambivalent attitude to publicity: on the one hand he shamelessly promoted himself, on the other he pleaded that he, too, was entitled to a private life and believed it harmed a writer's work

---

1   The interest of the academics, as I argue above, pitched him into a higher league entirely and set him on the road to being regarded as 'one of our greatest writers'.

if his readers knew too much about him. [1]

Hemingway was full of such contradictions. He had once loftily complained about writers who 'never learned how to say no to a typewriter', yet increasingly Hemingway himself found it impossible to say 'no to a typewriter': after Life magazine had commissioned him in 1959 for a 10,000-word feature on a series of Spanish bullfights, it later agreed, at Hemingway's request, to extend the length to 30,000 words. The piece eventually grew to 120,000 words. This was all a far cry from the often brutally concise style of his first four books which had so impressed the critics and helped to make his name. The manuscripts for his two posthumous novels, Islands In The Stream and The Garden Of Eden, were also exceptionally long – Eden reached more than 200,000 words – and both had to be drastically cut before they were published: this from the writer whose 'terse, precise and aggressively fresh prose' was once so admired. Yet arguably there is nothing hypocritical about Hemingway's attitude to the publicity he sought and the privacy he persuaded himself he was owed: as a man who sincerely believed he was always right about everything, he was possibly unaware of the obvious ironies.

According to Hemingway, he eventually agreed to the profile after Cowley pleaded that the money Life would pay him would allow him to send his son to the prestigious Phillips Exeter Academy in New Hampshire (and so much for Cowley's left-wing principles), though according to Cowley, quoted by Denis Brian in The True Gen, he wasn't quite as desperate for the money as Hemingway implied. He, his wife Muriel and his son Robert spent ten days in March 1948 in Havana, staying at the Ambos Mundos and enjoying the Hemingways' hospitality. Robert Cowley remembers that his mother was very impressed with Hemingway's 'extraordinarily good manners'; but he also recalls that

> *You could also tell [Hemingway] was an extraordinary hater, because once sitting in the living room he read aloud to everyone there a letter from someone he utterly despised. He'd read one sentence and comment, read another sentence and comment. I'd never heard anything funnier or more vicious. He was very funny . . . He looked very directly into your eyes when he spoke to you and held that look and spoke confidentially. He was an immense man, great broad shoulders, narrow hips, but a hell of a big gut.*

Cowley's profile eventually appeared in the second week of January 1949 under the title

---

[1] Given how throughout the 1950s he agreed to feature in photoshoots for several middle-brow and downmarket magazines – none of which paid much attention to his writing – one can only assume that he was wholly unaware of any contradiction in his belief.

A Portrait Of Mister Papa. It included much that Hemingway had asked Cowley to leave out – his 'counter-intelligence' activities and 'sub-hunting' on the Pilar which he felt might upset the Cuban government, and his 'fighting' in Europe. Cowley sent him a draft of the piece for his comments, yet with each letter to Cowley requesting this and that deletion, Hemingway added further details, many of which were complete nonsense: he volunteered the 'fact' that there 'was Indian blood in the family', that one of his sisters 'had been in love with him' and that he had been obliged to give up driving after five car crashes in which people had died or been badly injured. [iii] Michael Reynolds writes

> *Cowley must have been perplexed by Hemingway's frequent and contradictory letters, taking away with the left hand what the right had given. But this behaviour also kept Cowley asking questions, for each of Hemingway's responses would reveal some new piece of biography, some more fabulous than accurate, all provocative and sometimes paranoid.*

In these letters to Cowley and others, Reynolds adds,

> *Hemingway was rehearsing the biography, modifying here, exaggerating there, leaving a confusing trail of truths, half-truths and outright fantasies. At 48 he was saying outrageous things to complete strangers, things he would never have said earlier. What appears at times to be mania can also be read as his response to the canonization of his generation [of writers] already dead.*

Both Hotchner and Cowley accepted Hemingway's claims, even the more outlandish stories, without question. These included having an 'aluminium kneecap', 'having fought as a professional boxer', 'running away from home to live the life of a hobo' and 'being a star football player' at school. Yet it would be unfair to take Hotchner and Cowley too strongly to task: both had been commissioned to enlist Hemingway because he was, in 1948, one of America's best-known and most successful novelists (and this was before he wrote and published Across The River And Into The Trees). It would have been very unusual, not to say quite odd, for them to have listened politely to what he had to say, then concluded he was simply – as we now know – telling a string of complete whoppers. Those of his friends in Cuba who drank with him and knew him well were increasingly inclined to take most of his claims and stories with a large pinch of salt, especially when each 'achievement' became more spectacular with the telling; but new acquaintances such as Hotchner and Cowley could not have known. Talking to Denis Brian, friends and acquaintances of Hemingway suggested he was often sending people up and would tell his tale tales for a joke; this is certainly possible, but one does wonder why he would do so with Cowley for what was to be a serious profile. Hotchner had never before met Hemingway, though Kenneth Lynn points out that Cowley, in particular, was not as scrupulous in his reporting as he might have been. In his introduction to The Viking Portable Hemingway in 1944, he had even got the year of Hemingway's birth wrong. But, Lynn adds,

> *On boozy days and nights at the Finca [in the ten days interviewing Hemingway for his profile], the lord of the manor had undoubtedly grown expansive, and Cowley never seems to have wondered whether his host's fascinating yarns could be trusted. A Portrait Of Mr Papa not only took Hemingway's sub-hunting activities far too seriously, but grossly exaggerated the significance of his war service in France.*

Hemingway's reaction to Cowley's profile, says Lynn, was that is was 'OK' but 'not awfully accurate'. Lynn adds

> *Some years later, Cowley stoutly defended his reportorial reliability by pointing out that the only specific objection Hemingway had raised was about the anecdote of his carrying canteens of gin and vermouth at his belt during combat in World War II. In the first place, Hemingway had scoffed, good vermouth hadn't been available, and in the second place he would never have wasted a whole canteen on the stuff, no matter what.*

In view of Hemingway's protest, Cowley's canteen anecdote does begin to look more than questionable. In fact, the claim was also made in an interview with the New York Times' editor and writer C.L. Sulzberger by Col Lanham who was accompanied by Hemingway for several weeks at the front in the autumn of 1944. More seriously and curiously, why did Hemingway choose to play down the 'canteens of gin and vermouth' claim, but allow other equally fatuous claims – for example, running away to live as a hobo – to stand?

...

In the years after returning home to Cuba, Hemingway's health, which had increasingly taken a battering, went into a slow decline. He had a strong constitution when he was younger, but the two concussions he suffered in Europe in 1944, both of which went untreated, and his steady excessive drinking were taking their toll. Now in middle age, his metabolism was less able to deal with the stresses to which he subjected it, and age was slowly making itself felt. He was upset that the thick head of dark hair he once sported was getting ever thinner, and he had long been obliged to wear spectacles for his poor eyesight, although he rarely wore them in public and always removed them if he knew he was about to be photographed. His blood pressure was again dangerously high, he was overweight, and he now had to take a variety of medications to deal with his several ailments which included his chronic insomnia. He did make another effort to cut back on drinking and watch his weight, but by 1948 he decided an extended break in Italy might do him good. It would be a belated honeymoon for him and Mary and a trip down memory lane to revisit the various places he had known as a younger man, including the spot on the Pave River where he had been blown up by an Austrian mortar 30 years earlier.

He and Welsh set off in September 1948 and docked at Genoa after a four-week voyage across the Atlantic. They toured northern Italy, taking in Stresa, Bergamo and Cortina d'Ampezzo (which he had visited with Hadley and where he based his short story Out Of Season) where Welsh rented a villa for them for the following few months. Towards the end of October they reached Venice and settled themselves in the very expensive Gritti Palace hotel. Soon Hemingway was invited to go duck shooting on the small island of Torcello to the north-east of Venice in the Venetian Lagoon, and he and Welsh decided to base themselves there for a few weeks. In the November, Welsh went to see the sights in and around Florence, and Hemingway took off to the banks of the Piave.[1] This was his second trip to the area, and yet again Hemingway could discern nothing in the landscape he could identify. One irony, as Michael Reynolds points out, was that he was ignoring his own advice about 'going back'. After his first trip, with Hadley, to find that same spot in 1921 and failing to do so because the landscape had already recovered from the devastation of war, he had filed and sold to the Toronto Daily Star a short feature in which he advised readers

> *Don't go back to visit the old front. If you have pictures in your head of something that happened in the night in Paschendale [sic] or in the first wave working up the slope in Vimy, do not go back to verify them. It is not good . . . it is like going into the empty gloom of a*

---

1   He was accompanied on the trip by the writer and journalist Fernanda Pivano who was translating A Farewell To Arms into Italian, and he thought it would assist her in the task to see the area where it was all said to have taken place.

theater where the charwomen are scrubbing. [1]

It was while staying on Torcello in mid-December that Hemingway met Adriana Ivancich, the daughter of an impoverished family of Venetian nobility, at the home of his new hunting friends. Then just a month short of her 19th birthday, she was 30 years younger, but he was smitten, and after spending Christmas at the rented Cortina villa, he returned to Venice for two weeks – without Welsh – to meet her again. A few weeks later, an eye infection developed into erysipelas, and he was kept in hospital in Padua as a precaution, although his life was never in danger as was later claimed by Scribner's for publicity purposes. Then he and Welsh returned to the Gritti Palace in Venice. Before leaving Italy to return to Cuba, he saw Ivancich – and her chaperone who was always present at their meetings – several times. By then he had started writing a short story about her which soon evolved into his fifth novel, Across The River And Into The Trees. The short story had been started before he met Ivancich, and it was about a retired US military man who, as did Hemingway, was enjoying shooting duck and other birds on Torcello. The figure of 'Renata' was incorporated into the story only after Hemingway had met Ivancich and developed his crush.

Hemingway and Welsh set sail for Cuba in April and were back at the Finca Vigia by the end of May 1949. On the voyage home, which also took almost a month, Hemingway spent every morning working on his new novel and carried on writing it once back at the Finca. He also wrote Ivancich many letters declaring his love for her. By September Hemingway said he had written 13,000 words of the story, now well on its way to becoming a novel, and with the assistance of Hotchner had contracted with Cosmopolitan to serialise the opening chapters. [2] By the end of October another 13,000 words of his novel had been written, and a second trip to France and Italy was planned. By November when Hemingway and Welsh flew to New York to set off on that second trip, he had also agreed to spend the best part of three days there with the journalist Lillian Ross for a New Yorker profile.

...

Ross had first met Hemingway on Christmas Eve, 1947, in Ketchum when she was

---

1   A cynic might suggest that by mentioning Passchendaele and Vimy in his piece for the Toronto Star, both sites which witnessed World War I battles in 1917, Hemingway might, perhaps, have been hinting to his reader that he had taken part in the fighting there. He had not, of course. He did not get to Europe until a year later.

2   Of the two stories he had agreed to write for Cosmopolitan nine months earlier, he now claimed one had been written, but that he had not submitted it because it was 'too rough'.

writing a profile of Sidney Franklin, who had been with Hemingway in Spain in 1937 and 1938, and Hemingway had given her background details of his time and friendship with Franklin. After their New York meeting in November, Ross' long [1] profile, entitled How Do You Like It Now, Gentlemen? appeared on May 6, 1950, and caused a minor controversy. The title was taken from a nonsensical phrase Hemingway had for no apparent reason taken to repeating (and is said to have done so for the rest of his life, to Welsh's increasing irritation). Ross was accused of trying to make Hemingway look like a fool, and indeed in some ways he does come across as foolish, but it is odd to blame Ross. She simply reproduced what he had said and the jokey way he had adopted of speaking in a kind of pidgin 'injun' fashion. Many also felt Hemingway's continual use of sports analogies for writing and comparing himself to taking on past literary figures in the boxing ring was also silly. Hemingway had told her

> *I started out very quiet and I beat Mr. Turgenev. Then I trained hard and I beat Mr. de Maupassant. I've fought two draws with Mr. Stendhal, and I think I had an edge in the last one. But nobody's going to get me in any ring with Mr. Tolstoy unless I'm crazy or I keep getting better.*

Although Hemingway adopted a nonchalant air about Ross' feature and reactions to it once it had appeared, it did upset him, and he was, according to Meyers, 'shocked and felt awful'. In a piece she published in the New Yorker almost 50 years later, Ross denied that the profile showed Hemingway in a bad light. She also insisted that before publication the magazine had sent Hemingway proofs of her feature piece, and because he had raised no objections, she had assumed he was happy with the profile. To that claim A.E. Hotchner countered that the proofs had not arrived until the Monday of the week of publication – it was due to appear on the following Saturday – so there would have been no time to make changes. This is disingenuous: if Hemingway had been upset and had wanted the profile to be amended, a quick phone call to the magazine in New York would surely have been sufficient to delay publication: whatever difficulties that might have brought would have been the magazine's problem, not his: Hemingway was sufficiently prominent for the magazine to have accommodated him, whatever – certain – havoc it would have created with its production schedule. At the heart of it all was, as Meyers writes, that

> *Hemingway put on a performance for Ross, expected her to see*

---

1   . . . not to say rather dull and long-winded – Americans do seem to love long-winded.

> *through his act and show the highbrow readers of her magazine the man behind the rather transparent mask. Instead, she accepted the façade, repaid his generosity with meanness and established her reputation at his expense . . . Though [Hemingway] assumed the role of a dumb ox, constantly spoke with wisecracks and sporting metaphors, he was not as stupid or boorish as Ross' account suggested. She never recorded or revealed the serious and sensitive side of his character, and chose to portray him as a boring braggart who keeps punching himself in the stomach.*

In her 1999 New Yorker response, entitled Hemingway Told Me Things: Notes On A Decade's Correspondence, Ross reports that she and Hemingway had, in fact, kept up an 'unshakeable' friendship until his death and had written to each other regularly. Referring to the 'controversy', she wrote that in one letter he had urged her to ignore it. In another letter, she claimed, he told her

> *All are very astonished because I don't hold anything against you who made an effort to destroy me and nearly did, they say. I always tell them how can I be destroyed by a woman when she is a friend of mine and we have never even been to bed and no money has changed hands?*

Admittedly, Hemingway's forgiveness seems a little left-handed, but he also lets her off the hook. To others, though, Hemingway did indicate that he wasn't overly pleased with how Ross had portrayed him, though characteristically he held different positions on the issue depending upon to whom he was talking or writing. In her 1999 response Ross insisted that she

> *wanted to give a picture of this special man as he was, how he looked and sounded, with his vitality, his unique and fun-loaded conversation, and his enormous spirit of truthfulness intact. He had the nerve to be like nobody else on earth, stripping himself – like his writing – of all camouflage and ornament.*

In retrospect, her claim that Hemingway 'had the nerve' to 'strip himself' bare is ironic – by 1999 Ross must have been familiar with the rather less adulatory biographies that had appeared in the 1980s and 1990s which did a great deal of the stripping for him. Arguably Hemingway's lifelong efforts to present himself to the world as hard, stoic, tough, fearless and above all a 'real man' suggests on the contrary a fair degree of intentional camouflage and ornament. For example, he decided his novel The Garden Of Eden, which would certainly have stripped him of any camouflage, was 'too sexually adventurous to be published during his lifetime'. In the novel David Bourne, the main male protagonist in the heavily cut and edited published version and his alter ego, indulges in sexual games and gender reversal with his bisexual wife. We know – from Hemingway – that he and Welsh did the same: in bed, he sometimes became 'Catherine' and she was 'Pete'. [1] That he chose not to publish it suggests he certainly did not 'have the nerve like nobody else on earth'.

Ross' 'controversial' 1950 profile is a case in point of the confusing complexity that in Hemingway masqueraded as simplicity. Though Hemingway champions might jump in and claim that 'complexity' was and is the essence of his work, others might counter that the 'complexity' detected by academics is invariably speculative and the kind of 'knowledge' that can never be proved. Hemingway was certainly not 'stripping himself of all camouflage and ornament' when he chose to play the dumb ox in his encounter with Ross and expected her to see through the mask and describe to her readers the fine, sensitive artist beneath the surface: he was doing quite the opposite – camouflaging himself, something the essentially shy man he had done all his life. The obvious question is: why didn't he just play it straight? Why did he put on a performance for Ross? Quite apart from perhaps hoping to deflect scrutiny, another possible explanation is unexpectedly simple: as the friends Denis Brian interviewed for his book The True Gen continually point out, Hemingway was a great joker – he was always up for a laugh. He did put on a performance for Ross, but the po-faced New Yorker writer took it all at face value. In that light it is no surprise Hemingway felt rather stupid.

Seventy years on, it is almost impossible to sort out what was what and, frankly, it can now be seen as the trivial episode of little consequence it was. The 'controversy' it caused at the time among the chattering classes does, though, underline the extraordinary public status and fame Hemingway had at the time. It also highlights the rather silly, not to say dangerous, game Hemingway was playing with the public and the critics when he tried to control how he was perceived. On the one hand he wanted to be seen as a 'bad guy' – not many years later he often used the phrase 'we bad boys' – the no-nonsense kind who knew all about life and the dirty knocks it dealt. At no point in his life did he want to be thought of as an arty intellectual. Yet when, as in the Ross profile, he was taken by his word and portrayed as a simple, down-to-earth, rough and tough man, the antithesis of what conventionally was seen as 'the artist', he didn't like it at all, despite his disclaimer to Ross. That same ambivalence about who he was and,

---

1   Though no one has suggested Welsh was bisexual.

particularly, how he wanted to be seen, also permeated his dealings with a number of academics who contacted him and asked for his cooperation with various studies of his work they planned to complete. [1]

...

After that three-day meeting with Ross, Hemingway and Welsh, with Hotchner and two friends in tow, set sail for Europe. Six weeks in Paris were followed by two more months in Venice where the ageing, lovelorn, paunchy, short-sighted and balding Hemingway spent more time with – again always chaperoned – young Adriana Ivancich. Finally, after inviting her and her mother Dora to stay with them at the Finca Vigia later that year, he and Welsh sailed back to the US and travelled home. There, Hemingway revised the manuscript for Across The River And Into The Trees, and it was published by Scribner's at the beginning of September. He then turned back to continuing his work on his 'Bimini novel', part of the 'sea war' element of his 'big war book'. As with the 'air' element of that planned work, nothing more was to become of the putative 'land war' volume because he had used all his experience and the material intended for it in Across The River. Another complication was that after Hemingway first announced to Scribner's that he was writing a new novel but gave no more details, the house had assumed this was to be the 'big book' he kept talking about. They were disappointed when it was not. Fearing that the public, which had been primed to expect a grand 'war novel' from the famous Ernest Hemingway, might feel a little cheated, Scribner's cooked up an explanation: it hi-jacked the few weeks Hemingway had spent in hospital in Padua while his erysipelas was being treated and turned it into the fiction that he had been very ill. Thus, so the story went, Hemingway, 'almost at death's door', had temporarily abandoned writing the 'big book' and written a shorter novel which he felt confident he would have the time to complete.

The rumpus about Ross' profile might have underlined Hemingway's status as 'one of America's greatest contemporary writers', but his latest novel then damaged it badly. The critics, who Hemingway had long convinced himself hated him, were not at all impressed. Some were simply baffled that Across The River And Into The Trees was being presented as a serious work; others were prepared to write off Hemingway as a literary force, a man of the past. Hemingway's first biographer Carlos Baker, who two years later published the admiring Hemingway: The Writer As Artist, observed that

In spite of Ernest's high hopes and preliminary vauntings,

---

1   See p.203ff.

> *Across The River was received that September with boredom and dismay. The American reviews bristled with such adjectives as disappointing, embarrassing, distressing, trivial, tawdry, garrulous and tired. Many said that the book read like a parody of his former style.*

A lone – and quite odd – voice of praise came from fellow writer John O'Hara in the New York Times who claimed that

> *The most important author living today, the outstanding author since the death of Shakespeare, has brought out a new novel. The title of the novel is Across The River And Into the Trees. The author, of course, is Ernest Hemingway, the most important, the outstanding author out of the millions of writers who have lived since 1616.*

Like Hemingway, O'Hara was also an alcoholic and might well have been drunk when he wrote and submitted for publication his extraordinary claim. Far more typical of what the critics thought of Hemingway's novel – he was convinced it was the best thing he had written – was, also in the New York Times, from J. Donald Adams. He wrote

> *To me, Across the River And Into the Trees is one of the saddest books I have ever read; not because I am moved to compassion by the conjunction of love and death in the Colonel's life, but because a great talent has come, whether for now or forever, to such a dead end.*

In the New Yorker, Alfred Kazin recorded that

> *It is hard to say what one feels most in reading this book – pity, embarrassment that so fine and honest a writer can make such a travesty of himself, or amazement that a man can render so marvellously the beauty of the natural world and yet be so vulgar.*

Equally baffled by the novel was Maxwell Geismar in The Saturday Review of Literature. He wrote

> *This is an unfortunate novel and unpleasant to review for anyone who respects Hemingway's talent and achievement. It is not only Hemingway's worst novel; it is a synthesis of everything that is*

> bad in his previous work and throws a doubtful light on the future. It is so dreadful, in fact, that it begins to have its own morbid fascination . . . The ideological background of the novel is a mixture of True Romances, Superman, and The Last Frontier.

A year later in the Kenyon Review, Isaac Rosenfield began

> It is not enough to say that Across the River And Into The Trees is a bad novel, which nearly everyone has said (the fact is, a good deal of it is trash) or to ascribe its failure to Hemingway's playing Hemingway. Such judgments fail to go deep; they make an artificial separation between the man and the artist, and attribute to the former, as though these were superficial mistakes, shortcomings which are the very essence of Hemingway's art. It seems to me that no writer of comparable stature has ever expressed in his work so false an attitude toward life.

Rosenfield adds, though notably before Hemingway had written and published The Old Man And The Sea,

> For all these reasons, it seems to me that his reputation must soon decline, and while the excellent aspects of his style, at least in the earlier novels and some of the stories, the clear, clean writing that he does at his best, will retain their value, the deep moral significance that some critics (e.g. Cowley) have found or pretended to find in his attitude toward life has already begun to look like a hoax.

At a pinch, Hemingway might have been able to persuade himself that this was all just more of the same spite from those damned, nasty critics who were out to get him. But the standing of his novel did not improve with age. Writing 40 years later in Ernest Hemingway, his short review of all of Hemingway's work published before 1990, Peter L. Hays – notably an academic, not a critic – observed that the 'disastrous reviews'

> criticised the slackness and self-indulgence on the prose that seemed a bad parody of the early, taut Hemingway style

and, Hays adds,

> Critics have tried to redeem it from its own failings, praising

the denseness of allusions to such writers as Dante, Thomas Mann (Death In Venice), and Gabriele D'Annunzio, the symbolic resonance of nearly every scene, every word, but none of these make the novel work.

A slightly kinder, more sympathetic note of consolation was struck by Britain's Cyril Connelly (quoted by Jeffrey Meyers in The Critical Heritage) that

It is not uncommon for a famous writer to produce one thoroughly bad book.

We don't know whether Hemingway ever came across Connolly's rather left-handed claim, but it is unlikely much to have cheered him up. [iv]

. . .

Apart from the critical mauling Hemingway's new novel received, there were other reasons that made this a miserable time in his life. He had a ferocious long-distance argument on the telephone with Pauline Pfeiffer about their son Gregory, after which she died suddenly the following day and his youngest son Gregory blamed him for her death. His mother also died, though he had not seen her for 21 years, a grandson died and Charles Scribner (the II) head of his publishers Scribner's also died. Hemingway's blood pressure and weight were still very high, and as usual he slept very badly, if at all. Adriana Ivancich and her mother Dora had arrived two months after his new novel was published and were staying in the Finca's guest quarters. Adriana's brother Gianfranco was also holed up at the Finca – year earlier, Gianfranco had landed a job with a Havana shipping company while the Hemingways were in Europe and had been given free run of the Finca, and had not moved on. Hemingway was still plagued by his infatuation with Adriana, but not only did she not reciprocate his feelings but she fell for a good-looking Cuban. As for his latest novel, although Hemingway had asked for it not to published in Italy for a few years to forestall any possible scandal, Venice still got to hear about it and there was a shocked reaction. Adriana was easily identified as novel's 'Venetian noblewoman' [1] and for the sake of appearances Dora eventually decided she and her daughter should move out of the Finca and into a Havana hotel. To make it worse for Hemingway, Adriana was unimpressed with his novel and declared that it was 'unbelievable' that a young Venetian woman from a sheltered background would jump into bed with an older man – it would simply not happen. As usual, Welsh bore the

---

1   Though a friend of Adriana's claimed she had been the model.

brunt of Hemingway's anger and misery. At one point he threw his glass of wine over her in front of his guests. On another occasion when Welsh had offered to help Gianfranco by typing out a US visa application, Hemingway walked into the room and seeing them together, for no apparent reason became furious and threw the typewriter on the floor. Yet again Welsh simply rolled with the punches.

. . .

Hemingway insisted that Adriana was 'a muse' and that her presence helped him write, and while she and her mother were still staying at the Finca – and in the wake of the dismayed reaction to his novel – he began writing The Old Man And The Sea. He resurrected the story from one of his Esquire features that had appeared in April 1936. This in turn was based on a tale Carlos Gutiérrez, his first mate on the Pilar at the time, had told him. The new work is often referred to as a novel, but at just 27,000 words it is more a novella. Under a deal struck with Life worth $40,000 ($457,243 in 2023), the story was published in full in the magazine's Sept 1, 1952, edition of which all five million copies of sold out. It was also chosen as a Book of The Month for which Hemingway was paid $21,000 ($240,052). And when Scribner's published it a week after it appeared in Life, it had an initial print run of 50,000 copies. Eventually, producer Leland Hayward paid Hemingway $150,000 ($1,714,661) for the film rights and his help as an advisor. [1] The Old Man And The Sea certainly salvaged Hemingway's career as a writer and restored his reputation. Contemporary reviewers hailed it as a 'return to form', but praise was not universal and often rather muted. Fellow novelist William Faulkner, who was never best buddies with Hemingway, began his review with

> *His best. Time may show it to be the best single piece of any of us, I mean his and my contemporaries.*

In the New York Times Orville Prescott declared

> *The Old Man And The Sea is a short novel, only 27,000 words. It is much simpler and enormously better than Mr Hemingway's last book, Across The River And Into the Trees . . . Within the sharp restrictions imposed by the very nature of his story Mr Hemingway has written with sure skill. Here is the master technician once more at the top of his form, doing superbly what he can do better than*

---

1 It should be pointed out that although Hemingway was able to mitigate how much tax he paid because he lived outside the US, a great deal of the money went to the US Inland Revenue Service.

anyone else.

Yet in the Partisan Review Delmore Schwartz noted, perhaps a little tactlessly, that

> *The ovation which greeted Hemingway's new novel was mostly very nice. For it was mostly a desire to continue to admire a great writer. Yet there was a note of insistence in the praise and a note of relief, the relief because his previous book [Across The River And Into The Trees] was extremely bad in an ominous way, the insistence, I think, because this new work is not so much good in itself as a virtuoso performance which reminds one of Hemingway at his best.*

Writing in the Virginia Quarterly Review John Aldridge had some good words to say about the story before admitting

> *But one must take care not to push these generosities too far, if only because they spill over so easily into that excess of blind charity we all tend to feel for Hemingway each time he pulls out of another slump and attains to the heroism of simply writing well once again.*

He suggested the novella should be recognised

> *for the degree of its success in meeting the standards set down by his own best previous achievement as an artist. I have these standards in mind when I say that The Old Man and the Sea seems to me a work of distinctly minor Hemingway fiction.*

In sum Aldridge remained unconvinced and wrote

> *In the best of the early Hemingway one always felt that the prose had been forced out under great pressure through a tight screen of opposing psychic tensions . . . now the prose [in The Old Man And The Sea] . . . has a fabricated quality, as if it had been shipped into the book by some manufacturer of standardized Hemingway parts.*

Several decades on, critics and reviewers were even less kind. In the Atlantic Monthly in October 1983 James Atlas simply recorded that

> *The end of Hemingway's career was a sad business. The last novels*

were self-parodies, none more so than The Old Man And The Sea. The internal monologues of Hemingway's crusty fisherman are unwittingly comical ('My head is not that clear. But I think the great Di Maggio would be proud of me today'); and the message, that fish are 'more noble and more able' than men, is fine if you're a seventh grader.

In his biography of Hemingway 12 years later, Kenneth S. Lynn was almost brutal, though arguably his summing up The Old Man And The Sea is a fair one:

Today, there is only one question worth asking about The Old Man. How could a book that lapses repeatedly into lachrymose sentimentality and is relentlessly pseudo-biblical, that mixes cute talk about baseball ('I fear both the Tigers of Detroit and the Indians of Cleveland') with crucifixion symbolism of the most appalling crudity ('he slept face down on the newspapers with his arms out straight and the palms of his hands up') have evoked such a storm of applause from highbrows and middle-brows alike – and in such overwhelming numbers?

Fellow biographer, James Mellow, was a little kinder, but was also not as impressed by the novella as Hemingway hoped readers would be. He writes

Critics read [the sharks] as tropes for critics. In a letter to Edmund Wilson, Hemingway insisted on setting the record straight: 'You know I was thinking about actual sharks when I wrote the book and had nothing to do with the theory that they represented critics. I don't know who thought that up.' But Hemingway, with a new book in process [the anticipated sea war element of his 'big book'] and still smarting over the critical reception of Across The River, was promulgating his own metaphor of the artist at bay. In a letter to Harvey Breit, he spoke of the lobo wolf: 'He is hunted by everyone. Everyone is against him and he is on his own as an artist is.' There was no doubt that The Old Man And The Sea was a surrogate fable of Hemingway's own life as a writer who had dared to venture too far from the shore on the wide blue Gulf Stream, which had become Hemingway's major metaphor for the mysterious force of life . . . Hemingway, too, was a former champion trying for a comeback, as

Santiago was formerly El Campeon, not only a great fisherman, but rather awkwardly – it is one of the sentimental flaws of the novel – the champion arm wrestler of the island. The too easy identification of Santiago with Hemingway himself unavoidably taints the narrative with a kind of self-pity.

For years, not least because of Hemingway's simple and uncomplicated prose, The Old Man And The Sea was a staple in high school and college English literature syllabuses, and as such became part of the fabric of many a man and woman's early years in the 1960s, 1970s and 1980s. Many might thus remember the story fondly, although how much it would delight their rather more mature minds in later life is another matter. Hemingway's novella not only evoked a storm of applause (and some relief that 'Papa' was not yet passed it), but won him the Pulitzer Prize that had been denied him in 1940. It is also believed to have smoothed the path to being awarded the Nobel Prize in 1954. Also smoothing that path, some suggest, were the two plane crashes Hemingway had survived earlier that year at the conclusion of his African safari, which might also have decided the Nobel committee that perhaps the writer should be awarded the Prize before death carried him off.

1954-1961 – Terminal decline and suicide

Yet, details, the perjuries of personal recollection, the innocent or dishonest lies of friends, may not really constitute the life. If one knew everything there was to know about a writer's at some phase of his or her career (the moments say of Hemingway's brooding observations on life and writing and the Gulf Stream), would one know everything that might be known about the writing, its banal origins, its hidden motivations? Or, as in a photograph, is the angle of the light, etched in certainty, simply a matter of the moment and misleading?

**James R Mellow, Hemingway:
A Life Without Consequences.**

I met Ernest Hemingway at Sun Valley last week, and was taken totally by surprise. I had not been prepared by talk, photos, or interviews for a) that charm, and b) that beauty.

**Leonard Bernstein in a letter
to Martha Gellhorn, Jan 7, 1959.**

Mary was Hemingway's wife during the years of his greatest fame and most radical deterioration, of the Nobel Prize as well as the Mayo Clinic. She felt she had been an entity, and feared she would become an appendage. At the age of 36, she gave up her independence and professional career, adopted his sporting passions, entertained his coarse cronies, matched his numerous accidents with her own falls and fractures, and even tolerated his infatuation with two teenage girls, the 'vestal virgin' Adriana Ivancich and the flirtatious Valerie Danby-Smith.

Jeffrey Meyers, Hemingway: A Biography.

It is not likely that Hemingway was a brave man who sought danger for the sake of the sensations it provided him. What is more likely the truth of his own odyssey is that he struggled with his cowardice and against a secret lust to suicide all his life, that his inner landscape was a nightmare, and he spent his nights wrestling with the gods. It may even be that the final judgment on his work may come to the notion that what he failed to do was tragic, but what he accomplished was heroic, for it is possible that he carried a weight of anxiety with him which would have suffocated any man smaller than himself.

Norman Mailer, interview with Christopher Dorman-O'Gowan, quoted by James Michener, Iberia, 1968.

AFTER the Pulitzer Prize board accepted the jurors' recommendation to award the prize to Hemingway for For Whom The Bell Tolls in 1941, one influential board member insisted that the Pulitzer Prize could not and should not be associated with a novel with such profane and sexual content. The board decided not to award the prize Hemingway after all (though it did not award it to another author, either).[i] Twelve years later though, in 1953, he did succeed and was awarded the Pulitzer Prize for The Old Man And The Sea.

That same year Hemingway began planning his second safari in East Africa. When Look magazine heard about it, it struck a deal with Hemingway and contracted to pay him $10,000 ($114,310 in 2023) for a 3,500-word feature on the safari and another $15,000 ($143,571) for a series of pictures to be taken by their staff photographer Earl Theisen, at total of $25,000 ($239,285). Yet again those figures also counsel the caution necessary when we read a biography: according to Kenneth Lynn, Hemingway was to be paid double that sum: $25,000 for the feature and another $25,000 for posing for Theisen's pictures. So which is it? Who knows, although, frankly, it doesn't actually matter, but it will have boosted Hemingway's morale and ego a fair degree. [1]

He and Mary Welsh set off for Europe in June and planned to visit Paris and then Spain before carrying on to Kenya. It was the first time Hemingway was back in Spain since Franco's Nationalists defeated the Republicans, and he was apprehensive as to how he would be received. Their visit took in Valencia and Madrid as well as that July's Pamplona festival. As in 1925, Hemingway surrounded himself with friends for his Pamplona visit, but his return – another trip down memory lane – was not a great success. For one thing the town was now overrun with visitors, and he and Welsh could not find accommodation less then 25 miles away. In Pamplona Hemingway was reunited with Juanito Quintana, who had appeared as the hotel owner Juanito Montoya in The Sun Also Rises; yet again there are several versions of just how warm their friendship was. In The Sun Also Rises Jake Barnes – that is Hemingway – is acknowledged by Montoya – that is Quintana – as a man who shares the true *afficon* for bullfighting and he treats Barnes as an insider (the role Hemingway always liked to play), although he disapproves when the Barnes group seem to lead the young matador Pedro Romero astray. This is an exceptionally rosy account of Quintana's feelings according to Jeffrey Herlihy-Mera, of the University of Puerto Rico. Writing in the Hemingway Review Spring 2012 edition, he says that Quintana had mixed memories of Hemingway and his friends

> *[Quintana] said they were 'big drunks' who misbehaved and were so disrespectful that he once had an employee serve some of the Hemingway crew lobster water as if it were consommé. When asked if Ernest's behavior made him angry, the ever-polite Quintana replied 'close to it' and went on, 'when he was too drunk he would disturb the other guests and I couldn't put up with that'.*

. . .

At the beginning of August, Hemingway and Welsh finally set off for East Africa to embark on their safari. Once in Kenya, they linked up with Mayito Menocal, a friend from Cuba (whose father had been president for eight years), Life's photographer Earl Theisen and white hunter Philip Percival who had organised Hemingway's safari in 1934. (Jeffrey Meyers writes that the Kenyan government, dealing with the Mau-Mau

---

1   The point is that one set of figures is wrong (or even both are): so what else might a biographer have 'got wrong'?

insurgency which was scaring off tourists, hoped that the publicity generated by Hemingway's visit would persuade potential visitors that there was little danger and had persuaded Percival, by then 67, to come out of retirement for the visit.)

Like Hemingway's return to Pamplona after 28 years, his return to East Africa also fell a little flat. His alcoholism and ageing eyesight meant his shooting was often poor. In 1934 it had been Charlie Thompson, his Key West friend, who had outshot him and to Hemingway's immense irritation had bagged more trophies. Now it was Mayito Menocal who was besting Hemingway, and he did not like it. The incessant boozing certainly did not help: according to Kenya game warden Denis Zaphiro, who was assisting Philip Percival, Hemingway was drinking all the time. Quoted by Meyers, Zaphiro said

> *[Hemingway's] drinking would have killed a less tough man. Two or three bottles of hard liquor a day. Wines etc with meals. Gin a favourite drink. I suppose he was drunk the whole time but seldom showed it. Just became merrier, more loveable, more bull-shitty. Without a drink he was morose silent and depressed.*

Hemingway was once so drunk that he fell out of a fast-moving Land Rover driving through the bush. When at one point he began to apologise to Percival for his poor marksmanship, Percival was having none of it and cut him off, telling him simply 'Oh, Ernest, don't give me that nonsense, the whole thing has been a disgrace'.

Hemingway also became obsessed with the local Kenyan Maasai culture and began to ape the Maasai. While Welsh was away from the camp on a short pre-Christmas break in Nairobi, he shaved his head, dyed his clothes the colour of theirs and took up with a local young woman to whom he insisted he was now engaged. He claims he also had sex with her, but this is doubtful. [1] Welsh behaved stoically throughout as though she were unconcerned, and curiously, biographers report, Hemingway's odd behaviour acted as a stimulus to their sex life. Often quoted by biographers is a passage Hemingway added to the diary she kept – the former journalist in her always had one eye on eventually publishing a book on her life with Hemingway, which she finally did in 1976, calling it How It Was. In the diary he makes direct reference to their sex life, one night indulging in role reversal in bed. He wrote that

> *Mary had always wanted to be a boy and thinks as a boy without ever losing any femininity . . . she loves me to be her girls [sic],*

---

1   A good case might be made that this 'fling' was another example of outlandish behaviour while in the manic phase of a bi-polar cycle.

which I love to be, not being absolutely stupid . . . I loved feeling the embrace of Mary which came to me as something quite new and outside all tribal law.

. . .

More seriously, once the safari proper had ended, Hemingway was almost killed, although his drinking cannot be blamed. On his 1934 safari, he had contracted amoebic dysentery and had to be airlifted to Nairobi for emergency treatment. Nineteen years later, he was treating Welsh to several plane trips to see the country from the air and he almost died in the second of two crashes.

The first crash occurred on January 24, 1954, when their pilot, Roy Marsh, flew low over the Murchison Falls in Uganda along the Victoria Nile to allow his customers a better view. At one point he flew even lower to avoid a flock of birds, and his plane clipped a telegraph wire. Marsh managed to crash-land in the bush and no one was badly hurt, though Welsh was later found to have broken two ribs and Hemingway's dislocated shoulder was thought to have been caused in that first crash. However, the plane's rudder and, crucially, its radio antenna were disabled, and with radio communication out of service, the pilot could not call for help. To avoid crocodiles in the river, Hemingway, Welsh and the pilot took to higher ground for the night. When a BOAC airliner spotted the plane's wreckage but saw no sign of life and a search plane that was alerted could also spot no one, Hemingway was presumed dead; his 'death' made the headlines around the world. The following day the three were rescued by a passing river launch [1] and taken to a town on the east bank of Lake Victoria; there, a second pilot, T.R. Cartwright, was waiting to fly them on to Entebbe. However, the 'runway' they were to use was simply a stretch of very rutted baked earth, and the plane crashed on take-off, bursting into flames. Welsh, Marsh and Cartwright escaped through one of the plane's small windows, but Hemingway was trapped, too large to squeeze through the window, and the port door was jammed shut. With flames already engulfing the inside of the plane, he finally managed to force the door open by using his head as a battering ram. He and Welsh were driven inland to Butiaba where Hemingway received only perfunctory medical help – the doctor who attended simply bandaged his head and cleaned up superficial cuts, but examined him no further. The following day they were driven to Entebbe where Hemingway agreed to give a press conference – the world by

---

1   The launch's captain is reported to have charged Hemingway through the nose for taking his party back to safety.

now reassured that the famous writer had not died after all – and he played up to his image as the 'indestructible Papa Hemingway'. [ii] The media reported that he was 'in high spirits', but he was, in fact, in great pain, seeing double and intermittently deaf. After three days resting in a Nairobi hotel bed – and already drinking again – he was up and about, though he ears were still ringing and he was still seeing double.

Several weeks later he went on a fishing trip with his son Patrick and Philip Percival and others, but he was still in considerable pain and often irascible, so much, in fact, that after Hemingway shouted at Patrick's wife and made her cry, Patrick upped and left the party. To compound his already serious injuries, when Hemingway insisted on helping when a bush fire broke out, he fell into the flames and suffered second and third-degree burns. It wasn't until he and Welsh were back in Europe that, in Venice, he was given a proper and methodical examination, and the full extent of his injuries were established. Only then did he receive proper treatment. His injuries included two cracked discs in his spine, ruptures to his liver, spleen and a kidney and dislocations to his shoulder and right arm. His skull had broken open, and pressure on a nerve was paralysing his sphincter muscle (which meant he was obliged to defecate standing up). He had also suffered his fourth severe concussion in ten years. He spent a month in bed in Venice recuperating, and a friend who visited him was shocked by his appearance: his hair was now white and Hemingway looked 70 years old. He was still just 55.

. . .

By the spring of 1954, the years of heavy drinking, the several concussions Hemingway had suffered and the latest round of injuries were taking a severe toll. His terminal decline, mental as well as physical, over the following seven years was now underway. In addition to medication for his high blood pressure and insomnia, he was taking several other drugs and, crucially, it was not clear how they interacted. Depression was a known side-effect for several of them, and he certainly should not have been mixing his medication with alcohol. While he was being treated for his depression in Minnesota months before his death in 1961, his doctors also diagnosed haemochromatosis, a hereditary disease [iii] which stops the body from ridding itself of iron and from which he would have been suffering all his life. The slow but steady accumulation of iron causes damage to the heart and liver, as well as swelling of the arms, legs and feet and erectile dysfunction: these were all conditions from which Hemingway had suffered for many years. Mentally, he became ever more irascible and his mood fluctuated wildly, and, as was now usual, Welsh bore the brunt of his unpredictable and often manic behaviour.

1954-1961 – Terminal decline and suicide

In October, Hemingway was awarded his Nobel Prize for Literature. That he was finally honoured suggested to some biographers that his near-death in East Africa had persuaded the Nobel Committee that Hemingway might not be long for this world. He had the same ambivalent attitude to literary prizes as he did to the Book Of The Month Club: he always purported to disdain the Nobel Prize and other such baubles, but this was simply another pose. Years earlier, in a letter to Charles Scribner II, he was already hinting that he might be due to win it: in November 1941, Hemingway was awarded the gold medal of the 'Limited Editions Club' for his then new novel For Whom The Bell Tolls. He told Scribner's he would be unable to attend the award ceremony in New York and asked them to send a stenographer to record the presentation speech fellow writer Sinclair Lewis would be making. But someone at Scribner's slipped up, no stenographer attended and Hemingway was furious. In his letter to Charles Scribner expressing his anger – he had already hauled Max Perkins over the coals a few days earlier – he claimed Lewis' speech might have been printed as a pamphlet and could have secured him the Nobel Prize for Literature. His logic in making his claim is not clear, but what is clear is that even then he considered himself to be great writer who should be honoured by the Nobel committee. Eight years later [1] and despite his ostensible indifference, he was very put out when William Faulkner won the Nobel Prize. In a letter to a friend, the New York Books Review editor Harvey Breit, he wrote

> *You see what happens with Bill Faulkner is that as long as I am alive he has to drink to feel good about having the Nobel Prize. He does not realise that I have no respect for that institution and was truly happy for him when he got it.*

To which claim Evelyn Waugh's Mr Salter might again have responded 'Up to a point, Lord Copper'.

. . .

Since Hemingway had returned to Cuba from Europe in 1945 until the last year of his life, it became his habit to work on one manuscript and then carry on with, or even start, another. Writing Across The River And Into The Trees had interrupted his work on the 'big book' about World War II, and in the wake of Across The River's publication, he had written and published The Old Man And The Sea before returning to writing his 'big

---

1 Because of some Nobel Prize constitutional technicality, Faulkner was awarded the prize in 1949, but did not receive it until the following year.

book'. By then this had become just the 'sea' element of his planned trilogy as the 'air' and 'land' war volumes had both gone by the board. At some point between returning from Europe in 1945 and the mid-1950, he had also started to write what became The Garden Of Eden. Hemingway continued working on it intermittently before – no one knows why – abandoning it and depositing the manuscript at his bank in Havana. In 1956, he also began writing a 'semi-fictitious' account – Hemingway's own phrase – based on his second African safari, a book he apparently hoped would be something between a novel and reportage. This became True At First Light and was published in 1999 to mark the centenary of Hemingway's birth. Like almost all of the posthumously published work the original 200,000-word manuscript had to be extensively cut by more than half and edited before it was deemed to be in any commercially useful shape.

After he won his Nobel Prize, the peace and quiet Hemingway had enjoyed – and valued – at the Finca Vigia became increasingly elusive. He now became one of Havana's tourist sights, and coachloads of sightseers pitched up outside the Finca's gates to catch a glimpse of the legendary 'Papa' Hemingway. Quite apart from the tourist hoi polloi, the number of visiting friends – some old, many new, some invited, others not – grew. It seemed dropping in on Nobel Prize winner and famous writer Ernest Hemingway had become part of the social round. Hemingway was both irritated and pleased, but he made them all welcome. Then, in the summer of 1955, preliminary work began on filming The Old Man And The Sea, and to honour his contract with producer Leland Hayward to 'advise' with the script and shooting, Hemingway had to put aside his writing and he spent a great deal of time with the production team. He soon found it frustrating. For one thing he had disagreements with Hayward's screenwriter Peter Viertel, who wanted to alter one or two aspects of the story, and Hemingway was having none of it. Leland also began location shooting in Cuba, and Hemingway's 'assistance' was required for that. Once the film people had departed for the year, he returned to his African 'novel', but it was not to be for long: at the end of 1955 and early 1956 he was laid up in bed for three months with nephritis (once known as Bright's disease) and hepatitis. Once he had recovered, Hayward and his film people were already back in Havana and wanted his help filming the fishing sequences. All-in-all Hemingway, who had previously avoided being involved with the filming of any of his previous work, found the experience thoroughly dispiriting. Michael Reynolds records that Hemingway was

> *determined to have real sharks attacking and actual marlin in an authentic ocean. That was the Hollywood promise written down*

> *on paper; but as he was to learn, words written on the West Coast somehow had different meanings from standard English. Moreover, anything scheduled, promised or planned meant absolutely nothing in the movie business.*

It got no better:

> *Trying to coordinate the weather, film crew, blood bait and sharks was proving almost impossible. When the camera crew were ready, the weather was too rough to film. When twenty gallons of slaughterhouse blood and four tubs of fish heads were standing by, the film crew was somewhere else. One part or other never got to the right place on time. Days were wasted. Money was spent and spent again. If not the sharks, then the marlin would not cooperate – too small, too far away, not jumping enough. When not wasting time at the dock, they wasted time at conferences or waiting for Spencer Tracy to show up.*

Tracy was an alcoholic although he was then on the wagon; but when he did finally arrive in Havana, he started drinking again. Hemingway also thought that Tracy was miscast as 'the old man' because he looked too fat and healthy for the unlucky but stoic fisherman who had spent three days and nights at sea with no sleep whatsoever. Finally, unable to get the footage of marlin and sharks needed of the Cuban coast, Hayward, Hemingway and the film crew took off to Peru for just over a month to try their luck there. Yet their luck was out: the marlin caught were too small for the 'part' they were to play. Hayward eventually settled for using a large plastic model to represent the marlin the old man catches and straps to the side of his skiff where it is was then eaten by sharks. A plastic marlin was certainly not what Hemingway had in mind. He was not pleased.

...

By the summer of 1956, almost 30 months after the plane crashes, Hemingway's recovery was still incomplete and his health was suffering in new ways. In addition to his high blood pressure and excess weight, his cholesterol count became excessive, and both he and Mary Welsh were found to be clinically anaemic. As much to get away from the steady stream of 'celebrities' who kept dropping in as for their health, they decided to take another break in Europe and Africa, and set sail at the beginning of September. The conflict between Israel and Egypt (which had blocked the Suez Canal by sinking more than 40 vessels) put paid to any notions of visiting East Africa, but they were able to tour bullfights in Spain; however in Madrid Hemingway fell ill again and was laid up in bed for several weeks. Eventually returning home and stopping off in Paris in November, Hemingway is said to have been reminded by the Ritz Hotel of two small boxes he had supposedly stored in the hotel basement at the end of the 1920s.

. . .

The discovery of these small boxes was certainly serendipitous and some sceptics prefer to refer to it as their 'discovery'. The generally accepted account, first given by Leonard Lyons on December 11, 1957, in his gossip column in the New York Post, is that they contained old notebooks, newspaper clippings and manuscripts. In 1964 in the New York Times Book Review, Mary Welsh wrote that the

> *two small, fabric-covered, rectangular boxes, both opening at the seams . . . [contained] blue-and-yellow-covered pencilled notebooks and sheaves of typed papers, ancient newspaper cuttings, bad watercolors done by old friends, a few cracked and faded books, some musty sweat shirts and withered sandals. Ernest had not seen the stuff since 1927, when he packed it and left it at the hotel before going to Key West.*

Such an detailed description of the boxes and their contents might seem to be copper-bottomed proof of the veracity of the discovery; yet notably Mary Welsh's source of the details was Hemingway himself. The same was true of Lyons: he had been informed of the contents by Hemingway when he had lunch with him at the Finca and he based his account solely on what he was told.

Hemingway later wrote that finding the two boxes led him to reminisce about his years in Paris and had prompted him to write his memoir. Yet one sceptic, academic Jacqueline Tavernier-Courbin, then of the University of Ottowa, suggested that, on balance, it is more than possible the supposed discovery was just another Hemingway myth. Writing in the Autumn (Fall) 1980 edition of the journal College Literature and expanding her claim 11 years later in a full-length book, Ernest Hemingway's Moveable Feast: The Making Of A Myth, Tavernier-Courbin outlines the arguments for and against her scepticism. She attempts to demonstrate – and perhaps succeeds – that the 'discovery' was more probably what we might today call a public relations exercise. Tavernier-Courbin suggests revelation of the 'discovery' was a convoluted ruse by Hemingway to get himself off a hook: he had previously sniffed that writers who resorted to composing their memoirs were tacitly admitting they were at the end of their career and had more or less thrown in the towel. 'Finding' the two boxes and claiming they had caused him to reminisce might go some way of acquitting him of that charge. To substantiate her claim, Tavernier-Courbin describes several oddities and inconsistencies in the accounts provided by Lyons and Welsh. For example, she writes, the boxes were said to have been stored at the Ritz in 1927 when Hemingway travelled to Key West for the first time. In fact, he didn't do so until 1928. One of the boxes was said to have contained the original manuscript for A Farewell To Arms – but it could not have done: Hemingway had later presented that manuscript to his new wife's generous uncle, Gus Pfeiffer, as a gift. Storing the items would not in itself have been unusual: two suitcases had been stored at another hotel at about the same time. But the deposit of those two suitcases was referred to in several letters written by Hemingway in the late 1920s; no mention of the Ritz Hotel boxes was made at all until 30 years later in Lyons' column in 1957. One also wonders why Hemingway was not told of the boxes when he was based at the Ritz Hotel in the last few months of 1944 and the beginning of 1945. According to Welsh the Ritz had first asked Hemingway to remove the boxes in 1936, though yet again she could only have been told this by Hemingway; thus it can have no bearing either way on whether the story of the boxes is true. Such inconsistencies are, though, circumstantial and might well simply be down to misunderstandings and faulty accounts by Lyons and Welsh.

In fact, whether or not two small boxes were found and the discovery was the impetus for writing the memoir might be neither here nor there: Reynolds suggests that by late 1956 – many months before the apparent discovery – Hemingway had already begun musing on the past and, in letters to friends, seemed to be rehearsing various anecdotes. Certainly, from mid-1957 until his death he was writing and re-writing sketches – in tandem with other projects – for what became A Moveable Feast.[1] At one point he declared the memoir completed – Reynolds writes that Hemingway claimed the first draft was written in six months – and he delivered the manuscript to Scribner's; then he changed his mind and delayed publication. In a letter to Charles Scribner III the year before he died, he explained he wanted to re-write parts of his memoir and that he was also afraid of suits for libel.[iv] A Moveable Feast was eventually published in 1964 after Mary Welsh had edited it. She insisted she had not changed a word of what Hemingway

---

1   The title was not chosen by Hemingway.

had written, but had merely re-arranged some of the chapters and corrected grammar and spelling. That is not wholly true: when her edited version was compared to various drafts and manuscripts in the Boston JFK Library, it became obvious that Welsh had suppressed some parts of what Hemingway had initially submitted to Scribner's, including deleting flattering references to Hadley Richardson. Forty-five years later, in 2009, a new edition of the memoir, edited by Hemingway's grandson Sean, was published in which parts of the original manuscript were reinstated and the chapters were again re-arranged. The first edition was a best-seller – a month before it was published, Life magazine printed eleven of its twenty sketches, and Scribner's gave the book an initial print run of 85,000 copies. It featured on the US best-seller list for eight months and held the top spot for five of those months. The critics also liked it, and for many A Moveable Feast contained the best writing Hemingway had produced in years. Some did note, and did not like, what has been described as the settling of scores – Gertrude Stein, Scott Fitzgerald and Ford Madox Ford who had all promoted Hemingway in his early, unknown years were made to look either foolish or otherwise flawed. Scott Fitzgerald especially is made to look very silly. Though not named, Pauline Pfeiffer, John Dos Passos and Gerald and Sara Murphy are condemned as being responsible for the break-up of his marriage to Richardson: biographers repeatedly note that Hemingway always managed to shift the blame for his misdeeds on to others. Yet despite those sour observations the critics gave Hemingway a pass, perhaps relieved that the writing was not as bad as it had become over the last fifteen years of his life. Slightly more sceptical were several British critics: in the London Magazine Julian McLaren-Ross felt that Hemingway's adoring portrayal of Hadley Richardson seemed to be the model for all the 'far too admiring and acquiescent' women in his fiction and notes – tartly but honestly – that

> *A lot of nostalgic nonsense is often written about poverty and hunger by successful authors who no longer have to experience them.* [v]

In the journal Encounter the Cambridge academic Tony Tanner suggested that

> *The book is written with a good deal of arrogance: every episode is turned to leave Hemingway looking tougher, more talented, more honest, more dignified than anyone else.*

The verdict of Frank Kermode, another Cambridge academic, who was writing in the New York Review of Books is notable. He seemed to welcome the memoir – he wrote

1954-1961 – Terminal decline and suicide

in some ways, Hemingway's best book since the 1920s

– but he could also be understood tacitly to be admitting that a great deal of the work Hemingway produced since A Farewell To Arms appeared in 1929 more than 30 years earlier was really not up to snuff. [1] Referring to the blatant score-settling, Kermode also notes sardonically that Hemingway's famous built-in 'shit detector'

can purge not only your prose but your acquaintances.

Something of a mystery and still so far unexplained is the last line in Hemingway's preface that

If the reader prefers, this book can be regarded as fiction

and although he adds

but there is always the chance that such a book of fiction may throw some light on what has been written as fact

it is not at all clear how. The obvious, rather puzzling, question is: exactly why might a reader prefer the book to be regarded as fiction? Although A Moveable Feast did not appear until three years after Hemingway's death, he cannot have known its publication would be delayed when he wrote his preface, and presumably he expected it to appear in his lifetime. If he had concerns about possible libel suits, he would, or should, have known that these were unfounded: those men and women he named in his memoir who might have objected to what he wrote and sued for libel were long dead. Those who were not yet dead were not named. Some critics were charmed by Hemingway's descriptions of his 'we was poor, but we was happy' line about domestic bliss with Hadley, their toddler 'Bumby' and F. Puss their cat; others perhaps agreed more with McLaren-Ross' implication that it was all a little sentimentally unreal. In that respect it might well be regarded as fiction; and the dialogue from a writer whose gift for dialogue had long been championed is curiously stilted, artificial and, above all, cloying.

. . .

---

1   If this was the essence of what Kermode was saying, he was echoing Matthew Bruccoli's view, and as neither man will have had any reason gratuitously to belittle Hemingway's work, we are obliged to accept them at their word. It would be interesting to hear what other Hemingway champions, past and present – including the many contributors to the still-thriving Hemingway Review – make of that summing up of Hemingway's achievements since 1929.

Despite the break in Europe, Hemingway's health continued to decline. After substantially cutting back on his drinking, restricting himself to just two glass of wine a day and for a year drinking very little hard liquor, his consumption gradually increased again. Reynolds writes

> To visitors he claimed he was drinking only light wines and one or two whiskeys, but the numbers [recorded in the Finca 'liquor' bills as part of information submitted to the IRS] say that his need for alcohol was regaining control of his life. Combined with his continued daily intake of tranquillizers, antidepressants, heart medicine, testosterone steroids and large does of vitamins, Hemingway's drinking, which was forbidden with several of the drugs, contributed to his steadily deteriorating health.

Also worrying was the political situation in Cuba which throughout 1957 and 1958 was worsening. A few years earlier, Hemingway had put himself at risk from the authorities bolstering the rule of dictator Fulgencio Batista by seeming to support a group of revolutionaries who were training in Cuba to start an uprising in the Dominican Republic. He had written a small cheque as a donation for the revolutionaries and his Cuban doctor was astonished that Hemingway had been stupid enough to sign a cheque rather than give them cash.[1] He advised him to take off to the Rockies for the rest of the year to stay out of potential harm's way. Once back at the Finca, Hemingway wisely did mind his own business, but the violence was increasing. The bodies of men and women who had been tortured and killed by Batista's men were being found everywhere, including near the Finca. At one point, according to Reynolds, Hemingway, Welsh and his first mate Gregorio Fuentes took the Pilar out to sea

> where the men tore open bunks to take out 'heavy rifles, sawed-off shot guns, hand grenades and canisters and belts of ammunition for automatic rifles' and threw the arsenal overboard. Had the government discovered the cache [perhaps left over from the 'sub-hunting' days], Hemingway would have been hard-pressed to explain their presence.

With an eye to the future and the worsening situation in Cuba, Hemingway asked friends

---

1   We all make mistakes, but this piece of foolishness is rather at odds with what might be expected of the wise and canny cove Hemingway believed himself to be.

in Ketchum, Idaho, to rent him a house for the winter. Reynolds adds

> *He may have been a great friend of the Cuban people, but in the dark of night he was just another rich American exploiting the Cuban poor.*

For the last few months of 1957 and the first seven of 1958, Hemingway worked steadily on his memoir and The Garden Of Eden (which was thus growing ever longer). He returned to the Finca in the spring of 1958 after expressing his interest in buying the house in Ketchum which became his last home. The years at the Finca, Hemingway's home for the past 20 years, were coming to a close. He and Welsh spent the last few months of 1958 and the first of 1959 in Ketchum, with Hemingway working on one of his several manuscripts. At the end of December 1958, Castro's revolution succeeded and Batista fled the island. Concerned by the situation in Cuba, Hemingway bought the house in Ketchum for cash. In March 1959, he and Welsh set off for another tour of the bullfighting in Spain. When Charles Scribner heard of their plans, he suggested to Hemingway that Scribner's could publish a revised and updated edition of Death In The Afternoon with an addendum based on his most recent round of watching bullfights. Scribner also informed him the house would like to reissue a collection of his short stories for students. He asked Hemingway to submit a list of stories he might like to see included, write a preface for the new volume and a brief introduction to each featured story. When it became known that the tour of bullfights would also take in a series of one-to-one (*mano a mano*) encounters between matadors Luis Miguel Dominguin and his brother-in-law Antonio Ordonez, Life magazine's Madrid correspondent contracted Hemingway to write a 10,000-word feature. [1]

. . .

In Spain, the Hemingways were the guests of one Nathan 'Bill' Davis at his estate, La Consula in the hills outside Malaga. Davis was a very wealthy American with business interests in the US and Spain and who, according to some biographers, 'collected celebrities' – Noel Coward, Lauren Bacall, Vivien Leigh and Ava Gardner were among his many visitors. In Hemingway's case it might be unfair to suggest he, too, was being 'collected': Davis had known Hemingway at least since 1942 (and possibly as early as 1930) as a letter from Hemingway shows. Davis' wealthy family originated in Pennsyl-

---

1   This is the piece which grew remorselessly from the initially agreed word count to 30,000 words and then to 120,000 words as Hemingway began to lose control.

vania, and novelist Booth Tarkington is said to have based the wealthy Indiana family in his novel The Magnificent Ambersons on the family of Davis' mother.

Hemingway and Welsh arrived in May before the corrida season got underway, and Hemingway began writing the preface to the new collection of short stories he had promised Scribner.[1] In this he adopted an unusual persona, that of a lecturer addressing a class of students, and his preface does read as though he were giving a lecture. But this conceit does not come off at all, and when he completed his preface and showed it to Welsh, she was unimpressed. The attempted humour fell flat, she told him, it sounded condescending and much of it made little sense. When Hemingway sent the preface to Charles Scribner, the publisher was equally underwhelmed, but he had to more tactful than Welsh. Michael Reynolds records that Scribner did his diplomatic best

> *to draft his response to Ernest's preface which was clearly inappropriate for almost any audience. He agreed with Ernest's list of stories to be included, but wanted to do some judicious editing of the preface ... After digesting Scribner's response and weighing it in the same basket with Mary's less than enthusiastic critique, Ernest sent Scribner a brusque telegram [instructing him] to stop not only the preface but the entire short story project ... It was the first time that anyone at Scribner's had told him a piece of his writing was unpublishable.*

The standard of this preface was another indication that of Hemingway's continuing mental and physical decline. When the bullfight season got underway at the beginning of June, the non-stop travelling across Spain from north to south and east to west proved to be exhausting and will not have helped Hemingway's health; and although he kept it up, Welsh grew weary of it all, and she and Bill Davis' wife Annie passed on several bullfights and returned to the peace and comforts of the La Consula estate.

As usual Hemingway surrounded himself with an entourage of acolytes who were – and were expected to be – in almost constant attendance. It would be unfair to call them 'hangers-on' because they were all there at Hemingway's invitation and often at his expense – Hemingway did not just like to have an audience but needed one. Joining the entourage in Pamplona was Valerie Danby-Smith, a 19-year-old Irishwoman who had based herself in Madrid where she was combining nannying duties for friends with attempting to launch her career as a journalist. She had found occasional work as a

---

1   See Appendix, The Art Of The Short Story.

stringer for a Belgian news agency, and when the agency heard that Hemingway was in Madrid, it asked her to get an interview with the 'world-famous' writer. Hemingway almost always gave journalists seeking such a meeting short shrift, but he was taken with Danby-Smith. He did not agree to an interview, but he invited her to be one of his guests at the Pamplona festival due a few weeks later. Danby-Smith says she regarded the invitation as just a throwaway remark and gave it little thought until she was contacted by Juanito Quintana. Quintana had lost his hotel in the Civil War when it was commandeered by Francoists and was acting as Hemingway's agent in Pamplona; he wrote to Danby-Smith that he had reserved a hotel room and corrida tickets for her, and asked her to confirm she would be attending. She did and joined the party. Towards the end of the week in Pamplona, Hemingway asked Danby-Smith to accompany him to other bullfights. When she told him she didn't have the money and had to work, he and Bill Davis persuaded her to join them as their 'secretary' at $250 a month (about $2,603 in 2023). It was something of a sinecure: though Danby-Smith did occasionally take down letters dictated by Hemingway, her main role was simply to be in attendance. Yet Hemingway was again smitten, and much to Mary Welsh's irritation, Danby-Smith gained pride of place, being placed next to Hemingway at dinner and with him in the front seat of the car when travelling to the next bullfight. As had happened in Venice and Cuba when Hemingway believed himself to be in love with Adriana Ivancich, Welsh was again completely cast out and ignored by Hemingway who had eyes only for Danby-Smith. When at the end of the festival he took his entourage for a picnic to the spot on the Irati river north of Pamplona he had taken Hadley more than 30 years earlier, Welsh slipped on a stone in the river and broke a toe in three places. She got no sympathy or attention from Hemingway.

...

Forty-five years after that summer's tour of corridas with Hemingway, Valerie Danby-Smith wrote a memoir, in part chronicling the four months she spent with Hemingway in Spain and six months living at the Finca the following year. It was published as Running With Bulls in 2004 and is something of a curio. After Hemingway's death, Valerie had settled in New York and had a halfway successful career in publishing and magazine journalism before she married Gregory Hemingway and had her family. But she is otherwise unremarkable, and the only reason anyone would read her memoir is what it might tell us about Hemingway we did not already know; and it tells us nothing new. Apart from an overlong and quite detailed chapter on following the bullfights around Spain (which bores readers as Danby-Smith admits the tour began to bore her) and another chapter describing her time later at the Finca as Hemingway's by then bona fide secretary, most of the memoir does not involve Hemingway at all. More to the point, the picture Danby-Smith gives of Hemingway is quite at odds with what his biographers write. Although she says she grew fond of him, she also complains he was possessive of her and that the late-night meals she was obliged to attend as part of his entourage – at which Hemingway repeated the same anecdotes and jokes many times over – became tiresome. She does acknowledge that he lost his temper once or twice in Spain – although never with her – but she makes no mention of his fluctuating moods and the continual decline in his mental and physical health: she gives the impression there was nothing much wrong with him. His biographers and friends tell a very different story. A graphic account of the poor state Hemingway was in which might have been a little more accurate comes from his World War II friend 'Buck' Lanham. He was a guest at the 60th birthday party Welsh had organised for Hemingway at La Consula, and he had flown in from the US to attend. He told Denis Brian, as recorded in The True Gen,

> . . . [Hemingway] was a sick man. The plane crashes had ruptured his liver and ruptured his spleen. And he had very bum kidneys that he was treated for constantly. Of course, he was an absolutely incredible drinker. He could drink twenty-four hours a day. So he had a physical breakdown in all departments. He had lost a great deal of weight and was unhappy with himself. He was cursing his doctor every day, because although he was supposed to be with him the whole time, the doctor was doing a little sightseeing.

The doctor was George Saviers, Hemingway's friend and physician in Ketchum. He and his wife had been asked to join the touring entourage in Pamplona and were also guests at the La Consula birthday party. Lanham continues

> I went into Ernest's room the morning I arrived to see if he was all right, because I'd heard he was ill the night before. And, my God, I looked around his room and there were bottles of urine in every possible place, all labelled and dated, waiting for the doctor to analyse them. Ernest was furious when I came in. He was sitting, reading. He was never a hypochondriac, but now he was a very sick man. He couldn't write anything. Life had lost all meaning, all point for him.

Yet in Danby-Smith's memoir there is no hint at all of this quite obvious decline.

Just before leaving for the US and then for Cuba, Hemingway asked Danby-Smith to come back with him to work as his secretary at the Finca. He told her he relied on her completely and couldn't write without having her around. He even hinted that he might kill himself if she refused.[1] She told him she would think about it.

. . .

Welsh, thoroughly neglected and sidelined, not just in favour of Danby-Smith but by the other celebrity guests, had finally had enough and returned to Cuba a month early. Without consulting her, Hemingway had invited Antonio Ordonez and his wife to stay at the Finca and then at the newly-bought house in Ketchum, and Welsh ostensibly left to prepare the homes to accommodate their guests. Hemingway travelled with her to Paris to see her off and sensing her mood, he presented her with a $4,000 watch; but it did not assuage Welsh. Once back at the Finca, she wrote Hemingway a long letter complaining about how he had treated her and telling him that once their visitors were gone, she would find an apartment for herself in New York and end their marriage. Hemingway responded by telegram that he didn't agree with her decision, and when a few weeks later he was back in Cuba, he presented her with another very expensive gift, a diamond pin. Again she changed her mind about leaving him and decided to stay, yet his treatment of her did not improve. In Idaho, Ordonez and his wife had to return to Spain prematurely, and a little later, out hunting with Hemingway and George Saviers, Welsh slipped on ice and fractured her elbow. On the drive to hospital, according to James Mellow, she was groaning with pain, but was told by Hemingway *'You could keep quiet . . . Soldiers don't do that'*.

Hemingway and Welsh were back in Cuba by mid-January, and because her fractured elbow meant Welsh could no longer type up the Life bullfighting feature Hemingway was writing by hand, he contacted Danby-Smith and repeated his request for her to come over to Cuba to work as his secretary. This time she agreed and flew out from Europe, and according to Danby-Smith's memoir, the three of them – Welsh now apparently less jealous of her and taking Danby-Smith with her on shopping trips to Havana – enjoyed a quiet and peaceful time, with Hemingway writing in the morning while she typed up his work and letters he dictated. Hemingway had always wanted a daughter, but according to Danby-Smith his interest in her was not paternal and he regarded her as a

---

1 An echo of what Hemingway had told Hadley Richardson, Pauline Pfeiffer and Martha Gellhorn in the weeks before he married them.

possible new wife. At one point, she writes, he asked her to marry him, and though she did not take the proposal seriously, there is little reason to doubt Danby-Smith's claim. Six years earlier on the last occasion Hemingway saw Adriana Ivancich, in Paris where she was studying art, he had also suggested, although more obliquely, that he and she might marry. But in other respects Danby-Smith's account is too rosy – Hemingway was going downhill fast, yet Danby-Smith's account has nothing to say about that. She records walks she and Hemingway had enjoyed the evening air and visiting a local bar to sit and chat. Her memoir gives the impression that he was content and at peace. Yet there were increasing and unmistakable signs of his paranoia: later that year, in Idaho and at supper with friends, he noticed the lights were on in his local bank and insisted the FBI were in there going through his records. At the Finca Hemingway could not stop writing ever more of his Life feature; he asked Life to extend his deadline and told Scribner's not to count on the revised version of Death In The Afternoon being ready in time for publication later that year. Finally, in mid-summer and in something close to desperation, he summoned A.E. Hotchner to Cuba to help him cut the Life feature to the new length agreed with the magazine: by then it had reached 120,000 words, but Life were expecting just 30,000. Yet Hemingway then rejected every one of Hotchner's suggested cuts, for reasons that often made no sense to Hotchner. The piece was eventually brought down to just under 70,000 words – still more than double what Life wanted – and Hotchner took the manuscript to New York. Life were not at all pleased to get over twice what they had expected, but agreed to publish the feature in three parts for $90,000 ($923,487 in 2023) and to pay Hemingway another $10,000 when the piece appeared in the Spanish edition. Yet Hemingway still wasn't happy with it and told Scribner's that before it was published in book form, he would have to travel to Spain again to check one or two further details.

. . .

That trip marked the beginning of Hemingway's final decline which only ended when he shot himself. He flew to Europe unaccompanied and, says one biographer, because he had previously only flown across the Atlantic in turbo-prop aircraft and never in a civil jet aircraft, he was disconcerted by how much faster the journey was. Welsh, with Danby-Smith at the apartment she was renting in New York, was oblivious to the mental state Hemingway was in, but became very alarmed when Hotchner rang her one night a day or two after Hemingway had arrived in Spain to tell her that according to a news report Hemingway had collapsed in Malaga and might have died. He had not

– as Hemingway reassured her by cable – but he was far from well. Bill Davis and his wife were shocked to see how much his mental and physical condition has deteriorated since they last saw him ten months earlier. Hemingway asked Welsh to fly out to take care of him, but remembering the misery of the previous year, Welsh was reluctant and instead sent Danby-Smith; shortly afterwards Hotchner also flew to Spain. He had seen Hemingway just weeks earlier, but he, too, was shocked by the state he found Hemingway in. As biographer James Mellow put it

> *At La Consula the bewildered Davises [had borne] the brunt of Hemingway's breakdown. He kept to his bed for days, was stone silent whenever they drove him anywhere. (He told Hotchner that Davis was trying to kill him in a car accident, not having succeeded the year before.) It was clear to Hotchner that Hemingway was suffering from delusions.*

Back in the US by the beginning of October, Hemingway joined Welsh in New York, but he refused to leave the apartment because he was convinced he was being tailed by the FBI. Welsh wanted to get him back to Ketchum – by now 'home' – but she persuaded him to go there only with difficulty. His paranoid behaviour worsened. When they arrived by rail at Shoshone, he spotted two men in overcoats and claimed they were two FBI agents tailing him. Two college professors who arrived to see him were shocked by his appearance and, says Reynolds, later reported

> *. . . his face was pale and red-veined, not ruddy and weather-beaten. We were struck by the thinness of his arms and legs . . . he walked with the tentativeness of a man well over sixty. The dominant sense we had was fragility.*

He seemed to settle in at Ketchum and to get on with writing, but was constantly worrying – about his bank balance (which was exceedingly healthy) and that he did not have sufficient money to pay his various taxes; about potential legal trouble over getting Valerie Danby-Smith into the US; and, according to Michael Reynolds

> *He worried that a cottonwood tree blown across the Big Wood River [at the foot of the hill on which his house stood] formed a natural bridge across which 'anybody' could infiltrate his defenses. On either side of the front door he had crude glass portals built so that he could see whoever as at the door.*

It was clear to everyone that Hemingway was mentally in a bad way, and Welsh knew she had to get psychiatric help for him. But when Saviers suggested to Hemingway he check in at the Menninger Clinic which specialised in psychiatry, he refused point-blank – sixty years ago it was still an enormous stigma to be thought 'crazy'. He was finally persuaded to go to the Mayo Clinic in Rochester, Minnesota, and was admitted on the last day of November 1960, ostensibly for treatment for his hypertension. Initial medical tests confirmed for the first time that he was probably suffering from haemochromatosis, but the primary treatment was for his very poor mental condition and for, better or worse, it was at the Mayo that Hemingway was given the electro-shock treatment for his chronic depression. Such treatment did show positive results for some patients and medical protocols have been transformed since 1960. But given that over the past sixteen years Hemingway had been concussed several times and the concussions had never been treated, the electro-shock treatment is thought to have caused brain damage and done more harm than good. It did, though, bring about a short-term improvement, and he was discharged to return to Ketchum at the end of January.

Over the next few weeks he appeared to be a little better, but the electro-shock treatment seemed to have destroyed his memory which upset him a great deal. He was unable to carry on with completing the introduction to his memoir or even come up with a title. Then the paranoia returned and he became convinced his letters were being read and his phone was being tapped. He further despaired in mid-April when Cuban counter-revolutionaries launched their abortive invasion in the Bay of Pigs, and he feared the several manuscripts stored in a Havana safety deposit box were lost to him for ever.

A week later, Welsh rose one morning in Ketchum to find Hemingway downstairs with a shotgun and two cartridges. He had also a suicide note. She knew that George Saviers was due to make his daily call to measure Hemingway's blood pressure and she kept her husband talking for an hour until Saviers arrived and convinced Hemingway to be taken to the local hospital where he was sedated. A few days later he persuaded Saviers to allow him to go home to complete various unspecified tasks, and was taken back by a hunting friend and a hospital nurse. He got into the house before them and when they caught up with him, he was loading a cartridge into a shotgun. They managed to get the shotgun off him and took him back to hospital. The following day – and against his will – he was flown back to the Rochester's Mayo Clinic, but he was now intent on killing himself: when the plane landed to refuel and passengers got out to stretch their legs, he tried to walk into a spinning propeller.

Over the following six weeks Hemingway was subjected to more electro-shock treatment and his doctor thought he was responding well. But Welsh didn't when she arrived at the clinic to see him: he ranted at her, accused her of conspiring to have him locked away in the hospital, and she was puzzled and concerned that Hemingway's erratic mental condition was not apparent to his doctors. She contacted another respected psychiatric hospital – the Mayo clinic did not specialise in treating mental ill-health – which assured her it would be willing to admit Hemingway; but when she asked the Mayo to recommend that Hemingway be transferred, she was told that would not be necessary. When she went to visit her husband, she was astonished to find he had somehow persuaded his doctors that he was far better: he was sitting in his physician's office, she later wrote,

dressed in his street clothes, grinning like a Cheshire cat

and she was told he was ready to go home. At the end of June he was driven home to Ketchum and arrived on June 30. He seemed happier, but it became clear that he was still paranoid: the following evening Hemingway, Welsh and a friend were at a restaurant having dinner when he informed them that two men sitting nearby were FBI agents keeping an eye on him. The next morning Hemingway rose early and found the key to the gun cupboard in the basement. Although Welsh had locked the guns away, she had inexplicably refused to hide the key to the cupboard. Hemingway returned upstairs to the foyer with a shotgun, stuck the barrel in his mouth and blew off the top of his head.

APPENDICES

An Essay On Criticism

by Virginia Woolf

HUMAN credulity is indeed wonderful. There may be good reasons for believing in a King or a Judge or a Lord Mayor. When we see them go sweeping by in their robes and their wigs, with their heralds and their outriders, our knees begin to shake and our looks to falter. But what reason there is for believing in critics it is impossible to say. They have neither wigs nor outriders. They differ in no way from other people if one sees them in the flesh. Yet these insignificant fellow creatures have only to shut themselves up in a room, dip a pen in the ink, and call themselves 'we', for the rest of us to believe that they are somehow exalted, inspired, infallible. Wigs grow on their heads. Robes cover their limbs. No greater miracle was ever performed by the power of human credulity. And, like most miracles, this one, too, has had a weakening effect upon the mind of the believer. He begins to think that critics, because they call themselves so, must be right. He begins to suppose that something actually happens to a book when it has been praised or denounced in print. He begins to doubt and conceal his own sensitive, hesitating apprehensions when they conflict with the critics' decrees.

And yet, barring the learned (and learning is chiefly useful in judging the work of the dead), the critic is rather more fallible than the rest of us. He has to give us his opinion of a book that has been published two days, perhaps, with the shell still sticking to its head. He has to get outside that cloud of fertile, but unrealized, sensation which hangs about a reader, to solidify it, to sum it up. The chances are that he does this before the time is ripe; he does it too rapidly and too definitely. He says that it is a great book or a bad book. Yet, as he knows, when he is content to read only, it is neither. He is driven by force of circumstances and some human vanity to hide those hesitations which beset him as he reads, to smooth out all traces of that crab-like and crooked path by which he has reached what he chooses to call 'a conclusion'. So the crude trumpet blasts of critical opinion blow loud and shrill, and we, humble readers that we are, bow our submissive heads.

But let us see whether we can do away with these pretences for a season and pull down the imposing curtain which hides the critical process until it is complete. Let us give the mind a new book, as one drops a lump of fish into a cage of fringed and eager sea anemones, and watch it pausing, pondering, considering its attack. Let us see what prejudices affect it; what influences tell upon it. And if the conclusion becomes in the process a little less conclusive, it may, for that very reason, approach nearer to the truth. The first thing that the mind desires is some foothold of fact upon which it can lodge before it takes flight upon its speculative career. Vague rumours attach themselves to people's names. Of Mr. Hemingway, we know that he is an American living in France, an 'advanced' writer, we suspect, connected with what is called a movement, though which of the many we own that we do not know. It will be well to make a little more certain of these matters by reading first Mr. Hemingway's earlier book, The Sun Also Rises, and it soon becomes clear from this that, if Mr. Hemingway is 'advanced' it is not in the way that is to us most interesting. A prejudice of which the reader would do well to take account is here exposed; the critic is a modernist. Yes, the excuse would be because the moderns make us aware of what we feel subconsciously; they are truer to our own experience; they even anticipate it, and this gives us a particular excitement. But nothing new is revealed about any of the characters in The Sun Also Rises. They come before us shaped, proportioned, weighed, exactly as the characters of Maupassant are shaped and proportioned. They are seen from the old angle; the old reticences, the old relations between author and character are observed.

But the critic has the grace to reflect that this demand for new aspects and new perspectives may well be overdone. It may become whimsical. It may become foolish. For why should not art be traditional as well as original? Are we not attaching too much importance to an excitement which, though agreeable, may not be valuable in itself, so that we are led to make the fatal mistake of overriding the writer's gift?

At any rate, Mr. Hemingway is not modern in the sense given; and it would appear from his first novel that this rumour of modernity must have sprung from his subject matter and from his treatment of it rather than from any fundamental novelty in his conception of the art of fiction. It is a bare, abrupt, outspoken book. Life as people live it in Paris in 1927 or even in 1928 is described as we of this age do describe life (it is here that we steal a march upon the Victorians) openly, frankly, without prudery, but also without surprise. The immoralities and moralities of Paris are described as we are apt to hear them spoken of in private life. Such candour is modern and it is admirable. Then, for qualities grow together in art as in life, we find attached to this admirable frankness an equal bareness of style. Nobody speaks for more than a line or two. Half a line is mostly sufficient. If a hill or a town is described (and there is always some reason for its description) there it is, exactly and literally built up of little facts, literal enough, but chosen, as the final sharpness of the outline proves, with the utmost care. Therefore, a few words like these: 'The grain was just beginning to ripen and the fields were full of poppies. The pasture land was green and there were fine trees, and sometimes big rivers and chateaux off in the trees'—which have a curious force. Each word pulls its weight in the sentence. And the prevailing atmosphere is fine and sharp, like that of winter days when the boughs are bare against the sky. (But if we had to choose one sentence with which to describe what Mr. Hemingway attempts and sometimes achieves, we should quote a passage from a description of a bullfight: 'Romero never made any contortions, always it was straight and pure and natural in line. The others twisted themselves like corkscrews, their elbows raised and leaned against the flanks of the bull after his horns had passed, to give a faked look of danger. Afterwards, all that was faked turned bad and gave an unpleasant feeling. Romero's bullfighting gave real emotion, because he kept the absolute purity of line in his movements and always quietly and calmly let the horns pass him close each time.') Mr. Hemingway's writing, one might paraphrase, gives us now and then a real emotion, because he keeps absolute purity of line in his movements and lets the horns (which are truth, fact, reality) pass him close each time. But there is something faked, too, which turns bad and gives an unpleasant feeling—that also we must face in course of time.

And here, indeed, we may conveniently pause and sum up what point we have reached in our critical progress. Mr. Hemingway is not an advanced writer in the sense that he is looking at life from a new angle. What he sees is a tolerably familiar sight. Common objects like beer bottles and journalists figure largely in the foreground. But he is a skilled and conscientious writer. He has an aim and makes for it without fear or circumlocution. We have, therefore, to take his measure against somebody of substance, and not merely line him, for form's sake, beside the indistinct bulk of some ephemeral shape largely stuffed with straw. Reluctantly we reach this decision, for this process of measurement is one of the most difficult of a critic's tasks. He has to decide which are the most salient points of the book he has just read; to distinguish accurately to what kind they belong, and then, holding them against whatever model is chosen for comparison, to bring out their deficiency or their adequacy.

Recalling The Sun Also Rises, certain scenes rise in memory: the bullfight, the character of the Englishman, Harris; here a little landscape which seems to grow behind the people naturally; here a long, lean phrase which goes curling round a situation like the lash of a whip. Now and again this phrase evokes a character brilliantly, more often a scene. Of character, there is little that remains firmly and solidly elucidated. Something indeed seems wrong with the people. If we place them (the comparison is bad) against Tchekov's people, they are flat as cardboard. If we place them (the comparison is better) against Maupassant's people they are crude as a photograph. If we place them (the comparison may be illegitimate) against real people, the people we liken them to are of an unreal type. They are people one may have seen showing off at some café; talking a rapid, high-pitched slang, because slang is the speech of the herd, seemingly much at their ease, and yet if we look at them a little from the shadow not at their ease at all, and, indeed, terribly afraid of being themselves, or they would say things simply in their natural voices. So it would seem that the thing that is faked is character; Mr. Hemingway leans against the flanks of that particular bull after the horns have passed.

After this preliminary study of Mr. Hemingway's first book, we come to the new book, Men Without Women, possessed of certain views or prejudices. His talent plainly may develop along different lines. It may broaden and fill out; it may take a little more time and go into things—human beings in particular—rather more deeply. And even if this meant the sacrifice of some energy and point, the exchange would be to our private liking. On the other hand, his is a talent which may contract and harden still further, it may come to depend more and more upon the emphatic moment; make more and more use of dialogue, and cast narrative and description overboard as an encumbrance.

The fact that Men Without Women consists of short stories, makes it probable that Mr. Hemingway has taken the second line. But, before we explore the new book, a word should be said which is generally left unsaid, about the implications of the title. As the publisher puts it . . . 'the softening feminine influence is absent—either through training, discipline, death, or situation'. Whether we are to understand by this that women are incapable of training, discipline, death, or situation, we do not know. But it is undoubtedly true, if we are going to persevere in our attempt to reveal the processes of the critic's mind, that any emphasis laid upon sex is dangerous. Tell a man that this is a woman's book, or a woman that this is a man's, and you have brought into play sympathies and antipathies which have nothing to do with art. The greatest writers lay no stress upon sex one way or the other. The critic is not reminded as he reads them that he belongs to the masculine or the feminine gender. But in our time, thanks to our sexual perturbations, sex consciousness is strong, and shows itself in literature by an exaggeration, a protest of sexual characteristics which in either case is disagreeable. Thus Mr. Lawrence, Mr. Douglas, and Mr. Joyce partly spoil their books for women readers by their display of self-conscious virility; and Mr. Hemingway, but much less violently, follows suit. All we can do, whether we are men or women, is to admit the influence, look the fact in the face, and so hope to stare it out of countenance.

To proceed then—Men Without Women consists of short stories in the French rather than in the Russian manner. The great French masters, Mérimée and Maupassant, made their stories as self-conscious and compact as possible. There is never a thread left hanging; indeed, so contracted are they that when the last sentence of the last page flares up, as it so often does, we see by its light the whole circumference and significance of the story revealed. The Tchekov method is, of course, the very opposite of this. Everything is cloudy and vague, loosely trailing rather than tightly furled. The stories move slowly out of sight like clouds in the summer air, leaving a wake of meaning in our minds which gradually fades away. Of the two methods, who shall say which is the better? At any rate, Mr. Hemingway, enlisting under the French masters, carries out their teaching up to a point with considerable success.

There are in Men Without Women many stories which, if life were longer, one would wish to read again. Most of them indeed are so competent, so efficient, and so bare of superfluity that one wonders why they do not make a deeper dent in the mind than they do. Take the pathetic story of the Major whose wife died—'In Another Country'; or the sardonic story of a conversation in a railway carriage—'A Canary for One'; or stories like 'The Undefeated' and 'Fifty Grand' which are full of the sordidness and heroism of bull-fighting and boxing—all of these are good trenchant stories, quick, terse, and strong. If one had not summoned the ghosts of Tchekov, Mérimée, and Maupassant, no doubt one would be enthusiastic. As it is, one looks about for something, fails to find something, and so is brought again to the old familiar business of ringing impressions on the counter, and asking what is wrong?

For some reason the book of short stories does not seem to us to go as deep or to promise as much as the novel. Perhaps it is the excessive use of dialogue, for Mr. Hemingway's use of it is surely excessive. A writer will always be chary of dialogue because dialogue puts the most violent pressure upon the reader's attention. He has to hear, to see, to supply the right tone, and to fill in the background from what the characters say without any help from the author. Therefore, when fictitious people are allowed to speak it must be because they have something so important to say that it stimulates the reader to do rather more than his share of the work of creation. But, although Mr. Hemingway keeps us under the fire of dialogue constantly, his people, half the time, are saying what the author could say much more economically for them. At last we are inclined to cry out with the little girl in 'Hills Like White Elephants': 'Would you please please please please please please stop talking?'

And probably it is this superfluity of dialogue which leads to that other fault which is always lying in wait for the writer of short stories: the lack of proportion. A paragraph in excess will make these little craft lopsided and will bring about that blurred effect which, when one is out for clarity and point, so baffles the reader. And both these faults, the tendency to flood the page with unnecessary dialogue and the lack of sharp, unmistakable points by which we can take hold of the story, come from the more fundamental fact that, though Mr. Hemingway is brilliantly and enormously skilful, he lets his dexterity, like the bullfighter's cloak, get between him and the fact. For in truth story-writing has much in common with bullfighting. One may twist one's self like a corkscrew and go through every sort of contortion so that the public thinks one is running every risk and displaying superb gallantry. But the true writer stands close up to the bull and lets the horns—call them life, truth, reality, whatever you like—pass him close each time.

Mr. Hemingway, then, is courageous; he is candid; he is highly skilled; he plants words precisely where he wishes; he has moments of bare and nervous beauty; he is modern in manner but not in vision; he is self-consciously virile; his talent has contracted rather than expanded; compared with his novel his stories are a little dry and sterile. So we sum him up. So we reveal some of the prejudices, the instincts and the fallacies out of which what it pleases us to call criticism is made.

An Old Newsman Writes

by Ernest Hemingway,
Esquire, December 1934

YOUR correspondent is an old newspaper man. That makes us all just one big family. But the bad luck for the customers is that your correspondent was a working newspaper man and as such used to envy the way columnists were allowed to write about themselves. When the papers would come over your correspondent would read a long blob-blobs by his then favorite columnist on the columnist himself, his child, what he thought and how he thought it, while on this same day your correspondent's output would be something on this order: KEMAL INSWARDS UNBURNED SMYRNA GUILTY GREEKS, sending it at three dollars a word Eastern Cable urgent to appear as, copyrighted by Monumental News Service, 'Mustapha Kemal in an exclusive interview today with the correspondent of the Monumental News Service denied vehemently that the Turkish forces had any part in the burning of Smyrna. The city, Kemal stated, was fired by incendiaries in the troops of the Greek rear guard before the first Turkish patrols entered the city.'

    I don't know what was on the mind of the good grey baggy-pants of the columns when he used to write those I, me, my pieces but I am sure he had his troubles even before he took over the world's troubles and, anyway, it has been interesting to watch his progress from an herbivorous (out-doors, the spring, baseball, an occasional half-read book) columnist to a carnivorous (riots, violence, disaster, and revolution) columnist. But personal columnists, and this is getting to read a little like a column, are jackals and no jackal has been known to live on grass once he had learned about meat—no matter who killed the meat for him. Winchell kills his own meat and so do a few others. But they have news in their columns and are the most working of working newspaper men. So let us return to the ex-favorite who projects his personality rather than goes for the facts.

Things were in just as bad shape, and worse, as far as vileness, injustice and rottenness are concerned, in 1921, '22 and '23 as they are now but our then favorite columnist did not get around as much in those days or else he didn't read the papers. Or else we had to go broke at home before anybody would take the rest of the world seriously.

The trouble with our former favorite is that he started his education too late. There is no time for him, now, to learn what a man should know before he will die. It is not enough to have a big heart, a pretty good head, a charm of personality, baggy pants, and a facility with a typewriter to know how the world is run and who is making the assists, the put-outs and the errors and who are merely the players and who are the owners. Our favorite will never know because he started too late and because he cannot think coldly with his head.

For instance the world was much closer to revolution in the years after the war than it is now. In those days we who believed in it, looked for it at any time, expected it, hoped for it—for it was the logical thing. But everywhere it came it was aborted. For a long time I could not understand it but finally I figured it out. If you study history you will see that there can never be a Communist revolution without, first, a complete military debacle. You have to see what happens in a military debacle to understand this. It is something so utterly complete in its disillusion about the system that has put them into this, in its destruction and purging away of all the existing standards, faiths and loyalties, when the war is being fought by a conscript army, that it is the necessary catharsis before revolution. No country was ever riper for revolution than Italy after the war but the revolution was doomed to fail because her defeat was not complete; because after Caporetto she fought and won in June and July of 1918 on the Piave. From the Piave, by way of the Banca Commerciale, the Credito Italiano, the merchants of Milan who wanted the prosperous socialist co-operative societies and the socialist municipal government of that city smashed, came Fascism.

It is too long a story to go into here but our present literary revolutionary mouthpieces ought to study a little contemporary history. But no history is written honestly. You have to keep in touch with it at the time and you can depend on just as much as you have actually seen and followed. And these boys started too late. Because it isn't all in Marx nor in Engels, a lot of things have happened since then.

What the boys need, to play the races successfully, is past performances. They also need to have known horses for a long time, and to be able to tell them in the early morning around sun-up with no numbers, no colors, with blankets on them, and to be able to clock them, then, as they go by in the half-light and, thus, know what times they are capable of making.

If the men who write editorials for the New Republic and The Monthly Review, say, had to take an examination on what they actually know about the mechanics, theory, past performance and practice of actual revolution, as it is made, not as it is hoped for, I doubt if any one of them would have one hundredth part of the knowledge of his subject that the average sensible follower of the horses has of the animals.

France was whipped and ready for revolution in 1917 after the failure of the Chemin des Dames offensive. Regiments revolted and marched on Paris. Clemenceau came into power when practically every politician and all the sane people of the country were secretly negotiating or hoping for a peace and by shooting or frightening out of the country all his old political enemies, refusing to negotiate a peace, executing God knows how many soldiers who died without publicity tied to stakes before the firing squads at Vincennes, and holding on without fighting until the American effort arrived, had his troops fighting again by July of 1918. Because they ended up as winners, revolution was doomed in France and anybody who saw, on Clemenceau's orders, the Garde Républicaine, with their shining breastplates, their horse-hair plumes, and those high-chested, big-hoofed, well-shod horses, charge and ride down the parade of mutilated war veterans who were confident the Old Man would never do anything to them, his poilus that he loved, and saw the slashing sabers, the start of the gallop then, the smashed wheel chairs, men scattered on the streets unable to run, the broken crutches, the blood and brains on the cobble-stones, the iron-shod hooves striking sparks from the stones but making a different sound when they rode over legless, armless men, while the crowd ran; nobody who saw that could be expected to think something new was happening when Hoover had the troops disperse the bonus army.

Germany was never defeated in a military debacle. There was never any Sedan such as prepared the way for the Commune. There was no final complete bankruptcy of faith in what the war was fought for. U. S. troops took Sedan but the Army was retreating orderly. Germany had simply failed to win in the Spring and Summer but the army was still intact and there was a peace made before there was a defeat of the kind that makes revolution. True, there was a revolution but it was conditioned and held in check by the way in which the war had ended and those who had never accepted a military defeat hated those who had and started to do away with the ablest of them by the vilest program of assassination the world has ever known. They started, immediately after the war, by killing Karl Leibnecht [sic] and Rosa Luxembourg, and they killed on, steadily eliminating revolutionary and liberal alike by an unvarying process of intelligent assassination. Walter Rathenau was a different and better man than Roehm, the pervert, but the same men and the same system murdered both.

Spain got a revolution that corresponded exactly to the extent of her military debacle at Annual and those who were responsible for that terrible butchery lost their jobs and their thrones. But when they tried to extend that revolution three weeks ago the mass of the people were not ready for it and they did not want it.

Neither Austria nor Hungary were ever really defeated in the war in the sense that France was defeated in 1870. The war wore out before anyone won it with them and what has happened in both countries has reflected that. Too many people still believed in the State and war is the health of the state. You will see that finally it will become necessary for the health of the so-called communist state in Russia. But the penalty for losing a war badly enough, completely and finally enough is the destruction of the state. Make a note of this, Baggy-pants.

Now a writer can make himself a nice career while he is alive by espousing a political cause, working for it, making a profession of believing in it, and if it wins he will be very well placed. All politics is a matter of working hard without reward, or with a living wage for a time, in the hope of booty later. A man can be a Fascist or a Communist and if his outfit gets in he can get to be an ambassador or have a million copies of his books printed by the Government or any of the other rewards the boys dream about. Because the literary revolution boys are all ambitious. I have been living for some time where revolutions have gotten past the parlor or publishers' tea and light picketing stage and I know. A lot of my friends have gotten excellent jobs and some others are in jail. But none of this will help the writer as a writer unless he finds something new to add to human knowledge while he is writing. Otherwise he will stink like any other writer when they bury him; except, since he has had political affiliations, they will send more flowers at the time and later he will stink a little more.

The hardest thing in the world to do is to write straight honest prose on human beings. First you have to know the subject; then you have to know how to write. Both take a lifetime to learn and anybody is cheating who takes politics as a way out. It is too easy. All the outs are too easy and the thing itself is too hard to do. But you have to do it and every time you do it well, those human beings and that subject are done and your field is that much more limited. Of course the boys are all wishing you luck and that helps a lot. (Watch how they wish you luck after the first one.) But don't let them suck you in to start writing about the proletariat, if you don't come from the proletariat, just to please the recently politically enlightened critics. In a little while these critics will be something else. I've seen them be a lot of things and none of them was pretty. Write about what you know and write truly and tell them all where they can place it. They are all really very newly converted and very frightened, really, and when Moscow tells them what I am telling you, then they will believe it. Books should be about the people you know, that you love and hate, not about the people you study up about. If you write them truly they will have all the economic implications a book can hold.

In the meantime, since it is Christmas, if you want to read a book by a man who knows exactly what he is writing about and has written it marvellously well, read Appointment in Samara by John O'Hara.

Then when you have more time read another book called War and Peace by Tolstoi and see how you will have to skip the big Political Thought passages, that he undoubtedly thought were the best things in the book when he wrote it, because they are no longer either true or important, if they ever were more than topical, and see how true and lasting and important the people and the action are. Do not let them deceive you about what a book should be because of what is in the fashion now. All good books are alike in that they are truer than if they had really happened and after you are finished reading one you will feel that all that happened to you and afterwards it all belongs to you; the good and the bad, the ecstasy, the remorse and sorrow, the people and the places and how the weather was. If you can get so that you can give that to people, then you are a writer. Because that is the hardest thing of all to do. If, after that, you want to abandon your trade and get into politics, go ahead, but it is a sign that you are afraid to go on and do the other, because it is getting too hard and you have to do it alone and so you want to do something where you can have friends and well wishers, and be part of a company engaged in doing something worth doing instead of working all your life at something that will only be worth doing if you do it better than it has ever been done.

You must be prepared to work always without applause. When you are excited about something is when the first draft is done. But no one can see it until you have gone over it again and again until you have communicated the emotion, the sights and the sounds to the reader, and by the time you have completed this the words, sometimes, will not make sense to you as you read them, so many times have you re-read them. By the time the book comes out you will have started something else and it is all behind you and you do not want to hear about it. But you do, you read it in covers and you see all the places that now you can do nothing about. All the critics who could not make their reputations by discovering you are hoping to make them by predicting hopefully your approaching impotence, failure and general drying up of natural juices. Not a one will wish you luck or hope that you will keep on writing unless you have political affiliations in which case these will rally around and speak of you and Homer, Balzac, Zola and Link Steffens. You are just as well off without these reviews. Finally, in some other place, some other time, when you can't work and feel like hell you will pick up the book and look in it and start to read and go on and in a little while say to your wife, 'Why this stuff is bloody marvellous.'

And she will say, 'Darling, I always told you it was.' Or maybe she doesn't hear you and says, 'What did you say?' and you do not repeat the remark.

But if the book is good, is about something that you know, and is truly written and reading it over you see that this is so you can let the boys yip and the noise will have that pleasant sound coyotes make on a very cold night when they are out in the snow and you are in your own cabin that you have built or paid for with your work.

Who Murdered The Vets?

A Firsthand Report On The Florida Hurricane

This piece appeared in New Masses on 17 September, 1935.

I have led my ragamuffins where they are peppered; there's not three of my hundred and fifty left alive, and they are for the town's end, to beg during life.

Shakespeare.

WHOM did they annoy and to whom was their possible presence political danger?

Who sent them down to the Florida Keys and left them there in hurricane months?

Who is responsible for their deaths?

The writer of this article lives a long way from Washington and would not know the answers to those questions. But he does know that wealthy people, yachtsmen, fishermen such as President Hoover and President Roosevelt, do not come to the Florida Keys in hurricane months. Hurricane months are August, September and October, and in those months you see no yachts along the Keys. You do not see them because yacht owners know there would be great danger, unescapable danger, to their property if a storm should come. For the same reason, you cannot interest any very wealthy people in fishing off the coast of Cuba in the summer when the biggest fish are there. There is a known danger to property. But veterans, especially the bonus-marching variety of veterans, are not property. They are only human beings; unsuccessful human beings, and all they have to lose is their lives. They are doing coolie labor for a top wage of $45 a month and they have been put down on the Florida Keys where they can't make trouble. It is hurricane months, sure, but if anything comes up, you can always evacuate them, can't you?

This is the way a storm comes. On Saturday evening at Key West, having finished working, you go out to the porch to have a drink and read the evening paper. The first thing you see in the paper is a storm warning. You know that work is off until it is past and you are angry and upset because you were going well.

The location of the tropical disturbance is given as east of Long Island in the Bahamas and the direction it is traveling is approximately toward Key West. You get out the September storm chart which gives the tracks and dates of forty storms of hurricane intensity during that month since 1900. And by taking the rate of movement of the storm as given in the Weather Bureau Advisory you calculate that it cannot reach us before Monday noon at the earliest. Sunday you spend making the boat as safe as you can. When they refuse to haul her out on the ways because there are too many boats ahead, you buy $52 worth of new heavy hawser and shift her to what seems the safest part of the submarine base and tie her up there. Monday you nail up the shutters on the house and get everything movable inside. There are northeast storm warnings flying, and at five o'clock the wind is blowing heavily and steadily from the northeast and they have hoisted the big red flags with a black square in the middle one over the other that mean a hurricane. The wind is rising hourly and the barometer is falling. All the people of the town are nailing up their houses.

You go down to the boat and wrap the lines with canvas where they will chafe when the surge starts, and believe that she has a good chance to ride it out if it comes from any direction but the northwest where the opening of the sub-basin is; provided no other boat smashes into you and sinks you. There is a booze boat seized by the Coast Guard tied next to you and you notice her stern lines are only tied to ringbolts in the stern, and you start bellyaching about that.

'For Christ sake, you know those lousy ringbolts will pull right; out of her stern and then she'll come down on us.'

'If she does, you can cut her loose or sink her.'

'Sure, and maybe we can't get to her, too. What's the use of letting a piece of junk like that sink a good boat?'

From the last advisory you figure we will not get it until midnight, and at ten o'clock you leave the Weather Bureau and go home to see if you can get two hours' sleep before it starts, leaving the car in front of the house because you do not trust the rickety garage, putting the barometer and a flashlight by the bed for when the electric lights go. At midnight the wind is howling, the glass is 29.55 and dropping while you watch it, and rain is coming in sheets. You dress, find the car drowned out, make your way to the boat with a flashlight with branches falling and wires going down. The flashlight shorts in the rain and the wind is now coming in heavy gusts from the northwest. The captured boat has pulled her ringbolts out, and by quick handling by Jose Rodriguez, a Spanish sailor, was swung clear before she hit us. She is now pounding against the dock.

The wind is bad and you have to crouch over to make headway against it. You figure if we get the hurricane from there you will lose the boat and you never will have enough money to get another. You feel like hell. But a little after two o'clock it backs into the west and by the law of circular storms you know the storm has passed over the Keys above us. Now the boat is well-sheltered by the sea wall and the breakwater and at five o'clock, the glass having been steady for an hour, you get back to the house. As you make your way in without a light you find a tree is down across the walk and a strange empty look in the front yard shows the big old sappodillo tree is down too. You turn in.

THAT'S what happens when one misses you. And that is about the minimum of time you have to prepare for a hurricane; two full days. Sometimes you have longer.

But what happened on the Keys? On Tuesday, as the storm made its way up the Gulf of Mexico, it was so wild not a boat could leave Key West and there was no communication with the Keys beyond the ferry, nor with the mainland. No one knew what the storm had done, where it had passed. No train came in and there was no news by plane. Nobody knew the horror that was on the Keys. It was not until late the next day that a boat got through to Matecumbe Key from Key West.

Now, as this is written five days after the storm, nobody knows how many are dead. The Red Cross, which has steadily played down the number, announcing first forty-six then 150, finally saying the dead would not pass 300, today lists the dead and missing as 446, but the total of veterans dead and missing alone numbers 442 and there have been seventy bodies of civilians recovered. The total of dead may well pass a thousand as many bodies were swept out to sea and never will be found.

It is not necessary to go into the deaths of the civilians and their families since they were on the Keys of their own free will; they made their living there, had property and knew the hazards involved. But the veterans had been sent there; they had no opportunity to leave, nor any protection against hurricanes; and they never had a chance for their lives.

During the war, troops and sometimes individual soldiers who incurred the displeasure of their superior officers, were sometimes sent into positions of extreme danger and kept there repeatedly until they were no longer problems. I do not believe anyone, knowingly, would send U.S. war veterans into any such positions in time of peace. But the Florida Keys, in hurricane months, in the matter of casualties recorded during the building of the Florida East Coast Railway to Key West, when nearly a thousand men were killed by hurricanes, can be classed as such a position. And ignorance has never been accepted as an excuse for murder or for manslaughter.

Who sent nearly a thousand war veterans, many of them husky, hard-working and simply out of luck, but many of them close to the border of pathological cases, to live in frame shacks on the Florida Keys in hurricane months?

Why were the men not evacuated on Sunday, or, at latest, Monday morning, when it was known there was a possibility of a hurricane striking the Keys and evacuation was their only possible protection?

Who advised against sending the train from Miami to evacuate the veterans until four-thirty o'clock on Monday so that it was blown off the tracks before it ever reached the lower camps?

These are questions that someone will have to answer, and answer satisfactorily, unless the clearing of Anacostia Flats is going to seem an act of kindness compared to the clearing of Upper and Lower Matecumbe.

WHEN we reached Lower Matecumbe there were bodies floating in the ferry slip. The brush was all brown as though autumn had come to these islands where there is no autumn but only a more dangerous summer, but that was because the leaves had all been blown away. There was two feet of sand over the highest part of the island where the sea had carried it and all the heavy bridge-building machines were on their sides. The island looked like the abandoned bed of a river where the sea had swept it. The railroad embankment was gone and the men who had cowered behind it and finally, when the water came, clung to the rails, were all gone with it. You could find them face down and face up in the mangroves. The biggest bunch of the dead were in the tangled, always green but now brown, mangroves behind the tank cars and the water towers. They hung on there, in shelter, until the wind and the rising water carried them away. They didn't all let go at once but only when they could hold on no longer. Then further on you found them high in the trees where the water had swept them. You found them everywhere and in the sun all of them were beginning to be too big for their blue jeans and jackets that they could never fill when they were on the bum and hungry.

I'd known a lot of them at Josie Grunt's place and around the town when they would come in for pay day, and some of them were punch drunk and some of them were smart; some had been on the bum since the Argonne almost and some had lost their jobs the year before last Christmas; some had wives and some couldn't remember; some were good guys and others put their pay checks in the Postal Savings and then came over to cadge in on the drinks when better men were drunk; some liked to fight and others liked to walk around the town; and they were all what you get after a war. But who sent them there to die?

They're better off, I can hear whoever sent them say, explaining to himself. What good were they? You can't account for accidents or acts of God. They were well-fed, well-housed, well-treated and, let us suppose, now they are well dead.

But I would like to make whoever sent them there carry just one out through the mangroves, or turn one over that lay in the sun along the fill, or tie five together so they won't float out, or smell that smell you thought you'd never smell again, with luck. But now you know there isn't any luck when rich bastards make a war. The lack of luck goes on until all who take part in it are gone.

So now you hold your nose, and you, you that put in the literary columns that you were staying in Miami to see a hurricane because you needed it in your next novel and now you were afraid you would not see one, you can go on reading the paper, and you'll get all you need for your next novel; but I would like to lead you by the seat of your well-worn-by-writing-to-the-literary-columns pants up to that bunch of mangroves where there is a woman, bloated big as a balloon and upside down and there's another face down in the brush next to her and explain to you they are two damned nice girls who ran a sandwich place and filling station and that where they are is their hard luck. And you could make a note of it for your next novel and how is your next novel coming, brother writer, comrade s - - t?

But just then one of eight survivors from that camp of 187 not counting twelve who went to Miami to play ball (how's that for casualties, you guys who remember percentages?) comes along and he says, 'That's my old lady. Fat, ain't she?' But that guy is nuts, now, so we can dispense with him and we have to go back and get in a boat before we can check up on Camp Five.

CAMP FIVE was where eight survived out of 187, but we only find sixty-seven of those plus two more along the fill makes sixty-nine. But all the rest are in the mangroves. It doesn't take a bird dog to locate them. On the other hand, there are no buzzards. Absolutely no buzzards. How's that? Would you believe it? The wind killed all the buzzards and all the big winged birds like pelicans too. You can find them in the grass that's washed along the fill. Hey, there's another one. He's got low shoes, put him down, man, looks about sixty, low shoes, copper-riveted overalls, blue percale shirt without collar, storm jacket, by Jesus that's the thing to wear, nothing in his pockets. Turn him over.

Face tumefied beyond recognition. Hell he don't look like a veteran. He's too old. He's got grey hair. You'll have grey hair yourself this time next week. And across his back there was a great big blister as wide as his back and all ready to burst where his storm jacket had slipped down. Turn him over again. Sure he's a veteran. I know him. What's he got low shoes on for then? Maybe he made some money shooting craps and bought them. You don't know that guy. You can't tell him now. I know him, he hasn't got any thumb. That's how I know him. The land crabs ate his thumb. You think you know everybody. Well, you waited a long time to get sick, brother. Sixty-seven of them and you got sick at the sixty-eighth.

And so you walk the fill, where there is any fill and now it's calm and clear and blue and almost the way it is when the millionaires come down in the winter except for the sandflies, the mosquitoes and the smell of the dead that always smell the same in all countries that you go to – and now they smell like that in your own country. Or is it just that dead soldiers smell the same no matter what their nationality or who sends them to die?

Who sent them down there?

I hope he reads this – and how does he feel?

He will die too, himself, perhaps even without a hurricane warning, but maybe it will be an easy death, that's the best you get, so that you do not have to hang onto something until you can't hang on, until your fingers won't hold on, and it is dark. And the wind makes a noise like a locomotive passing, with a shriek on top of that, because the wind has a scream exactly as it has in books, and then the fill goes and the high wall of water rolls you over and over and then, whatever it is, you get it and we find you, now of no importance, stinking in the mangroves.

You're dead now, brother, but who left you there in the hurricane months on the Keys where a thousand men died before you in the hurricane months when they were building the road that's now washed out?

Who left you there? And what's the punishment for manslaughter now?

Ernest Hemingway,
Key West, FL.

The Art Of The Short Story

by Ernest Hemingway.

GERTRUDE STEIN who was sometimes very wise said to me on one of her wise days, 'Remember, Hemingway, that remarks are not literature'. The following remarks are not intended to be nor do they pretend to be literature. They are meant to be instructive, irritating and informative. No writer should be asked to write solemnly about what he has written. Truthfully, yes. Solemnly, no. Should we begin in the form of a lecture designed to counteract the many lectures you will have heard on the art of the short story?

Many people have a compulsion to write. There is no law against it and doing it makes them happy while they do it and presumably relieves them. Given editors who will remove the worst of their emissions, supply them with spelling and syntax and help them shape their thoughts and their beliefs, some compulsory writers attain a temporary fame. But when shit or merde — a word which teacher will explain — is cut out of a book, the odour of it always remains perceptible to anyone with sufficient olfactory sensibility.

The compulsory writer would be advised not to attempt the short story. Should he make the attempt, he might well suffer the fate of the compulsive architect, which is as lonely an end as that of the compulsive bassoon player. Let us not waste our time considering the sad and lonely ends of these unfortunate creatures, gentlemen. Let us continue the exercise.

Are there any questions? Have you mastered the art of the short story? Have I been helpful? Or have I not made myself clear? I hope so.

Gentlemen, I will be frank with you. The masters of the short story come to no good end. You query this? You cite me Maugham? Longevity, gentlemen, is not an end. It is a prolongation. I cannot say fie upon it, since I have never fie-ed on anything yet. Shuck if off, Jack. Don't fie on it.

Should we abandon rhetoric and realize at the same time that what IS the most authentic hipster talk of today is the twenty-three skidoo of tomorrow? We should? What intelligent young people you are and what a privilege it is to be with you. Do I hear a request for authentic ballroom bananas? I do? Gentlemen, we have them for you in bunches.

Actually, as writers put it when they do not know how to begin a sentence, there is very little to say about writing short stories unless you are a professional explainer. If you can do it, you don't have to explain it. If you cannot do it, no explanation will ever help.

A few things I have found to be true. If you leave out important things or events that you know about, the story is strengthened. If you leave or skip something because you do not know it, the story will be worthless. The test of any story is how very good the stuff is that you, not your editors, omit. A story in this book called 'Big Two-Hearted River' is about a boy coming home beat to the wide from a war. Beat to the wide was an earlier and possibly more severe form of beat, since those who had it were unable to comment on this condition and could not suffer that it be mentioned in their presence. So the war, all mention of the war, anything about the war, is omitted. The river was the Fox River, by Seney, Michigan, not the Big Two-Hearted. The change of name was made purposely, not from ignorance nor carelessness but because Big Two-Hearted River is poetry, and because there were many Indians in the story, just as the war was in the story, and none of the Indians nor the war appeared. As you see, it is very simple and easy to explain.

In a story called 'A Sea Change' everything is left out. I had seen the couple in the Bar Basque in St. Jean-de-Luz and I knew the story too, too well, which is the squared root of well, and use any well you like except mine. So I left the story out. But it is all there. It is not visible but it is there.

It is very hard to talk about your work since it implies arrogance or pride. I have tried to get rid of arrogance and replace it with humility and I do all right at that sometimes, but without pride I would not wish to continue to live nor to write and I publish nothing of which I am not proud. You can take that any way you like. Jack. I might not take it myself. But maybe we're built different.

Another story is 'Fifty Grand'. This story originally started like this:

' "How did you handle Benny so easy, Jack?" Soldier asked him. "Benny's an awful smart boxer," Jack said.' All the time he's in there, he's thinking. All the time he's thinking, I was hitting him.' "

I told this story to Scott Fitzgerald in Paris before I wrote 'Fifty Grand' trying to explain to him how a truly great boxer like Jack Britton functioned. I wrote the story opening with that incident and when it was finished I was happy about it and showed it to Scott. He said he liked the story very much and spoke about it in so fulsome a manner that I was embarrassed. Then he said, 'There is only one thing wrong with it, Ernest, and I tell you this as your friend. You have to cut out that old chestnut about Britton and Leonard.'

At that time my humility was in such ascendance that I thought he must have heard the remark before or that Britton must have said it to someone else. It was not until I had published the story, from which I had removed that lovely revelation of the metaphysics of boxing that Fitzgerald in the way his mind was functioning that year so that he called an historic statement an 'old chestnut' because he had heard it once and only once from a friend, that I realized how dangerous that attractive virtue, humility, can be. So do not be too humble, gentlemen. Be humble after but not during the action. They will all con you, gentlemen. But sometimes it is not intentional. Sometimes they simply do not know. This is the saddest state of writers and the one you will most frequently encounter. If there are no questions, let us press on.

My loyal and devoted friend Fitzgerald, who was truly more interested in my own career at this point than in his own, sent me to Scribner's with the story. It had already been turned down by Ray Long of Cosmopolitan Magazine because it had no love interest. That was okay with me since I eliminated any love interest and there were, purposely, no women in it except for two broads. Enter two broads as in Shakespeare, and they go out of the story. This is unlike what you will hear from your Instructors, that if a broad comes into a story in the first paragraph, she must reappear later to justify her original presence. This is untrue, gentlemen. You may dispense with her, just as in life. It is also untrue that if a gun hangs on the wall when you open up the story, it must be fired by page fourteen. The chances are, gentlemen, that if it hangs upon the wail, it will not even shoot. If there are no questions, shall we press on? Yes, the unfireable gun may be a symbol. That is true. But with a good enough writer, the chances are some jerk just hung it there to look at. Gentlemen, you can't be sure. Maybe he is queer for guns, or maybe an interior decorator put it there. Or both.

So with pressure by Max Perkins on the editor, Scribner's Magazine agreed to publish the story and pay me two hundred and fifty dollars, if I would cut it to a length where it would not have to be continued into the back of the book. They call magazines books. There is significance in this but we will not go into it. They are not books, even if they put them in stiff covers. You have to watch this, gentlemen. Anyway, I explained without heat nor hope, seeing the built-in stupidity of the editor of the magazine and his intransigence, that I had already cut the story myself and that the only way it could be shortened by five hundred words and make sense was to amputate the first five hundred. I had often done that myself with stories and it improved them. It would not have improved this story but I thought that was their ass not mine. I would put it back together in a book. They read differently in a book anyway. You will learn about this.

No, gentlemen, they would not cut the first five hundred words. They gave it instead to a very intelligent young assistant editor who assured me he could cut it with no difficulty. That was just what he did on his first attempt, and any place he took words out, the story no longer made sense. It had been cut for keeps when I wrote it, and afterwards at Scott's request I'd even cut out the metaphysics which, ordinarily, I leave in. So they quit on it finally and eventually. I understand, Edward Weeks got Ellery Sedgwick to publish it in the Atlantic Monthly. Then everyone wanted me to write fight stories and I did not write any more fight stories because I tried to write only one story on anything, if I got what I was after, because Life is very short if you like it and I knew that even then. There are other things to write about and other people who write very good fight stories. I recommend to you 'The Professional' by W. C. Heinz.

Yes, the confidently cutting young editor became a big man on Reader's Digest. Or didn't he? I'll have to check that. So you see, gentlemen, you never know and what you win in Boston you lose in Chicago. That's symbolism, gentlemen, and you can run a saliva test on it. That is how we now detect symbolism in our group and so far it gives fairly satisfactory results. Not complete, mind you. But we are getting in to see our way through. Incidentally, within a short time Scribner's Magazine was running a contest for long short stories that broke back into the back of the book, and paying many times two hundred and fifty dollars to the winners.

Now since I have answered your perceptive questions, let us take up another story.

This story is called 'The Light of the World'. I could have called it 'Behold I Stand at the Door and Knock' or some other stained-glass window title, but I did not think of it and actually 'The Light of the Would' is better. It is about many things and you would be ill-advised to think it is a simple tale. It is really, no matter what you hear, a love letter to a whore named Alice who at the time of the story would have dressed out at around two hundred and ten pounds. Maybe more. And the point of it is that nobody, and that goes for you, Jack, knows how we were then from how we are now. This is worse on women than on us, until you look into the mirror yourself some day instead of looking at women all the time, and in writing the story I was trying to do something about it. But there are very few basic things you can do anything about. So I do what the French call *constater*. Look that up. That is what you have to learn to do, and you ought to learn French anyway if you are going to understand short stories, and there is nothing rougher than to do it all the way. It is hardest to do about women and you must not worry when they say there are no such women as those you wrote about. That only means your women aren't like their women. You ever see any of their women, Jack? I have a couple of times and you would be appalled and I know you don't appal easy.

What I learned constructive about women, not just ethics like never blame them if they pox you because somebody poxed them and lots of times they don't even know they have It — that's in the first reader for squares — is. No matter how they get, always think of them the way they were on the best day they ever had in their lives. That's about all you can do about it and that is what I was trying for in the story.

Now there is another story called 'The Short Happy Life of Francis Macomber'. Jack, I get a bang even yet from just writing the titles. That's why you write, no matter what they tell you. I'm glad to be with somebody I know now and those feecking students have gone. They haven't? Okay. Glad to have them with us. It is in you that our hope is. That's the stuff to feed the troops. Students, at ease.

This is a simple story in a way, because the woman who I knew very well in real life but then invented out of to make the woman for this story, is a bitch for the full course and doesn't change. You'll probably never meet the type because you haven't got the money. I haven't either but I get around. Now this woman doesn't change. She has been better, but she will never be any better anymore. I invented her complete with handles from the worst bitch I knew (then) and when I first knew her she'd been lovely. Not my dish, not my pigeon not my cup of tea, but lovely for what she was and I was her all of the above which is whatever you make of it. This is as close as I can put it and keep it clean. This information is what you call the background of a story. You throw it all away and invent from what you know. I should have said that sooner. That's all there is to writing. That, a perfect ear — call it selective absolute pitch — the devotion to your work and respect for it that a priest of God has for his, and then have the guts of a burglar, no conscience except to writing, and you're in, gentlemen. It's easy. Anybody can write if he is cut out for it and applies himself. Never give it a thought. Just have those few requisites. I mean the way you have to write now to handle the way now is now. There was a time when it was nicer, much nicer and all that has been well written by nicer people. They are all dead and so are their times, but they handled them very well. Those times are over and writing like that won't help you now.

But to return to this story. The woman called Margot Macomber is no good to anybody now except for trouble. You can bang her but that's about all. The man is a nice jerk. I knew him very well in real life, so invent him too from everything I know. So he is just how he really was, only, he is invented. The White Hunter is my best friend and he does not care what I write as long as it is readable, so I don't invent him at all. I just disguise him for family and business reasons, and to keep him out of trouble with the Game

Department. He is the furthest thing from a square since they invented the circle, so I just have to take care of him with an adequate disguise and he is as proud as though we both wrote it, which actually you always do in anything if you go back far enough. So it is a secret between us. That's all there is to that story except maybe the lion when he is hit and I am thinking inside of him really, not faked. I can think inside of a lion, really. It's hard to believe and it is perfectly okay with me if you don't believe it. Perfectly. Plenty of people have used it since, though, and one boy used it quite well, making only one mistake. Making any mistake kills you. This mistake killed him and quite soon everything he wrote was a mistake. You have to watch yourself. Jack, every minute, and the more talented you are, the more you have to watch these mistakes because you will be in faster company. A writer who is not going all the way up can make all the mistakes he wants. None of it matters. He doesn't matter. The people who like him don't matter either. They could drop dead. It wouldn't make any difference. It's too bad. As soon as you read one page by anyone you can tell whether it matters or not. This is sad and you hate to do it. I don't want to be the one that tells them. So don't make any mistakes. You see how easy it is? Just go right in there and be a writer.

That about handles that story. Any questions? No, I don't know whether she shot him on purpose any more than you do. I could find out if I asked myself because I invented it and I could go right on inventing. But you have to know where to stop. That is what makes a short story. Makes it short at least. The only hint I could give you is that it is my belief that the incidence of husbands shot accidentally by wives who are bitches and really work at it is very low. Should we continue?

If you are interested in how you get the idea for a story, this is how it was with 'The Snows of Kilimanjaro.' They have you ticketed and always try to make it that you are someone who can only write about their self. I am using in this lecture the spoken language, which varies. It is one of the ways to write, so you might as well follow it and maybe you will learn something. Anyone who can write can write spoken, pedantic, inexorably dull, or pure English prose, just as slot machines can be set for straight, percentage, give-away or stealing. No one who can write spoken ever starves except at the start. The others you can eat irregularly on. But any good writer can do them all. This is spoken, approved for over fourteen I hope. Thank you.

Anyway we came home from Africa, which is a place you stay until the money runs out or you get smacked, one year and at quarantine I said to the ship news reporters when somebody asked me what my projects were that I was going to work and when I had some more money go back to Africa. The different wars killed off that project and it took nineteen years to get back. Well it was in the papers and a really nice and really fine and really rich woman invited me to tea and we had a few drinks as well and she had read in the papers about this project, and why should I have to wait to go back for any lack of money? She and my wife and I could go to Africa any time and money was only something to be used intelligently for the best enjoyment of good people and so forth. It was a sincere and fine and good offer and I liked her very much and I turned down the offer.

So I get down to Key West and I start to think what would happen to a character like me whose defects I know, if I had accepted that offer. So I start to invent and I make myself a guy who would do what I invent. I know about the dying part because I had been through all that. Not just once. I got it early, in the middle and later. So I invent how someone I know who cannot sue me — that is me — would turn out, and put into one short story things you would use in, say, four novels if you were careful and not a spender. I throw everything I had been saving into the story and spend it all. I really throw it away, if you know what I mean. I am not gambling with it. Or maybe I am. Who knows? Real gamblers don't gamble. At least you think they don't gamble. They gamble, Jack, don't worry. So I make up the man and the woman as well as I can and I put all the true stuff in and with all the load, the most load any short story ever carried, it still takes off and it flies. This makes me very happy. So I thought that and the Macomber story are as good short stories as I can write for a while, so I lose interest and take up other forms of writing.

Any questions? The leopard? He is part of the metaphysics. I did not hire out to explain that nor a lot of other things. I know, but I am under no obligation to tell you. Put it down to *omertá*. Look that word up. I dislike explainers, apologists, stoolies, pimps. No writer should be any one of those for his own work. This is just a little background, Jack, that won't do either of us any harm. You see the point, don't you? If not it is too bad.

That doesn't mean you shouldn't explain for, apologize for or pimp or tout for some other writer. I have done it and the best luck I had was doing it for Faulkner. When they didn't know him in Europe, I told them all how he was the best we had and so forth, and I over-humbled with him plenty and built him up about as high as he could go because he never had a break then and he was good then. So now whenever he has a few shots, he'll tell students what's wrong with me or tell Japanese or anybody they send him to, to build up our local product. I get tired of this but I figure what the hell he's had a few shots and maybe he even believes it. So you asked me just now what I think about him, as everybody does and I always stall, so I say you know how good he is. Right. You ought to. What is wrong is he cons himself sometimes pretty bad. That may just be the sauce. But for quite a while when he hits the sauce toward the end of a book, it shows bad. He gets tired and he goes on and on, and that sauce writing is really hard on who has to read it. I mean if they care about writing. I thought maybe it would help if I read it using the sauce myself, but it wasn't any help. Maybe it would have helped if I was fourteen. But I was only fourteen one year and then I would have been too busy. So that's what I think about Faulkner. You ask that I sum it up from the standpoint of a professional. Very good writer. Cons himself now. Too much sauce. But he wrote a really fine story called 'The Bear' and I would be glad to put it in this book for your pleasure and delight, if I had written it. But you can't write them all, Jack.

It would be simpler and more fun to talk about other writers and what is good and what is wrong with them, as I saw when you asked me about Faulkner. He's easy to handle because he talks so much for a supposed silent man. Never talk, Jack, if you are a writer, unless you have the guy write it down and have you go over it. Otherwise, they get it wrong. That's what you think until they play a tape back at you. Then you know how silly it sounds. You're a writer aren't you? Okay, shut up and write. What was that question?

Did I really write three stories in one day in Madrid, the way it said in that interview in The Paris Review and Horizon? Yes, sir. I was hotter than a let's skip it, gentlemen. I was laden with uninhibited energy. Or should we say this energy was canalized into my work. Such states are compounded by the brisk air of the Guadarramas (Jack, was it cold) the highly seasoned bacalao vizcaino (dried cod fish. Jack) a certain vague loneliness. I was in love and the girl was in Bologna, and I couldn't sleep anyway, so why not write. So I wrote.

The stories you mention I wrote in one day in Madrid on May 16 when it snowed out the San Isidro bullfights. First I wrote 'The Killers' which I'd tried to write before and failed. Then after lunch I got in bed to keep warm and wrote 'Today is Friday'. I had so much juice I thought maybe I was going crazy and I had about six other stories to write. So I got dressed and walked to Fornos, the old bullfighter's cafe, and drank coffee and then came back and wrote 'Ten Indians'. This made me very sad, and I drank some brandy and went to sleep. I'd forgotten to eat and one of the waiters brought me up some bacalao and a small steak and fried potatoes and a bottle of Valdepeñas.

'The woman who ran the Pension was always worried that I did not eat enough and she had sent the waiter. I remember sitting up in bed and eating, and drink the Valdepeñas. The waiter said he would bring up another bottle. He said the senora wanted to know if I was going to write all night. I said no, I thought would lay off fora while. Why don't you try to write just one more, the waiter asked. I'm only supposed to write one, I said. Nonsense, he said. You could write six. I'll try tomorrow, I said. Try it tonight, he said. What do you think the old woman sent the food up for?

'I'm tired,' I told him. Nonsense, he said (the word was not nonsense.) You tired after three miserable little stories. Translate me one.

'Leave me alone,' I said. 'How am I going to write it if you don't leave me alone?' So I sat up in bed and drank the Valdepeñas and thought what a hell of a writer I was if the first story was as good as I'd hoped.

I have used the same words in answering that the excellent Plimpton elicited from me in order to avoid error or repetition. If there are no more questions, should we continue?

It is very bad for writers to be hit on the head too much. Sometimes you lose months when you should have and perhaps would have worked well but sometimes a long time after the memory of the sensory distortions of these woundings will produce a story which, while not justifying the temporary cerebral damage, will palliate it. 'A Way You'll Never Be' was written at Key West, Florida, some fifteen years after the damage it depicts, both to a man, a village and a countryside, had occurred. No questions? I understand. I understand completely. However, do not be alarmed. We are not going to call for a moment of silence. Nor for the man in the white suit. Nor for the net. Now gentlemen, and I notice a sprinkling of ladies who have drifted in attracted I hope by the sprinkling of applause. Thank you. Just what stories do you yourselves care for? I must not impose on you exclusively those that find favour with their author. Do you too care for any of them?

You like 'The Killers'? So good of you. And why? Because it had Burr Lancaster and Ava Gardner in it? Excellent. Now we are getting somewhere. It is always a pleasure to remember Miss Gardner as she was then. No, I never met Mr, Lancaster. I can't tell you what he is really like but everyone says he is terrific. The background of that story is that I had a lawyer who had cancer and he wanted cash rather than any long-term stuff. You can see his point I hope. So when he was offered a share in the picture for me and less cash, he took the more cash. It turned out badly for us both. He died eventually and I retained only an academic interest in the picture. But the company lets me run it off free when I want to see Miss Gardner and hear the shooting. It is a good picture and the only good picture ever made of a story of mine. One of the reasons for that is that John Huston wrote the script. Yes, I know him. Is everything true about him that they say? No. But the best things are. Isn't that interesting.

You mean background about the story not the picture? That's not very sporting, young lady. Didn't you see the class was enjoying itself finally? Besides it has a sordid background. I hesitate to bring it in, on account of there is no statute of limitations on what it deals with. Gene Tunney, who is a man of wide culture, once asked me, 'Ernest, wasn't that Andre Anderson in 'The Killers'?' I told it was and that the town was Summit, Illinois, not Summit, N.J. We left it at that. I thought about that story a long, long time before I invented it, and I had to be as far away as Madrid before I invented it properly.

That story probably had more left out of it than anything I ever wrote. More even than when I left the war out of 'Big Two-Hearted River'. I left out all Chicago, which is hard to do in 2951 words.

Another time I was leaving out good was in 'A Clean Well-Lighted Place'. There I really had luck. I left out everything. That is about as far as you can go, so I stood on that one and haven't drawn to that since.

I trust you follow me, gentlemen. As I said at the start, there is nothing to writing short stories once you get the knack of it.

A story I can beat, and I promise you I will, is 'The Undefeated'. But I leave it in to show you the difference between when you leave it all in and when you take it out. The stories where you leave it all in do not re-read like the ones where you leave it out. They understand easier, but when you have read them once or twice you can't re-read them. I could give you examples in everybody who writes, but writers have enough enemies without doing it to each other. All really good writers know exactly what is wrong in all other good writers. There are no perfect writers unless they write just a very little bit and then stand on it. But writers have no business fingering another writer to outsiders while he is alive. After a writer is dead and doesn't have to work any more, anything goes. A son of a bitch alive is a son of a bitch dead. I am not talking about rows between writers. They are okay and can be comic. If someone puts a thumb in your eye, you don't protest. You thumb him back. He fouls you, you foul him back. That teaches people to keep it clean. What I mean is, you shouldn't give it to another writer, I mean really give it to him. I know you shouldn't do it because I did it once to Sherwood Anderson. I did it because I was righteous, which is the worst thing you can be, and I thought he was going to pot the way he was writing and that I could kid him out of it by showing him how awful it was. So I wrote 'The Torrents of Spring'. It was cruel to do, and it didn't do any good, and he just wrote worse and worse. What the hell business of mine was it if he wanted to write badly? None. But then I was righteous and more loyal to writing than to my friend. I would have shot anybody then, not kill them, just shoot them a little, if I thought it would straighten them up and make them write right. Now I know that there is nothing you can do about any writer ever. The seeds of their destruction are in them from the start, and the thing to do about writers is get along with them if you see them, and try not to see them. All except a very few, and all of them except a couple are dead. Like I said, once they're dead anything goes as long as it's true.

I'm sorry I threw at Anderson. It was cruel and I was a son of a bitch to do it. The only thing I can say is that I was as cruel to myself then. But that is no excuse. He was a friend of mine, but that was no excuse for doing it to him. Any questions? Ask me that some other time.

This brings us to another story, 'My Old Man'. The background of this was all the time we spent at the races at San Siro when I used to be in hospital in Milan in 1918, and the time put in at the track in Paris when we really worked at it. Handicapping I mean. Some people say that this story is derived from a story about harness racing by Sherwood Anderson called 'I'm a Fool'. I do not believe this. My theory is that it is derived from a jockey I knew very well and a number of horses I knew, one of which I was in love with. I invented the boy in my story and I think the boy in Sherwood's story was himself. If you read both stories you can form your own opinion. Whatever it is, it is all right with me. The best things Sherwood wrote are in two books, Winesburg, Ohio and The Triumph of the Egg. You should read them both. Before you know too much about things, they are better. The best thing about Sherwood was he was the kind of guy at the start his name made you think of Sherwood Forest, while in Bob Sherwood the name only made you think of a playwright.

Any other stories you find in this book are in because I liked them. If you like them too I will be pleased. Thank you very much. It has been nice to be with you.

June, 1959,
La Consula, Churriana, Malaga, Spain

ENDNOTES

Introduction   Pages 23-42

i   Maugham, who died in 1965 at 91, might be remembered by some, perhaps unfairly, as something of a monster: in his old age, he disinherited his only daughter and in his last few years was known for almost uncontrollable raging; yet according to his biographer Selina Hastings that picture is misleading. Hastings writes that in his dotage Maugham had most probably suffered from senile dementia, then not much acknowledged as an illness, and that throughout his life he had been known for his consideration, his kindness and his generosity, not least to younger aspiring writers.

ii It has been suggested by one biographer, Richard Bradford, that despite an apparent initial reluctance when he was approached, Hemingway always eventually agreed to assist those writing about him and his work. Bradford reasons that if some tall story Hemingway had concocted years before were finally discovered to be untrue, he could make sure he was in a position to explain away inconsistencies and contradictions.

iii It might be best here to add 'apparently'. There is a suggestion that Hemingway did not even bother applying to the US armed forces because he knew his bad eyesight would count against him and that he decided to try to enlist with the Red Cross because he knew its medical requirements were lower. Hemingway also wore glasses from quite an young age, but always made sure to remove them if a photographer was around.

iv Hemingway was dismayed when in the spring of 1923 his wife Hadley Richardson told him she was expecting a child. He complained bitterly and publicly that he was too young to be a father and was told by several friends to pull himself together and face up to the fact. By 1936 when he portrayed the death of the writer Harry 'corrupted' by his wife's money in The Snows Of Kilimanjaro and the death – or murder – of Francis Macomber by the wife who despised him, his marriage to Pauline Pfeiffer was just nine years old. It was already under strain: Pfeiffer refused all forms of contraception except *coitus interruptus,* and he had already had an affair, though there are those who doubt it. Nineteen months later he began his affair with Martha Gellhorn which ended his second marriage.

v   Robert McAlmon, who was Hemingway's first publisher, releasing Three Stories And Ten Poems under his imprint Contact Editions in 1923 in a limited 300-copy edition, summed it up well. McAlmon was an early Paris friend (or better, perhaps, acquaintance) and accompanied Hemingway to his first bullfights in Spain, but the two eventually fell out. McAlmon's acid, though apparently accurate, description of Hemingway was: '*He's the original Limelight Kid. Wherever the limelight is, you'll find Ernest with his big lovable boyish grin, making hay.*'

vi In parallel with Hemingway's nascent career in the mid-1920s, Sigmund Freud's nephew Edward Bernays was almost inventing single-handed what he called – and we now know as – public relations and coming up with new practices in advertising. Bernays' influence in many fields was remarkable. Utilising his uncle's ideas about the 'ego' and the 'self', he developed new advertising techniques. For example, until the 1920s it was decidedly infra-dig for women to smoke, especially in public. At the behest of tobacco firms Bernays fundamentally changed that perception by re-branding cigarettes as 'Torches of Freedom' and persuading women that by smoking they were 'expressing themselves' and striking a blow for 'emancipation' and 'equality'. Cigarette sales increased markedly. Meanwhile in Germany, Joseph Goebbels became fascinated by Bernays' work and techniques, and adapted some of them to produce his propaganda for the nascent Nazi regime.

vii There is more than enough scope for a thoroughly superficial psychological analysis of why Hemingway might have had an inferiority complex, but I am neither qualified nor, more to the point, at all interested in attempting it. Did his mother's practice of dressing him up as a girl when he was young and treating him and his older sister Marcelline as twins have any bearing on his pleasure in sexual role reversal as a – heterosexual – adult? Who knows and, frankly, who cares? Relevant here is that two women who knew him well were persuaded that he did have such an inferiority complex and said so.

viii As for that 'padding', true to form academia will always have a plausible explanation. Hemingway's eventual 'official' biographer, Carlos Baker, tried to persuade us in Hemingway: The Writer As Artist that such passages were included in the novel because 'a sense of place' (as well as 'a sense of fact' and a 'sense of scene') were important to Hemingway. That does, though, beg the question: for which writer, whether highbrow, lowbrow or middlebrow are they not important? Baker also insists that many of Hemingway's short stories are 'built with a different kind of precision – that of the poet-symbolist'. Fair enough, but the sceptic might then ask Baker: if Hemingway choose to employ 'poetic-symbolism' in some of his short stories, why did he not also employ it in his verse? His verse is flat, banal and almost adolescent in nature, and I have yet to come across any critic or academic who any of it amounted to more than a hill of beans. Surely, verse would be just the form in which to apply the 'precision' of a 'poet-symbolist'?

'Truth' in Hemingway — Pages 43-58

i One might also wonder why a man who certainly had a command of language and could write clear English when he wanted to do so often resorted to using words that by constant repetition became banal and lame. To describe a wine, a meal, a hotel, a town, a bridge and so on blandly as 'fine' tells us pretty much nothing except that it met with the writer's approval. Who hasn't visited a restaurant that a friend has praised as 'great', 'fantastic', 'amazing' – or even just 'fine' – and served what we thought was a very mediocre meal in uninteresting and unappealing surroundings? What, we wonder, is so 'fine' about the place?

ii In the third decade of the 21st century, one might point out that the notion of being 'chaste' is not just condescending and sounds rather quaint, but that in our more 'enlightened' times – it's always safest still to use the word 'enlightened' in quotation marks – there is no reason to assume that, for example, an unmarried woman enjoying a full and active sexual life can't in other respects 'be chaste', whatever that might mean.

iii By all accounts of his life, Gissing inclined more to Reardon's integrity and might well have spent sleepless nights in anguish about what might count as 'dishonest writing'. But he is thought not to have been quite as impoverished as he led others to believe, and although it took him several years to get his literary career started, he was able to support himself and his wives – he and his first wife separated in 1884 and she died in a 1888 and he remarried three years later – through teaching. Gissing was said to have been a very earnest youth and a conscientious, hard-working student who became an earnest and hard-working man with a distinctly bleak outlook on life. He died at just 46, perhaps a warning to us all.

iv That the Hemingways – or rather Hemingway, as he called all the shots – chose to live in a rundown apartment with no indoor toilet when they first settled in Paris puzzled their friends, who knew they certainly had the resources to pay for better accommodation. When they returned from Toronto in January 1924 for a second sojourn in Paris, they moved into a similarly down-at-heel apartment (above an active and noisy sawmill), and choosing again to live in such near squalid conditions was especially odd now that they had a three-month-old son.

v One does wonder why instead of renting that 'hotel garret' Hemingway didn't put the rent he might have been paying the hotel towards renting a slightly bigger and better apartment for himself and Hadley Richardson in which he might have had a private room to write.

vi Hemingway was taken up by the RAF several times on bombing missions as an observer and his claim is ambiguous: yes, he had 'flown' with the RAF, but he sometimes strongly implied that he had actually flown an RAF plane. As unlikely as his 'fighter pilot' story sounds, we should remember that he recounted with a straight face that after actually landing on a Normandy beach on D Day, he had taken control of a stranded US army unit and led it to safety. That account was almost certainly not told in light-hearted jest intended to amuse.

vii Biographer Mary Dearborn suggests that as Hemingway was probably bi-polar, many of these fantasies where produced while he was in a 'manic phase'. That is certainly more than possible. Dearborn was specifically referring to claims Hemingway made in the last 15 years of his life, but if it was true then, there is no reason why it should not have been true when he was a younger man. Hadley Richardson has given accounts of Hemingway's behaviour which could be described as manic. Such behaviour might well have presented when Hemingway was still in his teens: Ted Brumback, a fellow Kansas City star reporter, recalled how

Hemingway stayed awake all night reading Browning's verse aloud. Brumback fell asleep and when he awoke at 4am, Hemingway was still reading aloud and told Brumback he thought he might like it as he awoke.

viii I suggest that every artist, in whatever field she or he is working, is creating 'illusion', one which certainly does involve – in the broadest and strictly an amoral sense – 'deception'. The writers, painters and composers we admire most are perhaps those most adept at creating such 'illusion'. We might – semi-seriously – even consider 'art' to be a form of *'fregatura'* which I understand is an Italian word for 'scam' or 'rip-off'. Certainly, 'the artist' has – presumably – very different motives to the conman hoping to empty your wallet; but in the skill both demonstrate when they are going about their work, they are arguably close cousins. The sleight-of-hand of a stage magician might serve as a good example of what, in part, an artist gets up to.

ix Tavernier-Courbin was investigating the supposed discovery in the Paris Ritz hotel in the mid-1950s of two small suitcases deposited there 30 years earlier. They were said to have contained an assortment of items and included letters, drafts of stories and manuscripts. Hemingway said the discovery persuaded him to write A Moveable Feast, his memoir of the early Paris days. Tavernier-Courbin marshals the various 'facts' surrounding the discovery and concludes that, on balance, there was no such 'discovery'. Pertinently, all accounts of how the suitcases came to be found lead back to just the one source: Hemingway himself.

x Let me here play Devil's advocate and respond on behalf of Hemingway's champions: to understand what 'artistic truth' might be, I will point out that many, if not most, of us will acknowledge that when reading a book, watching a play or watching a film, we might feel that *this* 'rings true' whereas *that* 'doesn't ring true'. The work in question might concern, for example, a scene set in a specific locale or era or social background, say a middle-class Jewish household in Golders Green, London, or a down-at-heel black community in Louisiana of which the author has no direct experience and with the best will in the world might simply get crucial nuances wrong. For those familiar with that locale, era or social background, the scene as presented might jar; those unfamiliar with them most probably do not notice. That is not really what is meant by 'artistic truth', but perhaps the notion of something 'ringing true' helps to shed a little light on what 'artistic truth' might be.

xi I must concede that some apparent 'blank nonsense' might, ironically, prove itself to be a useful tool to spark further intellectual consideration; the notion of 'a paradox' might be thought to fulfil that role. Taoist meditations and sayings could be cited as an example of that 'paradox', but it would be crucial that we are aware of what we are doing.

xii The 'purpose' of 'art' seems to be a matter of fashion: what we insist art 'should do' varies from era to era. At one extreme is the purity of *'l'art pour l'art'* of the French philosopher Victor Cousin (which became the *'art for art's sake'* of the aesthetic movement). More recent preaching insists that 'art's purpose' is political or moral or a means of emotional expression or a form of therapy or . . . (cont p.94).

xiii Unhelpfully, 'literature' (like 'art') is one of these uncomfortably vague notions which invariably defy definition. Why is this piece of fiction 'a work of literature' but not that one? A pragmatist might suggest it would be simpler to regard all written work as 'literature' and then to distinguish between 'good' literature and 'bad' literature (although we would then be resorting to those two weasel words 'good' and 'bad'). The same might apply to 'art'. In that sense Hemingway's third novel To Have And Have Not would certainly qualify as 'literature', but would equally be regarded by many who have read it as 'bad' or even 'very bad' literature.

xiv It was a relief when I finally came to realise that a 'problematic' or hard-to-understand piece of writing was often simply poorly written. It was then that I understood that *'muddled writing invariably betrays muddled thought'*. So if something you are reading baffles you, it might not necessarily be your fault — it might even be a nonsense which the author him or herself is unclear about. As an example I offer The Emperor's New Critique by Hollis Robbins which considers Hans Christian Andersen's story The Emperor's New Clothes. Whatever Ms Robbins is trying to say, she certainly does not manage to say it clearly. See p.222ff.

xv Admittedly some books do. To this day, fifty years on, I get as much pleasure from reading Richmal Crompton's Just William books as I did at nine years old, and they are certainly far more than 'children's books'.

I argue that Crompton was a better writer than Hemingway. The novels – and humour – of Evelyn Waugh's novels, particularly Decline And Fall and A Handful Of Dust, have for me also not faded in the slightest.

xvi Just as the early 19th-century German Romantic movement wanted to embrace sentiment, 'idealism', 'the poetry of life', '*das Ich*', '*Symphilosophie*' and 'nature' and saw themselves as counteracting the scientific, rationalist 'tyranny' of the Enlightenment, it seems each age reacts to an earlier one. Thus at the time of writing we have for many years valued 'the intellect' and 'science' and their dictates over sentiment. But a certain irrationalism has been making itself felt. In the Western world one current 'debate' is over 'transgenderism' – whether or not an individual born 'a male/female' and assigned one or the other 'gender' at birth, but who 'feels' they belong to the opposite gender and 'transitions' accordingly is now a member of that 'sex'. The 'debate' is not just getting complicated, but quite rather nasty – in some circles you disagree at your peril. So who knows, the time might come when 'the intellect' is again cast out and disparaged as the German Romantics opted to cast out rationalism. It is an irony, and a very banal one, that our moral systems and *Zeitgeist* are as much a slave to fashion as skirts, jackets, hairstyles, pop music and interior decor.

Subjectivity: is objective judgment possible?   Pages 59-71

i A related question, which I shall not pursue here but which interests me, is why exactly do we have a compulsion to 'grade' writers (or painters, performers, businessmen and women, rich people, sports people and so on)? Would it in any way matter that 'Ben Johnson was not as "good" as Shakespeare but "better" than Webster', or possibly the opposite? Or that 'Prince was "more talented" than Michael Jackson'? That 'Pele was not as good as/was better than Messi'? When our 'serious' Sunday papers compile their interminable 'lists' (sometimes called 'power lists') – 'Up-and-coming young writers', '20 artists to watch out for', 'Our most influential gays' [sic], 'Best movies of all time' and so on, they are just filling column inches and know full well the kind of fluffy guff their readers want and so they set about providing it. But surely academia might care to take a more adult, less venal approach? You think they do? Me, I'm really not so sure. Read between the lines . . .

ii   The essence of the dilemma of having no universally accepted criteria by which to 'judge' works of 'art' presents itself in other areas of thought, for example in moral philosophy. Once atheists began to insist, inconveniently, that an all-powerful 'God' did not exist and thus could not be the 'fixed point' by which moral standards and virtue were gauged and set, moral philosophers faced a real problem: so what was the imperative to 'be good' and not to 'be bad'? It could be even worse: was it possible that without such an imperative 'good' and 'bad' simply did not exist? A telling consequence of 'God's' demotion and rather embarrassed that there was now no discernible 'fixed point' is the current insistence that, for example, human rights 'are universal' and that there the matter ends. It doesn't, of course; quite how they are 'universal' is never explained, and frankly it can't be. For 'God' now simply read 'are universal'.

iii   We might also note that the critics and academics could – in theory – be accepted as disinterested on the question of the 'worth' of a piece of literature; but when considering the judgment of publishers' readers and editors, on the other hand, a note of caution must be sounded: publishers' readers and editors are not necessarily, or even primarily, looking for 'good literature'; they are hoping to discover work that will sell. And it was that factor which helped to launch Hemingway's career – his first two novels, The Sun Also Rises and A Farewell To Arms, sold very well indeed. But were and are they 'good literature'? The amount of sales has no bearing on the matter either way.

iv   The commercial 'worth' of a work of art – or put more simply how much folk are prepared to pay for owning it – is, of course, an entirely different matter. In the literary industry the 'worth' of new work will certainly be determined by how many copies his or her publisher thinks they can shift. Those who 'care passionately' about literature might choose to disagree, of course, but – for the record – I don't 'care passionately' about literature; I just 'like reading'.

v   At the time of writing, Amis has been dead only a few days and the media have been full of fulsome praise for him. Notably, though, it was invariably his 'London trilogy' of novels which are cited in appreciations. These three novels were published and popular in the 1980s and early 1990s. His later work did not sell as well, though that might be more a reflection – perhaps a case in point – that Amis and other writers of his generation were no longer *dans la vent* and had been superseded by younger writers whose work had now become 'must-read' work for those who subscribe to that sentiment.

vi The Dial was founded in 1840 as a journal for those who subscribed to the philosophical principles of Transcendentalism, but it soon established itself as a political and literary publication. In the 1920s it concentrated on modernist works. T.S. Eliot's The Waste Land made its first appearance in print in the US in The Dial.

vii Typical of a stubbornness to defend Hemingway's status as 'a great writer' at almost any and every cost, there have been some attempts to spin Across The River And Into The Trees into being not quite as awful as to many it seemed. In his book Ernest Hemingway, Peter L. Hays puts paid to those attempts and records that '*Critics have tried to redeem [the novel] from its own failings, praising the denseness of allusions to such writers as Dante, Thomas Mann (Death In Venice), and Gabriele D'Annunzio, the symbolic resonance of nearly every scene, every word, but none of these make the novel work.*'

viii In my view and based on the two novels and the short stories I have read by O'Hara, he was a gifted writer and certainly better than Hemingway. But he was an odd bird: as an Irish-American, he always felt like an outsider in the affluent Pennsylvania WASP society in which he grew up, and when his doctor father died just before he finished high school, his family hit on hard times (thought these states are relative) and there was not enough money for him to attend college. This hit O'Hara hard, and he seems never to have overcome his disappointment at not going to Yale. He was a long-standing contributor to the New Yorker, but drank heavily and developed into a quick-tempered, cantankerous, alcoholic right-winger, and fell out of literary favour. Despite his oddly favourable review of Across The River And Into The Trees, he considered Hemingway as an arch-rival. One O'Hara biographer described him as '*An egomaniac who had mastered the art of the awful first impression. Easily wounded, a snob and a social climber, he was sometimes cruel, envious, a bully, and* *violent to women as well as to men.'* Many writers rate him, but he is not much known today, partly, it is suggested, because he refused to allow any of his stories to be anthologised.

ix   Bruccoli was writing in 1978 by which time the reappraisal of Hemingway's work was already underway. Yet even within a year of Hemingway's death, in July 1962 in the New York Times, Maxwell Geismar had described For Whom The Bell Tolls as *'a curious mixture of good and bad, of marvellous scenes and chapters which are balanced off by improbably or sentimental or melodramatic passages of adolescent fantasy development'*. Presumably Hemingway would have written off Geismar as 'just another critic out to get him'; but F. Scott Fitzgerald, his one-time best friend who did a great deal to get his career off the ground, might not be as easily dismissed. His view of the novel was that *'it is a thoroughly superficial book which has all the profundity of [Daphne du Maurier's] Rebecca.'* Anyone who has ploughed through the long passages of often banal dialogue and was wholly unconvinced by the 'love affair' in the novel might be inclined to agree with both assessments.

x   Another inconvenience is my strong suspicion that Hemingway's prime reason for writing The Sun Also Rises was simply 'to write a novel' in order to build on the publishing success of his first volume of short stories and kick-start his literary career. He could certainly have decided to try to give the work intellectual shape by introducing a 'theme', but if for a moment we disregard the grand claims made for The Sun Also Rises as some kind of 'masterpiece' and consider John Dos Passos' suggestion that it is more *'a cock and bull story about a lot of summer tourists getting drunk and making fools of themselves at a picturesque Iberian folk-festival'*, it does throw a rather different light on it all. As for that intellectual shape, the optimism of his biblical quotation is certainly completely at odds with what Hemingway is alleged to have intended doing in his novel.

What was it to be – 'artist' or 'celebrity'?   Pages 72-88

i   In 1923, the American Robert McAlmon – who had married into money and founded Contact Publishing – brought out Three Stories And Ten Poems. In the same year Hemingway was asked to contribute fiction

Endnotes

for a series of volumes conceived by Ezra Pound as an 'Inquest into the state of the modern English language'. The series was published by the British Paris-based journalist Bill Bird, who had set up Three Mountains Press after he acquired an old printing press. It appeared as *in our time* — lower-case initial letters throughout as befits ambitious modernists — and consisted of eighteen very short stories. These formed the basis of Hemingway's first commercial publication, the short stories collection *In Our Time* which was published in New York by Boni & Liveright.

ii By the 1920s, Scribner's — or to give the firm its full title Charles Scribner's Sons — had a respectable stable of writer, including Henry James and Edith Wharton, but was regarded as fusty and increasingly old-fashioned, and Perkins and other young editors were continually urging the board to rejuvenate the house's customer base. When Hemingway's The Sun Also Rises was considered for possible publication, Scribner's board of elderly men objected to the novel's subject matter and language, and Perkins fought hard to get them to change their minds. The orthodox view among Hemingway champions might be that Perkins 'recognised the book's literary worth'. It is far more likely that he calculated it was the kind of title that would bring Scribner's back into the younger generation of book-buyers' favour. He was right. Perkins had already been successful overcoming the board's reluctance to publish F. Scott Fitzgerald's first novel, This Side Of Paradise. It sold well, and Fitzgerald's second novel, The Beautiful And The Damned, was even more successful.

iii Both of Hemingway's maternal grandparents were English, and his mother Grace (neé Hall) was very proud of her English roots. Windemere Cottage was named after Lake Windermere in the north-west of England, though where, how and why the first 'r' got lost, no one has established.

iv A collection of some of the pieces he wrote for the Weekly Star and daily Toronto Star, then and later from Europe, was published on a website dedicated 'our former employee Ernest Hemingway' called The Hemingway Papers. (It was at *https://ehto.thestar.com* but seems to have disappeared, though it might be reinstated). These short pieces, as well as the longer 'Letters' he wrote for Esquire and the pieces for the short-lived political and news magazine Ken in the 1930s, suggest Hemingway was a far better journalist than he was a fiction writer. His journalism is very readable and often quite entertaining. The Toronto Star's tacit boasting of its connection with Hemingway is ironic: as a freelance it paid him peanuts – just one cent for every two words, though (as he writes in one feature filed from Paris) he was paid a little more and received expenses when he was specifically commissioned and had to travel. When he finally came on staff in Toronto from the beginning of October to the end of December 1923, he loathed every minute of his time there, not least because his overall boss Harry Hindmarsh decided early on that the young man who had arrived from Paris was insufferable. Although Hemingway was still only 24, he considered himself to be a veteran reporter and thought some of the tasks he was given were demeaning. A very entertaining account of Hemingway's disastrous three months on staff in Toronto can be found in William Burrill's Hemingway: The Toronto Years.

v The Cooperative Commonwealth was part of a scam by a crook called Harrison Parker. He conned savers out of a total $15m ($255m in 2023). Hemingway claimed he had soon got the measure of Parker, though he continued working for the publication.

vi Stein described the story as *inaccrochable* which – I don't speak French and am only reporting what I've read – usually means that the sexual content of a painting deems that it could never be exhibited (presumably 'in polite society'). Up In Michigan was rejected Boni & Liveright when the house agreed to publish the In Our Time collection. It was published in the original [lower-case] *in our time* collection, but commercial publishers repeatedly refused to publish it until Scribner's finally gave way and included it in Hemingway's 1938 collection The Fifth Column And The First Forty-Nine Stories. By modern standards the story is decidedly very tame indeed. *O tempora, o mores*.

vii Such 'agreement' does indicate that Hemingway had informed Richardson that 'he had a marvellous literary future', though in making such a claim, he will not have differed from several thousand other young and enthusiastic would-be writers worldwide who think they will make all the difference. As for Hadley Richardson, she was certainly no pushover according to her biographer Gioia Diliberto; but accounts all describe her as essentially a good-natured woman, and she might have been more inclined to give way and take her lead from Hemingway, especially as

Endnotes

she later reported that life with Hemingway could be 'exhausting'. Zelda Fitzgerald, Scott's wife, once told her *'I notice that in the Hemingway family you do what Ernest wants'*.

viii Reportedly, Y.K. Smith and his wife Genevieve, who was known as 'Doodles', had what is sometimes called an 'open marriage', but Hemingway didn't know that. It is often reported that despite 'the rebel' Hemingway liked the world to see him as, he was essentially deeply conservative and conventional. As they might say 'you can take the boy out of Oak Park, but you can't take Oak Park out of the boy'. It seems Y.K. knew of his wife's affairs and had several of his own. But he was very irritated when a flat-footed Hemingway condemned 'Doodles' behaviour, and Y.K. told him to find somewhere else to live.

ix There is, of course, more to 'literary' writing than just the words that go down on paper: there is also the thought being expressed, both overtly and tacitly, and the 'artistic' skill a writer demonstrates in organising how he or she chooses to convey that thought. Arguably there is, in that sense, as much real 'art' in journalism – especially in propagandistic journalism – and in advertising, however much 'purists' might recoil in horror from that suggestion.

x In a piece Hemingway wrote for Collier's, entitled Voyage To Victory reputedly on the night of June 6 as soon as he had returned to London after witnessing the invasion (which was, however, not published for another six weeks), he writes 'the day we took Fox Green beach was the sixth of June'. This is strictly true if 'we' refers to the Allies; but there is more than a hint in that phrase that he, Ernest Hemingway was part of the invading force which landed on the Normandy beaches. He goes on to describe how little-by-little Lieutenant Robert Anderson, the officer commanding the landing craft he was on (who very soon becomes 'Andy') asks his advice and how he then gradually takes charge to save the craft from potential disaster. Notable are that despite the fearful roar and noise of the wind and sea, and the racket made by artillery fired to and from the beaches – mentioned in the piece by Hemingway – he is able to reproduce, it would seem almost verbatim, conversations on the craft with Andy and his coxswain. Throughout, Hemingway, his experience and his sage advice are, as usual, centre stage.

xi I am conscious of sometimes repeating the same quotations in these pages, but that is because I hope that at each mention they will help to flesh out and underline a new point I am trying to make. So here I cannot resist repeating that mid-market publications wanting to shift copies on superstore news-stands by featuring 'Papa' Hemingway and stories about him all largely opted to work on the principle quoted by Maxwell Scott, a newspaper reporter in the film The Man Who Shot Liberty Valance that *'when the legend becomes fact, print the legend'*.

Personality, mental and physical health   Pages 89-105

i Denis Brian also quotes Henry 'Mike' Strater, a Hemingway friend from the Paris days, who claimed that Hemingway once got him very drunk in a bar while he only pretended to drink, then took him outside and knocked him out cold. The claim sounds not just fanciful but incredible, but a local barman confirmed to Brian that he was able to prevent a similar incident by threatening Hemingway with a baseball bat. Strater believes he had earned Hemingway's ire because when both were fishing off the coast of the Caribbean island of Bimini, one of the Bahamas island north-east of Key West, he broke a local record by snagging the biggest marlin that until then had been caught locally. Hemingway could never stand being bested and relegated into second place or worse.

ii As usual, there are conflicting accounts. It is also claimed that Hemingway's weak left eye, a condition he inherited from his mother Grace, persuaded him he would probably fail a medical if he tried to enlist in the army, navy or the marines, and so he didn't even bother and opted to join the Red Cross ambulance service because its medical standards for recruits were lower.

iii In his book The True Gen, Denis Brian writes that Alice Toklas, Gertrude Stein's life-partner, reported hearing – though even she admits it was just 'gossip' – that Hemingway had a short fling in Paris with the British painter Sir Francis Rose after they met in public baths in the late 1920s. According to the gossip, both men immediately broke off the liaison as soon as they discovered who the other man was. How much credence we should give to such 'gossip' is a personal matter. What might be relevant is that no other

Endnotes

'gossip' along the same lines has ever been reported. Sir Francis, who would have been in his late teens at the time, was, like Hemingway, a Stein protégé. He married when he was 33, but his sexual inclination was overwhelmingly homosexual and the marriage ended in divorce.

iv   Even though the memoir was written over 30 years after Loeb had been ridiculed by Hemingway in The Sun Also Rises and he should have known better, he still innocently repeats his former friend's explanation for the bad left eye, that it had been 'damaged in street brawl'. It had not: his eye had been defective since he was very young. But having people believe it had been 'damaged in a street brawl' was sexier, more macho and more in keeping with how Hemingway liked the world to see him.

v   We can no longer question Hemingway as to what he was saying, but how can one writer 'beat' another? Quite apart from all evaluations of writers being distinctly and wholly subjective – that word again – it is, to my mind, oddly philistine to regard achievement in 'the arts', whether as a writer, composer or artist, as some kind of contest. In that sense the regular lists produced by the 'serious newspapers' of, for example, 'The Decade's Best Writers', as well as the many 'literary prizes' awarded annually are essentially tacky nonsense. They are only respectable as ruses by publishers and their co-conspirators to bump up book sales. Whether Hemingway's claims were, like the 'injun' accent he adopted in the days he spent with Lillian Ross, intended humorously we can also now never know. For details of the 'fuss' caused by the profile – it was thought by many to have made Hemingway look ridiculous – see p.453ff.

The writer, journalist, 'insider' and expert — Pages 106-117

i   According to the Committee To Protect Journalists (*https://cpj.org*), in the ten years to 2023, 264 journalists were murdered while doing their job, the figure based on where a motive could be confirmed. A further 225 were murdered but the motive could not be established. Between 1992 and 2023, a total of 2,194 journalists and media workers have died in the course of their work. On the other hand in a 'journalistic career' of more than 44 years, one largely, though not exclusively, restricted to reporting on flower festivals and later making sure the correct cartoons were being printed in the following day's paper, I am glad to confirm my life was never in danger. That might give some context to the many popular notions of what 'journalism' and a 'journalist' are. If you do fancy training to become 'a hack' and you plan to do a more than just compile flower festival results, it's best not to ply your trade in China, Russia, Iran, Syria, North Korea, Mexico, Somalia, Saudi Arabia and many other countries. How many of those who died who also wanted to 'become a writer' is, unfortunately, not recorded.

ii An interesting research project, though one that would be impossible to undertake, would be a global investigation into the lives of those for whom 'great things' were predicted when they were young who then went on to achieve nothing at all of any significance or consequence.

iii The reality of covering such a conference is far more mundane than many might imagine – it is not 'exciting'. It consists more or less of writing up the various 'facts' the conference organisers want to publicise and release at press briefings and then filing 'a story'. If anything, whatever might be written up as a colour piece is likely to have been more interesting. As a rule journalists worked and work in packs, helping each other out, although on the understanding that if and when, it is every man and woman for him or herself. As an affable, relatively inexperienced, 23-year-old reporter, Hemingway would most certainly have been taken under the wing of more senior colleagues and given tips and advice.

iv Ironically, Hemingway might well have become a Star staff reporter based in Paris, but he blew the opportunity when he was presented with it. As William Burrill points out in Hemingway: The Toronto Years 1920-1924, at some point in 1920 while Hemingway was working for the Cooperative Commonwealth, he was contacted by the Star's managing editor John Bone who, on the recommendation of the Weekly Star editor Herbert Cranston, offered him the job. Getting a little to clever for his own good, Hemingway substantially exaggerated what he was being paid by the Cooperative Commonwealth and said he would only go if he were paid more than 'his current salary'. But the amount he demanded was too high for Bone who withdrew his offer. Later that year, when moving to Paris became the plan, Hemingway contacted Cranston who agreed to consider any freelance pieces he submitted to the Weekly Star. See p.323 for details

Endnotes

of why Bone contacted Hemingway – the offer of the job was not quite as straightforward as it might have been.

v   According to William Burrill, Hemingway also rather overdid the 'bohemian artist' in how he dressed when he turned up in Toronto; it did not go down to well on the straitlaced Toronto Star. However, Burrill, who had interviewed many of the, by then elderly, folk who had worked on the paper in late 1923, admits that their memories and recollections varied enormously. Drinking was a sacking offence on the Star, but there are many accounts of reporters turning up for work so drunk that their – sober – friends and colleagues would sit close to them on either side to ensure they didn't fall off their chairs or face first on to their desks.

'Rules on writing' and the 'Theory of Omission   Pages 118-128

i   In his comments on Hemingway's first novel, Fitzgerald accused him of being '*careless + ineffectual*' and '*of [embalming] in mere wordiness an anecdote or joke that casually appealed to [him]*'. He went on that the '*first chapter contains about 10 such things and it gives a feeling of condescending casuallness*'. He added '*there are about 24 sneers, superiorities, and nosethumbings-at-nothing that mar the whole narrative up to P. 29 where (after a false start on the introduction of Cohn) it really gets going*'. He also said the writing '*honestly reminded [him] of Michael Arlen*', and as Hemingway despised Arlen, he would not have been pleased. By ditching the first two chapters, Hemingway followed Fitzgerald's advice and improved the novel, but he subsequently always pretended it was he who had decided they were not needed. Pertinently, Hemingway always took criticism badly, and it could well have been at that point that for him their friendship was slowly coming to an end. Not many years later he regarded Fitzgerald as a friend in name only and was distinctly unpleasant about him, notably in the 1936 story The Snows Of Kilimanjaro and his memoir A Moveable Feast.

ii Fitzgerald had based Dick and Nicole Diver, the two protagonists of his novel Tender Is The Night, on his and Hemingway's rich friends Gerald and Sara Murphy, but his novel was certainly not intended as a portrait of the Murphys. The two Divers – Dick becomes an alcoholic and Nicole is mentally unstable – resemble Fitzgerald and his wife Zelda far more. Yet in Hemingway's comments on the novel, which are confused, confusing and often nonsensical, he apparently takes Fitzgerald to task both for inventing two fictional characters and not providing a 'true' portrait of the Murphys. Hemingway also takes another shot at Fitzgerald for writing fiction to make money, ignoring that by the time the novel was published, Fitzgerald had frittered away a large fortune, was obliged to pay for Zelda's psychiatric care as well as his daughter Scottie's school feeds, and was in poor health. He eventually found work as script doctor in Hollywood. Certainly, in view of the exceptionally generous rate Hemingway negotiated with Esquire for his 'Letters' and the lucrative Book of the Month Club deals he signed, his criticism about 'writing for money' looks very much like a very bad case of pots and kettles.

iii The first few stanzas of McGonagall's memorable poem The Tay Bridge Disaster run:

Beautiful Railway Bridge of the Silv'ry Tay!
Alas! I am very sorry to say
That ninety lives have been taken away
On the last Sabbath day of 1879,
Which will be remember'd for a very long time.

'Twas about seven o'clock at night,
And the wind it blew with all its might,
And the rain came pouring down,
And the dark clouds seemed to frown,
And the Demon of the air seem'd to say –
"I'll blow down the Bridge of Tay."

When the train left Edinburgh
The passengers' hearts were light and felt no sorrow,
But Boreas blew a terrific gale,
Which made their hearts for to quail,
And many of the passengers with fear did say –
"I hope God will send us safe across the Bridge of Tay."

There are another four (or five) stanzas of varying length.

Endnotes

The Sun Also Rises and the 'lost generation' — Pages 129-147

i Dos Passos and cummings [sic] chalked up more service in an ambulance corps than Hemingway's four weeks, yet Hemingway claimed for the rest of his life that he 'had gone to war' in 1918. Strictly speaking he had 'gone to war', though certainly not in the sense in which the phrase is usually used and understood. cummings had an awful time: he was imprisoned by the French for several months as a suspected spy. He described his experiences in his autobiographical novel The Enormous Room, published in 1922.

ii Dos Passos later apologised to Hemingway for his New Masses review, though whether he had changed his mind about the novel or simply decided he did not want to risk his friendship with Hemingway is not recorded. As for his review, telling your readers what you think your readers want to hear is a time-honoured journalistic principle which has sustained and still sustains many a publication and TV services. Dos Passos might well have assumed his left-of-centre to far-left readers very much wanted to hear that the group that joined Jake Barnes in Pamplona were nothing but privileged middle-class wasters. If we substitute 'viewers' for 'readers', any number of television pundits and their shows, whether of the Left or the Right, operate on the same principle.

iii It would also be unfair to describe Brett Ashley as 'a nymphomaniac' as Edward Wagenknecht does in Cavalcade Of The American Novel: From The Birth Of The Nation To The Middle Of The Twentieth Century. He writes: '*I am, I must confess, less inclined than many critics to prostrate myself in admiration before the nymphomaniac Lady Brett Ashley, when she decides to give up the bullfighter lest she should poison his youth with her corruption.*' Wagenknecht published that view in 1952, pertinently pre 'the Pill' and long before the advances feminism has achieved to date. Quite what Wagenknecht – who was born a year after Hemingway in 1900 and died in 1984 – or the US of the 1920s would have made of the sexual freedoms enjoyed and demanded by Western young women in the second decade of the 21st century is anyone's guess.

A modernist writer?   Pages 148-166

i   Harold Loeb, 'Robert Cohn' in The Sun Also Rises, published his first novel, Doodab, in the same year that Hemingway published In Our Time, and attempted to give it a 'modernist' slant by removing all definite and indefinite articles – 'a' and 'the' – from his text. These were all re-instated by his publisher, Boni & Liveright, before the novel was published. Loeb published only two more novels, The Professors Like Vodka (1927) and The Tumbling Mustard (1929), before he abandoned the 'literary life'.

ii   One or two characters in For Whom The Bell Tolls are a little more rounded, notably Pilar and Pablo, than in Hemingway's first three novels; but of the other protagonists – other members of Pablo's gang – though each does have a definite presence in the novel, it would be untrue to suggest Hemingway examined their 'inner lives' in any way. As for Maria, 'the love interest', she, like Catherine Barkley in A Farewell To Arms is almost a caricature and barely makes it into two dimensions.

iii   A novel that might be considered a modernist work in content and conception would be The Good Soldier by Ford Madox Ford, published in 1915. In it Ford, in a non-linear manner, deals with several varying accounts of three deaths and a broken relationship, and utilises the then fresh technique of the unreliable narrator.

iv   Hemingway was certainly not prolific. Anton Chekhov wrote more than 450 short stories and Guy de Maupassant – the 'de' was added by his father at his mother's insistence – wrote more than 300. Somerset Maugham could only manage around 100 short stories, but he did also manage to turn out more than 25 plays and 20 novels.

v   Hemingway, a keen angler and fisherman, could not help indulging himself in these passages, writing detailed descriptions of finding bait, trekking to the spot where the fishing will be done, storing the trout caught and eating lunch. Each reader must decide for him or herself how interesting and engaging these passages are; but some might agree they add nothing to a supposed tragic account of a 'lost generation' in despair, and the various scholarly justifications attempting to show how they might do not convince. Like several other passages, they come across as padding. The same point about Hemingway indulging himself can be made about his short stories Big Two-Hearted River and The Undefeated.

vi Some good examples of this are from Carlos Baker in Critical Readings: The First Forty-five Stories in his 1951 book Hemingway: The Writer As Artist. Hemingway's *'deepest trust was placed in the cumulative effect of ostensibly simple, carefully selective statements, with occasional reiteration of key phrases for thematic emphasis'* and that like *'any writer with a passion for craftsmanship, Hemingway not only accepts but also sets himself the most difficult experimental problems. Few writers of the past fifty years, and no American writers of the same period except James and Faulkner, have grappled so manfully with extremely difficult problems in communication'*. This is all very plausible, but is it really the case or possibly nothing more than academic waffle? Are sceptics such as me simply demonstrating our shallow philistinism or are we more in tune with the innocent lad in Hans Christian Andersen's tale The Emperor's New Clothes? Yet again, find that coin and toss it to help you decide. NB. The description 'experimental' always tends to sound impressive, but readers should bear in mind that though some 'experiments' succeed, not all do and some fail badly. Strictly, the description 'experimental' is neutral, although oddly to describe a work as 'experimental' does carry with it a vague suggestion that the attempt is somehow admirable. Then there's the divisive matter of agreeing on what has 'succeeded' and what has not. Room for more academic waffling?

Hemingway theology – Round and round   Pages 167-182

i   Of Hemingway's work, I have most recently re-read To Have And Have Not and For Whom The Bell Tolls, and frankly both novels justify Gore Vidal's catty observation, quoted in my preface, that *'American society, literary or lay, tends to be humorless. What other culture could have produced someone like Hemingway and not seen the joke?'* Vidal might have had more than one eye on the spotlight when he said that, but nevertheless it is – to these British eyes at least – spot-on.

ii Didion came to prominence as *'a leading exponent of the New*

Journalism' and, according to her New York Times obituary *'reflected Norman Mailer's prescription for "enormously personalized journalism in which the character of the narrator was one of the elements in the way the reader would finally assess the experience".'* The NYT adds that 'As a teenager, Ms. Didion typed out chapters from Hemingway novels to see how they worked,' and – Vladimir Nabokov might have taken note – *'She was deeply influenced by Hemingway's handling of dialogue and silence. Joseph Conrad was another formative influence.'* Didion was eventually celebrated as a grande dame of US letters, but she was not to everyone's taste. In a 1980 piece which is said to have angered Didion even years later, fellow essayist Barbara Grizzutti Harrison described her as 'a neurasthenic Cher'. Harrison added that she was *'disinclined to find endearing a chronicler of the 1960s who is beset by migraines that can be triggered by her decorator's having pleated instead of gathered her new dining room curtains.'*

iii Ironically, Hemingway's command of punctuation was at best sketchy and, at worst – for example in Death In The Afternoon – it rendered some passages quasi-incomprehensible. It is worth pointing out – as all too often many schoolteachers do not – that learning punctuation is not a matter of 'learning the rules' for their own sake, but of helping students acquire a facility that allows them to make what they write comprehensible or, alternatively, to guide the reader as to how to read a sentence. For example, the sentence *'the doctors who were better paid had bigger houses'* does not mean the same – and note the commas – as *'the doctors, who were better paid, had bigger houses'*. The first sentence doesn't refer to all doctors, just those doctors *'who were better paid'*. The second does refer to all doctors. The punctuation makes all the difference: each sentence is identical – each 'consisting of nine words' as Didion might chose to put it – save for the two commas, but convey something different. Whether in the passage quoted by Didion Hemingway consciously used commas to achieve the effect she admires is a moot point. This sceptic, noting Hemingway's flawed command on punctuation on too many other occasions, thinks probably not.

iv Sixty-odd years after Hemingway's suicide in 1961, it might be difficult – especially for those under 40 – to comprehend just how very famous he

Endnotes 541

had become by the mid-1950s. Yet his fame was so global that even the Pope and the Kremlin sent their condolences to his widow, Mary Welsh.

v Some might suspect that in play here was the tried and trusted newspaper practice of building up a personality in order then to take him or her down again – all in the interests of sales, of course – but I don't think that was the case. The print media might have played an important role in the rise and rise of Ernest Hemingway in the late 1920s, but his slow decline – in critical eyes – was all his own work. For newspapers and later the mid-market magazines, Hemingway – and his reputed prowess at everything – remained 'good copy' throughout his life.

vi The various streams of income generated by For Whom The Bell Tolls – book sales, film rights and becoming a Book of the Month choice – made Hemingway financially independent for the first time in his life. Married to Hadley Richardson and then Pauline Pfeiffer, it was their money – especially Pfeiffer's – that subsidised him and, in the 1930s, allowed him to engage in several costly pastimes. Hemingway did earn his own money, though notably – and ironically – from journalism, but it would not have been enough to live the life he enjoyed. He invested some of the proceeds from For Whom The Bell Tolls wisely in stocks and some property, and in 1961 he died a very wealthy man.

vii That play, The Fifth Column, features a very thinly disguised Hemingway as a cynical, hard-drinking and – of course – well-informed war correspondent and secret agent, and a very thinly disguised Martha Gellhorn as the hero's rather bubble-headed, Vassar-educated mistress, also a war correspondent. It takes place in the city's Hotel Florida where the protagonists are holed up, as were Hemingway and Gellhorn.

Hemingway theology – The tyranny of 'meaning' Pages 183-195

i When I was 17 and in my last year at an English Roman Catholic boarding school, a small group of us sixth-formers had our RI (religious instruction) classes with the headmaster. Mr W. was Irish and a nice man and I liked him – I took German with him and we got on well. Sadly, he had long lost

the respect of the rest of the school and was the continual butt of jokes. Though he was well-meaning, he was wholly out of his depth running an institution that liked to see itself as 'a leading RC public school'. Mr W. lasted about two years before he was sacked. Our group of five or six gathered once a week in his comfortable study, settling on his sofa and into armchairs (in the cold months before a large blazing log fire). As these things tend to evolve, one of us came to take on the task of engaging Mr W. in conversation for 45 minutes while the others dozed quietly until the end of class. One day, to get the ball rolling, I announced that I was having 'doubts'.
'What doubts?' Mr W. asked.
Well, I told him, I do chemistry, biology and physics A-level, and I just can't see how a 'virgin birth' is even possible.
'Do you believe in God, Powell?' he asked.
I told him that, yes, I did (as then I thought I did).
'Do you believe that God created the world?'
I told him that, yes, I did.
'Do you believe that God made the laws of nature.'
Well, yes, I told him, he must have done.
'Well, if he made the laws, he can break 'em, too, can't he?'
It is a similar kind of cock-eyed thinking which makes Prof Reinert's explanation fatuous and more than ridiculous. But as Reinert was then a professor in the Department of English at the University of Washington, I doubt anyone felt able to tell him so, least of all his students.

Caveat lector – Enter academia   Pages 196-212

i   One might cite Danielle Steel, Robert Ludlum, Wilbur Smith, Ian Fleming, Harold Robbins, Daphne du Maurier, Tom Clancy, John Grisham, Frederick Forsyth, Judith Krantz, Jackie Collins and, more recently, Stan Lee, Stephen King, Dan Brown, Neil Gaiman, J.K. Rowling as popular novelists whose success and standing the literary establishment might deign to acknowledge. But the establishment would be reluctant to concede these writers had 'anything important' to tell us about 'the human condition' – that is the task of 'serious writers'.

ii   Maugham was a shy man, and because he stuttered, he was very

Endnotes 543

self-conscious in public. The stutter developed after his mother died when he had just turned eight and his father then died, 30 months later. Maugham had grown up in Paris and French was his first language, but after his father's death, he was farmed out to live with an uncle, a rather severe Church of England (US Episcopalian) clergymen and a German aunt, and he was very unhappy. The stutter remained with him all his life.

iii Here's a reminder of what Woolf wrote to save you skipping back to find the passage: *'When we see [kings, judges and lord mayors] go sweeping by in their robes and their wigs, with their heralds and their outriders, our knees begin to shake and our looks to falter. But what reason there is for believing in critics it is impossible to say. They have neither wigs nor outriders. They differ in no way from other people if one sees them in the flesh. Yet these insignificant fellow creatures have only to shut themselves up in a room, dip a pen in the ink, and call themselves 'we', for the rest of us to believe that they are somehow exalted, inspired, infallible. Wigs grow on their heads. Robes cover their limbs. No greater miracle was ever performed by the power of human credulity . . . [the believer] begins to think that critics, because they call themselves so, must be right [and] begins to doubt and conceal his own sensitive, hesitating apprehensions when they conflict with the critics' decrees.'*

iv There is something very muddy in our thinking about 'art'. More than a few seem to believe that there is some kind of intrinsic, almost metaphysical, quality of 'being art' that works either possess or do not possess. This might be deduced by two judgments often made, that 1) *'this is art'* and 2) *'this is not art'*. Certainly, a 'work of art' might or might not 'interest' and 'engage' us; but that *you* are 'interested and engaged' in and by a work but *I* am not says more about you and me than much about the work in question. More useful and constructive might be to acknowledge that *all* works conceived and realised and intended 'as art' are bona fide 'works of art'; but that is otherwise saying very little more about the work in question and certainly not praising them. It would then simply be a question of considering each work *individually*, deciding whether one is 'interested and engaged' enough in and by a work to spend more time considering it, or would prefer to move on to consider another 'work of art'. That approach might also better cater for cultural differences and changing tastes and values: it would surely be a nonsense that this work '*is art*' today in my country but thought not to be so abroad or is no longer '*art*' in one hundred years' time.

v   A telling example of how a book's title could subtly indicate the bias of it contents might be the title of the English translation of Theodor Haecker's study of the Danish philosopher and writer Søren Kierkegaard, *Der Buckel Kierkegaards,* Haecker's last work before he died. In German *Buckel* means 'hump' and alludes to the curvature of Kierkegaard's spine. Haecker had converted to Roman Catholicism after he first translated Kierkegaard's work and came to dislike the Dane's often outspoken anti-clericalism. In his book Haecker examines how Kierkegaard's 'hunchback' and the ridicule if often attracted might have influenced the Dane's often satirical and sardonic take on life. Its English title was not, as it might have been, Kierkegaard The Hunchback but, oddly, Kierkegaard The Cripple. Although these days we would no longer refer to someone with a physical disability as 'a cripple' (assuming that Kierkegaard's hump might be regarded as a 'disability), the word might also subtly suggest rather more about Kierkegaard than simply his physical state: it might perhaps try to inform the reader what to expect from Haecker's analysis and how he had come to think of Kierkegaard and his work.

vi   For two weeks Hemingway drove a Red Cross ambulance, then volunteered to work closer to the front, running a rest and recreation station serving coffee, chocolate and cigarettes to Italian troops. It is now thought that he did not – as Baker also claims – help carry wounded from the trenches to a first aid post. When – unofficially – he started visiting the trenches to deliver his coffee, chocolates and cigarettes, he was blown up by an Austrian mortar bomb at the end of his fourth week. The rest of his 'war service' was spent in the Red Cross hospital in Milan. Eventually discharged in November to return to duty, he immediately contracted jaundice and a few days later was back in care. Discharged for a second time by Christmas, he returned to the US at the beginning of January, thus concluding his Great War 'war service'.

vii   The title of that omnibus edition of the short stories is disingenuous: yes, strictly these stories were the 'first' forty-five stories' written by

Hemingway; but 'first' tacitly implies there were many more. There were not, only about another nine or ten. By comparison – and Hemingway did like to compare himself with other 'great' writers – Maupassant wrote over 300 short stories and Anton Chekhov 500.

Caveat lector – Erich von Däniken takes a bow   **Pages 213-225**

i   Connoisseurs of the kind of pseudo-scientific and pseudo-archaeological, though lucrative, claptrap touted by Erich von Däniken might also care to check out the work of Michael A. Cremo, Robert K.G. Temple, Richard L. Thompson, Graham Hancock, Richard Leigh, Christopher Knight, Zecharia Sitchin, John A. Keel, Philip Coppens, Jim Marrs, Leslie Kean, Immanuel Velikovsky, Michael Baigent, Adrian Geoffrey Gilbert, David Hatcher Childress and David Icke.

ii   This might again highlight the necessary distinction between 'scientific disciplines' and those in the arts, such as English literature and especially philosophy; and a conscious distinction is necessary. At the most basic level, when a chemist refers to 'an alkali' or 'a metal' or a mathematician talks of 'addition' and 'subtraction', 'division' and multiplication', there will be no misunderstanding. If in time it becomes apparent that there has been some kind of misunderstanding along the line, it can easily be sorted out: at the end of the day chemists, mathematicians, physicists, biologists (and I don't doubt even practitioners of Thomas Carlyle's 'dismal science' economics) are able to 'speak the same language'. Not so, it would seem the many academics working in English literature or philosophy. From my limited knowledge of philosophy it seems often standard practice for a philosopher to come up with a new intellectual concept and often words and phrase to get an idea across, and then to use them widely, leaving his or her listeners or readers unsure of what he or she is trying to convey and whether they can be sure they even understand a certain philosophical notion in the way intended. The kind of chaos that can ensue is highlighted in the various suggested solutions to the 'insoluble problem' found in Hemingway's A Clean, Well-lighted Place.

iii   A quite comical insight into a certain over-earnestness which pervades much academic undertaking in the arts is this from a book review in the Hemingway Review of Autumn/Fall 2021: '*[David] Faris begins The Hemingway Industry with a definition of the term "industry." With that definition, we grasp what precisely Faris will be investigating in his book. In that introduction, Faris writes, "An industry is an organized productive activity in which labor and capital are brought to bear on raw materials to produce a desired output."*' I suspect most coming across the phrase 'the Hemingway Industry' would have a reasonably good idea of what is being suggested without needing chapter and verse; I would be very surprised if they did not. An irony is that rather than clarify, Faris' definition, rather muddies the waters and 'the Hemingway industry' involves neither capital, labour or raw materials.

Caveat lector – The Rorschach effect **Pages 226-240**

i   Fadiman had regarded The Sun Also Rises as the finest novel of its year, thought A Farewell To Arms was even better, but was less impressed by To Have And Have Not. He thought '*the best stuff in it should have been planed and chiselled into short stories and let go at that*'. As for Death In The Afternoon, which had preceded Winner Take Nothing, he unenthusiastically noted that is '*was perhaps something [Hemingway] simply had to get out of [his] system*'.

ii   Being just two paragraphs of Hemingway's writing and the rest simply the text of the letter, One Reader Writes has been criticised by some wonder whether it is even a bona fide short story. The opposing view, inevitably, might be that for that very reason it is 'modernist'. Who knows? Yet again you pays your money and you makes your choice.

The suspected inferiority complex. **Pages 241-247**

i   John Pudney, a British Royal Air Force public relations officer who met Hemingway in the early summer of 1944, felt '*he was a fellow obsessed with playing the part of the Ernest Hemingway and hamming it to boot, a sentimental 19th-century actor called upon to act the part of the 20th-century tough guy*'. Generally, there was a feeling that Hemingway,

Endnotes

all high spirits and bonhomie, was trying too hard to be 'Ernest Hemingway'. See p.439.

The linguist — Pages 248-253

i   I discovered this crucial point many years ago when I read Heinrich Mann's *Der Untertan* in German. I had learned to understand German on my German mother's knee and later to speak the language when I attended German schools, and for several years I was bi-lingual and culturally more German than English. Mann's *Der Untertan* is a sharp satire of Wilhelmine Germany of the first decade of the 20th century, and although it is certainly not 'a comedy', it is very funny – in German. The first time I read it – and often found myself laughing out aloud – I wondered how well the humour translated into English. Badly, as I discovered: the novel has variously been published in English as Man Of Straw, The Patrioteer, and The Loyal Subject – none of which do the German title justice – and when I eventually read a translation, it was as flat as a pancake, the satire wholly blunted and buried.

The unknown lover and sex roles in bed — Pages 254-262

i   Prudence Boulton was occasionally employed at the Hemingway Walloon Lake cottages to babysit and clean house. She died in a suicide pact with her boyfriend at 17. She is likely to have featured in two Hemingway short stories, Ten Indians and Fathers And Sons.

ii   Hemingway, now sold on marlin fishing, bought Pilar in 1934 and asked Arnold Gingrich for an advance on the 'Letters' he would write for Esquire to help pay for it. Pilar cost him around $7,450 ($169,051 in 2023). 'Pilar' had been Pauline Pfeiffer's 'code name' while his affair with her in Paris was still illicit. He also named one of the protagonists in his Spanish Civil War novel For Whom The Bell Tolls 'Pilar'.

iii   Hemingway's friend Charles 'Buck' Lanham couldn't stand Gellhorn and took a dislike to her when he, she and Hemingway once had dinner. He first met Hemingway after D Day who had attached himself as an accredited correspondent to the US Army 22nd Infantry Regiment which

iv Earlier, I mention a very tenuous claim that Hemingway had a brief affair in Paris with the British painter Sir Francis Rose. The only source was Alice Toklas, Gertrude Stein's partner, and even she dismisses it as nothing but vague gossip. Robert McAlmon, a nominal friend in Paris who privately published Hemingway's first work, also suggested Hemingway was a closet gay, but as both came to dislike each other intensely, his claim is regarded as a gratuitous piece unpleasantness.

A lifetime's work   Pages 263-281

i   According to biographers, the story was apparently intended to insult an acquaintance, the American poet and writer Chard Powers Smith, whom Hemingway had taken against, though why he had has not been established. It was originally called Mr And Mrs Smith, but Max Perkins advised Hemingway to change the title.

ii Although The Maltese Falcon by Dashiell Hammett, perhaps today one of the better known 'hard-boiled' pulp novels, wasn't published until 1930 and Raymond Chandler didn't publish The Big Sleep until 1939, the pulp genre was as old as the century and is said to have reached the peak of its popularity in the 1920s and 1930s.

iii In many ways the spat between Faulkner and Hemingway was reminiscent of – if I might briefly be incorrect – a hissy fit between two ageing queens. Faulkner sneered that Hemingway had *'never been known to use a word that might send the reader to the dictionary'*. Hemingway responded *'Poor Faulkner. Does he really think big emotions come from big words? He thinks I don't know the ten-dollar words. I know them all right. But there are older and simpler and better words, and those are the ones I use.'* Frankly, the only sane response to all of it is simple 'who cares (because, bots, it's the work we are interested in').

Work published posthumously   Pages 282-298

i   Ironically, after Islamic State (ISIS) terrorists struck at various points in

Paris on the night of November 13, 2015, in an attack in which 130 people were murdered, Hemingway's memoir became much in demand and climbed to the top of the French best-sellers' list, with many Parisians reportedly leaving a copy of the book with candles and flower as memorials throughout the city.

ii   According to Tom Jenks in his 2010 account of 'editing' The Garden Of Eden, Scribner's was by then very much on the back foot, and its new owner, Macmillan, had moved the house from its very prestigious Fifth Avenue premises to a 'modest building' in Nineteenth Street. A few years later what remained of Scribner's, now little more than a Macmillan imprint, was again uprooted, this time to Macmillan's own offices where it led a rather pokey, out-of-the-way existence. Ironically, ten years later Macmillan was itself swallowed up, by Simon & Schuster, which itself was taken over by Pearson in 1998 who then sold it to the German publishers Holtzbrinck in 2001. Of Scribner's there is now little left.

In sum: Chacun à son goût   Pages 299-309

i   . . . or possibly she: when we think of female poets from antiquity, to many the name Sappho of Lesbos might occur soonest; but in fact many women were active in literature, as well as in the sciences, medicine, history and philosophy. A quick net trawl will come up with the writers Aesara of Lucania, Perictione, Phintys, Ptolemais of Cyrene, Philaenis, Nicobule, Pamphile of Epidaurus, Aelia Eudocia, Cornelia Africana, Sulpicia I and Sulpicia II and Faltonia Betitia Proba, who were active between 2,500 and 1,500 years ago. Given the wars and fighting Homer describes, it is more probable that he was a man, but we ill-advised to take such a 'fact' as read.

ii   It is now accepted that the Hungarian novelist, writer and journalist, Arthur Koestler, was guilty of at least one rape (of the filmmaker and feminist Jill Craigie) and possibly several others. Although Koestler's official biographer, Michael Scammell, played down the charges, made by another writer, David Cesarani, saying it had been made fifty years after the rape was claimed to have occurred and that Craigie was the only woman to go public, he concedes that Koestler could be 'sexually aggressive'. Cesarani insists Koestler was a misogynist, and in his autobiography The Invisible Writing, Koestler admits he denounced a woman he was sleeping with to the Soviet secret police. But crucially and to the point: do any of these unsavoury details have any bearing on Koestler's fiction and non-fiction?

iii   Publishers, literary agents, the media and booksellers work hand-in-glove to try to ensure continuing sales by regularly producing 'lists' of every stripe: 'Most Promising Young Writers', 'Best Feminist Novels Of The 20th Century', 'Top Ten Gay Novels', 'Britain's Best-Loved Writers/Poets/Novelists' – that kind of thing. In their own way each of the publishers, agents, the media and booksellers benefits, and it's all harmless enough, of course and part of life's great tapestry; but one does wonder whether the literary industry is rather more 'passionate about money' than it is 'passionate about literature'.

iv   The work of Arnold Bennett, John Galsworthy and H.G. Wells was rather pooh-poohed by some of their 'modernist' peers, partly because all three were successful professionally and made a good living from their writing. That scorn seems to be an inelegant variation on the conviction that 'an artist must suffer for her or his art' and its unstated corollary that 'if an artist isn't suffering, the art can't be that good, can it?'

v   The insistence by some that William Shakespeare, the 'mere' glover's son from Stratford-upon-Avon who, according to his friend and rival playwright Ben Johnson, had 'small Latin and less Greek' and had only attended grammar school and so could not have been the author of that the verse and plays attributed to him is nothing but classic British snobbery. Notably, in Johnson's poem 'To the Memory of My Beloved Master William Shakespeare, And What He Hath Left Us' in which he had remarked '*though [Shakespeare had] small Latin and less Greek . . .* he was praising him, not dissing him: Johnson's point was that *despite* his lack of formal education, Shakespeare could be ranked highest among the greats: he writes '*I will not lodge thee by / Chaucer, or Spenser, or bid Beaumont lie / A little further off, to make thee room: / Thou art a monument without a tomb*'.

vi   Whatever one thinks of Hemingway's fiction, his place in literary history cannot be denied, although that, too, has no bearing on the artistic 'worth' of his work; and at second blush there might be rather less to 'having a

Endnotes

place in literary history' than seems to be implied: it depends upon what we understand by the phrase. In one sense, the Scottish poet William McGonagall arguably also had a place in literary history.

vii The American writer and political activist Mary McCarthy had built herself a reputation as a serious novelist in the 1940s and 1950s, but when she published her novel The Group in 1963, this was dented. Her novel featured in the best-sellers' lists, but alienated many in New York's Establishment and was written off as 'an awful fatuous superficial book', 'a trivial lady writer's novel' and a 'very labored, somehow silly Vassar affair'. What might have upset New York's artistic great and good – one of whom composed a parody of the novel for the New York Review Of Books – was perhaps less the novel's literary qualities but its subtly satirical tone and that McCarthy had more or less based her fictional group on own circle of friends at Vassar College where she enrolled in 1929.

viii I rather like the inscription Mrs Sabatini asked to have etched on the her husband's headstone, the first line from his novel Scaramouche – '*He was born with a gift of laughter and a sense that the world was mad.*'

1899-1921 – The early years   Pages 312-321

i Gamble might have been the 'homosexual visitor' Hemingway writes about in A Moveable Feast, who at some point made a sexual proposition, which, Hemingway declined, but that seems unlikely given that Hemingway spent a week with Gamble in Sicily. Although for some reason Hemingway didn't want his friends to know about his trip, there have been no suggestions that their relationship was not entirely platonic. The 'homosexual visitor' might have been just another Hemingway invention.

1921-1924 – Paris and life are sweet   Pages 322-332

i Accounts by Star reporters who had worked under Hindmarsh stress he was formidable and ruthless, worked his staff hard to get a story and did not tolerate failure. Yet with his father-in-law Joe Atkinson, he helped turn a failing newspaper into Canada's largest and most profitable news sheet. One Gwyn 'Jocko' Thomas, who began as a copy boy and worked his way up to become the Star's police reporter, remarked semi-seriously that *'if you had to lie, cheat or steal to get a story, you lied, cheated and stole'*. Hemingway remarked that under Hindmarsh life on the Star was like 'working in the Prussian army under a bad general' – a nice line, but Hemingway was not speaking from experience. Hindmarsh was remembered as being loyal to his staff, or better, to those staff who delivered. The Star was founded in 1892, but languished until Atkinson took it over seven years later. 'Holy Joe', Atkinson was a Methodist teetotaller and being caught drinking was a sacking offence, yet many staff are reported to have drunk – and been drunk – at work. Atkinson was said to be a bundle of contradictions: under his ownership the Star became left-leaning and campaigned on social issues, but he refused to allow staff to join a union. The star was respected as a serious newspaper, but was often sensationalist in nature, being one of the first papers to carry photographs on the front page and to employ big, bold headlines.

1924-1925 – Learning to be a success   Pages 333-342

i   Although Hemingway was often exceptionally generous in later life and helped out many friends, according to Scott Donaldson he gained a reputation in the early years in Paris of being slow to pay back money he had borrowed and sometimes simply did not even bother. Kitty Cannell, at the time Harold Loeb's girlfriend and who became Frances Clyne in The Sun Also Rises, is quoted by Donaldson as saying Hemingway had *'a Tom Sawyerish way of getting money from people and then saying they had embarrassed him by forcing it on him'*.

ii   Ford's father was a German who had settled in England before Ford was born in December 1873, and his mother was English, the daughter of the Pre-Raphaelite painter Ford Madox Brown. Until he changed his surname by deed poll in 1919, Ford was still Ford Herman Hueffer, but after World War I, he decided it best to have an English surname. Changing his name also allowed him to qualify for a small legacy. Ford was already 40 when war broke out, and he was recruited by the British War Propaganda Bureau. The following year he enlisted in a Welsh infantry regiment and took part in the Battle of the Somme. While on active duty he was gassed and repatriated.

iii A particular embarrassment to Ford was a piece Hemingway had written and published in the issue of the *transatlantic review* edited while Ford was in the US raising money. Joseph Conrad had just died, and Hemingway wrote a eulogy in which he insulted the poet T.S. Eliot by claiming he would grind Eliot to dust and sprinkle it over Conrad's grave if it would bring the novelist back to life. Ford was mortified.

iv In early 1925 when Hemingway signed his contract with Boni & Liveright and then realised Scribner's were also interested, Scribner's best-selling and 'name' authors were either dead or old. By 1925, Stevenson had been dead for 31 years, although at 44 he had died relatively young; James had died nine years earlier at 73; Burnett had been dead only one year, but was 75 when she died; Wharton and Galsworthy were still alive, but in 1925 they were, respectively, 63 and 58, and neither was producing the kind of fiction any of the young in Fitzgerald's 'jazz age' would have regarded as 'now'. Galsworthy died eight years later and Wharton in 1937.

v In a sense, possibly contentiously, Hemingway's decision to ditch the 'modern' publisher Boni & Liveright for 'safe and respectable' Scribner's sums up one contradiction in his character: the would-be rebel was fundamentally conservative. It is a point made by all his biographers and is perhaps reflected in how within very few years his seemingly 'modernist' writing style lost any claim to 'being modern' or 'cutting edge'. In his fiction, even of A Farewell To Arms the prose style is wholly conventional, although as it is rather 'bald' and un-showy nature, that might mislead some readers into identifying it as a 'modern' work.

vi Ironically, at the Finca Vigia near Havana, Hemingway's home for almost 20 years from 1940 on, he kept between 20 and 30 cats which were continually interbreeding and stinking the place out. Much to the disgust of Hemingway's third wife Martha Gellhorn, who was fastidious about hygiene, they had the run of the place and defecated everywhere. Eventually, while Hemingway was away on one of his 'sub-hunting', expeditions, Gellhorn had the males neutered to stop the inbreeding, much to Hemingway's fury.

vii In time, F. Scott Fitzgerald was also a victim. After singing Hemingway's praises to Perkins, encouraging his move from Boni & Liveright and facilitating his introduction to Scribner's, and advising him to ditch the opening several thousand words of The Sun Also Rise, he was ridiculed in Hemingway's The Snows Of Kilimanjaro. At Max Perkins' bidding Hemingway eventually removed Fitzgerald's name from the story. His portrait of Fitzgerald in his memoir A Moveable Feast, composed over several years in the late 1950s, is notably unkind. The valuable assistance Fitzgerald gave Hemingway when launching his career and the subsequent shabby treatment he received from his one-time close friend might underscore the truth of the cynical observation that *'No good deed goes unpunished'*.

1925-1926 – Finally on the literary map   Pages 343-352

i The process of converting to Roman Catholicism and being initiated as a member of the church usually involves instruction in the tenets of the RC faith and takes many weeks; and the RC church insists that a non-Roman Catholic must convert before being allowed to marry an RC and any children in the marriage are brought up as RC. In theory the RC church will never allow a divorcee to be married in an RC ceremony. In practice, ways are often are found to break the ostensibly unbreakable rules. Making substantial donations to the RC church is often effective.

ii I suggest it is distinctly odd that a writer 'who did not have ideas' should be regarded as 'a great writer'. Surely 'having ideas' or even 'having the germ of an idea' would be natural, especially in a young man quite possibly brimming with enthusiasm. The oddity is underlined when a decade later, under pressure to produce a third full-length work of fiction and bereft of inspiration, Hemingway recycled two short stories to become part of that third novel certainly indicates that the suggestion is not entirely fanciful. Thus cannibalising two previously published short stories to produce To Have And Have Not does not much speak of a fertile mind.

Endnotes

1926-1927 – Out with the old, in with the new   Pages 353-361

i   Hickok was the Paris bureau chief of the US Brooklyn Daily Eagle (and later a news editor at the Voice of America) and the trip was primarily intended for him to see fascist Italy for himself. Hemingway, who went along for the ride, published an account of their trip in The New Republic in May 1926, and then used that first non-fiction account – altering very little of it – for his short story Che Ti Dice La Patria? that appeared in Men Without Women six months later.

1927-1929 – Fame and a comfortable life   Pages 362-371

i   It is reported that towards the end of 1923, Fitzgerald stopped drinking and in a matter of months had completed ten short stories, which earned him $16,450 overall from the magazines and allowed him both to pay his outstanding bills and spend the summer of 1924 finishing up The Great Gatsby. Today – in 2023 – that $16,450 would be worth $293,079. However, he and his wife could not stop spending and in that same year they blew close to $36,000 ($641,390) when the average American earned $1,400 ($24,942). Fitzgerald's ineptitude with finances inspired him to write the self-mocking autobiographical account How To Live On $36,000 A Year.

ii   Uncle Gus' largesse was certainly boundless. He had arranged for a new Ford A Coupé to be on the quayside when the couple arrived in Key West (though other accounts claim the car was delayed on the mainland). When Hemingway and Pfeiffer decided to settle in Key West, Gus paid for the purchase, renovation and decoration of the splendid, but rundown, house they had chosen as their new home; and when in the early 1930s Hemingway announced he wanted to go on safari to East Africa, Uncle Gus gave Ernest and Pauline $25,000 ($358,037 in 2023) worth of stock to sell to pay for the two month-long trip.

iii   Whether Perkins did collect the manuscript on his visit or whether Hemingway later delivered the manuscript to New York in person is unclear: the biographers' accounts differ. Such discrepancies in the chronicles of Hemingway's life are not uncommon and his cavalier attitude to the truth cannot be blamed. Another example is that most biographers tell us Hemingway wrote the first draft of The Sun Also Rises by hand in 'blue' school exercise books, yet Mary Dearborn has Hemingway 'typing' the story in Spain and France. So which was it: did he write it by hand or type it? Such variations should alert us to tread carefully when reading a biography, which, as Debra Moddelmog points out, is essentially just a collection of available 'facts' selected to tell 'a story' in keeping with 'narrative unity and ideological consistency'.

1929-1934 – Becoming the legend   Pages 372-381

i   I agree that each book might certainly have a 'life of its own' – in fact those of us who try our hand at writing often find that in time the work can begin to run away with itself and becomes in need of a disciplined blue pencil. But I can't quite see how it would be necessary for the book to 'kill off a part' of the author to begin that life. To my ears it sounds more like the kind of hi-falutin' romantic twaddle that delights many who describe themselves as 'passionate about literature', but to which a down-to-earth man who could not abide bullshit – as Hemingway saw himself – would give short shrift.

1934-1936 – Poor sales and growing depression   Pages 382-398

i   One wonders whether Hemingway might not, like John Dos Passos, have drifted further and further to the right had he lived for another 20 years – 'small government' was never a Democrat or left-liberal demand. In the 1964 presidential election, Dos Passos campaigned from the Republican candidate, Senator Barry Goldwater. It would not be outlandish to speculate that the keen huntsman Hemingway might not eventually have thrown in his lot with the decidedly illiberal National Rifle Association and insisted it was every US citizen's right 'to bear arms'.

ii   As far as I know we are not aware of what Hemingway himself thought of the novel. It is arguably difficult to take a dispassionate and objective look at your own work, but he must have realised that the muddled and

Endnotes

inconsequential work that, to put it quite mildly, was eventually published came nowhere close to realising his plan.

iii This is reminiscent of the circularity of logic which blights much Hemingway scholarship and is described above in 'Hemingway theology'. Because for many Hemingway can do no wrong, the *'fragmented form'*, *'ham-fisted approach to politics'* and *'hard-boiled obsession with cojones'* – phrases borrowed from a Kent State University Press website plugging its publication of Reading Hemingway's To Have And Have Not by Kirk Curnutt – must in some way surely be admirable: so why don't we call it 'innovation'? According to the website Curnutt *'explicates dozens of topics that arise from this controversial novel's dense, tropical swelter of references and allusions. From Cuban politics to multifarious New Deal alphabet agencies', from rum running to human smuggling to byways, bars, and brothels, [and] delves deeply into the plot's rich textural backdrop.'* That's one way of putting it. There are others.

iv It will not be Hemingway's novel which still resonates with the public today: when we hear of To Have And Have Not, we are more likely to recall the Howard Hawks film starring Humphrey Bogart and Lauren Bacall. In fact, the only parts of the film has in common with Hemingway's novel are its title and the names of several protagonists. In his conversation with Peter Bogdanovich, Hawks admits that the only element he valued in Hemingway's 'bunch of junk' was the passionate relationship between Harry Morgan and his wife Marie.

1936-1940 – Cuba and a second divorce   **Pages 399-413**

i Rebecca, a psychological thriller first published in 1938 and filmed two years later by Alfred Hitchcock with Laurence Olivier and Joan Fontaine, is one of Daphne du Maurier's most successful novels. I don't know whether Hemingway was aware of Fitzgerald's verdict or not. By 1940, when Fitzgerald had less than four years to live, Hemingway had long moved on from their friendship.

1940-1943 – Trying and failing to settle Pages 414-423

i   Though 'living in sin' was still unusual, it was not unknown, and no one would have raised an eyebrow had Hemingway and Gellhorn lived together without getting married. Yet the essentially uptight Oak Park conservative in Hemingway, raised in a Congregationalist home where the household – family and servants – met every morning for prayers conducted by the paterfamilias and the family attended church twice on Sundays, again had the final say. His zeal to marry again recalls Pfeiffer's consternation when she declared '*I don't mind Ernest falling in love, but why does he always have to marry the girl when he does?*'

ii Ironically, in the last months of his life when Hemingway suspected the FBI were keeping tabs on him everywhere – trailing him in New York, going through his bank files in Ketchum – the Bureau had lost interest. It never closed its file in him, but that seems more to have been bureaucratic indolence. What is surprising is that Hemingway escaped attention from the fanatics on the House Un-American Activities Committee (HAAC) in the 1940s and 1950s. This is remarkable given the close cooperation between HAAC and the FBI, and the Bureau's well-documented fears about Hemingway's loyalties. His involvement with and support for the – Soviet-controlled – Spanish Republicans was well-known, yet at no point did HAAC, which saw Communist subversion everywhere, choose to summon him to appear and explain himself. If the claim by the former KGB man, Alexander Vassiliev, is true that Hemingway had been recruited by the NKVD in 1941, the HAAC would certainly have treated the matter as far more serious.

1943-1944 – Lonely and the third marriage ends Pages 424-432

i   Dearborn writes that Gellhorn was covering the war in Italy in the autumn of 1943 when she bumped into Robert Joyce, Hemingway's embassy contact in Cuba when he was running is 'counter-surveillance' operation ('the Crook Factory) to whom he had been submitting his 'counter-intelligence' reports. Embassy life had become dull for Joyce and he had joined the newly-formed Office of Strategic Services (OSS) which later morphed into the Central Intelligence Agency (CIA). Gellhorn told

Endnotes

him about her attempts to get Hemingway to move on from the silly spy network and sub-hunting and to involve himself seriously in the war effort. It was then, says Dearborn, that Joyce suggested to the OSS that it might care to consider enlisting Hemingway.

1944-1945 – Playing soldier and wooing again   Pages 433-441

i   Many accounts of the few days in Rambouillet when Hemingway was the nominal leader of a gaggle of French resistance fighters describe him as 'waging a private war'. This is hyperbolic rubbish, typical of how we like to build up our heroes and glamorise what is 'known' about them. He spent less than a week in Rambouillet, and though he certainly did have a substantial amount of weaponry in the hotels rooms he had commandeered, at no point were he and the resistance group ever involved in fighting or action of any kind. Accounts of his arrival in Paris are also largely fictional, and one should once again be reminded of the advice of Maxwell Scott in The Man Who Shot Liberty Valance *'when the legend becomes fact, print the legend'*.

1945-1954 – Fourth marriage and infatuations   Pages 442-464

i   Here is a list of titles – not necessarily complete – offered for sale since Hemingway's suicide: The Snows Of Kilimanjaro And Other Stories (1961), The Fifth Column And Four Stories Of The Spanish Civil War (1969), The Nick Adams Stories (1972), 88 Poems (1979), Complete Poems (1979), The Short Stories Of Ernest Hemingway (1984), The Complete Short Stories Of Ernest Hemingway (1987), The Collected Stories (Everyman's Library) (1995), Hemingway On Writing (1999), Hemingway On Fishing (2000), Hemingway On Hunting and Hemingway On War (2003), and Hemingway on Paris (2008).

ii   Three other suggested reasons as to why Welsh hung on in their relationship are that after her ectopic pregnancy in 1946 and she had been on the point of bleeding to death, it was reputedly Hemingway's quick thinking which pulled her through; for this she was always grateful. Some biographers suggest that as she was in her forties in the last decade of Hemingway's life and no longer a young attractive women, resuming her career as a journalist would not have been easy. Finally, one unkind suggestion is that she rather liked being the wife of the world-famous, wealthy and soon-to-be Nobel laureate Ernest Hemingway. Divorce would have put an end to that.

iii In view of such claims and Hemingway's son Patrick's insistence that from the mid-1940s on his father was a 'different man', it might well have be that his head wounds injured him far more seriously than was suspected. Relevant here would be the car crash in London in May 1944, for which he received just superficial treatment, whose damage was perhaps compounded by a new head wound a few months later. Nor can we know whether he was sober or drunk when he wrote to Cowley making those claims, though even had he been drunk, they were distinctly odd. It might even be possible that Hemingway was indulging in a private joke.

iv Cyril Connolly must have had some sympathy with Hemingway. As a young man, a product of Eton and Balliol College, Oxford, who had many literary contacts, he gained a reputation, as did Hemingway, as a writer to keep an eye on. In 1954, the theatre critic Kenneth Tynan described Connolly's style as 'one of the most glittering of English literary possessions', though beware the usual luvvie hyperbole. The general verdict on Connolly has been that he was full of a promise he never fulfilled. By the early 1950s, Connolly was over 50 and will have realised he had missed the boat. He blamed it on what he regarded as his natural indolence. In 1938 he had published Enemies Of Promise and he was perhaps already aware that a glittering literary future was not be his. In it he made two telling observations, that *'There is no more sombre enemy of good art than the pram in the hall'* and *'Whom the gods wish to destroy they first call promising'*. Perhaps when he read the Across The River And Into The Trees he felt a little Hemingway's pain, and chose to be kind.

1954-1961 – Terminal decline and suicide   Pages 465-487

i The board's influential member was its chairman, Nicholas Murray Butler, president of Columbia University under whose guidance over 42 years the college expanded enormously, from just 4,000 students at the

Endnotes

beginning of the 20th century to 34,000 students by mid-century. Butler had strong political connections and in the 1920s he twice attempted to secure the Republican presidential nomination. By 1941, when he took against Hemingway's novel and vetoed it as a Pulitzer Prize winner he was 79, but what might seem like an old man's reactionary stance against Hemingway's novel could be misleading. As a young man who earned his doctorate in philosophy at just 22, he had studied in Paris and Berlin. Later in life and unusually for an American of his era (and possibly even today) he was an internationalist and actively worked towards international peace. Unfortunately, we don't, however, have any record of why he did not rate Hemingway's novel and ruled that it should not get the 1941 Pulitzer Prize. Whether, like me, he thought it not at all very good we just cannot know. He died just four years later.

ii Ever the image-conscious showman projecting 'Ernest Hemingway' (as a rather unimpressed John Pudney had earlier noted) he felt the world wanted and needed to see, Hemingway arrived to 'meet the Press' carrying a bunch of bananas and a bottle of gin and quipped 'My luck, she is running very good'. Good copy, perhaps, though complete tosh. He had been very badly injured and the booze certainly did not help. It was at his point, when he was still just 55 years old, that his physical and then his mental health began to give way terminally.

iii Haemochromatosis is said to be prevalent among people with a Celtic genetic ancestry (not that Hemingway is reported to have any Irish or Scottish forebears – his ancestors were from Yorkshire, not usually claimed as a Celtic part of the world). It can be treated when diagnosed, but unfortunately many of its symptoms are common for other disorders and they are often first misdiagnosed and so treatment for haemochromatosis is delayed.

iv In keeping with the distinct lack of clarity which all too often attends 'facts' about Hemingway is the account by A.E. Hotchner of how the 'Ritz hotel' trunk and its contents came to be discovered. 'Ed' Hotchner was Hemingway's friend, confidant, business partner, travel companion and, frankly, bag-man who forged a good career out of his friendship with the writer. In his 2009 New York Times review of the revised edition of Hemingway's memoir A Moveable Feast, he writes that one day at lunch at the Ritz hotel in 1956 with Hemingway and Charles Ritz, the hotel's owner, Ritz reminded Hemingway that he had left a trunk at the hotel. The trunk, he wrote, had been 'especially made for Hemingway by Louis Vuitton' and 'Ernest had wondered what had become of it' (Presumably by the end of the 1920s and with Hemingway now married to his rich second wife Pauline Pfeiffer, the trunk was a one-off commission.) Hotchner's version of the discovery doesn't exactly contradict the accounts by Hemingway and the New York gossip columnist Leonard Lyons and Mary Welsh, but in their accounts – which are basically simply Hemingway's account as he was the source of what Lyons and Welsh retailed – the 'trunk' is not a smart Louis Vuitton number, but two small suitcases; and, of course, Jacqueline Tavernier-Courbin contends that the whole episode was invented to justify Hemingway writing his memoir. Hotchner was reviewing a revised edition of the memoir that had been edited by Hemingway's grandson Sean which Sean declared to be 'a truer representation of the book my grandfather intended to publish'. Welsh, Hotchner writes, had '*cobbled [her] manuscript together from shards of an unfinished work and [had] created the final chapter, There Is Never Any End to Paris*'. Welsh had died 23 years earlier, and she and Hotchner were by then not on the best of terms – she had sued him over his memoir of Hemingway he published in 1966.

v   Julian McLaren-Ross (born a more prosaic James Ross) knew what he was talking about. Born in 1912 into comparative wealth, be became increasingly penurious from the mid-1930s on. He had an acknowledged literary gift and made a small name for himself in the 1940s with a number of short stories, but his personality and lifestyle worked against him all his life. From the mid-1940s on, after he was court-martialled from the British army and relocated to London, he spent every afternoon and evening until the early hours in various bars and drinking clubs in North Soho (in an area nicknamed Fitzrovia) holding court to a circle of admirers. Once back where he was currently calling home and fuelled by amphetamines to keep himself awake, he wrote until well into the early morning – book reviews, fiction and later radio and film scripts – to earn a his living. He repeatedly obtained advances from publishers for novels he pitched, sometimes pitching the same novel to different publishers, but he hardly ever delivered and gradually squandered any goodwill his charm and small talent had won him. His drinking and lifestyle – he never used buses or London's underground railway (the Tube) and travelled everywhere by cab, even short distances – meant he rarely paid his rent or hotel bills and was repeatedly evicted. In the mid-1950s he was sometimes reduced to sleeping in the cubicles of a hotel's Turkish baths or even in a park. The chronic boozing and his diet of amphetamines and cigarettes led to his early death in 1964 from a heart attack at just 52.

BIBLIOGRAPHY

Bibliography

The Art Of Ernest Hemingway
– John Atkins

Ernest Hemingway, A Life Story
– Carlos Baker

Hemingway: The Writer As Artist
– Carlos Baker

Everybody Behaves Badly — The True Story Behind Hemingway's Masterpiece The Sun Also Rises
–Lesley M. M. Blume

Modernism, A Guide to European Literature
–Edited by Malcolm Bradbury and James McFarlane

The Man Who Wasn't There: A Life Of Ernest Hemingway
–Richard Bradford

The True Gen: An Intimate Portrait of Hemingway By Those Who Knew Him
– Denis Brian

Hemingway And The Mechanism Of Fame
–Matthew J. Bruccoli

Conversations With Ernest Hemingway
– Matthew J. Bruccoli

Ernest Hemingway And His World
– Anthony Burgess

Hemingway: The Postwar Years And The Posthumous Novels
– Rose Marie Burwell

A Second Flowering: Works And Days Of The Lost Generation
– Malcolm Cowley

Ernest Hemingway: A biography
– Mary V. Dearborn

Paris Without End: The True Story of Hemingways First Wife
– Gioia Diliberto

The Paris Husband
– Scott Donaldson

By Force Of Will: The Life And Art Of Ernest Hemingway
– Scott Donaldson

Hemingway vs Fitzgerald: The Rise And Fall Of A Literary Friendship
– Scott Donaldson

The Apprenticeship Of Ernest Hemingway The Early Years
– Charles A. Fenton

Four Lives In Paris
– Hugh Ford

Memoirs Of Montparnasse
– John Glassco

Along With Youth : Hemingway, The Early Years
–Peter Griffin

Crusade In Spain
– Jason Gurney

Hemingway
– Peter L. Hays

Bibliography

Running With Bulls
— *Valerie Hemingway (née Danby-Smith)*

Ernest Hemingway: A New Life
— *James M. Hutchisson*

Intellectuals
— *Paul Johnson*

Ernest Hemingway
— *Verna Kale*

The Hemingway Women Those Who Loved Him — The Wives And Others
— *Bernice Kert*

Hemingway And His Conspirators : Hollywood, Scribner's And The Making Of American Celebrity Culture
— *Leonard J. Leff*

Men Without Art
Wyndham Lewis

Hemingway
— *Kenneth S. Lynn*

Hemingway, A Life Without Consequences
James R. Mellow

Fame Became Him: Hemingway As Public Writer
— *John Raeburn*

The Young Hemingway
— *Michael Reynolds*

Hemingway: The Paris Years
— *Michael Reynolds*

Hemingway: The Homecoming

– Michael Reynolds

Hemingway: The 1930s

– Michael Reynolds

Hemingway: The Final Years

– Michael Reynolds

Hemingway And The Sun Set

– Bertram D. Sarason

In The Spanish Civil War

– Amanda Vaill

New Essays On The Sun Also Rises

– Edited Linda Wagner-Martin

Ernest Hemingway, A Literary Life

– Linda Wagner-Martin

Hemingway Goes To War

– Charles Whiting

Hotel Florida — Truth, Love And Death Ernest Hemingway: A Reconsideration

– Philip Young

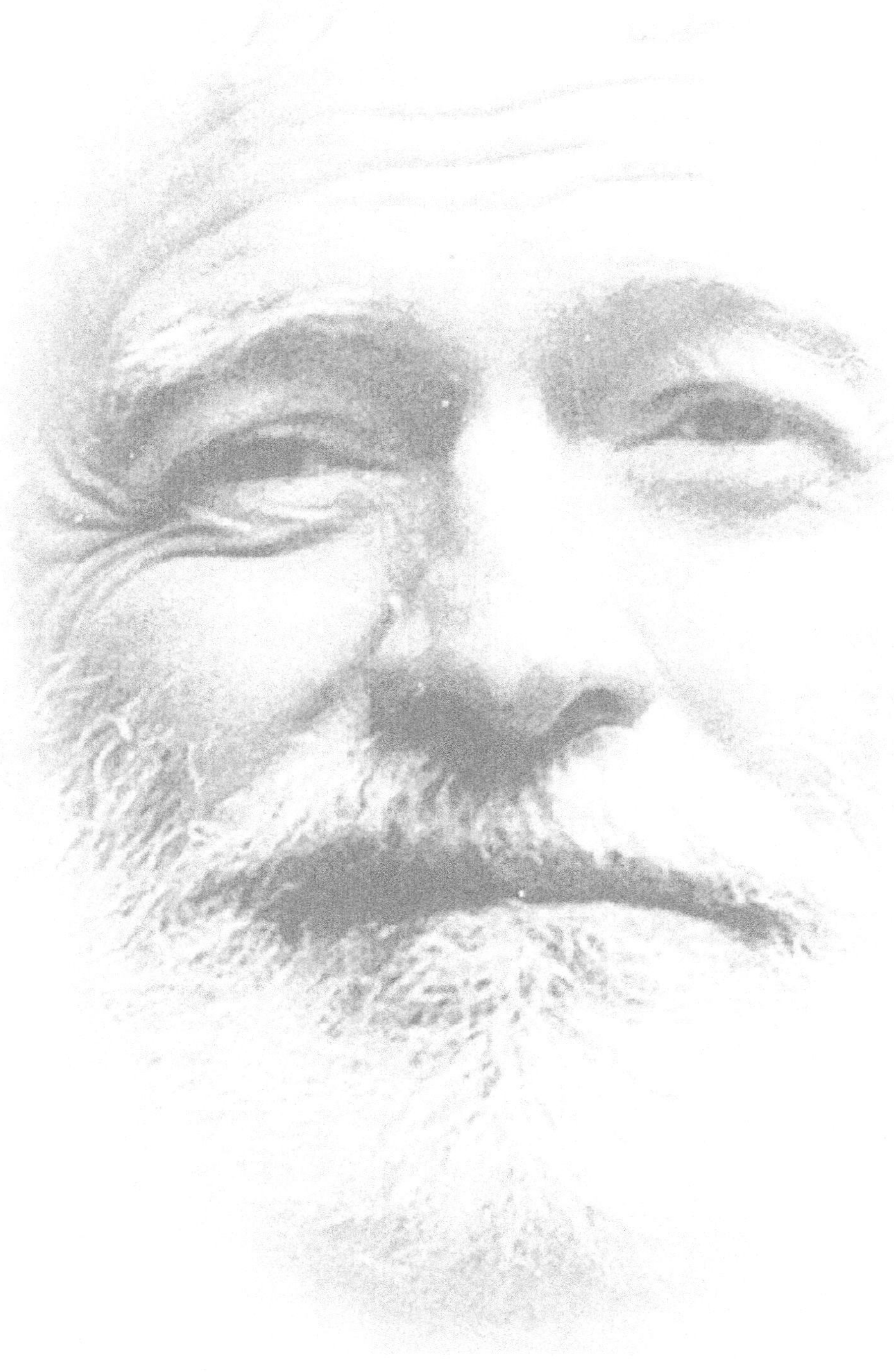

Printed in Great Britain
by Amazon